The Challenges of Business

Managing in the Canadian and Global Context

Len Karakowsky
York University

Captus Press

The Challenges of Business
Managing in the Canadian and Global Context

Captus Press Inc.
Units 14 & 15, 1600 Steeles Avenue West
Concord, Ontario L4K 4M2
Telephone: (416) 736–5537
Fax: (416) 736–5793
Email: Info@captus.com
Internet: http://www.captus.com

The publisher and the author gratefully acknowledge the authors, publishers and organizations for their permission to reproduce their work in this book. Care has been taken to trace ownership of copyright material contained in this book. The publisher will gladly take any information that will enable the rectification of any reference or credit in subsequent editions and apologizes for any errors or omissions.

Statistics Canada information is used with the permission of Statistics Canada. Users are forbidden to copy the data and redisseminate them, in an original or modified form, for commercial purposes, without the expressed permission of Statistics Canada. Information on the availability of the wide range of data from Statistics Canada can be obtained from Statistics Canada's Regional Offices, its World Wide Web site at http://www.statcan.ca, and its toll-free access number 1-800-263-1136.

Cover artwork by Deborah Karakowsky.

Library and Archives of Canada Cataloguing in Publication

Karakowsky, Len
   The challenges of business: managing in the Canadian and global context / Len Karakowsky.

Includes bibliographical references and index.
ISBN-13: 978-1–55322–132–6
ISBN-10: 1-55322-132-X

   1. Business—Textbooks 2. Management — Textbooks. I. Title.

HD31.K31 2007   658   C2006–905797–4

Canada ▪■ We acknowledge the financial support of the Government of Canada through the Book Publishing Industry Development Program (BPIDP) for our publishing activities.

0 9 8 7 6 5 4 3 2 1
Printed in Canada

Table of Contents

4   The Challenges of Change   339

Appendices

              379

Preface

The Canadian business landscape has changed dramatically in recent years. Bankruptcies, mergers and foreign takeovers are just a few of the common business events that we continue to witness. However, even more alarming are the increasing occurrences of scandals and corruption among businesses. What is going on?

Clearly, we live in a rapidly changing environment. Business is influenced by a host of factors that exist outside the walls of the company, including technological advances, the globalization of the workplace, the changing role of government and the continued "re-engineering" of organizational structures, to name but a few. What are the fundamental challenges facing us today, and in coping with these challenges, are there responsibilities that business must address? The aim of this text is to introduce the student to many of these critical concerns facing today's organizations. However, I hope that you find this book goes beyond a mere presentation of current issues affecting organizations.

A fundamental aim of any university education is to encourage critical thinking skills. I have tried to develop this book with that objective in mind. That is, this book is not so much a description of business practices or a "how to" of managing a business; rather, it is intended as a springboard for critically examining how organizations are designed, how they are managed and what central challenges they face. It presents the reader with questions, concepts, theories and ideas. And it is aimed at encouraging students to think about these concepts and assess how they might add value to an understanding of the nature of organizations and management.

As with the completion of any book, much thanks must be given to the many individuals who contributed directly or indirectly to the writing process. First, I wish to thank Randy Hoffman, Pauline Lai, Lily Chu, Jason Wormald, Jennifer Wong and all the staff at Captus Press for their tremendous effort in preparing this book for publication. Second, I would like to thank Professors Eytan Lasry and You-Ta Chuang for their chapter contributions. I am delighted that this text also contains sections written by a number of my graduate as well as undergraduate students, and I thank all of them for their wonderful contributions. I am grateful to Professor Diane Jurkowski, Julia Richardson, Eytan Lasry, Kelly Thomson, Peter Tsassis, Peter Modir and Vita Lobo, and the rest of my colleagues at York University for their input and suggestions. Finally, I must express my gratitude to my dear wife, Debbie, whose support and encouragement made all this possible.

Len Karakowsky
Toronto, Canada

Introduction

The central aim of this book is:

- To examine current issues affecting the management of organizations.
- To offer insight into the unique challenges present in the Canadian business context.
- To help generate conceptual frameworks for identifying and analyzing key issues within organizations and their environment.
- To encourage critical thinking regarding the nature of organizations and the challenges of managing in the workplace.

This book presents conceptual frameworks, ideas and theories drawn from the work of management scholars and organizational research. In order to enhance critical thinking skills, each chapter emphasizes concept application through the infusion of extensive "real-life" business illustrations, largely drawn from the Canadian popular press. Each chapter begins with **The Business World**, which reports current real-life business issues and themes explored within the chapter. The chapters are also filled with real-life business illustrations, summarized within the **Talking Business** exhibits. Each chapter also contains end-of-chapter **Concept Applications** with questions. These cases are also largely drawn from the Canadian popular press, and are intended to give you an opportunity to apply chapter concepts to real business contexts.

In addition to encouraging critical thinking skills, this book is equally concerned with relating ideas and issues voiced by practitioners and communicated through such popular press sources as *BusinessWeek*, *Canadian Business*, *Fortune*, *Report on Business*, *The Globe and Mail* and *The National Post*.

STRUCTURE OF THE BOOK
Part 1: The Challenges and Responsibilities of Business

Chapter 1 presents the broader context within which managers manage — the environment of organizations. This chapter helps us appreciate the challenges of developing managerial strategies to cope with the environment. It describes the context within which much of our examination of organizations and management occurs. The framework employed is one that underscores both internal forces and external forces directed at the organization. The ability to adequately address both types of forces will, ultimately, determine the organization's fate.

Chapter 2 identifies the fundamental responsibilities of business in terms of its relationship with society. This chapter considers challenges for practitioners with regard to managing organizations in a responsible and ethical manner. This relates to the underlying issue of business ethics and corporate social responsibility.

Part 2:   Internal Challenges of Business

Chapter 3 presents a glimpse into the world of managers. Any organization must be managed — that is, in very simple terms, an organization must generate a set of goals, and these goals must be accomplished. What is the role of the manager in generating goals and ensuring that these goals are fulfilled? What is the best way to manage people? The aim of Chapter 3 is to provide a better sense of what managing is all about, to offer insight into the different styles of managing, and to identify the various approaches or philosophies that have been generated with regard to managing people.

Chapter 4 outlines specific challenges to designing organizational features. Are the traditional methods of designing organizations still valid? What factors suggest whether certain structures will succeed or fail? Specifically, what is the relationship between strategy and structure? What new organizational forms are arising? These are among the issues addressed in this chapter.

Chapter 5 introduces the concept of business strategy. What does business strategy encompass? How is it formulated? What factors influence the success or failure of a business strategy? These are among the central questions addressed in Chapter 5.

Part 3:   External Challenges of Business

Part 3 presents critical issues that encourage you to reconsider the current status of organizations and their ability to adapt to the challenges of the present and future. Chapter 6 describes the competitive environment and identifies key issues in understanding prospects and challenges for any business. In addition, this chapter considers the role that technology can play in business success. Chapter 7 discusses organizations in the global or international context. This chapter explores the notion of globalization, and outlines a number of central considerations in any organizational efforts to expand internationally. Chapter 8 considers the roles that government can play with regard to business, and how these roles have been changing. Issues such as privatization, deregulation and the facilitation of trade agreements are discussed.

Part 4: The Challenges of Change

Chapter 9 explores the issue of change. What is change, and how do organizations experience change? We will consider factors that either create or reduce resistance to change in organizations. This chapter also discusses the notion of the learning organization, and addresses the question of whether organizations are capable of facilitating learning and development among their members. Current issues such as mergers, tipping-point change and the case of IBM are examined.

PART 1

The Challenges and Responsibilities of Business

The Challenges of Business: Managing the Internal and External Forces

What are the key factors that determine business success or failure? How, indeed, does one make sense of the current state of business? Assessing the prospects of organizations requires a careful examination of the contexts within which organizations operate. Much of this chapter and, indeed, this book is intended to address the internal and external context of organizations and those factors that critically impact the functioning and fate of business. The Canadian business context is given primary attention.

LEARNING OBJECTIVES

By the end of the chapter, you should be able to:

1. Define three internal characteristics of organizations that play a central role in their success or failure.
2. Identify the forces that comprise the specific and general environments of organizations.
3. Discuss the nature of the six external forces confronting organizations.
4. Explain the importance of each of the external forces within the Canadian business context.
5. Describe the framework that this text will use to examine the nature of organizations and management.

I would like to thank Josh Stern who contributed Talking Business 1.4 and 1.5 to this chapter.

The Business World —————————————————————————

How's Business in Canada?

Think of it as a good neighbor, with no fences. And like a good neighbor, there's nothing you can't ask it to do — like provide a home for your company's expansion or relocation project.

It's no wonder that more U.S. expansions and relocations are ending up in Canada. Enterprising corporate executives are recognizing the value of Canada's available, skilled work force, low cost of doing business, robust transportation system and access to domestic and global markets. Not to mention its available, cost-effective business real estate, favorable business climate and attractive quality of life. In most every area, Canada stands ready to compete with any U.S. or international site that you might be eyeing for your company's expansion project.

The Economist Intelligence Unit (EIU) rates Canada No. 1 among 60 countries for the years 2005 to 2009 in its general business environment ranking. "Canada is expected to be the best place in the world to conduct business during the next five years," according to EIU. "The country scores particularly high on the quality of its infrastructure, open regime for foreign trade and favorable market opportunities."

KPMG's latest Competitive Alternatives study rates Canada as the overall cost leader in its comparison of business operating costs in 11 industrialized countries. What's more, Canada's cities scored very well in Mercer Human Resource Consulting's latest quality of life rankings for cities worldwide.

But don't just take our word for it. Look at the numbers; do the math. When you are considering where to site an expansion or relocation project, don't forget to consider Canada. The Canada Ratings 2005 supplement gives you vital information you need on Canada's economy, people and business climate.

Inside this supplement, the latest in a series produced by Expansion Management's research team, you'll find data and statistics on our northern neighbor's work force, cost of doing business, tax rates and other critical success factors.

Business & Industry

Canadian businesses are the engines that drive the Canadian economy. Today, Canada ranks No. 11 among countries worldwide in its gross domestic product and per capita GDP. Manufacturing is a key part of the Canadian economy. More than 14 percent of all employed Canadians work in manufacturing operations. Transportation equipment, food, chemicals and petroleum products are the categories that led in value of shipments from Canadian manufacturers in 2004. "Canada is becoming an increasingly attractive option as a prospective site because of its favorable exchange rate and the fact that it's a safe alternative in terms of a stable government and in terms of insulation from security and political issues," said John H. Boyd, president of The Boyd Co., a Princeton, N.J.,-based site location consulting firm.

Employment & Labor
Canadian workers are highly skilled, motivated and are reasonably priced. Wages, for instance, have remained fairly steady up north. Alberta, the oil-rich province, has maintained its current $5.90 (Canadian) minimum wage rate since 1999. Among the provinces, Alberta has the lowest minimum wage. Innovative efforts like the Career Focus Program are helping biotech businesses staff their operations and help young Canadians start on the ground floor of the biotech industry. Through the program, businesses get cash incentives to create employment opportunities for new workers.

The program will produce dozens of work-experience jobs through 2005 with the help of a federal wage subsidy that offsets part of the cost of staffing new biotech positions. Subsidies will cover about one-third of salaries paid out to participants for a minimum six-month period.

Competitiveness
Canada is the overall leader in KPMG's Competitive Alternatives study, which compares business-operating costs in 11 industrialized countries, as well as 98 cities worldwide. "Labor costs are key to being cost-competitive regardless of industry, since they typically comprise anywhere from 60 percent to 80 percent of the costs of most business operations," said Stuart MacKay of MMK Consulting, which directed the study for KPMG. The Competitive Alternatives report measured the combined impact of 27 significant cost components. For more details on the report, access www.competitivealternatives.com. Later this spring, the Web site will offer an interim update to the 2004 Competitive Alternatives data.

Taxes & Spending
There's no shortage of incentives to assist business taxpayers in Canada. The Scientific Research and Experimental Development (SR&ED) program, for instance, is a federal tax incentive effort to encourage businesses of all sizes and in all sectors to conduct research and development that will lead to new, improved or technologically advanced products or processes. The SR&ED program is the largest single source of federal government support for industrial research and development in Canada.

In the latest fiscal year, corporate income taxes accounted for slightly more than 8 percent of federal, provincial, territorial and local government revenue.

Taken together, consumption and personal income taxes accounted for more than half of government revenues in the latest fiscal year, according to Statistics Canada.

MAKING SENSE OF ORGANIZATIONS AND MANAGEMENT

The preceding "Business World" article suggests that Canada offers a positive environment within which businesses can operate and succeed. However, what exactly can make the Canadian business context favourable or unfavourable for business? That is, what constitutes the business context or environment, and what factors play the strongest role in determining whether a business will prosper or fail? This question requires a closer examination of the environment of business and of those factors that constitute the environment of business — both internal and external. What determines the ultimate success or failure of an organization? How does one identify what possibly lies ahead? Perhaps the most productive way is to get a sense of how organizations are currently functioning, and identify some ongoing challenges they face. To understand the forces that act on business, we can look inside and outside organizations. That is, we can consider key issues that can be defined as existing within the boundaries of the organization; and we can examine issues that are part of the organization's external environment. This chapter sets the stage for that examination. The next chapter, Chapter 2, emphasizes the need to manage the different forces, particularly societal ones. This will be referred to as the stakeholder framework.

CHALLENGES INSIDE AND OUTSIDE ORGANIZATIONS

The Internal Context of Business

What goes on within the walls of an organization? That is, what comprises the internal context of organizations? In Chapters 3, 4 and 5 we will consider more closely the internal context of organizations. This book will focus, internally, on three fundamental concepts: people, structure and strategy. Looking inside organizations involves a consideration of how people within organizations are managed. Chapter 3 considers the notion of management, and discusses perspectives on managing people. Organizations' fates are intrinsically bound up with the quality of decisions that are generated inside the organization. Consequently, Chapter 4 looks inside the organization to consider how organizations are designed, and why they have decided to undergo dramatic change. Chapter 5 introduces the notion of business strategy and its relevance to organizational success or failure. Following, we will expand this description of our examination of organizations from the inside.

Effectively Managing People

Chapter 3 considers the nature of the members who comprise an organization and how they manage and are managed. It does not matter whether they are non-profit organizations, small businesses or a giant multinational corporation; any type of organization must be managed. Organizations are made up of people and, consequently, this factor is clearly one that we must carefully examine. (See Talking Business 1.1.) How do we manage people within the organization? Regardless of your role in organizations, no doubt at some point in your career you will be required to apply some sort of management or leadership skills in the conduct of your job. Simply working in organizations is a reason to be familiar with how organizational life operates and to understand what exactly is involved in the art or science of management. Given the importance of this issue, we will take a closer look at it in more detail in Chapter 3.

TALKING BUSINESS 1.1   **MANAGING IN CANADA**

Nearly half of all working Canadians would abandon their employer if they were offered a comparable job elsewhere, a new study has found. Based on a survey of 3,000 Canadian employees, human resources research company Watson Wyatt found 46 per cent were so unhappy they'd hardly think twice about switching jobs. That's an increase of almost 10 per cent since the *WorkCanada* study was last conducted two years earlier. And, when asked whether they thought their's was a good place to work, only 43 per cent said they did. That marks a 12 per cent decline in the same period.

According to the latest report, some of the growing willingness to leave a job can be chalked up to the well-known "grass is greener elsewhere" phenomenon. But the survey found many respondents' feelings were, in fact, grounded in a much more serious disenchantment. For example, the survey found that only 40 per cent of employees believe they are afforded opportunities for professional growth, development and advancement. And, perhaps even more disheartening were the mere 27 per cent who said they feel job performance is reflected in their pay.

Other highlights of [the] study include:

* A growing number (76 per cent) of workers said they understand their employer's goals, but four out of ten said they didn't know what specific steps are needed to achieve them.
* Just under half of employees (49 per cent) said their company hired people with the proper skills and knowledge to do the job.
* Only a few more (52 per cent) said they have the skills and training to do what they're paid to do.
* More than one-in-five of those surveyed (22 per cent) said they are routinely asked to do an unreasonable amount of work. That was up from 16 per cent in 2002.

Besides setting themselves up for future workforce troubles — when aging baby boomers leave jobs that no one else has been trained to step into, for instance — the report warns that employers are paying a price right now. "In an increasingly competitive environment, it is vitally important that organizations take full advantage of the considerable potential inherent in their people," Watson Wyatt Canada's Graham Dodd said in a

---

statement. "Utilizing a productive engagement model — that ensures employees are both engaged in and enabled to do their jobs — can provide organizations a significant competitive advantage, helping to enhance performance, drive productivity and create maximum value."

But the apparent perception among many employees — that the prospect of a "productive engagement model" remains a pipe dream — is bolstered by a new study from Statistics Canada.

According to the federal agency, hourly wages have grown little in the past two decades. And, while senior employees have seen median wages rise by 4 per cent since 1981, new hires actually experienced a wage decline. Besides the lowering of starting wages, StatsCan notes that [more] workers are being hired into temporary jobs than ever before, and fewer workers are being covered by registered pension plans.

The Statistics Canada report, *Are Good Jobs Disappearing in Canada?*, is based on data culled from various studies conducted between 1981 and 2004. Watson Wyatt's countrywide survey of workers' attitudes towards their workplaces and employers was conducted in mid-2004, and is considered accurate to within 3 percentage points.

Source: Reproduced with permission from CTV.ca, "Survey: Many Canadian workers ready to quit" (January 26, 2005), http://www.ctv.ca/servlet/ArticleNews/story/CTVNews/20050126/canada_workreports_20050126/Canada?s_name=&no_ads=

Developing a Suitable Organizational Structure

Chapter 4 considers the internal context of the organization with regard to how it is designed and the implications of organizational design and redesign. As we discuss in Chapter 4, organizational structure is a deliberately planned network or pattern of relationships that exists among individuals in various roles or positions. This includes the formal hierarchy of authority, the distribution or grouping of work (for example, into departments) and the rules or procedures that control and coordinate behaviour in the organization.

The structure of many organizations has been radically redesigned in recent years. Organizations in just about every industrialized nation have been undergoing change. (See Talking Business 1.2.) While some companies have reduced their levels of hierarchy or laid off employees at all levels, others have undergone a concurrent change in their whole business process, while other have simply closed down. In order to understand what is happening — and, more important, *why* it is happening — we need to understand more about the design or structure of organizations. This is the aim of Chapter 4 — to offer an insight into the anatomy of organizations and, ultimately, to explain why organizations are being redesigned.

TALKING BUSINESS 1.2 **CHANGING GM'S ORGANIZATIONAL STRUCTURE**

GM is changing its organizational structure to become more competitive. The aim is to reduce bureaucracy and the rigid rules that impede innovation in car design. In the past, a new vehicle would start with designers who created the concept. Next, it would go to brand managers for their input. Then manufacturing bosses would take their turn and decide what chassis, platform, and parts to use. Finally, engineers would make a few more alterations. Little communication would occur among the parties in the various departments. The design would also involve huge delays as it made its way through the myriad of approvals required at various levels in the GM hierarchy. Under the new organizational structure, GM can focus on making better vehicles, with those closest to the market making collaborative decisions regarding the model design ... Each new-vehicle program will boast a team of engineers, designers, accountants, researchers, and product planners working in concert....

Source: Based on David Welch, "At GM Bob Lutz maps a different route" *BusinessWeek* Magazine (February 1, 2002).

Generating a Winning Business Strategy

Deciding what strategies the organization should pursue is a key task of managers. Managers are continually faced with making decisions, both minor and major, on a daily basis. The aim of Chapter 5 is to describe the nature and purpose of strategic management. The chapter examines issues that are of critical importance to strategic management. What are the key forces in determining an industry's structure, and what are the strategic implications? We will consider the roles of organizational resources and capabilities in firm performance. Our exploration will also include a discussion of corporate strategy and an identification of three generic strategies, and how organizations go about implementing strategy. This examination reflects a central internal force that all organizations must contend with — the ability to generate a game plan in order to succeed. (See Talking Business 1.3.)

Exhibit 1.1 illustrates the framework we adopt in this book, and also identifies the environment of business, which we discuss next.

The External Context of Business

We can refer to the external context of organizations as their environment. Management scholars have typically defined the environment of an organization along two dimensions: the organization's *specific or task environment*, and the organization's *general environment*. Each factor in an organization's external environment can be considered as existing in two

***TALKING BUSINESS* 1.3   POP STRATEGY**

With sales of cola and other pop falling, cash-rich PepsiCo has put itself on a wellness workout as it tries to tilt its offerings toward fast-growing health-conscious snacks and drinks ... PepsiCo, more so than archrival Coca-Cola of Atlanta, has strategically diversified outside the soft-drink business in recent years as it looks for faster-growing markets, including health-conscious beverages and snacks and international markets. Having a greater assortment of offerings also gives PepsiCo more clout with grocers, who control prized store shelf space ... The non-pop strategy appears to be working ... That diversification has put PepsiCo in a stronger market position than Coca-Cola, whose sales and profit are much more dependent on soft-drink sales.

Source: Excerpted from Barrie Mckenna, "Is Pepsi a natural mix with Evian and yogurt?" *The Globe and Mail* (July 20, 2005), B1.

EXHIBIT 1.1   INSIDE AND OUTSIDE ORGANIZATIONS: FRAMEWORK FOR THIS BOOK

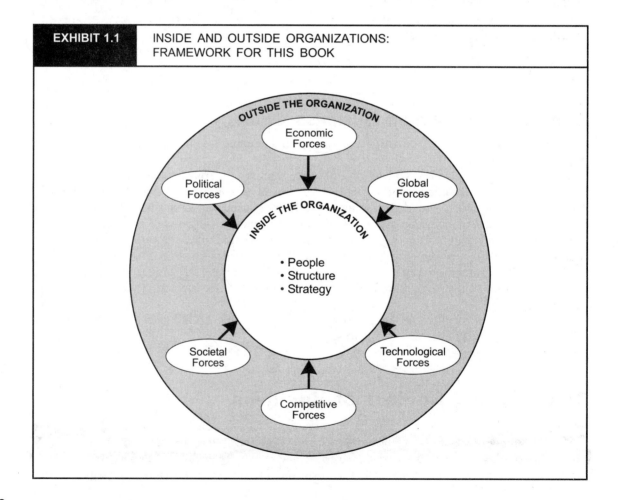

spheres: a specific sphere or environment within which the organization directly operates and a general sphere or environment that would encompass the external environments of all organizations in a society. The specific sphere has been referred to as the environmental domain of the organization. For example, changes in the international environment may be a common factor for all organizations with, say, trade agreements affecting Canadian industry in general. However, some industries may have been differentially affected by changes in the international environment via trade agreements. Not all organizations within an industry or within different industries are equally affected by changes in the environment. There are changes that affect all or some industries, and there are changes or factors that influence the direct sphere or environment of the organizations.

Specific or Task Environment

Any organization is surrounded by external stakeholders. These are parties or groups that have direct influence on the organization's ability to obtain resources and generate outputs. Stakeholders have some kind of stake or interest in the organization, and could include such parties as the organization's customers, suppliers, the labour pool from within which the organization obtains employees, competitors, unions, distributors, creditors, the local public and the government. (See Exhibit 1.2.) While not all of these stakeholders may exist or exert influence on every organization, they are the types of factors that potentially constitute the specific environment of an organization.

General Environment

The sphere surrounding the organization's specific environment is typically referred to as the **general environment**. The forces that make up the general environment ultimately shape the specific environment of the organization. Consequently, the general environment will also influence the organization's ability to obtain resources. General environmental factors typically include: economic, competitive, technological, societal, global and political forces. (See Exhibit 1.2.)

Economic Forces

Whether it is a recession or strong economic health in Canada, the economic environment acts as a strong influence on the present and future prospects of any organization. Moreover, given the strong global ties in Canada, we can also consider the international economic environment as exerting an influence on Canadian organizations. Certainly, we understand the strong influence that the United States and its economy exert on Canadian business.

Any organization, in considering how it will obtain resources from the environment, must ask the question, Is the economy healthy or weak? Organizations are continuously forced to adapt to changing economic conditions. Downsizings are more likely to occur in lean times than in rich. For example, the development of a temporary workforce was partly an outcome of the recession that occurred in the 1990s and the consequent introduction of massive downsizings and layoffs of permanent members of the workforce. Economic changes have also facilitated changes to the nature of the employer–employee

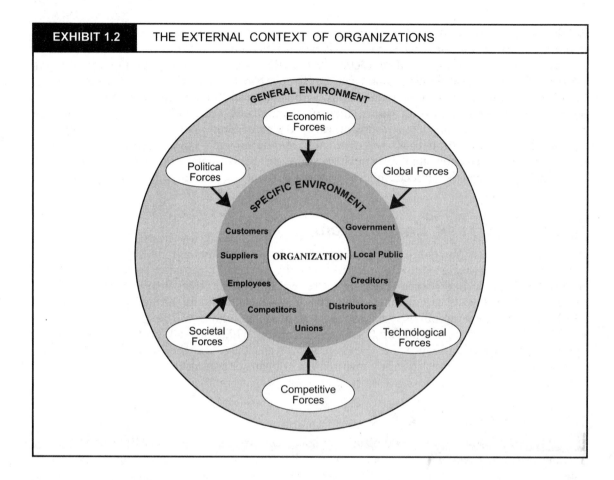

EXHIBIT 1.2   THE EXTERNAL CONTEXT OF ORGANIZATIONS

relationship. Lifetime employment appears to be a thing of the past. Consider the 1950s or the 1970s — those were times when employment actually meant security. In fact, the dominant model was long-term employment stability. However, a change to these implicit employment promises occurred sometime in the 1980s, when the age of downsizing began, with large, secure organizations beginning to lay off employees. Today, part-time and temporary work arrangements have become much more common than in the past.

Competitive Forces

Competitive forces operate at two levels for any organization. As mentioned, an organization will have its own set of competitors, yet the force of competition can be viewed from a more general level. For example, globalization, as discussed elsewhere in this book, opens the floodgates for competitors in many industries. Clearly, the number of competitors and the nature of competition will dictate changes in organization design and strategy. Competition, both domestic and foreign, certainly has demanded an acceleration in innovation among firms in many industries. Organizations, to compete effectively, must continually create new and better methods of serving customers. While globalization has opened up larger markets for businesses, it has also facilitated much higher levels of competition. Chapter 6 examines the nature of competitive forces and includes a consideration of the different stages of the industry lifecycle model. Chapter 6 also identifies the key drivers of industry evolution and how competitive forces change during the lifecycle. What are the key success factors for firms at each stage of the lifecycle? Innovation is a critical aspect of competitive forces, and we will consequently examine different types of innovations and explore the relationship between technological evolution and industry evolution. Furthermore, we will discuss the impact of technology on competitive business practices and technology lifecycle models.

Technological Forces

Chapter 6's discussion of innovation acknowledges the importance of technological forces that surround organizations. Technology plays a central role in how an organization functions, how it obtains resources and, ultimately, how effectively it competes. The technological environment exerts influence across industries. For example, in the case of Bell Canada, the increase in the number of competitors in the telecommunications industry was partly a consequence of the ability of smaller businesses to enter the industry with the increasingly sophisticated technology that formerly was the domain of big business, given its costly nature. However, with technological advances came reductions in operating costs which led to the ability to attract more competitors who could now afford to enter the industry.

Change in technology is a constant and is a force that permits and demands organizational change. (See Talking Business 1.4.) One benefits of technology is increased flexibility in work arrangements. Telework, or telecommuting, essentially means that, given today's technology, an employee can work from home. Typically, with the aid of a modem or fax machine, business need not be conducted from a formal office. This has also contributed to increased flexibility with regard to the hours of work. Clearly, organizations will continue to be affected by this environmental factor.

Societal Forces

Societal forces have an important impact on organizations. The nature of a society certainly is an entrenched part of any organization's general environment. For example, we have witnessed an increasing concern for individual welfare in the workplace as societies become more cognizant of human rights and how people should be treated. Consequently, the workplace increasingly emphasizes organizational justice — how employees are treated. This has translated into greater laws governing fairness in the workplace. One such area that has been dramatically affected is compensation. Pay equity has been among numerous issues examined in redressing inconsistencies in pay treatment among men and women, for example. We have also witnessed an increasing emphasis on merit-based pay and pay-for-performance — which all attempt to more closely link actual effort to performance instead of seniority-based pay, which bases pay on the number of years an employee has been with the organization.

Business must respond to society. Consumer tastes change, for example, and business must adapt to such changes. (See Talking Business 1.5.) Similarly, the types of organizations that serve societal demands can change. The aging population suggests that greater

TALKING BUSINESS 1.4   HARNESSING THE FORCE OF TECHNOLOGY

Downloading music illegally has been a problem for some time now. Napster pioneered the peer-to-peer technology that enabled file-sharers around the globe to instantly and illegally have access to thousands of songs. Mired in lawsuits, Napster was eventually prohibited from engaging in this activity (but it paved the way for other like-minded services such as Kazaa and Grokster). The music industry had no choice but to provide something that the consumer clearly wanted. Apple Computer, Inc. has led the way with its iPod and iTunes service. Currently making up only 2% of total revenue, digital downloading is expected to reach 25% by 2008. Clearly the music industry needs to stay innovative in order to combat sliding CD sales. The film industry is similarly attempting to harness the power of technology. Film studios are desperately trying to fight a decrease in ticket sales as well as an insurgence of technology that allows pirating to be conducted at a click of the mouse. One answer to this problem is to embrace the technology. Consumers want to download movies to their computers? Launch a pay-per-download movie site.

Technology has had a similarly powerful impact on the television industry. The life of a TV show has long been determined by the ratings. Recorded by Nielsen Media Research, each new show has to instantly prove itself, otherwise it will be cancelled, often with episodes yet to air never to be seen again. However, with the advent of TV shows on DVD, this perform-or-die ethos has been slowly changing. TV-DVD revenue has been steady, and the network heads are being forced to modify their strategy. For example, Joss Whedon's television show *Firefly*, was cancelled after only 14 episodes in 2002. Once released on DVD, it amassed a huge cult following, which allowed Whedon to bring the license over to Universal from Fox, and reunite the entire cast for the 2005 theatrically released film, *Serenity*.

Sources: "Music — Digital Downloading: Finally getting in on the act." *[London] Marketing Week* (September 1, 2005), p. 20.; Robert Poe, "BlingTones' Ringtones Crunk Out the Revenue." (June 1, 2005) <http://onlinenews.itu.int/americas2005onlinenews/article/articleDetail.jsp?id=172176>; "Movie same-time DVD releases" (2005) <http://p2pnet.net/story/6796>

emphasis needs to be placed on such industries as the health care sector. In addition, society has a certain set of ethics or values, and these can influence the type of behaviour that organizations will manifest in that society. From a societal standpoint, it is not difficult to understand the importance of adequately addressing the issue of the ethical behaviour of business organizations and their constituents. All sectors of society, including organizations themselves, are drastically affected by a variety of forms of unethical behaviour. There is a growing belief that organizations are social actors responsible for the ethical and unethical behaviour of their employees. Critics of business argue that organizational leaders must examine more closely the "moral sense-making" within organizations, or the moral conflicts that arise in routine operations and decisions, in addition to responsibilities to external constituencies. The tolerance of unethical behaviour in a society

***TALKING BUSINESS* 1.5   DISNEY CHANGES WITH THE TIMES**

In 2004–2005, the Walt Disney Company attempted to undergo significant change through the leadership of CEO Robert Iger, who planned a massive overhaul. The central aim was to re-establish Disney as the strong "brand" that it once was. One of the Disney Co.'s traditional strengths has been its commitment to family entertainment. However, Disney has recently been forced to reassess its strengths and consider riskier ventures. One such example is Iger's plan to become a bigger player in the electronic gaming industry. Up until now, all of Disney's games have adhered to the Disney values. Recognizing changing consumer tastes, Disney has plans to expand their titles to include more violent games. For example, Iger approved the production of "Turok," a dinosaur hunting game. The game contains graphic violence but it also may appeal to a wider audience. Consequently, Igor commented how the game will be distributed: "You're never going to see a Turok attraction in one of the theme parks."

As well, with the closure of their last hand-drawn animation facility in Sydney in mid-2006, Disney will branch out into computer animation (which began with 2005's *Chicken Little*) and embrace this new technology in order to remain relevant. Iger will also be looking at how the various properties will be delivered. "If we sit back and rely on old technology, the consumer is going to pass us by," Iger says. "It's extremely important as I enter this new role that I not let that happen to the Walt Disney Co. We're not a technology company, but we need to be the closest thing to that." Disney will move to bring hit TV shows, such as *Desperate Housewives* and *Lost* to the Internet, enabling consumers to download them at will on various devices such as Apple's iPod, or on the Sony Playstation Port (PSP) in the Universal Media Disc (UMD) format. There are also currently discussions taking place to bring various Disney titles to cell phones.

Sources: "Better Mousetrap: In Shakeup, Disney Rethinks How It reaches Audiences; Iger seeks High Tech Delivery of Movies, TV Shows; Theatre owners worry; 'Housewives' on a handheld" by Merissa Marr. *Wall Street Journal.* (Eastern Edition) (October 1, 2005) p. A.1; "Business: Restoring magic; Disney" *The Economist* (July 16, 2005) 376(8435): 59; "Disney to Close Last Hand-Drawn Animation Studio" (July 27, 2005) <http://www.cbc.ca/story/arts/national/2005/07/27/Arts/disneyanimation050727.html>

would seem to be a precursor to the acceptance of corporate unethical behaviour. This is an issue that we will more fully explore in Chapter 2, which also emphasizes the requirement for organizations to manage all forces and the stakeholders embedded in each force.

Global Forces

Global forces, in many ways, are forces that could be embedded in general economic, political, technological or societal forces — but are international in nature.

The tragic and devastating events of September 11, 2001, resulted in a chain reaction of international consequences, including changes in economic and political forces acting on organizations. Global events have an increasingly important impact on local organizations. While there is no universally agreed-upon definition of *globalization*, it is useful to consider this concept as a process: that is, a process involving the integration of world economies. The presence of trade blocs reflects the accelerating pace with which nations are integrating their economies. Globalization also includes the globalization of markets — the notion that consumer preferences are converging around the world. Whether it is for products made by McDonald's, Sony, Gap or Nike, organizations are increasingly marketing their goods and services worldwide. On the other side, production is increasingly becoming a global affair. Businesses will set up operations wherever it is least costly to do so.

Certainly, international trade agreements are global agreements among governments that are changing the nature and functions of many businesses. A Canadian organization may not simply consider consumers within the domestic borders, but may have a significant consumer market overseas; this demands a knowledge of global societies, global competitors and other forces that exist on an international level.

The global forces of the general environment underscore the increasingly tangled web of players in the global business context — domestic and foreign competitors, domestic and foreign workers, domestic and foreign industry, government, national cultures and economies. How business is conducted in light of trade agreements and global arrangements is a key issue for our entire society. And this is a theme we will explore more fully in Chapter 7.

Political Forces

Political forces can exert influence at both the specific and general levels. The government's push toward deregulating many industries was not solely aimed at the telecommunications industry, but rather was designed to welcome more competitors into the Canadian business sector and facilitate freer trade between Canada and the United States. The reduction in trade barriers worldwide has also opened the doors for increasing presence of foreign competition in many industries. Deregulation and privatization, discussed in another chapter, are clear examples of the importance of considering the effect of governmental changes on business strategy. Are government regulations facilitating, or restricting, certain business strategies? The political environment of business can dictate changes in how business competes, or what services it offers and how they can be offered. As we will discuss in a later chapter, the deregulation of protected industries in the 1980s and 1990s created competition for companies where no real competition had previously existed. Industries such as telecommunications, banking, energy and aerospace were dramatically affected by these governmental/regulatory changes. As the dominant companies in these industries were forced to compete in an open market, some responded by downsizing their workforce.

In a general sense, the traditional relationship of government with business is clearly undergoing change. The trend toward increased government involvement after World War II seems to have reversed by about 1980. In fact, some observers have suggested that this massive disposal of government-owned assets and the reduction of government controls in the business sector indicate a minor revolution of sorts. We will examine this issue in more detail in Chapter 8.

THE EXTERNAL ENVIRONMENT IN CANADA

From the above description of the environment, it can be observed that there is an overlap of factors between the general environment and the specific environment. An organization may have a specific market niche or set of consumers; but demographic changes in the general environment, such as an aging society, will certainly translate into changes to consumer tastes at the specific environment level. Similarly, as noted above, the government's aim to reduce trade barriers at a national level can translate into regulation within an organization's specific environment, or can result in increased competition within the organization's specific environment. This underlines the importance of understanding the impact of the general external environment or the specific environment of the organization. Let's revisit each of the external environmental forces with regard to the Canadian context of organization.

Economic Forces in Canada

What are some of the indicators of the current state of health of the Canadian economic scene? One indicator of the health of the economy is GDP — **gross domestic product**: the total value of a country's output of goods and services in a given year. The money that is earned from producing goods and services goes to the employees who produce them, to the people who own businesses and to the governments in the form of taxes. The general trend of governments worldwide is to reduce their share of GDP. Obviously, it is good for GDP to grow: from 1979–1989 Canada's GDP grew about 3.2% annually. By 2000, growth in Canada's GDP reached about 4%. In 2005, GDP grew by 2.9%. Currently, Canada's economy is expected to see compounded annual growth of 2.5% until 2025.[1] (See Exhibit 1.3 for GDP growth since 1999 and including the second quarter of 2006 which saw a 2.0% rise in GDP).

The future health of the Canadian economy, as in most economies, is continually the subject of speculation. It appears that economists are not necessarily more accurate in their predictions of economic well-being than are those looking into the proverbial crystal ball. It would seem crucial to understand what underlying forces are ultimately shaping the state of our business system in Canada. This amounts to distinguishing between short-term changes in the domestic economy and ongoing trends in the nature of the business enterprise system. It may be more manageable for us to consider what has been going on around us in recent years and assess what conditions will continue to persist in the coming years.

The unemployment rate increased sharply in the early part of the 1990s due to the severe 1991–1992 recession and the steepest drop in economic activity since the Great Depression of the 1930s. While much of the 1990s were not bright for employment, we have witnessed vast improvements in recent years. By 1999, the unemployment rate dropped to 7.6%; in 2005 it dropped to 6.7%, which was the lowest level achieved in three decades. This decrease in unemployment continued to drop in 2006, reaching a low of about 6%. The number of employed individual peaked at 16 million in 2005, which was about 63% of the working-age population. (See Exhibit 1.4.)

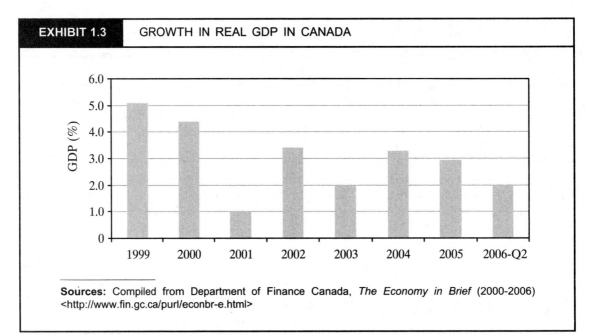

EXHIBIT 1.3   GROWTH IN REAL GDP IN CANADA

Sources: Compiled from Department of Finance Canada, *The Economy in Brief* (2000-2006)
<http://www.fin.gc.ca/purl/econbr-e.html>

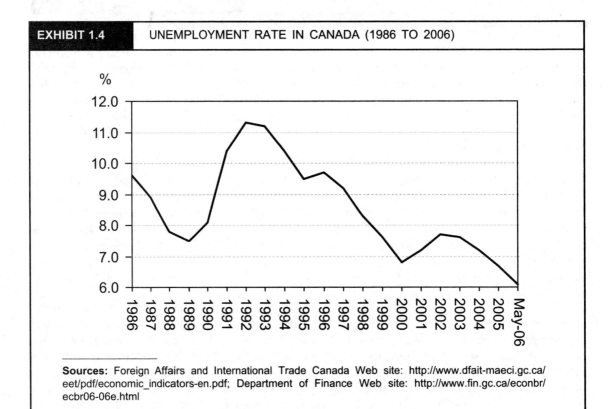

EXHIBIT 1.4   UNEMPLOYMENT RATE IN CANADA (1986 TO 2006)

Sources: Foreign Affairs and International Trade Canada Web site: http://www.dfait-maeci.gc.ca/
eet/pdf/economic_indicators-en.pdf; Department of Finance Web site: http://www.fin.gc.ca/econbr/
ecbr06-06e.html

Political Forces in Canada

The Canadian economic system has been described as a mixed system. This refers to the notion that while we possess a capitalist economy, government nonetheless plays an important role. In fact, historically, government has played a critical role in the Canadian economy. In Canada, we have a long history of government involvement in business in the sense of promoting and protecting our industries. Tariffs on imported goods were designed to protect our domestic business by making the cost of foreign goods more expensive relative to those of Canadian goods. It can be argued that a large portion of Canada's industrial development is due to protectionism through tariffs first imposed in 1879 by Sir John A. Macdonald's National Policy. Eventually, the government also offered direct incentives for industrial and resource development. "Incentive programs" were established to encourage managers to conduct business in a manner desired by the government.

Managers may decide to, say, invest in a new product development, or engage in greater export activities, or to locate in an underdeveloped region. Consequently, government incentives will be offered to engage in such activities. Receiving government financial support or reward for such activities would influence decisions to engage in these activities. (See Talking Business 1.6.)

Competitive Forces in Canada

When you think "Canadian business," what picture do you conjure in your mind? Looking back over Canada's past, it has been argued that we established a certain pattern for ourselves in terms of the type of business activity we emphasized here. During most of our existence, we have developed as a largely open economy, trading internationally, primarily,

---

TALKING BUSINESS 1.6   GOVERNMENT AID TO BUSINESS

In Canada, recent issues concern the degree to which government can or should help businesses compete — whether in the form of direct subsidies, tax incentives or some other forms of protectionism. For example, one recurring controversy in recent years is the level of government subsidies to businesses operating in the global marketplace and government support for research and development programs. One recent controversy involved an ongoing dispute regarding government subsidies to Canada's aerospace giant Bombardier and its main competitor in the jet market, Embraer SA (Empresa Brasileira de Aeronáutica S.A.) of Brazil. The recent lumber dispute highlighted in Talking Business 8.6 in Chapter 8 is another example of the difficulty in establishing the degree to which government should aid business. In Chapter 8 we will assess some of the ways government can or should be involved in business activity.

---

in resources. Specifically, Canada, for most of our existence, has focused on the extraction and processing of our natural resources. It has been suggested that our emphasis on the export of our natural resources, typically in a relatively unprocessed state, made us more akin to a simple supplier of raw materials, whether it has been logs and lumber, pulp and newsprint, unrefined minerals, agricultural crops, etc. In fact, it has been argued that our corporations are much more involved in the extraction and processing of natural resources than most other countries at comparable stages of economic development. This pattern has led critics to suggest that we have not developed the entrepreneurial and technological expertise of other nations, who used our "raw materials" and added value through their own technological resources. However, it would be unfair to suggest that this is the whole picture. The fact is, we have witnessed major changes in the nature of our economic sector, and we continue to see a major transformation in our economy and in the types of business competitors we have created. As with any capitalist-based system, Canada views competition as an important part of the business enterprise system!

Imagine a situation where there is only one provider of an important good. If society requires this good, then they must be willing to accept whatever price the provider demands. There is also no assurance regarding the quality of the good. There is little incentive for the provider of this good to be efficient in operations — any high costs can be passed on to the consumer in the form of high prices. Similarly, there is little need to innovate or produce higher quality products for the consumer, given that there is no risk of losing this captive market. Consequently, competition is considered to be an important element: this entails firms competing with each other to provide better products at lower prices in order to increase sales and profits.

Pure competition, sometimes referred to as **perfect competition**, exists when there are many small firms producing an identical product, and consequently no single producer has the power to affect the price of the product. Traditionally, the agricultural industry is an example of this type of competition, given the identical nature of the products and the fact that no single producer can influence prices. In fact, these companies are forced to respond obediently to prices set in the market. **Monopolistic competition** involves a large number of small firms whose product or service is perceived as slightly different. As a result, each firm has some influence on the prices, such as may be the case with retail operations. An **oligopoly** exists where there are a small number of producers with a different product. For example, car manufacturers have significant control over prices, and yet competition does play a role in the prices set. Finally, a monopoly exists where there is only one seller or producer.

Our economic system is based on the assumption that sufficient competition exists among business enterprises to ensure that business provides the goods and services required by society at a fair cost. Competition is the "invisible hand" that ensures the market works in this manner. However, if an industry is relatively concentrated, then businesses can act as price setters, not price takers. Of course, with extreme concentration, as is the case with a monopoly, then business can set the price itself or collude with other businesses. Observers suggest that Canada has not taken as strict a stance on industry concentration as the United States, where legislation has been aimed at preventing industry concentration. In Canada, government-legislated competition policy does attempt to discourage industry concentration, but also seeks to control the potential inequities created when a small number of firms dominate a particular market. (See Talking Business 1.7.)

***TALKING BUSINESS* 1.7   COMPETITION**

How does the Canadian corporate landscape shape up in terms of the relative numbers of business competitors? Well, looking across industries, what we tend to see is domination by a relatively small number of firms. That is, we have a relatively small number of corporations in any particular industry. This has been referred to as "industrial concentration in the economy." Statistics Canada recently estimated that the largest 25 firms in Canada are responsible for about 25% of total profits generated in the business sector and own about 41% of the total assets. Of course, some industries are more concentrated than others. For example, we have relatively few large players in the brewery industry, in banking and among department stores.

Technological Forces in Canada

Traditionally, Canada's economy has been resource based. This refers to our emphasis on industries like agriculture, mining, forestry, fisheries, minerals and energy. Natural resources have constituted the bulk of Canada's exports. Given the nature of our primary industries, one important implication is that prices for the output of these industries are very much influenced by the world market. That is, these natural resource industries are highly affected by any fluctuations in the global supply and demand for these commodities, suggesting that many of our industries are highly sensitive to changes in the global or world market. A general criticism that has been levelled at the Canadian business environment is that we need to catch up in the area of technology and innovation rather than relying on our natural resources in largely unprocessed forms.

However, the Canadian economy has been transforming. We have already seen significant changes in the sectoral composition of Canada's economy over the 20th century. At the beginning of the 20th century, there was a balance between employment in the primary sectors of the economy and the industrial and service sectors. What we mean by the primary sector is agriculture, mining, logging, fishing, hunting and trapping. The industrial sector is akin to the manufacturing or goods-producing sectors, while the service sector can include things like the hotel or restaurant industry. At the beginning of the 20th century, we had an abundance of employment in the primary sector, with most of this coming from the agricultural sector. However, even early in the century Canada witnessed a steady decline in agricultural employment right up until World War II — after which time this decline continued even more rapidly.

Canada's employment has clearly shifted away from the agricultural sector. Why? A number of reasons have been offered. Perhaps one of the most obvious reasons for the decline in agricultural employment is a reduced need for human capital: that is, part of the reason is simply due to technological advances that have made human labour obsolete. Many areas have become increasingly mechanized and, consequently, require far fewer workers to achieve the same level of output. Concurrent to this decline has been the increasing urbanization of the Canadian population: increasing numbers of Canadians continue to flock to cities from rural areas in search of employment, and it is the cities that attract the largest share of new immigrants.

If there has been a significant shift in employment away from the agriculture sector, the question is, Where has it shifted to? What we have seen happening in conjunction with that decline in Canada is great increases in the number of Canadians employed in goods-producing and service industries. The manufacturing sector produces tangible goods, such as clothes, oil, food, machines and automobiles. The service sector includes things like banking, insurance, information, marketing, accounting, hospitality and food services, recreation and so on.

The shift to the manufacturing and service sectors was particularly striking in the first 15 years following World War II, after which growth in these areas slowed, although it certainly continued throughout the sixties, seventies and eighties. However, what is particularly striking in the later post-war period is the simultaneous rise in service sector employment, and, at least since the 1950s, the rapid decline in goods-producing industries. We continue to witness this trend, albeit at a reduced rate. Consider this: in 1950, only 42% of Canadians were employed in service-producing industries; by 1993, the figure had risen to over 72%. Whereas at the turn of the century we shifted from an agricultural to an industrial economy, the second shift has been the transition from a goods-producing to a service-oriented economy. This shift is summed up in the observations in Talking Business 1.8.

TALKING BUSINESS 1.8   INFORMATION TECHNOLOGY

Canada's information technology sector will replace rocks and trees as the dominant force in the economy over the coming decade, according to a study from the Toronto Dominion Bank. Despite the recent weaknesses in the New Economy industries, their growth will continue.... By 2010, Canada's economy is expected to be even less resource-based, more heavily wired and more service-driven than ever before.... By that time the New Economy is expected to reach 12.6% of gross domestic product, effectively closing the gap with the resource sector. Currently, these industries account for 8% of GDP, triple the amount in the early 1980s.... The bank defined the New Economy as eight industries in the area of information technology — four in manufacturing and four in services. Those in manufacturing include communications and electrical equipment; office and business machines; communications, energy, wire and cable; and scientific equipment. Services include telecommunications — both broadcasting and carriers — computers and software sectors. Meanwhile the resource sector, which includes oil and gas, agriculture, forestry, fishing and logging, and resource-based manufacturing, continues to decline, currently accounting for 14.5% of the economy, down from 17% two decades ago....

Source: Excerpted from Marian Stinson, "New economy still seen as future" *The Globe and Mail* (May 31, 2001).

Why are we moving away from the natural resources and the manufacturing sector to the service sector? What is driving this shift? Well, there is not really one accepted reason for this transformation to a service economy. But probably the most often cited reason is technology: just as mechanization of agricultural production decreased the need for human capital, more generally the increasing mechanization of manufacturing facilities has similarly reduced the need for human labour in this sector. We can produce comparable levels of output with far less labour than we did in the past. This is referred to as a productivity improvement. And as far as productivity is concerned, what we have seen is labour productivity growth in manufacturing outpacing productivity growth in services. (See Exhibit 1.5.) Why?

Consider the nature of many service-oriented jobs: social workers who counsel youths, waiters who serve customers, and medical caregivers who treat patients are not easily replaced by machinery. Productivity growth in this sector is thus much slower than in the manufacturing sector. The result of this difference in productivity growth rates is that more Canadians need to be employed in services in order to maintain the relative levels of service and manufacturing output.

EXHIBIT 1.5	EMPLOYMENT BY INDUSTRY (IN THOUSANDS)				
	2001	**2002**	**2003**	**2004**	**2005**
All industries	14946.2	15310.4	15672.3	15947.0	16169.7
GOODS-PRODUCING SECTOR	3779.9	3878.6	3925.7	3989.8	4002.4
Agriculture	323.3	325.4	332.4	326.0	343.7
Forestry, fishing, mining, oil and gas	278.9	270.3	281.6	286.6	306.4
Utilities	124.4	131.9	130.5	133.3	125.3
Construction	824.3	865.2	906.0	951.7	1019.5
Manufacturing	2229.0	2285.9	2275.2	2292.1	2207.4
SERVICES-PRODUCING SECTOR	11166.2	11431.8	11746.6	11957.2	12167.3
Trade	2363.3	2409.3	2467.8	2507.1	2574.6
Transportation and warehousing	775.8	760.7	790.9	799.4	793.6
Finance, insurance, real estate and leasing	876.7	895.1	917.0	960.6	987.8
Professional, scientific and technical services	986.5	987.1	1003.6	1018.3	1050.0
Business, building and other support services[1]	537.2	579.6	608.7	630.2	654.4
Educational services	981.6	1007.4	1027.1	1035.7	1106.1
Health care and social assistance	1540.4	1617.3	1679.2	1733.4	1734.6
Information, culture and recreation	709.4	715.1	714.6	738.0	735.1
Accommodation and food services	943.2	985.1	1005.5	1012.4	1004.5
Other services	666.8	686.2	713.1	696.6	693.4
Public administration	785.4	788.9	819.0	825.5	833.1

1. Formerly Management of companies, administrative and other support services.

Source: Statistics Canada, CANSIM, table (for fee) 282-0008 and Catalogue no. 71F0004XCB. (Last modified: 2005-09-08.) <http://www40.statcan.ca/101/cst01/econ10.htm> [Accessed Nobember 7, 2006].

Whatever the source, there is little question that services are playing a much greater role in our economy than they have in the past. However, one final question that we can ask related to all this is, Is this shift a good thing? Let's consider several implications of this transition.

On an individual level, anyone planning on entering the job market or remaining employable must consider his or her skill set. Obviously, our workforce must be better educated and capable of attaining the relatively higher skill levels required in the highly paying service sector jobs (in comparison to the manufacturing sector). The notion of the **knowledge worker**, a relatively recent buzzword, underscores the increasing importance of higher education and the value of transferable skills.

But in broader terms, is the service sector better for our economy? Or is manufacturing still very much a critical element? A number of observers suggest that we should say "good riddance" to the old, outdated manufacturing sector and welcome the growing service sector with open arms. For example, economist Nuala Beck, in her popular book *Shifting Gears: Thriving in the New Economy*, referred to a "new knowledge economy" that is quickly replacing the old mass-manufacturing economy. Beck observed that these "knowledge workers" now make up 30% of North America's workforce, while only 10% are actually involved in production. Further, it is the more knowledge-intensive new industries (like the high-tech industries) that are creating most of the jobs and driving the economy.

Societal Forces in Canada

Demographics comprises the characteristics of a population (e.g., age, sex, income, employment status, etc.). What are some defining characteristics of our population? First, there are not many of us — relatively speaking. Canada's total population of approximately 31 million is among the smallest of the industrialized nations. It has been observed that our relatively small market has made it extremely difficult to develop more than a handful of domestic manufacturers of a stature capable of competing on the world markets. Moreover, it has been asserted that Canada has generated too many small operations that have been protected for too long by government. What are the implications of this? Many businesses see an urgent need to expand their markets beyond Canadian borders.

Demographic (population) trends have a significant effect on business planning and activities. In the 20 years following World War II (1946–1966), Canada witnessed an unusual phenomenon. Large numbers of war veterans, aided by government grants, got married and acquired housing for their families. In addition, the hundreds of thousands of immigrants who were entering Canada annually also needed housing. Four children per family was the norm. These were *baby boomers*. This explosive growth in population and family formation led to a 20-year boom in many industries (e.g., housing, furnishings, children's clothing, etc.).

Today, other important demographic trends have emerged that will have a great impact on the next few decades. For example, consider the *aging population*. (See Talking Business 1.9.) The demographics of the workforce have changed gradually over the years, and among these changes we have witnessed a graying or aging of the workforce. In 1921 the median age of the Canadian population was under 24 years; by 1993 it had risen to

***TALKING BUSINESS* 1.9   AN AGING WORKFORCE**

The challenges of dealing with a changing workplace demographic were also noted in a recent report by economist Bill Robson for the C.D. Howe Institute, entitled, *Aging Populations and the Workforce: Challenges for Employees.* The report suggested that over the next 20 years, both business and government will need to adapt numerous employment practices and social policies to meet the changing demands of an aging workforce, and a workforce that is more highly educated and largely female. Currently, the federal government has been initiating training and labour policy changes that recognize the aging of the workforce. Recently, the Minister of Human Resources and Development suggested, for example, that Canada accept more immigrants to replace retiring workers. According to the report, private-sector employers will also require new recruitment and training strategies to manage an older workforce and a greater immigrant population.

over 33 years. The median age continues to rise, and could be as high as 50 by the year 2036. In 1981, the largest age bracket was the group between 15 and 24. Population projections show that by 2006, the largest group will be the 40–49 age bracket, and by 2031 it will be the 70–74 age bracket. By 2011, the portion of the population over 65 and 75 will be about double what it was in 1981 (9.7%). At the same time, the portion of the population that is very young continues to decrease because of declining birth rates since the mid-1960s (e.g., in 1971 about 30% of the Canadian population was between 6 and 19; by 2001, it had dropped to about 20%). So businesses will cater to an older population: health care, recreation, travel are among the industries that are predicted to benefit from an older population.

One other major change in the makeup of the workforce is *women in the workforce.* The growing number of women in the workforce is another trend that will have a significant impact on business. In 1921 only 20% of the female population worked outside the home. By the 1990s the figure had risen to about 60%. Exhibit 1.6 shows trends in labour participation rates by gender and age group. There are also some interesting patterns to observe within the workforce. Now into the 21st century, we see the continued increase in the number of women in the workforce. We are also observing an increase in the cultural diversity of organizations — a greater heterogeneity of races and nationalities. The changing cultural mix of organizations demands that we place greater attention on efforts to effectively integrate the variety of cultures, along with men and women in the workplace.

Global Forces in Canada

The United States.   Clearly, our proximity to the United States is an element that influences the nature of our business environment. Keep in mind that the United States has a population that is approximately 10 times that of Canada. And though we possess

EXHIBIT 1.6	LABOUR FORCE CHARACTERISTICS				
	2001	**2002**	**2003**	**2004**	**2005**
	'000s				
Population 15 years and over	24,444.3	24,797.3	25,106.5	25,443.4	25,805.5
Labour force	16,109.8	16,579.3	16,958.5	17,182.3	17,342.6
Men	8,690.5	8,907.1	9,066.8	9,164.4	9,250.2
Women	7,420.2	7,673.0	7,887.2	8,019.0	8,097.7
Employed	14,946.2	15,310.4	15,672.3	15,947.0	16,169.7
Full time	12,242.5	12,439.3	12,705.3	12,998.1	13,206.2
Part time	2,703.7	2,871.1	2,967.0	2,948.9	2,963.5
Unemployed	1,163.6	1,268.9	1,286.2	1,235.3	1,172.8
	%				
Employment to population ratio	61.1	61.7	62.4	62.7	62.7
Participation rates (15 years and over)	65.9	66.9	67.5	67.5	67.2
15–24 years	64.7	66.6	67.4	67.0	66.0
Men	66.1	67.8	68.3	67.9	66.2
Women	63.2	65.3	66.4	66.1	65.8
25–44 years	86.3	86.9	87.1	87.4	87.1
Men	92.1	92.3	92.5	92.4	92.3
Women	80.4	81.3	81.7	82.3	81.8
45 years and over years	48.9	50.3	51.8	52.3	52.6
Men	56.8	58.1	59.2	59.6	59.9
Women	41.6	43.2	45	45.6	45.9
65 years and over years	6.1	6.7	7.5	7.7	8.1
Men	9.4	10.3	11.5	11.8	12.1
Women	3.4	3.8	4.2	4.5	5.0
Unemployment rate	7.2	7.7	7.6	7.2	6.8

Source: Statistics Canada, CANSIM, tables (for fee) 282-0002 and 282-0022. (Last modified: 2006-01-25.) <http://www40.statcan.ca/l01/cst01/econ10.htm> [Accessed November 26, 2006].

one of the largest countries in terms of land mass, the bulk of our population lives within 200 km of the Canada–U.S. border. In fact, the U.S. presence in the Canadian business sector is a defining characteristic of our environment. Moreover, the trade agreements we have entered into with the United States have critical implications for our business sector (an issue we will deal with later in this book).

Importance of international trade. Currently, Canada exports over 40% of its total annual production (GDP), compared to 25% a decade ago. This underscores the fact that Canada is considered to be a major trading nation. A key concern regarding our international business activity is whether we are selling more to other countries (exporting) than we are importing (buying from other countries). Other than the United States (our major trading partner, consuming more than 85% of our total exports), we have traditionally run

EXHIBIT 1.7	CANADA'S INTERNATIONAL TRADE (2001–2005)				
	2001	**2002**	**2003**	**2004**	**2005**
Total Exports					
ALL COUNTRIES (Total)	404,085	396,381	381,000	411,840	435,641
United States (U.S.)	351,751	345,366	326,700	348,142	365,800
European Union (Total)	18,728	17,867	19,902	22,833	24,543
Japan	8,340	8,360	8,183	8,558	9,119
ROW	25,266	24,788	26,215	32,307	36,179
Total Imports					
ALL COUNTRIES (Total)	343,111	348,957	336,104	356,056	379,577
United States (U.S.)	218,290	218,497	203,803	208,971	214,897
EUROPEAN UNION (Total)	39,339	39,891	40,114	42,001	45,530
Japan	14,641	15,428	13,818	13,511	14,460
ROW	70,841	75,141	78,369	91,573	104,690
Trade Balance					
ALL COUNTRIES (Total)	60,974	47,424	44,896	55,784	56,064
United States (U.S.)	133,461	126,869	122,897	139,171	150,903
European Union (Total)	−20,611	−22,024	−20,212	−19,168	−20,987
Japan	−6,301	−7,068	−5,635	−4,953	−5,341
ROW	−45,575	−50,353	−52,154	−59,266	−68,511

Source: Compiled from Industry Canada, Trade Data Online <http://strategis.ic.gc.ca/sc_mrkti/tdst/engdoc/tr_homep.html> [Accessed on 2006-03-15].

a trade deficit with most other countries (i.e., our imports have outweighed our exports), as illustrated in Exhibit 1.7.

A number of issues regarding our trade status have received much attention in the last decade or so: the Free Trade Agreement and the North American Free Trade Agreement (NAFTA) and the consequent increase in the degree of openness to international trade. As mentioned earlier, Canada's traditional reliance on trade in unprocessed natural resources has received much criticism, and its current reliance on U.S. trade has been scrutinized, as reflected in Talking Business 1.10.

Foreign ownership. How "Canadian" is Canadian business? In other words, what proportion of the corporations doing business in Canada are not actually controlled by Canadian sources?

While the level of foreign ownership varies among different industries (e.g., about 67% in chemical product and textile manufacturers, and only about 9% in communications), the average level of foreign ownership is relatively high by world standards. Annual foreign investment in Canadian companies means ownership of assets like factories, land, buildings, machinery, equipment and companies themselves. So, we have a pretty high level of foreign ownership, largely U.S.-based, in Canadian corporations — but what difference does that make to the nature of business in Canada?

TALKING BUSINESS **1.10   THE UNITED STATES AND CANADA**

... the critical importance that the United States holds for Canada as its largest trading partner, a relationship worth $1.3 billion a day in trade across the border.... Canada depends heavily on the United States as the prime market for its exported goods, and this dependency has increased in recent years. In 1995, the United States consumed 77.5 percent of all Canadian exports. By 1999, it accounted for 85.8 percent. Canada runs a large positive trade balance with the United States, but a negative trade balance with all other trading partners. If Canadian exports to the United States decline, Canada's overall balance of trade will slip into deficit territory.... Canada maintains relatively liberal trade policies and has provided favourable access to its markets for the least developed countries. However, high levels of protection still exist in some sensitive sectors, such as certain agricultural products and textiles and clothing. Eventually, Canada will have to accelerate the reduction of tariffs on these products and provide more duty-free access to improve resource allocation within Canada, and to end intermittent trade disputes with potentially important trading partners. With exports to the United States likely to decline, Canada will have to renew its efforts to build stronger trade relations with countries in the European Union and Asia, to stave off a downturn at home.

Source: Reproduced from Fay Hansen, "Canada weathers the slowdown," *Business Credit* (April 2001) 103(4): 46–49, with permission from the National Association of Credit Management.

What are the implications of foreign investment? There is much debate about this topic. In fact, Canadians have traditionally been ambivalent when it comes to the issue of foreign investment. For some, interest in the Canadian economy is a good thing. On the one hand, we want to attract investors to our country in order to help generate more business and more jobs. The source of ownership shouldn't make a difference when the results are the same — more jobs for Canadians and more money invested in the Canadian economy.

What impact does foreign ownership have on the personality of our corporate sector? Keep in mind that these foreign-owned corporations are largely subsidiaries of U.S.-based "parent" companies. One important consideration is the activity that the corporation carries on in order to conduct its business — i.e., strategic planning, research and development, marketing, etc. Many foreign-owned firms, like the car manufacturers or the multinational oil companies, operate Canadian subsidiaries largely to produce or simply market the product. These products are typically designed outside Canada, usually using imported components. These Canadian subsidiaries, then, do not perform the complete range of functions in order to offer a product in the marketplace. These are the traditional so-called **branch plants**.

Some observers believe that we will continue to see the rapid spread of branch plants in Canada, with progressively less important activities being allocated to the Canadian subsidiary. This has led many critics to suggest that these subsidiaries are nothing more than "sales offices" for the U.S. parent company. Mel Hurtig made the following critical observation regarding the significance of foreign ownership in Canada:

> In ... just over 20 years, there were 11,380 companies in Canada taken over by non-resident-controlled corporations. The total value of the takeovers was just over $548.494 billion. During the same years, new foreign investment for new businesses in this country was just over $18.040 billion. So, it was just over 96.8% foreign investment for takeovers, and a pathetic less than 3.2% for new business investment. Breaking down the numbers further: 11,380 companies over 20 years is 569 companies a year average. Or you can think of it as 3 companies every two days, and an average of 47 a month, EVERY month for the last 20 years![2]

Moreover, some critics argue that we have built up a dependence on foreign capital to supply us with the funds for business development. While this financial assistance was welcome, it brought a major cost with it — the establishment of these branch plants, and an economy that is approximately 30% foreign-owned. Moreover, it has been suggested that the presence of this branch plant economy has impeded the development of an innovative or entrepreneurial spirit in Canadian business. In other words, there is a sense that, historically, Canadian managers have not been challenged to do the strategic planning, to engage in the research and development and to develop the technological expertise to add value to the present supply of products or services. However, we are witnessing the increasing presence of Canadian-owned and global competitors, such as Bombardier and Nortel; it is important that Canada continue to move beyond its history and carve a bigger niche in the global environment.

CHAPTER SUMMARY

Understanding the context of business is the only way to get a sense of where we are headed in terms of future economic prospects. Whether you are currently a full-time student or in the workplace, an understanding of the context of organizations is a critical part of any intelligent person's portfolio. In many ways, the aim of the upcoming chapters is to shed more light on the internal and external contexts of organizations, and to consider the implications for the future of organizations. What are the prospects for business, and what are the challenges we must confront? This is the importance of the nature and context of business. This book takes an integrative approach with regard to the "inside-outside" framework. Rather than compartmentalizing the internal and the external issues affecting organizations, each chapter will consider both. Though some sections focus on the internal functions of organizations (such as Chapter 3, "Management Philosophies"), each chapter keeps the external context in mind. No organization operates in a vacuum, and so the real world surrounding the organization is also considered.

HBC: The Trials and Tribulations of a Great (?) Canadian Retailer

... Analysts are indeed finding "it's hard not to think of the Bay," as the tag line of its ad campaign goes, but not for reasons the company would like. Investors keep looking to the horizon for a white knight who has never shown up. Meanwhile, every year, management says the business is looking up; every year, earnings seem to fall further behind. "I think we have all lost patience and we're fed up," says Research Capital Corp. analyst David Brodie. "What is it they see that we don't see? Because it strikes me that [HBC's] strategies have done nothing for them over the past few years, and what's going to be so much better over the next few years?"

... Of course, Hudson's Bay Co., founded in 1670, is a survivor. From its roots as a fur trader and governor of a vast portion of what is now Canada, it has settled down to become "the dowager duchess of the Canadian retailing sector," to use Holden's words. Perhaps, as [George] Heller [CEO of HBC) and his management team promise, it will rise like a phoenix. HBC operates almost 550 stores under the Bay and Zellers banners, as well as smaller chains such as Home Outfitters and Fields. Its most profitable division is financial services, offering credit cards that can be used in HBC stores as well as Esso gasoline outlets. It had operating earnings before interest and taxes of $162 million last year — while the company as a whole had EBIT of $129 million. The retail operations have been losing money, and, says Holden, "things could start to snowball" if sales drop further, customer traffic falls, credit card receivables decline and losses increase.

In late 2003, Heller outlined a strategy to boost sales and profits, targeting earnings of $2 a share by 2006 and $2.85 by 2008, on sales, respectively, of $8.5 billion and $9 billion. To get there, the company added new product categories, such as pharmacy and convenience items, to boost traffic at Bay stores; it beefed up efforts to sell appliances, jewelry and electronics, relying less on the volatile apparel market; it pushed to improve its house brands, and signed exclusive agreements for clothing lines to make stores more of a fashion destination. It has also been busy trying to integrate its various divisions' management, back-office, marketing and distribution operations; it has made a concerted effort, through its credit cards and its loyalty programs, to get customers to spend more dollars within the HBC family. To do all that, Heller is relying on two executives he has worked with since the 1980s: Thomas Haig, formerly responsible for Zellers, is now president of HBC stores and specialty; Marc Chouinard, who was head of the Bay, is president of HBC merchandising group.

Now, the company has been forced to pull back on the growth targets Heller announced back in 2003. ... It's one thing to abandon unrealistic goals; it's another to contend, as HBC management has, that the plan in place to meet those now-abandoned goals is still working. "The current strategies with respect to Zellers and The Bay stores will remain in place and in fact be expanded upon," says a March report from analyst Jamie Spreng of Fraser Mackenzie Ltd. (Spreng has since moved to Sprott Asset Management.) "Having watched traffic counts at Zellers struggle over the years, and now seeing

The Bay stores also losing foot traffic," he adds, "this is discouraging." Sprang points out that Zellers' performance has been steadily declining despite its traffic-generating initiatives. Now, the Bay is suffering through the same problems — and the same initiatives to fix them. At the same time, both Zellers and the Bay have to deal with new players in the Canadian apparel business, such as Abercrombie & Fitch, and with the continuing encroachment of recent entrants like Old Navy, H&M and Zara.

... To a large extent, HBC's problems are those of the department store sector as a whole. "Consumers don't favour the traditional multi-storey department store anymore," says John Chamberlain, an analyst with bond-rating agency DBRS. Department stores, he adds, can "increase sales by dropping prices radically, or they're able to get margins up a bit by cutting costs, but they can't seem to do both." As for a discount player such as Zellers, it must contend with the phenomenon that is Wal-Mart. Since the Bentonville, Ark.-based retailer arrived in Canada in 1993, it has steadily gained market share — it now has more than half of the department store sector — and out-produces its competitors on a sales-per-square-foot basis. That only makes it stronger — making it harder for Zellers to catch up.

Not that it has never been done elsewhere. Hani Zayadi — former boss and mentor to Heller, Haig and Chouinard at HBC and at the now-defunct Woodward's chain back in the late 1980s and early 1990s — moved to Australia in 2001 to take on the job of turning around the Kmart division of Coles Myer Ltd., the country's biggest retailer. "The challenges weren't too dissimilar," says Zayadi, who was president of Zellers in its pre-Wal-Mart glory days. When he arrived, the most significant threat to Australia's Kmart (no relation to Kmart in the United States) was the Big W division of Australia's Woolworths Ltd. Big W had an "everyday low price" strategy like Wal-Mart, with which it has a strategic relationship.

Zayadi put in place a plan to lower prices, change the merchandise mix and build a team committed to improving Kmart's productivity. The strategy "didn't look too good" in its first year, says Zayadi, who is now head of Coles Myer's food, fuel and liquor division. But the improvements eventually clicked, and in three years Kmart was able to boost annual sales to more than A$4 billion, from about A$3 billion. Zayadi, who worked for Wal-Mart International in Canada before going to Coles Myer, admits that had his adversary actually been Wal-Mart, and not a clone, the recovery might have been more difficult. Wal-Mart "would have fought back" harder, he says. And he defends his former proteges still fighting it out in Canada. Heller and crew have strong leadership capabilities and have "earned their stripes," he says, noting the three have "managed reasonably well, under the circumstances," to keep HBC alive.

Source: Reproduced with permission from Zena Olijnyk, "Does He Know Something We Don't?" *Canadian Business* (Summer 2005) 78(10): 148–52.

QUESTIONS

1. What factors *inside* this organization may have contributed to the company's strengths or weaknesses? That is, to what degree do you think that the following areas might play a key role in the success or failure of HBC: managing people, strategy and organizational structure?

2. What factors *outside* the organization may have contributed to the company's strengths or weaknesses? That is, to what degree do you think that the following areas appear to play a key role in the success or failure of HBC: political forces, economic forces, global forces, technological forces, competitive forces, societal forces?

3. Which factor do you think played the greatest role in HBC's problems? Why?

7 Rules for Succeeding in the New Business World

Rule #1 Ally & Conquer

Global competition, a scarcity of capital and looming skills shortages are becoming major impediments to business success. ... Contracting out work to companies or individuals, locally or abroad, can help you expand while focusing on what you do best. Any task that isn't one of your company's core competencies — such as human resources, IT, distribution, sales' or marketing — could be outsourced. ... Using outside resources allows you to run lean yet bulk up when necessary. Collaborating with other businesses, whether through strategic alliances, joint ventures or research consortia, is also an increasingly vital way to grow your company. Partnerships can provide access to new markets and technologies as well as speed innovation and product development — at a lower risk and investment than doing it alone....

Rule #2 Be a Curious CEO

You wouldn't dare outfit your staff with Commodore 64s. As a CEO, you, too, must continually upgrade. Demographic, economic and social changes mean that certain skills and traits are becoming more important for CEOs; developing them is critical. The ability to build strong, independent teams is imperative as companies begin to take on higher-value-added activities to remain relevant. Especially if your company runs on intellectual capital, you require expert staff who have the capacity — and the freedom — to make important decisions; with so much information out there, it's impossible for one person to keep on top of everything. There's simply no room for the command-and-control structure anymore, says Middleton. "Having an organization waiting for orders is not using probably 85% of the intellectual capability of the organization," he explains. "It's also slow and demotivating. Everything moves faster today. If you're going to wait for your front-line troops to tell you of a change [in customer feedback] and it crawls its way up a hierarchy for a little group at the top to decide what to do about it, then by the time you've implemented the solution, you've missed the window of opportunity." The modern-day CEO must be able to lead a team and clearly communicate the company's direction and core values so staff can make "executive" decisions in line with business goals....... "We live in an era where change is constant," ... "With your organization, you have to make bets on technology trends, industry trends, macro demographic trends...

Rule #3 Be the Lifeguard at Your Talent Pool

Retirement is a dream for many 9-to-5ers, but it will soon become a nightmare for unprepared business owners. Major skills shortages are imminent as the country's largest demographic cohort — the baby boomers — gets set to collect its final paycheques. The coming wave of retirees could cause a loss of momentum that will have dire implications for business growth.... According to Statistics Canada, the population aged 45 to 64 has increased 36% in the past decade alone. The first wave of boomers will be turning 65 in 2011. So you'd better start preparing now. Herrmann suggests looking at where you want your company to go over the next several years and then determining whether you have the skills and people power to get there. "The same way you would say, 'Do we have enough computers? Do we have enough desks?' You must track when you're going to start losing people." Then, talk to your accomplished older employees about remaining with you beyond retirement age ...

Rule #4 Seek the Fountain of Youth

Generation Y — born in the 1980s and '90s — accounts for 19% of Canada's workforce, and that number is rising. In order to grow your business long term, you must uncover a new set of skills needed to attract, retain and motivate the 20-somethings of today and tomorrow. Gen Y as a group is short on commitment, thanks to an abundance of local and global job opportunities. A study by Hays, an Australian recruiter, shows that just 2% of Gen Y, also known as the Echo Boom, view a career as a job for life, compared with 12% for their senior generations. It also discovered that, on average, echo boomers anticipate staying with an employer for two to four years, compared with six years for their older colleagues. If you're not careful, you'll watch a steady stream walk out the door. If you are able to engage Gen Yers, your return on investment could climb off the charts. They're generally great multi-taskers, not to mention techno-savvy, highly educated, intelligent, team-oriented and adaptable. The key is figuring out what drives them ... But what about your older employees? A blanket strategy won't work, warns Michelle Ventrella, human resources director at Pivotal Integrated HR Solutions in Mississauga, Ont. Make your workplace as flexible as possible by allowing choices wherever you can (a menu of à la carte benefits, for example). "It's about awareness of who's in your group," explains Ventrella, "and then making the effort to find out what's more likely to be a hit or miss, as well as recognizing individual differences — within a [generational] cohort." ...

Rule #5 Keep Up with Kids

Understanding young people has never been easy, but marketing to today's under-25s is vital to your business. Seriously, dude. "It's important to keep an eye on this group because if it's not a viable market now, it's going to be in the future," says David Morrison, author of *Marketing to the Campus Crowd*. That's because it forms the largest generational cohort since the baby boomers ... This will take an appreciation of Gen Y's unique point of view. They're more sceptical of big brands and big marketing campaigns, and are increasingly sophisticated consumers because they've grown up with a huge amount of choice while having more control over their purchases than their predecessors. ... Take Burlington, Ont.-based West 49 Inc., for example. Targeting no one but echo boomers, the retailer of boardsports equipment and apparel enjoyed revenue of $87 million in 2004, up 753% over the previous five years. Grassroots marketing has been essential to West 49's success. The company sponsors professional athletes as well as 150 amateur skateboarders, and each of its 64 stores has a discrete budget with which it runs contests and sponsors local events or charities. Internet marketing is also an important way to reach Gen Y. "Online is a very effective way of talking to our audience on a cost-per-thousand basis," says Brent Laderoute, West 49's head of advertising. "Our customers spend a huge amount of time online, so we really put a lot behind the website." ...

Rule #6 Brand and Deliver

The global economy is increasing the competitive clutter, making it more important than ever to stand out. Branding is the way to do it — even if you're not Pepsi or Apple. A strong brand simplifies a customer's decisions by instantly conveying a product's or firm's distinct value proposition. A study conducted by Toronto-based Interbrand Canada Inc. determined that brand value accounts for an average of 33% of the intangible assets of publicly traded companies. "A huge amount of a corporation's value today is tied into their intangible assets," says Bev Tudhope, Interbrand Canada's CEO. "And brands are intangible assets that have real, quantifiable economic value." ...

Rule #7 Look Eastward and Upward

China and India's economic expansion creates some real threats, but even more opportunities for Canadian companies. ... These countries are set to become your biggest competitors, but they can also act as instruments to help you compete in the world market. Rapid growth in Asia shows no sign of slowing down. A report by the Goldman Sachs Group predicts that by 2041, China could surpass the U.S. to become the largest economy in the world; India could be third-largest. These countries are an enormous new source of direct competition. Thanks to lower wages, they can produce goods and provide services at a fraction of the cost achievable by Canadian firms. Two million Indians graduate from college each year, and most speak English; China and India together graduate 380,000 engineers per annum. The workforces in both countries are developing stronger technical and managerial skills. India is already a major destination for service outsourcing (mostly back-office services and call centres) and is becoming a hub of outsourced R&D and software design. ... That's where taking advantage of opportunities afforded by these emerging markets comes in. .. Using Asia as a source of cheap labour is becoming critical for Canadian companies. While wages are rising in the coastal areas of China, moving farther inland should provide low costs for decades to come. The potential for long-term growth in India is even higher ... Using both countries as sources of inexpensive labour — in manufacturing or the offshoring of white-collar work — can help you cut costs, boost productivity, bring products to market faster and focus on higher-value activities such as technical innovation. Falling telecom costs and the Internet make offshoring more feasible now than ever....

Source: Reproduced with permission from Jennifer Rivkin, "The New Rules of Growth," *Profit* (November 2005) 24(5): 58–62.

QUESTIONS

1. How are the internal forces of business illustrated in this article? Describe them.

2. How are each of the external forces illustrated in this article? Describe them.

3. Which forces are among the most powerful forces acting on business today, according to this author?

The Responsibilities of Business: Managing the Societal Force

2

What roles and responsibilities must business address in order to be successful? Managing the societal forces requires attention to stakeholder needs. This chapter defines and discusses the notion of stakeholders of business. We will look at the issue of corporate social responsibility, and analyze the debate regarding what role business should play in this area. The latter part of this chapter addresses the challenge of defining business ethics. We will examine models of ethical reasoning in organizations. The purpose of this chapter is to draw attention to the ethical dimension of business, and to encourage a more critical understanding of the ethical issues that you will no doubt confront at some time in your career.

LEARNING OBJECTIVES

By the end of the chapter, you should be able to:

1. Define stakeholders and corporate social responsibility.
2. Analyze the debate for and against the relevance of corporate social responsibility.
3. Understand the challenges of defining business ethics.
4. Explain the models for judging the ethics of decisions.
5. Discuss how organizations may contribute to unethical behaviour at work.

I would like to thank Imran Kanga, Paul Thompson, and Joseph Adubofuor, who contributed Talking Business 2.6, 2.7, and Concept Application "Mining for Responsibility," respectively, to this chapter.

The Business World ————————————————————————

The Canadian Company in a Global Mess

For 1.2 billion dollars, Talisman Energy is unloading the twenty-five per cent share it bought four years ago in a massive oil project in southern Sudan.

When Talisman moved into the East-African country, it became implicated in a long and bloody civil war between the Islamic dictatorship in the North and non-Muslims in the South — a conflict that has dragged on for nearly twenty years, killed more than two million people and displaced millions more. And those are conservative numbers.

Talisman's business partner in this endeavour was the country's government. (Sudan has been described by Washington as a "rogue" and terrorist state.) Dozens of religious and human rights groups accused the Canadian company of fuelling the civil conflict and helping to tip the scales in favour of the country's military.

That's because oil royalties earned by the government help to pay for things like gunships, bombers and "death squads" — the paramilitary goons who nailed spikes in the temples of people suspected of helping rebel troops.

It's also alleged by many human rights groups, including Amnesty International, that the Sudanese military has used a Talisman airstrip to launch aircraft for attacks on innocent civilians.

The company has insisted it was an instrument for positive change in Sudan, pointing to infrastructure improvements for which it is responsible, such as a health clinic and water wells.

But critics have blasted the Canadian company for providing "moral cover" for a corrupt and ruthless regime in Khartoum, saying that the Sudanese government was murdering and displacing innocent people so that more oil exploration could be done, more profits could be made and shareholders could get a healthy return.

The allegations cast a large shadow. Many people — and, indeed, many municipalities, the City of Edmonton being one of them — profited from investments in Talisman Energy.

One of Talisman's harshest critics is Eric Reeves, an English professor at Smith College in Massachusetts. The prof pulls no punches: "The sale by Talisman Energy of its twenty-five per cent stake in Sudan's Greater Nile oil project marks the end of a deeply disgraceful chapter in Canadian history. Canada's reputation as a stalwart defender of human rights and human security has been permanently stained by the complicity of a Canadian corporation in the ongoing oil-driven destruction of Sudan."

Reeves goes on to point fingers at both Canadian politicians and the Canadian media, saying they share some of the responsibility for allowing the company to "exacerbate massive human suffering and destruction." But, he says, final responsibility for this "moral catastrophe" must be borne by the CEO of Talisman Energy and the company's Board of Directors, as it was they who "failed to respond to the devastating indictment of Talisman's operations in Sudan, rendered by every single credible human rights report on oil development in this torn country."

But, of course, Talisman *was* forced to respond. The company's operations in Sudan had become a huge public relations nightmare, not only for the company but for those who invested in it. When all was said and done, it was the need to preserve profits and returns for shareholders that seems to have forced Talisman's hand.

Talisman CEO Jim Buckee put it this way, "Although I believe our presence in Sudan has been a force for good, we are ultimately in the business of creating value for our shareholders."

So Talisman is leaving Sudan, but its Sudanese headache will follow them. Skirmishes will continue in at least one courtroom.

Talisman and the Government of Sudan are defendants in a civil-suit launched in New York City this year by the Presbyterian Church of Sudan and a coalition of Sudanese refugee groups. The suit, filed in February, alleges Talisman and its business partner collaborated "in a joint strategy to use military forces in a brutal ethnic cleansing campaign against a civilian population."

The company vigorously denies the charges and is fighting to have the case thrown out.

Two Alberta-based groups, Freedom Quest International and the Federation of Sudanese Canadian Associations, are thinking about launching their own lawsuit in Canada.

Mel Middleton of Freedom Quest says they're waiting to see what comes out of the suit in New York. He thinks it might be possible to hold the Calgary company accountable under Ottawa's new "anti-terror" legislation. Middleton says he will continue to press for accountability and for reparations to be paid to the victims of Sudan's "oil-fuelled genocide."

Natalina and Morris Yoll of the Federation of Sudanese Canadian Associations say, "Talisman's past complicity is neither forgotten nor forgiven."

Source: Reproduced with permission from Byron Christopher, "No Graceful Exit," *RabbleNews* (November 5, 2002) <http://www.rabble.ca/news_full_story.shtml?x =16719>.

BUSINESS AND SOCIETY ———————————————

"The Business World" story underscores the issue of corporate social responsibility. What constitutes socially responsible business behaviour? In addition, should businesses be required to look beyond their profit objectives in order to help society? Unethical behaviour may be directed against the organization itself, or it may be consistent with the organization's goals but inconsistent with commonly accepted ethical principles. Whether unethical behaviour comes in the form of subtle discrimination against other employees, "padding" expense accounts, paying or accepting bribes, questionable advertising or other forms of fraudulent activity, there is little doubt that the costs of such behaviour eventually accumulate.

The media has increasingly reported a concern over the erosion of business responsibility, and unethical activities in organizations are estimated to cost industry billions of dollars a year.[1] It seems that much of what has been written in the popular press and reported in the news has tended to reflect poorly on the ethics of business. The recent phenomenon of corporate downsizings and massive layoffs has certainly contributed to the public's dim view of business. Other recurring issues that raise questions about the ethics of business include things such as misuse of natural resources, too close a relationship with government, not treating employees properly and corporations being too big and too powerful. All these perceptions, whether accurate or inaccurate, reflect a commonly held view that business and ethics do not go together.

Some scholars have suggested that there is a crisis of confidence in a variety of corporate activities.[2] Perhaps most of the blame for the current distrust of business can be traced to the recent flood of scandals that has permeated the news media reports. If anything has shaken the business-society relationship, it has been the countless, major headline-grabbing scandals, particularly within the past several years. For many observers, the rapidly expanding list of corporate wrongdoers has all but caused a breach in society's trust for business leaders.

Numerous companies worldwide have undermined public confidence in the integrity of business through their scandalous activities. The list of ethics violations is long and has been attributed to such companies as Enron, WorldCom, Tyco International, Conseco, Adelphia Cable and Global Crossing, Xerox and HealthSouth. Elsewhere, recent allegations of fraudulent activities have been levelled at the Dutch food distributor and retailer Royal Ahold, France's Vivendi, Britain's Marconi, SK Corporation in South Korea and Tokyo Electric Power Company in Japan.

Anyone who has attended to recent news reports understands that Canadian business is no less immune to corporate scandal and wrongdoing than any other business sector in the world. Consider the following recently reported events:

- Nortel fired a number of senior executives, including former chief executive officer Frank Dunn, for their connections to an accounting scandal in the company. The company was forced to restate its earnings, which had been falsely inflated.

- Canadian media mogul Conrad Black was fired as chairman of Hollinger International Inc., which, in turn, controls Hollinger newspaper assets such as London's *Daily Telegraph* and Chicago's *Sun-Times*. A US$200 million lawsuit directed at Black alleged that he was responsible for altering the company's financial records and for diverting company funds to himself, to an associate, and to other companies that he controlled.

- Canada earned the distinction of being home to a company that became the first multinational corporation to be fined ($2.2 million) for bribing a government official involved in a World Bank-funded dam project designed to provide water to South Africa. Acres International, an Ontario-based engineering firm, was found guilty of paying a bribe of $266,000 to the former chief executive of the Lesotho Highlands Water Project in Africa as a means to obtain a $21.5-million technical assistance contract for a multi-dam construction program.

- The Montreal family-entertainment company, Cinar, paid a total of $25 million in lawsuits stemming from fraudulent business ventures.

- The Canadian government, together with a number of Canadian businesses, faced charges of corruption stemming from a government advertising and corporate sponsorship program managed by the federal Public Works Department. The federal auditor general's report indicated that $100 million was paid to a number of communications agencies in the form of fees and commissions, and the program was essentially designed to generate commissions for these companies rather than to produce any benefit for Canadians.

- The Canadian Imperial Bank of Commerce agreed to pay a penalty of US$80 million to settle charges of aiding and abetting the Enron Corporation's accounting fraud.

Whether the business community will be able to adequately respond to society's expectations of greater accountability is largely dependent on the level of attention that business affords this issue. And, given the growing attention directed at corporate behaviour, the onus appears to be on business to develop a much better understanding of the status of ethics and integrity present within the walls of the workplace.

Managing the Forces of Business and the Stakeholders of Business

You will recall from Chapter 1 that this text is aimed at helping you understand the challenges of business. These challenges are conceptualized as the fundamental internal and external forces that all organizations must contend
these forces will be addressed in some manner thr
other layer of challenge within which all these for
to notions such as corporate social responsibility,
— all issues that are addressed in this chapter. As
considered as merely one of six external forces,
acting on business — both internal and external.

Managing Stakeholder Interests

Life in business organizations was once simpler
especially the modern corporation, is the instituti

> Our society today consists of many people with a multitude of interests, expectations, and demands as to what major organizations ought to provide to accommodate people's lifestyles.... In a society conscious of an always-improving lifestyle, with more groups every day laying claims to their pieces of the good life, business organizations today need to be responsive to individuals and groups they once viewed as powerless and unable to make such claims on them. We call these individuals and groups stakeholders.[3]

In their text *Business and Society*, Karakowsky, Carroll and Buchholtz emphasize the notion of managing the stakeholders of business. They suggest that in order to more fully understand the ethical dimension of business, it is critical to appreciate the concept of *stakeholders*. In fact, the stakeholder concept has become a central idea in understanding the business and society relationship. **Stakeholders** are individuals or groups with whom business interacts and who have a "stake," or vested interest, in the business. A stake can range from simply an interest in management's actions to a legal or moral right to be treated a certain way to a legal claim of ownership at the other extreme.[4]

Traditionally, we observe two broad groups of stakeholders — external and internal stakeholders. External stakeholders are composed of such parties as government, consumers and community members. Internal stakeholders can include business owners and employees among the principal groups. The notion here is that stakeholders have legitimate claims on the organization. Consequently, a fundamental responsibility of management is to address and manage the needs of differing stakeholder groups — in addition to the needs of the most obvious stakeholders, the owners/investors or shareholders of the business. Keep in mind that, just as stakeholders can be affected by the actions or decisions of the business firm, these stakeholders also can influence the organization's actions and decisions. Therefore, the management of stakeholder interests is critical to business success.

In addition to the owners/investors/shareholders, other obvious stakeholders include employees and customers, as well as competitors, suppliers, the community, special-interest groups, the media and society in general. Some observers would also view our environment and our future generations as important stakeholders in the activities of business. The importance of managing diverse stakeholder needs is evident in the following assertion by David Wheeler and Maria Sillanpää:

> In the future, development of loyal relationships with customers, employees, shareholders, and other stakeholders will become one of the most important determinants of commercial viability and business success. Increasing shareholder value will be best served if your company cultivates the support of all who may influence its importance.[5]

Managing the Challenges of the Societal Force

So what does it take to successfully manage the challenges of the societal force? An organization that adequately addresses the societal force will, by definition, fulfil its responsibilities to the variety of stakeholders. What is the connection between the societal force and fulfilling the responsibilities to various stakeholder groups? To answer that question we need to understand the concept of **corporate social responsibility** (CSR).

CORPORATE SOCIAL RESPONSIBILITY

The historical "ethical yardstick" for business has been profit — the "bottom line." Scholars such as economist Milton Friedman argued that the workings of the free and competitive marketplace will "moralize" corporate behaviour.[6] Therefore, business need only be concerned with the profit motive, since the "invisible hand" of the free market will produce a "systematic morality." Similarly, John Kenneth Galbraith argued that corporate responsibilities should be purely rational and economic.[7] However, according to Galbraith, it is the regulatory hands of the law and the political process, rather than the invisible hand of the marketplace, that turns these objectives to the "common good." Both views reject the exercise of independent moral judgment by corporations as actors in society. On the other hand, most scholars concerned with the study of business ethics[8] implicitly reject these views and instead argue that it is the responsibility of business organizations to develop a "moral conscience" and exercise ethical judgment or social responsibility.

The term *social responsibility* refers to those obligations or responsibilities of an organization that involve going beyond

- the production of goods/services at a profit
- the requirements of competition, legal regulations or custom.

Social responsibility involves an obligation to create policies, make decisions and engage in actions that are desirable in terms of society's values and objectives. (See Talking Business 2.1.)

We can elaborate upon this definition by referring to one of the most commonly cited definitions of CSR. Archie Carroll's four-part definition asserts that the social responsibility of business encompasses the economic, legal ethical, and discretionary (philanthropic) expectations that society has of organizations at a given point in time.[9] See Exhibit 2.1.

Carroll's definition indicates that there are issues above economic and legal ones that a business must confront. Obviously, a business must address economic responsibilities — it must generate goods or services that society wants. And further, a business must abide by the laws in order to fulfill its legal responsibilities. However, this definition suggests that just fulfilling these two areas of concern is insufficient. Ethical responsibilities include the standards or expectations that reflect what the societal stakeholders regard as fair. Finally, business has somewhat voluntary or philanthropic responsibilities that, while voluntary, do reflect part of the implicit agreement between business and society and can include such activities as corporate donations, volunteerism and any other kind of voluntary involvement of the business with the community or other stakeholders.[10]

Consider such acts of CSR as those demonstrated by Levi Strauss & Co., which has tried very hard to maintain strict work standards to protect employees in operations in different parts of the world. In addition, the company is consistently lauded for its efforts in the social sphere, an effort summarized recently in an article:

> Besides patching together jeans, Levi Strauss has a long history of funding projects that help patch together groups of people. Project Change, an independent nonprofit originally funded by the Levi Strauss Foundation (and still closely associated with it), combats racism in communities where the company has manufacturing operations. There are now sites in Albuquerque, El Paso, Knoxville, and Valdosta, Ga. In

---

TALKING BUSINESS 2.1   BEING SOCIALLY RESPONSIBLE

At its worst, a corporation can poison the water we drink, prop up brutal dictatorships, assassinate inconvenient indigenous leaders, kill 3,800 people with chemicals (Union Carbide in Bhopal, India, 1984), swindle billions from shareholders and governments through tax and accounting evasion, or bring proud men or women to tears by shattering their job security.

At its best, however, the modern corporation can be an incubator for human progress and wealth creation. A well-run corporation can help sustain the communities that sustain it by contributing to public programs through the payment of its full taxes and even picking up the slack or innovating public goods in space where the government cannot or will not.

...A well-run corporation can be a place where its workers — some of whom spend more waking hours at work than home — not only make a living wage, but a place where they build their self-worth and satisfy the most primordial of human needs: to be part of something bigger than one's self.... A well-run corporation can transfer know-how, capital, and culture to Third-world nations; a fusion that aids the impoverished and teaches us new perspectives that are essential to our long-term survival.... A well-run corporation not only strives to minimize environmental harm, but can help to wipe out the long trail of environmental degradation by developing new ways of doing things that are environmentally sound, such as fuel cells, wind power, water filtration without chemicals, and organic crop techniques ... A well-run corporation can make life less worrisome by providing products that meet only the highest safety and quality standards, even if it costs a little more in the short-term. ... A well-run corporation allows all its shareholders — no matter how small — to propose resolutions by providing transparency on the Triple-Bottom Line (financial, social, and environmental), and by compensating people based on the value they bring to the enterprise rather than their proximity to the firm's power brokers.

Source: Reproduced with permission from "Canada's Best 50 Corporate Citizens: An Introduction," *Corporate Knights.ca* <http://www.corporateknights.ca/content/page.asp?name=2002intro>.

Albuquerque..., research showed that people of colour were twice as likely as whites to be denied home loans, regardless of their income. Project Change established a Fair Lending Center to help customers comparison-shop among local banks and to encourage banks to lend in poor New Mexico neighbourhoods. In Valdosta, the project talked nine banks into funding mortgages for low-income first-time home buyers.[11]

This is certainly admirable corporate behaviour, but is it necessary? That is, does Levi Strauss & Co. have an ethical obligation as a business to do this? While we applaud the efforts of companies like Canadian Tire, Levi Strauss Co., Magna, Southwest Airlines, should we demand such behaviour from all organizations? And more generally, does business have a moral responsibility to us — whether we are employees, customers, creditors or society in general?

EXHIBIT 2.1	THE FOUR COMPONENTS OF CSR

CSR Responsibilities	Societal Expectation	Examples
Economic responsibilities	Society *requires* business to fulfill these responsibilities.	Generate rational business strategy, make profits, minimize costs....
Legal responsibilities	Society *requires* business to fulfill these responsibilities.	Honour all relevant laws and regulations governing business activities....
Ethical responsibilities	Society *expects* business to fulfill these responsibilities.	Engage in business practices that are in line with what society considers acceptable, fair, just....
Philanthropic responsibilities	Society *desires* business to fulfill these responsibilities.	Engage in activities that help the betterment of society — e.g., volunteerism, charity....

Source: Karakowsky, Carroll & Buchholtz, 2005

The CSR Debate

There is much diverse opinion regarding the degree to which business should practise social responsibility. Some argue that, at best, business should have very limited social responsibilities, while others argue that the social responsibilities of business should be extensive. What are the arguments for believing that business should take on extensive social responsibilities, and what is the rationale used by those who believe business should not be required to take on the mantle of social responsibility? Let's consider the cases first against, and then for, social responsibility. (See Exhibit 2.2.)

The Case Against CSR

1. Business Is Business

Probably one of the best-known arguments against social responsibility for business comes from the work of economist Milton Friedman, who argued, quite simply, that profit maximization is the primary purpose of business, and to have any other purpose is not socially responsible! Friedman points out that in a free enterprise, private property system, a manager is an employee of the owners of the business and, consequently, is directly responsible to them. In other words, Friedman and others argue that a business's primary responsibility is to the owners or shareholders. Clearly, owners and shareholders want to maximize profit, and so this should be the business's highest priority.

Some have argued that a regard for ethical values in market decisions might lead businesspeople to confuse their economic goals with altruistic goals so that they fail to fulfill the basic business function of operating efficiently. While most scholars in the field

EXHIBIT 2.2	THE CSR DEBATE

Against Social Responsibility	For Social Responsibility
1. Business is business. 2. Business plays by its own rules. 3. Business should not dictate morality. 4. Organizations cannot be held accountable for their actions.	1. Business should conform to societal expectations. 2. CSR is a practical strategy. 3. Must acknowledge network of stakeholders. 4. Long-term benefits.

advocate one form or another of corporate responsibility, they also acknowledge the difficulty of adopting an ethical corporate objective. Albert Carr argued that no company can be expected to serve the social interest unless its self-interest is also served, either by the expectation of profit or the avoidance of punishment.[12]

Consider the case of Bata. Here was a company, Bata Ltd., a Canadian-based national company, known for its socially responsible behaviour — including establishing a plant where no community formerly existed. Yet, recently, it chose to shut down its Ontario plant and move operations overseas. (See Talking Business 2.2.)

Is it socially responsible for a company to take away the jobs that it initially created? On the other hand, given the significant drop in annual profits, if the company did not move production overseas, where costs were much cheaper, the company would be in dire straits. Consequently, jobs were shifted from Canadian workers to those in China, where labour was much cheaper. Is this socially responsible? If you consider Bata's responsibility to its owners and its creditors, they would argue that it would have been irresponsible *not* to move production abroad.

2. Business Plays by Its Own Rules

This sentiment suggests that business cannot be judged by the same set of rules or standards of moral conduct that we apply outside of business. Carr, in a famous article written for the *Harvard Business Review*, raised the question of whether, indeed, we should expect that business managers apply the same ethical standards we might apply in our personal lives. Carr suggested that "bluffing" (i.e., lying), which may be viewed as an unethical practice in social relations, can be viewed as legitimate behaviour within the boundaries of business activity. Carr compared corporate activity to a poker game, whereby ethical standards within the boundaries of the "game" may differ from societal standards.[13] The "players" (business executives), therefore, may engage in activity that is acceptable within the "rules" of business, even though this activity may be viewed as unethical by the public (those outside the "game" of business). Therefore, individuals may employ ethical standards in business that differ from those generally employed in their non-working lives. That is, where "business bluffing" has been accepted as a form of business conduct, members come to believe in this behaviour as an accepted way of

---

***TALKING BUSINESS* 2.2   SHOULD THESE CORPORATE BEHAVIOURS BE MANDATED?**

CN	Established the CN Safe Community Fund, which offers an annual $25,000 incentive award to encourage communities across the country to incorporate rail safety initiatives and campaigns with local school participation.
Sears	Sears works together with the Boys and Girls Clubs of Canada to offer support and funding for youth-focused programs such as *I Can Swim* and the *Sears Ontario Drama Festival. Sears Young Futures* initiative has contributed over $3 million to youth groups across Canada
TELUS	Working in co-operation with the Alberta School Boards, TELUS provides a portion of the funding, office space and the technology to help teachers and educators develop the necessary skills to effectively use the Internet as a teaching tool and to develop online educational materials.
Petro-Canada	Provides financial support, and assists the Canadian Association of Food Banks with business planning and marketing communications directed at providing food to those in need and raising public awareness about hunger in Canada.
Home Depot Canada	Provides funding and materials to community-based organizations for the development and building of safe community playgrounds across Canada (in 2002 provided $1 million for this cause).

---

doing business. For example, union and management negotiations are subject to negotiator tendencies to demand more than what might otherwise be equitable, as a means of bargaining. Similarly, a company may convince customers that its product is worth significantly more than the cost of producing it, as a means to accrue a high profit. Members of organizations will engage in behaviour compatible with accepted beliefs, although these behaviours might otherwise be viewed as unacceptable.

Given this, why should we expect businesses to be good citizens in the same way as individuals? We might expect that a business will try to advertise its product in a manner that suggests it may be of much higher quality than it really is. That's part of the rules of business — which are largely focused on profit maximization and not necessarily on seeking the truth in advertising, for example.

Is business a game? Do you accept the notion that business is like a game and should be played by its own rules? Is it acceptable to leave our moral standards at the door, so to speak, when we enter the workplace? Recall the scenario earlier of the CEO and the gift in order to achieve the $22-million contract. Would you give the gift? Why, or why not? If this is considered a bribe and therefore unethical, why would you give the gift? The common response is because it is part of the "rules of the game." This is the expectation that, in business, this is a legitimate, commonly accepted practice. However, there is a danger in de-coupling behaviour — in avoiding scrutiny of business behaviour. First, it makes an assumption about what is and what is not acceptable in business. In this case, for example, businesses are increasingly frowning upon giving gifts to clients or customers. Consequently, what is acceptable for business and society is not necessarily a stable factor. In addition, for some individuals, it is unacceptable to trade off one's ethics in the "line of duty." The question becomes, What is acceptable for you?

3. Business Should Not Dictate Morality

Given that business enterprises are fundamentally responsible to the owners or shareholders, their mandate is to maximize profit, and that is their area of expertise. They are economic institutions, and they should leave the issue of social policy to the jurisdiction of government. Managers are simply not skilled in the area of social policy, and consequently should not be held responsible to carry out duties of social responsibility. If businesses enter the area of social policy, they are, in effect, expanding their power. How? Well, a corporation that is engaging in extensive social programs is essentially performing a political function in addition to its economic purpose. Some critics suggest that allowing business to have both economic and political power in its hands is potentially dangerous. As an article in *The Economist* argued:

> It is no advance for democracy when public policy is "privatized," and corporate boards take it upon themselves to weigh competing social, economic and environmental goals. That is a job for governments, which remain competent to do it if they choose. And when it comes to business ethics, it is worth remembering that managers do not, as a rule, own the companies they are directing. Their first duty is to serve the people who are paying their salaries, so long as they stay within the law and the canons of ordinary decency. In the political arena, the chief executive of the biggest multinational has just one vote — and that is how it should be.[14]

Consequently, those opposed to businesses venturing into the social sphere, for this reason, argue that government can simply enforce regulations to ensure that business is socially responsible rather than allowing business to take it upon itself to judge matters of social responsibility.

4. Organizations Cannot Be Held Accountable

While society may judge somewhat cynically the ethics of "big business," who exactly is to be held accountable for the actions taken by individuals on behalf of their company? It is not always easy to place blame when the entity responsible for an action is not an individual but, rather, a corporation. Many scholars have asserted that rather than observing organizations, it is the corporation's leaders and their constituents whose behaviour must be studied. Following this line of reasoning, Carroll argued that unethical business behaviour is the result of two ethical standards — personal and business. Carroll's research suggested that individuals under pressure compromise their personal standards in order to achieve the goals of the organization.[15] Similarly, Carr argued that "the ethic of corporate advantage invariably silences and drives out the ethic of individual restraint."[16]

Can we hold organizations responsible for their crimes? Should IBM be somehow held accountable for its alleged involvement in the Holocaust, as reported in Talking Business 2.3? What responsibility do organizations have to ensure their products are

---

***TALKING BUSINESS* 2.3   IBM AND THE HOLOCAUST**

A recent book by Edwin Black, entitled *IBM and the Holocaust*, offers compelling evidence that IBM played an important role in some of the most horrific events of the 1930s and 1940s in Europe. Specifically, IBM's production of hundreds of Hollerith machines, the precursor to the computer, played a central role in the first racial censuses conducted by the Nazis. Beginning in 1933, the Hollerith machine was used by the German government to identify its intended targets. As Black comments in his book:

> Nearly every Nazi concentration camp operated a Hollerith Department ... in some camps ... as many as two dozen IBM sorters, tabulators and printers were installed ... [I]t did not matter whether IBM did or did not know exactly which machine was used at which death camp. All that mattered was that the money would be waiting — once the smoke cleared.

The author suggests that IBM's involvement with Nazi Germany helps explain one mystery of the Holocaust — how so many people were killed in so little time. With the knowledge of top IBM management in the United States, IBM's European subsidiaries actually perfected the means for the Nazis to quickly collect census data for its murderous plans. Hitler awarded IBM chairman Thomas Watson a medal for his company's work.

Source: Based on Edwin Black, *IBM and the Holocaust: The Strategic Alliance between Nazi Germany and America's Most Powerful Corporation* (New York: Crown Publishers, 2001), p. 375.

---

not misused? Do businesses have a responsibility not to associate with countries that are violating human rights? Or, on the other hand, should business strategy be guided purely by profits?

The Case For CSR

Now that we have looked at some of the more common sources of support for ignoring social responsibility, let's consider the counterargument. Why should business be concerned with the issue of social responsibility? Why might business be obliged to take on social responsibility? Why should business go beyond its legal requirements or industry standards?

1.   Conform to Societal Expectations

Scholars in the field of business ethics have argued that business and society need not be seen as distinct entities but, rather, that business plays a role within society: fundamentally, businesses are created to serve public needs. It is for this same pragmatic reason that a business will not act in any way that will reduce its legitimacy in the eyes of the public. Given that the very existence of business enterprise is largely dependent on acceptance by society, there is an obligation not to violate societal beliefs regarding socially responsible behaviour — particularly if such violations would undermine the credibility of an enterprise's role in society. Scholars have suggested that the doctrine of corporate social responsibility can also be understood as part of an effort to reconcile the intentions and results of capitalism. Advocates of corporate social responsibility understand the importance of the profit motive; however, they view this as only part of the social responsibility of business.

Shareholders of major corporations have shown increased expectations that businesses behave responsibly. Shareholder proposals permit investors to present issues of concern to corporate management, and to other shareholders who can then vote in order to support or reject the proposals. Recent proposals were submitted to Hudson's Bay Co. and Sears Canada on the issue of sweatshop labour. Both Sears and the Bay have faced allegations that they purchase apparel from sweatshop factories in Lesotho, where child labour, unsafe conditions and sexual harassment have been reported. A 2002 shareholder initiative calling on Hudson's Bay Company to put in place a process to end alleged sweatshop abuses in its supply chain was supported by more than 36% of the shareholders voting at the annual shareholders' meeting. The resolution put forward at the meeting urged the board of directors to adhere to the International Labor Organization's Declaration on Fundamental Principles and Rights at Work and report to shareholders annually on compliance.

2. Adopt CSR as a Practical Business Strategy

A second, even more pragmatic, reason for businesses to be socially responsible is to avoid public criticism or scrutiny that might inadvertently encourage more government involvement or regulation. For example, we have recently witnessed a number of organizations accused of unfair business practices and attempting to create a monopoly. Other organizations, like Nike, have been heavily criticized for shutting down operations in America in favour of setting up business where labour is cheap, and in some cases where sweatshop-like conditions exist among the factories of the foreign contractors. A lack of concern for social responsibility may invite public scrutiny.

The practical side of being socially responsible can be seen in the realm of business-consumer relationships. The notion of exploiting the consumer for profits would be both socially irresponsible and unwise for any business. There are many cases of consumer lawsuits aimed at businesses who lacked responsibility for their treatment of consumers. For example, in 2002, an individual from British Columbia filed a class action lawsuit against Shell Canada. The suit alleged that Shell didn't do enough to notify consumers about a problem with its gasoline. Shell subsequently admitted that an additive in its gas was responsible for causing damage to fuel gauges or pumps in certain cars. The lawsuit also claimed that Shell continued to sell the product even though it was aware of the problem. A Shell representative issued a news release that offered a "sincere apology for any inconvenience this problem may have caused." Shell also had discreetly compensated consumers for months by offering Air Miles or free gas. In response to Shell's behaviour, a representative of the Automobile Protection Association, a consumer advocacy group, commented that "It's a longstanding principle that when you put out something that's defective, you put the word out. It would appear the company sort of ducked when they had a decision to make."[17] In a different case, in 2003, the Competition Bureau ruled that Sears Canada practised "deceptive marketing" by advertising false sale prices on five lines of automobile tires. The Bureau's commissioner said Sears intentionally deceived consumers by pretending to offer them special prices on major lines of all-season tires, while having little intention of selling substantial quantities of the tires at the regular prices.[18] These types of practices bring "unwelcome" public attention and scrutiny to the guilty businesses.

3. Acknowledge Membership in a Broader Network of Stakeholders

As described earlier, stakeholders refer to any individuals or groups who bear some type of risk as a result of the corporation's actions. Stakeholders might have financial, physical or human stakes or interests in the corporation. Who are the potential stakeholders in business activity? Among the list of stakeholders and the corporation's responsibilities to them, we can include those identified in Exhibit 2.3.

Among some of the other potential stakeholders in a business are **suppliers**, the **government** and **society** in general — each of whom may also be affected in some way by corporate activity and, consequently, must be considered in conducting business. In any actions a business takes, then, the business should consider the impact on any party that has a stake in its operations: i.e., that is affected by its behaviour. Aside from ethical considerations, there are practical reasons to attend to all the stakeholders' interests, even when they conflict: if management focuses on only the concerns of a minority of stake-

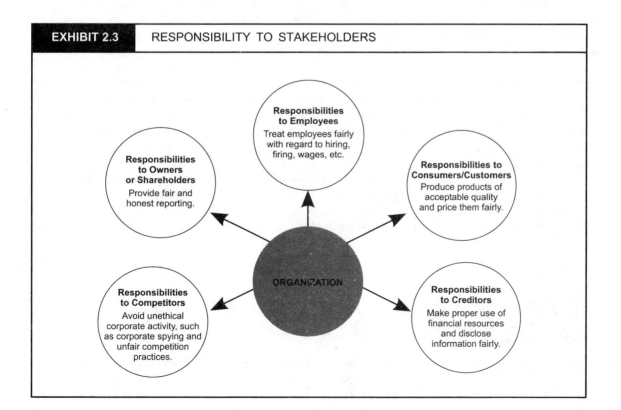

EXHIBIT 2.3   RESPONSIBILITY TO STAKEHOLDERS

Responsibilities to Employees
Treat employees fairly with regard to hiring, firing, wages, etc.

Responsibilities to Owners or Shareholders
Provide fair and honest reporting.

Responsibilities to Consumers/Customers
Produce products of acceptable quality and price them fairly.

ORGANIZATION

Responsibilities to Competitors
Avoid unethical corporate activity, such as corporate spying and unfair competition practices.

Responsibilities to Creditors
Make proper use of financial resources and disclose information fairly.

holders, such as the owners, other stakeholders may withdraw their participation with and support for the enterprise and, consequently, harm the business. Thus, to suggest that business need not be socially responsible is to ignore the fact that business enterprises regularly interact with, and affect, numerous stakeholders.

There are many examples of corporations making a difference in communities through volunteer activities. CIBC, Canadian National, Hewlett-Packard (Canada) Ltd., Suncor Energy Inc., and TransCanada PipeLines Ltd. joined together with the National Aboriginal Achievement Foundation in 2002 to establish a project called Taking Pulse. This private-sector effort is aimed at increasing the participation of Aboriginal people in the Canadian workforce. In the words of Rick George, the president of Suncor Energy Inc., "This is an excellent opportunity for involvement in creating a long-term strategy that will benefit Aboriginal people and indeed the great economy.... We are committed to corporate social responsibility and strongly believe our workforce should be reflective of the communities in which we work." Microsoft Canada engaged in a partnership with the non-profit organization Boys and Girls Club of Canada to increase computer accessibility for children who lacked the opportunity. Microsoft Canada received high accolades from Imagine Canada for its contributions to the community, including its financial donations in the millions of dollars, software, resources, online support and training by employee volunteers.

4. Gain Long-term Benefits of CSR

Advocates of corporate social responsibility suggest that even if an action does not result in immediate benefits for the enterprise, engaging in socially responsible behaviour is wise from a longer-term strategic perspective. This, perhaps, connects to the first point made — regarding the relationship of business with society. A business that fosters this relationship will more likely continue to receive acceptance from, and be considered legitimate by, the public. The notion of building and maintaining goodwill with the public and a positive image are certainly influenced by social responsiveness (see Talking Business 2.4). For example, Johnson & Johnson, the maker of Tylenol, was faced with major disaster in the 1980s after a number of tragic deaths were found to be the result of poisoned Tylenol capsules. While the cause was later found to be tampering at the retail location, not at the manufacturers' site, Johnson & Johnson took complete, extensive responsibility in withdrawing all their Tylenol capsules from the market (retail value of over $100 million) and running television commercials and establishing telephone hotlines urging the public not to use them. And this also prompted Johnson & Johnson to re-introduce the product in tamper-proof packages. While the company's social responsibility was costly, the company made up for that loss by restoring public confidence in its reputation.

IS CORPORATE SOCIAL RESPONSIBILITY ON THE RISE?

The central arguments that support the case against business enterprises taking a more active role in the area of social responsibility were outlined above. One remaining question is, Where are we now? That is, how have the views of corporate social responsibility

---

***TALKING BUSINESS* 2.4   CSR AT CANADIAN TIRE**

Ninety per cent of Canadians live within 15 minutes of one of 1,100 Canadian Tire retail outlets. This corporate giant is attempting to use its enormous capacity to reach the public to raise social awareness and affect change, according to the president of the Canadian Tire Foundation for Families.

Gordon Cressy spoke at the Rotman School of Management conference March 19 on Corporations in the Community: A Canadian View of Corporate Social Responsibility.

Corporate social responsibility is not just public relations but a new way of operating to rebuild trust between corporations and consumers in a post-Enron world ... At Canadian Tire, there are 450 independent retail dealers and the success of the company is due to their community involvement, he says. "Corporate social responsibility is about grassroots involvement." At the grassroots level, the company has a policy of double-matching local contributions to local projects and has aided more than 300 charitable projects across the country, Cressy says. In addition, the foundation plan calls for input at a time of crisis and provides disaster relief in such instances as floods and the fires in the Kelowna and Kamloops area. "We have the clothing, propane tanks and other things needed and we can supply them quickly," he says.

The Canadian Tire Foundation for Families has also developed a national program to encourage young people to become involved in sports and recreation. The foundation is partners with others including government and not-for-profit organizations to advocate for increased recreational opportunities for youth at a time when health issues and lack of exercise for young people are raising national concerns.

"This national signature program unleashes the power of the corporation behind a cause," Cressy says. "We have enormous capacity to reach the Canadian public and, working with partners, can leverage that power to affect social awareness and make changes."

Source: Reproduced with permission from John Driscoll, "Canadian Tire Foundation pushes company's CSR agenda," *Axiom News* (March 26, 2004). Web site: <http://www.axiomnews.ca/index.htm>.

---

changed over the years? What philosophy are more and more businesses adopting currently with regard to social or moral obligations? According to some observers, we are undergoing a gradual transformation that increasingly involves shaping organizations to reflect higher levels of social responsiveness. There is an increasing push for organizations to balance the profit objective with goals of social responsibility. In other words, business enterprises have begun to make greater efforts to recognize and balance the needs of different stakeholders.

How corporations govern and oversee their own behaviour has been a central issue. The long list of corporate scandals has drawn attention to this notion of "who safeguards" the interests of owners/shareholders of large corporations. Recent legislation has attempted to hold organizations more accountable for their behaviour and to offer greater disclosure of their activities to the public. One such major piece of legislation originated in the United States and is called the Sarbanes-Oxley Act.

The aftermath of the scandals in the early 21st century were the biggest impetus for change, which led to the enactment of such legislation as the 2002 Sarbanes-Oxley Act in the United States and the initiation of similar legislation in Canada. The Sarbanes-Oxley Act was introduced in the United States following the flood of accounting scandals at companies such as Enron and WorldCom. The Act was aimed at re-establishing corporate accountability and investor confidence. The Act's central purpose was to make public companies more accountable by increasing transparency or disclosure in their financial reporting. This required additional regulations governing public company accounting, corporate responsibility and investor protection. In order to accomplish this, increased requirements were also placed on CEOs (chief executive officers), CFOs (chief financial officers), and the functions that they oversee.

The significant impact of the Sarbanes-Oxley Act is evident to many observers, such as Megan Barnett, who made the following comments:

> More than just a buzzword born in the depths of the corporate scandals, good governance has turned into a new way of life for some company gatekeepers.... Under the new rule regime, boards find themselves under intense scrutiny. They have fired members who have conflicts of interest, possess thin credentials, or are past their prime. They have hired new directors they believe are beyond reproach, with no skeletons and talents more suited to the job. They have more meetings, more conference calls, and more questions to ask of senior management. They face the challenge of simultaneously beefing up controls to meet new regulatory requirements while remaining active in shaping the company's strategy. They consult more with their lawyers.... Boards must now comprise mostly independent directors, which means the individuals must not have any material ties (à la Enron) to the company or its management.[19]

While the Sarbanes-Oxley Act itself is not directed at Canadian jurisdictions, it does affect Canadian companies that trade on U.S. stock exchanges, and it has served as an impetus for similar Canadian legislation. In 2004, the OSC (Ontario Securities and Exchange Commission) presented 18 new corporate governance standards for boards of publicly traded companies. These standards are intended to make corporations more accountable for their behaviour and financial reporting methods.

Of course, how business responds to different stakeholders may be represented on a continuum from a purely pragmatic, self-interest approach to a socially responsible approach. The traditional pragmatic approach has been one that focuses on strategies that consider only the objectives of the owners or shareholders. It places emphasis on the needs of one group of stakeholders — the owners or shareholders. This reflects the notion that the primary orientation of business is to fulfill economic, as opposed to social, interests. On the other hand, there is a drive to adopt a more socially responsible approach. This approach does not ignore the responsibility of business to owners or to shareholders to maximize profits; however, this should not be accomplished at the expense of other stakeholders. Managers are challenged to use ethical principles to guide managerial actions when faced with competing interests among different stakeholders.

DEFINING BUSINESS ETHICS ————————————

Business ethics is not simply a societal concern — it has increasingly become an organizational issue that demands urgent attention. Managing ethical behaviour in business organizations requires an in-depth understanding of the many factors that contribute to employees' decisions to behave ethically or unethically. Talking Business 2.5 underscores the perceived deterioration of ethics in society as reflected in the lack of trust.

Before we begin to consider the issue of business ethics, a definition would clearly be helpful. Unfortunately, as numerous writers on business ethics have indicated, defining

---

TALKING BUSINESS 2.5 THE DISTRUSTFUL SOCIETY

Most Canadians say there is a decline in trust around the globe, yet many still agree that trusting is an integral part of Canada's national identity.

A poll released yesterday by the Toronto-based Centre for Ethical Orientation suggests that nine of 10 Canadians agree that trust is declining worldwide.

According to the survey of 2,000 people, most said they are losing trust in private businesses and government institutions.

"We found the results sobering," said Jim Allen, director of CEO. "Generally, in today's society it takes more to earn people's trust than it used to. The thing that is most troubling is Canada appears to be moving from a high-trust society to a low-trust society."

A key reason Canadians are less trusting of companies and the government, he said, is that they feel pressed by downsizing in both the public and private sectors, and mistreated and ignored as citizens and consumers.

"People have lost faith in the system," Mr. Allen said. He cited "disengagement" as a reason for the decline in trust, pointing to the proliferation of telephone voice mail and electronic transactions.

"Trust forms the very bedrock of our political and economic system," said John Hunkin, chairman and chief executive officer of Canadian Imperial Bank of Commerce, which sponsored the poll in association with McKinsey & Company, a global consulting management firm.

"Any erosion in public trust — be it trust in our political institutions and processes, trust in our capital markets or trust in our legal system — should be of concern to us all."

According to the survey, 88 per cent agree that it takes more to earn trust today, while 87 per cent agree people are less trusting now.

And Canadians are not very trusting of each other, the survey showed. About 86 per cent of respondents agreed that more people "are looking out for themselves," while 77 per cent agreed that respect for institutions is declining; 84 per cent "strongly agree" cynicism has increased.

In the survey, 56 per cent of respondents said Canadians are more trustworthy than Americans, while 66 per cent said Canadians are more trusting than Americans.

Source: Reproduced with permission from Kim Lunman, "Canada Less Trusting Now, Poll Finds," *National Post* (June 25, 2003), A8.

business ethics is extremely challenging. However, what we can do is examine what constitutes the topic of business ethics, and we can identify the models that people employ to try to judge what is ethical and what is unethical behaviour. A major weakness of much of the scholarly literature on the topic of business ethics is a failure to adequately define the construct of ethics. Often, ethics have been defined differently by theorists. Some scholars view ethics as an inquiry into theories of what is "good and evil" or into what is "right and wrong." Others have, quite simply, defined ethics as "the study of morality," the right standards of behaviour between parties in a situation,[20] and activity that we should or should not do.[21] Ethics is the study of morality or moral judgments, standards and rules of conduct.[22] The notion of business ethics has been considered as comprising the rules, standards, principles, or codes giving guidelines for morally right behaviour in certain contexts.[23]

A situation can have an ethical dimension, where the consequences of an individual's decision affects the interests, welfare or expectations of others.[24] Unethical behaviour has been defined as behaviour that in some way has a harmful effect on others and is "either illegal, or morally unacceptable to the larger community."[25]

Ethical Behaviour as a Social Phenomenon

One central implication is that ethical behaviour, by its very nature, occurs within a **social context**. That is, it is a social phenomenon and, consequently, must be evaluated in terms of the relationships among a potential network of players. The social aspect of ethics is also reflected in theories of ethics, such as Kant's **Categorical Imperative**.[26] Kant asserted that actions, to be moral, must respect others — to function in society, individuals recognize that they must restrict their actions, just as they expect others to restrict theirs.

As many scholars have observed, behaviour, in its abstract interpretation, has no values or ethical component. Therefore, what is defined as ethical or unethical behaviour represents a judgment based on a referent structure. It is further difficult to define what constitutes ethical or unethical behaviour within an organization. In very broad terms, business ethics requires the organization or individual to behave in accordance with some carefully thought-out rules of moral philosophy. While the term itself is not easily definable, one can readily think of examples of activities that could be considered unethical business practices, based on our views of what constitutes ethical or unethical behaviour. For example, types of activity that may be considered unethical behaviour include: misrepresenting the worth of a product or a business; engaging in forms of corporate spying; deciding to launch an aircraft that does not meet strict safety requirements; employee theft.

Certainly, behaviour that is illegal is, by definition, unethical; however, the reverse is not true: what is legal is not necessarily ethical. It is this latter issue that makes the study of business ethics much more compelling. That is, grappling with the "grey areas" of business presents a major challenge. What are the examples of behaviours that might be considered acceptable business practices, but might otherwise be considered unethical? Keep in mind that unethical behaviour may be directed against the organization, or it may be an activity that is consistent with the organization's goals but inconsistent with commonly accepted ethical principles. Later in this chapter we will identify these types of behaviour.

Business Ethics as Managing Stakeholder Interests

For the purpose of this chapter, we can consider one of the broader definitions of business ethics. In general terms, we can think of business ethics as the standards/rules/principles used to judge the rightness or wrongness of behaviour. Mark Pastin, a writer on business ethics, notes that, "Managers today manage interests as much or more than they manage people or assets."[27] That is a useful observation from a business ethics perspective. In fact, the workplace can be viewed, in Pastin's terms, as a "tangled web of conflicting interests vying for scarce resources."[28] A manager is required to balance the interests of many different parties: shareholders, employees, customers, creditors, etc. And a basic issue of business ethics is really all about balancing these interests, many of which may be competing (see Talking Business 2.6).

MODELS FOR JUDGING THE ETHICS OF DECISIONS

Employees at all levels invariably face decisions with some kind of ethical dimension. The decision to compromise personal ethics for the sake of organizational objectives can bring devastating results. Consider the case of Betty Vinson:

> Betty Vinson has always kept her life well ordered. ... In 1996, she took a job as a mid-level accountant at a small long-distance company. Five years later, her solid career took a sudden turn in a very sorry direction. Today Ms. Vinson, 47 years old, is awaiting sentencing on conspiracy and securities-fraud charges. She has begun to prepare her 12-year-old daughter for the possibility that she will go to jail. The long-distance company grew up to be telecom giant WorldCom Inc., which melted down [in 2002] in an [US]$11 billion fraud, the biggest in corporate history. Asked by her bosses there to make false accounting entries, Ms. Vinson balked — and then caved. Over the course of six quarters she continued to make the illegal entries to bolster WorldCom's profits at the request of her superiors. Each time she worried. Each time she hoped it was the last time. At the end of 18 months she had helped falsify at least [US]$3.7 billion in profits.[29]

Notoriety gained through unethical behaviour can be observed in press reports in recent years. For example, a number of years ago one of Canada's most prestigious law schools was shaken with the revelation that law students had lied to prospective employers about the academic grades achieved in their first year of law school. An inquiry launched by the dean of the University of Toronto's Law School indicated that approximately 30 of the 170 students were guilty of this offence. All those accused readily admitted that they had lied to prospective employers about grades earned for the purpose of gaining a potential advantage in securing employment. The shock of this offence is reflected in the words of the dean's legal advisor, David Scott: "They are enrolled in a program whose underpinnings depend on scrupulous honesty since, as lawyers, they will be expected to uphold the integrity of our system of justice by their own personal conduct. Honesty, in this context, involves acceptance of responsibility for one's acts."[30]

TALKING BUSINESS 2.6   **COCA-COLA AND CORPORATE SOCIAL RESPONSIBILITY**

In 1993 Coca-Cola entered the Indian market when the Indian government began to open up its borders to foreign direct investment and quickly gained a lead in the Indian beverage market. Over the past 12 years, Coca-Cola invested more than US$1 billion in India, making it one of the country's top international investors. The company directly employs approximately 6,000 local people in 76 bottling plants throughout India and indirectly creates employment for more than 125,000 people in related industries through an extensive supply and distribution structure.

While bringing many benefits to the local economy, Coca-Cola also presented significant problems. On April 22, 2002, more than 2,000 angry protestors assembled at the gates of the Coca-Cola factory in Plachimada, Kerala, claiming that the plant was destroying their livelihoods and taking away their right to clean water. The Coca-Cola factory in Kerala extracts up to 1.5 million litres of water daily from local wells in the region, creating hardship for local farmers due to reduced availability of water for irrigation purposes. These farmers, who depend heavily on groundwater for their livelihoods, discovered that their crop yield dropped dramatically as a result of Coca-Cola's actions.

According to observers, the indiscriminate mining of groundwater by Coca-Cola dried up many wells and contaminated the remainder, yielded undrinkable water, which devastated local communities. According to local estimates, Coca-Cola's water mining parched the lands of more than 2,000 people residing within 1.2 miles of the factory. On the other hand, company officials defended their behaviour and instead blamed the problems on area drought conditions. The local citizens were infuriated once again in August 2003 when tests on Coke beverages carried out by various accredited government and non-government laboratories found high concentrations of pesticides and insecticides in several beverage samples, making them unfit for consumption. Again, Coca-Cola denied much of the accusations and argued that the company adhered to both local and national laws for food processing and labelling. However, in June of 2005, the U.S. Food and Drug Administration (USFDA) rejected shipments of Coke beverages from India because they were deemed unsafe based on U.S. laws.

Sources: http://www.coca-colaindia.com/about_us/abo_coca_cola_india_int.html; Nityanand Jayaraman, "Coca Cola Parches Agricultural Lands in India," *CorpWatch India* (May 28, 2002); http://www.indiatogether.org/environment/water/drinkcoke.htm; Steve Stecklow, "How a Global Web of Activists Gives Coke Problems in India," *Wall Street Journal* (June 07, 2005); "Coke, Pepsi contain cocktail of pesticide residues, claims CSE" *Our Corporate Bureau* (August 6, 2003); http://www.coca-colaindia.com/quality/quality_technical.html

What guidelines does an individual rely on to grapple with ethical issues in the workplace? Clearly, a greater understanding of the ethical dimension of workplace decisions is required if one hopes to prepare to resolve workplace issues effectively and properly.

The literature on ethics is extensive and exists across a variety of disciplines, including philosophy, anthropology, sociology and psychology. However, until recently there have been few attempts to apply this theoretical framework to the specific area of business ethics. As Pastin pointed out, the challenge to scholars in the field of business ethics is "to apply what appears to be esoteric, philosophical concepts to the real concerns of business organizations."[31]

Business ethics is typically examined using normative theories — theories of how individuals should ideally behave. There are a variety of ways theories of ethics have been grouped. Among these classifications is the grouping of theories as utilitarian (consequential) or single-rule (non-consequential). We can consider two central models that have been used to describe the basis of judging the ethics of organizational decisions:

1. utilitarian, or end-point ethics
2. rule ethics

These two models identify potential methods of resolving conflicting interests within organizations. The models identify the logic or rationale a manager might employ in dealing with organizational issues that possess ethical implications.

End-Point Ethics

A major model of ethics used in the literature is end-point ethics. The dominant form of this view was articulated in John Stuart Mill's *Utilitarianism*, as a response to the Industrial Revolution.

Utilitarianism asserts that to determine whether an action is right or wrong, one must assess the likely consequences, including tangible economic outcomes (profit for shareholders), or intangible outcomes, such as happiness or friendship. For example, "What does it mean to be an ethical business person?" Utilitarianism posits that an ethical person acts so as to produce the "greatest ratio of good to evil." Consistent with this view, an ethical manager would ensure the owners, employees and customers all share fairly in the business's gain. Utilitarianism asserts that an action is ethical if it produces, or if it tends to produce, the greatest amount of good for the greatest number of people affected by the action.[32] In other words, actions themselves are neither ethical nor unethical; rather, ethics are judged based on the outcomes of such actions. That is, ethical behaviour is a behaviour that results in total benefits or utility exceeding total costs, or negative consequences. In this regard, utilitarianism ideally requires an examination of the fairness of the outcomes,[33] given that the consequences experienced by all affected parties ultimately determine whether or not an action is ethical. The "modern" counterparts of end-point ethics are cost-benefit and risk-benefit analyses.

The Consequences of Our Actions

In sum, end-point ethics is a model for ethical decision making that states that a person, organization or society should engage in the activity that results in the greatest balance of good over harm for all. In other words, where we have a number of different interests at play, we need to consider what action will benefit most of the parties. The focus is on judging the ethics of an action by considering its outcome for all potentially affected parties. It is not the process of the decision or the behaviour to achieve the outcome that are considered, but the outcome itself. As mentioned, the concept of end-point ethics is also referred to as utilitarianism. Why this strange name? Well, because we are talking about maximizing utility, or usefulness, of a decision for all stakeholders — those potentially affected by the decision. It is an ethical analysis that considers the relative gains and costs for all parties affected by a decision or action. If the benefits outweigh the costs, then we go ahead with the decision — or choose the decision that gives us this outcome.

In other words, according to utilitarianism, an ethical person will make a decision or act in a way that produces the greatest ratio of good to evil, so to speak. From a business perspective, this might suggest that an ethical manager will ensure that owners, employees and customers, for example, all share fairly in business gains. Now, how do we compare the relative benefit and harm to each stakeholder? That is difficult to answer. In broad terms, we compare the costs and benefits to each stakeholder by considering a number of possible factors, which might include social (i.e., how it affects society or the public as a whole), human (psychological or emotional impact) or economic (for example, what is the dollar impact of our decision?).

Limitations

Clearly, a major problem with this approach to ethical reasoning lies in the difficulty of estimating and comparing relative benefits and costs or harm to the stakeholders. Consider an example. Many Canadian businesses are increasingly conducting business globally. Should we be concerned if our Canadian business people are conducting business with a foreign country that has a record of human rights violations? For example, the Prime Minister of Canada has led trade missions to a number of countries with an infamous record of human rights violations in order to establish business relations. Is this ethical? Well, consider what end-point ethics suggests. Do overall benefits exceed overall harm? There are great potential gains for Canadian businesses by expanding their reach to foreign markets. This means potentially more jobs in Canada and a healthier economy. What harm arises? Those supporting such ventures argue that there is no harm generated and, consequently, they can ethically support such business. Those opposed might argue that we might be supporting oppressive regimes. So how do we judge whether, indeed, there are more benefits than harms arising from such business ventures?

A second fundamental problem with the end-point ethics approach is that, as the name implies, it looks just at the end-point, or result, without considering the implications of what it takes to achieve those results. It does not ask us to consider whether or not the manner in which the outcomes were achieved is ethical. This is the notion of the "ends justifying the means." So even if end-point ethics helped generate a solution that resulted in a maximization of the greatest good for all those affected, it ignores what happens "in-between," that is, to get to that point or outcome. End-point ethics says, start with a consideration of the consequences to judge the ethics of a decision. This involves asking at least two key questions:

1. Who will be significantly affected by this decision?
2. What is the impact of this decision as perceived by each of the affected groups?

In sum, end-point ethics gives managers a tool for analyzing business decisions. This line of thinking basically asks us to consider the following: Who counts most in our decision, and how are they affected by it? However, it doesn't tell us to examine the process or what to do about strategy.

Rule Ethics

A second major method of ethical reasoning is referred to as rule ethics. Deontological theories of ethics (that is, theories of ethics arising from the study of duty) refute the utilitarian assertion that the ethics of an action is based on its outcomes, and suggest that the ethics of an action is independent of the outcomes or consequences. **Rule ethics** is essentially the fundamental deontological perspective, which considers actions as ethical or unethical based on their relation to the rules and principles that guide behaviours.[34] Based on this perspective, ethical behaviour is behaviour that can be deemed as morally right regardless of the consequences. In the Western world, for example, Judeo-Christian religious and moral rules or values have played a major role in defining morality in society.[35] Of course, even within Western society, there are a variety of beliefs or rules regarding what is ethical, and society has tended to permit rules to change in many areas of behaviour.

Right versus Wrong

Rule ethics is the view that there are basic rules that determine the "rightness" or "wrongness" of actions. Stated quite simply, rule ethics asserts that an individual should do what is required by valid, ethical principles, and should not do anything that violates those principles. These are the fundamental notions of right and wrong. Given the diverse nature of society there is no one clear set of rule ethics that is followed by all individuals. This is, perhaps, one of the central problems in assessing whether behaviour can be deemed ethical — whose rules should apply?

Both utilitarian and rule ethics consider the social aspect of ethics: unethical behaviour is behaviour that has a harmful effect on others and is "either illegal, or morally unacceptable to the larger community."[36] How do these two models of ethical reasoning operate differently? Let's consider a business issue, and see what each model offers with regard to resolving a problem.

Applying the Models: A Scenario

You are a business person trying to win a $22-million contract for your company with a major corporation overseas. You learn that in order to gain the contract, you need to offer a substantial monetary gift to the CEO of the major corporation. What would you do?

This question is one that managers must increasingly ask themselves as we continue to conduct business on a global scale. And certainly, as many observers have pointed out, attitudes and customs regarding ethical business practices can vary widely among different countries.

From an End-Point Ethics Perspective

From this perspective we could not get any universal agreement as to the ethics of such a practice. Clearly, many countries have no problem with bribery. Reconsider the principles of end-point ethics: Do we achieve the greatest balance of good over harm for all potential stakeholders? First, who gains from a bribe? Well, clearly your company will benefit from getting the deal and, consequently, you benefit as well. Who is harmed by such a transaction?

You might consider three potential losers:

1. Does the bribe compromise your ability to do business with companies like this one in the future — will the perception of your company be negative?
2. Competent competitors who are otherwise deserving of the contract may lose because they refused to offer this bribe.
3. The bribe might permit inferior products or services to be purchased simply because the supplier bribed those in power to help get the product or service to market. Consequently, consumers may be harmed.

If, indeed, these three stakeholders are harmed in this way as a consequence of our decision, end-point ethics would likely guide us away from such a decision. However, end-point ethics does not necessarily condemn such behaviour as unethical. If the product or service is not inferior — that is, if the bribe helps us conduct business and sell a good product that is fairly priced — then consumers are not harmed. If the CEO will likely receive a bribe from some other supplier, regardless of whether you choose to bribe or not, then end-point ethics suggests that no one is "worse for the wear," so to speak, by having received the bribe. Depending on how it is applied, end-point ethics potentially could justify the giving of a bribe. Certainly, it does not uniformly condemn such a decision. Rather, the result depends on how rigorously the decision maker has identified all potential stakeholders, and carefully weighed the relative costs and benefits (both tangible and intangible) that arise from this action.

From a Rule Ethics Perspective

What guidance does rule ethics offer us in considering whether or not to bribe the CEO of this foreign corporation in order to gain the contract? Again, consider what rule ethics says. It says that we should do what our ethical codes or beliefs tell us to do. Now, in North America, at least, there are many organizations that have instituted strict codes of ethics that prohibit giving or accepting gifts of any kind. Perhaps that would be a guiding rule for some decision makers. On the other hand, perhaps an individual's personal or religious beliefs dictate honesty in all aspects of life; and this may also serve to act as a rule prohibiting engaging in a bribe. It may be our belief that no business person should pay a bribe to any company official, even though the ethical codes of some other countries do, indeed, tolerate bribery.

Does rule ethics generate a negative response to the question of gift-giving? Once again, this model does not generate universal responses to problems. For example, perhaps we have rules that advocate such gift-giving, and these rules guide our behaviour. Do we have any obligations that override our ethical prohibition of bribery? What if your company's survival depended on securing business with this foreign company? What if thousands of jobs would be lost in your company if the business was not obtained and that could not be obtained other than through the bribe? Could these issues offer compelling reasons to follow a rule that "all is fair in business"? Rule ethics may dictate overriding the general prohibition against bribery because of the greater urgency to protect the company and jobs. Consequently, even rule ethics does not provide a blanket condemnation of bribery. Modern society, it seems, has lost its ability to provide clear rules or guidelines to individuals that will enable them to resolve conflicting interests.

Lessons?

What lessons do we learn from an understanding of end-point ethics and rule ethics? Perhaps the greatest value of these models lies in what they demand of us. Both models are inherently flawed, as we discussed. They are limited by the degree of rigour that the user (decision maker) employs in their use. End-point ethics demands that we question the ethics of our actions in the following ways:

- Which stakeholders have we identified, and which have we not identified?
- Have we clearly acknowledged the harm, as well as the benefits, that may arise from our decisions?
- How have we determined the relative importance of each of the stakeholders?
- How have we determined the relative weight of the benefits and harms that will potentially arise from our decisions?

Similarly, rule ethics suggests we need to think more critically about what rules we employ in making decisions:

- Where did the rules that guide our behaviour and choices come from?
- Do we use these rules consistently, or only when it is convenient?
- Do we apply separate sets of rules to govern our professional and our personal lives? Why?

As you can see, the value of considering the models we use to make decisions is in demonstrating the fact that our decisions often have an ethical dimension. Without an understanding of the motivation behind our decisions, we may fall victim to making decisions on purely a business basis, even though they may have ethical implications. See Talking Business 2.7.

TALKING BUSINESS 2.7   THE ETHICS OF GLOBALIZATION: KILLING JAMAICA?

A recent documentary entitled *Life and Debt* produced by Stephanie Black vividly illustrates the devastating effects that globalization has had on Jamaica. The documentary examines the effect of the International Monetary Fund's (IMF) policies on developing countries through Jamaica's experience with the organization. After having gained its autonomy from Britain in 1962, Jamaica was struggling economically. It appeared that salvation would come in the form of financial assistance, a loan, from the International Monetary Fund (the IMF). However, there were several stipulations, including the requirement to devalue the Jamaican currency and reduce trade barriers by withdrawing local import restrictions. Jamaica would thus enter the world market — it was going global. The result was devastating. The local economy became flooded with foreign imports (cheaper than Jamaican goods), and consequently huge losses in jobs and economic self-reliance followed.

This kind of liberalization of policies meant huge benefits to the larger lender (developed countries such as the United States and Britain) but meant real hardship for Jamaica. In his article, "Who Is Aiding Whom," David Sogge speaks of the problems of the international trade liberalization in ways that raise questions in one's mind as to who benefits most — and is referred to as the "dual mandate of western aid." For example, the lender countries do not allow exports from the recipient (borrower) country to be bought and sold in the recipient country, and instead the opposite is done — the lender countries "dump" their exports on the developing (borrower) country. Other issues involved in these agreements include repayment of the debts, which are extremely strenuous and the interest rates are often inordinately high. Other problems include the brain drain in the developing countries where most of the trained professionals of these countries go to take up residence in the developed nations in search of a "better life" — a better standard of living.

With these kinds of imbalances in trade agreements and international relations, developing countries like Jamaica, other Caribbean countries and Latin American countries are at a disadvantage, and the playing field is not level.

Jamaica has been identified as the third most dangerous country in terms of crime and violence in the world today along with other countries including South Africa and Colombia.

According to an article published in the online *Observer* — "Crime, joblessness remain dominant concerns" (December 1, 2005). This article reports that unemployment and high economic price increases have led to the breakdown of community leadership and involvement, and have been replaced with crime.

Source: Stephanie Black, Dir. *Life and Debt in Jamaica*. Film. A Tuff Gong Pictures Production, 2001. (www.newyorkerfilms.com); Holger Henke, "Jamaica Decision to Pursue a Neo-liberal Development Stategy: Realignments in the State-Business-Class Triangle," *Latin American Perspectives* 26(5): 7–33; Hilary Nicholson, Dir. "Together Against Violence," *City Life* series. Videorecording. Oley, PA: Bullfrog Films Inc., 2001; David Sogge, *Give and Take: What's The Matter With Foreign Aid*, pp. 24–39. Halifax, NS: Fernwood Publishing, 2002.

DO ORGANIZATIONS MAKE US UNETHICAL?

The two models of ethical decision making outlined above help give us an understanding of the ways we may resolve conflicting interests in the workplace. Neither model guarantees we will make a sound, ethical decision. That depends on the level of rigour with which we analyze our choices and on the impact of our choices. When faced with decisions that involve ethical implications, why might we not "do the right thing"? Why do some individuals choose to engage in unethical behaviour, while others do not? There are countless theories that attempt to answer that question. Among the theories are suggestions that self-interest is a major influence on unethical behaviour. For example, based on **agency theory**, it is argued that when agents (employees) possess more information than principals (employers), and their goals conflict, agents may behave in accordance with their self-interest and, thereby, such individuals may deceive the principal.[37] Other scholars have accused individuals (human agents) of being "pure egoists"[38] whose behaviour typically reflects a desire to maximize their own utility.[39] This sentiment is also expressed in neoclassical economics and social exchange theory, which assert that individuals will engage in unethical behaviour if it is in their best interest to do so.[40] As an example of this self-interest connection, there is some research evidence to suggest that if individuals receive a personal gain or reward from giving a bribe to another party, they are very likely to engage in this form of unethical behaviour.[41]

From a normative perspective, business ethics advocates that individuals should be motivated by more than a complete focus on self-interest.[42] Some scholars have pointed out that a rational, economic focus on self-interest can be irrational — "rational agents approach being psychopathic when their interests are solely in benefit to themselves."[43] Certainly this criticism of self-interest makes sense from a social perspective. We live in societies where co-operation is expected, and a purely economic, self-interest focus would prove dysfunctional for society.

For many years researchers have attempted to discern the relative role of the individual's and the organization's characteristics in encouraging unethical behaviour in the workplace: the notion of distinguishing "bad apples or bad barrels."[44]

Managing ethical behaviour in business organizations requires an in-depth understanding of the many factors that contribute to employees' decisions to behave ethically or unethically. One key question that needs to be addressed is, Under what conditions will individuals, within their roles as employees, engage in behaviour that does not conform with commonly accepted standards of ethical behaviour?

What factors in the workplace might create an environment where unethical behaviour is acceptable? That is, when do employees willingly engage in what otherwise would be considered unacceptable behaviour? For example, why may an individual willingly engage in corporate "spying," or why may an individual willingly misrepresent a product's quality to a customer? The research and theory has acknowledged that organizations can present unique challenges to ethical behaviour for their constituents. Organizational factors play a role in ethical decision making and behaviour at two points: establishing moral intent, and engaging in moral behaviour.

Exhibit 2.4 summarizes the framework adopted to explain the impact of organizational context. The elements that play a critical role in individual ethical behaviour in the

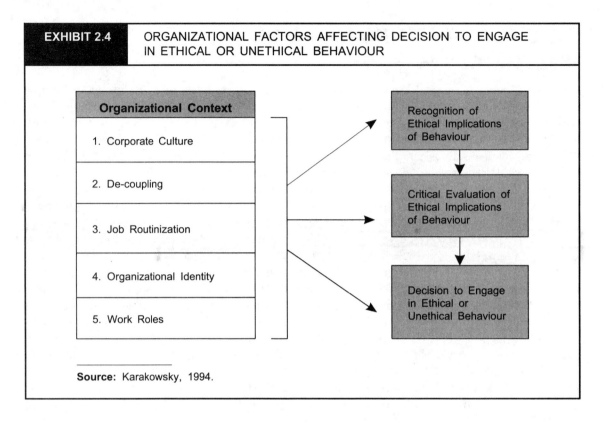

EXHIBIT 2.4 — ORGANIZATIONAL FACTORS AFFECTING DECISION TO ENGAGE IN ETHICAL OR UNETHICAL BEHAVIOUR

Source: Karakowsky, 1994.

organization are culture, organizational de-coupling, routinization of work, organizational identity and work roles. The influence of these factors on behaviour arises through their impact on the following:

- perceptions or recognition of the ethical dimension or ethical implications of the work situation
- critical evaluation of the ethical implications or consequences of work behaviour
- final decision to engage in the behaviour.

The elements of this framework, as outlines in Exhibit 2.4, are delineated in the following pages.

1. Unethical Behaviour as a Consequence of Corporate Culture

Business morality is essentially a social reality, as opposed to a physical reality, and therefore cannot be fully understood apart from the social system and organizational culture that are conceptualizing it.[45] What is organizational culture, and how can it impact my decision as an employee to engage in ethical or unethical behaviour?

Organizational culture has been defined as the bond or glue that holds an organization together. It encompasses a set of shared beliefs regarding how members of the organization should behave and what goals they should seek. In this sense it is an intangible, abstract component of any organization. There is an IBM culture, a Nortel culture, a McDonald's culture and a Harvard University culture. Every organization contains some kind of culture.

The notion that norms influence ethical behaviour has been suggested for many years. Specifically, organizational culture provides an organizational reality within which ethically relevant actions are discussed, judged and legitimized. For example, culture, through its transmission of organizational beliefs, can provide employees with *legitimate* (sanctioned) or *non-legitimate* approaches to ethical decision making and behaviour.

Rituals and Myths

Organizational researchers who consider culture to be a system of publicly and collectively accepted meanings also suggest that an organization is filled with organizational "rituals and myths."[46] Organizational rituals and myths contain messages that provide a shared experience and reinforcement of values for members of the organization. Myths specifically contain a narrative of events, often with a "sacred" quality attached. Both ritual and myth play a crucial role in the continuous processes of establishing and maintaining what is legitimate and what is unacceptable in any organizational culture.[47] The "myths" and "rituals" are simply the organization's established products, services, techniques and policies or rules that employees adopt/conform to.[48]

Organizational myths could be, for example, legends of corporate heroes and their deeds within the organization, which can provide guidance (positive or negative) for employees facing ethical decisions in similar circumstances.[49] This may permit individuals to legitimize their actions in ethical dilemmas.[50] That is, the culture, through its transmission of myths, can provide employees with legitimate (sanctioned) or non-legitimate approaches to ethical decision making and behaviour.

What's the Connection to Ethics?

How can managers generate a culture that encourages ethical behaviour? It has been suggested that a strong ethical culture can be generated through the areas of selection (choosing employees whose beliefs are consistent with those of the organization), socialization (conveying the organization's goals and norms effectively), and training and mentoring (reinforcing the organization's culture through training and personal role models).[51] Gatewood and Carroll suggested that the socialization of ethics, which occurs through a process of internalization of organizational ethical standards, is fundamental to the ethical conduct of organizational members.[52] Other authors have provided similar suggestions for encouraging ethical behaviour in organizations, including the development of corporate ethical codes of conduct,[53] and public discussions of ethical issues through formal meetings.[54] This sense of open confrontation and discussion of ethical concerns must be institutionalized before it becomes an effective means of resolving moral conflict. Corporate codes of conduct are one of the most common methods used by the business community as an attempt to improve ethical conduct. These rules are intended to reflect the general values of society. Codes of ethics are one means of "institutionalizing" ethics in corporations.[55] This involves incorporating ethics formally and explicitly into daily business life.

Corporate Codes of Conduct

Ethical codes are necessary because laws cannot prescribe the standard of ethical conduct for all situations.[56] However, it should be noted that many critics have suggested that these codes may become nothing more than "window dressing" — a means of appearing ethical that does not necessarily reflect actual practice. For example, it has been suggested that the lack of reinforcement of ethical behaviour reflected in management's "results orientation" can encourage employees to behave unethically.[57] "Good guys finish last" is the sentiment that propels this attitude in business. In other words, organizations that do not reward ethical behaviour are sending out the message that such behaviour is unnecessary. This can happen regardless of the presence of formal corporate codes of conduct.

Bureaucratic Cultures

Research support has been provided for the notion that moral atmosphere affects moral reasoning and moral judgment.[58] A number of research studies have attempted to explore this concept within the organizational context. Findings have indicated that when an informal or formal organization policy was present, ethical behaviour increased and unethical behaviour was deterred.[59] Weber examined the effects of size of the organization on a manager's stage of moral reasoning.[60] The results of Weber's study indicated that managers in smaller organizations appeared to be operating at a higher stage of moral reasoning. Weber suggested several reasons for these findings. Larger organizations often exhibit cultures with more complex bureaucracies and greater control over their employees through rules and regulations. Therefore, managers feeling isolated from the central decision-making authority will tend to rely on more immediate peers or supervisors for support or approval of their behaviour. On the other hand, smaller organizations tend to be less bureaucratic and possess fewer rules to govern employee behaviour. Subsequently, managers in this environment feel a greater sense of control over the decision-making process, along with a greater need to conform with social laws as a means to protect themselves from conflict with other stakeholders (i.e., customers, public, etc.). This reflects a higher stage of cognitive moral development. In other words, a democratic culture may encourage members to take responsibility for their actions, while an authoritative culture may dictate rules that replace individual discretion and, thereby, suppress development of ethical decision making.[61]

2. Unethical Behaviour as a Consequence of De-coupling

Organizations sometimes try to cover up inefficiencies by separating or de-coupling the behaviour from its evaluation. Specifically, "avoidance," "discretion" and "overlooking" of inefficiencies are acts that maintain the assumption that people are acting in good faith. This encourages confidence in the myths that legitimize an organization's activities. Organizations can protect themselves from public scrutiny by ensuring that any questionable activities are "de-coupled" from external evaluation in this sense.[62]

Corporate Language

The notion of de-coupling suggests that organizations can conduct themselves in ways that hide activities that would otherwise be considered unacceptable if they were subjected to closer scrutiny. Among the most infamous examples of conformity with organizationally legitimized, yet unethical, behaviour were the crimes of the Nazi Party during World War II. While a variety of theories have been applied to attempt to explain the atrocities committed by the Nazis, one can consider how the Nazis de-coupled behaviour from its evaluation. The use of accepted or legitimized symbols or practices can help to de-couple actual activity from evaluation of that activity. For example, the use of euphemisms by the Nazi perpetrators de-coupled actual behaviour from evaluation of that behaviour — the victims were not murdered, according to Nazi language, they were "selected." This language provided a sense of legitimacy to what would otherwise be viewed as inhuman behaviour. The ability to de-couple deeds from evaluation or scrutiny supported the notion that legitimized beliefs, perpetuated through the use of symbolic language, could help maintain conformity and allegiance to a brutal cause.

Meyer and Rowan argued that to maintain external legitimacy organizations adopt commonly accepted rules on the surface and incorporate them into their structure.[63] However, these rules may, in effect, be unrelated to how the activities are really conducted. The selective use of language to label various work practices is one method of disguising the unethical implications of workplace behaviour. For example, the unethical practice of corporate spying may be symbolically legitimized (to the organization and its employees) as a form of market analysis — a term that gives a sense of legitimacy to what would otherwise be considered unethical business practice. This use of corporate language or labels can de-couple the behaviour from moral evaluation of the behaviour. Consequently, this suggests that employees will be encouraged to engage in unethical behaviour where that behaviour has been legitimized through the adoption of the behaviour as accepted business practice, and where behaviour and evaluation of that behaviour are de-coupled.

3. Unethical Behaviour as a Consequence of Work Routinization

McDonald's is the most famous example of routinized work: that is, work that is governed strictly by rules and regulations, as scientific management advocates. However, McDonald's is not the only organization dependent on routinized work practices; in fact, to a degree, most jobs have some element of routinization. A number of scholars have recognized the pervasive existence of routinized work practices, or habitual routines, in organizations. This phenomenon has been described as concrete behaviour that is not governed by rational deliberation but, rather, by routinized performance programs.[64]

The notion of adopting routinized performance programs as accepted ways of doing work can be thought of in terms of institutionalizing behaviour on the job. For example, consider the airline pilot who follows clear procedures with regard to flying the plane, or the auditor who follows strict guidelines with regard to performing an audit. Clearly, both these jobs require a high degree of professional judgment or discretion. However, both also rely on some standards and commonly accepted methods for performing the work, also referred to as **habitual routines.** Gersick and Hackman suggested that behavioural norms that evolve in groups pressure individuals to adhere to habitual routines.[65] That is, once a routine has been established in a group, the behaviours involved in executing the routine will submit to normative control. Management scholars have suggested that once a behaviour is accepted as a legitimate means of accomplishing the work, its actual effects (efficiency or otherwise) are not readily questioned.

Habitual Routines

The legitimization of acceptable behaviour can extend to the actual job itself — how the work is performed. The organization may generate routinized work procedures that are viewed as legitimate since they follow an acceptable set of rules. For example, following the written guidelines of conducting an audit is viewed as a legitimate method of auditing. The proliferation of technical guidelines to govern work methods enhances the perceived legitimacy of the work. However, in actuality, these routinized work methods may be neither the most efficient, nor the most effective, way of conducting the work.

Gersick and Hackman identified both functional and dysfunctional consequences of routinized or habitual behaviour.[66] A major advantage of habitual routines is that they save time and energy, since they don't require active management: in this respect, they should improve efficiency. How much of our work constitutes simply "going through the motions" — that is, that portion of our work that does not demand constant mental scrutiny but, rather, can be performed with minimal attention to detail? Among the disadvantages identified were the tendency for routines to permit a misinterpretation of the situation to occur. That is, if a group fails to recognize a novel stimulus situation or changes that occur to familiar situations, then invoking a habitual routine will be inappropriate. What is the impact of such habitual routines on ethical behaviour in organizations?

Reduction of Critical Thought

A fundamental characteristic of habitual routines, the inability of habitual routines to adapt to change, has important implications for ethical behaviour in the workplace. For example, consider a situation involving an engineer who habitually performs a safety check on the construction standards of a building plan. The engineer performs all the checks in accordance with the professional or legal requirements, while neglecting to consider non-routine indicators of potential risk in the construction. Certainly, there is an ethical or moral dimension to decisions or practices that can affect the well-being of others: the duty of care in performance that exists beyond strict legal requirements can be considered an ethical concern. In the case of the engineer, strict adherence to habitual routines permits unethical behaviour to occur due to the failure to critically analyze the ethical implications of a workplace behaviour — i.e., to consider the welfare of all parties potentially affected by the behaviour.

4. Unethical Behaviour as a Consequence of Organizational Identity

Jackall argued that the bureaucratization of organizations has influenced "moral consciousness." According to Jackall, this transformation heralded,

> ... the decline of the old middle class of entrepreneurs, free professionals, and independent businessmen — the traditional carriers of the old Protestant Ethic — and the ascendance of a new middle class of salaried employees whose common characteristic was and is their dependence on the big organization.[67]

According to this view, corporate America destroyed ethical values. The Protestant Ethic emphasized the "stewardship" responsibilities associated with the accumulation of wealth. However, as Jackall argued, "the very accumulation of wealth that the old Protestant Ethic made possible gradually stripped away the religious basis of the ethic, especially among the rising middle class that benefited from it." In addition, organizational bureaucracies created their own "internal rules" and "social context" to guide individual conduct. Jackall argued the following:

> Bureaucracy ... breaks apart the older connection between the meaning of work and salvation. In the bureaucratic world, one's success ... no longer depends on one's own efforts ... but on the capriciousness of one's superiors and the market....[68]

Is Bureaucracy to Blame?

Based on this perspective, modern organizations encourage unethical behaviour largely as a result of the demise of the Protestant Work Ethic through the bureaucratization of these organizations. Why blame bureaucracy? Bureaucracies are considered guilty given their characteristics of requiring the subjugation of personal belief systems to the beliefs or goals of the organization. This is reflected in the notion of "working for the boss" — our futures are dependent on our ability to fulfill our organizational responsibilities, regardless of the consequences. To the extent that individual identities continue to become intrinsically bound up with organizational identities, the ethics of an individual employee may be tied to the ethics of the organization with which they identify. To the extent that our personal identity is bound up with our organizational identity, what organizations demand of us may dictate the ethics that we live by.

Social identity theory[69] posits that individuals classify themselves and others into social categories (e.g., organizational membership, age, gender) that are defined by the typical characteristics abstracted from the members. Organizational identification is a specific form of social identification.[70] Individuals can identify with elements of the organization that have been reified — i.e., that have become embodiments of the characteristics perceived as typical of its members: "I work for IBM," "I am a lawyer," etc. These are all statements of identity based on an organization or a profession. For example, an individual can identify with his/her membership as a professional accountant. What are the consequences of this process of social or organizational identification? One consequence of social identity is the tendency of the individual to support the values and actions of the group, and to internalize the perception of the group as more desirable compared to other groups.[71] Group members can enhance self esteem by increasing the desirability associated with their social categories.[72] The consequences of identification with the organization also have implications for ethical behaviour of group members.

In the Name of the Boss

When we identify with our organizations, we tend to become less critical of its policies and behaviour. The notion that identification with the organization restricts or discourages evaluations or perceptions that might reflect poorly on the organization has clear ethical implications. Ashforth and Mael suggested that identification can provide a mechanism whereby an individual can continue to believe in the integrity of the organization despite wrongdoing by senior management.[73] Individuals who maintain a strong organizational identity will not critically evaluate their behaviour on its own merits (i.e., actual consequences), but will judge behaviour based on perceptions of the social category to which they belong. For example, a public accountant who identifies strongly with her firm or professional body may avoid critical evaluation of her conduct when she perceives herself as acting on behalf of that firm or professional body, which upholds professional standards. Indeed, at the extreme, there is research to suggest that employees will engage in unethical behaviour at the request of authority figures.[74] In addition to the influence of authority figures, the research has explored the effects of peers on ethical behaviour. In fact, many researchers have suggested that unethical behaviour is learned in the process of interacting with persons who are part of intimate personal groups or role-sets: employees who have learned through differential association in their role-sets to be unethical and have the opportunity to engage in unethical behaviours will be more likely to do so.[75]

5. Unethical Behaviour as a Consequence of Organizational Roles

Organizational role theory proposes that individuals in organizations occupy positions or roles that involve a set of activities, including interactions with others, that are required or expected as part of the job.[76] Individuals fulfill role requirements based on internalized expectations concerning the responsibilities of the role. Roles have a psychological reality to individuals occupying them.

The presence of incompatible expectations of attitudes, beliefs and behaviours inherent in social roles will generate an ambivalence known as role conflict.[77] Kahn et al. identified several forms of role conflict, including inter-role conflict, which refers to the competing demands of two or more roles that an individual occupies.[78] For example, the demands associated with the role of employee may conflict with the demands associated with the role of family member. How do individuals resolve the inherent conflict of organizationally situated roles or identities? Ashforth and Mael summarized the methods individuals employ to cognitively resolve role conflict, including denying role conflict, compartmentalizing roles or identities, and prioritizing roles.[79] These types of coping mechanisms suggest that individuals do not necessarily engage in a critical, objective evaluation of competing role demands.

Role Conflict

What are the implications of organizational roles for the ethical behaviour of individuals occupying those roles? More specifically, what are the implications of these conflict resolution strategies for ethical behaviour? Consider the case of an employee in the role of salesperson who must decide whether the role responsibility of reaching the sales target at all costs should take priority over his role as honest citizen. The individual may rationalize that he is responsibly fulfilling role obligations, even though the behaviour required to fulfill the role of salesperson might be ethically unsound. Consistent with Ashforth and Mael's summary of responses to role conflict, the individual can resolve the role conflict by compartmentalizing or **prioritizing role demands** as a means to rationalize the behaviour. That is, the employee can adopt a different set of standards to judge what constitutes appropriate salesperson behaviour as contrasted with appropriate honest citizen behaviour. Essentially, this suggests that ethical conflicts among competing role demands can effectively be ignored by the individual through this cognitive process.

Conflict Resolution

What effect does the organization have on role conflict resolution? How an individual chooses to resolve the multiple role conflicts will depend largely on the organizational context. Returning to the previous discussion, the institutional elements, including culture, identity, de-coupling and routinization, will impact the individual's reactions to role conflicts and demands. For example, if the organizational culture ignores an ethical dimension to role requirements, individuals will not attempt to reconcile their role performance with ethical considerations; if the organization institutionalizes habitual behaviour and suppresses analytical thought, then evaluation of the ethical implications of role responsibilities and role conflicts will similarly be reduced. Clearly, organizational context will significantly influence how an individual resolves role conflict.

Judging the Ethics of Organizations

Earlier in this chapter, we considered two central models of ethical decision making: endpoint ethics and rule ethics. These prove to be useful models for critiquing the ethics of our everyday decisions. Can we judge the ethics of organizations as entities? That is, can we critique the nature of the organizational arrangements under which we function as employees? There is another ethical tool or model that speaks directly to the nature of organizations and the question of the conditions under which organizations conform to or violate ethical principles. One such tool for considering the ethical dimension of organizational issues is social contract ethics.

Social Contract Ethics

One version of rule ethics, **social contract ethics**, was articulated by John Locke.[80] This model posited that the rules by which people live are those that they would agree to live by if given the opportunity to make a choice based on reason or knowledge. Locke's idea of the social contract provided a basis for a new model of organizations that views them as networks of contracts. Immanuel Kant added that only rules that apply equally to everyone are ethical.[81]

Taken together, the social contract model of ethical reasoning views the ethical rules that we live by as products of an implicit contract. A social contract is an implicit agreement regarding basic principles of conduct. These social contracts are harboured by the cultures of groups or organizations and by our society. Organizational social contracts represent the ground rules regarding conditions of employment, rewards and performance expectations. Organizational management researchers have viewed organizations as a web of implicit contracts — every time you enter a new organization you are entering a web of contracts. Of course, the question is, Are these contracts or ground rules sound?

A contract is sound if all parties entering into it have entered into it freely and fairly. And fairness involves the notion that, regardless of your position, you would view the contract as equally fair from all perspectives. It is not unbalanced in favour of some interests over others. According to social contract ethics, then, an individual should do what a fair, voluntary contract would dictate: that is, the ethical guide for dealing with any issue. Social contract ethics is essentially about assessing the ethics or fairness of an organizational arrangement — whether that is how people are hired or fired; how they are evaluated; or how they are rewarded, among other things. So, any member of an organization attempting to address that test would ask at least three questions: Do I really agree with this contract, or am I just tolerating it? If I occupied a different position in this company, would I accept this contract?

An Example: The Ethics of Downsizing

Let's consider a pervasive issue that continues to affect the business landscape: organizational downsizings. What might the social contract model say about the ethics of downsizing? Consider the recent observations of a writer, who commented on the "new deal" between workers and the organizations:

> In the old manufacturing economy, blue-collar unemployment always rose and fell in lock step with factory inventories; now a similar thing is happening to the mostly white-collar workers in the sleek offices of the new economy. ...If this sounds like deja vu all over again, it is ... [Years ago] [c]ompanies began getting very explicit in their warnings to employees: Jobs were not for life. Harvard professor Rosabeth Moss Kanter was one of a chorus of academics and consultants arguing that since companies could no longer provide job security, they should do more to give workers "employability security" through training and skills counselling.[82]

We could consider the implicit contract between a number of different parties, but let's just consider the implicit agreements among employer and employee. Many critics have argued that what we have seen with the downsizing phenomenon is a violation of a number of implicit rules existing between employer and employee. No longer is there an implied agreement that you enter a company in your twenties, work hard, and retire some 20 or perhaps 30 years later. Throughout the 1990s we witnessed massive layoffs of employees who felt they had kept their end of the social contract by working hard for their organizations, yet were terminated in an organizational restructuring or downsizing.

This view of a violation of the social contract was expressed in *The Globe and Mail*'s article, "One Day You're Family, the Next Day You're Fired." The article recounted the events that preceded the termination of about 300 employees of a Canadian company as part of a downsizing. The article told how the terminated employees were locked out of the building and only permitted back inside to collect their personal belongings, under the watchful eyes of security guards who also escorted them out again. These kinds of stories were pervasive throughout the 1990s and, unfortunately, continue today.

What does the future hold? Will we see a decreased, or increased, emphasis on social responsibility? Well, we have been experiencing much turbulence in the corporate world in recent years. Part of the chaos, including the infamous spread of corporate downsizing, has left many people sceptical of the morality of business. On the other hand, there is a strong belief that business will place increasing emphasis on the recognition of the needs of different stakeholders. That is, many observers believe that more and more businesses will need to place more emphasis on their social responsiveness to maintain legitimacy and acceptance from the community at large. As Talking Business 2.8 indicates, many industries have yet to fully come to grips with the challenge of increasing social responsibility.

TALKING BUSINESS 2.8   IS WAL-MART GOOD FOR SOCIETY?

Wal-Mart Stores, Inc. would like you to know that it is not evil. It is not rabidly anti-union. It doesn't squeeze suppliers within an inch of their lives, and it does not pay employees starvation wages. It does not destroy local communities, nor does it condone the hiring of illegal immigrants just because they work cheap. It does not discriminate against women and minorities. And if it ever did any of that stuff, it is going to stop.

Whether you believe these assurances or not isn't really the point. The mere fact that Wal-Mart needs to make them tells all you need to know about the identity crisis facing the world's biggest retailer. It also provides a tough lesson in how quickly a company's public image can crumble, and how difficult it can be to pull out of a reputational nosedive once it has begun.

It was only four years ago that a survey conducted by Cone Inc./Roper found Wal-Mart to be Americans' top choice for "good corporate citizen." But that was before the U.S. government began to probe whether its contractors knowingly hired illegal immigrants to clean stores. It was also before a federal judge approved a class-action suit alleging sexual discrimination at the chain, a case that could affect up to 1.6 million current and former workers and cost the company more than a billion dollars in damages.

. . . .

On the surface, these all seem like relatively simple problems to fix. Just be nicer. Obey the law. Build someplace else. Oh, if only it were that simple. The Bentonville, Ark.-

based giant is facing a dilemma. It's the very same one that tripped up many huge transnational corporations in recent years — Microsoft, McDonald's and Coca-Cola, to name just three — as their rapid growth and massive wealth began to breed public resentment. What do you do when the secret to your success becomes your biggest liability?

Wal-Mart grew into the world's most dominant retailer by selling cheap stuff to average folks. It's a straightforward, apple-pie kind of business, except that to make it work you need to be big, and you need to keep costs down. In Wal-Mart's case, that has meant keeping a tight lid on wages and benefits, and moving aggressively to build new stores. For two decades, the company was an awe-inspiring success story, and through the '80s and '90s its stock marched steadily higher. Revenues topped US$256 billion last year, meaning that if Wal-Mart were a country, it would boast the world's 31st biggest economy, ahead of Saudi Arabia and Sweden.

But such success comes at a cost, and there is a growing group of critics eager to tally up the bill. Earlier this month, researchers at the University of California at Berkeley released a study pointing out that because Wal-Mart's 44,000 workers in California must rely on public assistance programs, the company's business practices end up costing taxpayers US$86 million a year. The study relied on data from a 2001 lawsuit against the company, which indicated that three-quarters of Wal-Mart employees make less than US$10 an hour, compared to the average of US$14 at large California retailers.

Wal-Mart said the study's conclusions were based on "faulty assumptions," but at this point it really doesn't matter much what the company says. It is the classic victim of its own astonishing success. After all, when you make a US$9-billion profit, as Wal-Mart did last year, your employees will likely read about it in the paper and think, "Hey, maybe I should get paid a little better." It's little wonder that workers in Jonquière, Que., were pleased when they recently became the first Wal-Mart employees in North America to get a union certified.

Wal-Mart is only too aware of its image problem. This past winter, the company produced television ads featuring happy workers talking about what a swell place it is to work. And in June, it took more substantive action. CEO Lee Scott unveiled an eight-point plan to improve employee relations, including an "office of diversity" to ensure women and minorities get a fair shot at promotions, and a new, more generous pay structure. The company is also reportedly in talks with the U.S. Justice Department to settle the issue of illegal immigrant workers.

But if history is any guide, Wal-Mart's problems won't go away so easily. Once the government and computer industry rivals began attacking Microsoft for predatory business practices, even Bill Gates's huge charitable donations couldn't remove the stigma from his company. The stock slumped in 2000 and has never recovered.

The market seems to be anticipating a similarly difficult future for Wal-Mart. After two decades of explosive growth, its stock has been flat as a pancake for five years, leaving Wal-Mart facing a tough decision: fundamentally change its approach to appease its critics, or press on with business as usual and deal with challenges as they come up. Either way, Wal-Mart's best days among America's most admired companies are past.

They say it's lonely at the top, and now Wal-Mart knows why.

Source: Reproduced with permission from Steve Maich, "Wal-Mart's Mid-Life Crisis: What happens when being big and cheap becomes your Achilles heel," *Maclean's Magazine* (August 23, 2004).

■ CHAPTER SUMMARY

This chapter attempted to underscore the ethical dimension of organizational decisions and behaviour. How managers balance the different needs of stakeholders demands knowledge of the ethical implications of otherwise typical business decisions. Ethics is central to the managerial task. Management educators have been expanding the realm of management literature to consider the relationship of ethics and management. An understanding of the social responsibility of business organizations and their constituents may help create a more productive and trusting relationship between business and society.

Mining for Social Responsibility

Historically, decisions to permit mining industries in less developed countries (LDCs) have been made by the central government of the local region in the less developed country. Often, this development is undertaken with the support and encouragement of international development agencies, who are seeking to encourage private investment in order to generate such benefits for the underdeveloped host country. Jobs are created, technology can be introduced and poverty can be alleviated in many cases. Unfortunately, there are also negative consequences at times.

One of the most significant and problematic consequences can be the impact on the physical, economic, cultural and social environment. A case that illustrates this issue is the story of two groups of people, the Teberebe and Bogoso, who live in the Wassa West District of Ghana, West Africa.

For generations, the Teberebe and Bogoso were land owners who farmed the land that surrounded them. Now, their entire community has been displaced and resettled in an unfamiliar environment. The decision that brought about this harsh change was made by a local chieftain, who, on behalf his people, placed a thumb print in lieu of a signature on a document, not knowing the implications it would have on his people. This document has changed not only a culture, but also a way of life and has greatly impacted the region.

The mining companies have not made any real efforts to provide the people with adequate resettlement training to adjust to their new environment. Instead of providing the citizens with an adequate transition into the now industrialized environment via education and training, the citizens have been left to fend for themselves, on land that was once their own. The mining companies view this as purely a business transaction. The mining companies have not broken any laws. They have legally acquired the land and they have created jobs where no jobs existed in prior years, which can help reduce poverty. In addition, the mining companies feel they have no obligation beyond paying for this purchase.

Supporters of the mining companies suggest that this situation is consistent with any intelligent business practice — does any business consider its social impact? Does Wal-Mart avoid setting up business where it might interfere with local competitors? No. Consequently, how can these mining companies be expected to consider the social plight of the region? That, according to the mining companies, would simply be unfair and costly to the company.

The mining company, in an effort to provide housing for the people of the Wassa West District, erected a new housing project, which fails to meet the needs of the people. The mining company paid little attention to the traditional cooking, living and relation patterns of this once proud people. Instead of constructing traditional housing units with kitchen and bathroom, the housing unit provides a common living space with communal kitchen and bathrooms, where residents must wait in single file to cook and wash. This reduces any privacy for individuals, but it is the most cost-efficient way to build the premises.

There is no medical evidence to suggest what the long-term effect of dust inhalation from the mining will be on the people in the area as well as what will be the long-term impact of drainage and underground reservoirs. Have mining companies taken advantage of the local lack of expertise and sophistication in negotiating resettlement contracts?

There is increasing pressure from many human rights groups to make the mining industry more socially responsible. To achieve this, there will need to be an expanded understanding and awareness of the human impact of the mining industry; a willingness to include in the decision-making processes the interests and concerns of those who lack political power and who are without economic resources; and a commitment to considering new and alternative approaches to mining industry.

QUESTIONS

1. Describe how well (or how poorly) the mining agencies have addressed corporate social responsibility.

2 (a) With specific reference to the definition of CSR, explain how this case reflects the notion of CSR. Is the mining company being socially responsible or not? Explain.

   (b) Why should the mining companies not be forced to go beyond purchasing the land at a fair price and making profits in this case (i.e., not be forced to be socially responsible)?

   (c) Why should the mining companies be forced to accommodate the needs of the local citizens in addition to purchasing the land at a fair price and making profits (i.e., be forced to be socially responsible)?

3. Applying the six external forces framework of our course, outline the potential impact of each of these forces on the mining companies. At the end of your discussion, indicate which of these forces will likely have the greatest impact on the future of the mining companies and explain why. Throughout your answer, use specific examples/references to this case, and make any assumptions that you require.

Corporations Giving (Till It Hurts)

Canada's three largest credit-card companies announced yesterday they will forgo and repay all fees extracted from on-line tsunami-disaster contributions to the principal aid groups and donate the money to the mounting relief effort.

The move, retroactive to Dec. 26, follows similar initiatives in Europe and elsewhere, and will add hundreds of thousands of dollars to the coffers of nine designated charities carrying out relief work in Asia.

Visa Canada, MasterCard Canada and American Express Canada had all already made sizable corporate donations to the cause.

But yesterday's decision, ostensibly reached independently by the big three, means the charities will no longer be charged the fees normally deducted from contributions.

These fees range upward from 2 per cent. The retroactive provision means the recipients will be getting a refund.

Derek Fry, president of Visa Canada, said because of the volume of charitable contributions flowing through the company, it would not be possible to itemize each one.

As a result, he said, Visa and its member banks can for the moment only estimate how much money will be refunded to the charities.

"We're pretty comfortable it'll be more than half a million dollars. But whatever it is, we will give it back — we'll make a donation equivalent," he said.

Visa's exemption will apply at least until Jan. 31.

It is the banks, rather than Visa, that levy the fees. Proclaiming a refund — rather than, for instance, increasing the banks' own donations by an equivalent amount — reflected a collective wish to demonstrate that none of the financial institutions are profiting from the tragedy, Mr. Fry said.

"Is that optics? Yes, it's optics, I can't argue with that. We want Canadians to make contributions and know that we're donating the fees back to the Red Cross and others."

MasterCard Canada president Kevin Stanton said his company decided to waive the fees "because it's the right thing to do. Canadians have responded in an unprecedented generous way and we wanted to help maximize the effect of that generosity — that their dollars go as far as possible."

Mr. Stanton said he expected the additional yield for the charities benefiting through MasterCard "to be in the six figures."

His company, too, has made the exemption effective until at least Jan. 31 and he added "this has been in the works since the event."

David Barnes of American Express said the company's fee-exemption policy will be in effect until April 30.

When asked why the change is taking effect now — more than a week after the killer tsunamis struck — he said it was a matter of logistics. "It's simply a case of getting things together and getting organized," he said.

The nine designated charities are the Canadian Red Cross, CARE Canada, Development and Peace, Doctors Without Borders, Oxfam Canada, Oxfam Quebec, Save the Children, Unicef Canada and World Vision Canada.

Source: Reproduced by permission of The Globe and Mail from Timothy Appleby, "Credit-card companies turn fees into contributions," *The Globe and Mail* (January 6, 2005), A4.

QUESTIONS

1. In what ways are the issues presented here issues of business ethics?

2. In what way is corporate social responsibility an issue here? Should these companies be forced to be socially responsible? Why? Why not?

3. Would it have been unethical for the credit card companies to make a profit in this situation? Consider rule ethics, end-point ethics and social contract models.

PART **2**

Internal Challenges of Business

Managing the Workforce

3

Organizations that succeed can only do so with the support of their organizational members. In this chapter we will examine the roles of managers and the fundamental philosophies underlying different management styles. You will become familiar with the classical approaches and the behavioural approaches to management. As well, we will consider if any management lessons can be learned from the "military model." We will also identify current challenges of managing a diverse workplace, along with the issue of employment equity.

LEARNING OBJECTIVES

By the end of the chapter, you should be able to:

1. Describe the types of roles managers play within organizations.
2. Identify the underlying philosophies of management within the classical school of thought.
3. Discuss the underlying philosophies that comprise the behavioural school of thought.
4. Consider the managerial lessons offered through the military model of managing.
5. Identify the importance of managing diversity in the Canadian workplace, including the issue of employment equity.

I would like to thank Orlando Carlos Lopez who contributed Talking Business 3.4 to this chapter. I would also like to thank Melanie Gammon who authored the section entitled "The Military Model of Managing — Can It Still Work?," for this chapter.

The Business World

The Toxic Workplace

When Steve Jones was just two years from retirement, he quit his job as vice-president of human resources at one of Canada's largest banks, walking away not only from a high salary but also from a fat pension. He'd spent his entire career in banking, and had no idea what to do next. A change of management two years earlier had replaced a people-friendly way of doing business with one more cutthroat and focused on the bottom line — an approach diametrically opposed to what Jones believed in. The new leaders systematically dismantled programs he'd put in place. The level of pressure he experienced at work went through the roof. Not only was he sleeping badly, he'd developed diabetes, which he says may have been triggered by high stress. He'd tried, unsuccessfully, to get laid off. "I was a 53-year-old, overweight white guy," says Jones, who asked that his real name not be used, "and I figured, if worst comes to worst, I can always deliver pizza."

You know things are bad when delivering pizza beats hanging in for another 24 months. Besides, Jones had a high-paying job — he was making $180,000 a year as a corporate exec with a swish office in a downtown high-rise. But realizing "there wasn't much value in a pension if I was dead," he knew he couldn't stay. "I felt absolutely out of step," he says. "There'd be conversations in meetings that made me feel I was in a foreign country where I didn't understand the rules or the principles."

In *The Corporation*, the hit 2003 documentary film, businesses are portrayed as psychopaths that can wreak havoc in the communities where they operate. Human resource experts are finding the same kind of havoc can be wreaked inside a company as well, and can have disastrous effects on the people working there. It's a phenomenon that's become increasingly prevalent, they say, so much so there's now a new moniker to describe the situation: the toxic work environment. In Jones's case, there was nothing wrong with *him*; rather, his workplace was so poisonous, he was unable to function. And in today's business world, where there's an unprecedented focus on next quarter's earnings, the toxic company is becoming increasingly commonplace. "This is an unchecked phenomenon," says Sussannah Kelly, who is building an executive search business after two decades in corporate human resources. As part of the global search firm Boyden International, Kelly and her business partner Michael McInerney have established a Toronto consulting business called the Boyden Institute, which aims to identify and weed out toxic leaders. "There's a lust for unreasonable profits," Kelly says.

That lust creates a culture inside an organization where the pursuit of short-term profits towers above all else, including the company's own long-term health. Often, the CEO's remuneration — and ego — is closely linked to those quarterly profits, and boosting all three replaces what's best to sustain the company's growth and survival. McInerney points out that with the average tenure of today's CEOs shrinking, they have only a small window in which to make a mark. Often, the result is an absence of humanity in the workplace, Kelly says.

Relentless demands, extreme pressure and brutal ruthlessness are all trademarks of a toxic company, as is a twisted disconnect between what a firm says it does for employees and what it actually is doing. People are looked at as costs, rather than assets. On its books, a company might have progressive policies regarding work-life issues, but in fact employs no part-time workers, a key option for those who are struggling to balance career and family. Fear and paranoia, and anxiety to the point of panic, are other characteristics of a toxic workplace. "You can tell as soon as you walk into an office that it's toxic," says Barbara Moses, a consultant in career management and author of *What Next? The Complete Guide to Taking Control of Your Working Life*, among other employment-related books. "People are rushed; they have that harried look," she says. "Conversations are curt and abrupt; there's no chance for thoughtful, rich conversation."

There are multiple reasons why the toxic workplace is proliferating, Kelly says. With mega-mergers and globalization, some corporations are becoming more vast and impersonal, while simultaneously recurring waves of job cuts have left companies lean and left individuals with workloads greater than is reasonably feasible over the long haul. Instead of rewarding long-term planning, expediency is demanded. Add in a leader who ignores the human toll, and the result is likely a toxic workplace. Creative and innovative ideas — ironically, the factors that drive the best corporations — are stifled; employees are alienated; people get sick.

As of yet there aren't studies focusing directly on the toxic workplace, but other stats provide an interesting backdrop. An overwhelming 90 per cent of Canadian companies polled last summer said the workload of their employees has increased, says a report by Mercer Human Resources Consulting. At 64 per cent of them, "emotional tension is prevalent among employees," and absenteeism is up at 68 per cent of the firms. Another study, conducted by a different HR consulting firm, Towers Perrin, shows most Canadians are barely turned on by their work. While one in five say they are highly engaged, almost the same proportion (17 per cent) say they are disengaged. Three out of five claim to be moderately engaged.

.   .   .   .

Culture matters, stresses McInerney, and it's almost always set by the person at the top. "If there's a healthy culture, an organization can survive tumultuous times," he says. "If it isn't innovating, it's not going to survive." Nor will employees. Jones, now working as a consultant, says that while he makes far less money than he used to, his health is pretty good. "I wouldn't trade the money," he says, "to ever go back into that again."

Source: Reproduced with permission from Katherine Macklem, "The toxic workplace: A poisoned work environment can wreak havoc on a company's culture and its employees," *Macleans* (January 31, 2005) <http://www.macleans.ca/topstories/ business/article.jsp?content=20050131_99562_99562>.

WHY STUDY MANAGEMENT THOUGHT? ———————

As "The Business World" illustrates, managing people is clearly central to an organization's success in today's context. What is the best way to manage people? Are there actually philosophies of managing?

Regardless of whether we are looking at a small business or a giant corporation, any type of organization must be managed. When we refer to the notion of "a manager," who are we referring to? A manager can be an individual at any level of the organization. For example, *top management* could include the chief executive officer (CEO) or president, along with vice-presidents; *middle managers* could include such figures as departmental or division heads, plant or branch managers, deans; *supervisors*, or first-line management, might include department heads, foremen or supervisors. Individuals can take on formal or informal managerial roles. For example, a "team leader" may or may not be formally assigned a managerial role, though that person may have much of the responsibilities of a manager. Regardless of your profession, or your role in organizations, no doubt at some point in your career you will be required to apply some sort of management or leadership skills.

The field of management can, indeed, be systematically studied, and a consideration of it is of benefit to anyone who wishes to understand the philosophies that have guided managers for the past century. Below, we will consider the body of knowledge that attempts to identify principles employed by managers in their daily practice. However, before we embark, we need to ask a simple question: What do managers do?

WHAT DO MANAGERS DO? ———————

What exactly does it mean to manage? What are the functions or roles of a manager? Management has been defined in many ways, including the following:

> "The art of getting things done through people." (Mary Parker Follett)
> "Managers give direction to their organizations, provide leadership and decide how to use organizational resources." (Peter Drucker)

To be a little more systematic, management has also been described as:

> The process of administering and coordinating resources effectively and efficiently in an effort to achieve the organization's goals.

This last definition needs a little more explanation. The term *efficiency* refers to using the fewest inputs to produce a given level of output. The term *effectiveness* refers to the pursuit and achievement of goals that are appropriate for the organization.

We need to be a little more specific about what exactly it is that managers do. Here's a somewhat more detailed definition:

> Managing includes the process of planning, organization, leading and controlling organizational resources in the effort to achieve organizational goals.

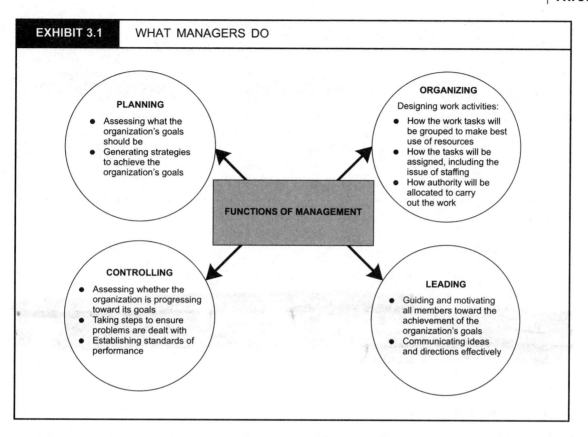

EXHIBIT 3.1 WHAT MANAGERS DO

PLANNING
- Assessing what the organization's goals should be
- Generating strategies to achieve the organization's goals

ORGANIZING
Designing work activities:
- How the work tasks will be grouped to make best use of resources
- How the tasks will be assigned, including the issue of staffing
- How authority will be allocated to carry out the work

FUNCTIONS OF MANAGEMENT

CONTROLLING
- Assessing whether the organization is progressing toward its goals
- Taking steps to ensure problems are dealt with
- Establishing standards of performance

LEADING
- Guiding and motivating all members toward the achievement of the organization's goals
- Communicating ideas and directions effectively

Exhibit 3.1 outlines each element of this definition — or what have commonly been considered the four central functions of management: planning, organizing, leading and controlling.

The Roles Managers Play in Organizations

Henry Mintzberg, a management scholar, conducted an in-depth study of managers in the 1960s. His observations have stuck with us today, and seem to present a useful account of the many roles that managers can potentially play. Among the interesting results of his study is the fact that Mintzberg's work contradicted the then dominant view of the role of managers.

The traditional view of the role of managers was that managers were able to reflect systematically on information before making decisions and that their job was relatively clear and narrow. Mintzberg's study of managers found that managers engaged in a variety of unpatterned short-duration activities, and the constant interruptions suggested that there was little time for systematic reflection. Most important, Mintzberg offered a classification

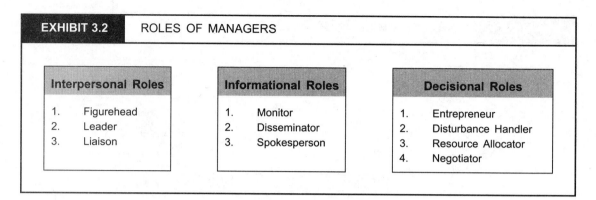

of the various roles that managers play. (See Exhibit 3.2.) Let's consider briefly each of the roles that Mintzberg identified.

Mintzberg presented 10 roles classified within three broad categories: **interpersonal roles**, **informational roles** and **decisional roles**. Essentially, these reflect three key areas of managing: developing and managing interpersonal relationships, dealing with the transfer of information and making decisions.

Interpersonal Roles

Interpersonal roles include those managerial tasks that arise from the manager's formal authority base and involve relationships with either other organizational members or external parties. **Figurehead** roles are typically ceremonial or symbolic in nature. For example, in the role of a figurehead, the supervisor might hand out "employee of the month" awards at a company banquet. In the **leader** role, the manager may serve as a motivator, a communicator and a coordinator of her subordinates' activities. This might include conducting performance appraisals, offering training to a new recruit, etc. A final role within the interpersonal grouping is that of **liaison**, which includes those managerial activities that involve developing relationships with members of the organization outside the manager's area of authority. This could include anything from a sales manager's relationship with the production department to a university dean's networking relationship with the city council.

Informational Roles

Mintzberg's second broad category of managerial roles, referred to as informational roles, reflects the importance of managers as communication sources for the organization — whether this involves gathering or giving out important information to other organizational members, or to parties outside the organization.

First, we can consider the manager as a **monitor** of sorts. That is, managers must constantly monitor the internal and external environments of their organization in order to gather information that is useful for organizational decision making. For example, the marketing manager may be responsible for assessing consumer demand for a newly proposed product.

Second, managers are also **disseminators** of information. That is, they may share or distribute the information that they have gained in their role as monitors, for example. Obviously, managers must ensure that subordinates have all information that they require in order to perform their job effectively. This might include offering clear information regarding company expectations of performance standards and performance appraisal criteria.

Third, the manager may act as **spokesperson**. Managers can also transmit information to individuals outside their area of authority. For example, a marketing manager might provide the engineering department with the latest report of consumer preferences regarding product design. Or the company president may report to a government regulatory board regarding the company's environmental policy.

Decisional Roles

Mintzberg's final category is referred to as decisional roles, and highlights the fact that managers must process information and act as decision makers. There are four classes of roles described here. First is the notion of the manager as **entrepreneur**. That is, the manager may, for example, develop and initiate new projects. This might include the personnel manager developing a new performance appraisal system, the marketing manager developing a new product, etc. Generating new projects and new ventures is a highly valued trait among today's managers.

Managers might also play the role of **disturbance handlers**. Dealing with and attempting to resolve conflict can include things like resolving a dispute between two employees, dealing with a difficult or unco-operative supplier, etc.

A third role that managers can play is that of **resource allocator**, which involves deciding how resources (money, equipment, personnel, time) will be allocated. So, a department head might decide how to allocate a limited financial budget among the different areas. Deciding how much time the division should invest in a new project is also a decision about resources.

The final decisional role identified by Mintzberg is the manager as **negotiator**. Indeed, numerous research studies have underscored the great degree to which managers are engaged in some form of negotiation throughout their activities. Whether this involves negotiating with customers, employees or other departments, a manager often bargains over issues that affect the operation of his or her department, unit or organization. For example, the production purchasing manager might negotiate with the supplier in an effort to speed up the supply of raw materials for the company's production department. A personnel manager might negotiate with a representative of the union to resolve a conflict.

Now that we have outlined the notion of managing and the roles of managers, in the next section we will take a more systematic look at how the role of manager is changing. We'll start with the oldest approach, and then consider more recent philosophies of managing people in organizations.

MANAGEMENT PHILOSOPHIES

If you have ever taken a trip to Disneyland, you will notice the great level of care and professionalism with which Disney employees (referred to as "cast members") conduct their jobs. In fact, Disney has even offered management training programs through its "university" for countless other organizations. What is so special about Disney's management approach that has helped it achieve worldwide fame and success? The answer — nothing is unique about its approach. However, what is rare is its ability to make sure the management philosophies employed are suitable for the nature of their organization. While a lot of what Disney is doing may make common sense, common sense alone won't get you very far when it comes to selecting and implementing a system of managerial practices that is suitable for today's organization. Clearly, not all organizations are created equal — from the McDonald's of the fast food industry to the Microsoft of the high-tech world, what works for one organization with regard to management philosophy may be deadly if applied in another environment. So the question is, what are the ranges of management philosophies that exist, and upon what principles are they based? Let's answer these questions as we consider the elements of two fundamentally different schools of management thought: the classical and the behavioural approaches. (See Exhibit 3.3 for a comparison of the two approaches.)

CLASSICAL APPROACHES TO MANAGEMENT

The oldest of the formalized perspectives of management has come to be known as the classical school of management, and it arose during the late 19th and early 20th centuries. This view originated during a time of rapid industrialization of the United States and European business sectors. Three streams that are central components of this school are:

1. scientific management
2. administrative management
3. bureaucratic management

We will look at each of these perspectives, and attempt to understand the contributions they have made to the field of managing, but first we must consider the environment surrounding the evolution of management thought.

The Social Context

Understanding the social context of late 19th and early 20th centuries sheds light on the logic of the management approaches that were generated.

One of the major driving forces behind the formalization of management thought was the **Industrial Revolution**. While management concepts have been around practically since the dawn of civilization, it was not until the 18th century, as a consequence of the intel-

EXHIBIT 3.3	MANAGEMENT PHILOSOPHIES

I. Classical Approaches to Managing

1. Scientific Management
2. Administrative Management
3. Bureaucratic Management

II. Behavioural Approaches to Managing

1. The Human Relations Movement
2. Mary Parker Follett and Chester Barnard
3. Modern Behavioural Science and Motivation-based Perspectives

lectual and scientific accomplishments of the Renaissance period, that the systematic development of management principles and practices began.

The Industrial Revolution, as the name implies, was a major transformation in work processes that began in the 18th century with the replacement of hand production by machine and factory production. For example, a new energy source, the coal-driven steam engine, was created to run the machines. The introduction of new work processes and machinery culminated in the factory system of production that eventually led to the mass production processes. Certainly, the factory system brought with it many benefits, including a higher standard of living. It also brought with it extensive changes in management, given that work was no longer conducted in workers' homes, but in factories.

The philosophy that fuelled the Industrial Revolution was the notion of "laissez faire," a term used by the economist Adam Smith in his book, *The Wealth of Nations*. This term essentially meant that business or manufacturers should be free to make and sell what they please and, consequently, reflected the notion that government should not interfere with the economic affairs of business. Businesses should be allowed to pursue their own self-interest. The economic view of labour was a straightforward one — the employer buys the labour, and the employee provides the labour. There was no long-term obligation on either side. That reinforced the notion that employees were not valued. With a great supply of labour and jobs involving little skill, it became clear that all power rested with the employer. It was in such an environment that philosophies like Scientific Management eventually arose.

1. *Scientific Management*

Frederick Taylor (1856–1915) was an American engineer who sought to help American industry deal with the challenges of improving productivity. Keep in mind that in Taylor's time there were no clear concepts of management and worker responsibilities. Taylor thought the problem was a simple one to solve — improve management practices, and you'll improve productivity. So, Taylor sought to better manage workers.

For most of his working life, Taylor was employed in steel mills, first as a labourer, eventually as foreman and, ultimately, as chief engineer. While working as a foreman at Midvale Steel Company in Philadelphia, and later as a consulting engineer at Pittsburgh's Bethlehem Steel, Taylor observed what he thought were significant inefficiencies in the conduct of work. The results of his observations and studies were eventually reported in a series of papers, *The Principles of Scientific Management*, published in 1911.

What was Taylor's philosophy? Taylor stated the fundamental objective of management: "Securing the maximum prosperity for the employer coupled with the maximum prosperity for each employee." This sounds reasonable; but what, specifically, does it mean and how do you go about achieving that apparently admirable objective? To answer the second question, Taylor believed that the way to improve things was through scientific management. What is scientific management?

There are at least three central features of Taylorism, or scientific management. Taylor proposed a number of important guidelines. Among them were the following principles:

(a) Standardizing the Work

During Taylor's days with Midvale Steel in Philadelphia, he made some interesting observations of workers whose task it was to shovel coal and iron during the manufacture of pig iron. He decided to experiment with different sizes of shovel, and varied the size of the load scooped in order to minimize fatigue. He also arranged for the workers to have varying work time and rest intervals so that he could experiment with recovery rate. Taylor closely analyzed the range of motions involved in shovelling. Based on his observations and recommendations, the average daily output of workers was tripled, and also the number of shovellers required for the job was reduced from 600 to 140! The science of shovelling was indeed born, and scientific management was a hit!

Scientific management, or Taylorism, then, was based on careful observation and measurement in order to determine the most efficient methods for performing a task. This essentially involves the scientific and systematic study of how work is done in order to improve the work process. Work can be studied objectively, and tasks can be broken down into their simplest steps. The scientific analysis of jobs required **time and motion studies**. This involved using a movie camera and a stopwatch to closely scrutinize the elements of performing a task. For example, bricklayers could be observed and timed in order to assess precisely which movements were most efficient for laying bricks.

All this was based on Taylor's belief that there is one best method for performing the job — and the job of management is to discover that method, and train workers and ensure that they use that method. This resulted in specializing or **compartmentalizing** the job into its basic parts: breaking the job down into its most fundamental steps and, where feasible, allowing workers to perform the most basic tasks. This kept the job simple, made it easy and inexpensive to train workers, and ensured a cheap and ready supply of labour to perform the job. **Standardizing** the work meant that there were clear rules regarding how to perform it, which left little or no room for individual discretion. There is no better way of ensuring consistent performance than through the creation of strict guidelines.

According to Taylor, the purpose of managers, then, is to help set proper standards for work performance. Managers must also train the workers in these standards, and direct their performance in order to achieve the most efficient and least fatiguing manner of working. Other responsibilities of management include selecting workers with the abilities that make them most suitable for the job.

(b) Supervising the Workers

Taylor believed that a manager can't be expert in everything. He therefore suggested that managers take charge only of their area of expertise. As a first-level supervisor, you should be responsible for workers who perform a common function with which you are familiar. Of course, it is the supervisor or foreman who would do the planning, time motion studies, scheduling, etc. More generally, what Taylor did was make clear the separation of the mental work of managers from the physical work of the labourers. The managers directed workers to do the work according to the standardized manner. Keep in mind that Taylor's views arose at a time when American industry had at its disposal a vast supply of labour, with a huge segment of new immigrants who, it was felt, were not fully capable of managing themselves.

Taylor's views have been criticized as denigrating employees and treating them as machines. However, Taylor did contribute to the creation of management as a "profession." Think of it: managers' skills became specific not to the manufacture of the product, but, rather, are to manage — regardless of the organizational context, managers could be trained to coordinate the activities of large numbers of people.

(c) Motivating the Workers

Taylor's philosophy about motivating the workers was quite simple: money motivates! While that may seem obvious to most of us, Taylor's views were interestingly consistent with the rest of his philosophy. In a sense, Taylor advocated a system that has recently been revisited by many different types of organizations. Taylor believed that compensation must be closely tied to performance. A paycheque for simply "walking through the door" is not motivating. It must be clear in workers' minds that they only get a "good day's pay" for a "good day's work." So, a **piece-rate system** was desirable, whereby workers' pay was directly tied to their output. If you produced at a standard level of production, you received a standard rate of pay; if you produced above average, you were paid at a higher rate.

How far-reaching are Taylor's views, and does Taylorism exist today? Scientific management continues to influence the management of work. From the manufacturing sector to the service industry, this philosophy, in many ways, guided organizations for much of the past century. For example, consider the teaching profession. Believe it or not, Taylor and the principles of scientific management had a profound impact on the education system. The industrial expansion of the early 20th century demanded a system of mass education that would educate huge numbers of formerly rural people, as well as new immigrants. The system required a rapid increase in the number of able though inexpen-

---

TALKING BUSINESS **3.1   TAYLORISM — ALIVE AND WELL**

Taylorism certainly remains alive and well across many different industries. You can prob-ably think of some real-life organizations that are managed according to the principles of scientific management. For example, UPS (United Parcel Service) has built its success in the delivery service on the principles of Taylorism. This company designed time and motion studies to ensure that the work of its delivery team is based on maxi-mum efficiency and performed under strict standardized guidelines. However, there is likely no better example of the modern application of scientific management than McDonald's.

The success of McDonald's is obvious, and largely based on the duplication of its service across diverse areas. Their management system has been adopted not only by other fast-food chains, but has spread to retail and other industries. McDonald's achieved fame by making the dining experience reliable and predictable for consumers — by the application of the principles of scientific management. Standardization guaranteed that customers continually received what they expected — both in the design of the store and in the system. Employee jobs are compartmentalized and standardized: cooking and cus-tomer service are broken down into a series of simple, standardized tasks performed according to strict detail.

Source: Based on George Ritzer, *The McDonaldization of Society: An Investigation into the Chang-ing Character of Contemporary Social Life* (London, England: Pine Forge Press, 1995).

---

sive teachers. Taylorism facilitated such a transition in the education system. Managers, who were typically male, became the supervisors or principals of the teachers, who were mostly women and less powerful and less well paid. The nature of teaching, too, became subject to the principles of scientific management. Remember the need to break the job down into its simplest components? Teachers were now specialized by grade and by subject; just as manufacturing work became specialized or compartmentalized, the task of teaching became standardized — what you taught and how you taught it were all part of a common plan. Clearly, then, Taylorism was adopted widely in industrial as well as non-industrial settings. Taylor's ideas also spread beyond North America to Russia, Japan, Germany and elsewhere. (See Talking Business 3.1.)

2.   *Administrative Management*

A second sub-school of the classical perspective of management is closely associated with the work of Henry Fayol (1841–1925). As the name implies, this approach focuses specifically on management and the functions that managers should perform. Fayol, like Taylor, had some compelling views of how organizations should be managed. An engineer for a mining company in France, Fayol applied his principles with much success; revitaliz-

---

***TALKING BUSINESS* 3.2   IS FAYOL ALIVE AND WELL?**

Some of Fayol's assertions have gone out of vogue. For example, in today's environment many organizations do not view centralized decision-making authority as being as efficient as allowing authority to reside at lower levels in the organization. In addition, the rights of workers certainly are no longer subordinated to organizational goals, and considerable attention is placed on satisfying individual interests and needs at work. However, some of Fayol's principles are quite compatible with contemporary management views. For example, Fayol's notion of team spirit is certainly considered in many workplaces that are attempting to facilitate team work.

Japanese management practices have been viewed as an application of many of Fayol's principles, including the emphasis on the collective good or general interest, as well as the emphasis on teamwork.

---

ing an ailing company certainly helped Fayol's management approach gain attention. However, whereas Taylor's work was largely aimed at guiding managers at the lower levels, Fayol's work focused on upper levels of administration. Fayol developed a number of principles of management that he believed could serve as universal principles that could be taught to managers regardless of their specific organizational environment.

Like Taylor, Fayol supported the notion of *division of work*: that is, by breaking work down into its simplest components and assigning these separate elements to workers, the work can be conducted more efficiently and productively. Similarly, Fayol believed that a manager's role is to give orders and to discipline employees. Fayol also advocated the notion of **unity of command**: that is, each employee should report to only one boss in order to avoid confusion and conflicting instructions. In addition, this authority should be concentrated at the upper levels of the organization.

Fayol believed that employees should subordinate their individual interests to the common good or general interest of the organization. In other words, the goals of the overall organization must take precedence over any individual interests of employees. Finally, among Fayol's stated principles was the concept of *esprit de corps* — that is, team spirit and harmony should be encouraged among workers in order to generate organizational cohesiveness and unity. Are Fayol's views still with us? See Talking Business 3.2.

3.   *Bureaucratic Management*

Max Weber (1864–1920) was a German sociologist whose work became most closely affiliated with the school of thought eventually known as bureaucratic management. This perspective is broader in its focus than scientific and administrative management, in that Weber's focus is on the nature of the organization as a whole. As was the case with Taylor and Fayol, Weber's beliefs came from observations of his environment.

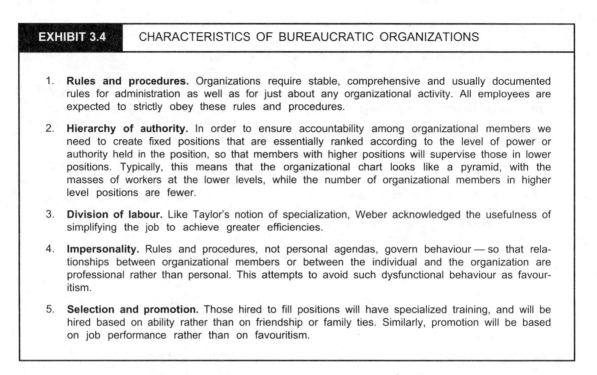

| EXHIBIT 3.4 | CHARACTERISTICS OF BUREAUCRATIC ORGANIZATIONS |

1. **Rules and procedures.** Organizations require stable, comprehensive and usually documented rules for administration as well as for just about any organizational activity. All employees are expected to strictly obey these rules and procedures.

2. **Hierarchy of authority.** In order to ensure accountability among organizational members we need to create fixed positions that are essentially ranked according to the level of power or authority held in the position, so that members with higher positions will supervise those in lower positions. Typically, this means that the organizational chart looks like a pyramid, with the masses of workers at the lower levels, while the number of organizational members in higher level positions are fewer.

3. **Division of labour.** Like Taylor's notion of specialization, Weber acknowledged the usefulness of simplifying the job to achieve greater efficiencies.

4. **Impersonality.** Rules and procedures, not personal agendas, govern behaviour — so that relationships between organizational members or between the individual and the organization are professional rather than personal. This attempts to avoid such dysfunctional behaviour as favouritism.

5. **Selection and promotion.** Those hired to fill positions will have specialized training, and will be hired based on ability rather than on friendship or family ties. Similarly, promotion will be based on job performance rather than on favouritism.

Weber observed that many 19th century European organizations were, in a number of ways, very poorly managed. One critical observation was that numerous organizations were managed on a personal basis, with employees guided more by personal loyalties to other individuals' agendas than by professional loyalties to organizational goals. This often resulted in the misuse of resources for personal means.

Weber believed that an alternative organizational structure was required, and this structure would improve the operations of the organization in a number of ways; this was the origin of the notion of the bureaucratic organization. Weber identified several fundamental elements of such an organization, including those in Exhibit 3.4.

What was behind Weber's principles? Consider what is potentially accomplished through these elements. Weber believed that an organization possessing these characteristics could best maintain consistent, dependable and reliable performance by its members. By having rigid rules and procedures and insisting on conformity to these guidelines, organizations ensure that the goals of the organization are perpetuated and are not dependent on the individuals who populate the organization at any one time.

The impersonality of a bureaucracy was also intended to avoid arbitrary and biased decisions of individuals that might be based on favouritism or personal agendas. Weber wanted to see an organization with a clear administrative structure so that employees would conform to these rules and regulations and understand that they must answer to the boss for their actions. Without these characteristics, Weber believed that organizational behaviour could be neither reliable nor predictable, and decisions might become arbitrary or biased. So, how much impact did Weber have? See Talking Business 3.3.

***TALKING BUSINESS* 3.3   IS WEBER ALIVE AND WELL?**

Ironically, while Weber's work was based on observations of European organizations, his views (translated into English in the 1940s) had a profound impact on North American organizations. Certainly, we have witnessed, over a good part of the past century, the growth of bureaucracies. In fact, it is only more recently that we have come to question the utility of the bureaucratic organization with its emphasis on rules and regulations.

Rigid bureaucratic rules work well when the environment is stable: that is, where consumer needs are unchanging, where technology is fixed, and where other environmental factors, such as political and social forces, are relatively constant. In that type of environment, the need to have comprehensive rules and regulations governing organizational activity, to ensure that authority rests with well-trained managers, all make sense. However, business environments have increasingly undergone rapid change and, consequently, organizations have been moving away from bureaucratic structures and the traditional rules and regulations that might now be outdated. On the other hand, some of the features of bureaucracies remain as strengths for almost any organization. For example, the notion of applying rules and procedures equally to all individuals across the organization would appear to support fairness and dependable behaviour in organizations.

The Classical Approaches in Perspective

The three classical approaches (scientific, administrative and bureaucratic) share a basic philosophy regarding what is required to manage effectively. The classical approaches all indicate a clear role for managers: the job of managers is to plan, control and direct the actions of their subordinates in order to obtain the greatest efficiency from their workers. Scientific management advocated the construction of tasks in a way that minimizes their complexity, and emphasized a machine-like approach to managing workers. The administrative management perspective highlighted the view that fundamental principles should guide the role of manager, regardless of the context. Finally, the belief in the benefits of bureaucracy reflects the view that organizations must be run according to a strict set of rules, with a clear hierarchy of authority to ensure accountability and adherence to the rules.

Now the question is, Is this the best way to manage? Let's reconsider the context within which this perspective was born. As mentioned, these approaches arose at a time when industry was rapidly expanding and relatively unskilled labour was in abundance. These approaches, in fact, all worked quite well from the time of their conception through the Great Depression of the 1930s. But times do change. And over time, the weaknesses of the classical approach became more and more apparent in some organizations. One major element absent in this approach is the role of human behaviour — the employee. These approaches assume that the worker will respond passively to his or her designated role in the workplace, and increasingly managers found that the assumption of the classical approach can break down in practice. Talking Business 3.4 clearly illustrates that employees' concerns cannot be ignored.

***TALKING BUSINESS* 3.4   STRANDED BY STRIKES**

Over 70,000 passengers found themselves stranded in the Heathrow airport, and several other airports on August 11, 2005.

This was the result of disagreements between employers and employees. The two companies involved were in-flight caterers Gate Gourmet (GG), and British Airways (BA). The conflict was sparked by GG's restructuring plans, which included staffing reductions, changes to overtime payments and the flexible deployment of staff to boost productivity. The Transport & General Worker's Union refused to accept these changes and called for a strike. Management then gave workers the ultimatum of going back to work or losing their jobs. The workers did not oblige, and over 600 employees were fired. This prompted the workers of British Airways, members of the same union, to go on an unofficial strike in support of the fired workers.

BA workers went on strike because they didn't believe Gate Gourmet had just cause for the firings. British Airways has unfortunately had three major strikes in three years.

This recent strike was not a direct result of BA's actions, and their management had very little control over the situation. However, it does reveal the precarious relationship that can exist between management and employees and the potential for such a relationship to be easily damaged.

BEHAVIOURAL APPROACHES TO MANAGEMENT

What we observed during the early part of the 20th century was that employees were managed pretty much the same way as the company managed their physical or financial resources: as another piece of capital to serve the organization's objectives. Over this century, approaches to managing people have changed dramatically. What caused us to change our philosophy of managing? The impetus for change arose through a variety of sources. Some of the initiatives came from business itself, some from government, some thorough union action and some through broad social changes. Whatever the source, what we witnessed in the second and third decades of the 20th century was the beginning of a more humane way of managing — a recognition of employees not simply as another resource to be managed, but as individuals with certain needs that must be addressed. The **behavioural approaches** focus on the nature of the employee and on what factors encourage employees to maximize their effort. Consequently, the behavioural school ultimately has led us to a consideration of what lies beneath the surface. That is, what is the driving force behind our decisions to put effort into our jobs or careers? What factors determine how much "blood, sweat and tears" employees are willing to expend in work performance?

The behavioural approach to management refers to managerial perspectives that consider the social or human side of organizations and address the challenges of managing human beings. This approach assumes that to achieve maximum productivity requires an understanding of the human factor of organizations and an ability to create an environment that permits employees to fulfill social, as opposed to simply economic, needs. The ongoing conflicts observed between management and employees are not necessarily a consequence of purely financial interests. Salary is obviously an important factor in employer-employee relationships. However, employees also require treatment that respects their dignity and work efforts. Recent strikes, such as that documented in Talking Business 3.4, reflect the broader concerns that employers hold, beyond simply "money matters." As with the classical approach, the school of thought that has come to be known as the behavioural approach is actually composed of a number of different perspectives. In sum, this school of thought calls upon managers to consider at least two critical features of organizations:

1. Organizations are designed to produce a good or service efficiently and effectively (a view shared by the classical school).

2. However, unlike the classical school, consideration must also be given to the fact that organizations are *social systems* through which individuals attempt to satisfy their personal and social needs, as well as their economic needs.

We can consider four broad perspectives that constitute the behavioural approach: the work of Elton Mayo and the human relations perspective; the assertions of Mary Parker Follett and Chester Barnard; and, finally, another sub-school that has been referred to as modern behavioural science.

1. The Human Relations Movement

Elton Mayo (1880–1949) conducted studies at Western Electric, in Hawthorne, Illinois, around 1924 that drew great attention to the importance of the social dimension of work. Among Mayo's studies was an investigation of the effects of lighting on worker productivity. To test the effects of lighting, Mayo chose one group of workers to be the experimental group: the "guinea pigs," so to speak. A variety of lighting conditions were manipulated. A control group was also used whereby this group of workers worked under constant lighting conditions. If better lighting improved productivity, then the group of workers working under better lighting conditions should outperform the control group. The results were puzzling, however. For example, the productivity of both the control and the experimental group increased. In fact, even when lighting was worsened for the experimental group, their productivity nonetheless increased. How to explain these results?

Mayo had inadvertently discovered what came to be known as the **Hawthorne Effect**. The experimental results (the productivity increases) were not, in fact, caused by the intended experimental manipulation (the increased lighting), but by other factors — here, by "human nature." Specifically, Mayo uncovered that the true source of the great productivity increase was the employees' receiving some special attention. That is, all subjects realized that they were the focus of attention for the study, and that itself increased their motivation to do a good job.

Surprisingly, social factors had thus had a greater impact on productivity than had actual working conditions. The Hawthorne Effect had a major impact on management thinking; and, in fact, it has been viewed as marking the transition from scientific management to the human relations approach. This approach focuses on organizations as social systems, and not simply formal structures. It stresses the need for managers to recognize that managing involves social interaction — that "employees are people, too!"

2. Mary Parker Follett (1868–1933)

Mary Parker Follett was a social philosopher who made a number of significant contributions to the field of management in the first decades of the 20th century. Based on Follett's observations of real-life managers, she identified a number of elements necessary for effective management. Among the factors she emphasized as critical were coordination, self-management and collaboration.

First, Follett argued that *coordination* was central to a manager's function. That is, Follett suggested that the manager's job of encouraging workers to maximize their productivity should come about not through force or coercion, but through involvement in coordinating and harmonizing group efforts. This requires managers being closely involved with subordinates in the daily conduct of their work, rather than simply being people who make and enforce rules.

Second, Follett stressed the importance of **self-management** and **collaboration**. Follett felt that decisions regarding how work is done can often be made by those performing the work, rather than by managers who may not be as familiar with the task. Consequently, subordinates should be involved in the decision-making process in matters that affect their work and how they should perform their work. Moreover, she felt that individuals would much prefer managing themselves than being led by a boss. Managers and workers should view themselves as collaborators or partners. Follett advocated her views at a time when Taylor was considered the leading management scholar. Follett's views were largely ignored, and have only gained acceptance in more recent times. Some observers suggest that the practice of management for the past 100 years might have looked very different had Follett been given more attention than Taylor.

3. Chester Barnard (1896–1961)

Chester Barnard was a practitioner who served as president of New Jersey Bell Telephone Company. Like Weber, he was interested in organizational structure; but Barnard, unlike Weber, with his impersonal idea of organizations, considered organizations as social systems. Among Barnard's contributions were his notions of communication and authority. Barnard felt that the two most critical functions of managers were:

1. To establish and maintain a communication system with employees. Barnard felt that organizations, as social systems, required continual communication and co-operation among all members to be effective.

2. Management must clearly establish the organizational objectives and ensure that all employees are motivated to help attain these objectives.

In terms of the notion of authority, Barnard contradicted the then-popular view of traditional authority, which reflected the notion that those in power have an absolute right to receive compliance from those at lower levels in the hierarchy. Barnard felt that authority of management over subordinates must be earned — that is, workers will only follow orders to the extent that:

- They understand what is required.
- They see how they relate to organizational goals.
- They believe that they will gain some benefit from accomplishing these goals.

Fundamentally, Barnard, like Follett, believed that a **collaborative** approach to management would be most effective for organizations.

4. Modern Behavioural Science and Motivation-Based Perspectives

Look around your workplace, and you will see some individuals who are completely committed to fulfilling the expectations and responsibilities of their employer. Continue looking, and you may also find someone asleep at his or her desk, or maybe surfing the Web for interesting vacation sites, while the boss's back is turned. What distinguishes these two workers? Is it a personality difference? Is it a difference in work ethic? Is it pay? Is it the boss? Is it the work environment? What variables play a critical role in determining the level of effort or motivation that employees bring to the job? Clearly, this question is critical for any organization aiming to maximize the potential of its workforce.

Another category of management theories that should be considered as an important part of the behavioural approach can be referred to as modern behavioural science. This school of thought arose largely in the 1950s, and continued the systematic study of the human element of organizations. Researchers came from academic backgrounds in sociology, psychology and anthropology, and became known as behavioural scientists and industrial psychologists. One underlying theme of this work is the issue of motivation. That is, rather than considering the primary role of management to be one of control (the classical approach), these theories consider the role of management as one that must foster a motivated workforce. Consequently, the underlying aim of much of this school of thought is to consider factors that influence the motivation of employees — a key issue for many of today's organizations.

THE BEST MANAGEMENT PHILOSOPHY? A CONTINGENCY APPROACH ——————————

Now that we have considered two very popular schools of management thought, the question is, Where are we today? What approaches are guiding leaders in management of organizations? The approaches described above have both strengths and weaknesses.

Experts agree that there simply is no one best way to manage. Instead, what has been advocated is referred to as the contingency approach to management.

As the name implies, this approach assumes that the best style of management depends on many contingencies: different conditions and situations require the application of different approaches or techniques. Essentially, this approach argues that there are few, if any, universal truths governing management techniques. Consequently, contingency management theories continue to examine different factors that dictate different requirements for managing people.

How to manage at UPS will differ from managing at Microsoft, which will differ from managing at a local hospital, etc. This is a central challenge for any managers — fitting their management philosophy to suit the organizational context. Think about the nature of different organizations and the type of work performed, and you will begin to see the importance of understanding the contingencies of management.

What are some contingencies of management philosophies? (See also Exhibit 3.5.)

1. Organizational size. Large organizations with hundreds of employees cannot be managed in the same manner as small organizations with few employees. The need for control and the challenge to achieve it in massive organizations may tend to encourage an approach that relies on elements of the classical school, such as the need for rules and regulations and the importance of an administrative hierarchy to ensure control. On the other hand, small, entrepreneurial organizations might function more effectively with a minimal number of rules and regulations.

2. Routineness of task technology. Some organizations may require employees to work in an assembly-line fashion, while their work is governed by machinery. Other jobs may not involve any significant level of technology: retail sales or being a bank teller are jobs that do not necessarily require technological expertise. These jobs are more easily subject to routinization — the standards advocated by Taylor, and the rules on which such workers can consistently rely. On the other hand, jobs that must continually adapt to changing technology require employees who are equally adaptive. High-tech organizations that employ "knowledge workers" are keenly aware that it is difficult to standardize the jobs of these workers, given the high rate of change within the present technology.

3. Environmental uncertainty. An organization that exists within a volatile environment must be prepared for continuous change. Change is the antithesis of the classical approaches, which emphasize stability and order. Consequently, organizations functioning in rapidly changing environments are less likely to find extensive application of the classical school useful in managing their workforce.

4. Individual differences. In any organization, employees differ with regard to their ability and motivation. Some people function better when given clear guidance: rules and regulations regarding how their job should be performed. Others perform better when the rules governing their performance are minimal. These differences suggest that a blanket application of either the classical or behavioural schools may risk ignoring the fact that the labour force is not homogeneous in terms of responses to the nature of work and management style.

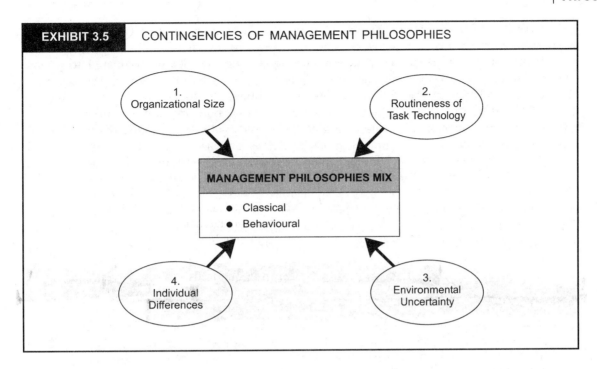

EXHIBIT 3.5 CONTINGENCIES OF MANAGEMENT PHILOSOPHIES

1. Organizational Size

2. Routineness of Task Technology

MANAGEMENT PHILOSOPHIES MIX

- Classical
- Behavioural

4. Individual Differences

3. Environmental Uncertainty

THE MILITARY MODEL OF MANAGING — CAN IT STILL WORK?

Organizations today are facing a fundamental crisis. Globalization has certainly created its own tests for organizations along with the usual challenges, such as achieving profit and growth targets, creating value, security, privacy, diversity and managing change. Many companies are failing to uphold basic business principles such as leadership and trust. Combine this with the fact that the labour force is rapidly declining while the demise of employee loyalty is rapidly increasing. The result is a fundamental crisis. Organizations are faced with the struggle of improving elements that contribute to organizational success. The search for the next successful model to guide managers continues unabated. In searching for guidance, it may be necessary to look in some familiar but largely ignored places.

Many books have been written on successful business models required to achieve organizational effectiveness. Traditional management research has largely condemned the military model of leadership and culture as outdated and old-fashioned. The military model conjures up words such as *dictatorship, command and control, chain of command, hierarchy* and *regimented,* which are often words associated with the manner in which the military runs its business. However, arguably, the military is the ultimate model for achieving organizational effectiveness. The military is extremely proficient at developing high-performance work teams, fostering trust and producing great leaders. In fact, companies such as General Motors, Home Depot, General Electric and Johnson & Johnson all target members from the military to work for their organizations.[1]

There exists an argument that the military organization cannot be compared to private business because the only time the military operates in its full context is during war.[2] However, the challenges faced by business and business leaders are the same as those faced by the military. Commonalities include the fact that both military and private organizations have specific measurements and goals, budgets, motivated leaders, discipline problems, established structures, communications processes and are under pressure to produce results.[3] In fact, the military is under much greater scrutiny than private organizations because of the amount of money funded by the public. In addition, as opposed to all other professions, military members are subject to unlimited liability. No other profession in the world requires the sacrifice of life that the military demands from its members. For this reason the military must be extremely adept at managing its human capital in order to ensure organizational effectiveness.

The **military ethos** plays a critical role in unifying the attributes of responsibility, expertise and identity. *Ethos* is defined as the disposition, character or fundamental values peculiar to a specific person, people, culture or movement. The military ethos is the foundation that encapsulates how the military operates on a daily basis. The military ethos is comprised of values, beliefs and expectations that reflect core Canadian values, the imperatives of military professionalism and the requirements of operations. It is referred to as the "centre of gravity" and the "ethical framework" with the sole purpose of bringing all members of the Canadian Forces together, regardless of rank, occupation or branch of service.[4] Therefore, the military ethos is universal to all military members. Trust is a major component of the military ethos. The ethos is intended to establish trust between the military and Canadian society, guide the development of leaders, create and shape the military culture, establish the basis for policy, enable professional self-regulation and assist in identifying and resolving ethical challenges.[5] The fundamental beliefs and expectations of the military and military values are an integral part of the military ethos. There is a shared vision inherent within the ethos.

The fundamental beliefs and expectations of the ethos include *unlimited liability, fighting spirit, discipline* and most importantly *teamwork*.[6] Accepting *unlimited liability* is a concept that refers to the belief that mission and troops, in that order, supersede over self. It refers to service before self or the "greater good" of the mission over that of individual life. Unlimited liability requires leadership that places the good of the mission and those led over the self-interest of the leader. *Fighting spirit* refers to the commitment to strive for excellence with a focus on moral, physical and intellectual qualities in order to achieve operational effectiveness. Members are expected to exemplify this spirit not only during war but also on a daily basis. The fighting spirit creates a bond between all members of the military regardless of rank or branch. *Discipline* refers to the self-discipline required in order to maintain a high standard of professionalism. It builds cohesion between members that allows individuals and units to achieve their objectives which could not be achieved by military skills alone. It also allows compliance with the interests and goals of the military while instilling shared values and common standards. Discipline builds self-assurance and self-confidence. A high standard of military discipline is generated, in part, through the knowledge of fellow members and trust in leaders. The military ethos places a high value on *teamwork*. Teamwork builds cohesion and allows the military to

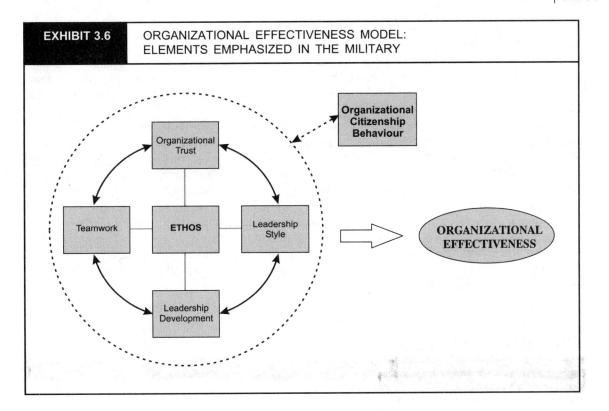

EXHIBIT 3.6   ORGANIZATIONAL EFFECTIVENESS MODEL:
ELEMENTS EMPHASIZED IN THE MILITARY

execute high level tasks through the integration and synthesis of the skill sets of all its members.[7]

The military ethos is the framework on which the behaviours of the military members are governed and conducted. The values and belief system exemplified by this ethos equate to honour for the military member, which comes from the loyalty and faithfulness to other members. The military ethos embodies the central concepts critical to the success of the military — i.e., in the attitudes toward organizational trust, leadership style and development, and teamwork and citizenship behaviour. We discuss these elements following, and suggest how an organization manages effectively by attending to these central issues — trust, leadership style and development, teamwork and citizenship. See Exhibit 3.6.

Key Management Best Practices in the Military: What Business Managers Should Know

There is little doubt that every single member of the military is aware of the organization's vision and mission. This is not only because it is specifically written in organizational doctrine, but because the military has ensured through organizational practices that all members are aware of what it takes to achieve this mission. The military has clearly defined the basic principles necessary for the organization to succeed. Trust, leadership and teamwork are vital in achieving the mission. These principles are consistently reinforced through written doctrine, human resource policies and practices (i.e., induction and training) and the day-to-day tasks of the military member. All members play an integral part in achieving the mission, and all members are well aware of the role they must play.

Contrary to common belief, the military fosters an open culture where people are encouraged to engage in broad inquiry, to think critically and to venture and debate new ideas in the interests of contributing to the collective effectiveness. An open culture embraces the notion that people in positions of authority are receptive to upward influence and that everyone, irrespective of rank or position, is expected to lead and does not require permission to do so.[8] The military HR strategy doctrine includes culture as part of the strategic plan. This plan includes the fostering of a culture that "ensures the integrity of the profession of arms, promotes the development of effective leaders, encourages life-long learning, supports innovation, understands and promotes diversity and provides the foundation for a leadership team."[9] It is this open culture that allows key elements such as trust to be created and fostered.

Organizational Trust

Organizational trust is crucial. Organizations must focus on creating a culture of trust in order to maximize effectiveness. Most important, trust can provide an organization with a competitive advantage that cannot be easily duplicated. Trust is an integral aspect of the psychological contract that exists between the employee and the employer. Trust refers to one's perception of others' integrity and openness, one's comfort with the expected actions of others, one's faith in other reactions and one's willingness to become vulnerable to the actions of others.[10] Employees want to feel that the organization has their best interests in mind. Although it is now rare to find the worker who remains with one company for an entire career, companies are rediscovering the value of loyalty. Organizations cannot build loyalty in the absence of trust. Research consistently supports the idea that organizational trust has an impact on organization effectiveness. For example, numerous studies have linked trust with a variety of desirable work behaviours such as organizational citizenship behaviour, performance, intention to turnover, problem solving, level of openness within a top management team, support for authorities, satisfaction and organizational commitment.[11] Similarly, trust has been linked with better task performance, openness in communication, information sharing, reduced conflict between partners in inter-organizational relationships and better acceptance of organizational decisions and goals.[12]

Equally, the absence of organizational trust can create serious challenges for an organization. Where there is a lack of trust, there will be failings in communication, delegation, empowerment and quality.[13] A corporate culture of mistrust causes employees to focus on survival and self-preservation by pursuing defensive values such as control, power, expediency and manipulation, which have a negative effect on productivity and morale.[14] Organizations must strive to create a culture of trust. As the military model illustrates, the critical factors needed to create a culture of trust are effective communication, leadership and human resources practices and programs that establish and reinforce the value of trust.

Organizational trust is of paramount importance in the military setting. There can be no greater context than war where individuals must expose vulnerability and trust the person beside them. Trust is reinforced through several mechanisms: an open culture (which has already been discussed), social structures, effective communication mechanisms, leadership, teamwork and human resource policies and practices. The military reinforces trust through a shared purpose, vision, mission and ethos. The organizational belief system is communicated through the profession of arms doctrine and by integrating beliefs through organizational structures and practices.

The military believes that trust is formed when people get to know each other on a personal level as well as on a professional basis. Military messes and institutes provide a social structure where common experiences can be shared and where storytelling occurs. Members of the military at all levels of rank and structure integrate in this social setting, where members can get to know each other on a personal level. A senior officer (Colonel) commented, "We tend to deal with people that we trust in preference over those who we don't know." Thus, the military provides and supports this social structure for its members.

Effective communication is implemented through formal and informal mechanisms. Formal mechanisms include briefings, the use of an "Orders Group" (O Group), the Intranet and mediation centres. The chain of command is used for passing along information in an efficient and effective order. In an operational setting, "orders" are passed along in meetings held with subordinates at each level. This mechanism is also used in administrative settings and ensures that information is passed along to all members. The military is also very specific in terms of how correspondence and documents are written and meetings conducted. For example, acronyms are commonly used in the military to expedite information. The use of mediation and conflict resolution is also advocated in the military as a means to effectively communicate and resolve friction before it escalates. Informal mechanisms include town halls and "walking around."

Leadership Style

The findings in the literature are consistent: leadership does have an impact on organizational outcomes such as individual performance, job satisfaction, innovation and organizational effectiveness. However, the literature is mixed regarding which leadership style is most effective. This may be partly due to the fact that there are varying definitions of *leadership*. Leadership has been defined in terms of individual personality traits, leader behaviours, responses to leader behaviours, interpersonal exchange relationships, interaction patterns, role relationships, follower perceptions, task goals, organizational culture and nature of work processes.[15]

Situational leadership theory suggests that leaders who want the best results should not rely on one single style of leadership.[16] Rather, for the best results, leaders should take a situational approach to leadership. This theory recommends using different styles as the situation permits or dictates, including directing, coaching, supporting and delegating. The type of style used depends on the best match to the follower's readiness, ability and willingness. As the readiness of the follower increases, the need for direction from the leader decreases. The academic literature is mixed with respect to support of this theory and the impact on organizational effectiveness.[17]

The military advocates situational-based leadership style. Each leader must find what works for him or her and take into consideration the developmental levels of the subordinate as well as the context. Leadership in the Canadian Forces is formally defined as "directing, motivating, and enabling others to accomplish the mission professionally and ethically, while developing or improving capabilities that contribute to the mission success."[18] A distinction is made between leadership at the junior level and leadership at the senior level of ranks. Junior level leaders are expected to engage, direct, motivate and enable subordinates in order to accomplish day-to-day tasks, which is referred to as "leading people." Senior level ranks are expected to "lead the institution," which entails sustaining military capabilities and systems through strategic planning, command and activity.[19]

The military philosophy of leadership is based on two key principles: distributed leadership and values-based leadership. Distributed leadership supports the theory that functions of leadership should be shared to varying degrees with peer and subordinate leaders and that leadership development is essential not only for those in leadership positions but also for everyone. Therefore, leadership is an essential component for all members. However, the military also recognizes that not every member is at the same level of capacity. Therefore, distributive leadership also takes into account the fact that the authority given to subordinates must be appropriate and must match the level of readiness. It is essential that when subordinates are given the opportunity to lead (referred to as "stretch assignment"), their performance be monitored, assessed, evaluated and corrected through feedback.

The second key principle of leadership is values-based leadership, meaning that leaders are to be guided in their decisions and actions by the values that are embraced by the organization.[20] For example, the military advocates the relationship between leadership style and accountability. Leaders are accountable for demonstrating ethical behaviour and acting in accordance with the military ethos. In addition, the military views trust as an important element of leadership and thus a climate of trust between leaders and followers is essential. Leaders are expected to build and maintain trust relationships with all members through the following: demonstrating a high level of competence through performance and enhancement of professional development, exercising good judgment, involving subordinates in decision-making processes and giving them additional authority, demonstrating a concern for the well-being of subordinates, treating subordinates with fairness and respect, leading by example and honouring promises and commitments.[21]

One of the ways the military demonstrates its practice of leadership is by embracing the concept of *mission command* which is largely founded on trust. Mission command has been adopted as a result of the changes in warfare. There is a greater emphasis on accelerated decision making, initiative and coordinated independent action. Commanders on the ground are most able to interpret the situation, assess the threat and take decisive action. Mission command follows the principle that commanders are given a task and provided the resources and constraints with which to execute the task. Mission command allows the member freedom of action to perform the task (mission) and report back any exceptions. This is opposite to the myth that decisions in the military are centrally controlled at high levels and executed without any freedom of judgment. In essence, leaders are given a great deal of freedom in how they execute tasks, and all personnel have a strategic impact on what they do or do not do. Mission command is meant to exploit success, not reinforce failure.

Leadership Development

There are many different forms of leadership development initiatives, such as classroom training, corporate universities, on-the-job training, mentoring (formal and informal), community service, challenging assignments, critical reflection, use of teams, job rotations, job sharing and formal coaching. Potential candidates for these programs or initiatives may be selected through various means, such as the succession-planning process, formal internal processes under which managers recommend individuals, the use of performance management tools, such as 360-degree feedback, executives or senior management selecting potential candidates — with or without input from other managers or hiring leadership talent from outside the organization. However, best practice organizations view leadership development as a component of all jobs at all levels.

Leadership development programs have an impact on organizational effectiveness. In order for the leadership development program to be effective, the organization must determine what exactly leadership entails for that specific organization. After this has been determined the organization must connect leadership development to the organization's culture, goals and strategy. The most effective leadership development programs should encompass intra-personal qualities, training, real life experience, work/life programs and mentoring.

Leadership development is a critical organizational practice in the military and can be found in both formal and informal formats. The military views leadership as a critical component for all members regardless of rank. All military members are responsible for achieving the organization's mission. Therefore, all members are expected to be leaders. Leadership development begins immediately for the military member and is the single thread woven through all training in the member's career. Leadership development programs in the military encompass operational training, classroom training, experience, critical reflection, mentoring and work/life programs.

Operational training is a major component in the military and serves many purposes, including leadership development. During their careers, members of the military are routinely assessed on leadership ability. For example, during basic officer training, members are put into leadership roles in small groups and given a task to execute (referred to as "small party tasks"). The nature of the task is not relevant compared to the way in which a leader conducts him- or herself. The member in the leadership role is assessed and evaluated on aspects such as time management, execution of the task and leadership ability. Members learn leadership skills through these types of exercises. This model of performance assessment, evaluation and feedback is a common and consistently applied management practice.

Formal leadership development programs are highly structured. Each program contains a developmental period, which occurs when the member first joins the organization. Next, there are four subsequent developmental tiers for officers and five tiers for non-commissioned members of the military. Each development tier contains core education and training programs that are consistent with the skills, values and attitudes considered essential for the military. Members must complete the courses and training in each tier in order to advance in the military. For example, one requisite in the Officer Developmental Period 2 is referred to as the OPME (Officer Professional Military Education), which provides a common body of knowledge to all officers and encourages a continuing evolution in self-reflection, decision making and leadership skills. The curriculum includes courses such as leadership and ethics as well as technical courses.[22] Succession Planning is formalized and based on factors such as education, bilingualism, experience, performance review, leadership ability and leadership potential.

Key leadership principles are taught in classroom training format based on preparation and work with the use of case studies, modelling, syndicate discussions, open forums and critical reflection. Storytelling is also used as an informal leadership development method — experiences are shared, and members learn from each other. The military regularly recommends reading lists for members in order to promote self-development. Formal mentors are brought in to pass on information based on real life experiences. More informal sessions take place with leaders and their subordinates where an open forum is advocated to promote discussion. Informal mentors are also used in the military — often in the form of a senior and junior member and are normally based on shared and common experiences. Experience also plays a key role in leadership development. The military places members in different jobs every two to three years, which provides the opportunity for new and challenging work assignments and to constantly upgrade skills and knowledge.

Finally, critical reflection is essential in leadership development. Critical reflection is used during classroom training but is also much more formalized. The military has adopted a process called the After Action Review (AAR), which takes place "during and immediately after any major activity such as an attack during a training exercise, a patrol during an operation in Canada or some other part of the world or a day-to-day activity such as setting-up and conducting a sporting event."[23] The Army has also established an organization called the Army Lessons Learned Centre, where a knowledge-based management system has been implemented to "collate, analyze and disseminate Canadian and Allied full spectrum operational experiences in order to support the Army Learning Process."[24]

Teamwork and Citizenship

Although the research supports the positive effects of the use of teams, the existence of high-performance teams is stated to be rare.[25] High performance teams "frequently outperform the teams that produce similar products and services under similar conditions and constraints."[26]

There appears to be a common theme among the research with respect to the effectiveness of teams. The key factors for effective teams include a shared vision, empowerment, and trust among team members. Teamwork creates a community because everyone must accept ownership and responsibility for a project's success or failure.[27] In order for team-based structures to be effective the organization must provide a culture that supports collaboration and a highly involved workforce. The culture should be based on empowerment, creativity, shared vision, participation, learning ability, trust and a shared consensus.

Teamwork is of paramount importance in the military. Teams are built to succeed in the mission. The mission cannot be accomplished individually and thus teamwork is a critical part of the military ethos. Teamwork is required to foster the cohesion necessary to achieve the organizational mission. The military stresses the importance of team over the individual, and teamwork is reinforced through doctrine, training and exercises.

The concept of teamwork can be found throughout military doctrine. Team is one of the main principles of the military ethos. The importance of the mission is understood, and completion of the mission depends on teamwork. The fact that all members share and understand this mission is a key enabler of teamwork. As previously discussed, teamwork is a fundamental component of basic training. Members are placed in small groups and given tasks to execute as a team. Members must work together in order to achieve the goals established for them. Individual strengths and weaknesses are identified, and members work together to overcome the weaknesses of the individual and capitalize on the strength of the collective team. These types of exercises continue well past basic training and reinforce values such as trust, selflessness and conscientiousness. These exercises in teamwork build trust through adversity and humility and reinforce selflessness, a sense of belonging and respect for peers. Teambuilding exercises such as the ruck march are a common organizational practice used to reinforce the importance of team and trust.

Many non-military companies use job descriptions to outline the expected tasks and responsibilities of an employee's position. In essence, each job description is linked to the specific output necessary to accomplish organizational goals and remain effective and competitive. However, it is the actions of employees performed outside of these standardized job descriptions that can have a profound impact on organizational effectiveness. Successful organizations need employees who will do more than what is stated in the job description and extend themselves beyond normal requirements and expectations. Organizational citizenship behaviour describes the actions taken by employees that demonstrate a willingness to go "above and beyond" the duties outlined in their job description.

The military culture, which reinforces a shared purpose and values, is also accountable for building and fostering organizational citizenship behaviours that are commonly demonstrated by military members. The focus on teamwork throughout the career of the military member reinforces the greater good of the team before self as well as a focus on going above and beyond what is expected. Members of the military consistently perform duties above and beyond their terms of reference, such as volunteering to organize sports days, sitting on committees or helping out a fellow soldier. The military as an organization is largely involved in supporting volunteer organizations such as United Way and perform these volunteer duties as well as accomplish daily tasks and responsibilities. Other organizational practices in the military that elicit citizenship behaviours, such as work/life benefits and work/family programs, will be discussed under the next section.

CURRENT ISSUES IN THE WORKPLACE: MANAGING WORKFORCE DIVERSITY

Business needs to recognize the diverse nature of the labour pool. Statistics Canada shows that over 5 million Canadian citizens were foreign-born, comprising nearly 20% of the total population.[28] This diversity is increasingly reflected in the Canadian labour pool. Immigrants who came to Canada in the 1990s have accounted for approximately 70% of the total growth of the labour force in recent years. Women also comprise a significant component of the Canadian labour force and account for about half of both the employed workforce and all union members. Visible minorities and people with disabilities, together with women, make up over 60% of Canada's labour force.[29] Diversity in our workforce is also reflected in the growing presence of older workers. At the start of the 21st century,

EXHIBIT 3.7	REPRESENTATION OF DESIGNATED GROUPS IN THE LABOUR FORCE

	Representation in	
	Canadian Population	Workforce
Women	50.90%	47.3%
Aboriginal people	3.30	2.6
People with disabilities	5.10	5.3
Members of visible minorities	13.40	12.6

Source: Human Resources and Social Development Canada, "Fact Sheet on Members of Designated Groups, 2001 Census <http://www.sdc.gc.ca/asp/gateway.asp?hr=en/lp/lo/lswe/we/ee_tools/data/eedr/annual/2001/facts-2001.shtml&hs=lzl> [Date accessed: 2006-10-31].

Canadians 37–55 years old made up about 47% of the labour force, and by 2011, half of these workers will be 55 or over.[30] Recruiting workers from all groups of society is critical. It is clear that organizations must attend to the rights of a diverse group of individuals.

Challenges in the Labour Pool

There are four groups in Canada that traditionally have not received equitable treatment in employment: women; Aboriginal peoples; people with disabilities; visible minorities. Exhibit 3.7 identifies their relative presence in the population and the labour pool. Ironically, while these groups represent 60% of the total workforce, they have historically been denied fair treatment at work. These designated groups have faced significant obstacles related to their status in the labour force, including high unemployment, occupational segregation, pay inequities and limited opportunities for career advancement. We have come to expect that organizations will help address the challenges faced by these groups.

The Four Designated Groups

Women

Women have been segregated in occupations that are accorded both lower status and lower pay. According to Statistics Canada, while women represented 46.7% of the total workforce in 2005, they were clearly not equally represented across occupations. Women have been underrepresented in such areas as semiprofessional occupations, management and board positions, supervisors in crafts and trades, and sales and service personnel.[31]

Women's failure to achieve higher-level corporate positions has been attributed to a variety of sources, including lack of mentoring opportunities, lack of female role models, stereotyping and preconceptions of women's roles and abilities, exclusion from informal networks of communication, and failure of senior leaders to assume accountability for women's advancement.[32]

In a recent survey in Canada, the majority of women executives surveyed believe they have to work twice as hard as men to achieve success. Respondents also indicated that they continuously find themselves hitting the "glass ceiling," and are not accepted into the executive-level culture, which includes participation in "the boys club." The findings also revealed a concern that women continue to face more barriers to career advancement than men with the same qualifications, and are often presented with fewer opportunities. Among the greatest career barriers identified was the "the lack of comfort on the part of men in dealing with women on a professional level." Gender-based stereotyping was also indicated as a career barrier. In addition, many respondents felt that they are paid less than men with similar qualifications and they receive less credit and recognition for accomplishments.[33]

Aboriginal or First Nations People

Aboriginals (representing about 3.3% of the population) are one of the fastest-growing populations in Canada, and yet they remain vastly underrepresented in the workforce, with their unemployment rate hovering at the 20% range. Researchers have estimated that the Aboriginal population "baby boom" will result in 350,000 Native people reaching working age in the next few years, and this underscores the growing need for Canada to absorb more Native people into its workforce.

In addition to the need for improved access to education, another barrier to improved employment is the geographical distribution of the Native community. Employment opportunities on or near the Aboriginal reserves are limited. In addition, while over half the Aboriginal population live in the four Western provinces, these provinces account for a relatively small percentage of the total jobs in Canada, compared to Quebec and Ontario.[34] Sadly, in many urban contexts, Aboriginal workers have typically been largely segregated in low-wage, unstable employment. Among the biggest barriers faced by the Aboriginal community may be perception — with many Aboriginal Canadians feeling that they do not "fit" with the corporate environment.

Individuals with Disabilities

Individuals with disabilities have experienced a higher unemployment rate compared to the national average. Among the challenges faced are attitudinal barriers in the workplace, physical demands unrelated to the job requirements and inadequate access to the technical and human support systems. The Canadian Health Network notes the importance of acknowledging this segment of the population and of the labour pool:

> In the coming decades, people with a disability will comprise a larger percentage of the population in Canada than ever before. The math is pretty straightforward. As the baby boom generation grows older, the overall age of the population will increase.

And because the incidence of disabilities is strongly correlated to age, these numbers will rise together. The degree of accessibility available to this aging population will play a key role in determining their level of health or of hardship, just as it plays a critical role in the daily lives of the more than four million people currently living with a disability in Canada.[35]

A major challenge faced by persons with disabilities is the issue of accessibility. This can entail a variety of obstacles. While physical barriers may be the most visible obstacle to full accessibility, economic barriers, social discrimination, and obstacles to communication can all prevent someone from having equal access to a building, a service, or a job.[36]

Visible Minorities

In the last decade, almost 70% of the growth in the labour force was accounted for by newcomers who arrived in the 1990s. In addition, as the baby boom generation retires, immigrant workers will play a greater role in the labour pool. It is estimated that by 2011, new immigrants will comprise most, if not all, of the labour force growth.[37] Workplace obstacles faced by visible minorities include culturally biased aptitude tests, lack of recognition of foreign credentials and excessively high language requirements. A study released by the Canadian Race Relations Foundation indicated that desirable jobs and promotions elude many visible minorities and Aboriginal people, who believe that subtle forms of racism permeate the workplace. The report, prepared by Jean Lock Kunz, Anne Milan and Sylvain Schetagne from the Canadian Council on Social Development (CCSD), examined the experiences of visible minorities and Aboriginal peoples in cities across Canada. Among the findings were the following:

- Aboriginal peoples, visible minorities and immigrants to Canada encounter more challenges in finding employment in all regions in Canada.
- Foreign-born visible minorities experience the greatest difficulty finding desirable work, and only half of those with a university education have high-skill jobs.
- Compared to white Canadians, visible minorities and Aboriginals who possess a university education are less likely to hold managerial and professional jobs. Among those visible minorities who do hold managerial jobs, over 50% are self-employed, compared with only 30% of white Canadians.[38]

Employment Equity

The Department of Justice Canada defines equity as "treating people fairly by recognizing that different individuals and groups require different measures to ensure fair and comparable results."[39] The notion of equity is equated with fairness and impartiality. Employment equity refers to the treatment of employees in a fair and non-biased manner. This term was developed by Judge Rosalie Silberman Abella, Commissioner of the Royal Commission on Equality in Employment (1984) to reflect a distinct Canadian process for achieving equality in all areas of employment.

Under the authority of the Commission, a process was developed to deal with systemic discrimination in the workplace. According to the Commission, "systemic discrimination" was responsible for most of the inequality found in employment. Employment equity was designed as an ongoing planning process used by an employer to accomplish a number of objectives, including:

- Eliminating employment barriers for the four designated groups identified in the Employment Equity Act — women, persons with disabilities, Aboriginal people and members of visible minorities.
- Redressing past discrimination in employment opportunities and preventing future barriers.
- Improving access for the designated groups and increasing their distribution throughout all occupations and at all levels.
- Fostering a climate of equity in the organization.
- Implementing positive policies and practices to ensure the effects of systemic barriers are eliminated.[40]

A 2005 progress report indicated the following changes in labour representation among the four groups since 1997: for women, from 40.9% to 43.4%; visible minorities, from 5% to 13.3%; Aboriginal peoples, from 0.7% to 1.7%; and persons with disability, from 1.6% to 2.5%.[41] Employment equity is an issue for all individuals regardless of their sex, religion, age, national origin, colour or position in an organization.

The Legal Basis of Employment Equity Act

Employment equity covers a number of activities, including identifying and removing systemic barriers to employment opportunities that adversely affect the four designated groups and implementing special measures to remove any barriers and provide reasonable accommodation.

The Employment Equity Act was passed in 1986. Its purpose includes the following mandate:

> ... to achieve equality in the workplace so that no person shall be denied employment opportunities or benefits for reasons unrelated to ability and, in the fulfillment of the goals, to correct the conditions of disadvantage in employment experienced by women, Aboriginal peoples, persons with disabilities, and visible minority people by giving effect to the principle that employment equity means more than treating persons in the same way but also requires special measures and the accommodation of differences.[42]

The second Employment Equity Act received royal assent in 1995 and came into force on October 24, 1996. It built upon the earlier legislation and clarified and enforced employer obligations as outlined in the act. The act governs private sector employers under federal jurisdiction as well as almost all employees of the federal government.[43] The Employment Equity Act (1995) requires employers and Crown corporations that have 100 employees or more and that are regulated under the Canada Labour Code to implement employment equity and report on their results. Under the Act, the employer must:

TALKING BUSINESS 3.5: EMPLOYMENT EQUITY IN IBM AND SHELL CANADA

- In 2003, *IBM* launched the Canadian Women's Leadership Council, involving the participation of women executives and senior leaders to become active in the development of high-potential women in IBM Canada. This program mirrors the goals of a similar body created in 2002 to increase development of visible minorities.
- For the past five years, IBM Canada's visually impaired employees have mentored students at the Canadian National Institute for the Blind's Summer Camp to acquaint them with technology.
- *Shell Canada* provides diversity awareness training to all employees, including management, and has implemented an Ombuds office to facilitate fair and equitable resolution of workplace issues.
- In 2001, Shell completed a review of their progress related to diversity and implemented various initiatives, including hiring a full-time diversity advisor and developing a diversity gap analysis to help identify priority areas of action.
- The company offers a disability management program to assist ill or injured employees.
- Shell Canada supports the recruitment and retention of Aboriginal employees through participation in Aboriginal community outreach programs, funding of educational initiatives, and offering scholarships through the National Aboriginal Achievement Foundation.

Source: Excerpted from Human Resources and Social Development Canada, "Employment Equity Awards 2003 <http://info.load-otea.hrdc-drhc.gc.ca/workplace_equity/fcp/merit_awards/2003/> [Date accessed: 2006-08-29].

- Distribute to employees a questionnaire that allows them to indicate whether they belong to one of the four designated groups.
- Identify jobs in which the percentage of members of designated groups is below their relative representation in the labour market.
- Disseminate information on employment equity to employees, and consult with employee representatives.
- Scrutinize the current employment system in order to assess whether any barriers exist that may limit the employment opportunities of members of designated groups.
- Generate an employment equity plan directed at promoting an equitable workplace.
- Endeavour to implement the employment equity plan.
- Monitor, assess and revise the plan in a timely fashion.
- Complete an annual report on the company's employment equity status and activities.

Increasingly, businesses have begun to recognize that employment equity is "good for business," and Canada continues to strengthen its programs in order to exploit the

118

strength of an increasingly diverse workforce. Among the numerous organizations that focus on employee equity is the Bank of Montreal Group of Companies (BMO). BMO recently received accolades from the Conference Board of Canada for its employment equity and diversity initiatives, including its employee-led diversity action teams, internal employee assistance program and its recently launched project to help identify workplace barriers among persons with disabilities.

Numerous businesses have increased their efforts to assist the Aboriginal community in gaining greater self-sufficiency and participation in the workforce. There are a number of companies that have been actively involved in boosting the presence of Aboriginals in the workplace. As well, many businesses have proven that they can work with Aboriginal communities, educational institutions and government to enhance employment prospects for Aboriginals. A common recruitment method for companies is to offer support for educational institutions, training initiatives and scholarships for Aboriginal students. For example, 3M Canada contributes to bursaries given through the Department of Indian and Northern Affairs Canada for Aboriginal students who are pursuing careers in fields related to health care. In addition, recruitment strategies that reach out to Aboriginal communities and organizations are also used.[44]

CHAPTER SUMMARY

We have discussed the nature of managerial roles and considered what the job of a manager entails. This chapter also identified the central schools of management thought that have guided our thinking for over a century. We also considered the elements of managing that contribute to success and, ironically, how these elements are actually originated from a military ideology. Finally, we examined the issue of demographic diversity at work. We identified a number of protected groups in the Canadian workplace, discussed the issue of equity and human rights protection. The chapter ended with a look at the responsibility of managing a diverse workforce and the rights that must be afforded to such employees.

Managing the Workforce at Home Depot

Every retailer knows that motivated and passionate store-level employees are the key to ensuring customer satisfaction and financial success. The challenge of creating, maintaining and growing such a culture was the topic of last month's International Mass Retail Convention's general session, which featured Annette Verschuren, president of The Home Depot Canada.

She offered IMRA attendees insight into how the home improvement retailer has achieved its tremendous growth during a session titled "Behind the Orange Apron."

"The greatness of our company is the sum of the actions of our people," Verschuren said. Strategy, leadership, creativity and the ability to execute are all necessary, she added, but "if you don't have a team of people with a passion to win, you will never be great."

Home Depot has to be considered one of retailing's great companies because of the financial success the company has achieved.

Verschuren said when she became president of The Home Depot Canada in 1996 there were only 19 stores doing approximately $1 billion in annual sales. Now, annual sales are approximately $4 billion and the 83rd Home Depot store in Canada is scheduled to open this week.

Home Depot's success in Canada has mirrored its success in the United States. In 1997, Home Depot's total sales were $24.2 billion and by the end of last year they had increased to $53.6 billion. And more growth is expected. "We will be a $100 billion company by 2005, easy," Verschuren said.

To get there will require the addition of 40,000 new employees each year, all of which also have to be highly motivated and passionate about the business. "You have to make your full team business partners with you. They are your competitive advantage," Verschuren said. "Take care of your people and they will take care of your company. I know it is a cliche, but it is so true."

Verschuren highlighted six areas that are essential for ensuring a culture of performance. There has to be an emotional appeal so that the employees feel good about the company. "Many of our most successful hires are customers that have fallen in love with the company," she said.

There also must be a high level of trust in the products and services that are being sold. Senior management must have vision and leadership and the workplace environment has to be favorable; that means sharing in the success of the store.

The Home Depot Canada offers even part-time employees health care benefits and a potentially lucrative bonus program whereby a cashier can receive an annual bonus of between $400 and $800. To further ensure the store is a positive workplace environment, human resource professionals also were recently hired in each store.

"I can tell you within two seconds of entering a store whether morale is good," Verschuren said. "With an unhappy workforce you have nothing and you will never be great."

Financial performance and social responsibility were other factors she cited. If the company is socially responsible, employees can feel good about working there and, in turn, are inclined to be very supportive of the communities in which they reside. That is the case with many Home Depot employees who are heavily involved in community service and last year devoted six million hours.

Source: Reproduced with permission from Mike Troy, "Motivating Your Workforce: A Home Depot case study," *DSN Retailing Today* (June 10, 2002) 41(11): 29.

QUESTIONS

1. Discuss in detail which elements of the behavioural school of management are applied at Home Depot.

2. How might the classical school of management also be applied effectively here?

3. Would all organizations be better managed by focusing on the behavioural as opposed to the classical school of management? Why or why not?

Connecting Employment Engagement to Business Success

Historically whenever companies wanted to improve business results, management dealt with specific business issues. But, by changing that focus to deal with employment engagement, corporate issues can be resolved and business success achieved.

. . . .

The third objective relates to people. It ensures that everyone involved in the company is doing what they need to do, when they need to do it, to ensure the success of the financial and operations objectives.

Every business issue and challenge involves people. As much as they drive the strategic effectiveness of a business, when they are not engaged in their work, they adversely affect operational imperatives and financial stability. This is nothing new. What is new is taking the approach that, in addition to people having a role in contributing to management's challenges, they can also play an essential role in identifying business issues and helping resolve them. Facilitating an environment of employment engagement can bring the answers an organization needs.

What Is Employment Engagement?

Engagement in the workplace is not one-sided. After all, "it takes two to tango" in any situation.

The term "employee engagement" implies that just the employees need to be engaged and that their committed efforts will go a long way towards meeting the company's objectives. This is true, but it's not the whole story.

The total picture is captured by the term "employment engagement." Employment engagement implies a mutual aspect to engagement. Both the employees and the employer need to be committed to supporting each other in meeting the organization's objectives. With this approach, the onus is not just on the employee. Rather, it recognizes that both the employer's and the employees' needs must be equally in sync.

Employer's Needs

First of all, employers need staff to "be" at work. This is not just about physically being at work and on time, it's about attentiveness, attitude and focus on the job.

With written job descriptions, managers specify what they need an employee to do in any given job function. Each job has a specified degree of operational requirement and expectation. Beyond this employees must do their jobs well, going above and beyond. It's about employees putting some of their selves into the role. It's bringing passion to the job, being dedicated, exceeding expectations.

If every employee was at work when they were needed, did the job according to what was required, and did that job well, then employer needs would be met.

Employees' Needs

Ah, here's the rub ... employees want something in exchange. Employees really only want three things.

The right level of total remuneration: Employees want to be rewarded with an appropriate quantifiable value for the work they do. These days employers can choose from a whole host of different components for the total remuneration package. Whatever is included in this basket, the levels of compensation need to be adequate. It's not necessary to offer the highest level, it just has to be at the right level for employees to feel they're adequately valued and treated fairly.

Tools and support: Employees will do their jobs more readily if they have the right tools and support. At a very basic level, this includes things like air conditioning, an ergonomic chair, phone and computer. But tools and support can also include access to supportive leadership, mentoring, training programs, job rotation, career opportunities, clearly defined performance measurement standards and an understanding of how a job fits within the larger business context.

Responsibility with corresponding authority, recognition: In terms of driving functionality and engagement, responsibility, authority and recognition are so closely interrelated that it is appropriate to bundle them together into one category. To do their job well, employees need to be given responsibility; they need to have ownership. Any given responsibility needs to be matched with corresponding authority so that the employee feels they are being supported to succeed, not being set up to fail. Finally, the employee who meets the employer's requirements wants to be appreciated for accomplishments and adequately recognized. This is not about money; it's about being appreciated and respected for efforts.

The Business Connection

Securing an environment of mutual employment engagement is the catalyst to resolving business issues at their foundation.

If every business issue and challenge involves staff, then it stands to reason that employees have the answers. In its simplest form, the employee who has a problem articulates it only because she is also the keeper of the solution. So, it's in management's best interest to pay attention to employees who are vocal about their concerns, who speak out about problems — they are doing the organization a favour. To resolve business issues and challenges, ask employees the right questions in the right way, and they will provide the answers.

·   ·   ·   ·

Employees want to care. They want what is best for the company — after all, they have a vested interest. Secure an environment of employment engagement, and involve employees in business-issue resolution, and you'll find that they are the best source for business success.

Source: Reproduced with permission from Daphne Woolf, "Connecting Employment Engagement to Business Success," *Canadian HR Reporter* (September 12, 2005) 18(15): 6–7. Copyright HR Reporter, September 12, 2005, by permission of Carswell, Toronto, Ontario, 1-800-387-5164. Web site: www.hrreporter.com

QUESTIONS

1. What is employee engagement?

2. Which management philosophy or philosophies is/are most closely associated with the practice of employee engagement?

3. Do you think engagement is a big issue in most organizations? Why or why not?

Designing Organizations for Success

4

Organizations in just about every industrialized nation have been undergoing change. Many companies have reduced the number of levels in their hierarchy; others have undergone a concurrent change in their whole business process, while others have simply closed down. The aim of this chapter is to examine some of the approaches that organizations have adopted with regard to structure and design, including re-engineering, downsizing and going virtual. We will also examine the reasons behind these changes, and consider more generally the question, What determines how an organization is designed?

LEARNING OBJECTIVES

By the end of the chapter, you should be able to:

1. Identify four broad trends in the changing nature of organizational design.
2. Discuss the relevance of metaphors used to describe organizations.
3. Identify the contingencies of organizational structure.
4. Explain the concept of re-engineering.
5. Describe the notion of the virtual organization.
6. Discuss the phenomenon of downsizing and its rationale, methods and objectives.

I would like to thank Amy Bitton, who contributed Talking Business 4.8 and the "Pixar: No Mickey Mouse Organization" Concept Application case to this chapter.

The Business World ———————————————————

Are We Reinventing Organizations or Are We Destroying Them?

I was sitting in the lounge of a nearly empty restaurant recently in Boston with two former associates, reminiscing about the "good old days" and the wonderful business team we had back then. When one of them speculated about what it would be like to pull that team back together again, I instinctively remarked: "It wouldn't be the same."

As I drove back to my hotel, a nursery rhyme kept flirting through my head: "Humpty Dumpty had a great fall. All the king's horses and all the king's men couldn't put Humpty Dumpty together again." That nursery rhyme crept into my mind again later during a discussion on what happens after the ravages of reengineering/downsizing.

Countless companies have reengineered/downsized, tearing apart organizations like a mad gardener uprooting plants in an overgrown flower bed. The result, for the very short term, improved profitability resulting from lower expenses. In the long term, it is often remission, decline, and failure. Recognizing this, some companies have tried to reconstruct the dismantled organization, or what was left of it, only to find that nothing works quite the same anymore.

Fortunately, the reengineering/downsizing rage seems to have run its course. The originators of reengineering, Michael Hamler and James Champy, along with their earlier cohort Thomas Davenport, have "confessed" to the failure of reengineering/downsizing. In essence, they've said: "We forgot the people." But what are the reengineering gurus to do now? Can they put the corporate Humpty Dumpties together again?

Probably not, at least not as they once were. We might have learned this from both personal experience and the laws of nature. For example, many of us have gone back to visit places where we once lived, only to find them [somehow] diminished by time and perspective. Scientists have tried to recreate natural systems, like the prairies that once covered thousands of square miles of middle America, [a]lso to no avail. They may plant the seeds of the same strains of grass, at the same latitude and longitude, but it [n]ever comes out the same. They cannot quite put [nature], Humpty Dumpty together again.

What made the old days so good was a group of talented people, working together to achieve worthy goals, in the face of fearsome competition. The spirit of the organization was one of collaboration, cooperation, competition, conflict, culture, and relationships. Those relationships endure to this day. We had fun. We worked hard, often frantically and always with the knowledge that, if we didn't, one or more of the competitors breathing down our necks would catch us or pass us. That simply would not do. Our collective pride and spirit said "No way!"

What about the role of compensation in all of this? Was it an incentive, a motivator, or a reward? I think it was much more of a reward than a motivator. We worked together, competed together, won together, and celebrated together. The pay was recognition for a job well done. If this sounds like a sports analogy, it is. Even the most crassly commercial professional athletes who play for pay want to win the World Series or the Super Bowl. They want it not for the extra money that they'll earn, but for the sense of achievement and team pride that it creates. After "dynasty" teams are broken up, they can't be put back together again, either. New teams, with a new winning chemistry, must be built.

Why should business be any different? Maybe organizations that are recklessly torn apart can't be put back together again, at least not quite the way they once were. But new ones can be built on the same principles. A sense of achievement, recognition, pride in accomplishment, and rewards are the main ingredients. Leaders who know this create an environment where these elements come together naturally and often.

Maybe we can't "put Humpty Dumpty together again," but we can remember what worked well in the past and attempt to replicate it, perhaps a little differently — and, hopefully, a lot better.

The competition is always getting tougher. Markets are always changing. But people remain pretty much the same. They will respond if you create the right environment. In the process, you may discover that nursery rhymes were full of hidden management wisdom.

Source: Reproduced with permission from Jerry R. Mitchell, "January 2005 President's Message" <http://www.gss.net/mef/january_2005_president.htm>.

THE CHANGING NATURE OF ORGANIZATIONS

It is an obvious fact that we are a society of organizations. From our hospitals, to our schools to our multinational organizations, it is hard to imagine life without organizations. And, for better or worse, those very institutions and organizations that we have grown up with are continuing to undergo dramatic change. To understand what is going on out there, we need to first consider several things. What exactly are organizations? What constitutes the structure or anatomy of an organization? Why do different organizations have different structures? These are among the key questions addressed in this chapter. The last two decades have witnessed tremendous change and turmoil that we have witnessed across the organizational landscape. From the massive reductions in the workforce of many well-known organizations like Nortel, GM, and Bell Canada, to changes in how organizations are designed and operated — fundamentally there has been a rethinking of how organizations should be designed. Organizational theory has been trying to make sense of the revolution we have observed in the organizational world.

Some observers have suggested that what is going on is a shift away from the classical, traditional, bureaucratic model (see Exhibit 4.1). Recall our earlier discussion of perspectives of management and Weber's notion of the bureaucratic organization: a central stream of classical management thought. This philosophy of organization design guided many of our organizations for most of the 20th century. The traditional, bureaucratic organizational structure emphasizes factors such as job specialization, a formal hierarchy of authority, a clear system of control and rules and regulations to guide behaviour.

Why do we need the bureaucratic design? Because it achieves the fundamental goals of organizations: predictability and reliability — rules and standardized jobs ensure workers are doing what the boss wants; and control — the formal hierarchy ensures that how the work is conducted is clearly controlled. Ironically, these very strengths of the bureaucratic structure can also become weaknesses when the environment changes. For example, increasing competition, demands for better products and services, improved customer service, and more sophisticated processes of generating the product all suggest that the stability of bureaucracies impedes any chance for innovation. The philosophy of organizational struc-

EXHIBIT 4.1	GOODBYE BUREAUCRACY

Traditional Bureaucracy	Modern Organizations
• tall/hierarchical	• flat
• rigid, rule-oriented	• fluid
• buffered from environment	• integrated
• narrow market	• global

ture that emphasized job specialization, the narrow division of labour, standardization, rules and the like is simply not suitable to a changing environment.

Believe it or not, the traditional or classical approach to organizational structure, which arose in the time of the Industrial Revolution, dominated our thinking about the nature of organizational design right up until the 1980s. It was not until then that organizations began to realize that the bureaucratic structure needed to be replaced with new designs. Most of the shifts in organizational design essentially aimed to move away from the bureaucratic paradigm. Among the important trends in the redesign of organizations, the adjectives identified in Exhibit 4.1 best describe the new approaches and the shift away from the bureaucratic design.

1. Flat Organizations

If there is any consistent pattern in the sweeping changes to corporate architecture, it has been the de-layering of organizational hierarchies. Tall organizations have narrow spans of control and flat organizations have wider spans of control. The shift we have observed in organizational redesign has been from the former to the latter. Certainly, one of the most pervasive phenomena to hit the organizational landscape since the 1980s has been downsizing, which often involves flattening the organizational hierarchy. We will address this issue in more detail later in the chapter. It is difficult to read the newspaper without reading some report on an organization flattening its hierarchy through downsizing. As mentioned earlier, Toyota eliminated three of its seven layers of management, and IBM Canada cut its levels from ten to about four in the 1990s, and these trends continue today among many organizations.

Flattening the hierarchy accomplishes a number of things. Among the benefits are increased speed of decision making: decisions and information take much less time to travel across levels of bureaucracy. This allows organizations to react much faster to the demands of a changing environment. In addition, the de-layering of layers of management means that much more responsibility and self-management is coming from the lower levels of the organization, so that employees and those who are closest to serving customers or producing the product are now more involved in the decision-making process.

2. Fluid Organizations

The bureaucratic organization is obsessed with control and facilitates control largely through strict adherence to rules and standards for how work is done. Again, think back to our discussion of the purposes of organizational structure. When organizations exist in dynamic environments, being able to adapt to change is critical. Bureaucratic rules tend to impede such adaptiveness, given that rules must be changed to fit new circumstances. The organic organization that we identified earlier derives some of its strength from its ability to avoid being bogged down in rules that govern how work must be performed. Later in this chapter we will examine a very fluid or organic form of organization — the virtual organization.

129

TALKING BUSINESS **4.1   THE FLUID ORGANIZATION**

Lifetime employment was once a goal that both companies and individuals hoped for, but today the idea is dead. Few people will ever achieve it. In fact, prospective employers are suspicious of candidates who possess a recent, lengthy tenure. If a "lifer" loses a job, he or she must counteract doubts about his or her ability to adapt quickly to a new workplace environment. As it is, many individuals in their 20s are changing jobs every year and would apparently have it no other way. Employees and communities were once critical factors in companies' long-term strategic decisions. Moving factories and jobs to another area of the country was unthinkable because of the damage it would do to the local community. In recent years, thousands of companies — including UPS, J.C. Penney, and Boeing — have moved their headquarters or operations from cities where they had deep roots. The old business structure — with a dominant CEO, a largely ceremonial board of directors, and employees willing to put the goals of the company first — is nearly extinct.

Source: Excerpted from John A Challenger, "The transformed workplace: How can you survive," *The Futurist* (Nov./Dec. 2001) 35(6): 24–28. Originally published in the Nov./Dec. 2001 issue of *The Futurist*. Used with permission from the World Future Society, 7910 Woodmont Avenue, Suite 450, Bethesda, Maryland 20814. Telephone: 301/656-8274; Fax: 301/951-0394; <http://www.wfs.org>.

Fluidity or flexibility in the functioning of an organization has been reflected in other ways, such as the notion of just-in-time inventory, which emphasizes the ability to generate inventory as needed through flexible manufacturing/supplier relationships, and consequently minimize costs. These just-in-time inventory principles have also been applied to the work relationship, where we now have a just-in-time labour pool, so to speak. That is, organizations have recognized that they no longer need to maintain a fixed supply of labour. If revenues at any time are diminishing, so too can the labour pool be diminished via downsizing, and that pool can be increased when revenues increase. Consequently, by the 1980s and throughout the 1990s we witnessed growth in temporary or contract-based employment. This adds immensely to the fluidity of an organization, since a temporary workforce can be easily adjusted to meet the upswings and downturns of a less predictable environment. This fluidity has, of course, profound implications for individuals within organizations, because it also underscores attitudes toward the permanence or lack of permanence of jobs within the "new" workplace, as observed in Talking Business 4.1.

3.   Integrated Organizations

The traditional bureaucratic organization advocates clear lines of authority and control. However, the newer organizational designs are less focused on the need for unity of command and clear lines of authority. It is unimportant to maintain distinct boundaries between levels in the hierarchy, between individuals and departments, and between organizational members and individuals external to the organization. In fact, just the opposite is now emphasized — aiming to create more integration among the formerly disparate units in the organization. For example, the new approaches to organizational design typically focus on teams of workers rather than on individuals. Cross-functional teams are quite popular work groups that bring together members from various parts of the organization.

Typically, work teams are given the power to manage themselves and make decisions without the approval of formal management — hence the name, *self-managing work teams*. Thus, GM's Saturn plant brought individuals from the legal department to marketing, to engineering, in order to be involved in the production of the Saturn car. Shell Canada has achieved much success with its use of self-managed teams, as have numerous other companies. Information sharing is a big part of this team-based approach — that is, having management give over information that once was solely their domain. This is much more common in today's organization than in the traditional bureaucratic model, where those in power held the information and did not share it with the lower levels.

The integration of units or members within the organization is one major trend. Another trend includes integration of the organization with players outside its boundaries. Organizations are increasingly building closer connections with their external environment. For example, an organization may attempt to establish close relationships with suppliers, integrating them into the manufacturing process, and generally creating an interdependent relationship. Other organizations are even creating alliances with other companies in order to develop new products or services. There are even cross-functional teams that include participants from outside the organization, such as suppliers, or distributors or even competitors.

The Japanese term for networking of major enterprises is *keiretsu*. These are loosely affiliated collections of companies, and have been quite common in industry and banking in Japan. Creating an organization out of a network of organizations is an issue we will address later in this chapter.

Of course, not all integration of organizations has been of such a loosely coupled nature. We have also witnessed recently the trend toward building collections of organizations through mergers and acquisitions. The spate of mergers and acquisitions that occurred in the 1990s seems to be continuing in the new millennium.

4. Global Organizations

Perhaps the most profound recent trend in the changing nature of organizations is the drive to "go global." Many organizations in today's world must focus on the global environment. The issue of globalization of business will be discussed in detail in a later chapter. Globalization can be considered one of the leading forces behind organizational change since the 1980s and 1990s. Globalization has brought with it many implications, including the increase in competition and greater access to more markets. Industries that were traditionally "protected" by tariffs, such as auto manufacturing, faced intense competition from foreign competitors for the first time, and with serious consequences.

Just about every sector of business is no longer insulated from competitors, customers or suppliers outside of their home country. Consequently, the notion of integration or networking can include relationships with suppliers, or even competitors, outside of local boundaries. Moreover, these members may exist in other countries. An organization may have networks of members across the world. For example, Canadian Company X might be selling a product it had designed by its team in Sweden, engineered in the United States and manufactured in Japan. In the global marketplace, businesses are also selling to customers all over the world. Consider, for example, Bata Ltd. whose head office is in Toronto. This is a company that has approximately 6,000 shoe stores in about 65 different countries. Given its large size, it is a challenge for Bata to ensure it is flexible and responsive to local market needs. Consequently, it employs a geographic form of departmentation, with independent divisions operating in Europe, Africa, South America and the Far East. Just think about the challenges this company faces in terms of responding to the variety of consumer preferences within these different locations. For Bata, decentralized decision-making authority is required to permit these divisions to focus on and quickly respond to local market needs.

THINKING ABOUT ORGANIZATIONS ———————

What Is an Organization?

What do you think of when you think of an "organization"? We can identify three broad categories of organizations:

1. public/governmental organizations that provide goods and services without necessarily generating a profit;
2. private/non-governmental organizations, including voluntary organizations, that offer goods or services without necessarily generating a profit; and
3. private organizations that produce goods or services with the intent of making a profit for the benefit of their owners or shareholders.

Though we can observe such diverse organizations that operate in these very different sectors, we can also identify underlying characteristics that are common to all organizations. In fact, it is useful to consider a very fundamental question as a starting part in our examination of the nature of organizations. What is an organization? How do we define it? Nortel, GM, Microsoft, your high school, St. John Ambulance — what do all these entities have in common? Organizations may be large corporations or small non-profit organizations; they might be housed within a large skyscraper; or they could simply be composed of members who are spread across a wide location. What makes all these things organizations?

So What Is an Organization?

Given the implications of the systems approach to organization, we can generate the following definition of organizations:

1. **Organizations are social entities.** Clearly, all the examples cited above have at least one common element — they are made up of people! They are entities that have been generated and are maintained by people. They involve some level of human interaction.

2. **Organizations interact with the environment.** Can you think of any organization that is not somehow linked to its external environment? Think about it. An organization obtains inputs from its environment, whether in the form of people, raw materials, technology or financial capital. All these inputs are transformed by the organization and become outputs: the goods, services or knowledge that the organization generates.

3. **Organizations are created to achieve goals.** That is, they are goal directed. Whether it is a profit-making organization or a non-profit organization, all organizations have some kind of goal or objective they were designed to achieve.

4. **Organizations possess some sort of structure.** All organizations need some kind of structure to ensure the work is properly allocated and coordinated. Of course, it is not so straightforward to define precisely what organizational structure is. What do we mean when we say that organizations possess a structure? How are organizations structured? We will address these questions below.

Using Metaphors to Describe Organizations

One helpful method of understanding the nature of organizations is through the use of metaphors. According to Gareth Morgan, a management scholar and author of *Images of Organization*, we can consider the notion of an organization as, essentially, a social construction. That is, we are giving a tangible name to something that we take for granted. Words, names, concepts, ideas, facts, observations, etc., do not so much denote external "things" as conceptions of things activated in the mind. They are not to be seen as a representation of a reality "out there," but as tools for capturing and dealing with what is *perceived* to be "out there."[1] Hence, we understand the usefulness of metaphors. A metaphor is often regarded as no more than a literary and descriptive device for embellishment, but more fundamentally it is a creative form that produces its effect through a crossing of images. A metaphor proceeds through assertions that "subject A is like B and . . ." Through the processes of comparison, between the images of A and B, we generate new meaning. The use of metaphors serves to generate an image for studying a subject. Different images of a subject guide and, ultimately, shape what is seen.

In more practical terms — what are the common features of these things that we call *organizations*? Why does this label fit a variety of entities, from non-profit to for-profit contexts? Metaphors are useful to help us describe and, ultimately, understand these social constructions. Consider dictionary definitions of the term *organization*. The Oxford English Dictionary has defined it as a term used primarily to describe the action of organizing or the state of being organized, particularly in a biological sense. Also, the term has been considered as referring to an organized body, system or society. The state of being organized in a biological sense was the basis of the metaphor of arranging or coordinating.

The term *organization* as a depiction of a social institution is relatively new, and creates a new meaning through metaphorical extension of older meanings. Ultimately, the importance of the metaphors we use to describe our hospitals, businesses, places of worship, etc., are important because they lead our thinking about the nature of these places, how they should be designed and how they should function. Let's consider an example of how metaphors guide our thinking in the area of management philosophy.

The Machine or Mechanistic Organizational Structure

In many ways, the different schools of thought with regard to organizational theories arise from insights associated with different metaphors for the study of organizations. Consider, for example, the theories of management, discussed in another chapter. The classical schools of management thought, including scientific management, administrative management and bureaucratic management, can be viewed as arising from a specific conceptualization or metaphor of what organizations represent. Arguably, the classical school of management thought is based implicitly on a conception of organizations that employs a "machine metaphor." Machines are perceived as entities that function in a prescribed, rational manner. They are devised to perform work toward specific goals, structure and technology. Consequently, some organizational scholars, implicitly drawing on such a conception or metaphor of organizations as machines, emphasize an analysis and design of the formal structure of an organization and its technology. These scholars have explained the purpose of organizations as they would a machine — to function in an orderly, prescribed and controlled manner. The aim, then, is to design organizations as if they were machines.

Taylor's notion of "economic man," and Weber's notion of the "faceless bureaucrat," are natural extensions of the principles of the machine metaphor of organizations. Scientific management encompasses the notions of control and efficiency — objectives well fitted to a machine metaphor of organizations. Of course, managers or management scholars whose philosophy is based on a machine metaphor will be led by such a metaphor. Consequently, the classical schools of management thought focused only on those issues pertinent to this metaphor: rules, regulations, a bureaucratic structure, etc. Human needs had no relevance in such a metaphor or model.

The Organic Organizational Structure

Of course, management thought has also been affected by other metaphors. For example, the "organism metaphor" encompasses a conception of organizations as systems of mutually connected and dependent parts constituted to share a common life. This metaphor suggests that we can conceive organizations as living organisms that contain a combination of elements differentiated yet integrated, attempting to survive within the context of a wider environment. The open-systems approach of organizations, discussed on the following page, is based on this metaphor. And with regard to management philosophies (see

EXHIBIT 4.2	WHAT DOES *ORGANIZATION* MEAN TO YOU?

- Organization as machine
- Organization as living organism
- Organization as political system
- Organization as theatre
- Organization as sports team
- Organization as family

Chapter 3), the behavioural school of management thought is, in fact, based on this metaphor. Consequently, these schools are concerned with sustaining human motivation and treating organizations as social systems. In other words, the organizational metaphor implicitly underlies and, ultimately, guides thinking of how organizations should be designed and managed.

Certainly, we can apply myriad metaphors to try to advance our understanding of what organizations really represent. Among some of the more popular conceptions of organizations in terms of metaphors are organizations as political systems;[2] organizations as loosely coupled systems;[3] organizations as theatres;[4] organizations as a collection of cultures.[5] (See Exhibit 4.2.) No one metaphor can capture the total nature of organizational life. New metaphors can be created for viewing and understanding organizations. Indeed, the very nature of the study of organizations and the field of organizational theory is metaphorical — that is, it is subjective in many ways. The notion of "organizations as systems" is one such metaphor whose implications we will explore in more detail below. This metaphor has guided organizational theories regarding structure and design.

Organizations as Systems. Scholars who have studied organizations have generated countless perspectives on the nature of these entities. One useful perspective involves the view of organizations as systems. How might the metaphor of an organization as a "system" guide our understanding with regard to how organizations operate and sustain themselves?

A system can de defined as interdependent elements working together to achieve a goal or goals. The interdependence of the elements creates an entity that is more than just the sum of its parts — something is achieved beyond the mere putting together of these separate components. The notion of organizations as systems is intended to guide our understanding of what organizations are all about and how they function and survive.[6] Specifically, the notion of an **open system** asserts that organizations are entities that are embedded in, and dependent on exchanges with the environment they operate within. In addition, organizations can be viewed as social systems, with people constituting the basic elements.

Interestingly, there have been times when organizations have been viewed as closed systems, with the belief that how organizations function and survive depends on their ability to remain divorced from their environment. Closed systems have been defined as

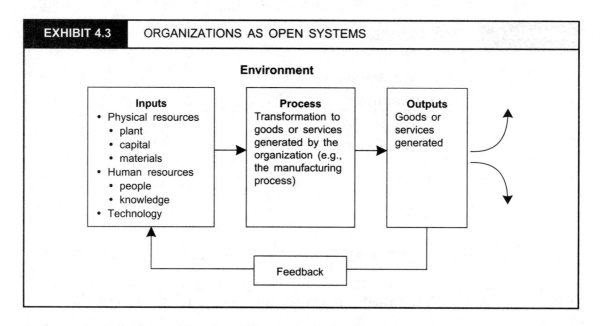

fully self-sufficient entities requiring no interaction with the environment, and this clearly makes this metaphor difficult to find in practice. This guiding metaphor led much organizational thinking to focus on the organization's internal environment with regard to dealing with organizational functioning and survival. At the same time, this approach failed to recognize the role that the external environment can have in the organization's operations.

It was only when the environment became sufficiently volatile and complex that theorists recognized the futility of viewing organizations as closed systems. It became necessary to embrace the open systems metaphor and further acknowledge the critical importance of the notion that organizations are embedded in their environment, requiring resources from and generating outputs to their environment. This also underscored the importance of further understanding the nature of the organization's external environment. (See Exhibit 4.3.)

An organization's environment represents all elements that exist outside the organization and that, potentially, influence or affect the organization in some way. As mentioned elsewhere, the open-systems perspective of organizations emphasizes the importance of the environment and interaction with the environment. Clearly, organizations are dependent on the environment for their survival and success. Without obtaining the necessary environmental inputs, whether they are suitable employees or the raw materials for production, organizations cannot function effectively. Similarly, if organizations fail to generate the types of products or services sought by the environment, then, too, these organizations will cease to exist. As suggested earlier, organizations are created in response to societal or environmental needs; and ultimately, it is the environment that will determine the organization's fate.

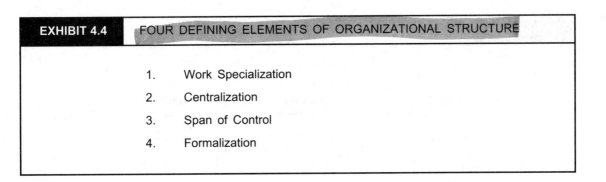

EXHIBIT 4.4   FOUR DEFINING ELEMENTS OF ORGANIZATIONAL STRUCTURE

1.   Work Specialization
2.   Centralization
3.   Span of Control
4.   Formalization

THE ANATOMY OF AN ORGANIZATION

What is organizational structure? The image of an organizational chart might come to mind for some of you. And, in fact, the organizational chart is a reflection of the underlying structure of an organization. However, there is a more specific notion of organizational structure. Organizational structure has been defined as a deliberately planned network or pattern of relationships that exists among individuals in various roles or positions. This includes the formal hierarchy of authority, the distribution or grouping of work (for example into departments), and the rules or procedures that control and coordinate behaviour in the organization. However, we can move beyond this definition and attempt to examine more systematically the dimensions along which organizational structure can be described (see Exhibit 4.4).

What Constitutes an Organization's Structure?

1.   *Work Specialization*

One fundamental question that must be addressed in designing organizational structure is, how are we going to divide up the work that must be done to achieve organizational goals?

Horizontal differentiation represents the degree of differentiation between horizontal (as opposed to vertical) units of the organization, based on things like the orientation of the members, the nature of their jobs and their education or training. The greater the number of occupations in an organization that require specialized knowledge and skills, the more complex the organization. One obvious dimension of horizontal differentiation is job specialization. The term *specialization*, or *division of labour*, refers to the degree to which organizational tasks are subdivided into separate jobs. There are fundamentally two different kinds of specialization: functional and social specialization (see Exhibit 4.5).

Functional specialization refers to the division of jobs into simple, repetitive tasks. If you recall the discussion (Chapter 3) of Frederick Taylor's scientific management, his phi-

EXHIBIT 4.5	JOB SPECIALIZATION

FUNCTIONAL	**SOCIAL**
Division of jobs into simple tasks	Level of professionalism among employees

losophy of managing advocated a high degree of job specialization: that is, Taylor argued that to maximize worker efficiency, jobs should be divided up into their smallest components, so that workers perform simple, specific and repetitive tasks. More recently, there has been a dramatic shift in beliefs regarding the degree of job specialization that should be implemented at work. Approaches to job redesign, like job enrichment, essentially advocate a low degree of job specialization: that is, rather than performing one narrow task, employees in some organizations perform a wide range of tasks. Job enrichment involves providing employees with more challenging and meaningful work largely by allowing them to increase the variety of work they perform, and the level of autonomy or freedom they have in performing the work.

Social specialization refers to the specialization of individuals, rather than the specialization of jobs. Social specialization is accomplished through the employment of professionals whose skills cannot be easily routinized. For example, an accountant who performs an audit does so through the application of specialized, trained skills. Similarly, engineers, nurses, doctors and professors are specialized professionals whose skills have been developed in a specific area or specialty.

2. Centralization

Where does authority rest within the organization? That is, what level in the organizational hierarchy has decision-making authority? This raises the question of centralization–decentralization.

Fundamentally, decision-making power can rest at the top of the organizational hierarchy. For example, if top management makes all the important decisions, with little or no input from lower levels of the organization, this would be considered a highly centralized decision-making structure. On the other hand, if decision-making authority is not concentrated at the top level, but rather is spread to the lower levels, this is referred to as decentralized decision making. As with the other elements we have discussed to this point, the 20th century also witnessed great changes in the relative concentration of decision-making authority. Essentially, many organizations chose to move from centralized to more decentralized structures. Largely, this move was intended to make organizations more efficient and speedier in their decision-making ability. Centralized organizations typically require longer time frames for decisions to be made. For example, it takes much longer for the head office of a geographically diverse operation to make decisions about its operations in another corner of the world than it would if that operation had authority to make its own decisions.

The notion of worker empowerment is a move toward shifting much greater levels of responsibility back to employees, so that, in a sense, they are at least partly their own bosses. One popular example of the trend toward less emphasis on one boss is the use of self-managing work teams. These essentially are collections of workers who work together on a project or task and largely manage themselves. Some organizations that have employed self-managing teams include GM's Saturn division, Motorola, Frito Lay, Shell and Microsoft, to name but a few. The need to have one all-powerful boss is no longer considered the best way of designing organizations.

3. Span of Control

How many levels of those in charge do we have? To address this issue, we can consider the notion of hierarchy of authority. The hierarchy is very much connected to something called the span of control. The span of control refers to the number of employees reporting to a supervisor. Obviously, it can vary from organization to organization, depending on how many subordinates an organization feels a manager can effectively direct.

The span of control is important because it really determines the number of managers and levels there are in the organizational hierarchy, something also referred to as **vertical differentiation**. How does the span of control determine the number of managers and levels? Consider the following examples. (See Exhibit 4.6.)

Imagine two organizations with the same total number of seven members, but with different spans of control, so that in Organization X, there is an average span of control of two with three levels of hierarchy (the president, two managers and four subordinates). In Organization Y, which also has a total of seven members, the span of control is six — there are only two levels in the hierarchy. (This organization might be considered as having one central leader, with all employees as one self-managing team who only report to one boss: the president.)

We can describe Organization X as having

- a relatively narrower span of control (two) compared to Organization Y, which has a wider span of control (six).
- a taller hierarchical structure (three levels of hierarchy), compared to Organization Y, which is relatively flatter (two levels of hierarchy). That is, the span of control clearly determines how "flat" or how "tall" an organization is.

In general terms, a narrow span of control tends to reflect a tall organization, while a wide span of control tends to reflect a flat organization. What difference does it make how many subordinates a supervisor oversees? What difference does it make how many levels of hierarchy exist within an organization? First, it has been argued that maintaining small or narrow spans of control improves a manager's ability to manage. Think about it — a manager who oversees, say, a handful of employees is much more capable of maintaining close supervision than a manager with a wide span of control who is responsi-

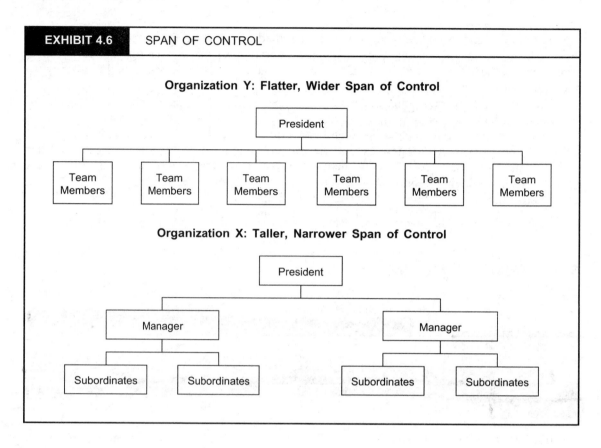

EXHIBIT 4.6   SPAN OF CONTROL

Organization Y: Flatter, Wider Span of Control

President

Team Members | Team Members | Team Members | Team Members | Team Members | Team Members

Organization X: Taller, Narrower Span of Control

President

Manager | Manager

Subordinates | Subordinates | Subordinates | Subordinates

ble for a large number of employees. However, there are also downsides to the narrow span of control: it is costly! Why? Quite simply, because it adds layers of management, and more management means more expenses to cover. Second, a narrow span of control (or tall structures) makes vertical communication more time consuming. Why? Again, consider what a narrow span of control creates. It creates more levels in the hierarchy, so that any information that must be transmitted from the top of the hierarchy to the bottom takes longer than it would to communicate if there were fewer levels. One other potential disadvantage of narrow spans of control, or tall structures, is that the close supervision such a system encourages also tends to discourage employee autonomy and self-management.

We have seen changes in the span of control in organizations over the past century. Certainly, the trend in recent years is to widen the span of control or, in other words, flatten the organizational hierarchy. From IBM to Toyota, we have seen significant de-layering of organizational hierarchies. Why? This has occurred for most of the reasons cited above: cutting costs and speeding up the communication or decision-making process. (See Talking Business 4.2.) Typically, widening the span of control or flattening the hierarchy includes spreading decision-making authority down to the lower levels of the organization.

> ### TALKING BUSINESS 4.2   DECISIONS MADE IN A JIFFY
>
> Jiffy muffin and biscuit mixes, produced by Chelsea Milling of Chelsea, Mich., have become so familiar that it's easy to overlook how amazing the brand's success really is. Recent market data indicate that Jiffy is the leader in the $230 million muffin-mix category, with 30.6% of the market as measured by revenue and 55.3% share as measured by unit sales. This performance is particularly impressive given that Chelsea Milling is a family-run operation competing with such corporate giants as General Mills and Pillsbury. Just how has Chelsea Milling beat the big players at their own game for more than 70 years? Part of the secret of their success is in their organizational structure. The firm is a simple operation that replaces corporate bureaucracy with lean efficiency. The decision-making process of their larger competitors is considerably more complicated. In this company, it's done by three or four people, as opposed to three or four departments. Most of Chelsea Milling's 350 employees are in manufacturing. The company mills and stores its flour, and everything except the printing of the little boxes is done on-site.
>
> ---
>
> **Source:** Based on Paul Lukas, "Jiffy's Secret Recipe" *Fortune Small Business* (December 3, 2001).

4.   *Formalization*

To what degree will rules or procedures be used to guide organizational members? The answer to that question is addressed in the notion of formalization. The level of formalization in an organization refers to the degree to which rules, regulations, procedures and the like govern how work is performed. In other words, **formalization** reflects the degree to which jobs within the organization are standardized. A high level of formalization means highly standardized work — i.e., clear rules regarding how the work should be performed. Highly standardized work, or work that is very much rule-directed, suggests that there is little individual discretion in how that work can be performed. In this regard, high formalization is what scientific management advocated in its assertion of standardizing work. And, if you recall, this was intended to ensure that performance was consistent and reliable — i.e., workers know what is expected of them and how, exactly, they should be performing their jobs. In addition, the greater the degree of formalization, the less reliance on individual discretion.

Can you think of any organizations that are highly formalized? Where you have an organization that has explicit job descriptions, numerous rules or procedures governing the work process, you've got a highly formalized organization. Like the other elements of structure, attitudes toward formalization in organizations changed dramatically throughout the 20th century. Essentially, what we have witnessed in many organizations is a shift from high formalization and standardization of work practices to less formality. Why? Given the need to adapt to the rapidly changing external environment, organizations have found they must be willing to scrap the old way of doing things in favour of methods that better accommodate the changing demands of their environment, whether the sources of change come from competitors, consumers, technological changes, etc.

WHAT DETERMINES ORGANIZATIONAL STRUCTURE? A RATIONAL PERSPECTIVE

Now, in broad terms, we can consider why organizations take on different structures, and we can consider sources of influence on organizational design. To simplify our discussion, we can consider the two extreme opposites, in terms of the organizational configuration identified previously: the mechanistic organizations and the organic organizations. Each can be defined using the four elements of structure (see Exhibit 4.7).

Organic and mechanistic organizations are polar extremes in structure. Machine bureaucracies, or mechanistic organizations, maintain jobs that are narrow in scope; decision making is centralized at the top of the organizational hierarchy and work is conducted within highly formalized rules and procedures. On the other hand, organic organizations tend to have jobs that are enriched with more variety and task responsibilities; typically, there is a team-based approach rather than a "top-down" approach to authority and control decision-making is decentralized throughout the organization. The worker is less restricted with fewer rules and regulations. While there are a variety of influences on the design of organizations, perhaps among the most significant sources of influence on the structure of organizations are strategy, size, technology and environment.

1.   Strategy

Clearly, an organization's structure is intended to help achieve its organizational objectives or strategy. In other words, structure should follow strategy. For example, if an organization's central mission is to be innovative, to pursue new product designs or services, then its structure should help achieve that goal. Clearly, from what we have discussed earlier, the characteristics associated with the organic organization would best suit that objective. Few rules and decentralized decision making encourage flexibility and adaptiveness to environmental demands. And these are, consequently, useful for encouraging innovation. If, on the other hand, efficiency or cost minimization is a central strategy, then the mechanistic organization is the better-suited structure (see Exhibit 4.8).

EXHIBIT 4.7	MECHANISTIC VS. ORGANIC ORGANIZATION		
		Mechanistic	**Organic**
1. Division of Labour / Work Specialization		narrow	wide
2. Centralization		centralized	decentralized
2. Span of Control		narrow	wide
4. Formalization		high	low

EXHIBIT 4.8	STRATEGY AND STRUCTURE

	Types of Organizational Strategies	
Elements of Structure	**Focus on Innovation**	**Focus on Cost and Efficiency**
1. Division of Labour	wide	narrow
2. Centralization	decentralized	centralized
3. Span of Control	wide	narrow
4. Formalization	low	high

2. Organizational Size

If you observe the organizational landscape, it is hard not to see some kind of connection between the size of an organization and its structure. In terms of our organic-mechanistic classification, there is a tendency for larger organizations to shift toward a more mechanistic structure — largely because of the need to control and coordinate many more employees. When you have masses of employees whose performance must be directed, it would seem beneficial to standardize or routinize the work, and ensure clear rules and regulations to guide performance. It is difficult to maintain the informality of the organic structure when organizations grow. However, that is not to say that many large organizations do not try to retain an organic structure, even in the face of significant growth. For example, although Microsoft is a large organization, it prides itself on innovation and has attempted to divide itself into manageable units that use team-based approaches and where informality frees up the entrepreneurial spirit. Similarly, Johnson & Johnson prides itself on being a decentralized empire. The top managers are given much decision-making power for their units, and there is a great effort to maintain a flat organizational structure, even though the company itself is quite large (see Exhibit 4.9).

3. Technology

Technology essentially refers to how an organization transforms its inputs, such as financial capital and physical and human resources, into services or products. For example, the assembly-line approach has been used to produce output in the car manufacturing industry. Among classifications within technology is how routine or non-routine that technology is. Routine technology refers to automated and standardized operations typical of mass production operations, while non-routine technology is not standardized, and might include anything from conducting genetic research to custom-made furniture. As you might have guessed, standardized, mass production technologies are more compatible with mechanistic

143

EXHIBIT 4.9	ORGANIZATIONAL SIZE AND STRUCTURE	

Four Elements	Small Organization	Large Organization
1. Division of Labour	wide	narrow
2. Centralization	centralized	decentralized
3. Span of Control	wide	narrow
4. Formalization	low	high

structures where such standardization or routinization of work is part of the main objective. Non-routine technologies, on the other hand, are better suited to the innovative, organic structures that do not allow formality and rules to govern activity.

4. Environment

Among the main elements we might consider as composing an organization's environment are suppliers, customers, competitors, the government and the general public. When might an organization's structure be affected by its environment? Again, if we can use a broad classification, you can think of an organization's environment in two broad classes: **dynamic** or **static** environment. Static environments, as the name suggests, exhibit little if any change — no new competitors, no new technologies, no government regulatory changes, etc. In such an environment of certainty, the mechanistic structure would be quite suitable: it generates rules and methods of performance based on environmental needs and, once established, does not change. A dynamic environment contains much uncertainty and undergoes much change. Clearly, an organic structure is much better suited, given its higher adaptiveness to change. Competition alone has accounted for much change in the environment of business.

All of these factors are useful to keep in mind when considering the range of changes we have witnessed in recent years.

The Importance of the Environment

In order to understand why organizations are designed in a certain way, it makes sense to consider the environment within which they operate. There are numerous theories and models that have attempted to identify those factors that determine the structure of organizations. Contingency theory is a natural outgrowth of systems theory,[7] and it recognizes that all organizations are open systems that can only survive through continuous and successful interaction with their environment.

What factors influence whether a tall bureaucratic organization or a simple flat structure is suitable? In what contexts does a centralized decision-making structure, as opposed to a decentralized structure, make sense? Contingency theory focuses on the contextual factors that can influence the structure and management of organizations, with a particular emphasis on organizational design. Why do some organizations benefit from centralized decision making? Why do some organizations require a high level of formalization with regard to employee job responsibilities? Contingency theories seek to explain what factors in the organization's environment influence these organizational design choices.

A central philosophy underlying contingency theory is that there is no one ideal way to organize. That is, there are no universal principles of what constitutes the best form of organization. The optimal organizational structure is dependent on, or is contingent on, the nature of its operating environment. Consequently, this implies that managers should seek to achieve a fit or alignment among the major elements of their organization's environment and its internal organizational design. Therefore, while contingency theory suggests that there is no one best way to organize universally, it does assert that there is one best way to organize, given a specific type of operating environment or organizational context.

Contingency theory is based on the assumption that organizations are able to adapt to changing environmental conditions. Given the need for organizations to design their structure in reference to their environment, successful organizations must adapt to any changes in that environment via structural change. This also assumes that organizations behave as rational entities that are able and willing to make internal structural changes to achieve a compatibility with their environment as a means for survival and success. According to contingency theory, there are a number of specific contingency factors that can influence organizational design. One of the most widely studied factors is the notion of environmental uncertainty.

Environmental uncertainty has been defined as the rate at which market conditions and production technologies change. There is no doubt that environmental uncertainty is an important dimension that may vary among organizations and industries. For example, some organizations operate within relatively static environments — few, if any, new competitors, unchanging technology, few changes in governmental regulations, etc. Other organizations may exist in very dynamic environments — constantly new competitors, rapidly changing technology, new governmental regulations, etc.

Researchers by the names of Burns and Stalker were among the first, in the 1960s, to systematically study the influence of the environment on organizational structure. Among their studies was a comparison of organizations existing in two fundamentally different environments: one set of firms operated within a dynamic, changing industry; another set operated in a stable, established industry. The researchers found that there were a number of significant structural differences in these two sets of organizations. (See Exhibit 4.10.) In essence, the results of this research suggested that an organization's structure is dependent, or contingent, on the type of environment within which the organization operates.

Lessons for managers. The contingency approach presents some important lessons for managers. Among these lessons is the need for managers to take great caution in the

| EXHIBIT 4.10 | DYNAMIC VS. STATIC INDUSTRY | |

Organizational Characteristics	Static Industry	Dynamic Industry
Rules and Procedures	• reliance on formal rules and procedures to carry out most organizational activities	• relatively fewer rules
Decision Making	• highly centralized	• more decentralized
Levels of Administration or Supervisory Control	• greater number of levels	• fewer levels

way they interpret the organization's environment. Managers must accurately define those environmental factors that have significant impact on their organizations in order to generate a suitable organizational structure — one capable of responding to environmental demands and the characteristics for which it was designed. By the mid-1980s, managers found that their assumptions about the environment largely no longer held. Organizational characteristics regarding the different kinds of hierarchies, organizational practices and strategies developed in the past were suddenly incapable of dealing with changes in the organizational environment.

RE-ENGINEERING

A management consultant by the name of James Champy was asked to observe the operations of an insurance company in an effort to improve its efficiency. Among his observations, Champy discovered that it took 24 days to obtain a policy after the client purchased it. Champy was curious to understand what work was done on these insurance policies during the 24 days it took to reach the purchaser. After following the trail of these policies, Champy found that only about 10 minutes of work was actually performed on these policies during that 24-day period. The additional time arose because the policies were transferred through 14 different departments. Was this necessary? Champy discovered that while there was no real need for policies to travel through this long and winding road, it nevertheless had become a tradition: "This is how we do things here." There had been no assessment, however, of whether, indeed, this method was still necessary.

James Champy and one of his colleagues, Michael Hammer, engaged in many more observations of different types of organizations, and they, along with a number of other experts, advocated a rethinking of organizational design, detailed in their best-selling book, *Reengineering the Corporation*. *Re-engineering* became one of the hottest business buzzwords of the 1990s; but what exactly is it? Fundamentally, re-engineering asks the question, If I were creating this company today, if I could start over, given what I know and given current technology, what would it look like? A more systematic definition includes the following elements:

> The fundamental rethinking and radical redesigning of business processes to achieve dramatic improvements in measures of performance (cost, quality, service, speed).[8]

In examining the definition of *re-engineering*, we can understand its essence and its basic contributions to organizational design. Let's consider each element of this definition.

1. Fundamental rethinking of the organization's structure and functions. Re-engineering involves a critical examination of the traditional method of structuring work. An organization will examine how it performs its functions in order to assess whether, indeed, this method makes the most sense. This examination of work processes is done with a focus on how to best serve customer needs. Two fundamental questions that any re-engineering effort must ask are: "How do we improve quality of our product/service?" and "How can we reduce costs?" One central aim is to eliminate any company practice that is not adding value to the process of generating a product or service for the customer. The notion of focusing on the company's "core competencies" implies that the aim is to concentrate on what the company does best and eliminate unnecessary functions or practices.

2. Radical redesign of organization processes and structure. The thrust of re-engineering is to "re-invent" the organization according to the current objectives. Hammer and Champy suggested that a lot of organizations that claim they are making changes to become more efficient are really just trying to do "worthless tasks" more efficiently. What re-engineering advocates is a "quantum leap." However, it is important to note that while the radical redesign of an organization is the fundamental rationale behind re-engineering, it is difficult to achieve in practice.

Accomplishing the goal of redesign typically involves organizing around process rather than around functions. For much of the 20th century, beliefs about organizing focused on specializing jobs, compartmentalizing them into the simplest elements, therefore ensuring work was standardized (as advocated in scientific management and Weber's notion of bureaucracy). Re-engineering advocates the collection of individual tasks into more whole jobs. This relates to the distinction between process and functions. It is reflected in the notion of moving away from a focus on specialized tasks to a focus on process. Consider an example offered by Hammer and Champy, the case of a credit agency, in Talking Business 4.3.

The illustration reflects the notion of organization around process — in other words, designing the organization in a way that considers the actual jobs that need to be performed. This is in contrast to a blanket approach to organizational design that would simply advocate the creation of different departments that jobs will be organized in. Often the bureaucratic structure becomes preoccupied with administrative levels of hierarchy, rules and regulations. The machine bureaucracy and the professional bureaucracy are

> ***TALKING BUSINESS* 4.3   THE CREDIT AGENCY**
>
> This organization found that the task of processing a credit application was extremely slow and inefficient, taking anywhere from six days to two weeks to complete. After a credit request was received by phone it was recorded on a piece of paper. This paper was then passed along to credit checkers, pricers (who determined what interest rate to charge), and to many other individuals who performed single, compartmentalized tasks. Credit applications typically were bounced around to different areas before they were properly completed. Now after much scrutiny, it was discovered that the time actually required to complete such an application shouldn't take more than 90 minutes! Consequently, it was time to re-engineer — "scrap" the traditional method organized around specialized, compartmentalized tasks and redesign the work around the process itself of completing a credit application. This did not require numerous specialists but simply required a few generalists. That is, one person could process an entire application without passing it on to others. So this work was re-engineered, resulting in a decrease in the four-hour application time, an enormous increase in the number of applications processed and fewer employees required to do the job.

examples of these popular forms of organizational design. What re-engineering advocates is to move away from a preoccupation with organizing work based on tasks, jobs, departments and administrative levels of hierarchy, and instead to focus on processes — the activities required to transform inputs into outputs. This fundamental logic of re-engineering was recently observed, as shown in Talking Business 4.4, by management scholar William Kettinger.

With regard to the nature of the job, re-engineering also advocates combining several jobs into one. This, too, was reflected in the credit agency example above. This is akin to the notion of job enrichment: that is, enriching the responsibility and challenge of jobs by allowing workers to do more of the task rather than one narrow, highly specialized piece of the work. Certainly technology has helped facilitate the integration of jobs and the ability of fewer people to perform a greater variety of tasks. In fact, it has been observed that among the leading factors contributing to the proliferation of re-engineering activity in the early 1990s were advances in information technology. Technologies including shared databases, client-server architecture and imaging could be efficiently applied to facilitate processes that cross different functional departments.[9]

The above suggests that re-engineering may result in the view that work can be performed efficiently with fewer employees. Typically, re-engineering means *cutting* the size of the workforce, and often involves flattening the organizational hierarchy. Examples abound, including organizations like Pepsi-Cola North America, which cut seven layers of its hierarchy to four in order to focus on designing itself around serving customers rather than simply maintaining a hierarchical bureaucracy. This also presents a major challenge for organizations attempting to re-engineer: the threat of job loss for many employees. Management scholar Varun Grover recently observed the following:

148

TALKING BUSINESS **4.4   LESSONS IN RE-ENGINEERING**

Typically in an early lecture in one of my classes, I ask a student to come to the board and draw a picture of a company where she or he has worked. Inevitably, they draw a hierarchical organization chart — the student is typically on the bottom, and the bosses are on top. I respond that if this is a picture of a company, then where are the customers, and how do products and services get produced, delivered, and improved? This pushes them to draw a horizontal, or process-based representation, of the company which explains these relationships. Soon the board is covered with every conceivable business process — order fulfillment, product development, quality assurance, and on and on. These students quickly see that a business process is nothing more than logically related tasks that use the resources of a company to achieve a defined business outcome. This is a simple, but powerful, concept! Within a few classes, these students have internalized a process view (or "process think," as we refer to it) that helps them conceptualize new ways to improve operations, satisfy customers, and make the best use of the latest information technologies. Similar to the way these students learn process thinking, employees at all levels have grown to incorporate a process view into all aspects of their work. As process thinking has become mainstream, re-engineering has lost its radical tone. We have seen reconciliation with more incremental process change methods such as TQM. Today we recognize that we must broaden the business change tent to accommodate radical business objectives, incremental implementations, and both top-down-driven and bottom-up-driven process change.

Source: Reproduced with permission from Varun Grover, William J. Kettinger, and James T.C. Teng, "Business process change in the 21st century" *Business and Economic Review* (Jan.–Mar. 2000) 46(2): 14–18.

Perhaps the biggest challenge associated with the success of the re-engineering phenomenon may be that of selling such a major change to the employees of the organization and getting them to "buy into" the strategic changes that must be undertaken for the firm to survive and prosper. For example, outsourcing activities that don't contribute to core competencies or technology to other firms that can perform them better may be a legitimate outcome of a good re-engineering effort. It would lead to work force reduction, but only with the purpose of making the firm leaner and more responsive. Time-based competition and the creation of "agile" corporations may not even be possible without such changes in work force size and composition. As companies emphasize the notion of capturing and leveraging "knowledge" as a source of value, a broader focus on process change management may perhaps be the only way to avoid skill obsolescence of employees and encourage horizontal career paths. The extent to which top level management can sell such a vision of change and its impact on the employees is critical. We found that often information technology problems are considered critical before the project, but it's the management of people and change that really makes the difference.[10]

TOWARD A VIRTUAL ORGANIZATION

If downsizing has become one of the most feared business buzzwords in recent years, a much more benevolent yet popular buzzword is the *virtual organization*. How does an organization become virtual? And equally important, Why would an organization want to become virtual? The virtual organization underscores how far we have come from the traditional notion of organizations. According to our old philosophy, the bureaucratic structure is typically large. The virtual organization, on the other hand, is not dependent on size for its functions. In fact, the virtual organization attempts to maximize its fluidity, flatness and integratedness with the environment — i.e., building off, many of the structural trends we identified earlier. Let's consider the ways a virtual organization attempts to achieve these characteristics.

Outsourcing. Outsourcing (or contracting out) involves hiring external organizations to conduct work in certain functions of the company. For example, payroll, accounting and legal work can be assigned to outsourced staff. The organization typically will retain its core functions or competencies — that is, those areas that it is in business to conduct. In other words, it sticks to what it does best and outsources functions that it doesn't wish to focus on. While the buzzword *outsourcing* may seem relatively recent, the practice of outsourcing has, in fact, been with us for many years. Consider the extensive list of "suppliers" of expertise to industry — lawyers, public accountants, independent insurance adjusters, contractors, appraisers, health care professionals and independent medical specialists. Perhaps what is also more recent is the trend toward building businesses with a consideration of which activities are required "in-house" and which functions can simply be outsourced. For example, CIBC outsourced a major portion of its human resource administrative functions to Electronic Data Services (EDS). The move is consistent with the philosophy of outsourcing: shedding business activities that do not reflect the organization's core competencies. Obviously, managing human resource functions, such as payroll or pension plans, are not part of CIBC's core competencies. These functions can be outsourced to a company whose core competency is in such areas. EDS specializes in these areas. CIBC gains by having an expert company deal with these functions, and at the same time the company has cut costs through the elimination of almost half its human resources department.[11]

A good example of the potential benefits and, often, necessity of outsourcing is found in the popular trend of outsourcing the payroll function. There are a variety of reasons for choosing to outsource the payroll function, including dealing with increased human resource demands that may be caused by employee population growth, mergers, acquisitions, spinoffs, consolidations and downsizing. As Heather Erickson points out in a recent article, outsourcing can often be used to help in special or unique circumstances. As an illustration, Erickson offers a number of possible circumstances that have encouraged the outsourcing of the payroll function in Exhibit 4.11.

Networking. We have increasingly been observing organizations limiting themselves to fewer activities in which they have expertise and assigning specialists to handle all other functions. This is also associated with the notion of integrated or networked organizations that we identified earlier. That is, organizations can engage in co-operative relationships with suppliers, distributors or competitors. The aim is to improve their efficiency and flexi-

---

EXHIBIT 4.11	OUTSOURCING PAYROLL: WHY?

1. **Mergers:** Following consolidation, the payroll function may be outsourced in order to permit the HR function and accounting function to focus on making changes that reflect the pay and benefit policies of the new corporation.

2. **Foreign acquisitions:** When a foreign buyer acquires a Canadian company, the unique nature of tax laws may not mix well with the new parent company's payroll system. Outsourcing the Canadian subsidiary payroll function avoids this conflict.

3. **Closing down a division:** In cases where a company is shutting down a division, complex severance packages paid over an extended period of time to a diverse group of former employees may be required. The demanding nature of these packages may not be efficiently dealt with by the internal payroll function, but may be better served by being outsourced to an external party while allowing the internal payroll department to focus on existing employee accounts.

4. **Confidentiality:** Salaries are typically a sensitive issue requiring high security. Some organizations may prefer to outsource the work done on particularly high security salaries, such as for senior executives, and on performance and incentive compensation plans in order to ensure that no organizational member becomes privy to this information.

5. **Entrepreneurial firms:** Small companies that are experiencing rapid growth in numbers of employees may find that outsourcing can offer a faster, more cost-effective way to manage the increasing demands of payroll. The outsourcing of the payroll function allows the business managers to focus on managing business growth and the core functions of the business rather than becoming preoccupied with the peripheral yet demanding function of payroll. For example, a small business that grows rapidly from three employees to 150 in 12 months found that when there were only the three owners to pay, writing cheques was easy. On the other hand, at 150 employees, the owners realized it was a function they no longer had time to manage. By outsourcing, the owners avoided hiring a full-time payroll person, and consequently the cost was much less than the cost of salary and benefits for a new full-time employee.

Source: Based on Heather Erickson, "Maybe organizational insider: Outsource payroll? Makes sense" *Canadian HR Reporter* (September 10, 2001) 14(15): G8.

---

bility in meeting new consumer needs. For example, a close relationship with a distributor might offer the supplier company more information about the changing needs of customers. The Japanese version of networked organizations called *keiretsu* could, in fact, really be considered the first form of the virtual organization.

Typically, a *keiretsu* involves a large bank or financial institution, a large industrial organization and a number of smaller firms. This integrated network of relationships allows the large industrial organization to produce the product with financial assistance from the bank. The role of the smaller firms may be to supply parts to the manufacturer, conduct research or, perhaps, distribute the final product. What we observe in virtual organizations are only those activities that are central — they are kept in-house, so to speak, and all other functions are outsourced to separate companies or individuals who are typically coordinated by a small head office. Or, each company is simply involved in some kind of network where each brings its own expertise to the collection of companies.

Shed non-core functions. The outsourcing aspect, again, is a central feature of the virtual organization. Clearly, organizations can become more "virtual" by shedding some of their non-core functions and outsourcing these to affiliated organizations. Companies that use information technology (IT) need to become as flexible as the virtual organizations, given the rapidly changing face of technology and its applications. For organizations whose core competency is not IT or all its elements, there is much to be gained from partnering with other organizations, in the virtual sense. A growing number of IT departments are considering outsourcing models to address all or part of their needs. "Small component" or discrete outsourcing service providers include such specialized offerings as storage and Web hosting. Application management has become a high-growth area in outsourcing service markets in Canada. Those seeking such services have a range of services to choose for outsourcing, including desktop or infrastructure services to various business functions. Network management can be outsourced, along with backup and recovery, as well as data centre services. Such examples are noted in Talking Business 4.5.

A virtual organization might be composed of simply a small group of business executives who form the core of the organization. Their responsibility is to oversee and co-ordinate the activities that might be done in-house as well as those functions that are outsourced — which might involve coordinating relationships among the companies that develop, manufacture, market and sell their products. Many more companies have found that they can become quite profitable without actually having to own their entire operation. Certainly, the traditional bureaucracy is structured so that production occurs in company-owned plants; research and development are conducted by in-house experts; sales and marketing are performed by the company's own sales and marketing department. This is not the case for the virtual organization, which doesn't believe you need to own everything. For example, Dell Computer owns no plants, and simply assembles computers from parts whose manufacture has been outsourced. Similarly, Apple Computer subcontracted the manufacture of its first Notebook to Sony as a means to speed entry into the market. Companies like Nike and Reebok have achieved success by focusing on what they do best — designing and marketing their products. They outsource almost all their footwear manufacturing to outside suppliers. Obviously, the virtual organization doesn't just outsource the peripheral function of the company; it outsources whatever costs less than conducting it in-house.

There are a number of *gains* potentially achieved by going virtual:

1. **The cost savings are significant.** A virtual organization need not own its own plants, nor employ its own research and development teams, nor hire its own sales staff. This means the virtual organization also doesn't need to hire the extra staff to support all these functions — such as personnel specialists, company lawyers, accountants, etc. The virtual organization can outsource most of these functions, and focus on what it does best. So there is little, if any, administrative overhead, so to speak, because work activities are largely contracted. Costs savings arise in areas such as training, purchasing of work-related tools, benefits, downtime and educational requirements. All these requirements are typically obtained with the arrival of the external or "outsourced" experts.

2. **The virtual organization is a great alternative for entrepreneurs.** That is, individuals seeking to start up a new business or venture may face huge startup costs. The net-

---

TALKING BUSINESS 4.5   GOING VIRTUAL: OUTSOURCING INNOVATION

You likely have never heard of HTC, Flextronics or Cellon. However, these companies design some very famous products. They represent the new trend in outsourcing — outsourcing innovation! Companies such as Dell, Motorola, and Philips are purchasing complete designs from Asian developers, making minor adjustments their own specifications, and putting their own brand names on the label. This type of outsourcing may also involve "offshoring" — relying on different regions of the world to provide this expertise.

Why is this trend occurring? Companies gain tremendous cost savings from this type of outsourcing. The outsourcing of manufacturing, technological support, and back-office work is not the only way to cut costs. Now, even outsourcing core competencies such as innovation can make financial sense! However, it also raises some risks. Who "owns" the final innovation? That's one reason why Apple Computer, for example, insists on developing its major products "in-house." On the other hand, companies such as Nokia no longer insist on developing everything itself. Because of the complexities of changing technologies, outsourcing may permit Nokia to focus on other areas while deferring to innovators for assistance on some projects.

Source: Based on Pete Engardio and Bruce Einhorn, with Manjeet Kripalani in Bangalore, Andy Reinhardt in Cannes, Bruce Nussbaum in Somers, N.Y., and Peter Burrows in San Mateo, California, "Outsourcing Innovation" *Business Week* [New York] (March 21, 2005), p. 84.

---

work of arrangements can exploit the expertise of different companies while not requiring the initiator of the business to buy everything and start a business from scratch.

3. **For a mature company, going virtual can be a fast way to develop and market new products.** Relying on the expertise of partners means that no huge investment is required to enter a new product or service territory.

4. **Fast and flexible are adjectives to describe the virtual organization.** The flexible arrangements of those parties involved can be of a temporary nature to produce a good or service. Resources can be quickly arranged and rearranged to meet changing demands and best serve customers. Management isn't getting bogged down in peripheral functions, but is simply focusing only on central functions.

Among the *risks and challenges* of becoming virtual are the following:

1. **Probably the biggest sacrifice is the notion of control.** Control has traditionally been a key goal of any organization. The structure of the bureaucratic organization is fundamentally based on the notion of control — control through standardization of work, control through hierarchy of authority, control through rules and regulations, control

through clear division of labour. However, the virtual organization doesn't provide such control. Think of it — how can you monitor all activity when it may not even be occurring within the walls of one building? Among the fears of going virtual and outsourcing is that we are "hollowing out" the organization and making it extremely dependent on external sources. The employees are not all ours; outsourcing to independent contractors doesn't carry with it the same level of control as staffing our own employees to do the work. Difficulties in control can particularly occur when a variety of subcontractors are involved in the work. This lack of control may also generate a lack of control over costs — once a company becomes dependent on a supplier, it may be unable to refuse an increase in the supplier's prices.

2. **Another potential disadvantage is the lack of employee loyalty.** If our organization is largely composed of temporary workers and subcontractors, who is really committed to perpetuating the goals of this company? Can a virtual organization really develop a sense of identity or culture that is the "glue" that binds everyone to a common purpose? This is an issue that virtual organizations must deal with. In fact, turnover in many virtual organizations tends to be high, because employees are committed only to the task for which they are hired, and in addition, employees may be working under temporary contractual arrangements and could be dismissed in favour of another contractor.

3. **A final significant risk in going virtual is the potential to sacrifice competitive learning opportunities.** Outsourcing involves the strategic decision to "let go" of some aspect of the organization — the decision could be to permit the manufacture of the footwear, as in the case of Nike, while retaining the core competencies (such as the marketing function, also, as in the case of Nike). The question is, Is there a danger in "letting go" of functions that may currently appear peripheral, but could become important functions of the organization should the organization's strategy change in the future? Clearly, if a function is outsourced, the experience or learning of this function as a skill is lost to the internal organization. Is there an inherent danger in such a situation? That is, Is there a danger in outsourcing, given the risk of losing key skills that could be needed for future competitiveness? Read Talking Business 4.6 for the risks of outsourcing.

DOWNSIZING

In terms of business buzzwords, probably the most dreaded buzzword of the 1990s was the term *downsizing*. While the 1990s have been referred to as the "lean, mean 90s," the trend toward leanness via downsizing has not gone away in the new millennium. In recent years, across Canada thousands of workers have been losing their jobs.

In broad terms, **downsizing** refers to the planned reduction in the breadth of an organization's operations. Typically, it entails terminating relatively large numbers of employees and/or decreasing the number of products or services the organization provides. It seems that if you think of just about any large corporation, it has likely experienced some kind of downsizing: from AT&T to Bell Canada, to Air Canada, to IBM, to General Motors,

TALKING BUSINESS 4.6 OUTSOURCING CORE COMPETENCIES?

Some companies claim they can do it all. Need an application that does X, Y and Z? No problem, they can do everything, and bigger and better than anyone else.

But not everyone wants to be a jack of all trades. Some companies realize the limitations of their capabilities. And where their expertise ends, they enlist the help of outsourcers.

That's why the Canadian Pacific Railway (CPR) outsources the maintenance of applications that it doesn't want to develop the expertise for in-house. Nine years ago, it outsourced the maintenance of some legacy apps to RIS and a year ago, decided to outsource its mainframe infrastructure to IBM.

. . . .

"We were looking for someone who could come in with some expertise and take this part over and basically make the headaches go away."

. . . .

"Sometimes we outsource to gain expertise that we don't want to develop in-house. Secondly, we will outsource because [its] technology we no longer wish to maintain."

The first step to determining whether or not to outsource IT is to determine if it's critical to the core business, says Graham McFarlane, a certified management consultant and a director at Western Management Consultants in Calgary.

. . . .

CPR, however, has outsourced the management of applications it considers critical to its business, Forte says. It outsourced the management of applications used to manage its train yards because the suite it acquired ran on Sybase technology, something it didn't use internally.

"We didn't want to dilute our technology base," he says. "We didn't want to [ ] go through the whole gauntlet of coming up to speed on a new database engine and new development tools. So we hired that expertise."

Because the application was critical, CPR took extra care with the governance structure surrounding the outsourcing deal, Forte says.

This is something companies often forget when outsourcing IT to a third-party, says Shawn McCray, a partner for the sourcing management practice at TPI in Houston, Tex.

"The major thing people overlook is that they have to continue to manage the outsourcer on an ongoing basis. Some companies think they don't have to worry about anything anymore. But you don't outsource leadership." ...

Source: Reproduced by permission of Computing Canada from Poonam Khanna, "CP Rail jumps aboard outsourcing train," *Computing Canada* (December 10, 2004) 30(18): 30.

to Northern Telecom — all have experienced massive cuts in their workforce. Consequently, most of us associate downsizing with the reduction of the workforce. However, we can be more specific, given that organizations can downsize in a variety of ways. For example, does reducing an organization's ownership of assets amount to downsizing? Does a reduction in the number of employees constitute downsizing?

> One definition of downsizing that has been offered is: "downsizing is a set of activities undertaken on the part of management and designed to improve organizational efficiency, productivity, and/or competitiveness. It represents a strategy implemented by managers that affects the size of the firm's work force, the costs, and the work processes.[12]

Based on this definition, there are three fundamental types of strategies for downsizing: workforce reduction, work redesign and systematic change. Workforce reduction typically involves a short-term strategy that is aimed at reducing the number of employees through such programs as attrition, early retirement, voluntary severance packages, layoffs, or terminations. Downsizing approaches have largely been directed at workforce reduction rather than the more detailed and longer-term strategies of job redesign and systematic change.[13] Following, we can more clearly identify the common approaches to downsizing. That is, we can be more specific about what exactly an organizational downsizing may entail. This will allow us to briefly identify the potential benefits as well as potential pitfalls of an organizational downsizing.

Methods of Downsizing

Management scholar Martin Evans provided a summary of the forms of downsizing, and he also identified the potential benefits and consequences of these different approaches to it. The most common forms of downsizing include any one, or a combination, of the following strategies (and the pros and cons of each of these approaches are shown in Exhibit 4.12):

1. **Across-the-board cutbacks.** Cutting a fixed percentage of the workforce across all departments or units.

2. **Early retirement and voluntary severance.** Those nearing retirement take early retirement, voluntarily as opposed to a forced leave — typically as the first stage in a downsizing process.

3. **De-layering — cutting a level or levels of the organization.** Termination or reassignment of the middle managers who are not replaced, flattening the organizational hierarchy by removing horizontal slices.

4. **Contracting Out (also referred to as outsourcing).** Lay off staff in areas that perform specialized functions and contracting out this work to agencies that can staff those areas with temporary workers. Types of activities that are typically contracted out include payroll, data entry, public relations and clerical work, as opposed to the core activities of the organization.

5. **Dropping product lines.** Discontinue some programs or product lines provided by the organization.

EXHIBIT 4.12 POTENTIAL BENEFITS AND RISKS OF DOWNSIZING

Potential Benefits

1. **Across-the-Board Cuts.** "Shares the pain," spreading it across the organization — all levels are equally affected.

2. **Early Retirement and Voluntary Severance.** Concentrates the terminations among those who are willing to leave.
   - May help achieve the reduced cost objective by encouraging the more senior and more highly paid staff to leave.

3. **De-layering.** Because the organization is cut horizontally, all areas are equally affected, and the "pain" is shared across all departments.
   - To the extent that decentralized decision making is desired, this approach allows the shift of responsibility to the lower and, perhaps, more appropriate levels in the organization.

4. **Contracting Out.** Immediate costs savings.

5. **Dropping Product Lines.**
   - Decide what areas may not be productive to continue to maintain.
   - A closer connection to long-term strategic planning compared to other approaches.
   - Concentrates the disruption in one or a few business units, as opposed to the entire organization.

Potential Risks

1. **Across-the-Board Cuts.** Efficient parts of organization are hurt. This form of downsizing ignores how well or how poorly the units are managed.
   - Typically conducted when there is no strategic plan — it simply cuts staff throughout the organization.

2. **Early Retirement and Voluntary Severance.**
   - Not necessarily guided by a strategic plan.
   - Encourages voluntary exits from all parts of the organization.
   - "Loss of corporate memory" — that is, a company may lose highly experienced, valued members who have been an intrinsic apart of what the organization is all about.

3. **De-layering.** A loss of corporate memory with the removal of middle managers. There may also be an overload of responsibility to top management, who now may need to fill the role of some middle management as well.
   - There may be significant costs attached to the transition from a taller organization to a flatter one where lower level employees must be trained to take on additional roles and responsibilities.

4. **Contracting Out.** Difficulties of dealing with the new suppliers of this labour and avoiding future cost increases.
   - The general loss of control with these temporary workers.

5. **Dropping Product Lines.** Pain is concentrated and not shared across the entire organization — a few people will carry the burden of this type of downsizing.

Consequences of Downsizing

The strategy of downsizing that started in the mid-1980s has now become commonplace. In the early stages, downsizing strategies were viewed as a panacea for the ills of organizations, providing organizations with a method of cost reduction, productivity and profitability improvement and, consequently, a higher competitive ability. Unfortunately, there is vast evidence that the anticipated benefits of corporate downsizing have largely failed to materialize. It is of interest to reconsider the anticipated benefits of downsizing and in what way these benefits have not been realized.

As the Wyatt report and numerous other studies have indicated, there are a host of benefits that organizations feel they can achieve through downsizing, including reduced bureaucracy, lower overhead costs, improved decision making, improvements in productivity and a stronger ability to innovate. But does downsizing contribute to a better "bottom line"? That is, does this activity enhance the organization's financial performance? There is research evidence that suggests that a downsizing or layoff announcement often leads to a drop in the organization's share price, particularly if that announcement was related to financial concerns or a massive and permanent cutback of employees.[14] There is also evidence to suggest that investors respond negatively to layoff announcements.[15]

Does downsizing improve organizational performance as measured by return on assets and common shares? There is research evidence indicating that organizations that engaged in an employee downsizing (i.e., termination of at least 5% of the workforce combined with little change in plant and equipment costs) did not outperform other organizations in their industry.[16] Similarly, a CSC Index survey found that less than 33% of all downsizing initiatives had achieved their anticipated productivity or profitability goals.

In a large-scale study conducted in Canada, data were collected from 1,907 Canadian organizations with at least 75 employees. This study examined how a permanent workforce reduction affects employer efficiency, employee satisfaction and employee–employer relations. The findings indicated that a permanent workforce reduction was associated with negative consequences. This echoes the findings in the United States and elsewhere, and underscores the consistent failure of downsizing to live up to its expectations.[17]

Added to the lacklustre results of downsizing is the wealth of evidence of the costs of downsizing in terms of human consequences. Needless to say, those individuals who are victims of a downsizing can be subjected to intense psychological trauma. However, there is ample research evidence to indicate that the *survivors* of a downsizing may also experience trauma. According to numerous studies conducted, survivors of a downsizing typically report greater levels of stress, burnout, reduced self-confidence and self-esteem and lower job satisfaction.[18] Studies have also found that a downsizing can have adverse effects on employee commitment to the organization, performance, customer and client needs, and reduced morale and trust.[19] See Talking Business 4.7.

Why Has Downsizing Failed to Achieve Anticipated Results?

If the cost reduction results are inconsistent, if there is no evidence that productivity, profitability and competitiveness improve as a result of downsizing, what is going wrong?

TALKING BUSINESS 4.7 **THE COST OF DOWNSIZING**

Downsizing is a fact of life. The question is will this phenomenon help or hinder the success of Canadian business in the long run?

Downsizing strategies employed by cash-strapped governments and companies alike ... have burdened Canada's health-care system with up to $14 billion a year in additional costs, a new federal study concludes.

The Public Health Agency of Canada report said increased workload, or "role overload," has driven costs higher and said doctor visits could be cut by 25 per cent and hospital stays by 17 per cent if the issue was properly addressed. "These numbers are a wake-up call to employers and governments," the study said.

"The data presented in this report paint a frightening picture of how inattention to workplace health and work-life issues is impacting Canada's health-care system."

Whatever savings realized from reduced corporate and government payrolls may well have already been wiped out by substantial increases in costs for health benefits and by more employee absenteeism, it said.

"Simply put, Canada's ability to be globally competitive in the future depends on our ability to address this issue."[1]

Source: [1] Keith Leslie, "Increased workload burdens health care," Canadian Press (November 10, 2004).

There are at least three fundamental issues that have been repeatedly linked with the failure of downsizing. These issues reflect shortcomings in the planning for and execution of organizational downsizings, rather than an outright condemnation of the practice itself.

1. Lack of strategic planning. Many downsizings have not been guided by a long-range strategic plan, but rather have been a short-term response to environmental pressures. The poor performance of downsizing has been associated with the tendency of downsizing programs to be hastily formulated and not linked with the organization's strategic plans.[20] While downsizing is by no means going away, by the end of the 1990s organizations were looking more critically at downsizing as a method of organizational change, and many reconsidered its role without the broader framework of organizational planning. Moreover, a *Fortune* magazine article expressed the growing sentiment that downsizing by itself provides no answers for organizational ills without a strategic plan. That sentiment is reflected in the observation made in Talking Business 4.8.

2. Lack of concern for, and involvement with, employees. Many downsizings do not involve those who are affected in the planning stages. That is, those in charge of the

---

TALKING BUSINESS 4.8   DOWNSIZING AND STRATEGY?

It is true that the workforce is not what it was for our parents or grandparents. The boss who held their hands and guided them up the hierarchical ladder is now nearing extinction. As corporations struggle to survive in this worldwide competitive war, costs must be minimized, and labour expenses are just the way to do that.

Labour represents approximately 60% of overall company costs. Cost cutting is consequently often tied to cutting human resources. And therefore, downsizings continue to dominate business behaviour. For example, in an effort to increase measures of performance and compete with other car manufacturers like Toyota, Ford Motor Company has reduced the salaried workforce in North America, in recent years, by 2,700. This is a fraction of Ford's future de-layering plans, which include the expansion of those cuts to approximately 10,500 people in the coming years.

All this begs the question — is downsizing really the answer to a company's performance "woes"? The answer depends on how closely these downsizing plans are matched with a proper strategic plan. In the case of companies like Ford, only time will tell whether downsizing was a rational or non-rational response to external forces faced by the company.

Sources: M. Belcourt, G. Bohlander, S. Snell & A. Sherman. (2004). *Managing Human Resources*, 4th Canadian Ed., Chapter 6: Training and Development. Toronto, Ont.: Nelson Canada; CBS News, "Ford Cuts Yearly Outlook, Plans New" (2005, August 19). Available online: http://www.cbsnews.com/stories/2005/06/22/ap/business/mainD8ASCP2G1.shtml [Retrieved: August 20, 2005]; N. Shirouzu. (2005, July 22). "Ford job cuts may be deeper than expected: White-collar staff warned 30% could go," *The Globe And Mail*, p. B9.

---

downsizing do not expect to get objective feedback or advice from those who will potentially be terminated, and so many employees are cut off from the actual planning of the organizational downsizing. It is important to note that the adverse effects of a downsizing may be mitigated through suitable communication of the downsizing to employees,[21] employee participation in the planning of the downsizing, a thorough analysis of tasks and perceived employee support from the organization,[22] as well as through advanced planning and coordination of outplacement services.[23] Attention needs to be given to both the terminated employees and those remaining. However, research evidence has suggested that insufficient attention has been given to the survivors of a downsizing.

3. Careless removal of corporate memory. Downsizings can eliminate individuals who are a central part of the organization's knowledge base — the notion of corporate memory. While intangible, the cost of corporate memory loss to an organization can be very significant. This can go beyond simply losing the expertise of a valued, experienced employee. This significance has been expressed by many observers:

> Downsizing devastates social networks. When a person is laid off, an entire personal network of internal and external relationships is lost as well. Downsizing destroys

informal bridges between departments, disrupts the information grapevine, severs ties with customers, and eliminates the friendships that bond people to the workplace.[24]

It has also been suggested that the loss of corporate memory can be particularly devastating to the organization's ability to innovate.

For better or worse, downsizings continue to reshape the corporate landscape; and, given that they are unlikely to disappear in the very near future, one can only hope that they will be planned carefully in order to bring about some of the improvements for which they are intended. To this point, the results of downsizing do not appear to be largely positive for many organizations, and yet we have witnessed the pervasive acceptance of downsizing as a legitimate organizational practice. The question naturally arises: Why have so many organizations agreed to adopt a practice that is not proven to be effective? If there is no significant proof that downsizing offers the results organizations are struggling to achieve, the question arises, Why do companies continue to downsize? In order to make sense of why organizations engage in restructuring themselves, it is useful to consider why organizations adopt such trends as downsizing. In terms of a rational explanation, the evidence is weak. Consequently, researchers have also considered non-rational approaches to explaining the phenomenon of downsizing. This requires an understanding of how non-rationality can influence organizational structure. See Talking Business 4.9.

Downsizing as a Non-rational Approach to Organizational Structure

How can organizational structure be non-rational? A perspective of organizations called **institutional theory** argues that organizations are driven to incorporate practices and procedures defined by current concepts of work and those accepted or institutionalized in society. Institutional acts, or the rules that govern organizational activity, are simply taken-for-granted means of "getting things done." They represent shared norms or expectations within or across industries. These rules dominate thinking with regard to how organizations should be designed. The implications are that accepted norms or rules, rather than a set of rational reasons based on clearly identifiable and measurable objectives, can encourage the creation or maintenance of organizational structures and processes. Institutional rules have little to do with efficiency, but they give organizations that conform to them a sense of legitimacy. That is, organizations can have, embedded in their structure, elements that are simply taken-for-granted ways of doing things — which may not, in fact, be accomplishing any specific organizational goals.

According to institutional theory, organizations may conform to institutionalized beliefs as a means to achieve legitimacy, resources and survival capabilities. The shared beliefs provide order through their institutionalization into organizational procedures and their direct influence on the behaviour of individuals. Consider such diverse organizations as IBM, Ben & Jerry's, McDonald's, Procter and Gamble and Bell Canada. All these organizations have risen within society. They have gained success and longevity through their ability to adapt their operations to the needs of society. Specifically, the organization

***TALKING BUSINESS* 4.9   MINTZBERG ON DOWNSIZING**

Question: You've criticized the "lean and mean" philosophy of job cuts. What are the consequences of a decade of downsizing?

Mintzberg: All the productivity gains by business may turn out to be productivity losses, because those gains came from firing people left and right. Say you're running a company and you have a warehouse full of stock; you fire everybody and then ship inventory for the next year. The productivity figures look really good, because you're getting all these sales with no employees. And within a year you'll close down.

It takes time for a business to train people, to gain people who believe in you. There is a contract between employers and employees. All these things are destroyed by downsizing. And, by the way, customer satisfaction indexes are going down because customers are being badly treated.

Question: Isn't downsizing the only hope for struggling companies like Nortel?

Mintzberg: There's been a lot of downsizing that wasn't driven by losses. In the telecom sector, they have been, but in other sectors, a lot of it was just because they didn't meet their earnings targets for a quarter. It's mindless.

Source: *McGill News*, Fall 2002 <http://www.mcgill.ca/news/2002/fall/mintzberg/>

---

becomes filled with various cultural forces: e.g., political rules, occupational groups and professional knowledge. In other words, as these organizations have grown, they have instituted acceptable ways of conducting business.

The ideas generated from institutional theory draw attention to the notion of the forces that act on an organization and encourage the adoption and maintenance of those activities that are viewed as legitimate. This perspective suggests that organizational structures and processes can arise not simply due to rational objectives for control and coordination, but because of adherence to non-rational, but institutional or socially accepted, rules. Meyer and Scott described a "continuum" — from organizations dominated by technical criteria (e.g., manufacturing organizations) to those dominated by institutional criteria (e.g., schools). What we have seen since the mid-1980s is a questioning of many of the fundamental institutional rules governing how organizations should be designed. In other words, at one time, the machine bureaucracy was the socially accepted structure for most organizations. Recently, this rule has been called into question, and increasingly the phenomenon of re-engineering, downsizing and going virtual seem to be the established trend in organizational design.

The continued use of downsizing by organizations, even though it has not lived up to its reputation, appears to be non-rational. Organizations do not, in fact, always act purely rationally. Institutional theory asserts that organizational structures and policies can become institutionalized and persist, even when they are no longer efficient.[25] This theory emphasizes the fact that an organization's functions can become established or embedded in social networks. These functions, whether they are how organizations are designed or simply how they behave, are affected by the pressures of conformity and legitimacy, which arise from the organization's environment.[26] Meyer and Rowan[27] defined **institutionalization** as "the processes by which social processes, obligations, or actualities come to take on a rule-like status in social thought and action."

The notion of downsizing has come to represent more than a reduction in an organization's workforce. It has come to reflect a longer-term, organizational evolution. Numerous organizations, by the 1990s, felt obligated to downsize given the intrinsic connection between being "lean and mean" and being highly competitive. Institutional theory offers some insight. Such institutional theorists suggest that the spread of corporate downsizing has been facilitated through: conforming to institutional rules that define legitimate structures and management practices; copying the actions of industry leaders; and responding to the legitimization of downsizing practices as accepted management practices via the media and popular press.[28] Why do organizations persist in conforming to the "rules" of downsizing?

Addressing this question can be accomplished through addressing the question of why organizations conform to institutional rules. At least three social factors have been cited. These factors include the notions of **constraining**, **cloning** and **learning**. We can briefly consider each factor in order to get a better understanding of how they influence adherence to the institutional rule of downsizing. In this regard, we can understand how these factors can make organizations follow rules or ideas that are not necessarily rational.

1. Constraining Forces

These forces represent those practices that come to define what are perceived as legitimate management structures and activities and that consequently place pressure on organizations to conform to these institutional rules. An example given[29] involves the relationship between large U.S. corporations and the stock market. Interestingly, studies have found that layoff announcements made by large corporations that were undergoing restructuring and consolidation were followed by increases in share prices. In other words, we have seen the tendency for public reactions to downsizings to be favourable — the notion of becoming "leaner and meaner" has become an accepted business strategy, and one apparently favoured by shareholders. Consequently, since the markets respond positively to such news, organizations have become constrained to perceive downsizing as a positive outcome and one to be sought. Of more interest is the finding that this constraining force was found to be even stronger when executives' compensation packages and bonuses were linked to share values.

2. Cloning Forces

These are forces or pressure for organizations to imitate the behaviours of industry leaders. Revisiting the downsizing example, some observers have suggested that organizations have been "jumping on the bandwagon." That is, many organizations downsize to demonstrate they are in tune with modern business trends, and consequently downsizing has been viewed as a way of "keeping up with the corporate Joneses."[30] This action represents a clear reduction in rationality — i.e., a move away from objectively defined criteria for downsizing and toward strict adherence to institutional rules. It has also been found that downsizing among industry members is more likely to occur when industry leaders downsize. The risks of failure are obvious given that this approach lacks a careful evaluation of the costs and benefits of this strategy.

3. Learning Forces

These forces are the result of institutionalized management practices. The lessons we teach future managers and businesses leaders are embedded in the courses taught in universities and professional associations. As an example of the biases generated in business schools, researchers like McKinley and his colleagues point out the case of cost-accounting techniques used in business strategy education.[31] From a purely cost-accounting perspective, the practice of outsourcing appears infinitely superior to maintaining a full-time workforce. Specifically, the method of allocating overhead costs clearly draws attention to the cost efficiencies gained by outsourcing; and, by definition, those units remaining as a permanent fixture for the organization appear more costly. According to McKinley, this perceived cost reduction gained from outsourcing increases the preference to outsource and can, consequently, become the driving force for a series of outsourcings and downsizings. This, then, is an example of how an emphasis on certain approaches toward business strategy that are spread through business education can come to play a role in rationalizing downsizing as a legitimate activity.

CHAPTER SUMMARY

You will remember that **contingency theory** asserts that organizations continually adapt to "fit" the environment. This implies that organizations will respond to changes in economic and environmental conditions by looking for alternatives to the traditional hierarchical organizational structure. Recent years have been marked by increasing threats to the survival of many organizations stemming from sources such as technological change, global competition, and the emergence of a knowledge-based economy. And in response to these threats, many organizations attempted to redesign and initiate fundamental changes in their organizational forms and management practices. According to many observers, the accumulation of changes in the organizational environment has demanded a shift in thinking with regard to organizational design. This shift has involved the movement away from the traditional, large, rigid, bureaucratic structure. Current practices now include outsourcing, re-engineering, going virtual and downsizing.

Call-Centre Outsourcing Is an Opportunity

New low-cost telecom technology is creating a major new service industry in Canada. These white-collar jobs are migrating in large numbers from America to newly established Canadian centres.

The term "call centre" is an umbrella description for a wide range of services — including travel reservations, technical support for customer service, customer contact centres, order entry, customer acquisition and retention capabilities, emergency response, online sales and multiple other solutions tailored to the needs of the U.S. customers.

A recent Export Development Canada publication forecasts 800 new call centres will be established in Canada by 2008. This represents a significant increase from the 450 centres operating today.

Large American firms have established their call-centre support north of the 49th parallel. They include Ford Credit, Dell Computers, Lehman Brothers, Neiman-Marcus in Alberta; eBay in British Columbia; IBM and AmeriCredit — a consumer finance company — in Ontario.

This trend will continue. According to the EDC report, a Deloitte Research survey of 100 financial services companies indicates they plan to shift $356 billion worth of operations and about two million jobs to other countries by 2008.

Why should Canada be considered? In order to be sustainable in an ever-increasing competitive global economy, U.S. firms must cut costs. They need suppliers who can deliver a similar level of service at a cheaper rate. As a supplier, Canada does this in spades.

Canadian call centres provide quality service at lower costs. However, the most significant advantages are the similar culture, common language, political and economic stability, lower employee turnover rates, lower payroll taxes and a well-educated workforce.

According to a 2004 KPMG study, Competitive Alternative, Canada's business costs are the lowest of the G7 countries — from five to 20 per cent lower than those offering similar services in the U.S.

Site Selection Canada, which provides consulting services to companies seeking Canadian and U.S. site locations for expansion or re-location, reported that in the 18 months ending Sept. 30, 2003, more than 37,495 customer service-representative positions were created. A further 118 customer-contact centres were established across Canada, with about 98 per cent coming from U.S.-based customers.

So, are we creating "fertile soil" for this wonderful opportunity to take hold? No.

We can do, and must do, much more to compete with the strength of our growing list of competitors — Mexico, India, Malaysia and the Philippines. These countries have lower labour costs and are actively adjusting their economic climate to attract this expanding industry.

We must ask ourselves whether we have the right financial and tax incentive programs to attract companies to Canada. We did this for the movie industry successfully.

165

Are we investing in the technology and infrastructure needed to support this industry? Our competitors are.

This is not only a big-business story. Small entrepreneurs can undertake strategic thinking about their business activities to determine whether some parts of it can be outsourced.

For example, many small firms find that their accounting, payroll, tax records and T4 slips are fertile ground to be provided outside their operation. The services of call centres in your area will also offer an opportunity to wring pennies out of your value chain.

The test you must apply is if the outsourcing can be undertaken more cheaply while maintaining quality, and you are not passing over your core competencies (the things you do well) to outside organizations, then you should give strong consideration to outsourcing. Your competition is.

In an era of rapid globalization, jobs, like water, will flow where there is the least resistance and the greatest opportunity to "pool" in the best global location.

Source: Reproduced with permission from Terrance Power, "Call-centre outsourcing is an opportunity," *Business Edge* (April 14, 2005) 1(7) <http://www.businessedge.ca/aboutus.cfm>.

QUESTIONS

1. What is the benefit of outsourcing "Call centers" as described here?

2. How are different geographic locations more or less beneficial for outsourcing?

3. Is this trend "good" for Canada and for Canadian business?

Pixar: No Mickey Mouse Organization!

Behind every amazing creation there is an even greater creator. As expected, behind the innovative phenomenon Pixar is Dr. Ed Catmull, an extraordinary 59 years old. Ed Catmull, with a vast education in the field of computer sciences and a passion for animation, has revolutionized the way films are made. Ed Catmull has had Disney as a customer and has won over many former Disney employees including one of Disney's former presidents. Not only has Pixar broken ground in the field of computer graphics and animation but it has also proven itself to be an exemplary organization.

Step by step Catmull built his empire. In the beginning there were the commercials and short films that would eventually get the attention of the former head of Disney's animation unit, Peter Schneider. Taken with the creative ability and talent seen in the ads and short films by John Lasseter, a ground-breaking animator, Disney sponsored a full-length feature, expenses and even some production people were offered up into what Peter Schneider had seen as a worth-while and low-risk investment. The hard work obviously paid off because, just as Peter Schneider predicted, the backing of a full-length feature proved to be a wise choice as *Toy Story* and its follow-up, *A Bugs Life*, went above and beyond what anyone could have hoped for; yet, these were just a preview for the blockbusters that Pixar would produce shortly after, such as *Finding Nemo* and *The Incredibles*.

Ed Catmull's vast array of talents is responsible for the creation of such a strong animation studio. Making animated films, particularly the 3-D computer generated kind is more like software design, than it is live-action film making. Cartoon editing takes place simultaneously with the storyboard process. As the script is mapped out into scenes that are then drawn and animated, the cartoons and individual scenes are fine-tuned. For example, Nemo, the loveable clownfish, may have stripes added or removed from his scaly orange skin. This collaborative editing is comparable to the way programmers optimize features in a piece of software. Differences between live-action films and animated ones lie in their procedural organization. An animated film benefits from having the same team work together many times and collaboration is a must. By way of collaboration and the freedom or flexibility of change, computer animation studios already possess inherent qualities necessary for a successful corporation.

Catmull's creation consists of 3 equal groups that are consistently working together in order to achieve the organization's impressive goals. To begin with, there is the technology development group which is generally responsible for the supply of computer-graphics tools. There is the creative development group which conceives and animates the stories and characters and, the production group that coordinates the entire filmmaking process. Aside from the crucial aspect of communication and collaboration, the freedom given to each group to work directly with one another and avoid going through higher-ups is, in effect, attracting organizations such as the U.S. Navy to send their organizational experts into Pixar and take notes on how to improve their own organizations.

Animated films have always used technology, even in Disney's earlier days. Today, artists' easels have been replaced by computers and Pixar has a small army of employees whose professions consist of ambitiously inventing and innovating technology to improve the appeal and increase efficiency throughout the company. In its consistent efforts to develop, Pixar has created a motivational flow and balance between art and technology, where creativity in art provokes advances in technology, and advances in technology inspire the art.

Source: Based on Brent Schlender, "The Man Who Built Pixar's Incredible Innovation Machine," *Fortune* (November 15, 2004) 150(10): 206–210.

QUESTIONS

1. How would you describe Pixar's organizational structure?

2. In what way does the organizational structure contribute to Pixar's success?

3. How might the contingencies of structure influence the design of Pixar?

Developing Business Strategy

5

How does a business create and sustain its competitive advantage? One of the fundamental internal forces that organizations must address is the issue of strategy. This chapter examines the nature and role of strategic management and the challenges it presents.

LEARNING OBJECTIVES

By the end of the chapter, you should be able to:

1. Describe the nature of strategic management.
2. Identify key forces in determining an industry structure.
3. Describe the roles of organizational resources and capabilities in firm performance.
4. Describe three generic strategies.
5. Explain what corporate strategy is.
6. Describe how to implement strategy.

I am grateful to Professor You-Ta Chuang, York University, who served as author of this chapter, and Ania Czyznielewski, who contributed the section entitled "Strategy in Action: The Case of McDonald's" to this chapter.

The Business World

Bleeding Continues at Battered HBC

Hudson's Bay Co.'s financial performance continues to deteriorate, with a $41-million quarterly loss that prompted some analysts to wonder whether the Canadian retailing institution will ever get its house in order.

The country's oldest merchant, which has been considered to be a potential takeover target, attributed its poor first-quarter results to a number of unusual factors, including a restructuring charge, the closing of some of its Zellers stores and a computer systems snag. The company also pointed to higher costs and tighter profit margins, although it said the costs should be offset in the rest of the year. The systems problems, tied to selling furniture and appliances, will mostly be ironed out in the second quarter and ultimately help boost the bottom line by the end of 2005, it said.

"All in all, the quarter was kind of mixed," George Heller, president and chief executive officer at HBC, told analysts during a conference call. "We don't take any pride in the bottom line ... But from a trend point of view, we do see some positive things coming out of this." Mr. Heller has persistently stuck by his long-term strategy, even though he acknowledged earlier this year that the company couldn't meet its five-year financial targets.

For the three months ended April 30, 2005, the loss almost doubled to $41.3-million or 60 cents a share from $22.8-million or 33 cents a year ago. Sales slipped to $1.48-billion from $1.5-billion. The company also said that its systems troubles led to about $10-million of lost sales of furniture and appliances. Same-stores sales, a key retailing measure of sales at outlets open a year or more, fell 0.6 per cent in the quarter.

John Chamberlain, an analyst at Dominion Bond Rating Service Ltd., said he could find no silver lining in the first-quarter results. He expressed concern that HBC's financial services division — the company's chief profit generator — had weakened. Mr. Chamberlain said it may be time to refine the strategy, because it hasn't been working. "It's hard to tell if it's the execution of the strategy or the strategy itself — but it's not coming together." He said discounter titan Wal-Mart Canada Corp. as well as Canadian Tire Corp. were able to make first-quarter gains in same-store sales, even though the quarter is historically a weak one for retailers.

Mr. Heller insisted that HBC is seeing the benefits of key initiatives, such as the off-price business and the updated and renovated Zellers stores. At Zellers, same-store sales rose 0.4 per cent. However, the operating loss widened to $25.3-million in 2004 from $6.9-million in 2003, while sales fell to $903.2-million from $917.6-million. The Bay's same-store sales slid 2.1 per cent. Its operating loss grew to $11.6-million from $2.9-million, and sales slipped to $553.2-million from $563.6-million. HBC has 294 Zellers, 98 Bay and 48 Home Outfitters stores.

Source: By Marina Strauss. Reproduced with permission from *The Globe and Mail* (May 25, 2005) B1 [edited].

WHAT IS STRATEGIC MANAGEMENT?

Why was Hudson's Bay Co. struggling with its poor performance, such as operating loss and decline in sales? Why were Wal-Mart Canada and Canadian Tire Corp still able to increase their sales while other retailers were suffering from seasonal weak sales? Of course, there are many factors contributing to differences in firm performance and retailers' sales in particular. In this chapter, we will be focusing on one of the key factors — strategic management.

Strategic management consists of the analysis, decisions, implementations and evaluations a firm undertakes in order to create and sustain its competitive advantages. As such, strategic management can be an ongoing process where managers of a firm constantly analyze their external and internal environments, make decisions about what kinds of strategies they should pursue, implement the strategies and evaluate the outcomes of the implementations to make any change if necessary. The ongoing process of strategic management is critical to firm performance and survival in that an effective process of strategic management can allow a firm to sustain its competitive advantage, which in turn enhances its performance and survival chances. As shown in "The Business World," Hudson's Bay was struggling with which markets it should compete in and how it should compete with other retailers like Wal-Mart and Canadian Tire. As a result, most of its product divisions suffered declining sales and low profitability. The turnover rates of Fortune 500 corporations shown in Talking Business 5.1 further illustrate the importance of strategic management.

But what is strategy? Most can agree that much of the success of Wal-Mart, Canadian Tire, or even highly profitable corporations can be attributed to, in part, the strategies these firms have pursued. However, there is no consensus on how to actually define the concept of a firm's strategy. Some definitions are long and complex; others are deceptively simple. Throughout this chapter, strategy is defined as the plans made or the actions taken, in an effort to help an organization/firm obtain its intended purposes. Such a definition corresponds to our prior discussion on the process of strategic management, where managers assess their external and internal environments to plan and take actions to pursue organizational goals, either short term or long term. Putting both strategy and strategic management together, a firm can be viewed as a goal-directed entity. By and large, the goals of most publicly traded firms are normally to maximize shareholders' returns through various means.

Although strategy is goal-directed and -intended, it sometimes can unintentionally evolve with either the internal or external environment. Henry Mintzberg argues that, due to the unpredictability of environments, managers in organizations cannot thoroughly plan out any strategy that would achieve the long-term goals of their firms. As such, some strategies would never be carried out, and managers would pursue strategies that they had not planned at the beginning of the strategic management process. For example, the recent SARS crisis in Canada led firms in the hospitality industry to pursue many different strategies in attempt to win back tourists, including cutting prices and seeking financial and non-financial supports from provincial governments. The unexpected crisis forced managers in these firms to change their strategies in response to a decline in their performance. Another example, Microsoft's entry to the Internet browser market (i.e., Internet Explorer) was not intended by its top management team. It was an idea forwarded by one of its software engineers.

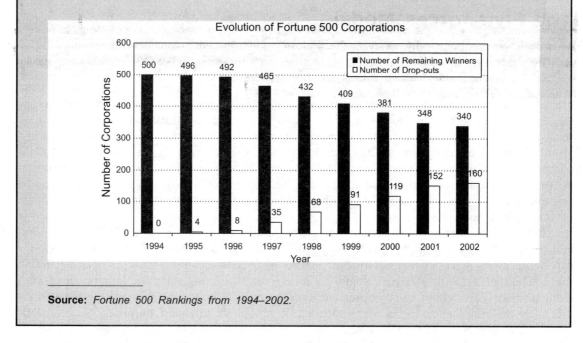

TALKING BUSINESS 5.1   WILL YOU BE ALWAYS ON THE TOP OF THE WORLD?

Firms need to constantly examine their internal and external environment in order to sustain their performance. As shown in the graph, during the period between 1994 and 2002, the turnover rate of Fortune 500 corporations (measured by firm's revenue) is near 32%. It shows the importance of strategic management in firm performance. Without effective strategic management, firm performance and its survival are at stake.

Source: *Fortune 500 Rankings from 1994–2002.*

In the next two sections, we will survey different approaches to strategy analysis, which is often the first stage of strategic management. Throughout the chapter, we will discuss different types of strategies and how to implement the strategies that are identified in the early stages of strategic management processes.

ANALYZING THE EXTERNAL ENVIRONMENT

By external environment, we will be focusing on five major groups associated with an industry. Before we look at each group in depth, we first need to define *industry*. *Industry* has been defined in many different ways. The definition used throughout this chapter is a group of organizations/firms that share similar resource requirements. The resource requirements range from raw materials, to labour, to technology, to customers. For example, Air Canada, Westjet, Jetgo, and Harmony Airways operate in the airline industry, where the four airline carriers share similar technology (e.g., aircrafts), labour (e.g., flight attendants) and customers (e.g., people who prefer air transportation). FedEx and UPS, however, are not in the airline industry because the customers those two companies serve are different from those of Air Canada, Westjet, Jetgo and Harmony Airways, although all of them share similar technology (e.g., aircrafts).

The Five-Forces Model

How can we systematically analyze the industry environment? Michael Porter drew upon research from industrial organization economics to propose a powerful, prescriptive model — **the five-forces model**, which allows us to systematically assess the industry environment. The thrust of the model is that the relationships between these five forces and the incumbent firms determine the attractiveness of the industry environment, which in turn helps us make strategic decisions in terms of how to achieve organizational goals or to find a position in the industry where we can best defend ourselves against competition. The five forces include threats of new entrants, bargaining power of suppliers, bargaining power of customers, threats of substitute products or services, and rivalry among existing firms (see Exhibit 5.1). These forces can either independently or jointly affect the attractiveness of the industry. Let's examine each force in more detail.

1. *Threats of New Entrants*

New entrants can take two basic forms, such as new startups and diversification of existing firms in other industries. Regardless, the entrants bring new capacity, desire to gain market share and substantial resources and capabilities. Prices can be bid down or incumbents' costs inflated as a result, reducing profitability. As such, the new entrants may impose significant threats to incumbents. Thus, incumbents need to consider how to create entry barriers to deter potential new entrants. There are five major sources of entry barriers from the potential new entrants' point of view.

Economies of Scale

Economies of scale refer to spreading the costs of production over the number of units produced. The cost of a product per unit declines as the number of units per period increases. From the new entrants' point of view, the entry barrier is increased (the threat of new entrants is reduced) when incumbents enjoy the benefits of economies of scale. Economies of scale can provide the incumbents cost advantages to compete with new entrants on the price, if necessary.

Capital Requirements

For some industries, such as airline and mining industries, the required capital to establish a new firm is significantly high. Accordingly, the level of required capital for entering the industries creates the barriers to potential new entrants. Thus, the threat of new entrants is reduced as the level of required capital increases.

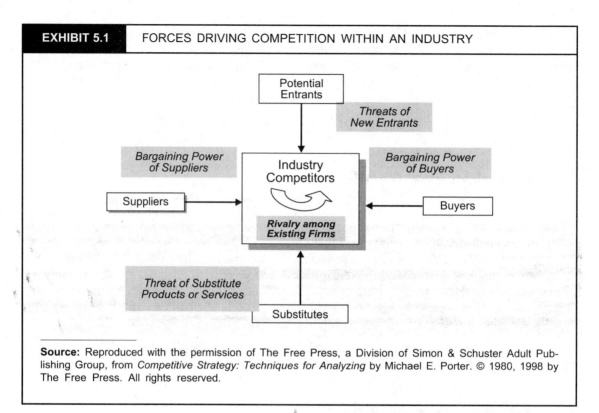

EXHIBIT 5.1 FORCES DRIVING COMPETITION WITHIN AN INDUSTRY

Switching Costs

Switching costs refers to the costs (monetary or psychological) associated with changing from one supplier to another from the buyer perspective. When the switching costs are minimal, customers can easily switch buying products from one firm to another. This creates an opportunity for potential new entrants in that the new entrants can easily acquire customers from incumbents. Thus, the threat of new entrants (the barrier of new entrants) increases (decreases) as the switching costs decreases.

Access to Distribution Channels

Accessibility to distribution channels can be an entry barrier for potential new entrants. In the situation where incumbents control most of the distribution channels, potential entrants would find it difficult to distribute their products or services, which in turn defers new entry. Accordingly, the threat of new entrants (the barrier of new entrants) decreases (increases) as accessibility to distribution channels decreases.

Cost Disadvantages Independent of Scale

The prior four sources are primarily associated economic advantages. However, sometimes, some advantages incumbents hold over potential entrants are independent of economic factors. Such advantages include governmental policies, legal protection (e.g., patents and trademarks) and proprietary products. These advantages create the barriers for potential new entrants, which defer their entries.

2. *Bargaining Power of Suppliers*

When considering supplier power, our focus is on the firms, organizations, individuals that provide raw materials, technologies, or skills to incumbents in an industry. Suppliers can exert bargaining power over incumbents in an industry by demanding better prices or threatening to reduce quality of purchased goods or services. Therefore, the power suppliers hold direct impact on the industry profitability as well as the incumbents' performance. There are two major factors contributing to suppliers' power in relation to incumbents in an industry.

The first one is the criticality of resources the suppliers hold to the incumbents. Quite often, when the raw materials suppliers provide are critical to incumbents in an industry, the suppliers are in a good position to demand better prices. The second factor is the number of suppliers available relative to the number of incumbents in an industry. Specifically, when the number of suppliers relative to the number of incumbents is low, the incumbents compete against each other for the relative small number of suppliers. As such, this gives suppliers power in that suppliers would have opportunities to negotiate better prices between incumbents. These two factors can independently contribute to supplier powers. And suppliers will have the highest power when these factors couple together.

Looking at the personal computer manufacturing industry, for example, there are many incumbents, like Dell, Hewitt-Packard, IBM and others. However, there are only two major firms, Intel and AMD, that supply the processor chips. Thus, the suppliers hold significant bargaining power over computer manufacturers because the processor chips are critical components of personal computers, and there are only two firms that supply this key component.

3. *Bargaining Power of Buyers*

When we consider buyer power, our attention focusses on the power held by individuals or organizations that purchase incumbents' products or services. Buyers can affect industry performance by demanding lower prices, better quality or services, or playing incumbents against one another. These actions can erode industry profitability as well as firm performance. There are many factors contributing to buyer power in relation to incumbents in an industry.

Switching Costs

Similar to the role of switching costs in threats of new entrants, the bargaining power of buyers increases as switching costs decrease. Specifically, when buyers can easily switch incumbents with little cost in terms of products or services, the incumbents would have little power over the buyers to enhance their performance.

175

Undifferentiated Products

Relatedly, when incumbents provide similar products or services to buyers, they would not be in a good position to negotiate with the buyers. Undifferentiated products allow buyers to find alternatives from other incumbents. They can also provide an opportunity to buyers to play against incumbents to get a better price, quality or service. Then, the bargaining power of buyers is enhanced.

Importance of Incumbents' Products to Buyers

Similar to our discussion on bargaining power of suppliers, when products or services that incumbents offer are important or critical to buyers, the power of buyers would be diminished.

The Number of Incumbents Relative to the Number of Buyers

The bargaining power of buyers could be diminished when there are relatively few incumbents offering products or services the buyers need, since the buyers do not have many alternatives to choose from.

Looking at grocery retailers in Canada, for instance, Loblaws, Dominion, Sam's Club, Sobey's and others are the key players in the industry. They are the buyers in relation to the grocery producers. The grocery producers do not hold significant bargaining power over these retailers because the number of producers is relatively high compared to the number of retailers, the switching costs for retailers are minimal, and the degree of differentiation among produces is relatively low. As such, the retailers enjoy significant bargaining power over the grocery producers.

4. Threats of Substitutes

All firms in an industry often compete with other firms in different industries, where the firms provide substitute products or services with similar purposes. For example, the traditional form of newspapers faces the substitutes, including the Internet, radio stations, television stations and so on. Such substitutes would gain newspaper subscribers and advertising revenues that might have belonged to the newspaper industry. As such, they threaten the profitability of the newspaper industry as a whole.

5. Rivalry among Existing Firms

The final force that affects industry structure is rivalry. The rivalry among incumbents in an industry can take many different forms. For example, Canadian insurance providers compete against each other by using different strategic actions, including cutting prices, providing new insurance products, improving operational efficiency, advertising, and through mergers and acquisitions. More broadly, rivalry can be intensified by several interacting factors.

Lack of Differentiation or Switching Costs

When products are significantly differentiated or switching costs of customers are minimal, customer' choices are often based on price and service. Under this situation, incumbents may experience pressure to launch more strategic action in an attempt to attract more customers or keep existing customers by enhancing their short-term performance. Accordingly, the rivalry among incumbents is intensified.

Numerous or Equally Balanced Competitors

When there are many incumbents in an industry, the likelihood of mavericks is great. Some firms may believe that they can initiate strategic action without being noticed. As such, their strategic action intensifies the rivalry among incumbents. In addition, the rivalry between firms tends to be highest when the firms are similar in size and resources. The firms similar in size and resources often target similar market niches and share similar resources requirements. These lead them to compete hand to hand.

High Exit Barriers

Exit barriers refer to economic, strategic and emotional factors that keep firms competing even though they may be earning low or negative returns on their investments. Examples of exit barriers include visible fixed costs, specialized assets, escalating commitment of management and government and social pressures.

Overall, the five-forces model provides managers with an assessment of the industry structure to help get some sense of industry attractiveness. Specifically, from the potential entrant point of view, the five-forces model helps the potential entrants understand the potential competitive environment of the industry and to make the entry decision. From the incumbent point of view, the model helps managers to assess their position in the industry relative to their rivals'. Sometimes, it also provides an overall picture of industry attractiveness to allow managers to make any exit decisions.

Each model has its limitations, however. Although the five-forces model offers a powerful tool for managers to examine an industry's attractiveness, it exhibits some shortcomings. First, the model does not explicitly take roles of technological change and governmental regulations into consideration. Specifically, it does not address how technological change and governmental regulations affect the power relationships between forces. Second, the focus of this model is primarily on the power relationships between each force at a given point in time. As such, it may have limited implications for future strategic decision making. Finally, the model assumes that all incumbents experience the same power relationship with each force. However, incumbents differ in terms of their resources and firm size, which can give them more or less power in influencing their suppliers or customers. (See Talking Business 5.2.)

Given the above limitations, in order to have a precise assessment, managers need to use the model with great caution. Specifically, they need to anticipate the effects of technological change, governmental regulations and industry trends on industry structure and their firm positions in the industry.

***TALKING BUSINESS* 5.2   WHY SOME FIRMS DO SO WELL WHILE OTHERS FOUNDER IN THE SAME INDUSTRY**

If we look at firms in the same industry, we will find some firms are doing pretty well, like Pfizer, GlaxoSmithKline, while others are doing poorly. This suggests that the internal resources and capabilities that firms have can also significantly influence firm performance.

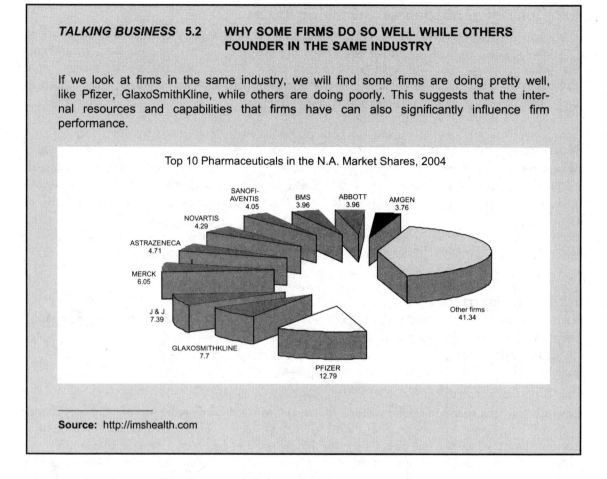

Top 10 Pharmaceuticals in the N.A. Market Shares, 2004

- SANOFI-AVENTIS 4.05
- BMS 3.96
- ABBOTT 3.96
- AMGEN 3.76
- NOVARTIS 4.29
- ASTRAZENECA 4.71
- MERCK 6.05
- J & J 7.39
- Other firms 41.34
- GLAXOSMITHKLINE 7.7
- PFIZER 12.79

Source: http://imshealth.com

ANALYZING THE INTERNAL ENVIRONMENT ———

After discussing how to analyze the industry environment, let's look at strategy analysis from another viewpoint — the internal environment. Indeed, research shows that the effects of the industry environment on firm performance are smaller than those of a firm's internal environment. Furthermore, if we look at all firms in an industry, we will see some firms are doing much better than others. This implies that how managers organize firm resources and capabilities plays a critical role in firm performance and survival. In order for managers to effectively organize firm resources and capabilities to enhance firm performance and survival, they need to know what kinds of resources and capabilities the firm has in the first place. Jay Barney provides a prescriptive VRIO (value, rareness, imitability, organization) model that can help managers examine the resources and capabilities in a systematic way. Before we discuss the model, we will first talk about what resources and capabilities are.

**TALKING BUSINESS 5.3   IN SUNNY SILICON VALLEY, TALENT-HUNGRY
WATERLOO BECKONS**

In today's business world, companies have tried every effort in attracting and recruiting talented employees all over the world to enrich their human capital in order to build and sustain their capabilities. One's been the exporter of highly skilled computer talents, Canada seems to reversing the trend, as telecom reporter Catherine McLean reports:

... So maybe Ontario's Waterloo region doesn't have the warm weather, or the mountains, or a flock of tech industry giants like Cisco Systems Inc., but as expatriate Canadians in Silicon Valley gather for the annual Canada Day picnic this year, recruiters will be pitching them to move back north. Over hot dogs and Molson under the California sun, potential recruits will be told about the career opportunities that await them in Waterloo, where technology companies are hungry for talent.

The June 26, 2005 picnic in Woodside, Calif., south of San Francisco, is an annual event for the Digital Moose Lounge, a networking group for Canadians in Silicon Valley. This year, however, it is being sponsored in part by Communitech, an association of Waterloo tech companies that is spearheading efforts to drum up recruits. Fifty partners, including Research In Motion Ltd., Sandvine Inc., Open Text Corp., Sun Life Financial Inc., and the cities of Waterloo, Kitchener and Cambridge have contributed $70,000 to develop a website and support marketing efforts.

Companies there are looking to fill more than 800 jobs, as both well-established players and upstarts experience major growth spurts. Sandvine, for example, aims to add 20 jobs right away. RIM wants to hire at least 1,500 workers this year. "The community can sustain a certain level of growth naturally, but when everyone is going through a growth phase, that's when we need a concerted effort to try and broaden or deepen the pool within the community," said Iain Klugman, president of Communitech ...[1]

Source: [1] Excerpts, reproduced with permission from *The Globe and Mail* (June 20, 2005), B1.

A firm's resources and capabilities include all of the financial, physical, human and organizational assets used by the firm to develop, manufacture and deliver products or services to its customers. Financial resources include debt, equity, retained earnings and so forth. Physical resources include the machines, production facilities, plants and buildings firms use in their operations. Human resources include all the experience, knowledge, judgment, risk-taking propensity and wisdom of individuals associated with a firm. (See Talking Business 5.3.) Organizational resources include the history, relationships, trust and organizational culture that are groups of individuals associated with a firm, along with a firm's formal reporting structure, management control systems and compensation policies.

The VRIO Model

Barney suggests that managers need to look inside their firms for competitive advantage. In order for a firm to achieve high performance, managers need to look at their resources and capabilities and ask four important questions: (1) the question of value (V), (2) the question of rareness (R), (3) the question of imitability (I), and (4) the question of organization (O).

The Question of Value

Managers need to ask if their firm's resources and capabilities add any value to capture market share or enhance profitability, either through exploiting emerging opportunities or neutralizing threats. Some firms do have such resources and capabilities. For example, NeoSet, a Canadian furniture maker, specializes in customized designs of home and office furniture. Its capability in customization of high-quality furniture allows the firm to obtain profitability from a small market, where other large furniture retailers, like IKEA, The Brick, and Leon's, do not compete.

The Question of Rareness

Although valuable resources and capabilities help firms to survive, those resources and capabilities need to be rare. In other words, they will have to be controlled by only a small number of firms in order for the firms to obtain competitive advantage. Thus, managers need to assess if their valuable resources and capabilities are unique among their competitors. For example, for many years, Wal-Mart's skills in developing and using point-of-purchase data collection to control inventory gave it a competitive advantage over its competitors, like K-Mart, a firm that has not had access to this timely information technology. Thus, during those years, Wal-Mart's capability to control inventory gave the company its competitive edge over its major competitor, K-Mart.

The Question of Imitability

Valuable and rare resources and capabilities can provide firms with competitive advantage; however, how long the advantage lasts depends on how *quickly* imitation could occur. When imitation occurs, it diminishes the degree of rareness, which may further erode the value of the resources and capabilities. Thus, managers need to ask themselves if their resources and capabilities are difficult to be imitated by other firms and then determine how to create the barriers for imitation.

The Question of Organization

The last question managers have to consider is whether their firms can be organized in effective and efficient ways to exploit their valuable, rare and difficult-to-imitate resources and capabilities to maximize their potentials. Organization of a firm is critical for firm success. Quite often, firms with valuable resources and capabilities experience a decline in performance because they do not have appropriate organizational structure and design, compensation policies, and organizational culture to exploit their resources and capabilities.

EXHIBIT 5.2	VRIO MODEL				

	Question of Value	Question of Rareness	Question of Imitability	Question of Organization	Competitive Advantage
A particular set of resources and capabilities	In favour of the firm	In favour of the firm	In favour of the firm	In favour of the firm	Sustainable competitive advantage
A particular set of resources and capabilities	In favour of the firm	In favour of the firm	Not in favour of the firm	In favour of the firm	Temporal competitive advantage
A particular set of resources and capabilities	In favour of the firm	Not in favour of the firm	In favour of the firm	In favour of the firm	Temporal competitive advantage

These four questions provide managers with important guidelines to assess their competitive advantage relative to their competitors. If the answers to these questions are all in their firm's favour, then the firms will have sustainable competitive advantage over competitors (see Exhibit 5.2). If any of the answers to these questions are not in their firm's favour, then the firm would only have temporal advantage over competitors. In this situation, the firm's performance may be threatened by the competitors at any time in the near future. Managers will have to act quickly to develop or acquire new resources or capabilities that help them to create sustainable competitive advantage.

SWOT Analysis

At this point, we have discussed two basic and important models that managers can apply to assess their firm's position in the competitive environment. To some extent, these two models complement and supplement each other to tell us about where opportunities and threats are situated in the external environment and how good or how bad we are in terms of the resources and capabilities we have. In other words, the conclusions of analyses from these two models can be summarized by **SWOT analysis** (strengths, weaknesses, opportunities and threats). The strategic logic behind SWOT analysis (see Exhibit 5.3) is that firms that strategically use their internal strengths in exploiting environmental opportunities and neutralizing environmental threats while avoiding internal weaknesses, are more likely to increase market share, sales or profitability than other firms.

Specifically, managers could use the VRIO analysis to identify what kinds of resources and capabilities their firm has that provide sustainable competitive advantage and what kinds of resources and capabilities present the firm's weaknesses. Managers could also

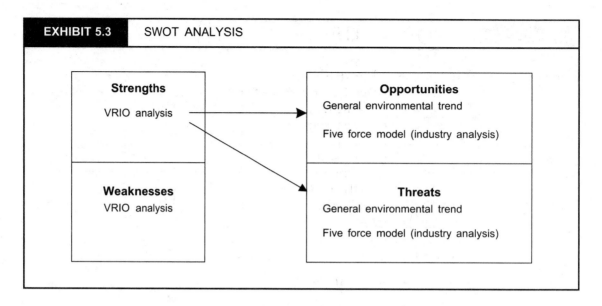

EXHIBIT 5.3   SWOT ANALYSIS

examine the trends of general environments and analyze industry structure (i.e., five force model) to assess opportunities and threats in the external environment. As such, the conclusion from the SWOT analysis can provide insights for managers into strategy formulation for the future.

For example, Starbucks, a specialty coffee retailer, realized that high quality of coffee beans are sensitive to environmental conditions (e.g., weather) and that the coffee-beans suppliers have great power over specialty coffee retailers because the coffee beans are critical inputs for the retailers. Starbucks used their capability in effective supply-chain management to naturalize the threats imposed by specialty coffee-beans suppliers through diversifying their suppliers and through precise inventory control. At one point, the number of Starbucks' suppliers reached over 1,500 worldwide. In addition, Starbucks understood that its brand reputation and image are valuable, rare and costly to imitate in the industry. It quickly harvested its brand reputation and image through entering the international markets and selling its Starbucks coffee in grocery stores. As such, Starbucks enjoyed enormous success for quite a long period of time.

The recent Google mania is another example. Google used its strengths in search engine and operation-system design capabilities to compete in the highly competitive computer industry. It identified the opportunities situated in the Internet search-engine market and the personal computer operation systems market by analyzing the weaknesses of incumbents' products. Google then used its capabilities in product design to capture the opportunities, which in turn gave it great success and challenged Microsoft's market positions in these two markets.

Both Starbucks and Google clearly understood how to use their sustainable competitive advantage (e.g., strengths) to capture opportunities in the marketplace (e.g., opportunities) or to neutralize the threats embedded in the industry environment. As such, both firms captured a significant portion of market share in their particular industry.

DIFFERENT LEVELS OF STRATEGIES ——————

To this point, we have discussed how managers can perform strategic analysis to identify opportunities and threats situated in their industry environment and strengths and weaknesses embedded within their firms. In addition, managers need to know whether or not their strengths are sustainable for long-term performance. In this section, we will discuss what kinds of strategies managers can pursue given the opportunities, threats, strengths and weaknesses they have identified.

Conceptually, we can categorize strategies into two levels — business and corporate levels. Business-level strategy is the strategy a firm chooses to compete in a given market. As such, which market a firm intends to operate in is a given. Corporate-level strategy is about how a firm allocates its resources in different markets to create synergy in order to achieve its organizational goals.

Business-level Strategy

There are three business strategies that have been widely discussed in the literature and have sometimes been called generic business strategies. They are cost leadership, product differentiation and focus (see Exhibit 5.4).

Cost Leadership

The purpose of cost leadership is to gain competitive advantages by reducing economic cost below that of all competitors. It often requires aggressive construction of efficient-scale facilities, vigorous pursuit of cost reductions from experience, tight cost and overhead control, avoidance of marginal customer accounts, and cost minimization in areas like R&D, service, sales force, marketing and adverting, general administration and so on. Accordingly, a great deal of managerial attention to cost control is necessary to achieve these aims. There are three sources of cost leadership: (1) economies of scale, where firms can increase their production volume to reduce marginal costs; (2) learning curve economies, where firms can reduce marginal costs by experience, such as learning-by-doing,

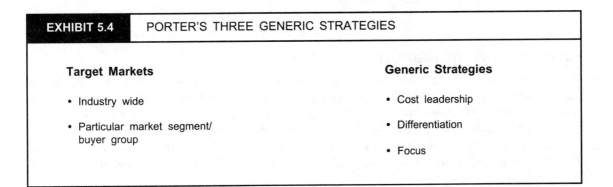

EXHIBIT 5.4	PORTER'S THREE GENERIC STRATEGIES

Target Markets

- Industry wide
- Particular market segment/ buyer group

Generic Strategies

- Cost leadership
- Differentiation
- Focus

and decreasing defects of productions or services; (3) low-cost access to factors of productions, referring to access to low costs of raw materials, labour, location and so on. Although each of these sources could be relatively easily imitated by competitors, a combination of these three can make imitation difficult, which in turn gives firms competitive advantages.

There are two major advantages associated with cost leadership. First, being a cost leader gives a firm the highest profit margins in the industry, which allows the firm to obtain abnormal returns, at least for the short term. The second advantage is that it gives firms flexibility in response to pressures coming from five forces in the industry environment. This is particularly critical in the situation where an industry becomes less attractive to competitors. More specifically, when competition among firms moves toward price competition, like what happens in mature industries, a firm with a cost leadership strategy would be likely to survive the competition because the firm can reduce its price and still obtain positive profit margins. Such a firm can also ensure increases in cost of raw materials when suppliers charge higher prices; its competitors might not be able to absorb the higher prices from the suppliers; as a result, they may have to transfer the costs to customers. As such, the firm would be able to win its competitors' customers over by charging lower prices. Furthermore, in a situation where buyers demand lower prices, the firm, compared to its competitors, could more flexibly respond to customers' demand by reducing its price to maintain or even expand its customer base. Finally, the threat of new entrants would be lower for the firm, compared to other incumbent firms. Since the firm has advantages of economies of scale, learning curve economies and low access to production factors, the new entrants are unlikely to able to charge the same price as the firm does. Accordingly, the new entrants are not likely to impose immediate threat to the firm in terms of its short-term performance.

Numerous firms have pursued cost-leadership strategies. For example, Wal-Mart, a retailer giant, is famous for its lowest prices in the marketplace. If you look at Wal-Mart closely, you will find it not only has the lowest prices in the marketplace, but is also the cost leader in the retailer industry. Wal-Mart obtains its economies of scale by high volume of purchasing and services. It also locates its stores in areas where the rents are not expensive. Furthermore, Wal-Mart uses state-of-the-art information technology to monitor its inventory in order to reduce inventory costs. Although these are small activities, the cumulative cost savings can be huge. Most important, the organization of these small activities makes it difficult for competitors to imitate Wal-Mart's operation. The managerial attention to cost reduction from various activities gives Wal-Mart a competitive edge in the highly competitive retailing industry.

Product Differentiation

Product differentiation is about firm's attempts to gain competitive advantages by increasing the perceived value of their products or services relative to that of other firms' products or services. The other firms can be either competitors in the same industry or firms from other industries. For example, Starbucks provides high-quality flavoured and specialty coffees as well as high-quality store design to differentiate itself from Tim Horton's and Country Style. As such, Starbucks is able to charge high-price premiums to customers given the value created.

EXHIBIT 5.5	EXAMPLES OF PRODUCT DIFFERENTIATION

Ways to Create Value	Examples
• Product features	Apple's Mac vs. PC
• Linking between functions	Traditional televisions vs. Televisions with DVD players
• Location	Pusatari's, a high-end grocery chain, locates its stores in expensive neighbourhoods
• Product mix	McDonald's combo, including burger, soft drink and fries
• Link with other firms	American Express credit card links with Air Miles
• Service	Staples' next-business-day delivery service

Firms can create value for their products or services to differentiate themselves from other firms in many ways, including product features, linkages between functions, location, product mix, links with other firms, and service (see Exhibit 5.5 for examples). However, managers need to keep in mind that the existence of product differentiation, in the end, is always a matter of customer perception. Sometimes, products sold by two different firms may be very similar, but if customers believe the first is more valuable than the second, then the first product has a differentiation advantage. Therefore, the firm with that product may be able to charge a higher price than the other firm.

For firms that obtain competitive advantages by pursuing product differentiation, they are often in good positions to defend the pressures from the five forces. More specifically, the threats of new entrants and substitutes for the firms would be lower than for others since the firms have imposed switching costs for their customers. In a situation where the suppliers pressure to increase the prices of raw materials, the firms could transfer the increased costs to the customers as long as the new prices do not exceed the value the firms created. When rivalry among firms becomes fierce, the firms would be unlikely to trap into price competition since the value they provided could protect them from the price wars.

That being said, managers who intend to pursue product differentiation need to consider if the value they are going to create is sustainable, at least for a certain period of time. As we discussed in the previous session, in order to achieve abnormal returns, firms need to obtain sustainable competitive advantages. Therefore, managers need to think about how to create value that is rare and difficult to imitate or substitute. For example, Apple successfully created an MP3 player, iPod, which it then sold nearly 2 million of in a relatively short period of time. Although Apple's success invited imitation from Creative, Sony, iRiver, Samsung and others, Apple has built up its brand loyalty through its product differentiation (e.g., unique product designs). Even though these competitors offered MP3 players with different functions and lower prices, the differences in price and functionality did not significantly attract customers' attention. As a result, Apple could continue to harvest its iPod's success.

Focus

While cost leadership and product differentiation are oriented to broad markets, focus strategy targets a particular buyer group, a segment of the product line or a geographic market. Specifically, the focus strategy rests on the premise that a firm is able to compete efficiently or effectively by targeting a particular narrow market. The firm thus can achieve either differentiation by better meeting the needs of a particular buyer group or lower costs in serving this group, or both. Accordingly, the firm may potentially earn above-normal returns by adopting either focused low-cost strategy or focused differentiation strategy.

For example, before 2003, Westjet's strategy was an example of focused low-cost strategy. Westject primarily served the markets in western regions of Canada, such as British Columbia and Alberta. The company also focused on achieving cost advantages in which it emphasized reducing costs through all value chain activities. IKEA is another example of a focused low-cost strategy adopter, where it targets the buyers, including young families and frequent movers, and it is able to sell knockdown furniture with low pricing through its efficient value-chain management. Companies like Godiva chocolates, Haagen-Dazs, and Hugo Boss employ differentiation-based focused strategies targeted at upscale buyers wanting products and services with world-class attributes. These firms focus on the high-income buyers and differentiate their products from other firms in terms of quality. As such, they are able to achieve high performance.

Corporate-level Strategy

In contrast to the business-level strategy that concerns how to compete in a given market, corporate-level strategy addresses two related challenges: (1) what businesses or markets a firm should compete in, and (2) how these businesses or markets can be managed so they create synergy. (See Talking Business 5.4.) In other words, the issues managers deal with concern determining which markets their firms should diversify into, in an attempt to create maximum synergies for the firm and then to achieve high performance. These are critical issues for managers because continuing to grow in a single market has become very difficult in today's business world, and the globalization trend also presents new market opportunities. Successfully managing diversification can give a firm enormous profitability and competitive advantage. In this section, we will discuss motives of diversification, types of diversification and the means to diversify.

But first, we need to define *diversification*. Diversification refers to a situation where a firm operates in more than one market simultaneously. The market can take many different forms. For example, Rogers operates in three major markets: cable provider, cellular phone service provider and Internet service provider markets. Canadian Imperial Bank of Commerce, Bank of Nova Scotia, Bank of Montreal and TD Canada Trust have all diversified into international markets. Most large Canadian insurance companies are highly diversified in terms of their insurance products and where they sell their products. In fact, if we look at the top 300 corporations in the *Financial Post* 1000, we will find the majority of the 300 corporations are highly diversified.

***TALKING BUSINESS* 5.4   MERGERS, ACQUISITIONS AND STRATEGIC
ALLIANCES ACTIVITY IN NORTH AMERICA**

Faced with intense competition, firms have tried various corporate strategies in response to competition and to sustain their performance. As shown in the table below, the biotech and pharmaceutical firms have been using mergers and acquisitions as well as strategic alliances in an attempt access to others' resources and capabilities in order to enhance their performance and survival chance.

**The Numbers of Mergers, Acquisitions and Strategic Alliances
in the North American Biotech and pharmaceutical Sectors,
1986–2003**

Year	Mergers and Acquisitions	Strategic Alliances
1986	70	25
1987	76	30
1988	66	30
1989	89	39
1990	96	102
1991	133	167
1992	118	386
1993	128	412
1994	151	451
1995	187	308
1996	162	205
1997	180	299
1998	178	164
1999	176	98
2000	176	69
2001	170	49
2002	169	64
2003	195	43

Data source: The numbers are generated from the SDC database.

Motives for Diversification

Why are the majority of the top Canadian corporations highly diversified? More generally, why do firms pursue diversification? There are many motives driving managers to pursue diversification. We can group these motives into two major categories: intra-firm and inter-firm dynamics.

The motives derived from intra-firm dynamics include means to growth and managerial self-interests. Firms operating in single markets, up to a point, will face some difficulties to continue growth in the markets even if they have sustainable competitive advantage. The difficulties may come from market saturation and intense competition within the markets they operate in. Accordingly, diversifying to new markets provides them with opportunities to sustain growth and increase revenue. By diversifying into new markets, firms have opportunities to share related activities, which in turn achieve economies of scope and then increase profitability and revenue. **Economies of scope** here refers to the situation where the total costs for serving two markets or producing the products for two markets are less than the costs for serving them or producing them alone. Such cost savings may derive from sharing production facilities, personnel or marketing activities. In addition to benefits from economies of scope through sharing activities, diversification allows firms to leverage their core resources and capabilities to explore growth opportunities in new markets.

For example, Bell Canada, competing in cellular phones and Internet service provider markets, provides retailing service through its retail stores, where customers can purchase both cellular phone products and Internet bundles. Through single store services, Bell Canada saves the costs associated with physical facilities and duplicated personnel. Second Cup diversified into different markets in the specialty coffee industry by using its core capability — producing high-quality flavoured coffee. It sells its coffee through its coffee houses and other distribution channels (e.g., Harvey's and Swiss Chalet).

The motive of growth rests on the assumption that CEOs and top executives are rational human beings — that is, they act in the best interests of shareholders to maximize long-term shareholder value. In the real business world, however, that assumption is tenuous. Quite often, CEOs and top executives act in their own self-interest. Specifically, there are huge incentives for executives to increase the size of their firm, and many of these are hardly consistent with increasing shareholder wealth. In particular, when executives' compensations are based on their firm's short-term performance, they are likely to pursue diversification in an attempt to boost their compensation at the cost of putting their firms in vulnerable positions in the long term.

The motives driven from inter-firm dynamics include market power enhancement, response to competition and imitation. When a firm pursues diversification and related diversification (see the definition of related diversification following), the firm can increase its market power within the industry it operates in. In this case, market power can come from increases in market share or revenue. As such, the firm can be in a better position to negotiate better prices or higher quality with its suppliers due to higher volume of purchases. The firm can therefore have more leverage to compete against its competitors. Similarly, diversifying into different markets can be due to the intense competition a firm experiences. When competition within an industry intensifies, a firm can either diversify into related markets or pursue vertical integration (see the definition of vertical integration following). Diversifying into related markets allows the firm to sustain growth or enhance revenue. Pursuing vertical integration provides a means for the firm to secure and control their raw materials or distribution channels. Finally, diversification can be driven by inter-firm imitation that can be independent of economic motives (e.g., growth, profitability, securing supply). Research has shown that firms are likely to adopt the diversification strategy when highly successful firms, large firms, or their comparable firms have adopted the strategy; even other firms pursuing diversification have experienced poor performance. Such imitation can lead to firms in dangerous positions in that diversification may not be consistent with either their short-term or long-term objectives. Eventually, it could fail the firms in the marketplace.

Types of Diversification

There are three major types of diversification — related, unrelated and vertical integration. Related diversification refers to the situation where a firm expands its core businesses or markets into related businesses or markets. Such an expansion usually involves horizontal integration across different business or market domains. It enables a firm to benefit from economies of scope and enjoy greater revenues if these businesses attain higher levels of sales growth combined than either firm could attain independently. By diversifying into related markets, a firm can create synergies through sharing activities (e.g., production facilities, distribution channels, sale representatives) and leverage its resources and capabilities. Related diversification also potentially gives a firm greater market power to compete against its competitors and greater bargaining power over its suppliers and customers.

The recent announcement of Lowe's entry to Canada is an example of related diversification. Lowe is a home renovation components retailer. It is a market leader in the U.S. home renovation market and has a reputation of excellent service and product quality. By entering Canadian markets, Lowe creates synergies for its own firm through leveraging its resources and capabilities. Its bargaining power over suppliers is also enhanced in that its potential high volume of purchases would enable Lowe to demand lower prices or higher quality of its suppliers. Similarly, one of the core capabilities embedded in Procter & Gamble is marketing competence. Many times, Procter & Gamble has successfully used its marketing competence to promote different but related products to increase customer loyalty and then increase customers' psychological switching costs, which in turn give Procter & Gamble more bargaining power with customers and help increase its revenues.

The second type of diversification is unrelated diversification, where a firm diversifies into a new market that is not similar to its current market domains. This kind of unrelated diversification tends to provide little synergies for a firm, given that there are few opportunities for sharing activities or leveraging resources and capabilities. An extreme example of such diversification is holding companies. Onex Corporation, one of the biggest holding companies in Canada, is involved in different industries, ranging from electronic manufacturing, health-care insurance, consumer care products, to transportation and logistics. Then, why do firms pursue unrelated diversification? A firm pursuing unrelated diversification tends to have (or believe) the synergies created (or to be created) through corporate office's management skills. Specifically, management skills in restructuring and financial controls allow a corporation to potentially maximize financial returns of each business unit and the corporation as a whole. When a particular business unit no longer provides financial returns to the corporation, it would be divested by the corporation in order to ensure the corporation's overall profitability.

The final type of diversification is vertical integration. Vertical integration refers to an extension or expansion of firm value chain activities by integrating preceding or successive productive processes (see Exhibit 5.6). That is, the firm incorporates more processes toward the source of raw materials (backward integration) or toward the ultimate customers (forward integration). For example, M&M Meat Shop, instead of selling its products through grocery stores, has its own retail stores to serve its customers. Ben & Jerry sells its ice cream products both through its own retail stores and Loblaws, Sobey's, and other supermarkets.

189

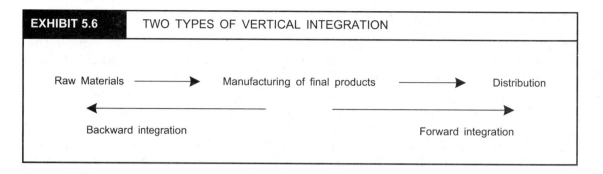

EXHIBIT 5.6	TWO TYPES OF VERTICAL INTEGRATION

Raw Materials ⟶ Manufacturing of final products ⟶ Distribution

⟵ ⟶

Backward integration Forward integration

TALKING BUSINESS 5.5   APPLE RETAIL STORES

On May 20, 2005, Apple Computer opened its first retail store in Canada at Yorkdale Mall, Toronto, Ontario. Although opening its own store triggered significant reaction from Apple's retailers in Ontario, Apple has not been completely satisfied with customer services provided by its retailers. Most important, Apple's intention is to provide a complete Apple experience. As stated in its press release, part of Apple's philosophy in founding the stores is that it wants customers to touch its products, feel them, experience the products before they buy them. In its more than 100 retail store locations over the world, Apple provides various classes that allow customers to get as educated as they choose to be in any given area. Such a forward integration enables Apple to have better control over its customer service and to secure and enhance its market position in the highly competitive personal computer market.

Clearly, vertical integration can be a viable strategy for many firms. It provides firms with benefits including securing raw materials or distribution channels, protecting and controlling over valuable assets, and reducing dependence on suppliers or distributors. By absorbing preceding or successive processes into a firm, the firm has better control over the prices and quality. Sometimes, it can increase the profit margins, especially when suppliers' or distributors' markets are highly profitable. Most important, the firm would have strategic control in terms of its overall strategic direction. As shown in Talking Business 5.5, Apple intends to offer Apple's experience to its customers through its own retail stores. This is consistent with the overall strategy Apple has been pursuing. Relying upon other means of distribution fails to deliver a complete Apple experience to its customers, which in turn may erode Apple's market performance. That said, there are risks associated with vertical integration. One of the major risks is increasing administrative costs associated with managing a more complex set of activities. As a firm absorbing new activities into its internal structure, the complexity of administration further increases. The increases in complexity can come from additional physical facilities; coordination between units, departments, or divisions; monitoring employees; and so on. Accordingly, carefully managing vertical integration is needed.

Means to Diversify

There are many ways to achieve diversification, either related or unrelated. Each way has its own advantages and disadvantages. The first is diversification through internal development. For example, Microsoft entered the video game market through its internal development of Xbox, while Sony and Apple opened their own retail stores to compete in the retailing sectors. Through internal development, firms have full control of the process of diversification and solely capture the potential revenue and profitability. That said, internal development has two major disadvantages. First, quite often, diversifying into new markets requires significant resource commitment. If firms do not have slack resources, then they might find it difficult to pursue internal development for diversification. Furthermore, internal development also requires time to develop the capability unique to the new markets. When the time window for the new market opportunity is narrow, firms might miss the opportunity, after developing the capability, to compete in the new market. The second disadvantage is the risk associated with diversification. While internal development allows firms to solely absorb the potential returns, it also implies that the firms have to bear alone the risk associated with diversification.

The second way to achieve diversification is through mergers and acquisitions. In general, mergers refer to two firms merging together to create a new firm with a new identity. Acquisitions refer to a firm's acquiring the majority of shares of another firm. In some cases, the acquired firm will become a division of the acquiring firm. In other cases, the acquired firms still operate independently or retain their brand or firm identity. For example, Johnson & Johnson, one of the leading pharmaceutical and consumer care companies, has pursued many acquisitions in the past decade (including ALZA Corporation, Tibotec-Virco N.V., 3-Dimensional Pharmaceuticals, Egea Biosciences, Inc.). One of its recent acquisitions is Neutrogena, which retained its brand identity. In fact, acquisition has been viewed as one of Johnson & Johnson's capabilities. Through its acquisition experi-

EXHIBIT 5.7	MERGERS AND ACQUISITIONS IN CANADA

**Number of Mergers and Acquisitions in Canada
Across All Industries, 2000–2004**

Year	Number of Mergers and Acquisitions
2000	2,244
2001	1,796
2002	1,695
2003	1,199
2004	1,491

Source: SDC database.

TALKING BUSINESS 5.6   MERGERS AND ACQUISITIONS ACTIVITY IN CANADA

Activity in Canadian corporate mergers and acquisitions is showing "ongoing strength," albeit at lower levels than a year ago and in the wider world, according to the financial advisory practice of KPMG. It estimated that mergers and acquisitions worldwide in the first half of this year will total $771-billion (U.S.), 14% above the volume in the first six months of last year. In Canada, transactions from January to June 6 were valued at $39.2-billion (U.S.), down 13% from $45-billion in the first half of 2004. KPMG Corporate Finance said the number of Canadian deals that closed in the first half stands at 638, compared with 649 in the first half of last year.

The top Canadian deals in the first half of 2005 were TD Bank's acquisition of 51% of Banknorth Group Inc., the merger of Adolph Coors Co. with Molson Inc., the takeover of Masonite by Stile Acquisition Corp. and Noranda Inc.'s consolidation of its ownership of Falconbridge Ltd.

Canada's 2005 numbers have not matched bullish hopes but are "consistent with the current backdrop ... characterized by stable capital markets and a number of transactions in the form of income trust IPOs instead of traditional M&A activity," commented Steve Smith, a partner in KPMG's corporate finance advisory practice in Toronto.

Globally, the Asia-Pacific region experienced the greatest upturn in investment flows during the first half, up 39% in deal value — and by 52% in Japan. Western Europe has closed 3,897 deals worth $298-billion, up 24% from a year ago and ahead of the United States, which recorded 3,652 deals worth $279-billion, down 27%.

Source: Based on Canadian Press, "M&A activity falls: KPMG" (June 20, 2005).

---

ence, Johnson & Johnson has developed specific capabilities to handle issues associated with acquisitions. Merger and acquisition has been one of the popular ways to diversify into new markets or to enhance market power. As shown in Exhibit 5.7, the number of mergers and acquisitions in Canada has been over 1,000 in each year since 2000. (See also Talking Business 5.6.) Mergers and acquisitions certainly provide firms with quick access to new resources and capabilities to compete in the new markets. They also allow the firms to increase market power or market share in a relatively short period of time. However, mergers and acquisitions share the same disadvantages as internal development — risk in the new market. Moreover, mergers and acquisitions have their own unique disadvantages or challenges. Quite often, managers face significant challenges in massaging two firms into one in terms of administrative issues and organizational culture. Failure in managing the processes of mergers and acquisitions can create significant employee turnover and can erode firm performance.

Mergers not only provide means for firms to increase market power and acquire new capabilities, they can also help two merged firms save enormous costs, which in turn increases their profit margins, like what Cineplex Galaxy expected in its merger with Famous Players Inc.:

Cineplex Galaxy LP expects to save as much as $20-million a year in operating costs once its proposed merger with rival Famous Players Inc. is complete, chief executive officer Ellis Jacob said yesterday. Speaking to analysts on a conference call, Mr. Jacob said the merged movie exhibitor will save money by combining its purchasing clout, cutting workers and renegotiating contracts with suppliers, after the deal closes some time in the third quarter of this year. ... "Our goal is to choose the best of the best from the people in both companies," he said. The company will also save money by trimming what it pays in professional fees. For example, "we'll only need one audit, not two," Mr. Jacob told the analysts. There might also be opportunities to renegotiate theatre leases when they come up for renewal, he said.

In 2004, the two companies collectively spent $42-million on administrative and management costs — $15-million at Cineplex Galaxy and $27-million at Famous Players. After the merger process is complete, in six to 12 months, Cineplex Galaxy hopes to benefit from a boost in revenue, as well as cost cutting. For instance, the new entity should be able to increase advertising revenue by installing, in many Famous Players theatres, the digital projectors that are now used for "preshow" advertising in Cineplex Galaxy theatres, Mr. Jacob said. ... Cineplex Galaxy also officially launched its selloff of 35 theatres in the combined group, a process required by the federal Competition Bureau when it granted permission for the merger. Even after the sale of those theatres, the combined company will be by far the biggest movie exhibitor in Canada, with 132 theatres and about 1,300 screens, in six provinces from Quebec to British Columbia.[1]

The third way to achieve diversification is through strategic alliances. **Strategic alliances** refer to two or more firms or organizations working together to achieve certain common goals. Strategic alliances can take various forms and serve various purposes. There are three major forms of strategic alliances: non-equity alliances, equity alliances and joint ventures. Non-equity alliances refer to the participating firms working together based on contractual agreements. Equity alliances refer to one firm having partial ownership in the other firm and the two firms working together to pursue common goals. Finally, **joint ventures** refer to two or more firms contributing to certain resources to form an independent entity. The purposes of strategic alliances can range from marketing activities, to manufacturing production, to distribution arrangements, to research and development.

Generally, strategic alliances provide firms with quick access to new resources and capabilities contributed by alliance partners. (See Talking Business 5.7.) As such, strategic alliances can be less costly and less of a resource commitment. Firms also share risks associated with diversification with alliance partners. On the other hand, firms will have to share potential revenue or profits with alliance partners. Furthermore, there are some specific risks associated with strategic alliances, with the partner selection in particular. Since alliance partners play a key role in success of strategic alliances, firms need to carefully select the partners in order to achieve their purposes in pursuit of diversification. Quite often, firms choose wrong partners due to the following: (1) the firms misperceive the partners' resources and capabilities; (2) the partners mispresent their resources and capabilities; and (3) the partners behave solely based on their own interests. Altogether, these could significantly impair strategic alliance operations, which ultimately fail to achieve the common purposes.

193

TALKING BUSINESS 5.7 **USING ALLIANCES TO OBTAIN NEW RESOURCES AND CAPABILITIES: EVIDENCE FROM BIOVAIL CORPORATION**

Biovail Corporation, one of the leading biotech and pharmaceutical firms in Canada, has recently initiated many strategic alliances in an attempt to quickly diversify into different market segments. The following are three of its alliance initiatives. Through strategic alliances, Biovail is able to access resources and capabilities of its alliance partners in expanding its market reach.

In April 2002, Ethypharm announced that Biovail had made an equity investment to acquire a minority stake in Ethypharm. This strategic investment will help finance Ethypharm's growth strategies, and further enhance the commercialization of its product portfolio, while giving Biovail access to complementary drug delivery technologies. Biovail has invested approximately € 74 million (US$65 million) to acquire 15% of the issued and outstanding shares of Ethypharm.

In December 2002, Biovail Corporation announced that it had entered into an agreement with Glaxo Group Limited of England (Glaxo) to acquire the Canadian rights to Wellbutrin® SR and Zyban®. Through this agreement and upon marketing approval from Canadian authorities, Biovail has the option to market Wellbutrin® XL, a once-daily bupropion product for the treatment of depression. Wellbutrin® SR is usually prescribed twice daily for the treatment of depression and Zyban® is administered for the treatment of nicotine addiction as an aid to smoking cessation. Both products are formulations of bupropion hydrochloride.

In July 2002, DepoMed entered into a development and license agreement with Biovail that granted to Biovail an exclusive license in the United States (including Puerto Rico) and Canada to manufacture and market DepoMed's Metformin GR(TM). Under the terms of the agreement, DepoMed will be responsible for completing the clinical development program in support of Metformin GR.

IMPLEMENTING STRATEGIES

Thus far, we have surveyed and discussed two major components in strategic management: strategy analysis and formulation. From time to time, managers need to assess both external and internal environments to identify opportunities, threats, strengths and weaknesses in order to change their strategic initiatives to sustain firm performance and survival. After setting out strategic initiatives, the next task managers face is determining how to implement the strategies. In this section, we will discuss strategy implementation from the management point of view: that is, through effective organizational design.

To implement strategies successfully, firms must have appropriate organizational designs. These include the processes and integrating mechanisms necessary to ensure that boundaries among internal activities and external parties, such as suppliers, distributors and alliance partners, are flexible and permeable. The performance of strategies will suffer if managers do not deal with various attributes of organizational design carefully.

As discussed in Chapter 4, organizational design refers to both formal and informal patterns of interactions that link together a firm's people, tasks and technologies. Organizational structure, one of the organizational design properties, is designed to ensure that resources are most effectively used by employees to accomplish organizational goals. Organizational structure tends to evolve with the organizational lifecycle in that organizational structure changes as an organization grows, expands or declines. Moreover, there is a debate about whether strategy follows organizational structure or organizational structure follows strategy. Regardless, a firm's organizational structure and strategy need to fit with each other in order to achieve good performance.

Let's consider business-level strategy and organizational structure. For a firm pursuing the cost leadership strategy, managers need to adopt an organizational structure that enables the firm to produce its products or services with minimum costs. A functional structure may be able to help the firm to implement the cost leadership strategy to achieve its goals. As discussed in Chapter 4, a functional structure helps a firm efficiently uses managerial and technical skills embedded in each functional group. It therefore offers the firm benefits of economies of scale, which in turn reduces costs of production and operations. It also provides learning opportunities for employees within each functional group. These further help to reduce production and operations costs. More broadly, a firm with the cost leadership strategy may consider adopting the design elements associated with mechanistic structure in that a mechanistic structure enables a firm to centralize decision-making processes, enable effective strategic control, and formalize and standardize operational procedures. As such, the firm would be able to achieve cost reduction and increase efficiency.

For a firm pursuing product differentiation strategy, its organizational design and structure will have to depend on the attributes of its product differentiation. For example, if a firm attempts to differentiate itself from its competitors based on product innovation, it should design its structure in a way that it can enable its employees in research and development areas to exercise their creativity and gather information on competitors' products in order to continue to generate unique ideas in the marketplace. For firms with traditional functional structure, product differentiation is possible but requires more attention to the differences between functional groups. To facilitate product innovation, an organic structure will be suitable for the functional group of research and development. Moreover, interfunctional group linkages will have to be created in order to facilitate information transfer between functional groups to enhance informational control. In other words, organizational structure needs to enable the functional group that is embedded with the selected attribute (e.g., innovation capabilities) to pursue product differentiation, while other functional groups serve as supportive activities and focus on cost savings. As such, a firm will be able to fully capitalize the benefits of product differentiation strategy.

Up to this point, our discussion on effective organizational design has been centred on firms with single or few products or services. For firms that are diversified into different markets, effectiveness of organizational design and structure can be critical for their performance and survival. However, their organizational design and structure can be complicated and complex in that they require well-crafted relationships between business units or divisions. In the current business world, diversified firms tend to adopt divisional or multi-divisional structures. The divisions can be organized by product lines or geographical locations. (For instance, Novartis AG, a Swiss company, diversifies into animal health, pharmaceuticals and vision care markets. It adopts a multi-divisional structure based on both product lines *and* geographical locations.)

In addition, firms adopting divisional or multi-divisional structures tend to decentralize decision-making processes from corporate level to business or market levels in terms of how to compete in each market. In grouping divisions based on products or geographical locations and decentralizing decision making, the divisions will be able to respond to competition in a timely manner. However, divisional or multi-divisional structures create duplicate roles or positions across divisions, such as marketing personnel and human resources management staffs. Such duplication can impose significant costs to firms, which erode the potential benefits associated with economies of scope. Accordingly, firms should carefully design their divisional or multi-divisional structures toward their diversification strategy. In fact, many successful, diversified corporations have made every effort to minimize duplication across divisions and to centralize standardized activities, such as manufacturing production.

STRATEGY IN ACTION: THE CASE OF McDONALD'S

McDonald's Corporation is the largest restaurant company in the world.[2] Formed in 1954, it now operates more than 30,000 restaurants worldwide and has had a tremendous impact on culture and society. It is estimated that McDonald's is responsible for 90% of new jobs in the United States; it hires about one million people annually; it is the largest purchaser of beef, pork and potatoes, and the second largest purchaser of chicken in North America. It is also the largest owner of retail property in the world, while its logo, the "Golden Arches," is more widely recognized than the Christian cross.[3]

Throughout most of its corporate life, McDonald's has been unrivalled in the fast-food industry. However, when stock prices hit a seven-year low in 2002 and the organization posted its first-ever quarterly loss in 2003,[4] it became apparent that the fast-food giant's long run as a growth company had ended, and that it needed to change or risk organizational death. The pressures from drastic changes in market demand have forced McDonald's to transform its leadership, business strategies and corporate culture in an effort to revive the mature brand so that it can continue to effectively compete in today's global economy.

McDonald's big wake-up call for change came in March of 2002. The company was on the brink of disaster. Shares were trading at $13 — well below the 52-week high of $30.72; and restaurants were being closed as franchisees saw their profit margins dip from 15% to 4%. At its lowest point, an estimated 20 franchisees left McDonald's every month.[5] In addition to its financial troubles, the company was also struggling with quality issues and poor performance in customer satisfaction. For nine consecutive years, the company ranked dead last in the American Customer Satisfaction Index,[6] and was feeling the consequences of lost market share to its competitors.

McDonald's long-time rivals were turning up the heat and were posting increased earnings and profits during the same period that McDonald's market share was eroding. For example, Wendy's saw its stock soar 57%, and Tricon Global, owners of KFC, Pizza Hut and Taco Bell, enjoyed 65% increases in 2002, whereas shares in McDonald's only rose 4% since April 2001.[7] In addition, new competitors like Quizno's were entering the marketplace, making "fast-casual" the largest growing segment in the restaurant industry.[8]

In an attempt to revive the organization and remain competitive in the industry, the board of directors at McDonald's staged a management shakeup. On December 5, 2002, they ousted chief executive officer Jack M. Greenberg and brought veteran executive Jim Cantalupo out of retirement to turn the company around.[9] Despite shareholders' general preference for an outsider, Cantalupo was the only candidate the board seriously considered, because members felt they needed someone who knew the company well and who could move quickly to respond to the challenges of expanding a mature company in what was a fast-changing consumer landscape.

Cantalupo was a fearless leader who was quick to recognize that "[t]he world has changed. We have to change too."[10] He echoed analysts who argued the organization lacked direction and focus, and that "the McDonald's way" failed to adapt quickly enough to match changing taste patterns.[11] Joined by a younger team of executives, Cantalupo quickly set about to re-energize the mature organization and presented a revitalization plan to decrease capital expenditures, scale back global expansion, raise dividends and lower growth targets.[12]

Under Cantalupo's vision and leadership, the turnaround at McDonald's was to begin by removing company initiatives that didn't successfully focus on the organization's restaurants or customers. This included a movement away from the "Made For You" food preparation system, originally launched in 1998 to improve product quality, but that resulted in doubled waiting times in restaurants.[13] His main focus was to get back to "speed at the drive-through, friendly service, marketing leadership, and product innovation."[14]

To achieve these goals, Cantalupo introduced a revitalization strategy, called "Plan to Win,"[15] which called for sweeping operational changes at the restaurant level. The plan included several initiatives: cutting more than 80 menu options; adjusting prices so that each ended in a zero or a five, for ease of computation on the customer's part; switching to an automated beverage-dispensing system to cut seven hours of labour per week; retrofitting fryers with a device that automatically cleans and changes oil, for a savings of 14 crew hours per week; packaging burgers in boxes instead of wrapping them, to cut serving time; and adding more premium menu options such as a new grilled-chicken sandwich on a whole-wheat bun and the McGriddle breakfast sandwich.[16] Many of these changes were aimed at achieving "restaurant optimization" and also focused heavily on reducing serving times at the restaurants. In the fast-food industry, promptness of service is a critical component that has a direct impact on the bottom line. According to former CEO Greenberg, saving six seconds at a drive-through increases sales 1%.[17]

The operational changes from Cantalupo's optimization program resulted in dramatic improvements to McDonald's service speeds. Wait times at the drive-through were reduced from 130 seconds to 99 seconds, while walk up customers got their orders in 30 seconds.[18] Although these operational improvements were a step in the right direction, Cantalupo realized that a successful transformation could not be achieved without changing McDonald's corporate culture.

According to Cantalupo, first and foremost, McDonald's has had to change the way that it viewed growth:

> For the past 49 years, the company lived by building new restaurants and changing that into a culture and perspective of bringing more customers into your existing restaurants — it's a whole culture change and then accepting the fact you might not be a 15% growth company and setting more realistic growth targets.[19]

To facilitate this change in growth perception, at a meeting between analysts, investors and journalists, McDonald's admitted that it was all grown up rather than trying to convince investors that it could maintain its history of powerful growth. In April 2003, the company announced that store openings would be pared to 360 from a high of 2,585 in 1996.[20] Its sales growth estimates were slashed from 15% to only 2%, and only 250 new outlets were planned for the United States — 40% fewer than in 2002.[21]

The logic behind these unprecedented moves was to bring more customers into restaurants that were already up and running instead of spending billions each year to open new ones[22] — the latter of which reduces both market share and profits from existing locations. According to Cantalupo, "We have to rebuild the foundation. It's fruitless to add growth if the foundation is weak."[23] For that reason, McDonald's management is pouring money back into *existing* stores, cleaning up their appearance, extending hours and speeding up service.[24] All of these improvements are expected to attract "more customers, more often" while encouraging them to be more brand loyal.[25]

Another piece of this optimization strategy has been to reinstate a tough grading system that will kick out underperforming franchisees. The decline in McDonald's service and quality can be traced to its rapid expansion in the 1990s when headquarters stopped grading franchises for cleanliness, speed and service, and to when training declined as a result of a tight labour market.[26] As a result, McDonald's is now enforcing a program that uses mystery shoppers and unannounced inspections to assess restaurants on these key areas. Owners that fail the rating and inspection system will be given a chance to clean up their act, but, if they don't improve, they will lose their franchises.

The final and perhaps most critical component of McDonald's revitalization strategy has been to instill a customer perspective that focuses on and responds to changing customer demands. This is a very common strategy often used by mature organizations that are trying to achieve renewal. Cantalupo best expressed McDonald's commitment to focusing on customer needs, when he stated the following:

> We are a mass marketer. When you are that, or decide to be that, you have to broaden your appeal ... Our focus is going to continue to be on our customers and what they're looking for. We're going to listen to them. We're going to give them choice and variety and try the best we can to satisfy as many of their needs as we can because that's what's going to build our business.[27]

The most significant change in consumer demands that has affected McDonald's resulted from the dramatic change of societal attitudes toward the fast food industry in recent years. For example, fat has become a major concern not only in North America but globally as well. In 2001, the Surgeon General declared a public health crisis and announced that 61% of the American population was overweight, causing 300,000 deaths a year.[28] In Europe, obesity was reported as the single biggest health challenge of the

21st century by the International Obesity Taskforce, which recommended that restrictions be placed on the targeting of young children to consume inappropriate food and drink.[29] At the request of national governments needing to reduce the burden on their health services, the World Health Organization also published a wide-ranging report on obesity and nutrition. Among its recommendations were reducing the demand for high-sugar and high-fat foods; increasing the use of recommended daily amounts of nutrients on packaging; and more controversially, the idea that governments consider levying taxes to control the sale of foods deemed unhealthy.[30]

Negative media reports have also compounded this situation. McDonald's has been forced to deal with the fallout of events such as the "Government's War on Obesity,"[31] the 2002 class action lawsuit brought against McDonald's by a group of overweight children seeking compensation for obesity-related problems,[32] and most recently, the release of the documentary, *Super Size Me*, which details the dangers of what can happen if someone were to eat nothing but fast food for an entire month.[33]

The overall results of these events have led to the restaurant industry changing its ways due to fears that it could become the next foodservice version of "Big Tobacco," with hefty lawsuits to match.[34] McDonald's has specifically responded to the changing consumer demands with a host of healthy initiatives, including the introduction of a line of premium salads,[35] developing more "wholesome food choices," such as substituting apple slices for fries in Happy Meals,[36] and producing ads on children's TV that star Willie Munchright to advise kids on balanced eating and exercise.[37]

The organization has also decided to shrink its menu as part of a broader initiative to streamline choices and provide customers with healthier alternatives. This includes phasing out 2% milk, 1.25-litre soft drinks and the 400-gram fruit-and-yogurt parfait.[38] Other recent efforts include eliminating the "super size" option from menus, using white chicken meat in McNuggets, and introducing a "Go Active! Adult Happy Meal" featuring a salad, a bottle of Dasani water and a "stepometer" to track the daily steps to measure physical activity.[39] The company is also using a new oil that reduces trans-fatty acids by 48% and saturated fats by 16%.[40]

McDonald's healthy lifestyle plan also includes partnerships with nutrition and fitness experts to fulfill a commitment to help consumers lead healthier, active lives. For example, in April 2004 the company launched an exercise and diet marketing campaign with Bob Greene, Oprah Winfrey's personal trainer.[41] Other global marketing initiatives have included a new tagline, "I'm lovin' it," with MTV-style commercials that are targeted at women, and regional advertising, ranging from billboards to ads in magazines like *O* and *Marie Claire* that recommend McDonald's salads, milk and juices to women who are concerned with nutrition.[42] These new menu choices are McDonald's attempts to change its image of offering only junk food, and are a way of appealing to women, who are considered to drive change with regard to eating patterns.[43]

Furthermore, in response to increasing pressures from politicians and lobbyists, McDonald's responded to the changing environment by retooling its corporate Web site to provide consumers with fat and calorie profiles of whole meals rather than individual items. Consumers can now select up to five menu items and place them in a virtual bag where a nutritional profile is calculated. McDonald's is also considering adding nutritional information to all its wrappings and is thinking about integrating healthy-eating messages into its ads as part of a plan to tackle the obesity allegations levelled against it.[44]

To date, the outcome of McDonald's multi-pronged turnaround strategy has been very positive. The company posted a fourth-quarter profit in 2004, one year after its first-ever quarterly loss,[45] and sales at stores that have been open for more than a year rose 7.4%, while same-store sales rose 2.4% compared with a decline of 2.1% in 2002.[46] It is reported that McDonald's sold more than 150 million orders from its new salad menu,[47] accounting for up to 6% of the company's increased sales.[48] According to Mary Vega Nichols, a McDonald's franchisee, "[McDonald's] is seeing a big sales increase from the additions to the menu. Frequency has increased because [customers] can come and eat every day. They have a choice now."[49]

Although McDonald's turnaround strategy appears to have resulted in a successful rebound of the fast-food giant, the company still needs to prove to its customers that it has transformed. For example, while McDonald's customer ratings are up overall, its outlets still trail competitors in critical areas such as line waits, order accuracy and store cleanliness.[50] Food quality also continues to be a problem and still comes in last for taste and quality of ingredients.[51]

In addition, the company has recently experienced hardship concerning its leadership team, which has stakeholders wondering whether McDonald's can keep the turnaround on track. Only 16 months into his leadership term, Cantalupo died unexpectedly of a heart attack in late April 2004. Two weeks later, the company was forced to disclose that its new CEO and president, Charles H. Bell, Cantalupo's right-hand man and successor, had colorectal cancer.[52] The revelations have shaken investor and franchisee confidence in the organization's ability to continue the revitalization process and have resulted in flat share prices since the announcements.

However, even in the face of this adversity, McDonald's is continuing to press forward with its efforts to revitalize the organization. For 2004, fast, accurate and friendly service remained a key issue for CEO Charles Bell. He is planning to remodel as many as 1,800 of 13,600 U.S. restaurants to create a more welcoming and contemporary ambience, and keep them open 24 hours.[53] He is also introducing a new payment system that will allow customers to make purchases by credit card at more than 8,000 restaurants by year-end. These initiatives are intended to boost sales and speed service.

The company is also continuing to follow the three key strategies outlined in Cantalupo's revitalization plan: to right the ship by returning McDonald's to the operational excellence and leadership marketing for which it was once famous; to align the system around the company's "Plan to Win" program, as a way to revitalize the brand and make it more relevant to a broader group of people by consistently delivering exceptional customer experiences; and to manage for financial strength by reducing capital spending and using the money remaining to pay down debt and return cash to shareholders.[54]

Although McDonald's journey toward organizational change began only a little over two and half years ago and there are still many challenges that lie ahead, it is clear that there is a firm commitment at McDonald's to re-energize the mature organization and transform it into one that will grow and sustain itself well into the 21st century. The company has taken many positive steps toward changing its leadership, business strategies and corporate culture in order to achieve its objectives of attracting new customers, encouraging repeat sales, building brand loyalty and creating enduring profitable growth. Only time will tell in terms of whether McDonald's can continue to adapt itself successfully to a changing environment.

CHAPTER SUMMARY

How to develop strategy is a critical task that managers face. Managers need to constantly assess both the internal and external environments to formulate appropriate strategy in order to sustain their firm performance and survival. In this chapter, we discussed two models that help managers to effectively assess the environment — Michael Porter's five-forces model and Jay Barney's VRIO model. In using these models, managers can identify opportunities and threats in the external environment as well as strengths and weaknesses embedded within their firms. As such, managers can formulate appropriate strategy in order to sustain their firm's performance and survival. We have also discussed the strategy options available for managers — business- and corporate-level strategies. Business-level strategy focuses on how to compete in a given market, including cost leadership, product differentiation and focus. Corporate-level strategy emphasizes creating synergies through diversification, such as related and unrelated diversifications and vertical integration. In massaging various types of strategies, managers would be able to enhance their firm's performance and survival. That being said, it is also critical for managers to adopt appropriate organizational structure and design to execute the strategies they want to pursue. Without effective organizational design and structure, the efforts put into strategy analysis and formulation will be wasted.

Viacom Buys Neopets

Nine-year-old Lane Kovich spends part of her day, every day, playing with her on-line virtual pet Kewl Dude on the website Neopets.com. Little does she know her green friend — which looks like a cross between a dragon and a lion with a horn jutting out of its nose — is part of a $160-million (U.S.) gamble by Viacom Inc., as the media conglomerate gobbles up the private Glendale, Calif.-based Neopets Inc.

The strategic move put Viacom in charge of Neopia, a mythical on-line world full of frolicking Neopets species such as Gelerts, Wockies and Scorchios. That world beckons Lane and many of her grade 3 classmates, who rush home from school to log on to the website, where they feed and play with their on-line friends, earning a virtual currency called Neopoints. "He's cute," Lane said, describing Kewl Dude. "He looks sort of like a dinosaur but he's a lion. He has brown eyes."

At first glance, virtual pets and New York-based Viacom — parent company of MTV Networks Inc., CBS Corp. and Paramount Pictures Corp. — appear to be an odd combination. But Neopets pulls in a staggering five billion website page views each month, and 79 per cent of its 25 million users are children under the age of 17.

Viacom's purchase gives it access to a marketer's dream demographic of fickle and often elusive kids. Neopets chief executive officer Doug Dohring said his virtual pet company should fit well with Viacom children's entertainment properties, such as Nickelodeon, and provide a future for television and direct-to-video deals. "The media companies are all looking for content, because that's what drives viewership and ultimately drives advertising revenue and other revenue," he said in an interview. "I think we just wound up being a perfect fit for Viacom."

Mr. Dohring founded Neopets in April, 2000, just after the dot-com bubble burst. He declined to offer specific financial information for the company, but said "we've been profitable and cash-flow positive for some time now." By comparison, Viacom is a media juggernaut that owns, among other things, VH1 musical network, Nickelodeon, Infinity Radio and book publisher Simon & Schuster Inc. In 2004, Viacom chalked up revenue of $22-billion, but posted a loss of $13-billion, reflecting writeoffs in its radio and outdoor advertising businesses.

"If you look at [Neopets] demographics, they are perfectly aligned with the MTV demographics," said Jeffrey Dunn, president of Nickelodeon Film and Enterprises. "We love it from a creative approach, we love it from an audience approach and when you add it together with the other space we have on the Web, it's a perfect one-two punch from an advertising point of view."

The sale of Neopets came at a time the company had reached a critical mass in the on-line youth market, Mr. Dohring said. Its website has been translated into 10 languages, its product licensed to retailers such as Minneapolis-based Target Corp., and its characters inked to a motion picture deal with Warner Bros. in March.

The private business's two main revenue streams are on-line advertising and licensing, but an emerging offshoot is polling the consumer traits of oblivious youngsters playing with their Neopets. The company then sells consumer results to companies looking to target children under the age of 12, answering questions like "how much free time do you usually have per day after you are done with your daily chores?"

Children like Lane, entranced with Kewl Dude in Nanaimo, B.C., are likely unaware of these kind of business deals as they play games such as "the wheel of excitement" with their virtual friends. So far, Lane has collected 3,779 Neopoints that can be used to buy virtual food. For the site's 25 million other users, yesterday's sale and its many numbers boil down to one question: what happens to the virtual creatures at Neopets? Nothing, Mr. Dunn said. The Neopets site is doing well enough on its own without interference from Viacom, he added. "They're unique within the company; we don't have anything that looks like this," Mr. Dunn said. "They do something that's different, and we're going to continue to allow them to do that."

More information on Neopet

What is a Neopet?
A Neopet is an on-line virtual creature that needs to be cared for, played with and fed on-line. Users select a character from among 49 different species, give their character a name and unique characteristics, and plunk them down in a virtual world known as Neopia.

What does it do?
A Neopet travels around Neopia's fantasy locations, such as Mystery Island, talking to other creatures, winning games and collecting virtual currency called Neopoints that is used to buy food and items.

What does it cost?
Registration is free.

Why does Viacom want it?
Neopets strikes at the heart of a fickle youth demographic and Viacom Inc. hopes to add the popularity to its MTV and Nickelodeon brands. One of Neopets Inc.'s emerging revenue streams is on-line market research, where the company boasts "unparalleled" access to young people.

How does the site make money?
Neopets Inc. has two major revenue streams: on-line advertising (which accounts for roughly 60 per cent of revenue) and product licensing. The company has also signed a movie deal with Warner Bros., and licences for plush toys in stores such as Target Corp. Sony Corp. is developing video games.

How many Internet hits a month?

A total of 25 million registered users generate a staggering five billion page views a month. Users have created 140 million virtual creatures and generate 60,000 new creations each day.

Source: By Rob Shaw. Reproduced with permission from *The Globe and Mail* (June 21, 2005).

QUESTIONS

1. What level of strategy is Viacom pursuing?

2. What are the reasons Viacom is acquiring Neopets?

3. In your view, does this acquisition fit into Viacom's overall strategy?

Home Reno Giant Lowe's Readies Move into Canada

Retailing and real estate insiders are bracing for the arrival of Lowe's Cos. Inc., a U.S. home improvement powerhouse whose entry into Canada could further shake up an already competitive retail landscape.

Two consultants have been quietly talking to Canadian landlords over the past few weeks, discussing possible deals for superstore sites, and industry sources believe Lowe's, the second-largest U.S. home improvement merchant, is the prospective tenant.

Lowe's could make an announcement about its plans for Canada as early as next week, real estate sources said. A number have been told to expect an announcement on June 6. Lowe's said it does not comment on rumours, but confirmed it has a global growth strategy.

"We have said for a number of years that we are evaluating international opportunities. At some point we will be a global company," said Chris Ahearn, a spokeswoman for Lowe's in Mooresville, N.C.

The chain has been a rival to Home Depot Inc., the world's biggest home improvement retailer, which already operates in Canada.

Lowe's has ridden the wave of women's growing interest in tackling home improvement projects. With annual sales of about $36.5-billion (U.S.) and more than 1,100 stores in the United States, Lowe's courts women by pushing home decor and other related items.

It has designed its mega-outlets in a more inviting manner, with wide aisles and bright lights to ease the stresses of shopping.

In Canada, Rona Inc. of Boucherville, Que., has become a powerful contender to the No. 1 Home Depot also by catering to women's tastes. As well, Rona has grown rapidly in recent years by swallowing rivals.

Now, industry insiders suggest that Lowe's may eventually try to snap up Rona, if it hasn't already attempted such a move.

When Robert Nibock took over as chief executive officer in January, he told analysts that he was interested in international growth.

"Certainly there's a lot of opportunity on the international side, and it's something that we will, over the next year or two, be in the process of assessing," Mr. Nibock said.

Retail consultant John Williams of J.C. Williams Group Ltd., said it may be difficult for Lowe's to establish itself quickly in this country without eventually making a big acquisition.

He pointed to the huge head start of both Rona and Home Depot. "It's a very difficult market," Mr. Williams said. "Rona and Home Depot are so well positioned now ... They're really duking it out."

Home Depot has 120 superstores here while Rona has 530 outlets of varying sizes.

Sylvain Morrissette, a spokesman for Rona, said he couldn't comment on rumours. But he insisted that Rona has developed a strong strategy to ensure its future.

Rona differs from Home Depot in that it has a wide array of store types, from uber-sized big boxes to small outlets. Lowe's may only be interested in Rona's superstores.

The rumours about Lowe's possible arrival in Canada have created a buzz in the industry. One retailing source said he had heard that Lowe's representatives have tied up as many as a dozen sites for its mega-outlets, and that is has set up a Canadian office. It is expected that the first stores will be in Southern Ontario by next year.

Real estate officials said Michael Goulais and Alan MacKenzie of M. Goulais Consultants in Toronto have been meeting with them to discuss locations for a U.S. retailer entering Canada. "They are producing letters of intent," one official said.

Reached this week, Mr. MacKenzie did not comment on whether he and his partner represent Lowe's and are trying to find store locations for the retailer.

One real estate source said Mr. MacKenzie expressed interest in some of his company's locations, and he is waiting to hear back about offers for the sites.

"We've been told it's an existing American organization that's looking for anywhere from 10 to 15 acres," the source said. "There's not that many, even in the States, American guys that take that size unit. Most of the ones that do take it are already here."

U.S. discounter Target Corp. has also been interested in coming to Canada. But Target CEO Bob Ulrich said last month [May] that it has no immediate plans to expand outside the United States.

Roger Plamondon, regional operations manager for Eastern Canada at Home Depot Canada, said he has heard the rumours about Lowe's but "for us, it's business as usual ...

"We have been in Canada for 11 years. We are very proud of our performance in Canada. We know the Canadian marketplace very well," Mr. Plamondon said.

Source: By Marina Strauss — Retailing Reporter. Reproduced with permission from *The Globe and Mail* (June 2, 2005), B1.

QUESTIONS

1. Which level of strategy does Lowe's initiate, business or corporate level?

2. What are the motives behind Lowe's entry to Canada?

3. In your opinion, how should Rona and Home Depot respond to Lowe's entry?

External Challenges of Business

The Competitive and Technological Environment

6

Why do industry-leading firms sometimes lose their market position to rivals? Why do some entrepreneurial firms fail to survive and grow following early marketplace successes? These questions can be addressed through the study of industry evolution and change. Industries are an essential backdrop for the analysis of how competitive forces affect the viability and performance of organizations. An industry's stage of evolution is a critical determinant of the degree and type of competition faced by organizations. This chapter focuses on how the nature of competition changes over the course of an industry's lifecycle.

LEARNING OBJECTIVES

By the end of the chapter, you should be able to:

1. Describe the different stages of the industry lifecycle model.
2. Identify the key drivers of industry evolution.
3. Explain how competitive forces change during the lifecycle.
4. Describe the key success factors for firms at each stage of the lifecycle.
5. Identify different types of innovations.
6. Understand the relationship between technological evolution and industry evolution.
7. Describe the key features of technology lifecycle models.

I am grateful to Professor Eytan Lasry, York University, who served as author for this chapter.

The Business World ———————————————————————

CRTC Turns Radio on Its Head with Landmark Ruling

OTTAWA — A landmark ruling yesterday by the federal broadcast regulator is expected to lead to a major shakeup of the Canadian radio industry, with consumers on the verge of being offered scores — perhaps hundreds — of new stations.

The Canadian Radio-television and Telecommunication Commission announced that it had approved all three applications for subscription-based digital radio, although consumers will have to get used to monthly fees.

The two satellite-based applicants said following the ruling that they expect to proceed with their plans and will be selling services in Canada in the coming months, perhaps as soon as the end of this year. Those behind an all-Canadian proposal involving the use of terrestrial transmitters instead of satellites said the decision was unfair because their competitors won't have to operate under as many rules and obligations.

"It should have been more equitable," said Paul Ski, executive vice-president of radio for Toronto-based CHUM Ltd., which offered a joint proposal with Astral Media Inc. of Montreal. "We've got to go back and review it."

Analysts said the ruling would almost certainly usher in a new era in Canadian radio, with one analyst saying that it could lead to the death of the entire AM band. Eamon Hoey, a telecommunications analyst in Toronto, said digital technology and subscriptions services will shake up the radio industry the way it already has done to television. "It will have the same effect as when cable took television beyond 24 channels and they started digitizing their networks," Mr. Hoey said. "For $10 [a month], you get a lot."

In setting up the rules for the nascent industry, however, the CRTC stuck to its old ways by imposing tight domestic content restrictions on the three service providers. The CRTC imposed a different set of restrictions on the two satellite-based providers. Among other things, Canadian Satellite Radio Inc. and Sirius Canada Inc. must produce at least eight original channels in Canada and one francophone channel for every three English-language stations.

The two companies, each of which has ownership ties to both the United States and Canada, must also give 5 per cent of their gross annual revenue toward funds dedicated to the development of Canadian artists. Those contributions will be divided up equally between English and French-language talent.

Gregg Terrence, president of Indie Pool Inc., which represents independent Canadian artists, said the ruling went beyond their hopes. Radio station operators will now have to play more, newer artists, Mr. Terrence said. "They'll have to dig deeper beyond the top 40."

Both satellite companies said they expect the commission's ruling will be good enough for them to go ahead with their plans. "We're celebrating," said Kevin Shea, chief executive officer of Sirius Canada. John Bitove Jr., who heads the Canadian Satellite Radio (CSR) proposal, said the regulator's various conditions will mean more work convincing investors. "We're going to have to relook at our business plans."

The growth in subscription radio could be driven by auto makers, which plan to include satellite-based radios in some upcoming models. Many analysts and industry officials had said they expected the CRTC ruling to lead to appeals to the federal cabinet or the courts, although none of the applicants suggested yesterday that they expected to do so.

Both satellite players had proposed offering their roster of stations for $12.99 a month. The CRTC also approved the CHUM-Astral licence for the provision of 50 homegrown channels, including at least 20 per cent in French. The service is expected to be available for $9.95 a month.

CHUM and Astral have also told the commission that they intend to provide five channels geared toward the aboriginal, Chinese, German, Italian, and South Asian communities. Those channels will also have to meet CRTC guidelines, including at least 35 per cent Canadian content.

The CHUM-Astral operation, which offers much more Canadian content than its rivals, would only have to contribute 2 per cent of gross annual revenue to the development of domestic talent. The CRTC's Charles Dalfen said the ruling should be great news for Canadian artists and consumers.

Source: By Simon Tuck. Reproduced with permission from *The Globe and Mail* (June 17, 2005).

THE INDUSTRY LIFECYCLE MODEL

How will the CRTC ruling change the Canadian radio broadcasting industry? Which organizations will benefit and which will need to adapt to the new satellite radio technology? Will satellite radio change the listening habits of Canadians? What entrepreneurial opportunities are created by these events? This chapter addresses these important questions by taking a macro-level, long-term view of industries and their evolution. Industries both old and new are not static and change in dramatic ways over time. It is, therefore, critical to examine how some of the key competitive and technological forces shape the external environment of organizations.

While it seems obvious to even the most casual observer that the nature and intensity of competition is quite specific to each industry, it is nonetheless remarkable how very different industries follow very similar and predictable paths in how competitive pressures evolve over time. Research in the fields of economics, strategic management and organization theory has highlighted how, like biological organisms, virtually all industries evolve along particular trajectories and through specific phases from their early emergence and growth to their eventual maturity and decline.

This is commonly known as the **industry lifecycle model**. Given a long enough period of observation, almost all industries exhibit an inverted U-shaped growth pattern, with the number of organizations rising initially up to a peak, and then declining as the industry ages (see Exhibit 6.1). The pace of an industry's evolution along its lifecycle is closely related to the evolution of technology within the industry. Technological innovations will often trigger the start of a new lifecycle or the creation of an entirely new industry.

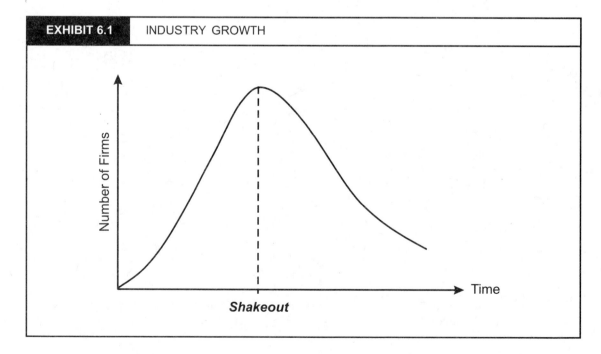

| **EXHIBIT 6.1** | INDUSTRY GROWTH |

Shakeout

The industry lifecycle model divides industry evolution into four distinct phases: *introduction, growth, maturity* and *decline*. According to the model, new industries tend to be highly fragmented (i.e., with many small competitors) and characterized by experimentation with novel technologies and business models. This *introductory* phase sees many entrepreneurial firms enter the industry, hoping to emerge as a market leader. As the industry coalesces around a particular approach and this dominant model is adopted by customers, suppliers and other key constituents, the firms whose approach does not conform to the emerging standard exit the industry during a shakeout. The widespread diffusion of an industry standard or *dominant design* is a critical step in facilitating an industry's transition to the *growth* phase.

Over time, the industry reaches the *mature* phase, where the market stabilizes and sales grow more slowly. Firms must then become more efficient producers to lower costs and compensate for slower revenue growth. This is often achieved through mergers and acquisitions that result in higher industry concentration. In the *decline* phase, aggregate sales drop and rivalry further heats up as the industry undergoes greater consolidation through more mergers and the exit of inefficient firms. Exhibit 6.2 shows the typical S-curve pattern of how sales volume grows, stabilizes and declines as an industry develops.

Understanding which phase of the lifecycle an industry is in is therefore critical for effective management at all levels of the organization. The lifecycle phase affects the degree of competition firms face, the type of organizational structure, the kind of strategy and the appropriate management approaches needed to survive and grow. The key success factors and sources of competitive advantage for firms are very different from one stage of the lifecycle to the next. Being successful when facing many small entrepreneurial com-

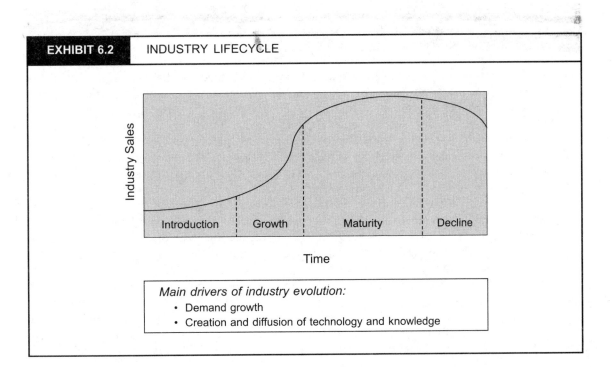

EXHIBIT 6.2 INDUSTRY LIFECYCLE

Main drivers of industry evolution:
- Demand growth
- Creation and diffusion of technology and knowledge

petitors with no clear leader in a fast-growing and technologically innovative market requires a very different approach than being part of a highly concentrated industry with a few large, established incumbents and slow or declining growth. Different types of firms tend to be market leaders at different stages given the difficulties organizations experience when they must adapt to a different environment and make the transition from one type of organizational structure or strategy to another.

While different industries move along the lifecycle at a different pace, the remarkable regularity of the pattern across a very wide spectrum of different industries makes the lifecycle model a powerful tool for managers and entrepreneurs. In addition, the industry lifecycle is a complementary approach to Porter's five forces framework, presented in Chapter 5. The five forces framework is essentially a static model that provides a valuable snapshot of an industry's attractiveness *at a specific point in time*. The lifecycle model, however, is inherently dynamic and shows how evolution affects industry structure and thus the forces of rivalry, potential entrants, customer and supplier power and substitute products described in the Porter model. In conjunction, both models can provide managers with a more complete set of tools for analyzing industries and understanding the forces of competition. We will now examine each of the different phases of the lifecycle in greater detail.

THE INTRODUCTION PHASE: ———————
INDUSTRY EMERGENCE AND CREATION

New industries emerge as the result of changes (usually technological or regulatory) that create opportunities for entrepreneurs to leverage novel combinations of resources to develop innovative products, services or processes. These opportunities are not always exploited immediately and some remain untapped and unrecognized for many years until someone decides to start a new firm that will take advantage of the resources and create a new market. Some industries are the result of important technological breakthroughs such as the biotechnology industry that emerged following the discovery of recombinant DNA by scientists Stanley Cohen and Herbert Boyer. (See Talking Business 6.1.)

Some industries are the outcome of government regulation (or deregulation) that creates markets for new products or services. For example, the Environmental Protection Act and a variety of companion state laws enacted in the United States in 1970 specified guidelines for organizations' behaviour toward the environment. As a result, an industry of consultants, lawyers, lobbyists and even a market for trading pollution credits through brokers has emerged to enable firms to comply and adapt to the new legislation. In Canada, the Supreme Court's decision of June 9, 2005, overturned the ban on private health insurance in Quebec. Many analysts regard this ruling as opening the door to the creation of a private health care industry in Canada. Whether this will in fact happen, what this potential industry will look like and how it will operate remains, however, very unclear at this point.

The early years of an industry are generally a tumultuous period where there is tremendous uncertainty about the future of the market. There is no dominant technology or business model and it is far from certain that the market will ever grow sufficiently to

TALKING BUSINESS 6.1   THE BIRTH OF BIOTECH

The biotechnology industry was born of a scientific discovery made in 1973 by Herbert Boyer, professor at the University of California at San Francisco (UCSF), and Stanley Cohen of Stanford University. At the time, many scientists were working on the idea of recombinant DNA but Cohen and Boyer were the first to perfect a technique for snipping out DNA — the blueprint molecules that cells use to make proteins — and combining it with fragments of DNA from another organism.

A scientific breakthrough, no matter how important, is not itself sufficient to trigger the birth of a new industry. This requires entrepreneurs who have the dream and the drive to commercialize technological innovations and develop marketable products. This is where Robert Swanson, an ambitious 29-year-old venture capitalist, comes in. In 1976, Swanson wanted to commercialize a new way of engineering drugs based on splicing DNA from one organism into the genome of another so he called Boyer and dropped by his lab at UCSF. As the pair sketched out their business plan over beers in a San Francisco bar, they were about to change the drug industry forever by creating the field of commercial biotechnology.

To turn this invention into a business, Boyer and Swanson incorporated under the name Genentech Inc. In 1982, the company won Food & Drug Administration (FDA) approval for the first genetically engineered drug, human insulin. Soon many more entrepreneurial scientists created new biotechnology firms, using recombinant DNA techniques to develop drugs aimed at diagnosing and treating everything from anemia to cancer.

Herbert Boyer's fascination with James Watson and Francis Crick's groundbreaking 1953 revelation that DNA was a double helix is what led him to a career in biochemistry. "The whole structure was so beautiful, and it explained so much about genetics," he says. Boyer and Swanson, who studied chemistry and management at the Massachusetts Institute of Technology (MIT) and began his career as a venture capitalist, shared a great love of science. The pair made a perfect team and complemented each other perfectly in their roles as businessman and scientist. Swanson, the CEO, was the front man dealing with potential investors, strategic partners and clients while Boyer was the internal operations chief who supervised the scientists on staff. As an academic, Boyer understood the Genentech scientists' need to communicate and disseminate their discoveries and persuaded Swanson to let them publish their results, even at the risk of exposing the firm's trade secrets.

Today, Swanson and Boyer are widely recognized as the founding fathers of the global, multibillion dollar biotechnology industry. Genentech, which was started during that fateful meeting in 1976 and has since spawned a slew of competitors — 1,400 firms in the United States alone — is now worth more than $100 billion. Boyer, who retired in 1991 as vice-president of Genentech and has remained on the board of directors ever since, says he and Swanson couldn't fathom the impact their innovation would have on the world. "When he walked into my office, it changed my life," he says, along with the lives of millions of people around the world. Just three years after retiring as chairman of Genentech's board in 1999, Swanson died of brain cancer at the age of 52.

Source: Based on "Robert Swanson and Herbert Boyer: Giving Birth to Biotech" in *Business Week* (October 18, 2004).

provide attractive financial returns and growth opportunities. At the same time, this is also a period of unbridled optimism among entrepreneurs jockeying for position as the future of the market unfolds. Early entrants into an industry tend to be small entrepreneurial firms excited by the prospect and potential growth of a new market. Large, established firms tend to lag smaller ones in entering new industries for two reasons. First, a nascent market is usually too small and risky to justify the entry of large firms burdened with high overhead costs and the need to generate more certain, even if lower, financial returns. Second, older incumbent firms usually have bureaucratic organizational structures that inhibit their ability to move quickly and flexibly into new markets. Smaller and more nimble firms rely on simpler structures and lower startup costs to capture a first-mover advantage. Entrepreneurial startups are inherently more tolerant of ambiguity and risk because they have much less to lose than established firms and are therefore more willing to gamble in the hopes of generating a very large payoff.

This introductory phase is one of great technical uncertainty where producers experiment with very different and novel combinations in the hopes of discovering a superior approach that will dominate those of other firms. Firms are intensely focused on research and development (R&D) activities during this period. This results in a high degree of product innovation with many different versions of products incorporating different features and technologies (see Talking Business 6.2). This also leads to confusion for customers and other stakeholders, which prevents the market from taking off into the growth phase. The types of customers who tend to purchase in the introduction phase of the lifecycle are early adopters willing to pay a premium for the privilege of owning a product before most anyone else, despite its early flaws and glitches. Conservative and price-conscious customers will usually wait until the mature stage before buying.

Despite (and partly because of) the uncertainty inherent in a new industry, the introduction phase of the lifecycle is a period of extraordinary creativity and innovation. An industry is rarely as vibrant as in its early years, when hope and optimism fuel the dreams of entrepreneurs and inventors. This period is the "gold rush" era of the industry where everyone can still make it big, given that nobody has yet.

In addition to the large upsurge in entry, new markets are extremely volatile. They may have no clear boundaries, and segments are not well defined. The market shares of the different producers are highly unstable and many entrants fail shortly after entering. It is nearly impossible to predict which firms will survive and grow, and it is often not all that obvious whether the industry itself will emerge as a viable entity able to sustain a group of producers. While we tend to study only those industries that did develop viable markets because we can observe the entire lifecycle, there are numerous examples of industries that began their lifecycle with much promise yet never made it past the introductory phase.

In the 1990s, several highly ambitious ventures planning to provide wireless telecommunications and broadband Internet services through satellite networks were launched with much fanfare. Iridium, backed by the wireless firm Motorola, and Teledesic, which was funded by McCaw Cellular and Microsoft owner Bill Gates, were two such ventures, along with Globalstar, ICO and others. Teledesic planned to blanket the earth's atmosphere with 288 low-earth orbit (LEO) satellites to build an "Internet in the sky." A combination of technical difficulties, financial troubles, mismanagement and slow customer adoption, due to the very high cost of satellite communications led to the demise of these ventures and of the nascent satellite communications industry — though not before they had lost billions

TALKING BUSINESS 6.2   THE EARLY YEARS OF THE AUTOMOBILE INDUSTRY

While it is hard to imaging the modern automobile industry with its few large, established firms as a hotbed of entrepreneurial activity, the early years of the American auto industry were indeed very dynamic and entrepreneurial activity was rampant. Between 1899 and 1923, the industry experienced a large surge of market entry with over 3,000 recorded attempts at automobile production launched during this period. Many of these firms failed within a year of entering and over 68% exited the industry within two years. While perfectly consistent with the industry lifecycle theory, the sheer abundance and diversity of producers and early designs is quite astonishing in light of today's highly concentrated and standardized industry. Consider, for example, the following early cars and their makers:

- The Roberts Electric was a two-seat electric car powered by two 60-volt motors, one for each rear wheel, and was made in 1897 by C.E. Roberts of Chicago.
- Kent's Pacemaker, a steam-powered car with three rear wheels and a single wheel in front for steering, was made by the Colonial Automobile Co. of Boston from 1899 to 1901.
- The Luxor, a gasoline-powered vehicle that resembled a Roman chariot, was designed by C.R. Harris of Pennsylvania, who never managed to get it into production.
- The Cotta Steam was a steam automobile with four-wheel drive and steering. It was produced in very limited numbers by the Cotta Automobile Co. of Rockford, Illinois, in 1903.
- The Rotary, a gasoline-powered car with a single-cylinder engine and two crankshafts, was made in Boston by the Rotary Motor Vehicle Co. in 1904 and 1905.
- The Pratt was a car with four rear wheels and two front ones and was powered by a 75-horsepower engine. It was built by Pratt Chuck Works of Frankfurt, New York, in 1907.
- The Menkenns, a three-wheeled car powered by a front-mounted airplane propeller was made in 1937 by Willie Menkenns of Hillsboro, Oregon.

While many of these designs may seem bizarre today, they highlight the uncertainty faced by the pioneers of the automobile industry. It was far from clear at the turn of the century what basic features the successful car would have. For example, a critical decision involved the type of engine or propulsion system to use. Steam, electric and gasoline-powered engines were all potential candidates and many producers used technologies and fuel other than gasoline. In fact, many early analysts believed that steam was a superior technology to power car engines.

Around 1920 however, the dominant design of the automobile had emerged — an all-steel enclosed body mounted on a chassis and a gasoline-powered internal combustion engine. This is the fundamental architecture of a car that remains (save for material innovations in the steel body) unchanged to this day. The adoption of this dominant design for cars was accompanied by the failure of many car manufacturers and a dramatic reduction in the number of new entrants. From a peak of 350 car makers in the United States in 1915, there were fewer than 50 by 1930 and less than 20 by 1940 (see Fig. 10–5 Carroll and Hannan, 1995). Today there are only two car makers left in the

continues

United States (GM and Ford) and the global industry is highly concentrated with 10 manufacturers controlling more than 80% of the worldwide market.

The first cars produced were quite expensive and affordable only by the very rich. By 1923, however, 50% of U.S. households owned an automobile. The diffusion of the automobile was accelerated by Henry Ford's introduction of the Model T in 1908 for an affordable $850; and by Ford's development of one of the most significant industrial innovations of the 20th century — the moving assembly line in 1913. This revolutionary process brought the product to the workers for the first time rather than having workers moving around a factory to perform tasks. Inspired by Frederick Taylor's principles of specialization and standardization, Ford had workers perform a single repetitive task rather than whole portions of automobile assembly. The new Ford plant in Highland Park, Michigan, produced over 300,000 cars in one year, 1914 — more than in the entire history of the company. The increases in productivity allowed Ford to continually drop the price of the Model T to as low as $290 in 1927, making cars truly affordable for the masses and paving the way for the massive changes brought on by the automotive industry we now know.

Source: Based on Glenn R. Carroll and Michael T. Hannan, *Organizations in Industry: Strategy, Structure & Selection* (New York, NY: Oxford University Press, 1995); and George Constable and Bob Somerville, *A Century of Innovation: Twenty Engineering Achievements that Transformed our Lives* (Washington, DC: Chapter Joseph Henry Press, 2003).

of dollars in the process (more than $9 billion in Teledesic's case). Iridium filed for bankruptcy in 2001 after having launched 66 satellites into space at a cost of more than $6 billion. An Iridium satellite now hangs in the Smithsonian National Air and Space Museum as a testament to the technological ability (and commercial failure) of this venture. While some of these firms have emerged from bankruptcy protection in a different form, the satellite communications industry has clearly not lived up to the high expectations of its early pioneers. Perhaps the technology was ahead of its time and it will eventually take off and grow. Nevertheless, this case illustrates that new industries can suffer quite severe growing pains and may never develop into mature industries. There are other industries that are still in the early stages of development and currently struggling to make it into the growth phase.

The Quest for Legitimacy

Organization theorists studying industry emergence and evolution have focused on the institutional and social conditions that affect the changing nature of markets and competitive forces. One of the most important contributions to emerge concerns the concept of

---

TALKING BUSINESS   6.3   GREY GOO AND THE PROMISING FUTURE OF THE NANOTECHNOLOGY INDUSTRY

Nanotechnology is the science and technology of building electronic circuits and devices from single atoms and molecules. These devices are typically less than 100 nanometers in size (one nanometer equals one millionth of a millimeter). This burgeoning industry is expected to make significant contributions to the fields of computer storage, semiconductors, biotechnology, manufacturing and energy. While the concept of nanotechnology was first introduced by the physicist Richard Feynman in 1959, advancements truly began to accelerate after Richard Smalley's discovery of carbon nanotubes won the 1996 Nobel Prize. In 2001, following large increases in U.S. government funding for nanotechnology research and the publication of an entire issue of the influential magazine *Scientific American* on the topic, the U.S. National Science Foundation predicted the newly defined "nanotechnology market" would grow to $1 trillion by 2015.

These events triggered significant investments by venture capitalists and entrepreneurs in a variety of nanotech startups. According to some scientists, the future of nanotechnology is one of astonishing possibilities, where diseases will be wiped out and we will live for hundreds of years. Envisioned are all kinds of amazing products, including extraordinarily tiny computers that are very powerful, building materials that withstand earthquakes, advanced systems for drug delivery and custom-tailored pharmaceuticals as well as the elimination of invasive surgery (because repairs can be made from within the body). Nano-sized robots will be injected into the bloodstream and administer a drug directly to an infected cell. Because they are composed of biological elements such as DNA and proteins, the nanobots can easily be removed from the body.

The promise of a technological and industrial revolution of unprecedented magnitude based on the science of nanotechnology rests on many underlying assumptions of technical advances that, while theoretically possible, remain unproven. The emerging industry also has to contend with fears, stoked by science-fiction films and novels, that there are great risks involved with nanotechnology. One of these is that self-replicating nanobots run amok will devour the earth in three hours, turning it into "grey goo" — a phenomenon called global ecophagy. More realistic concerns point to the potential toxicity of certain nanosubstances that are so small they can penetrate cell walls and membranes and disturb the immune system. Nevertheless, the high degree of uncertainty and controversy has not deterred entrepreneurs from entering the fray in the hopes of eventually "cashing in" on the upcoming nanotech revolution.

---

the legitimacy of new industries and organizational forms. Suchman defines organizational legitimacy as "...a generalized perception or assumption that the actions of an entity are desirable, proper, or appropriate within some socially constructed system of norms, values, beliefs, and definitions."[1] Other researchers have distinguished between two forms of legitimacy: sociopolitical and cognitive legitimacy.[2] **Sociopolitical legitimacy** refers to the endorsement of an industry, activity or organizational form by key stakeholders and institutions such as the state and government officials, opinion leaders or the general public. **Cognitive legitimacy** refers to the level of public knowledge of a new industry and its conformity to established norms and methods reflected in the extent to which it is taken for granted as a desirable and appropriate activity.

All organizations require legitimacy in order to acquire from external stakeholders the resources they need to survive and grow. Because organizations must extract resources from their environments, failure to conform to societal and institutionalized norms and beliefs results in a lack of legitimacy that will hinder their ability to recruit employees, obtain financial and material resources, sell products and services to customers, etc. There are many reasons why an organization's actions may not be perceived as desirable, proper or appropriate. Failure to comply to legal rules or to the ethical norms of society is one of them, as is pioneering a new type of firm or way of doing business.

Being new, small, unknown or unrecognized can cause a firm to lack legitimacy as it must prove to outsiders that it does conform to institutional norms. Even in existing industries, startup firms face higher risks of failure than incumbent firms with established track records and relationships with customers, suppliers and other stakeholders. In entirely new industries, the lack of legitimacy is even more pronounced, given how business models and organizational forms are novel and have yet to acquire sufficient legitimacy as desirable and appropriate entities. Entrepreneurs operate in a murky and ambiguous environment where there are few, if any, precedents available to determine what is considered a desirable and appropriate business activity. Stakeholders will therefore question the viability, not only of the specific venture, but of the nascent industry itself. Society's lack of understanding, acceptance and familiarity with the industry leads to even greater difficulties in marshalling resources so that new firms in new industries are even more likely to fail than new firms in established industries. (See Talking Business 6.3.)

To illustrate this idea, contrast the situations of an entrepreneur deciding to start a restaurant and another deciding to start a wireless text message advertising firm. A potential restaurateur need not convince external stakeholders of the virtue of the restaurant as a business model. It is a tried and true concept, and we have well-known templates for what they should look like. Everyone the entrepreneur speaks to will know what a restaurant is, how it will operate and make money. It is taken for granted that customers sit down and make choices from a menu, that food is prepared and served and that payment is tendered. With minor variations in menu, location or pricing, virtually all restaurants operate this way and have for hundreds of years. Entrepreneurs who conform to these institutional norms will have an easier time gathering the needed resources for their new venture. While the legitimacy of the individual venture needs to be overcome, the legitimacy of the restaurant industry is not an issue.

On the other hand, entrepreneurs launching a wireless text messaging advertising firm will need to explain to stakeholders exactly how this business will operate and generate revenues. They will also need to convince stakeholders of the potential viability of this concept as the text message advertising industry is still so new that, unlike restaurants, there are no institutional norms for how this business should be organized. It is not clear how and to whom ads should be sold and delivered. Will consumers accept them or find them intrusive and resent them? Is the technology proven? At the organizational level, entrepreneurs must establish the legitimacy of their specific venture, and at the industry level, they must collectively demonstrate that their novel organizational form or business model is desirable and appropriate.

While there may be intense technological competition between early entrants in an industry, there is also a high degree of collaboration for the greater good through the establishment of trade associations and standards-setting bodies that facilitate the pursuit of industry legitimacy. So-called "institutional entrepreneurs" play a critical role in helping to ensure the survival and growth of a fledgling industry by promoting its interests and coordinating efforts to gain institutional support and legitimacy. Linus Torvalds, the Finnish engineer who developed the Linux open source operating system, Jeff Bezos, the founder of Amazon.com, and Richard Smalley and Eric Drexler in the nanotechnology field are among the entrepreneurs who have become advocates and evangelists for the cause of the industry they pioneered in order to mobilize resources and legitimize it in the eyes of society. The collective action strategies pursued by institutional entrepreneurs often bear a striking resemblance to social movements. Successful institutional entrepreneurs are adept at presenting themselves as revolutionaries rebelling against the established order of large corporations, even though most of them actually aspire to grow their organizations and industry to replace the large firms.

In an industry's formative years, intra-industry rivalry is less intense as new organizations collaborate in the pursuit of legitimacy. New markets that have yet to achieve a sufficient degree of acceptance benefit from the endorsement of recognizable players. Smaller startups therefore often welcome the entry of established incumbents into the new market. When a large organization with a known track record enters the new industry, all firms benefit as this acts as an endorsement that signals the industry's viability and attractiveness, which helps it grow. This was the case when IBM entered the personal computer industry, for example, or when Wal-Mart entered the online retail market. When a large and successful retailer like Wal-Mart launches an e-commerce Web site, this signals to various stakeholders that the new market is important and worthy of Wal-Mart's attention. Wal-Mart's online presence attracts consumers to online shopping as well as attention from the media, the financial community and other stakeholders, all of which contribute to the establishment of cognitive legitimacy for the e-commerce industry.

THE GROWTH PHASE: ——————
DOMINANT DESIGNS AND SHAKEOUTS

In the introduction stage, the objective is to find the new industry's dominant model and get it accepted and institutionalized; although sales are important and contribute to this purpose, they are subordinate to the main goal of legitimization. As we will discuss, in the industry growth stage, the game becomes all about sales and market share. The growth stage begins when the market converges around a single dominant design or approach. A *dominant design* is defined by Anderson and Tushman as "a single architecture that establishes dominance in a product class."[3] In some cases, technical standards are specified and must be adhered to by all firms wishing to enter the market. When a standard is legally mandated and enforced by a government or standards organization, it is called a **de jure standard.** For example, the gauge of a railroad track, a light bulb socket, an electrical outlet, are all based on standards that have been explicitly specified by a standards organization — usually to ensure compatibility. A company wanting to produce light bulbs must make them to the correct specifications or they will be useless to consumers. A **de facto standard**, on the other hand, arises by virtue of common usage and is not officially sanctioned by any authority. It is a standard "in fact" or "in practice," rather than in law. Microsoft Windows is the *de facto* standard for personal computer operating systems because over 90% of the market uses Windows. Software developers must therefore write programs that are compatible with Windows if they want to reach the majority of the market.

As the standard or dominant model spreads across the industry, the producers that persist with a different approach usually exit the industry. This is one of the main causes of industry shakeouts. A **shakeout** in an industry is defined as a large number of exits from the market at the same time as the aggregate output of the industry increases. A large number of failures in a declining market is *not* a shakeout. A shakeout is a natural and healthy — albeit painful — process for an industry as it simply purges and weeds out the weaker competitors. The firms remaining after the shakeout emerge as strong competitors able to scale up production and serve the needs of a growing market. Nevertheless, there are cases of firms pursuing the path of a proprietary standard not in line with the rest of industry and remaining successful, though on a much smaller scale. Apple Computer, which pioneered the personal computer market, has been able to maintain its small share of loyal customers over the years. By not adhering to the Windows standard, Apple effectively restricted its market to small niches of graphic designers, academics and other consumers dissatisfied with Windows' quasi-monopoly. This, as Apple's troubles over the years can attest, is a very risky strategy. A firm must provide a significant benefit for a consumer to be willing to overcome the problems of incompatibility with 90% of the market.

Most other personal computer firms from the early 1980s, such as MITS, Commodore, and Tandy, did not survive. Prior to 1981, when IBM launched the IBM PC, and real commercial growth began, the different computer firms all had their own proprietary hardware and software platforms. Most of the exits from the industry occurred between 1987 and 1993. This period coincides with the introduction of Intel's 386 processor in 1986 and the release of Windows 3.0 in 1990, which had graphical interfaces that made computers more user-friendly. These versions of the Intel X86 line of microprocessors and of the Windows operating system firmly entrenched the so-called Wintel standard, which replaced the IBM PC as the dominant architecture for personal computers. Once this design was institutionalized as the standard, personal computers assembled and sold by clone manufacturers had to conform and include an Intel chip and Windows in order to be accepted by the market. When the vast majority of other users have a Wintel PC, few consumers are willing to deviate from the norm. Although there are newer versions of these components, the fundamental architecture of the PC with an Intel central processing unit (CPU) and Windows OS running application software has remained virtually unchanged for the past 15 years.

The adoption of a dominant design greatly accelerates the growth rate of new markets. As with automobiles, after about 20 years of industry evolution, 50% of U.S. households in 1999 owned a computer. Growth in demand is significantly related to the falling prices for products during the second phase of the lifecycle. The diffusion of a dominant industry model allows firms to standardize products and processes, resulting in dramatic costs savings that push prices lower. Standardization creates incentives for other firms to offer complementary products and services, such as software that runs on Windows or gas stations to fuel cars. The development of an industry infrastructure stimulates even more demand for the products in a cycle that leads to growth rates that increase during this stage. Products now appeal to a much wider mass market rather than just early technology adopters or the wealthy. As output grows further, economies of scale allow producers to generate more cost savings that drive prices even lower. This is another important cause of industry shakeouts. As product prices fall, inefficient producers come under significant competitive pressures and exit. Firms that are unable to match the economies of scale, production process improvements and lower prices of the most efficient producers will be driven out of the market. Also, high volume producers can afford to operate with lower profit margins while smaller firms are forced to exit.

Despite fierce competition and many exits, the high growth and reduction in uncertainty attracts many new entrants to the industry. Established firms from other industries that may have lagged the startups in entering now see the new industry as either potentially lucrative or threatening to their own assets and markets. They often enter by acquiring a firm already in the market rather than going through the trouble of starting a new division or subsidiary from scratch. Large firms bring tremendous resources to invest in distribution, marketing and advertising to capture a greater share of the market, as well as expertise in efficient production and the capacity to withstand fierce price competition. This is the case, for example, with many pharmaceutical firms that acquired promising biotech ventures rather than developing their own internal R&D capabilities in biotechnology.

In the introduction phase, product innovation and R&D were critical skills for organizations. After standardization, however, process innovation and sales and marketing become more important. This is a critical difference between the early and middle phases of the lifecycle and explains why large firms with greater resources and expertise in production processes and sales and marketing can displace entrepreneurial startups that fail to capture a meaningful first-mover advantage through property rights (e.g., patents, trademarks), customer loyalty or technological leadership. In the early market, organizations were more likely to collaborate to increase aggregate sales and achieve legitimacy. In the growth phase, rivalry is much more intense and firms try to build brand recognition and position themselves for when the market will cease to grow as rapidly.

THE MATURITY PHASE: ———————————
A CRITICAL TRANSITION

In the mature stage, the third in the lifecycle, growth in aggregate demand begins to slow. Markets start to become saturated as there are fewer new adopters to attract and so competition intensifies even more. This can, nevertheless, be a very profitable period for the surviving firms as the industry enters a period of relative stability. For example, between 1980 and 2000, the U.S. beer brewing industry was in a mature phase and was dominated by three large firms that controlled over 80% of the market (Anheuser-Busch: 47%; Miller: 23%; Coors: 10%). Over the 20 year period, market shares were very stable, and no firm gained or lost more than about a single share point in any one year.

Despite the high degree of concentration in mature markets, rivalry is fierce. A single point of market share can mean millions of dollars in revenue so firms spend large amounts on advertising and sometimes enter into damaging price wars to lure customers from the competition. Because technological knowledge has diffused to the far corners of the industry and patents may have expired, firms focus their innovative efforts on incremental improvements to products. (See Talking Business 6.4 on the British chocolate bar market.) This is the era where firms market the "new and improved" versions and the 25 different scents and flavours in the hopes of differentiating their products ever so slightly from the competition's. Incremental innovations also provide opportunities to extend the lifecycle in order to delay the inevitable arrival of the decline stage. As consumers accumulate knowledge of the industry and its products over time, they become much more sophisticated and demanding buyers. This influences the industry's trend toward the

---

TALKING BUSINESS 6.4   BLOCK CHOCOLATE — BREAKING THE IMPASSE

In a mature, largely commoditised market subject to heavy discounting by supermarkets and at odds with a preoccupation with healthy eating, block chocolate faces a battle for growth. Until last year, sales had been almost stagnant for five years, despite a short-term boost in 2002 following the launch of Nestle's premium chocolate Double Cream. The retail value of sales grew from $1.276 billion in 1998 to just $1.278 billion four years later, according to Euromonitor.

"We eat 2.5 kg of chocolate per person every year, and it would be hard — not to mention politically incorrect — to drive the market above that," says Datamonitor consumer analyst John Band. But the scale of the challenge hasn't stopped confectionery manufacturers looking for ways to boost value in their market. These include line extensions, premium launches, rebranding and refocusing promotional spend on the most successful brands.

In the UK block-chocolate market, Cadbury is the most successful player. It extended its lead over main rivals Nestle and Mars last year through a major relaunch of Cadbury's Dairy Milk, fuelling growth in the sector from $1.278 billion in 2002 to $1.456 billion — a rise of 14%. The relaunch brought products such as Fruit & Nut, Whole Nut, Wispa and Caramel Bar under the Dairy Milk umbrella. Variants, including Dairy Milk with mint chips and with crispy pieces, were added to the range, which has created a distinctive "purple patch" on supermarket shelves.

Sales of the line grew 13% last year, according to a Cadbury spokesman, and Euromonitor puts the company's market share at 53.1%, up from 50% last year. Of individual brands, Dairy Milk now has a commanding lead in share of the market, with 30.9%, well above its nearest rival, Masterfoods' Galaxy, which owns a 9.8% share.

Growing Pains

While Cadbury's success demonstrates there is scope to grow the block-chocolate market through new product development and innovation in branding, rivals have struggled to emulate it.

Mars relaunched Galaxy as a range, including products such as Minstrels and Ripple, with a $35 million campaign last year. Sales of Galaxy rose more than 10%, with

continues

Galaxy Milk Block sales soaring by 12% in the four months following its launch in September 2003. But an analyst from ACNielsen questions whether Galaxy's success is sustainable, given that it was achieved largely on the back of heavy promotional activity.

Nestle's strategy, meanwhile, has been to try to consolidate its position in the premium sector, with the recent launch of Double Cream: Double Chocolate and Double Berry. Double Cream, which contains Ecuadorian cocoa beans, was Nestle's first brand launch in five years, and aims to bridge the gap between Dairy Milk and Lindt by offering a hint of luxury at a price that is only marginally premium. [...] But sales of Double Cream, described by Nestle Rowntree managing director Chris White as "a product that re-establishes Nestle's chocolate credentials," have so far been disappointing. Analysts are sceptical about the ability of manufacturers to change the tastes or price expectations of British consumers for whom Dairy Milk represents the taste, price and quality standard.

"There is not much scope for a premium market in the UK at the moment, and the big three producers' fortunes will depend largely on their success in promoting their core ranges," says Jeremy Cunnington, UK senior research analyst at Euromonitor.

Nevertheless, there is a discernible rise in sales of chocolate containing between 70% and 80% cocoa solids, such as Lindt and Green & Black's. "Sales of Lindt Excellence rose by about 15% last year, but are still worth less than $44 million," says Cunnington. Sales of Green & Black's, which has 90% of the total UK organic chocolate market, were up 70%, albeit from a low base, and the company owns 3% of the block-chocolate market.

Band says that even if Green & Black's does manage to convert consumers to stronger chocolate, its ethical credentials would curtail its ability to capitalise on growth, while its super-premium positioning prevents it from leveraging its name on "middlebrow" products.

It is a mistake the Day Chocolate Company, which dominates the market in fair trade chocolate, with brands such as Divine and Dubble, has been careful to avoid. Sales of fair trade chocolate and cocoa products rose from $2.2 million in 1998 to $24 million last year, according to the Fairtrade Foundation. [...]

Health Kick

Despite their small overall share of the block-chocolate market, organic and fair trade brands may capitalise on the trend toward healthier eating. A high proportion of the products are dark chocolate, with a lower milk content, while the high level of cocoa solids makes them richer and more difficult to consume in volume. "You can buy a bar of Green & Black's, eat a bit and put the rest in the fridge for another day," says marketing director Mark Palmer. "We are not a snack food, but a considered eat, and operate on the premise that less is more."

Maybe, but less chocolate also means less profit, and none of the manufacturers has a ready solution to the battle that exists with healthy eating. As the ACNielsen analyst puts it: "Obesity concerns are not good for the market." Band concludes: "If someone could come up with a cheap, tasty and healthy chocolate bar, it might do OK. But chocolate is obviously so indulgent that a healthy version is missing the point — like low-alcohol beer."

continues

commoditization of its products and makes consumers even more price conscious, which in turn forces firms to continuously squeeze out more cost savings from their production processes.

When there is very little product differentiation and consumers have become notoriously fickle, power once held by the manufacturers now shifts to the distribution channel firms that control access to the customer. This is why shelf space is so critical in mature packaged goods markets like laundry detergent. When customers see very little difference between Tide and the competition, they will essentially grab whatever they have access to or what happens to be on sale. Retailers who control and allocate shelf space have more bargaining power than they did in earlier phases where customers would seek out a particular product because it possessed features not shared by others.

Given the scale required to compete efficiently, there is very little, if any, entry at this stage of the lifecycle. The sources of competitive advantage for firms reside in process engineering to derive greater manufacturing and production efficiencies and reduce costs even more. This often means outsourcing and shedding activities that can be subcontracted more efficiently. In some industries, production will shift from advanced to developing countries during this stage in order to benefit from lower labour costs. In terms of the generic competitive strategies described in Chapter 5, whereas differentiation was the favoured approach in the earlier stages, organizations that adopt a cost leadership strategy in mature markets tend to outperform their peers.

The shift from a dynamic and technologically innovative environment with many small firms to a stable and cost-efficient market with few large rivals also requires a change in the type of organizational structure, as described in Chapter 4. In the high-flying and uncertain early market, entrepreneurial startups need to be innovative, dynamic and flexible. The organic structure, with its decentralized approach, limited hierarchy and low formalization, is better suited to the environment of the introduction and early growth phases. In a mature market where efficiency and cost-cutting matter more than innovation, the mechanistic structure, with its stricter rules, chain of command and narrow division of labour, is more appropriate. Making the transition from one structure to the next is very difficult when organizations have been conditioned to behave a certain way. This is the main reason why few firms are able to remain industry leaders throughout the entire lifecycle.

THE DECLINE PHASE: ———————————
DIFFICULT CHOICES

An industry enters the decline stage when sales begin to fall. It is difficult to predict when this will happen, and the time it takes for industries to reach the decline stage varies widely. Nevertheless, industry sales typically decline as a result of one of the following:

1. *Changes in demographics:* e.g., Toward the end of the baby boom in the 1960s, demand for baby food dropped and rivalry among the leading firms — Gerber, Heinz, Beech-Nut — intensified considerably.

2. *Shifting consumer tastes and needs:* e.g., Social trends and health considerations have resulted in declining demand for cigarettes and tobacco products since the 1980s.

3. *Technological substitution:* e.g., Word processing software led to the decline of the typewriter industry; DVDs have replaced VHS cassette tapes as the medium of choice for movies, and sales of VHS tapes and video cassette recorders (VCR) are thus in decline.

Competition becomes especially fierce in the decline stage as firms face tough choices regarding the future. A decline, though, does not necessarily equal the demise or death of the industry, and there are a number of strategic options available to organizations for dealing with a declining market. These choices are often highly dependent on the actions of rivals, however. If many competitors decide to exit the industry and liquidate their assets, this may lead to profitable opportunities for the remaining firms. If other firms merge, however, their increased market power may reduce opportunities for the remaining competitors.

Organizations have five basic alternatives in the decline phase:

1. *Maintain a leadership stance:* This approach requires a firm to continue investing in marketing, support, product development, hoping that competitors will eventually exit the market. Despite declining sales and profit margins, there may still be opportunities to generate above-average returns for firms that remain the industry leaders during this phase.

2. *Pursue a niche strategy:* The objective is to find a specific segment of the industry that may not decline as rapidly as the rest and where the firm can expect to possess some form of competitive advantage to discourage direct competition in the niche. For example, a tobacco firm facing declining cigarette sales may decide to focus exclusively on the more robust cigar market and defend that niche heavily against competitors by investing in marketing and sales support.

A firm can ultimately choose to switch to a harvest, exit or consolidation strategy after having pursued a leadership or niche approach; the reverse is not true.

3. *Harvest profits:* This strategy requires squeezing as much remaining profit as possible from the industry by drastically reducing costs. The firm must eliminate or severely restrict investments in the industry and take advantage of existing strengths to generate incremental sales. This strategy is ultimately followed by the firm's exit from the industry.

4. *Exit early:* This approach allows firms to recover some of their prior investments in the industry by exiting the market early in the decline phase, when assets may still be valuable to others and there is greater uncertainty concerning the speed of the decline. Some firms also choose to exit the industry during the mature phase to truly maximize the value from the sale of its assets. Once decline becomes evident, assets are worth much less to potential buyers, who are in stronger bargaining position. The risk of exiting so early is that an organization's forecast for decline will prove inaccurate.

An important point to remember is that just as there are barriers to entering an industry, there are also barriers to exiting a market. A firm may have specialized assets, such as plants and equipment, that cannot be easily redeployed by other businesses. This greatly diminishes their resale value and acts as an exit barrier. Firms may also face high costs due to labour settlements if they exit an industry. The social cost of closing a plant in a region that is economically dependent on the industry can also hinder a smooth exit. Finally, there are non-rational exit barriers linked to the cognitive and emotional barriers that managers face in divestment decisions. Exiting an industry can be perceived as a sign of failure, and managers that have a strong emotional identification and commitment to an industry are understandably reluctant to admit defeat when they have worked hard at being successful.

5. *Consolidate:* This strategy involves acquiring at a reasonable price the best of the remaining firms in the industry. This allows the acquirer to enhance its market power and generate economies of scale and synergies to further reduce costs and make up

for declining demand. For example, in the online brokerage industry, sales and profits have been declining since the market crash of 2000. Fewer people are trading stocks online, putting pressure on companies like Ameritrade and Etrade to compensate. While Etrade has responded by entering the growing banking and mortgage markets to diversify its sources of revenue, Ameritrade has been on an acquisition binge. Starting with its 2001 acquisition of National Discount Brokers, Ameritrade has devoured several of its smaller competitors: Daytek in 2002; Mydiscountbroker.com and National Brokerage in 2003; Bidwell and J.B. Oxford in 2004; TD Waterhouse for $2.9 billion so far in 2005. Analysts claim that the only way for discount brokers to survive the decline in online trading — besides another unlikely stock market bubble — is to merge to generate economies of scale and become more efficient. Ameritrade is claiming that it can generate more than $500 million in savings by merging its operations with TD Waterhouse.

Exhibit 6.3 shows a summary of the key characteristics of the different industry lifecycle stages.

TECHNOLOGICAL FORCES —————————
Types of Innovation

As our discussion of industry lifecycles suggests, technological innovation is a key driver of industry evolution. Radically new innovations or *technological discontinuities* can create entirely new industries as automobiles or wireless phones have done, or seriously disrupt existing ones such as jet engines in the aircraft industry or digital cameras in the photography industry. *Radical or breakthrough innovations* embody significantly new technical knowledge and represent a major departure from existing practices. They are often referred to as discontinuous (as opposed to continuous) innovations, given that they build on a new base of knowledge that discontinues the previous technological regime. The shift to jet engines in aircrafts did not build on or continue along the same technological trajectory laid out by propeller-based engines; it thrust the aircraft industry on an entirely new path. Digital cameras are discontinuous innovations in photography because they do not build on existing chemical photography technology and threaten to render obsolete the technological infrastructure of the industry based on film processing. *Incremental innovations*, on the other hand, make relatively minor changes or adjustments to existing practices. For example, having a larger, higher resolution colour screen on a cell phone represents an incremental improvement to the current technology. Making internal combustion engines in cars more fuel-efficient is another example.

Another way to classify innovations relates to the systemic nature of products and how their components interact. Most products can be thought of as a system of components that interact based on an architectural design in order to achieve a desired purpose. There are thus two aspects of systems here, the type and nature of the components, and how they are organized — the system's architecture. Innovations that involve changes to the product's components but leave the overall configuration of the system relatively intact are

EXHIBIT 6.3   CHARACTERISTICS OF THE INDUSTRY LIFECYCLE STAGES

Characteristic	Stage			
	Introduction	Growth	Maturity	Decline
Market Growth	Slow	Very rapid	Moderate	Negative
Customers	Affluent, early technology adopters	Niche markets, increasing penetration	Price-conscious mass market, repeat buyers	Late adopters, knowledgeable users, residual segments
Rivalry	Low; technological competition	Increasing; entry and exit; shakeout	Intense; increased concentration; exit	Price wars; exit; mergers and acquisitions; asset liquidation
Critical Functional Areas	Research & Development	Sales and Marketing	Production and Manufacturing	General Management and Finance
Products	Very wide variety of designs	Standardization	Commoditization	Continued commoditization
Technological Development	Rapid product innovation	Product and process innovation	Incremental innovation	Very little innovation
Organizational Structure	Organic	Organic	Mechanistic	Mechanistic
Generic Strategies	Product differentiation	Product differentiation	Cost Leadership	Cost Leadership / Focus
Key Objectives	Increase awareness; achieve legitimacy; specify dominant design	Create demand; capture market share	Cost efficiency; extend lifecycle	Market or niche leadership; cost reduction; consolidation; exit

called *component or modular innovations*. Changes in the materials used in automobile bodies from steel to lighter-weight aluminum composites are component innovations. An innovation that alters the system's architecture or how the components interact and are linked with each other is an *architectural innovation*. Most architectural innovations, however, also require changes in the modules or components. A laptop computer is an architectural innovation given that it changes the standard configuration of a personal computer by making it portable, yet the components — microchip, operating system, keyboard, screen — remain essentially the same. Researchers have shown that organizations have a much more difficult time integrating and adapting to architectural innovations compared to modular innovations.

From an organizational perspective, it is useful to think of innovations in relation to an organization's skills and competencies. Technological innovations that build on a firm's existing knowledge and skills in certain areas are called *competence-enhancing*. Conversely, a *competence-destroying innovation* is one that renders obsolete an organization's technical skills and capabilities. A key point to remember is that whether a technological discontinuity is competence-enhancing or -destroying is often a matter of perspective. The same innovation can be competence-destroying to one organization and competence-enhancing to another, depending on their current knowledge base. Electronic calculators replaced slide rules as the tool of choice for engineers and mathematicians in the 1970s. This discontinuous innovation did not build on the knowledge of making slide rules and forced the largest U.S. slide rule manufacturer, Keuffel & Esser, out of the market. The calculator did, however, build on the electronics capabilities of firms like Hewlett-Packard (HP) and Texas Instruments (TI) that came to dominate the market. The calculator was thus competence-destroying for slide rule makers yet competence-enhancing for firms like HP and TI.

The Evolution of Technology

Joseph Schumpeter (1883–1950), an Austrian economist and professor at Harvard, was among the first to emphasize the role of technical progress and entrepreneurship as the driving forces of capitalist economies. In his work, he stressed the evolutionary and cyclical nature of industries that were periodically disrupted by the introduction of revolutionary innovations. In his most popular book, *Capitalism, Socialism and Democracy*, he coined the colourful, and now famous, expression of **creative destruction** to explain how innovations swept away old technologies, skills, products, ideas and industries and replaced them with new ones:

> ...this process ... that incessantly revolutionizes the economic structure from within, incessantly destroying the old one, incessantly creating a new one. This process of Creative Destruction is the essential fact about capitalism. It is what capitalism consists in and what every capitalist concern has got to live in.

In recent years, researchers have built on Schumpeter's ideas to further understand the process of technological innovation and evolution. The Abernathy-Utterback model, based primarily on their study of the automobile industry, forms the basis for most of the work that has followed on the technology lifecycle concept.[4] It states that technologies

231

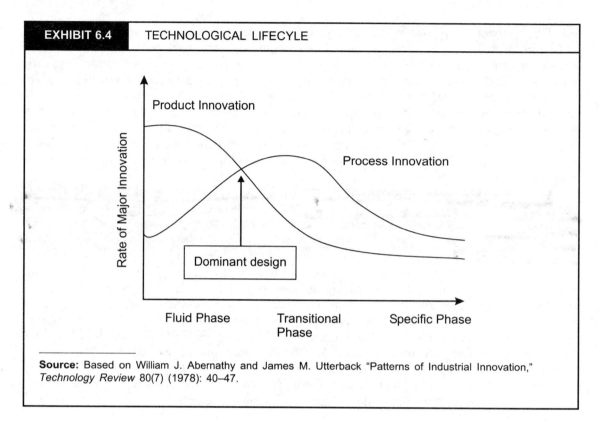

EXHIBIT 6.4	TECHNOLOGICAL LIFECYLE

Source: Based on William J. Abernathy and James M. Utterback "Patterns of Industrial Innovation," *Technology Review* 80(7) (1978): 40–47.

evolve from a fluid phase through a transitional phase to a specific phase (see Exhibit 6.4). When a new technology is initially introduced, it is still in a state of flux and there are a lot of technical as well as marketplace uncertainties. As the industry grows, a dominant design emerges and competition shifts from introducing new product features to meeting the needs of specific customers, which are by then well understood. A dominant design allows the standardization of parts and the optimization of organizational processes for volume and efficiency; therefore, in the specific phase, competition is based more on price than product features.

Anderson and Tushman build on this model to introduce the evolutionary notion of **punctuated equilibrium** to the study of industry evolution.[5] They study several industries over long periods and show that technological discontinuities tend to appear at rare and irregular intervals. These discontinuities trigger an *era of ferment*, a period of substantial product-class variation that ends with the emergence of a dominant design. Once a dominant design emerges, future technical progress consists of incremental improvements elaborating the standard. The *era of incremental change* (usually coinciding with the industry maturity stage) is a much longer period of relative stability and equilibrium. These long periods of incremental change are punctuated by technological discontinuities, hence the reference to a punctuated equilibrium (see Exhibit 6.5).

232

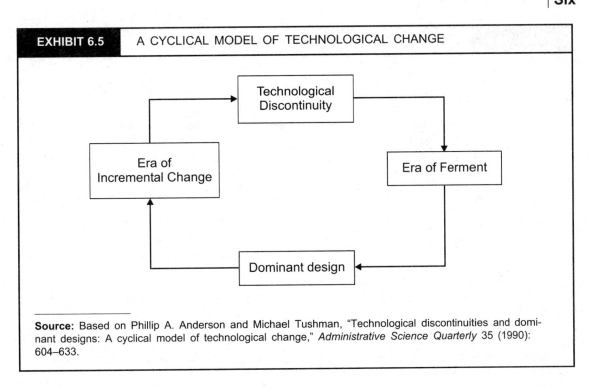

| EXHIBIT 6.5 | A CYCLICAL MODEL OF TECHNOLOGICAL CHANGE |

Source: Based on Phillip A. Anderson and Michael Tushman, "Technological discontinuities and dominant designs: A cyclical model of technological change," *Administrative Science Quarterly* 35 (1990): 604–633.

Technological Forecasting

One of the problems with the Abernathy-Utterback and Anderson-Tushman models is that, while useful descriptions of technological evolution, they do not help in predicting when a discontinuity will occur. Although it is virtually impossible to accurately predict when a technological discontinuity will appear, we can make more informed analyses of technological trajectories using **S-curves**. Foster introduced the concept of the S-curve to explain the rate of advance of a technology.[6] (See Exhibit 6.6.) When a new technology emerges, progress starts off slowly, then increases very rapidly as the technology is better understood and firms pour more efforts into research and development. As the physical limits of the technology are reached and the returns to engineering efforts start to decrease, the rate of technical progress begins to diminish. A new technology able to overcome the physical limits of the old one will then trigger a new s-curve so that performance keeps improving with successive generations of S-curves. (See Exhibit 6.7.)

Technological progress of the last 30 years in the computer industry has been driven in large part by what has become known as Moore's law, for Intel co-founder Gordon Moore. In 1965, Moore predicted that the power and performance of microchips would double every 18 months as a function of semiconductor manufacturers' ability to double the number of transistors on a chip. This prediction has proven fairly accurate, and the rate of technical advance in microprocessor technology has in fact been exponential. These technological achievements are based on a strategy of continually shrinking the size of the

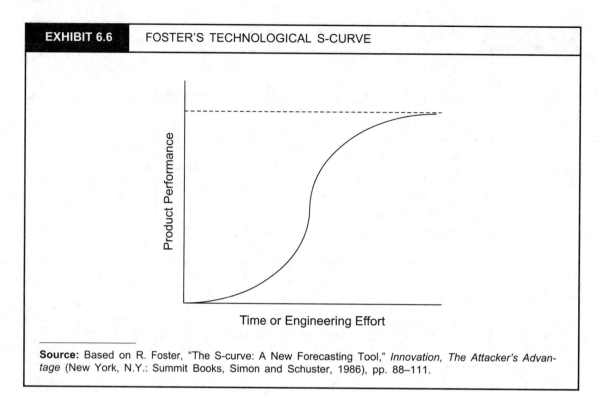

EXHIBIT 6.6   FOSTER'S TECHNOLOGICAL S-CURVE

Source: Based on R. Foster, "The S-curve: A New Forecasting Tool," *Innovation, The Attacker's Advantage* (New York, N.Y.: Summit Books, Simon and Schuster, 1986), pp. 88–111.

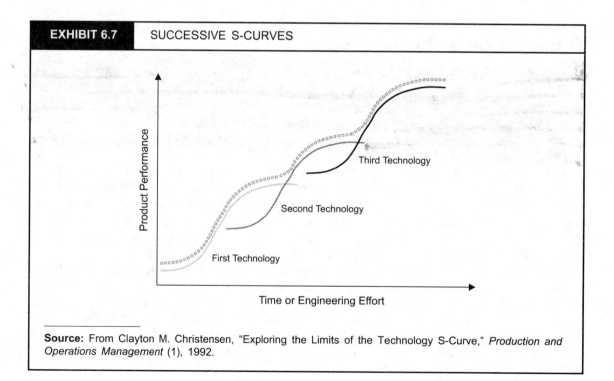

EXHIBIT 6.7   SUCCESSIVE S-CURVES

Source: From Clayton M. Christensen, "Exploring the Limits of the Technology S-Curve," *Production and Operations Management* (1), 1992.

transistors on chips so that electrons have less distance to travel, thereby speeding up the processing of data. As circuits get packed closer and closer on chips, however, they begin to overheat and performance suffers. This drop in performance signals that the current microchip technology is reaching the peak of its S-curve as the physical limits to shrinking transistor sizes are attained. In order for semiconductor firms like Intel and AMD to continue to generate performance improvements in line with Moore's law, a new technological discontinuity will have to replace the current strategy of miniaturization.

Several innovations are already in the works. One involves replacing a single high-speed processor with two or three that don't need to be as speedy, linked together on the same chip. A second, even more radical innovation entails stacking circuits in a three-dimensional manner and arranging chip functions vertically, rather than in a flat, horizontal design as current chips are configured. This technique promises to generate dramatic performance gains — some claim quantum leaps — and even reduce power consumption. Even though these innovations will require overhauling all the software running on chips and devising new methods for chip design and assembly, they may ultimately allow manufacturer to make the jump to the next technological S-curve and resume the phenomenal progress of Moore's law.

◼ CHAPTER SUMMARY

Competitive processes evolve in a remarkably predictable manner in most industries. Understanding what to expect and what drives evolution along the lifecycle of an industry is critical for managers needing to steer their organizations through turbulent times. In this chapter, we have identified the major phases and milestones that mark an industry's evolutionary path from introduction and growth to maturity and decline. At each stage of the industry lifecycle, the skills and capabilities needed to survive and grow change in significant ways. We have examined the nature of these changes as competition evolves in markets that go from fragmented and fast-growing to concentrated and declining. We have also considered the role played by technological innovation in the shaping of industry evolution. We have identified different models for the evolution of technology and discussed some tools for predicting the path of technological progress.

Trouble Brewing in Beer Industry

Under attack from wine and spirits makers, and chasing a shrinking customer base, brewers are waging a pitched price battle to stay alive.

Just before Christmas, John Sleeman, the man who runs Canada's third-largest brewery, committed an act he'd once hoped he would never be forced to do. He slashed the cost of his beer.

Ever since he dusted off a page from his grandfather's recipe book to start Sleeman Breweries Ltd. in 1988, he has tried to avoid the gutter price wars of the Canadian brewing industry. Better, not cheaper, was the Sleeman mantra. He put his brew in a stylish clear bottle and waxed on about his family's heritage and knack for making quality suds. There were no miniature plastic Stanley Cups to be found in cases of Sleeman Cream Ale.

[...] in October, Sleeman tried to raise the price of some of its flagship brands to nearly $42 for a case of 24 bottles. It quickly backtracked and put the price down to $40. Then, in December, it chopped the cost to $36. The sale ended after the holiday, but Sleeman temporarily brought back the discount in March to stimulate sales before Easter. "We're not in the cheap beer game," Mr. Sleeman says. But, he adds: "We found ourselves with not too much of an option there."

The Canadian beer industry has always had price battles, but they've rarely been quite like this. Under attack from wineries and liquor manufacturers, chasing after a shrinking customer base, brewers have elevated their fight for market share, with predictable effects on the bottom line. [...] The problems are numerous and, in some respects, intractable. Wine and hard liquor are gaining in popularity, partly because of demographics. Spirits manufacturers are taking advantage of relaxed government regulations with clever advertising and packaging that appeal to young people, the beer maker's core audience.

The two major domestic brewers, Molson Coors Brewing Co. and Labatt Brewing Co. Ltd., at first did what they always do to make up for lost volumes: They raised prices. But they raised them so high that they allowed discount brands to capture one-quarter of the Canadian market, by some estimates. A once-comfortable oligopoly now finds itself fighting regular skirmishes against smaller competitors who enjoy special tax advantages from provincial governments. [...] With beer sales stagnant — Bear Stearns thinks the U.S. market will grow less than 1 per cent this year, and Canada will be about the same — brewing is more than ever a market share game. As much as beer executives hate to cut prices, it's often a better option than cutting production.

The current dynamic is dangerous for Molson Coors, because its chief competitors in the United States and Canada — Anheuser-Busch Cos. Inc. and Belgium's InBev NV, Labatt's parent company — are larger, more efficient and capable of being vicious when it comes to keeping their customers. [...] But Molson Coors, like all beer makers, is fighting population trends as it tries to get bigger. A crucial customer segment — young men — is shrinking. In Canada, there are 325,000 fewer males between 20 and 34 than there were

15 years ago. Men in that age bracket now constitute just 10.5 per cent of the Canadian population, according to Statistics Canada, down from 13.5 per cent in 1989.

The result has been a shift in preferences, one that has boosted other forms of alcohol and more expensive imported beers such as Heineken. But diet has had an impact, too, and the perception exists that beer is the unhealthiest of the three major categories of booze.

Mr. Sleeman says part of the change can be traced back to a 1991 story by *60 Minutes* (on CBS) that documented the so-called "French paradox," which suggests the French live longer and suffer less heart disease because of their love of a fine Beaujolais. Wine sales began to climb "the next morning," recalls Mr. Sleeman, and they haven't stopped. In 2003, the average Canadian of legal drinking age consumed about 14.4 litres of wine, up 31 per cent from a decade earlier. Average beer consumption fell 5.5 per cent in that period.

If the wine makers had CBS on their side, liquor manufacturers benefited from changing laws and social mores. In 1995, the Federal Court of Canada struck down as unconstitutional a regulation banning hard liquor advertising on TV. The next year, Seagram Co. Ltd. broke a decades-old voluntary ban by American distillers, promoting its Crown Royal whisky on a Texas TV station. Still, it took a few years for the barriers to crumble. In 2001, NBC became the first major network to accept liquor ads. [...]

In Canada, liquor companies used to have to go to their provincial government for permission to sponsor an event at a bar. Those rules have been loosened, and spirits makers can even give out free samples of new products at liquor stores — which has aided sales of new inventions such as cranberry-flavoured vodka. "You can be 21 years old and you've got martini advertising that you never used to have before in bars and restaurants," Mr. Sleeman says. "The beer guys, we've all gotten lazy. We, as an industry, let them get ahead of us and now we're playing catch-up."

Then there's what Mr. Laboy of Bear Stearns calls the "*Sex and the City* effect." To have four attractive women drinking cosmopolitans on HBO's hit program had a meaningful impact on liquor's new appeal, the analyst says. And it continues even though the show is no longer making new episodes. Last month, Bacardi USA Inc. signed Kim Cattrall, who played a nymphomaniac named Samantha on the show, to promote a new line of "light spirits."

If the liquor industry has succeeded in creating a sexy image that attracts both men and women, beer makers have mostly stuck with their advertising formula of babes with large breasts and minimal clothing, with the result that most beer brands remain stuck with their narrow male demographic. "I love great-looking women in bikinis," Mr. Sleeman says. "But when half the population are great-looking women, why would you offend them?" Yet even Sleeman, which uses minimal sex imagery in its advertising, has struggled to capture the female drinker. Men still constitute at least 80 per cent of the buyers for even its most successful brands.

Some industry watchers argue that brewers have themselves to blame for their downbeat image. Accountants may love the Canadian brewers' deal to use the same, long-necked brown bottles for most of their brands because it saves millions in packaging costs. But since every bottle looks the same (with few exceptions), and the liquid often tastes the same, who can blame beer drinkers for concluding that most beers *are* the same, and buying the cheapest one?

"The Canadian brewers have been commoditizing themselves for 20 years," says Peter Holden, an analyst at Veritas Investment Research Corp. in Toronto. Bob Scott, a Toronto consultant who tracks the beer trade, is even more blunt: "There's been no innovation to talk of in the beer industry."

Slowly, this is changing. Molson, for example, is making a big bet on different packaging (Molson Canadian Cold Shots, a high-alcohol version of its biggest brand in a small silver can) and on Molson Kick, a lager with a caffeine additive that's available in an aluminum bottle. But it's not yet clear that these will be any more lasting than other beer inventions that sold well for a summer or two, then virtually disappeared. (Anyone for a Labatt Ice?)

An aluminum bottle won't address the domestic brewers' most serious problem, the cannibalization of higher-margin brands by cheap discounters like Hamilton-based Lakeport Brewing Corp. "We basically advertise that you can get a great-tasting beer at $24 for 24 plus deposit," says Lakeport CEO Teresa Cascioli, who this week filed documents with regulators to take her company public.

It's not that Lakeport is more efficient than the mega-brewers. Rather, it is small enough to qualify as a microbrewery under Ontario law, and gets preferential tax treatment. A micro that ships about 1.2 million cases a year in the province will pay a basic production tax of $3.1-million. Sleeman, Molson Coors and Labatt pay nearly $5.6-million to sell the same number of cases. [...]

There's no sign this will change. In fact, two years ago the Ontario government tweaked the tax regime to make it more favourable to small breweries. For the established beer companies, the options are to spend more on advertising or cut prices — or, in some cases, both. The only sure thing is that profit margins will get squeezed. "We've never had to do this before so it's a bit of a learning experience," Mr. Sleeman says. "But you really don't have much choice unless you're prepared to lose market share."

Source: By Derek DeCloet. Reproduced with permission from *The Globe and Mail* (May 7, 2005).

QUESTIONS

1. What stage of the lifecycle is the beer brewing industry in? Please explain and justify.

2. What strategies are available to Molson-Coors for dealing with declining sales, and what do you recommend they do?

3. How can Sleeman Breweries respond to discount beer competitors like Lakeport Brewing?

Fuel Cell: Juice for Buses, and Laptops?

In the next 20 years, it is still possible that fuel cell technology will help to revolutionize the transportation sector by replacing the internal combustion engine in both cars and buses.

Ballard Power Systems Inc., the world's leading fuel cell developer, is sticking to previous forecasts that the technology it is preparing for the global automotive sector will be commercially viable by 2010.

But even major players like Burnaby, B.C.-based Ballard say it is more likely the public will be using fuel cells for backup power in their homes and to recharge their laptop computers and cellphones before they are driving around in fuel cell cars.

The mood of caution marks a departure from the rosy predictions made eight years ago when Ford Motor Co. and DaimlerChrysler AG bought a 30-per-cent stake in Ballard, vowing to have 100,000 fuel cell vehicles on the road by 2005.

The shift can be attributed to a number of factors, including the relatively high cost of fuel cell stacks in comparison to existing technology, the need to ease public concerns about the safety of hydrogen fuel, and the challenge in overcoming regulatory hurdles barring the use of such devices in homes and businesses. "What is still missing is a fundamental breakthrough on the issue of costs," said Felix Pilorusso, a Toronto auto industry consultant who has written on the subject.

Ballard and its auto industry partners have proven that they can build cars and buses powered by fuel cells that yield electricity, heat and water by catalyzing the reaction of oxygen and hydrogen.

What they have yet to do is produce a fuel cell with the right combination of features that would enable it to fit under the hood of a car, yet still be capable of delivering power, acceleration and durability at a cost that drivers can afford. The 150 Ballard-powered fuel cell cars and buses that are expected to enter field trials around the world by the end of next year would cost over $1-million each if they were available to be bought in showrooms.

Even if they can deliver on promises to be in a position to start commercial production in 2010, firms like Ballard and General Motors Corp. still face challenges associated with producing the hydrogen fuel. That includes replacing the existing network of gasoline stations with a hydrogen refuelling infrastructure, at an estimated minimum cost of around $500-million.

Industry analysts are betting that fuel cells are more likely to become widely used in applications such as backup power and cellphone recharging, where convenience takes precedence over the cost of the energy being consumed. "Widespread adoption of fuel cells, and their long-term commercial viability, depend heavily on their rate of adoption in the portable market," said Jim Balcom, president of PolyFuel Inc., a Mountain View, Calif., maker of fuel cell membranes.

As a result, he said, the rate of commercialization depends on consumer demand for longer run times on their portable devices, and the manufacturing of increasingly power-hungry applications such as wireless connectivity in notebooks, and full-motion video into cellphones. Portable power applications could operate using disposable cartridges that would provide fuel to the fuel cell, therefore eliminating battery recharge time and reliance on an electricity source.

Meanwhile, Ballard is working on what it terms the commercial launch of one-kilowatt co-generation units that the company is supplying to Tokyo Gas for use as a replacement for a hot water boiler in Japanese homes. "We have high expectations for this product in the next five years," said Ballard spokesman Mike Rosenberg.

As Japan moves to diversify its energy resources sector by subsidizing the use of the fuel cell power generator, Ballard said it expects to have thousands of co-generation units in the field by 2007, ramping up to tens of thousands by 2008.

Source: By Peter Kennedy. Reproduced with permission from *The Globe and Mail* (May 26, 2005).

QUESTIONS

1. Is the hydrogen-powered fuel cell a technological discontinuity? According to the Anderson and Tushman model, at which stage of the cycle are fuel cells in? Please explain and justify.

2. Are fuel cells competence-enhancing or competence-destroying? For whom?

3. Draw an S-curve diagram showing the technological transition from internal combustion engines to fuel cell stacks in automobiles.

4. What phase of the industry lifecycle is the automobile industry in, and how will fuel cells affect its evolution?

The Global Environment

7

What are some of the fundamental sources of influence on the decision to engage in global business? In addition to addressing this question, this chapter will identify the different types of global business activity. We will examine one of the central controversies of globalization: the multinational corporation. This chapter will also explain why nations desire, or do not desire, to promote international trade, including an examination of the pros and cons of Canada's free trade agreement with the United States.

LEARNING OBJECTIVES

By the end of the chapter, you should be able to:

1. Define the notion of globalization.
2. Identify factors that have encouraged the globalization of business.
3. Describe the central channels or forms of global business activity.
4. Discuss the importance and consequences of multinational and borderless corporations.
5. Explain the purpose of protectionism and its relationship with international trade.
6. Identify the types of regional economic integration.
7. Discuss the purpose of NAFTA and its consequences.

I am grateful to Elena Varavina and Shu-Hui Huang, who contributed Talking Business 7.1 and Talking Business 7.2, respectively, to this chapter.

The Business World ─────────────────────────────

Is Canada for Sale?

Maybe we should just put a big "Canada For Sale" sign in the middle of the country. More and more, we seem to be losing ownership and control of our businesses to foreign acquisitors and there seems to be little concern. Right now, there are three bids for well-known or promising Canadian companies:

Vincor International Inc. is one of the world's top 10 wine companies, with significant production in the wine country of the Niagara Peninsula and the Okanagan Valley. It also has wine-producing operations in the U.S., New Zealand and South Africa. Now, a U.S. company, Constellation Brands Inc. wants to take it over. But why does Vincor need to be sold to a giant U.S. corporation instead of continuing to grow as a successful Canadian company?

Then there's ID Biomedical Corp., the high-flying Vancouver-based vaccine company whose flu vaccine, Fluviral, is likely to win U.S. approval for sale there in 2006.

One of the very few success stories in Canada's efforts to build a life sciences industry, ID Biomedical is now the takeover target [of] GlaxoSmithKline PLC, one of the world's largest pharmaceutical manufacturers. But what's the point of Canadian taxpayers providing more than $1 billion to support life sciences research in Canada if this money simply provides new products for foreign life science companies instead of building Canadian enterprises?

Hudson Bay Co., whose holdings include two of the shrinking list of national Canadian retailers, The Bay and Zellers, is the takeover target of U.S. financier Jerry Zucker. Clearly the company needs help, but where are the MBAs graduating from our business schools?

According to Investment Canada, 9,751 Canadian companies have been acquired by foreign investors since mid-1985 for just over $300 billion; in contrast, there have been only 3,495 instances where foreign investors have invested to start new business activities in Canada — the kind of foreign investment we really want, such as Toyota's recent decision to build a new plant in Canada — for a total investment of only $18 billion over 20 years.

In an era of globalization, every country will have a mix of domestically controlled and foreign-controlled companies. But few countries have such a high level of foreign takeovers as Canada. When a Canadian company of promise is sold to a foreign investor, it loses its potential to become a world-scale leader and instead becomes just part of a foreign corporation that aspires to global leadership.

For example, one of Canada's leading high-tech companies, Creo Inc., had positioned itself to be a world leader in digital printing systems. But it was taken over earlier this year by Eastman Kodak Co. in the United States. Kodak stressed that its takeover of Creo marked "another significant step in our journey to become the global leader in graphic communications." Creo is now just a branch of someone else's global aspiration instead of becoming the global leader itself.

Much of the action on takeovers is in Canada's energy industry, where for-eign, mainly American, investors have been buying control of an array of Cana-dian oil and gas companies. Much of Canada's oil-sands activity could end up under foreign control.

If Canada is to become a global player, active in China and India, as well as Europe, Russia and Latin America, then it must have business ventures and business executives in Canada with real decision-making power to develop as global players. When they become subsidiaries of foreign corporations, compa-nies in Canada lose real decision-making power. This was evident in the 2002 takeover of Westcoast Energy Inc. by Duke Energy in the U.S. Westcoast was a growing Canadian multinational, with energy projects in Mexico and China, as well as in Canada. But since its takeover, the Canadian subsidiary is relegated to running just its Canadian assets.

Canadian-controlled companies are also important because Canadian head-quarters support a wide array of business and other services, providing good jobs in our cities, and because they enable talented Canadians to pursue mean-ingful high-level jobs in Canada. So if we want a successful economy that can participate in the 21st century global economy, Industry Minister David Emerson should strike a task force to investigate why we are losing control of many of our most promising businesses and to identify what can be done about it.

Source: Reproduced with permission from David Crane, "Ottawa should probe loss of so many promising firms," *The Toronto Star* (November 4, 2005).

WHAT IS GLOBALIZATION?

"The Business World" highlights the new business world — one that involves many more players than local business and its domestic market. Business in the global context involves many stakeholders, including domestic and foreign competitors, workers, industries, governments, national cultures and economies. How business is conducted in light of trade agreements and global arrangements is a key issue for our entire society. And this is a theme we will explore more fully in this chapter.

While you may have heard or read about this popular buzzword, many of you may not be completely familiar with what it represents and its implications. What is globalization? While there is no one, universal definition, it is useful to consider this concept as a process.

Globalization is a process involving the integration of world economies. The presence of trade blocs reflects the accelerating pace with which nations are integrating their economies. For example, NAFTA, the North American Free Trade Agreement, discussed later in this chapter, is a free-trade bloc consisting of Canada, the United States and Mexico. The EU (European Union) groups 25 countries, while APEC (Asian Pacific Economic Cooperation) consists of 21 nations forming a free-trade zone around the Pacific.

Globalization is a process involving the integration of world markets. This reflects the notion that consumer preferences are converging around the world. Whether it is for products made by McDonald's, Sony, Gap or Nike, organizations are increasingly marketing their goods and services worldwide. Though local modifications may be made to tailor the product to the local consumers, there is a push toward global products. On the other side, production is increasingly becoming a global affair. Businesses will set up operations wherever it is least costly to do so.

In sum, the recurrent themes raised in any discussion of globalization tend to include elements of the following:

- Globalization can be considered a process that is expanding the degree and forms of cross-border transactions among people, assets, goods and services.
- Globalization refers to the growth in direct foreign investment in regions across the world.
- Globalization reflects the shift toward increasing economic interdependence: the process of generating one, single, world economic system or a global economy.

SOURCES ENCOURAGING GLOBAL BUSINESS ACTIVITY

Why have we witnessed a tremendous surge in business activity on an international scale? From giant multinational corporations to small businesses, in recent years the drive toward global business has accelerated. A number of fundamental factors have encouraged the move to "go global." Some factors can be considered **pull factors**, and are the reasons a business would gain from entering the international context. Other factors are **push factors** — these are forces that act upon all businesses to create an environment where competing successfully means competing globally. (See Exhibit 7.1.)

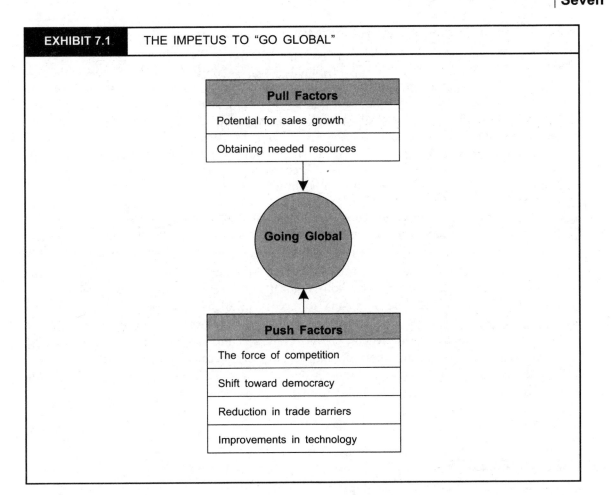

| EXHIBIT 7.1 | THE IMPETUS TO "GO GLOBAL" |

Pull Factors

Potential for sales growth

Obtaining needed resources

Going Global

Push Factors

The force of competition

Shift toward democracy

Reduction in trade barriers

Improvements in technology

Pull Factors

Potential for Sales Growth

A fundamental reason for engaging in global operations is to help a business expand its markets. Increased sales are typically the central aim behind a company's expansion into international business. A significant portion of sales among the world's largest firms are generated from outside the home country. For example, U.S.-based specialty coffee chain, Starbucks Corp., began expanding operations in Europe almost a decade ago (especially in Vienna). The potential for increased sales was clearly a pull factor, a key question was, Would consumers in this European culture be attracted to this American business? Starbucks' aim was to provide a more modern version of the relaxed atmosphere of the Viennese café in order to attract this new consumer segment. Clearly, having the world as your market offers almost limitless potential beyond domestic consumers. Having

245

access to foreign consumers also may mitigate the negative effects of domestic downturns in demand for the businesses' product or service. Consider, for example, the case of Avon Products Inc. This organization faced declining sales in North American markets, largely due to its traditional marketing channel (door-to-door sales), which failed to address the increased entry of women into the workplace and away from the home. On the other hand, Avon was able to successfully transfer its approach globally to over 20 emerging markets, including China, Brazil, South Africa and Mexico.

Obtaining Needed Resources

Businesses may choose to engage in global business activity in order to obtain resources that are either unavailable or too costly within the domestic borders. Acquiring foreign imports is a case of obtaining needed resources. It could be the case that a textile manufacturer imports its raw materials from a foreign supplier because these materials are not available locally. As well, the decision to locate businesses or plants in developing or underdeveloped nations may be a means to access inexpensive labour. For example, to access less expensive energy resources, a number of Japanese businesses have located in China, Mexico and Taiwan, where energy costs are not as high. Both Canadian and U.S. firms continue to expand their operations overseas because they can achieve higher rates of return on their investments, largely due to lower labour costs. (See Talking Business 7.1.)

Push Factors

The Force of Competition

Many domestic economies have become inundated with competing products or services. Typically, a business that seeks to grow needs to consider the markets beyond its domestic borders: this is where new, and potentially untapped, market opportunities still exist. Ironically, domestic economies are increasingly being filled with foreign competitors in many industries. The fact is, a business may find that it must compete against not merely domestic competitors, but foreign competitors as well. By default, a business may be *pushed* into becoming a global business by the simple fact that it is forced to compete with a foreign competitor. Moreover, for some businesses it seems foolhardy not to combat the foreign competition by attempting to go after the competitor's market overseas. In other words, the drive to "go global" may be a response to competitors' actions.

In addition, other domestic competitors may be expanding their markets overseas, which creates additional incentive for the business to follow suit. The notion of **first mover advantage** is a philosophy that underscores the benefits of being among the first to establish strong positions in important world markets. Later entrants into a foreign market may have more difficulty establishing themselves, and may even be effectively blocked by competitors.

TALKING BUSINESS 7.1   MADE IN CHINA

China's role is increasingly important in the world economy, and its growing role raises questions for the country itself and the world. China sees globalization as a key to its economic development and a better future for its people. Rapid growth has had a dramatic impact on the lives of millions of Chinese citizens. The success can be measured by tens of millions of people who have escaped poverty in China in the past decade or more. China's sheer size, coupled with its rapid growth, makes it a major player in the global economy. In nominal terms, China currently accounts for almost 4% of world output. By the end of 2004, China had attracted a total of $562.1 billion in foreign direct investment, approved the establishment of more than 500,000 foreign-funded enterprises in China, and created a huge import market of about $560 billion annually. As *The Economist* (August 5, 2005) reported, "Beijing, not Washington, increasingly takes the decisions that affect workers, companies, financial markets and economies everywhere." Consequently, both the United States and Canada have to come to terms with the emergence of China as a major nation. China's fast development has brought not only great opportunities for China but challenges for the rest of the world. Some producers see Chinese competition as a threat. They worry about competitive Chinese exports flooding their markets and destroying jobs. However, this is what globalization is about: a major realignment of power and capacities in the world, as not only China but other countries become more important, and more influential. The world's economies are becoming increasingly interdependent.

Shift Toward Democracy

The shift toward democracy among many societies that were formerly economically and politically repressed has contributed to the creation of new market opportunities. Numerous totalitarian regimes have been transformed in Eastern Europe and Asia, for example, which has created new economic opportunities for businesses in other parts of the world. Countries like Russia and Poland have shifted toward a more capitalistic and democratic approach. Perhaps one symbol of this acceptance was the success of the North American McDonald's in entering the Russian marketplace years ago. Similarly, there has been a great interest in foreign investment in China since its move toward privatization — reduction in government ownership — in many areas.

Reduction in Trade Barriers

In recent years it has been observed that global business activities have been growing at a faster rate than in previous years, and in comparison to growth in domestic business. This acceleration may be largely due to the general push toward freer trade. In fact, probably the most powerful source of influence encouraging increased international business is the reduction in trade and investment restrictions. For example, the North American

Free Trade Agreement (NAFTA) was established as an agreement to remove trade barriers between Canada, the United States and Mexico. This agreement essentially aimed to produce a common market among the members. Later in this chapter we will consider in more detail the nature of NAFTA, as well as a number of other important trade agreements.

Improvements in Technology

Another fundamental source of influence on globalization has been technology. Advancements in technology have more efficiently facilitated cross-border transactions. Innovations in information technology, as well as advances in transportation, have made it increasingly easy to transfer information, products, services, capital and human resources around the world. E-mail, the Internet, teleconferencing, faxing and transatlantic supersonic travel were among the activities that were not available until the late part of the 20th century.

Electronic commerce, or e-commerce, has been relatively free from government control, and this flexibility has contributed to the rate of globalization and the generation of virtual global organizations. Virtual organizations increasingly exist at the global level, where the geographic sources of the product or service and the location of the workforce are unimportant.

CHANNELS OF GLOBAL BUSINESS ACTIVITY

There are a variety of ways that businesses engage in global business. While practically any connection a business has with a foreign country essentially constitutes a form of global business, the degree of involvement of a business with a foreign country can vary. Below, we highlight various channels or forms within which businesses operate in the global sense. At a lower level of interconnectedness, a business can simply export or import goods or services to or from other countries. At a somewhat higher level, a company may choose to outsource some aspect of its business operations; it may choose to license some aspect or, perhaps, even arrange for franchise operations in foreign territory. Forming a strategic alliance or creating a joint venture with a foreign company requires the business to become more fully entrenched in the global context via directly investing in a foreign country. This can take the form of a merger, acquisition, the creation of a subsidiary or some other forms of direct investment in foreign operations. Each of these possible channels is discussed following. (See Exhibit 7.2.)

Exporting and Importing

Businesses that engage in international business are more likely to be involved in importing and exporting than in any other type of global business activity. In addition to selling our goods or services to other countries, Canadian businesses may also purchase goods or

EXHIBIT 7.2	CHANNELS OF GLOBAL ACTIVITY

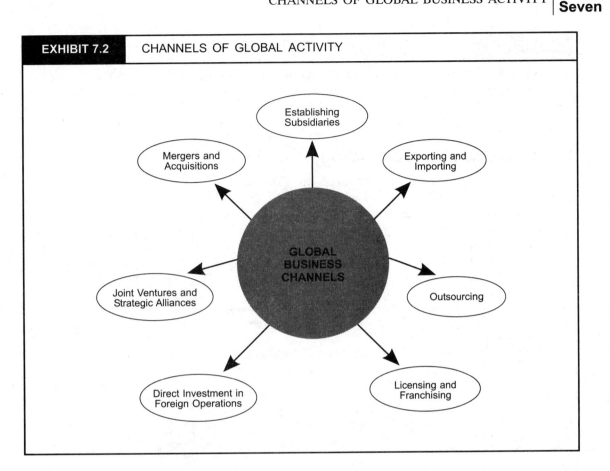

services from foreign countries for resale to Canadians. Merchandise exports are tangible goods transferred out of the country, while merchandise imports are goods brought into the country. On the other hand, businesses might deal in service exports or imports of services. For example, banking, insurance or management services can be performed at an international level. Another type of service export or import can involve the use of a company's assets, including things like patents, trademarks, copyrights or expertise. The use of such assets constitutes a service rather than the provision of a tangible good, and is typically arranged through a licensing agreement. We discuss this channel of global business later on.

Exporting certainly offers much additional profitable activity for businesses, and the business opportunities available through exporting are significant. While there are about 30 million potential customers within our Canadian borders, there are over 6 billion potential customers across the world, increasing by about 95 million people annually. Many Canadian businesses have taken advantage of the benefits of exporting. Canada exports over 40% of our production, making us a major trading nation. (See Exhibits 7.3 and 7.4 for recent trade patterns.)

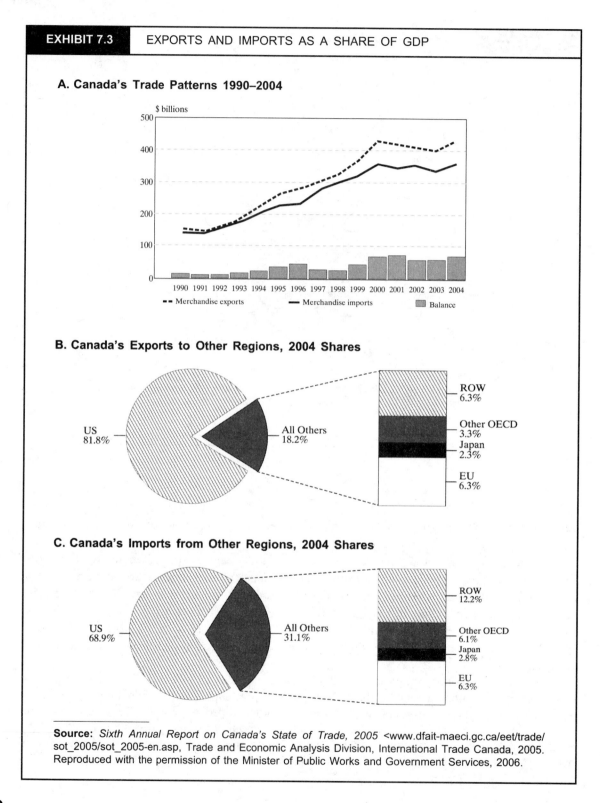

EXHIBIT 7.3   EXPORTS AND IMPORTS AS A SHARE OF GDP

A. Canada's Trade Patterns 1990–2004

$ billions

- - Merchandise exports   — Merchandise imports   ▨ Balance

B. Canada's Exports to Other Regions, 2004 Shares

US 81.8%

All Others 18.2%

ROW 6.3%

Other OECD 3.3%

Japan 2.3%

EU 6.3%

C. Canada's Imports from Other Regions, 2004 Shares

US 68.9%

All Others 31.1%

ROW 12.2%

Other OECD 6.1%

Japan 2.8%

EU 6.3%

Source: *Sixth Annual Report on Canada's State of Trade, 2005* <www.dfait-maeci.gc.ca/eet/trade/ sot_2005/sot_2005-en.asp, Trade and Economic Analysis Division, International Trade Canada, 2005. Reproduced with the permission of the Minister of Public Works and Government Services, 2006.

EXHIBIT 7.4	CANADA'S INTERNATIONAL TRADING PARTNERS

	Exports to	Imports from	CDIA*	FDI**
U.S.	348.2	208.9	164.9	228.4
Japan	8.5	13.4	9.1	9.7
U.K.	7.6	9.6	40.7	27.1
China (excl. HK)	6.6	24.1	0.5	0.4
Mexico	3.0	13.4	2.8	0.1
Germany	2.7	9.4	7.8	7.3
France	2.4	5.3	11.6	31.6
Italy	1.7	4.6	1.6	1.0
Brazil	1.0	2.3	7.6	0.8
India	0.9	1.6	0.2	0.1
Chile	0.4	1.3	5.9	n/a
Korea	2.3	5.8	0.6	0.3
Australia	1.6	1.7	7.8	2.0
World	411.4	355.2		

Merchandise exports and imports from 2004, CDIA/FDI from 2003
All data in billions of Canadian dollars

* Stock of Canadian Direct Investment Abroad; ** Stock of Foreign Direct Investment in Canada
CDIA — Canadian direct investment abroad; FDI — foreign direct investment in Canada

Source: *Canada's International Policy Statement: A Role of Pride and Influence in the World — Commerce* <http://itcan-cican.gc.ca/IPS/IPS-commerce03-en.asp#13>, International Trade Canada, 2005. Reproduced with the permission of Her Majesty the Queen in Right of Canada, represented by the Minister for International Trade, 2005.

According to International Trade Canada:

> Canada is the most open of the globe's major economies. We are the world's fifth largest exporter and importer-trade is equivalent to more than 70% of our gross domestic product (GDP). Exports account for almost 40% of our economy, and are linked to one-quarter of all Canadian jobs ... Exports allow Canadian companies to keep generating jobs and remain productive and competitive by selling their goods and services more broadly than in our relatively small domestic market. Imports give our consumers choice and reduce costs, and provide our farmers and manufacturers with inputs and productivity-enhancing technologies. Investment and the movement of people in both directions favour innovation, business and personal growth, and competitiveness. International commerce is the lifeblood of our economy.[1]

Statistics Canada reports indicate that Canada is the United States' most important trading partner, and for many years, the United States has been Canada's largest trading partner. Since 1989, Canada–U.S. trade has almost tripled from $235.2 billion to $677.8 billion in 2002. By the 21st century, the United States accounted for over 80% of Canada's total exports, compared to 71.1% in 1989. Currently, Canada exports more of its manufacturing output to the United States than it consumes domestically. While Mexico

251

still accounts for a relatively small share of our trade, trade with that country has grown greatly, and Mexico is now Canada's fourth largest trading partner.[2]

Observers have noted that while the bulk of our exports continue to go to the United States, distributing patterns of change have emerged. As a 2006 *Maclean's* magazine report noted:

> In 1993, 74 per cent of all Canadian exports went to the United States; by 2005, that figure had risen to 84 per cent. And yet ... even as our U.S.-bound exports have gone up, their profile has been changing, and not for the better: we are becoming more hewers of wood and drawers of water, not less so. We are sending the Americans more and more raw commodities (oil, natural gas, metals and other resources) and a smaller proportion of manufactured goods. Trade in services (everything from call centres to financial services), never strong to begin with, has also seen a relative decline. Services exports now stand at 12.5 per cent of our total, well below the OECD average of 22 per cent. This trend is particularly worrisome: the services sector now makes up two-thirds of our domestic economy, yet we haven't figured out how to export it. A whole segment of potential export growth and wealth creation is going unfulfilled.[3]

Outsourcing

Contracting out, or outsourcing, was discussed in an earlier chapter of this book. As you may recall, outsourcing involves hiring external organizations to conduct work in certain functions of the company: so, for example, payroll, accounting, and legal work can be assigned to outsourced staff. The organization typically will retain its core functions or competencies: that is, those areas that it is in business to conduct. Nike is well-known for its use of outsourcing on an international basis. Nike has typically entered into contractual arrangements with manufacturers in developing nations to produce its footwear while it focuses largely on marketing its product. In fact, this has been a major underlying source of controversy with regard to businesses "going global" — the fear that relatively higher-paying North American jobs will be lost as business decides to outsource manufacturing functions to cheaply paid labour in Third World countries. (See Talking Business 7.2.) Countries can be contracted for the production of finished goods or component parts, and these goods or parts can subsequently be imported to the home country or to other countries for further assembly or sale.

India is one example cited as a major offshore or outsourced location. As observed by one writer:

> Globalization has played a significant role in India's rise as an economic force. It is also the foundation behind the country's success in the outsourcing industry ... One of the biggest beneficiaries of this "openness" is the outsourcing industry. Today, no company with outsourcing plans does not have India on its laundry list. India was able to achieved self-sufficiency not by closing its doors to the world. Rather, it spread the word across the world of how easy it is to do business in India.[4]

Offshoring and Canada. The following *Globe and Mail* article by David Ticoll offers an interesting and disturbing insight into outsourcing in Canada:

TALKING BUSINESS **7.2   MADE IN TAIWAN**

Dell and Hewlett-Packard outsourced high-tech work to Taiwan that valued $10 billion and $21 billion respectively in 2005. Currently, Taiwanese engineers offer innovative solutions for customers seeking design and manufacturing outsourcing. In fact, Taiwan has become so strong in this field that some observers suggest that it is really the Taiwanese who are outsourcing the marketing and branding of their products to the rest of the world. Taiwan has developed dramatically from the poor and lowly provider of components and assembled machines to that of a leading innovator in the electronics industry. Currently, its companies are increasingly expert at original design, and they typically dominate manufacturing in central categories such as LCD screens, notebook computers, and modems. Taiwan's success has been attributed to several sources, including its lower pay scales. For example, its engineering costs are approximately one third of comparable services in the United States. In addition, assembly line wages average about $120 a month in Taiwan-owned factories on the mainland. However, many observers are quick to point out that Taiwan's strength is not simply based on cheap labour but on its entrepreneurial culture combined with effective government involvement. Taiwan has grown from a provider of cheap labour and products to one of the most talented sources of high-tech expertise in the world.

Source: Based on Bruce Einhorn, with Matt Kovac in Taipei, Pete Engardio in New York, Dexter Roberts in Beijing, "Why Taiwan Matters" *Business Week* (May 16, 2005) 3933: 76.

It looks like Canada may soon join the growing political firestorm raised by the transfer of information technology jobs to places such as India and the Philippines. Last week, offshore outsourcing, as the phenomenon is called, was among several issues that placed U.S. President George W. Bush on the campaign defensive. The topic is also hotly debated in Britain and Australia. Anecdotal evidence suggests that Canada will be next.

Companies elect to go with outsourcing — and offshore outsourcing in particular — for good business reasons. They enjoy cost savings on application development, for example, ranging from 35 to 70 per cent. They gain access to staff with specialized skills that they may lack internally. Thanks to strong project management disciplines, outsourcing firms often deliver quality results, and fast. The downside, of course, is the impact on a company's staff. Sometimes workers are protected, because the outsourced work is incremental to what they already do. Other times, the outsourcing firm hires a company's staff as part of the deal. But there are also times when people lose their jobs. One widely quoted 2002 estimate, from Forrester Research, predicted that 3.2 million U.S. services jobs would move offshore over the next 15 years.

A striking — and heretofore unreported — clue to the rise of outsourcing in this country comes from Industry Canada's quarterly statistical report on the information technology and communications sector. The latest study, published in December, shows services employment in the sector fell for the first three quarters of 2003, by a total of 2.6 per cent. This loss of about 7,000 jobs is unprecedented, and occurred during a job boom in the economy. Consulting and technical support by IT firms has consistently been a growth business. Never before have so many IT services jobs vanished, nor have such losses occurred over such an extended period.

Industry Canada analysts aren't sure why. But they suspect offshoring may have something to do with it. They plan to investigate this theory over the coming months.

If this theory turns out to be true, it will be striking evidence. After all, most jobs that migrate offshore aren't exported by IT firms, but by their clients in other sectors — banking, manufacturing, and so on. A bank, for example, concludes it can save call centre costs in India. It hires a North American or Indian IT services firm to handle it.

... What's the right thing to do? The answer is neither simple nor obvious. The anti-offshoring camp decries firms for caring only about profit. They shamelessly dump loyal employees. They submit them to the humiliation of training their own replacements. On a larger scale, the argument goes, we moved manufacturing jobs to China based on the theory that our economy needs more knowledge-intensive professions. Now that such jobs are moving offshore, it looks scary. We may all end up working at Wal-Mart.

The pro-offshoring camp has answers. Offshoring delivers a multiple return on investment. This creates capital for more promising ventures and demand for the next wave of innovative jobs. Consumers will pay less for goods and services. Places such as India prosper and grow as export markets for North American goods. Another line of argument says: Hey — why should rich countries have all the good jobs? Offshoring is a step in the direction of global justice. This is free trade at its best ...[5]

Licensing and Franchising Arrangements

The licensing agreement is an arrangement whereby the owner of a product or process is paid a fee or royalty from another company in return for granting permission to produce or distribute the product or process. How could this be a type of global business activity? For example, a Canadian company might grant a foreign company permission to produce its product; or conversely, perhaps a Canadian company wishes to distribute a foreign-made product in Canada and requires a licensing agreement.

Why might a business enter into licensing agreements? Essentially, companies that don't wish to set up actual production or marketing operations overseas can let the foreign business conduct these activities and simply collect royalties. Whether it is for licensing fees or for management consulting services between two companies from different countries, the fees paid to foreign firms in return for the performance of a service would constitute service imports. Fees earned by businesses through providing such services would constitute service exports.

Franchising shares some of the advantages of licensing, in that both are relatively lower risk forms of global business. Franchising is, of course, a common type of business activity in Canada and elsewhere. This becomes a global business activity when the franchises are scattered in different locations around the world. (See Exhibit 7.5 for a list of global franchises.) While franchising is discussed elsewhere in this book, it is sufficient to note here that franchising involves drafting a contract between a supplier (franchiser) and a dealer (franchisee) that stipulates how the supplier's product or service will be sold. The franchisee is the dealer (usually the owner of a small business), who is permitted to

| EXHIBIT 7.5 | AMERICA'S TOP 10 GLOBAL FRANCHISES FOR 2006 |

1. Subway
2. The Quizno's Franchise Co.
3. Curves
4. The UPS Store
5. Jackson Hewitt Tax Service
6. Dunkin' Donuts
7. Jani-King
8. RE/MAX Int'l. Inc.
9. 7-Eleven Inc.
10. Liberty Tax Service

Source: *Entrepreneur Magazine* Web site <http://www.entrepreneur.com/franchise500/index.htm>l

sell the goods/services of the franchiser (the supplier) in exchange for some payment (e.g., flat fee, future royalties/commissions, future advertising fees). Probably one of the best-known international franchises is McDonald's, which licenses its trademark, its fast-food products and operating principles to franchisees worldwide in return for an initial fee and ongoing royalties. In return, McDonald's franchisees receive the benefit of McDonald's reputation, its management and marketing expertise.

A recent *Entrepreneur Magazine* article observed:

> With all that's going on in the world, with all the anti-American sentiment, with all the anger directed toward U.S. franchises specifically, are there any people who are still interested in buying and opening franchises internationally? In a word, yes. Even after 9/11, the war in Iraq and the general global unease, one truth still holds: Franchising has proven to be one of the best marketing and expansion methods ever created. And while American franchises may be seen by a few as symbols of American greed, the majority still associates franchise brands with business success and economic development — even hope — worldwide. Why the popularity of international franchising? ... More than simply liking the concepts, these franchisees desire the advantages U.S. franchises provide. "The consumer perception gives the international franchisee a better base to start with, as many American brands enjoy universal brand recognition" says Bob Kendzior, vice president of international marketing and retail concepts for Allied Domecq Quick Service Restaurants, franchisor of Baskin-Robbins, Dunkin' Donuts and Togo's.[6]

Direct Investment in Foreign Operations

Foreign direct investment (FDI) involves the purchase of physical assets or an amount of ownership in a company from another country in order to gain a measure of management control. Capital can be invested in factories, inventories and capital goods or other assets.

255

**TALKING BUSINESS 7.3   CANADA'S CLOSE RELATIONSHIP WITH
THE UNITED STATES**

Our close relationship with the United States is reflected in the following observations
from Internal Trade Canada:

- Canada and the United States exchange some $1.8 billion in goods and services
  every day of the year — well over $1 million a minute.
- A truck crosses the border every two seconds.
- On average about 300,000 people cross the border each day.
- The United States is the largest source of foreign direct investment for Canada,
  responsible for over 65% of total FDI in Canada.
- The United States is the principal destination of Canadian direct investment abroad,
  accounting for over 43% of the total.
- The Government assists more than 16,000 companies annually in the U.S.
  marketplace, the vast majority of them small and medium-sized firms.

Source: *Canada's International Policy Statement: A Role of Pride and Influence in the World — Commerce* <http://itcan-cican.gc.ca/IPS/IPS-commerce02-en.asp#3>, International Trade Canada, 2005.
Reproduced with the permission of Her Majesty the Queen in Right of Canada, represented by the
Minister for International Trade, 2005.

Control of a company can be achieved without necessarily owning 100%, or even 50%, interest. A direct investment can be done through acquisition of an already existing business in the host country or through a startup built "from scratch," so to speak. The choice may be dependent on a number of factors, including the availability of suitable businesses in the host country. If a suitable business already exists in the host country, it may prove more efficient than starting up a business there from scratch. It is no surprise that the vast majority (about 90%) of all FDI stems from developed countries, given that business in these countries will more likely have sufficient resources to invest overseas. Foreign direct investment in Canada is the second highest in the G7 as a share of GDP. (See Talking Business 7.3 regarding Canada's relationship with the United States.) In addition, Canadian investments abroad are the third largest in the G7 as a share of GDP.[7] (See Exhibit 7.6 for an illustration of foreign direct investment in Canada.)

Throughout the 1990s, we observed a growth in foreign ownership in the Canadian business context. Toward the end of the 1990s, foreign firms controlled about 22% of assets in Canada, which is a modest growth from 20.5% in 1994. In 1998, foreign firms accounted for 31.7% of all corporate operating revenues, compared to 29.4% in 1994. More recently, a report in Statistics Canada noted the following trends:

> Canadian firms acquired foreign companies at a faster pace than foreign firms were acquiring companies in Canada. Between 1997 and 2002, Canadian firms acquired 447 foreign companies, transactions which are called "outward," while foreign compa-

EXHIBIT 7.6	FOREIGN DIRECT INVESTMENT IN CANADA, 1994–2003 CUMULATIVE AT YEAR END

Year	$Cdn Billions
1994	154.6
1995	168.2
1996	182.1
1997	194.3
1998	219.4
1999	252.6
2000	319.1
2001	341.0
2002	348.9
2003	357.5

Notes:

- Direct Investment represents the investment which allows an investor to have a significant voice in the management of an enterprise operating outside his own economy. For operational purposes, a direct investor usually has an ownership of at least 10% in an enterprise.
- An enterprise comprises Subsidiaries (direct investor owns more than 50%), Associates (direct investor owns 50% or less) and Branches (wholly or jointly-owned unincorporated enterprises).
- Control generally includes subsidiaries and branches, but may also include enterprises, on a case-by-case basis, with between 10% and 50% ownership by one company, group or individual where Statistics Canada ascribes the exercise of effective control.
- Direct Investment is measured as the total of the equity, long-term claims and the short-term claims of non-bank enterprises of the direct investor in the enterprise. It does not include bonds, bank loans or portfolio investments.

Source: Excerpted from "Foreign Investors Choose Canada" <www.2ontario.com/welcome/bcin_500.asp>. Reproduced with permission.

nies acquired 345 Canadian companies, so-called "inward" transactions. ... Between 1997 and 2002, foreign companies acquired $144 billion worth of Canadian companies, while Canadian firms acquired $124 billion of foreign companies. ... Europe edged out the United States as the largest acquirer of Canadian companies during the six-year period. ... in all years other than 2000, the United States invested significantly more through acquisitions in Canada than did Europe. The United States was the primary destination for acquisitions, accounting for over two-thirds of all outward mergers and acquisitions. Canada was a net acquirer of U.S. companies over the six-year period.[8]

Why would businesses wish to engage in foreign direct investment? Controlling companies can obtain access to a larger market or needed resources via the FDI. Earlier in the process of globalization, direct investment was, in a sense, a substitute for trade. That is, while companies traded commodities that they had in abundance or that they could produce more competitively, they would also directly invest in countries where they needed to secure their source of raw materials or to manufacture their products inside the domestic market and, thereby, avoid tariffs or other import barriers. In that way, foreign investment occurred as a substitute for trade. More recently, however, with the liberalization of trade, foreign investment exists alongside trade. This is clearly seen in the fact that about one-third of world trade is conducted between members of the same organizations — i.e., between a parent company and its subsidiary, and between two subsidiaries of the same company. For example, a foreign subsidiary may require resources or supplies from the home country and, consequently, will import them.

Consequently, although FDI increases in a country, employment levels do not necessarily rise because of this increased investment. For example, mergers often result in the consolidation and elimination of some common functions: this can entail layoffs and, therefore, reduced employment levels. This relates to a more general concern about FDI: Does it benefit, or harm, the host country? That question continues to be debated.

Joint Ventures, Strategic Alliances

A joint venture involves an arrangement between two or more companies from different countries to produce a product or service together, or to collaborate in the research, development, or marketing of this product or service. This relationship has also been referred to as a strategic network. These organizations develop an arrangement whereby they share managerial control over a specific venture, such as seeking to develop a new technology, gaining access to a new market, etc. For example, Canadian-based Northern Telecom has formed strategic alliances with numerous foreign-based organizations, like Daewoo in Korea, Mitsui in Japan and Ascom Hasler in Switzerland. Strategic alliances often aim to: extend or enhance the core competencies of the businesses involved; obtain access to the expertise of another organization; and generate new market opportunities for all parties involved. The level of ownership and specific responsibilities can be unique to that particular joint venture created among the partners. It has been observed that a high number of international joint ventures have failed largely due to the inability of the partners to find a proper "fit" with regard to their approaches and managerial styles. As in any relationship among partners, it must be given special attention, particularly when the partners are culturally diverse.

A typical arrangement may exist between a multinational corporation (MNC) and a local partner, since this facilitates the MNCs quick entry into a new foreign market through the joint venture with an already established local business. Consequently, the international joint venture has proven to be an efficient way of entering foreign markets rapidly and easing entry where local requirements have been implemented with regard to a degree of domestic ownership and participation in the production or distribution of the good or service.

Mergers and Acquisitions

A Canadian-owned company could actually merge with a foreign-owned company and create a new jointly owned enterprise that operates in at least two countries. The newspapers have been littered with reports of mergers and acquisitions on a global scale. It

TALKING BUSINESS 7.4 **GLOBAL MERGERS AND ACQUISITIONS**

There is still much debate over who should control Canada's corporations. We have witnessed bank mergers in the late 1990s, airline mergers in 2000, and we for some time have seen the acquisition of Canadian companies by foreign (particularly U.S.) multinationals. Are these purely corporate events, or should the public and government be concerned about who owns corporate Canada?

Way back in the 1970s, the Canadian government felt obligated to restrict the levels of foreign ownership in numerous sectors (particularly oil and gas, mining and manufacturing) via the Foreign Investment Review Agency (FIRA), whose job it was to assess whether the acquisition of a Canadian company by foreign investors would "harm" Canada.

However, FIRA discontinued its operations after 10 years. While the Canadian government still scrutinizes mergers and acquisitions departments, the federal concern over foreign domination has been largely replaced by simple competition concerns (e.g., proposed bank mergers), though regulation of foreign ownership within some industries (e.g., airlines) has continued.

On the "brighter side" it is also useful to note that the "typical" cross-border transaction no longer simply involves a U.S. multinational "swallowing up" a smaller Canadian firm. Current reports indicate that Canadian acquisitions of foreign companies outpaced foreign acquisitions of Canadian companies by wide margins in 2002, 2003 and 2004.

Source: Based on CBC News Online, "Canadian corporate takeovers that made news" (January 28, 2005), http://www.cbc.ca/news/background/mergers/

makes sense that, to the extent that globalization is a process of increasing the connectedness among economies, there is a further consolidation of markets and companies. For example, the Montreal-based commercial printing and book-publishing business, Quebecor World Inc., was able to expand rapidly in Latin America in recent years, largely through acquisitions and partnerships with local companies in Argentina, Chile and Peru. More recently, in 2004, the Canadian brewery Molson announced plans to merge with U.S. Adolph Coors Co. in a "merger of equals" valued at more than $8 billion, creating a new "Canadian–U.S." company called Molson Coors Brewing Co. (See Talking Business 7.4 for a discussion of Canadian mergers and acquisitions.)

Why do such mergers occur? A number of factors typically generate the drive to merge, including the goal of obtaining new markets for the business and the effort to obtain new knowledge and expertise in an industry. The notion of achieving economies of scale in production may also be a source of influence on the decision to merge. Companies that merge on a global scale may be doing so in order to generate world-scale volume in a more cost effective way. Specifically, economies of scale in production are obtained when higher levels of output spread fixed costs (overhead, plant, equipment, etc.)

over more produced units and, consequently, reduce the per unit cost. It is, in a sense, the ability to achieve cost efficiency through larger-scale production that is made possible through the creation of a bigger organization.

Establishment of Subsidiaries

Another well-known type of global business activity is the creation of subsidiaries or branch operations in foreign countries, through which the enterprise can market goods and services. Where possible, a business may choose to maintain total control of its product or service by either establishing a wholly owned subsidiary or by purchasing an existing firm in the host country. Acquisitions of local companies have become increasingly popular. These types of acquisitions allow efficient entry into a market with already well-known products and distribution networks. On the other hand, establishing a subsidiary from scratch in the host country may also be a viable option. For example, shortly following the import quota placed on Japanese cars in the 1980s, Japanese-based car manufacturers set up operations in North America and captured an even greater segment of the consumer market. Toyota, Honda and Nissan are among the companies that have successfully employed this strategy.

What are the benefits of such types of global arrangements? If the foreign country is a high source of sales for the enterprise, it may make sense to establish a presence in that country, in order to be more responsive to local consumer needs. Among the risks is the fact that much more is at stake when the company has invested in a wholly owned subsidiary: they have invested time, effort and expense to create this operation. Subsidiaries may face the threat of political instability, as evidenced in the past in places like China or South Africa. Subsidiaries may also face adverse environments that might turn hostile toward foreign ownership. For example, Toyota's presence in Canada has not been without controversy. In recent years Toyota's Canadian subsidiary argued that it was being unfairly slapped with import tariffs on parts, making it more difficult to compete with North American-based car manufacturers.

THE MULTINATIONAL CORPORATION ───────

In terms of global types of business activity, the multinational corporation is a type of global business that has been receiving increasing attention, for better or worse. What is a multinational corporation, and why are we seeing its presence increasing across the globe? Observers have noted that such corporations are breaking down borders among countries and creating, in essence, borderless corporations. What are the implications of multinationals in terms of the costs and benefits they bring to the countries in which they set up business? We will address these questions in this section.

The first place to start is to offer a definition. What exactly are multinational corporations, and in what way are they "global business"? A global business is a business that engages directly in some form of international business activity, including such activities as exporting, importing or international production. A business that has direct investments (whether in the form of marketing or manufacturing facilities) in at least two different countries is specifically referred to as a multinational corporation (MNC). In other words, multinational organizations, or MNCs, are business enterprises that control assets, factories, etc., operated either as branch offices or affiliates in two or more foreign countries. An MNC generates products or services through its affiliates in several countries, and it maintains control over the operations of those affiliates, and manages from a global perspective. MNCs may also be referred to as global companies when they operate in myriad countries across the world.

Typically, MNCs are very large organizations and, in terms of their relative role in the world setting, it has been estimated that the 600 largest MNCs account for about one-quarter of the activity of the world's economies. Technically, it may be more accurate to refer to such organizations as MNEs (enterprises), given that such organizations could, in fact, possess partnership status, for example, rather than being incorporated: a business can be multinational without being a corporation per se. Further, MNEs can be divided between those businesses that are globally integrated and those that are multi-domestic. Globally integrated companies are companies that integrate their geographically diverse operations through decisions centralized at head office. Consequently, all areas might be given the task of developing and selling a single global product; or perhaps each region is contributing to the manufacture of a certain product. A multi-domestic company, on the other hand, permits its geographically diverse components to operate relatively autonomously. For example, the Canadian division will focus on *its* market, and the U.S. division will focus on *its* market. (See Talking Business 7.5 for another example.)

TALKING BUSINESS 7.5   **IKEA IN CHINA**

For a truly global experience, try stepping off the streets of Shanghai into one of IKEA's largest outlets. IKEA Group, a franchisee of Inter IKEA Systems BV, entered China in 1998 when it opened its first store in Shanghai. A new, redesigned Shanghai store opened in 2003, replacing the original outlet. IKEA expects to have 10 large stores up and running in China by 2010. Supporting this physical expansion is revenue expansion: sales were already up 50% in the first three months of 2004. Ulf Smedberg, marketing manager of IKEA China, says that IKEA's mission is to provide smart solutions for homes by implementing three criteria: good design, functionality, and low price. IKEA offers a range of 8,000 to 10,000 products depending on each store's size. But the company adapts the layout of the store, presentation of the goods, home solutions offered, and prices according to national economic and cultural conditions.

Source: Based on Paula M Miller, "IKEA WITH Chinese Characteristics" *The China Business Review* (July/August 2004) 31(4): 36–38. Also available from http://proquest.umi.com/pqdweb?index= 14&did=677544231&SrchMode=1&sid=6&Fmt=4&VInst=PROD&VType=PQD&RQT=309&VName=PQD& TS=1116623733&clientId=5220

TALKING BUSINESS 7.6   WHAT'S THE THIRD WORLD?

With regard to the globalization debate, it is useful to note that the term *Third World* was originally intended to describe the poor or developing nations of the world. In contrast, the first and second worlds were composed of the advanced or industrialized countries. The developed worlds were viewed as including the United States, Canada, and most of the countries of Eastern and Western Europe, as well as Australia, New Zealand and Japan. Within the broad territory described as the Third World, there are actually countries that are developing either rapidly (e.g., Brazil, Hong Kong, Israel, Mexico, Singapore, South Africa, South Korea and Taiwan) or modestly (including many countries of Africa, Asia and Latin America, in addition to India, Indonesia, Malaysia, and China) and others that have remained underdeveloped (e.g., Somalia, Sudan, sub-Sahara Africa). According to recent estimates, the Third World contributes most to the world's population growth, but is able to provide only about 20% of the world's economic production. A major controversy with regard to global business revolves around the fate of these underdeveloped nations: will they be purely exploited for the economic gain of MNCs, or will they benefit from the presence of increased industry?

So who, exactly, creates these organizations? Most MNCs have headquarters in developed countries — the *home* country. More specifically, over half of the MNCs have headquarters in the United States. France, Germany, the United Kingdom and Japan are among the other countries that are home to headquarters for most of the remaining MNCs. MNCs maintain branch plants or subsidiaries in two or more foreign countries — these are the *host* countries, and they are either developed, developing or Third World countries. (See Talking Business 7.6.) Among some of Canada's well-known MNCs are Bata Corp., which operates footwear manufacturing and distribution facilities in about 60 countries, and Bombardier Inc., which similarly is very much a part of the global market. This company has operations that include transportation equipment and aircraft production. While its head office is in Montreal, nearly 90% of its sales are in markets outside of Canada. It has production facilities in locations including Canada, the United States, France and Austria; and it markets products on five different continents.

The Borderless Corporation

Anthony Spaeth commented in a *Time Magazine* article: "The machinery of globalization is already integrating financial systems, dismantling territorial frontiers and bringing people closer together."[9] This comment is perhaps best illustrated in the new term for MNCs — *borderless corporations*.

Borderless corporation refers to the increasing ability of MNCs to ignore international boundaries and set up business just about anywhere. In fact, more and more MNCs are taking on the appearance of borderless corporations. Many of today's organizations that operate globally are, perhaps, less accurately referred to as MNCs than as TNCs, or trans-national corporations; and in fact, these two terms are often used interchangeably. The term *TNC*, as well as the term *borderless corporation*, is also being applied to MNCs, given the increasing tendency of not simply setting up branch plants in foreign countries but of organizing management, investment, production and distribution as if the world were one country.

The term *multinational* is a bit inaccurate, given that many of these companies do not claim any specific nationality but, in fact, gear their planning and decision making to global markets. For example, goods could be designed in one country, raw material obtained from a second country, manufactured in a third country and shipped to consumers in a fourth country. Consequently, top management can be composed of international members, reflecting the international composition of the organization. The headquarters of MNCs can often be quite irrelevant. For example, while Nestle Food Corp. is head-quartered in Switzerland, fewer than 5,000 of its over 200,000 workforce are actually working in the home country. Nestle has manufacturing facilities in over 50 countries and owns suppliers and distributors all over the world. Other similar examples of borderless or stateless corporations would include Coca-Cola, which, although headquartered in the United States, operates independent facilities around the world. In fact, Coca-Cola has seen the bulk of its profits generated in the Pacific and in Eastern Europe rather than in the United States, as have companies like General Motors. Other companies are equally transnational and almost borderless: Phillips, Nissan and Canada's Northern Telecom (Nortel), which has increasingly moved beyond the title of being a "Canadian business." (See Talking Business 7.7.)

The term *borderless corporation*, as opposed to *multinational*, emphasizes the notion that an enterprise can be a global company without any clear nationality. Often, the com-

---

***TALKING BUSINESS* 7.7   THINK GLOBAL, ACT LOCAL**

There is no better way of serving the needs of a geographically diverse market than by locating in the different geographical regions. This is reflected in the motto well-known among today's MNCs: "Think global, act local!" It has been suggested that many MNCs, such as Coca-Cola, Sony, Motorola and Nestle, have decentralized decision making among their geographically dispersed locations. For example, in IBM each subsidiary has its own local management, its own culture and its unique market focus. What this does is ensure that, for example, a Canadian client of IBM Canada sees the company as, indeed, IBM Canada, and not as simply a subsidiary of another U.S. MNC. This same philosophy is increasingly being employed by just about every MNC. Consider Nestle, which is headquartered in Switzerland, and yet which seems to many to be a U.S. company. Consider also the car industry — is a Ford car an American car? Well, not exactly, if you can imagine that it might be assembled in Brazil with parts from Europe and the United States. Like many other MNCs, in the new global economy the idea is to think global but act local. Regardless of where they operate, MNCs aim to reflect the local market tastes.

| EXHIBIT 7.7 | THE POTENTIAL BENEFITS AND THREATS OF MNCs |

Potential Benefits

- Encourages economic development.
- Offers management expertise.
- Introduces new technologies.
- Provides financial support to underdeveloped regions of the world.
- Creates employment.
- Encourages international trade through a company's access to different markets: it is relatively easy to produce goods in one country and distribute them in another country through a subsidiary or foreign affiliate.
- Brings different countries closer together.
- Facilitates global co-operation and worldwide economic development.

Potential Threats

- MNCs do not have any particular allegiance or commitment to their host country.
- Profits made by an MNC do not necessarily remain within the host country but may be transferred out to other locations depending on where the MNC feels the funds are most needed.
- Decision making and other key functions of MNCs may be highly centralized in the home country, so that even though other operations are performed in the host country, they do not necessarily include things like research and development and strategic planning.
- Difficulty in the ability to control and hold MNCs accountable can create serious ethical concerns for the host country. (See Talking Business 7.8.)

---

pany has international ownership and international management. Headquarters do not necessarily belong to one home country.

Borderless companies are very mobile across borders with regard to the transfer of financial capital, materials and other resources. They set up business where it is profitable, rather than creating a branch plant whose head office is in another corner of the world. Decision making is local and decentralized. This underscores their focus in addressing the local needs of the market within which they operate.

Reduction in trade barriers is said to give rise to borderless corporations. However, borderless corporations can be equally effective in circumventing any trade barriers. Borderless corporations typically pledge no allegiance to any one country or location; business is simply set up wherever profits can be maximized. Consequently, countries refusing to conduct trade with another country may not view a borderless corporation as a problem.

Currently the rapid rise of these MNCs, or TNCs, or borderless corporations, is raising many questions and concerns. For example, at a time when many countries are concerned with their competitiveness in the international market and their status in terms of trade, should we be concerned with who is generating the bulk of our exports? Does it matter what a company's nationality is, as long as it is providing jobs? Which government, and whose set of rules, will govern the behaviour of MNCs, or borderless corporations? Critics view the globalization of business as bringing with it as many threats as it does opportunities. (See Exhibit 7.7.)

264

TALKING BUSINESS 7.8 THE ETHICS OF MNCs: SWEATSHOPS

Sadly, manufacturing sweatshops are still rampant across the globe. In 2005, a pilot project sponsored by six anti-sweatshop groups and eight global apparel makers (including Nike and Gap) attempted to contribute to the demise of sweatshops. Called the Joint Initiative on Corporate Accountability & Workers' Rights, the project aimed to help establish a single set of labour standards and common plant-inspection guidelines at dozens of factories in Turkey that manufacture apparel and other goods.

Other such efforts have been growing and there are currently approximately 100 large, mostly Western companies actively involved in the anti-sweatshop movement. However, observers note that the efforts are modest at this point, with thousands of manufacturers yet to participate. The critical need is to generate some kind of consensus around fundamental universal standards for particular industries (e.g., apparel or consumer electronics). Without such industry-enforced standards, companies ask themselves: Why should I, as a manufacturer, incur the cost of upgrading and monitoring my workplace standards if I have to compete with other companies that don't have the same obligations? Consequently, the involvement of huge multinational retailers like Wal-Mart Stores Inc., is a crucial part of any sweatshop solution. Multinationals like Wal-Mart purchase goods from thousands of plants globally, and so any workplace standards they establish for their suppliers have a critical and significant impact on many manufacturing industries.

Source: Based on Businessweek, "Stamping out sweatshops" (May 23, 2005), p. 136 <http://proquest.umi.com/pqdweb?index=1&did=841653771&SrchMode=1&sid=11&Fmt=3&VInst=PROD&VType=PQD&RQT=309&VName=PQD&TS=1116624207&clientId=5220>.

INTERNATIONAL TRADE

The globalization of business may be a relatively new buzzword, but one of its fundamental forms has been around for a long time: the notion of international trade. International trade essentially involves the purchase, sale or exchange of goods or services across countries. This can be distinguished from domestic trade, which involves trade between provinces, cities or regions within a country.

Certainly, the trend of globalization has included the gradual reduction in trade barriers among many nations of the world as a means to promote greater international trade. You have probably heard about the Free Trade Agreement and the debates surrounding it, but perhaps you are not very familiar with the issues. What are the implications of promoting freer trade across nations, and what are the implications of barriers to trade?

In order to understand some of the critical implications of free trade, it is useful to consider the nature of international trade. Why might countries want to trade? Why might countries want to engage in protectionism? Below, we will consider a brief history with regard to the issue of international trade.

The Logic of Trade

One fundamental argument is that since some countries can produce certain goods or services more efficiently than others, global efficiency and, hence, wealth can be improved through free trade. Clearly, it is not advantageous for citizens of a country to be forced to buy an inferior quality, higher-priced domestic good if they can purchase a superior, lower-priced, foreign-produced import. Consistent with this view is the belief that trade should be permitted to continue according to market forces and not artificially restricted through trade barriers. Freer trade would allow countries to trade as they deemed appropriate, rather than trying to produce all goods domestically. Consequently, each country can specialize or focus on producing those goods or services in which it maintains an absolute advantage, and simply trade with other countries to obtain goods or services that are required, but not produced by domestic suppliers.

Free trade is based on the objective of open markets, where a level playing field is created for businesses in one country to compete fairly against businesses in other countries for the sale of their products or services. The aim reflects the fundamental principles of comparative advantage. Each country expects to take advantage of each other's strengths, and thereby be permitted to focus on their own strengths. In simplistic terms, it is relatively inefficient for Canada to try to grow coffee beans or bananas, given the climate. Rather than wasting effort and money, these items can be imported from countries more suited to such endeavours, while Canadians can focus their efforts in areas where they can produce relatively more efficiently.

Mercantilism

The trade theory underlying economic thinking from the period ranging from about 1500 to 1800 is referred to as **mercantilism**. Specifically, the fundamental view was that a country's wealth depended on its holdings of treasure, typically in the form of gold. Mercantilism, essentially, is the economic policy of accumulating this financial wealth through trade surpluses. **Trade surpluses** come about when a country's exports exceed its imports and, consequently, more money is entering the country (from foreign consumers buying these exports) than is leaving the country (from domestic consumers buying foreign imports). This policy was particularly popular in Europe from about the late 1500s to the late 1700s, with the most dominant mercantilist nations including Britain, France, Spain and the Netherlands.

Countries implemented this policy of mercantilism in a number of ways. Foremost, the government would intervene to ensure a trade surplus by imposing tariffs or quotas, or by outright banning of some foreign imported commodities. Typically, the governments would also subsidize domestic industries in order to encourage growth in their exports. Another strategy employed by mercantilist nations was colonialization: acquiring less developed regions around the world as sources of inexpensive raw materials (such as sugar, cotton, rubber, tobacco). These colonies would also serve as markets for finished products. Trade between mercantilist countries and their colonies resulted in large profits, given that the colonies typically were paid little for their raw materials but were forced to pay high prices to purchase the final products. Obviously, the colonial powers benefited to the detriment of the colonies. In addition, mercantilist countries aimed to become as self-sufficient as possible with regard to domestic production of goods and services. This also served to minimize reliance on foreign imports.

Given this brief historical description, it is easy to see why, today, countries that endeavour to maintain a trade surplus and expand their wealth at the expense of other countries are accused of practising mercantilism or neo-mercantilism. Japan has often been viewed as a mercantilist country because of its typically high trade surplus with a number of industrial nations, including the United States.

Trade Protectionism

Essentially, **trade protectionism** is about protecting a country's domestic economy and businesses through restriction on imports. Why might imports be a threat to a country's business and economy? Two fundamental reasons can be considered:

1. Low-priced foreign goods that enter the country could compete with goods already produced here and, in effect, take business away from domestic producers. The ultimate consequence may be loss of sales and loss of jobs for domestic industries that are unable to compete with these lower-priced imports.

2. A country that imports more than it exports will have a negative balance of trade, or a trade deficit — which often results in more money flowing out of the country (to buy the imported goods) than flowing in (for our exports).

Among the best-known government responses to address these potential risks are the imposition of tariffs and import quotas. A **tariff** is essentially a tax placed on goods entering a country. Specifically, protective tariffs are intended to raise the price of imported products in order to ensure that they are not less expensive than domestically produced goods. This, of course, discourages domestic consumers from buying these foreign imports by making them more expensive to purchase.

Another common form of trade barrier or restriction is the **import quota**, which limits the amount of a product that can be imported. The reasons for this restriction are the same: to help ensure that domestic producers retain an adequate share of consumer demand for this product. For example, in the 1980s, both the U.S. and Canadian governments were concerned with the growing popularity of Japanese-made cars in Canada and the United States. These cars were higher quality and less expensive than the "Big Three" North American car manufacturers. After pressure from the automakers, both the U.S. and Canadian governments negotiated deals with the Japanese government and the Japanese automakers to "voluntarily" restrict the number of vehicles they would export to Canada and the United States for the following three years. Ironically, this strategy was short-lived, given that Japanese automakers eventually built auto plants in Canada and the United States and achieved an even greater share of the North American market.

More recently, a number of Canadian businesses have asked the Canadian government to protect them against foreign competition. See Talking Business 7.9.

TALKING BUSINESS 7.9   CANADIAN BICYCLE MAKERS PLEAD FOR PROTECTION

Canada's two largest remaining bicycle makers — their factories threatened by lower-cost foreign imports — begin a last-ditch effort today in Ottawa to seek emergency protection from Asian rivals. Procycle Group Inc. and Raleigh Canada Ltd. are asking the federal government to slap a 48-per-cent tariff on foreign bike imports to stop the bleeding of manufacturing jobs to China, Vietnam and other Asian nations. They warn a failure to get temporary safeguard protection could spell the end for "the vast majority" of bike manufacturing in Canada.

The case should set a precedent for how Ottawa responds to the new economic reality where Canadian factory owners are trying to decide whether to keep production going locally or move it offshore themselves. "The manufacturing industry is watching this with considerable attention," said Larry Herman, a trade lawyer with Cassels Brock in Toronto who is not acting for either side in the case.

Procycle and Raleigh appear at the Canadian International Trade Tribunal this morning seeking the rarely used "safeguard" shelter from foreign competitors. This is allowed under global trade rules if an industry faces serious injury from a sudden, unexpected flood of imports. The case may turn into a political hot potato for Ottawa because Finance Minister Ralph Goodale, not the independent and quasi-judicial CITT, must ultimately approve safeguard actions. Procycle and Raleigh say the imports in question — teen and adult bikes — have almost doubled in recent years to 1,063,768 units in 2004 from 538,523 in 2000. Mr. Goodale may be forced to choose between angering Beijing — Canada's top new trade priority — or voters in Quebec, where the biggest bike manufacturing plants are located and where hundreds of textile jobs have already been lost to Asian competitors such as China.

The retail bicycle market in Canada is worth as much as $300-million in annual sales, but market share held by Canadian producers has plummeted in recent years, sliding to 30 per cent in 2004 from 58 per cent in 2000. Imports now control 70 per cent of the market. Canada's largest retail stores are fighting the requested safeguard, warning it would drive up bicycle prices, erode selection and send Canadians cross-border shopping to the United States for better deals.

"It would make it much more difficult to [import] the products that are in demand, and if and when those products were brought in, they would be a hell of a lot more expensive in Canada," says Diane Brisebois, president of the Retail Council of Canada. "Retailers are shaking their heads. You don't get safeguards if you are a retailer. If a retailer decides to come in from the United States to compete with you ... you've got to compete." She said retailers have told her that Canadian bike makers should be focusing on more specialized niches to stay competitive. "You don't just continue producing commodity products ... especially when there's an incredible demand for specialty products in that sector and we are importing them from Spain, Italy and France. We would rather buy them from a Canadian supplier."

Retailers say the situation facing Canadian bike makers does not meet the test for safeguards because manufacturers have themselves to blame for lost sales. They also note that Canadian bike makers have enjoyed some government protection against low-priced imports from various countries for a long time. "With the exception of a few years,

continues

TALKING BUSINESS 7.9 continued (continued)

they have had anti-dumping protection since 1978. Since 1992 there has been steady protection," said Darrel Pearson of Gottlieb & Pearson, whose client is the Retail Council of Canada. "This is a very, very small industry which has had a tonne of time to adjust to imports," he said of Raleigh and Procycle. The CITT will render its decision on the case Sept. 1. If it agrees with bicycle makers and recommends safeguards, then Prime Minister Paul Martin's government will have to decide whether to enact them.

Both companies' significant operations are in Quebec: Procycle's in St. Georges-de-Beauce and Raleigh's in Waterloo. Between them, Raleigh and Procycle employ approximately 600 people. Both build their own frames, as well as some handlebars and other parts such as rims and they assemble the wheels from Canadian and imported parts. Their domestic competitors include Canadian importers, companies that assemble bikes from wholly-imported parts and some smaller manufacturers. Ken Morrison, Raleigh's vice-president of finance, said the company does not want to shut down its Waterloo factory. "We are the major employer in our town. Many of our employees have been with us for over 20 years. There are no other places where they can readily seek employment if the factory was to close."

Bike makers say that if Ottawa doesn't want to slap a 48 per cent tariff on imports, it could instead impose quota restrictions, limiting imports to 600,000 units — half of the total bikes entering Canada. Opponents of the safeguards warn it will anger China, which is a major bike exporter to Canada. "This is like the finger in the dyke approach to trade policy," said Peter Clark, a trade consultant acting for an importer opposed to the safeguards.

Two-wheeled flood
Procycle Group Inc., and Raleigh Canada Ltd. are asking Ottawa to slap a 48-per-cent tariff on foreign bike imports to stop the bleeding of manufacturing jobs to China, Vietnam and other Asian nations.

- $300-million: Annual sales of bicycles in Canada.
- 111%: The rate at which bicycle imports rose between 2000 and 2004.
- 969,300: The number of foreign-made bicycles that hit the Canadian market in 2004, up from 460,425 in 2000.
- 30%: The market share held by Canadian producers in 2004, down from 50 per cent in 2000.
- 70%: The share of the bicycle market now made up of imports.

Source: By Steven Chase. Reproduced with permission from *The Globe and Mail* (June 20, 2005), B1.

TALKING BUSINESS 7.10   THE FUTILITY OF PROTECTIONISM

Restrictions on imports can be self-defeating, given that other countries will act in a similar manner and reduce their imports. Consider the case of Canada, where a large portion of our raw materials are exported. Can it restrict imports from countries who are similarly purchasing our exports?

The Great Depression of the 1930s was largely due to the protectionist policy passed by the U.S. government at that time. The government placed tariffs on many goods entering the United States in order to protect U.S. industry. However, the result was that many other countries raised their tariffs and caused a sharp drop in U.S. exports and, in fact, hurt trade among almost all countries.

What's Wrong with Mercantilism and Protectionism?

A trade surplus, as opposed to a trade deficit, certainly seems like a desirable aim, and is, in many respects, a benefit for any nation. The issue, though, is whether a policy of mercantilism is feasible, given its dependence on restriction of foreign imports. Perhaps the most significant criticism of mercantilism is that the central assumption upon which this policy is largely based is inherently flawed. Mercantilism assumes that trade involves a **zero-sum gain** — that is, the world's wealth is a fixed pie, and a nation can only increase its share of the pie by forcing other nations to reduce their shares of the pie. Based on this logic, one can understand the drive to minimize imports while maximizing exports. The flaw in this logic, however, is readily apparent. The practice creates a "one-way street" of trade, so to speak. That is, a mercantilist country aims to maximize the goods/ services it sells to other countries, yet it expects to restrict the goods/services that these same countries attempt to sell to it. Even in the time of colonialism, the policy was ultimately self-defeating: colonies that received little payment for their raw material exports could not accumulate sufficient wealth to afford the high-priced imports that the mercantilists offered. (See Talking Business 7.10.)

Promoting International Trade

Whether it is tariffs, or quotas, or other forms of protectionism, we have seen a gradual lifting of trade restrictions as part of the wave of globalization. Most countries are endeavouring to eliminate trade barriers.

One of the most ambitious programs designed to encourage free trade was established way back in 1948 with the founding of GATT (the General Agreement on Tariffs & Trade), which was an agreement among approximately 100 countries to reduce the level of tariffs on a worldwide basis. And it did encourage a gradual reduction in trade barriers. In 1995 the World Trade Organization (WTO), in effect, took over the management of the global trade system from GATT. Its mandate is, essentially, to develop and administer agreed-upon rules for world trade, and discourage protectionist laws that restrict international trade.

Other organizations exist whose purpose is also to assist nations of the global economy. For example, the International Monetary Fund (IMF) was established after World War II to provide short-term assistance in the form of low-interest loans to countries conducting international trade and in need of financial assistance. The World Bank was established at the same time to provide long-term loans to countries for economic development projects. Typically, the World Bank will borrow funds from the more developed countries and offer low-interest loans to underdeveloped Third World nations. So, both these organizations, by assisting less prosperous nations, help to facilitate trade and investment between countries.

Countries themselves have been pursuing trading blocs and other forms of economic integration as part of the general thrust toward a more integrated world economy. This issue of economic integration is discussed below.

Facilitating Global Business: Regional Economic Integration

Regional economic integration means bringing different countries closer together by the reduction or elimination of obstacles to the international movement of capital, labour, and products or services. A collection of countries within such an integrated region is typically referred to as a regional trading bloc. Why do countries endeavour to integrate? It is, largely, a logical conclusion to maximizing the benefits of international trade, as discussed earlier, with regard to greater availability of products, lower prices and increased efficiency or productivity. Trading blocs increase international trade and investment, with the central aim of improving their economy and living standards for their citizens.

Regional integration can occur at different levels of intensity, so to speak. These include, from the lowest to the highest levels of integration, free trade areas, customs union, common market and economic union. It is worthwhile to briefly examine each form.

1. Free trade area. This form of economic integration involves the removal of tariffs and non-tariff trade barriers (i.e., subsidies and quotas) on international trade in goods and services among the member countries. Given that this form involves the lowest degree of regional economic integration, there is greater member autonomy with regard to such issues as how it chooses to deal with non-members and what types of barriers it should construct against non-member countries. Examples of this form are the North American Free Trade Agreement and APEC, both of which are discussed later in this chapter.

2. Customs union. This form of economic integration involves the removal of trade barriers on international trade in goods and services among the member countries. However, given that this form involves a somewhat greater degree of economic integration, there is less member autonomy with regard to such issues as how it chooses to deal with non-members, and what types of barriers it should construct against non-member countries. Members will typically generate a uniform policy regarding treatment of non-members. One example of this type of integration is the MERCOSUR customs union, which is a major trade group in South America. This customs union was established in 1991, and its partners include Argentina, Brazil, Uruguay and Paraguay; it grants associate status to Chile and Bolivia. By 1996 the members had eliminated tariffs on goods accounting for 90% of trade between the member countries and, eventually, largely abolished trade barriers. In 1995 MERCOSUR implemented a common external tariff: which, by definition, makes it a more highly integrated trading bloc than NAFTA. These countries represent an attractive market for foreign companies because of the large population and high proportion of middle-class consumers. However, tariffs for non-members have ranged from 16% to 32% and, consequently, have made it challenging for outsiders. Countries like Canada and the United States are awaiting further agreements like the FTAA (The Free Trade Area of the Americas) that would allow greater access to the Latin American markets for North American exports.

3. Common market. This form of economic integration builds on the elements of the two previous forms, including the removal of trade barriers and the implementation of a common trade policy regarding non-members. In addition, members of a common market will typically also generate a freer flow of labour and capital across their borders. Given the requirement of co-operation in economic and labour policy, this level of economic integration is, consequently, more difficult to achieve than the previous two levels. The European Union, discussed below, is one such example of a common market arrangement.

4. Economic union. This form of economic integration builds on the previous three forms and, in addition, involves a coordination of economic policies among the member countries. It requires a higher level of integration than a common market, because it involves the harmonization of fiscal, monetary and tax policies. In addition, it often includes the creation of a common currency. Consequently, member countries in such an arrangement maintain much less autonomy compared to the lesser forms of economic integration. In the following discussion of the EU, it can be noted that the members are moving toward greater integration of economic and political policies, which would, essentially, move them closer to a genuine economic union.

A significant portion of total world trade occurs within three regional trading blocs, also referred to as the Triad market of North America, Europe and Asia. Given the importance of these trading blocs, it is worthwhile to highlight each. Following is a relatively brief description of the trading blocs in Europe and Asia, followed by a lengthier discussion of the North American trade agreement and its implications for the Canadian business environment.

European Union (EU)

In 1992, 12 nations of Europe established a common market, called the European Community (EC); and in 1994, after adding several new members, it became known as the European Union (EU). The European Union is a common market with a single currency, a free flow of money, people, products and services within its member countries. Currently, there are 25 member states within the EU, with 12 members also adopting a common currency (the Euro) and monetary policy. The members include Austria, Belgium, Cyprus, Czech Republic, Denmark, Estonia, Finland, France, Germany, Greece, Hungary, Ireland, Italy, Latvia, Lithuania, Luxembourg, Malta, Poland, Portugal, Slovakia, Slovenia, Spain, Sweden, The Netherlands, United Kingdom. Four other countries have been invited to join, including Bulgaria, Croatia, Romania and turkey. In total, the EU is currently the largest integrated common market in the world, with approximately 457 million consumers.

Common market is a term that refers to a group of countries who remove all tariff and non-tariff barriers to trade. Indeed, the aim of the EU is to create a borderless Europe, so to speak. In fact, the bulk of the advanced regions of Europe exist in essentially one giant market, with the free movement of goods and services, as well as people and financial capital. Businesses that operate outside the boundaries of the EU can achieve the benefits of membership if they have a subsidiary in at least one member country. For example, U.S.-based companies like 3M, Hewlett-Packard and GE have already established a European presence, and consequently enjoy the same benefits as businesses who are part of the member European countries. Those not yet established in Europe are developing strategies to exploit this large market.

The EU can be a double-edged sword for non-members. It can generate protectionist policies for its members, like tariffs or quotas, to bar the United States or Japan from entry, for example. On the other hand, the EU could also create opportunities for non-members — they comprise a huge market for North American exports, for example. A number of U.S.-based companies have chosen to engage in joint ventures with European-based companies as a means of obtaining some kind of presence in the European market.

Does this common market matter to Canada? It certainly does. The EU is one of Canada's most important trading partners. Clearly, this large market cannot be ignored. Aside from the United States, five of Canada's top ten export markets are in Europe. Consequently, observers view Europe as a potentially strong market for Canadian goods, if tariff and non-tariff barriers can be reduced. In addition, many critics feel that there is currently too high a reliance on one market (the United States) for Canadian exports (approximately 84%), and increased trade with other markets is preferable.

Asian Trading Bloc

Another region of growing importance to Canada has been the Asia-Pacific region. This region has a total population of about two billion — approximately twice that of the European community. In addition to the drive for greater economic integration and free trade in Europe and North and South America, Asia has also sought to create trading blocs. Singapore, Hong Kong, Taiwan and South Korea (also referred to as the Four Tigers), together with the relatively dominant partner, Japan, have grown to become an increasingly integrated economic region.

ASEAN. The Association of South-East Asian Nations (ASEAN) was established in 1967 and became the first major free-trade bloc in Asia. Its aim was to promote greater co-operation in areas such as industry and trade among the members, including Singapore, Malaysia, Indonesia, Thailand, Vietnam, the Philippines, Brunei, Cambodia, Laos and Myanmar. At the same time, member countries are protected by trade barriers from non-members. There is a move to create a greater East Asian trade and economic grouping, consisting of the Association of Southeast Asian Nations (ASEAN) countries, plus Japan, China and South Korea.[10] The process of creating a trading bloc has been slower in Asia partly because, unlike NAFTA and the EU, there is a very wide disparity between the economic infrastructures and the GDPs of Japan, South Korea and China. While disparities exist among members in the EU, they are not as great. For example, a number of current EU members, like Portugal and Greece, have remained behind such members as Germany, France and Britain. In addition, much of Mexico's southern region lives in essentially Third World conditions. However, the disparities in the economies of China, South Korea and Japan are much greater. All this contributes to a greater difficulty in integrating the regions for trade purposes.

APEC. The Asia-Pacific region has also set out to facilitate greater economic co-operation and freer trade through the establishment of the Asia-Pacific Economic Co-operation (or **APEC**), formed in 1989. Among the members of APEC are the People's Republic of China, Hong Kong, Japan, Indonesia, Malaysia, South Korea, Canada and the United States, to name some of the 21 members. It is viewed as a significant economic force, given that its members generate over 50% of the global output and about 50% of its merchandise trade. APEC was established to promote economic co-operation among members in the areas of trade and investment. Its relatively diverse mix of countries is, in effect, an effort to counter the narrower regionalism of such arrangements as the EU and NAFTA. In fact, APEC includes three of the traditionally largest economies — the United States, China and Japan. NAFTA was included in APEC largely as a means to forge stronger economic links between North America and Asia.

How important is APEC to Canada? Canada's central aim in joining APEC was to expand trade opportunities with the region. This region has a total population of about two billion — approximately twice that of the European community. This represents a large market for Canadian exports. Next to the United States, Japan has been one of Canada's largest trading partners; and Japan, along with other member nations, represents a high potential as consumers for our exports. The suggestion is not necessarily to decrease the level of trade and investment that Canada has established with the United States; but rather, to pursue similar levels of access to other major regions, such as Asia. As business writer David Crane recently observed:

> Globalization in the 21st century is more likely to have an Asian face than an American one, as China and India boost their investments in education and research and development, building their own multinationals and expanding their economic reach. What will this mean for Canada? ... Canada's capacity to play the global role that Canadians aspire to will depend on many factors, including creating and allocating the resources that allow it to do so. This means Canada has to be an economic, social and environmental success at home. In particular, Canada has to make the transition to a knowledge-based society, with a high level of literacy and capacity for innovation.[11]

| EXHIBIT 7.8 | IMPACT OF NAFTA |

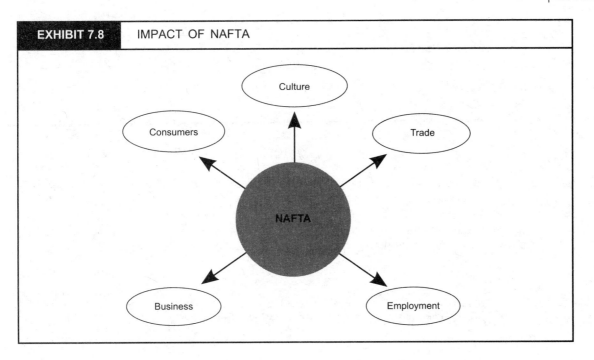

North America Trading Bloc and NAFTA

The Canada–U.S. Free Trade Agreement (FTA) came into effect January 1, 1989, and was largely aimed at reducing, and eventually eliminating, tariff barriers on almost all goods and services traded between Canada and the United States, as well as at further facilitating cross-country investments. Among the other provisions of the agreements are rules regarding government subsidies, the imposition of countervailing duties, standards of health and safety, and the environment. Essentially, for Canadian exporters this agreement offered better access to the huge American market for Canadian goods and services. In 1994, the North American Free Trade Agreement (NAFTA) was established and this, similarly, was an agreement to remove trade barriers between Canada, the United States and Mexico. This agreement, which replaced the FTA, essentially aimed to produce a common market among the members. There has been much written regarding the impact that NAFTA has had on Mexico, the United States and Canada. Before we identify some of the major arguments supporting or condemning free trade, let's consider some of the area that have been impacted by this free trade agreement: Trade, employment and business, culture, competitiveness and the consumer (see Exhibit 7.8).

NAFTA's Impact on Trade

Advocates of free trade say:

- NAFTA achieved its most fundamental objective: to increase the level of trade between Canada and the United States. (See Talking Business 7.11.) Canada and U.S.

***TALKING BUSINESS* 7.11   NAFTA QUICK FACTS**

- NAFTA is the largest trade agreement in the world.
- 96% of Canada–U.S. trade is hassle-free.
- One in three Canadian jobs is linked to trade, and NAFTA supports 5.2 million U.S. jobs.
- A truck crosses the Canada–U.S. border every two seconds; more than 300,000 people cross the border every day.
- Every day, more than $1.9 billion exchanges hands between the United States and Canada — that's $1 million every 15 minutes.
- More than 39 U.S. states have Canada as their primary market.
- Canada imports more goods from the United States than from any other country — more than all of the European Union members combined.

Source: Excerpts reproduced with permission from John Cooper, "NAFTA at eleven. Despite growing pains, it's still seen by some as a valuable tool for Canadian business," *CMA Management*, October 2005 <http://www.management mag.com/index.cfm/ci_id/2397/la_id/1.htm>

trade increased by about 75% since the establishment of the FTA. Of course, the United States continues to be Canada's major trading partner, accounting for almost 80% of Canada's total trade. (See Exhibit 7.9.)

- Canada's merchandise trade with the United States increased by 80% in the first five years of the NAFTA, and Canada's trade with Mexico increased by 65%, reaching $271.5 billion and $1.4 billion, respectively, in 1998.

- One measure of the relative significance of trade to a country is to observe the volume of an economy's trade relative to its total output (percentage of GDP). Exports of Canadian goods to the United States were approximately 17% of GDP in the 1980s, prior to NAFTA. With the implementation of NAFTA, exports and imports grew significantly over the period from 1990 to 1999. Specifically, as a proportion of GDP, exports grew from 25.7% to 43.2%, while imports grew from 25.7% to 40.3%. In contrast, for the 10 years prior to the Free Trade Agreement, exports and imports as a proportion of GDP were practically constant. Total Canada–U.S. trade in both goods and services rose from $425 billion in 1995 to $700 billion in 1999.

- The Government of Canada Web site has underscored what it views as many positive consequences of NAFTA, including the following:

  NAFTA has helped transform the three economies while creating synergies that go far beyond economic prosperity. As with any trade liberalization initiative or other economic change, NAFTA affected some sectors positively and others adversely, but there is little doubt that on the whole, the agreement produced real net benefits for workers and consumers of the three countries ... Some 70 million passengers cross the US–Canada border

| EXHIBIT 7.9 | GEOGRAPHIC DISTRIBUTION OF IMPORTS AND EXPORTS — MERCHANDISE TRADE |

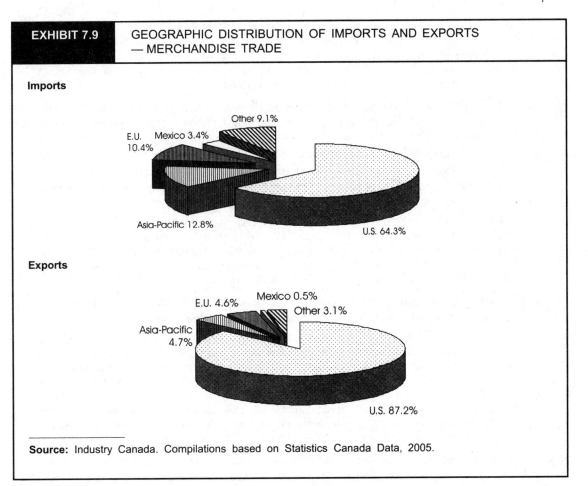

Imports

Other 9.1%
E.U. 10.4%
Mexico 3.4%
Asia-Pacific 12.8%
U.S. 64.3%

Exports

E.U. 4.6%
Mexico 0.5%
Other 3.1%
Asia-Pacific 4.7%
U.S. 87.2%

Source: Industry Canada. Compilations based on Statistics Canada Data, 2005.

each year (twice the population of Canada), along with 7 million commercial trucks, and 1.3 million rail containers. This contributes to a total two-way trade of $394 billion in 2003 ($1.08 billion a day). Since NAFTA's implementation in 1994, total merchandise trade between the US and Canada has grown by over 120%, and when you include trade in services, the growth has been closer to 140%. US trade with Mexico has shown even more significant growth (nearly tripled) over the same period. The total trade between the United States, Canada and Mexico has more than doubled, rising from $306 billion in 1993 to over $621 billion last year. United States exports to Canada and Mexico have surged 85% from $142 billion to $263 billion in the same period, significantly higher than the 41% increase of United States exports to the rest of the world.[12]

Critics of free trade say:

- Any trade improvements witnessed over the last decade may be more attributable to Canada's relatively low dollar than due to the results of NAFTA. The fact that for years, the U.S. dollar was stronger than the Canadian dollar may have been a stronger help for Canadian exports. As one writer observed:

Much has been made of Canada's NAFTA-driven trade success, but the reality does not live up to the hype. Canada's merchandise trade surplus with the U.S. — which grew from $48.6 billion in 1996 to $124.6 billion in 2005 — is less than meets the eye. ... a federal Industry Department study found that by far the largest factor — accounting for 90% of the 1990s export surge — was the low Canadian dollar.[13]

- While the quantity of Canada–U.S trade itself may have improved, there have not been any improvements in the quality or nature of Canada's export patterns. As noted earlier, Canada had been far too reliant on exporting our raw materials ("low-technology exports"), in relatively unprocessed form, to the United States. More "added-value", "higher-tech" exports needs to be generated so that we can become stronger in more valuable types of exports and engage in more research and development in order to do so. As one critic indicated:

   ... Although there was an increase in some high-tech sectors, notably telecommunications (until the 2001 meltdown) and aerospace, the trade deficit in high-tech products remains high ... and Canada's poor record in private sector R&D persists. Relative to GDP, Canada's exports of higher value-added products — including autos, machinery and equipment, and consumer goods — have fallen by one-quarter since 1999....[14]

- NAFTA has encouraged us to become too dependent on trade with the United States. This point is driven home by such observations as the following:

   Meanwhile, outside NAFTA, the world economy has undergone a vast metamorphosis. China has grown into a trading giant. India is becoming a global leader in the services trade. The European Union is bringing growth to once-perennial underperformers such as eastern Europe and Spain; the latter's economy has grown to roughly the same size as Canada's. The United States has made a higher priority of trading bilaterally with emerging players, and some of their trade agreements may prove more comprehensive than NAFTA, putting Canada's preferred status in the United States at risk. Indeed, China will soon supplant us as America's top trading partner.[15]

- We need to expand trade with other nations rather than relying soley on NAFTA. NAFTA may have caused Canada to become too complacent in the global market. Consequently, many observers note the need for Canada to place much greater effort on establish strong trade ties with other countries. As Phillip Preville commented in his recent *Maclean's* report:

   Our share of global exports and investment to China has actually been on the decline, and we are no longer among China's top 10 trading partners. .. Trade policy should be geared towards facilitating exports of services, and also importing components to reduce the cost of goods manufactured in Canada — a way of making China's manufacturing prowess work for us. ... also recommends pursuing trade with India and other emerging nations in Asia and Latin America, as well as renewing relationships with old partners in Europe and Japan.[16]

NAFTA's Impact on Canadian Employment and Business

NAFTA's impact on employment and wages has not been clearly determined to date. Different groups have offered different information as to whether jobs have been lost or created as a result of free trade. The key controversy surrounding NAFTA is the issue of jobs. Do open trade and increases in foreign presence in a country result in job creation or job loss? If countries allow products or services to freely enter their borders, what happens to the domestic producers of such products or services?

Advocates of free trade say:

- Foreign competition forces domestic businesses to improve their operations and improve their products or services.

- Protecting domestic business amounts to discouraging competitiveness and innovation and, ultimately, will lead to job losses, given the inability to remain competitive in world markets.

- Free trade encourages countries to abort inefficient operations and focus on the relatively stronger commodities or services in which they have a competitive or comparative advantage.

Critics of free trade say:

- Many Canadian manufacturers cannot compete with U.S. imports, and are forced out of business.

- Job losses arise from U.S. companies deciding to shut down their Canadian subsidiaries and exporting their tariff-free goods to Canada.

- Many manufacturing jobs are lost to Mexico, given that country's relatively cheaper labour and, hence, lower-priced goods.

  > Free trade was sold as a solution to Canada's persistent unemployment problem. Though there are other factors at play, the record does not bear this out. Average unemployment during the last 15 years has remained about the same as the average rate during the previous 15 years. Canada's unemployment rate was 6.8% in 2005, modestly lower than the 7.6% in 1989 (1.2 million workers are currently looking for work). This compares with U.S. unemployment, which was 5.1% in 2005, slightly below the 5.3% level in 1989. Nor has the promise of increased employment quality — high skill, high-wage jobs — under free trade materialized. On the contrary, displaced workers in the trade sectors have moved to lower-skill, lower-wage jobs in the services sector. Precarious forms of employment (part-time, temporary, and self-employment) have also increased....[17]

NAFTA's Impact on Canadian Culture

Advocates of free trade say:

- The agreement is not signing away Canada's cultural heritage, any more than the European Community forced European nations to lose their individual cultures.

- According to Statistics Canada, Canadian cultural exports exceed $4.5 billion, and more royalty money for music is coming into Canada than is leaving.

Critics of free trade say:

- Free trade will encourage the destruction of a unique Canadian culture.

- Increasing foreign domination of the Canadian economy will transform Canada into a pure economic subsidiary of the United States.

- Publishing and broadcasting industries are threatened by American competitors and the increasing presence of American-based media.

- The presence of the United States in areas like the Canadian entertainment industry would pose a serious threat to the transmission of Canadian culture.

NAFTA's Impact on Canadian Competitiveness and the Canadian Consumer

Advocates of free trade say:

- One of the central objectives of the FTA was to encourage Canadian businesses to become more competitive through exposing Canadian businesses to greater competition from American business.

- Canadian consumers are given more choice and are exposed to competitive products with free trade. That is, they will have access to potentially less expensive goods or services — whether they come from the United States, or from increasingly competitive Canadian businesses.

- Canadian companies that require inputs from U.S. businesses can now obtain them more cheaply, and pass these savings on to the consumer.

- Canada cannot afford to ignore the U.S. market. If Canadian companies wish to become more competitive, they also need to serve a larger market — and the United States certainly offers a huge market for Canadian goods. Free trade gives Canada greater access to selling goods and services to this market through the reduction of trade barriers.

Critics of free trade say:

- NAFTA has not encouraged any increase in productivity. Canadians have been unable to match U.S. productivity rates for the past 20 years, and have produced at rates that are equal to about 80% of the output of workers in the United States.

- NAFTA has not reduced the productivity gap between Canada and the United States:

  > As for the productivity gap with the U.S. that was, according to proponents, supposed to narrow under free trade, it has instead widened. Canadian labour productivity (GDP per hour worked) rose steadily in relation to U.S. productivity during the 1960s and 1970s, peaking at 92% of the U.S. level in 1984. Thereafter, it slid to 89% in 1989 and by 2005 had fallen to just 82% of U.S. productivity — below where it was in 1961.[18]

- Our good record of exports has come about largely because the relatively low value of the Canadian dollar has made our goods cheaper. In other words, it is not that we are producing cost-efficient goods, but rather it is an artificial reduction in the value of our dollar that has made them cheaper on foreign markets. Consequently, a higher Canadian dollar might result in decreased exports, given that Canadian goods would then likely be more expensive in foreign markets. What is needed, arguably, is real improvements in productivity coming from things like updating equipment, retraining workers and building competitiveness.

Should We Praise or Condemn NAFTA?

NAFTA, like other trade agreements, facilitates globalization — the mobility of resources across borders, the freer flow of goods and service, the increase in foreign investment and the growing interdependence of economies. Such instruments bring potential benefits and threats. While many observers see dangers in the outcomes of freer trade, only time will tell us whether Canada ultimately gains or loses. Talking Business 7.12 presents excerpts from the recent popular press that also attempt to identify the pros and cons of NAFTA.

***TALKING BUSINESS* 7.12 NAFTA, A DECADE LATER**

Praising NAFTA[1]

In supermarkets and department stores from coast to coast, Canadian consumers are faced with almost endless choices. But few are likely to be aware that both the range and affordability of products are linked to Canada's membership in the world's largest trading arrangement.

That's been increasingly so in the decade since Canada, Mexico and the United States entered into the landmark North American Free Trade Agreement, or NAFTA.

With a combined gross domestic product of US$11 trillion among its members, representing about 30 percent of the world's total, NAFTA ranks as an economic and diplomatic success. The access it has provided to the vast U.S. market has made Canada the envy of trading nations around the world.

... Both agreements have eliminated tariffs on most merchandise, set out clear-cut trading rules and created a larger, more integrated market. This makes North America one of the most efficient regions in the world in which to conduct business. Among the biggest winners of all have been Canadian consumers.

"Canadian shoppers win two ways," says John Curtis, the senior economist with International Trade Canada. "First, they have more choice because more goods and services are being imported. Second, prices are lower because NAFTA has made all three trading partners more competitive."

But it's not only consumers who benefit from freer flowing trade: it's the economy overall. Through NAFTA, Canada has consolidated its position as the largest trading partner of the U.S. In 2003, nearly 80 percent of Canada's total exports went south of the border, up from 71 percent in 1989. The importance of the U.S. as an export market has increased for most Canadian provinces and nearly every industry.

Consumer boon: NAFTA has eliminated tariffs on most merchandise, set out clear-cut trading rules and created a larger, more integrated market, making North America one of the most efficient regions in the world in which to conduct business.

"NAFTA has been a powerful force for Canadian manufacturers," says Perrin Beatty, President of the Canadian Manufacturers & Exporters, adding that predictable trade rules and the elimination of tariffs have created greater demand in the U.S. for Canadian-made parts and merchandise. "While there was a period of adjustment for manufacturers, NAFTA on balance has been enormously positive for Canada and has proven that we can compete."

continues

. . . .

Spurred on by NAFTA's success, Canada has been pursuing further trade opportunities throughout the hemisphere and beyond. Bilateral free trade agreements took effect in 1997 with Chile and in 2003 with Costa Rica. Canada is currently negotiating agreements with El Salvador, Guatemala, Honduras and Nicaragua. As well, Canada, Mexico, the U.S. and the other 31 democratic countries of the hemisphere are now working toward establishing a Free Trade Area of the Americas.

Such agreements can only be good for Canada, with its relatively small population and the importance of trade for its economic prosperity.

"There is very little doubt that our country's fiscal health is linked to freer international trade and investment," Curtis adds.

Condemning NAFTA[2]

Not too long ago, the Investment Review Division of Industry Canada reported a record number of foreign takeovers of Canadian companies in the same year.

After the House of Commons Industry Committee recently proposed dropping restrictions on foreign ownership of telecommunications and cable companies, our two national newspapers and some of the Asper dailies bubbled over with lavish praise. That this is happening in a country that already has such a terribly high degree of foreign ownership and foreign control is not only difficult to comprehend, but dismaying for those of us who value Canadian sovereignty and independence.

Even more dismaying is the likelihood that ... the sale of Canada to foreign owners will accelerate. Today, over thirty-five per cent of corporate profits in Canada already go to foreign companies. ... At what point would you say that enough is enough? And then, exactly what would you do about it? Of course, you do recognize ... that under the investment provisions of NAFTA we must continue allowing Americans to buy up our country, whether we like it or not. What would you then do about NAFTA...?"

. . . .

For example, the suggestion was made that "Canadians, it seems, have got used to the idea that we don't have to control companies to benefit from them. After all, foreign owners pay taxes and employ thousands of Canadians too." Moreover, while "Many Canadian energy companies have disappeared in recent years, often into the corporate arms of foreign competitors ... few concerns were raised that resources critical to our economy were being sold off to foreign companies."

The suggestion that Canadians find our unusually high level of foreign ownership acceptable is nonsense. Public opinion polls consistently show exactly the opposite. Earlier this year, a Decima poll showed that 72 percent of Canadians opposed foreign ownership in the media and telecommunications industries, 60 percent in the telephone industry and 66 per cent in newspapers. In a Maclean's poll, 81 percent agreed that Canadian ownership of businesses operating in Canada was necessary "in order to maintain a strong Canadian identity" and ... the Globe reported that 70 percent said they were opposed to more foreign control and three in five said that they were angry that the government wasn't doing more to stop foreign takeovers.

continues

TALKING BUSINESS 7.12 (continued)

Other recent polls have shown that 89 percent of Canadians believe that U.S. take-overs of Canadian companies is responsible for the Americanization of Canada (Ekos), three in every five Canadians say we are losing our independence from the U.S. (Maclean's), and 75% say Canadians should have the right to curtail and regulate foreign ownership (Vector).

Perhaps most dismaying of all, one poll showed that only a quarter of Canadians are confident that there will be an independent Canada in 25 years.

As for the Globe's contention that Canadians are not concerned about the increasing foreign control of our natural resources, another poll shows that 83% say "it is very important that Canada remains sovereign in the area of natural resources." As well, last year an Ipsos Reid poll showed that 80 percent of Canadians said that they were concerned about the foreign ownership of Canadian energy resources.

· · · · ·

Today, most manufacturing and oil and natural gas operating revenues in Canada already go to foreign owners. Dozens of key sectors of the Canadian economy are majority foreign-owned and controlled. As I have indicated in the past, in the United States there's not one single industry majority foreign owned. Not one!

Why do virtually all other developed countries resist massive foreign ownership of their economies? Here's a quick and very partial short list. Foreign corporations employ sophisticated transfer pricing and debt-loading schemes to transfer profits to their own countries or to tax havens before they are taxable in the host country. Foreign firms import much higher levels of parts, components and services than equivalent domestic companies. As a result, employment ratios to sales are invariably well below that for domestic firms. (One recent study showed that foreign firms in Canada import five times as much as domestic firms on a comparative basis.)

Excessive foreign ownership leads to hollowing out.... Head office jobs transferred out of the country result in truncated management, and key corporate decisions are made by people who live in another country and care little if at all about the welfare of the host country.

No self-respecting country would allow foreign corporations to control so many industries and so much of their economy as we do in Canada. The greatest irony of all continues to be that our own banks, pension funds and other financial institutions have for years been putting up most of the money that foreigners use to buy up our country.

... [O]f all the hundreds of billions of dollars of foreign direct investment monitored by Industry Canada, 96.6 percent has been for takeovers and only a pathetic 3.4 percent has been for new business investment. During this period just under 10,500 companies in Canada have been taken over by foreign buyers.

Welcome to what will soon be the colony of Canada.

Sources:

[1] From "A decade after the North American Free Trade Agreement was signed, its effects are being felt throughout Canada's economy — and supermarkets," *Canada World View*, Issue 24, Winter 2005, Foreign Affairs Canada. Reproduced with the permission of Her Majesty the Queen in Right of Canada, represented by the Minister of Foreign Affairs, 2005. <http://www.dfait-maeci.gc.ca/canada-magazine/issue24/06-title-en.asp>

[2] Reproduced with permission from Mel Hurtig, "Welcome to what will soon be the colony of Canada," *ABC theorists* (May 22, 2003) <http://canadianleaders.abctheorists.com/modules.php?op =modload&name=News&file=article&sid=50&mode=thread&order=0&thold=0>

Still Grappling with NAFTA

Though it has been over a decade since NAFTA has been in effect, its members are still struggling to understand and deal with a number of controversies that NAFTA has presented (see the softwood lumber case in "Concept Application" at the end of this chapter). For many critics, the benefits of NAFTA accrue largely to corporations rather than to individuals. As one observer comments:

> ... the North American Free Trade Agreement was sold to the people of the United States, Mexico and Canada as a simple treaty eliminating tariffs on goods crossing the three countries' borders. But NAFTA is much more: It is the constitution of an emerging continental economy that recognizes one citizen — the business corporation. It gives corporations extraordinary protections from government policies that might limit future profits, and extraordinary rights to force the privatization of virtually all civilian public services. Disputes are settled by secret tribunals of experts, many of whom are employed privately as corporate lawyers and consultants. At the same time, NAFTA excludes protections for workers, the environment and the public that are part of the social contract established through long political struggle in each of the countries.[19]

The concern that the rights of corporations are paramount in NAFTA is clearly illustrated in the growing number of lawsuits aimed at governments accused of discriminating against foreign-owned corporations. A recent case in point is that of UPS versus the Canadian Government (see Talking Business 7.13). Specifically, this controversy has largely

---

TALKING BUSINESS 7.13   WILL NAFTA FORCE PRIVATIZATION OF CANADA POST?

Why Is UPS Suing the Canadian Government?[1]

UPS claims that Canada's publicly funded network of mailboxes and post offices gives Canada Post an unfair advantage over private sector courier companies. It claims that Canada Post is unfairly subsidizing its competitive courier and express services by using a network that was built to provide its letter service. In fact, the post office is legally mandated to provide a broad range of postal services to everyone in the country, no matter where they live.

UPS wants Canadians to pay $160 million US in damages over its complaint involving Canada Post. If this weren't scary enough, the case could set a dangerous precedent. Most Crown corporations and public agencies deliver some services that are in competition with the private sector. The suit that UPS has launched could just as easily be launched over public education or health care.

Going Postal on NAFTA[2]

That's the problem with trade laws. No matter how nefarious they may be, all those clauses, numbers and government suits (not to mention the complete absence of any splashy 6 o'clock news villains) make us yearn for nap time. Or MTV.

continues

But in the 11 years since NAFTA was signed, more and more of us have come to realize we have good reason to stay awake. Secret trials. Outlandish billion-dollar damage claims. And the freakiest lawsuits imaginable, like the one that forced us to drop our ban on toxic gasoline additive MMT, apologize to the poor company that wanted to keep selling it to us, then write it a cheque for $20 million. All thanks to one little NAFTA clause that grants foreign corporations the power to sue governments if investors don't like what they are doing — Chapter 11.

Now, over a decade after the trade deal between Canada, America and Mexico was put to work, three groups have banded together to launch the first case in history that actually questions Chapter 11's lawfulness.

Why now? It seems the camel's back has been broken. An American corporation is using Chapter 11 to go after one of our public service pillars, Canada Post. It's something activists take very seriously, warning that if the company in question, United Parcel Service (UPS), wins its case (the first-ever NAFTA suit against a public service in this country), the fallout could be devastating.

The details sound fairly run-of-the-mail: UPS sues the Canadian government because Canada Post has somehow taken advantage of its letter mail monopoly to fund its parcel and courier services. The case is still pending. But if UPS wins, Deborah Bourque, national president of the Canadian Union of Postal Workers (CUPW), says the government will likely order Canada Post to get out of the parcel delivery biz, as the European Union's antitrust watchdog basically ordered Germany's national postal service to do after UPS successfully sued it back in 1994. "The problem," says Bourque, "is that Canada Post needs the profits it gets from the parcel business to ensure it can provide universal [letter] service in rural communities," something UPS obviously does not offer.

UPS spokesperson Cristina Torelli says the company isn't trying to interfere with the mail service monopoly. "[The suit] just requires that there be fair competition and that [Canada Post's] infrastructure be used for the purpose of mail [and not courier services]."

Ottawa-based trade lawyer Steven Shrybman says the argument sounds harmless enough: "'You can't compete with us [UPS] if you're providing a service in the public sector.' The problem for the public sector is that there are few, if any, pristine services where there isn't a competitive dimension." Adds Shrybman, "This could spell disaster for public services and encourage a lot of litigation by private companies seeking to break into the health care or water service markets in Canada."

"This is not about abrogating NAFTA as a whole," says Jean-Yves Lefort of the Council of Canadians, which along with CUPW and the Charter Committee on Poverty Issues has launched the constitutional challenge. "We're saying that the chapter that allows foreign corporations to sue governments directly, giving them rights over the rest of society, is wrong and should be shut down."

In fact, of all three NAFTA countries, Canada has lost the most — doling out $27 million in damages. The U.S., on the other hand, has never actually lost a Chapter 11 case, a reality that has many critics crying foul ...

Sources: [1] Excerpts, reproduced with permission from Canadian Union of Postal Workers Web site (May 10, 2002) <http://www.cupw.ca/pages/document_eng.php?Doc_ID=250>; [2] By Adria Vasil in *NOW Magazine* Online Edition, 24(1) (January 20–26, 2005) <http://www. nowtoronto.com/issues/2005-01-20/news_feature.php>>. © 2005 Now Communications Inc.

stemmed from one section of NAFTA legislation referred to as Chapter 11. Chapter 11 of NAFTA asserts that foreign corporations are permitted to sue the federal government for compensation if that government's legislation, policy, or the delivery of public services interferes with present or future profits of the foreign corporation.

■ CHAPTER SUMMARY

There is little doubt that the phenomenon of globalization will have profound effects on businesses and societies across the world. In this chapter we tried to make sense of this phenomenon — what it entails and what its implications are. Specifically, we considered why organizations may "go global," and we identified the different types of global business activity. We examined the significance of multinational and borderless corporations. We also considered why nations desire, or do not desire, to promote international trade, including an examination of the pros and cons of Canada's free trade agreement with the United States. Is all this good or bad? That is, will the trend toward an increasingly integrated world economy benefit societies, or generate greater harm? What are the challenges and opportunities for managers in the global workplace? It is hoped that the material in this chapter has encouraged you to think more critically about these questions.

Softwood Lumber & NAFTA

Canada scored what should be a knockout legal victory in the softwood dispute yesterday, but the U.S. government quickly dismissed the unanimous NAFTA ruling as irrelevant, a stalemate that observers warn could undermine respect for the 11-year-old trade deal. The U.S. lumber lobby, which started the timber battle in 2001, responded to the NAFTA judgment by calling the trade treaty's dispute resolution process "constitutionally defective."

The Coalition for Fair Lumber Imports announced it's preparing a constitutional challenge to try and scrap this section of the North American free-trade agreement. Yesterday, a last-ditch NAFTA appeals panel rejected Washington's claims that an earlier string of softwood rulings in favour of Canada broke trade rules.

NAFTA panels have three times concluded that the United States failed to prove that Canadian softwood poses a material threat of injury to U.S. producers. Under trade rules, if Washington can't prove Canadian timber injures or threatens to injure U.S. producers, it is obliged to scrap the duties on Canadian lumber imports. Yesterday's decision should end the dispute immediately. But the United States said the extraordinary challenge committee ruling was inconsequential and that it had no intention of scrapping the duty on Canadian softwood that can exceed 20 per cent or refunding the $5-billion in levies collected over the past few years. "We are, of course, disappointed with the [NAFTA panel's] decision, but it will have no impact on the anti-dumping and countervailing duty orders," said Neena Moorjani, spokeswoman for U.S. Trade Representative Rob Portman.

The United States says it found a fresh justification for the softwood duties in November, 2004.

Washington says yesterday's NAFTA ruling only applies to the U.S. International Trade Commission's 2002 finding of injury. It says the new justification for the duties came after the ITC reinvestigated the case in 2004 and again found Canadian timber poses a threat of injury to the U.S. market.

Ottawa said it believes the United States is now obliged under international law to scrap the softwood duties and refund the levies collected since 2002. "The world is watching," International Trade Minister Jim Peterson said.

Trade experts say the United States is eroding respect for NAFTA by ignoring yesterday's decision.

"For the U.S. government to deny the effect of this process weakens respect for the NAFTA and for the rule of law internationally, something the U.S. espouses when it suits its purposes," said trade lawyer Lawrence Herman of Cassels Brock in Toronto. While they disagree about yesterday's ruling, both Canada and the U.S. are trying to steer the conflict to the negotiating table in the hopes of finding a settlement that would end legal wrangling. Canada's Trade Minister said he thinks the NAFTA ruling enhances Ottawa's negotiating position "because the panel decision was final and unanimous."

Senior officials from both countries have been meeting since March and another negotiating session is planned as early as Aug. 22. Ontario's Natural Resources Minister

David Ramsay called on the U.S. to reconsider its dismissal of the NAFTA ruling. "How much longer are they going to continue, basically, to ignore an international treaty? That's something they need to ask themselves," he said. "They'd be pretty upset with us if we decided ... just to ignore decisions such as NAFTA panel decisions."

The U.S. timber lobby signalled that its members have lost patience with the dispute resolution system. "The process does not work," said lumber coalition chairman Steve Swanson. "NAFTA panels consistently act beyond their authority under U.S. law and the NAFTA."

Timber battle

Yesterday's NAFTA ruling ends another round in the 23-year-old softwood lumber feud between Canada and the U.S.

APRIL, 2001: U.S. Commerce department launches probe into American timber lobby allegations that Canadian wood is heavily subsidized and dumped in the U.S.

AUGUST, 2001: U.S. government's initial probe concludes Canadian softwood is subsidized; a countervailing duty is slapped on shipments.

OCTOBER, 2001: Initial probe also concludes Canadian lumber [is] being dumped at discounted prices; an anti-dumping duty is added.

MARCH, 2002: Softwood duties are finalized after further Commerce Department investigation.

APRIL, 2002: Canada challenges duties at NAFTA panels.

MAY, 2002: The U.S. International Trade Commission finds its lumber industry threatened with injury from Canadian shipments.

AUGUST, 2004: NAFTA panel rules in Canada's favour for the third time on threat of injury. It orders the U.S. to stop fighting rulings and take action to end the trade battle.

NOVEMBER, 2004: U.S. launches a last-resort appeal of NAFTA softwood rulings.

AUGUST 10, 2005: NAFTA extraordinary challenge panel rules in favour of Canada on injury, rejecting U.S. appeal of an earlier ruling that Washington failed to justify imposing duties on Canadian shipments.

Source: Reproduced with permission from Steven Chase, "U.S. brushes off Canada's NAFTA softwood victory," *The Globe and Mail* (August 11, 2005).

QUESTIONS

1. How are the elements of globalization present in this case, and why is NAFTA relevant here?

2. How does the Canadian government's involvement allegedly violate the spirit of NAFTA?

3. How does the U.S. response to this situation allegedly violate the spirit of NAFTA?

Do Our Foreign Investment Laws Still Have Legs?

December 1, 2004 — Foreign investment in Canada, which amounted to $358 billion in 2003, brings clear benefits to our national economy. For this reason, our federal legislation is designed to promote a welcoming, low-barrier environment for foreign investors. Since the introduction of the Investment Canada Act in 1985, hundreds of billions of dollars have been directly invested here without any foreign investor being rejected under the Act. Internationally, Canada has long pushed for a more liberalized global trade and investment regime, backing agreements that encourage foreign investment into our market and accord fair treatment to Canadian investors abroad.

However, national consensus on the virtues of foreign investment was broken by last month's announcement that China Minmetals, a company owned by the Chinese government, intended to purchase mining giant Noranda for approximately $7 billion. The news provoked exceptional levels of domestic opposition from all parts of the political spectrum. Those demanding that Ottawa put a stop to the deal voiced objections including concerns about foreign ownership of a national icon, questions of resource security and human rights, and worries about letting a foreign government own a piece of Canada.

As it turns out, Noranda will now likely go to a buyer other than Minmetals, or may not be sold at all. Nonetheless, the objections that were raised to the deal demand reflection in order to anticipate future cases. Should the criteria by which foreign buyers are judged be broadened beyond strictly economic ones? Should foreign governments be specifically barred from controlling Canadian firms? Do such issues demand a rewriting of Canadian rules governing foreign investment?

Some of the objections to the Noranda-Minmetals deal can, upon reflection, be dismissed. With revenues of $4.7 billion U.S., it is Canada's 36th largest company, employing 15,000 people worldwide. However, the size of the firm in question is not itself relevant, since Canadian companies of comparable size have long been owned, bought and sold by non-Canadians; think of Labatt, MacMillan Bloedel or Imperial Oil, to name a few. In such cases, foreign direct investment is widely regarded as a net positive for the Canadian economy and Canadians.

As for concerns that a foreign government investing here might not meet Canadian standards on labour, health and safety or the environment, the answer is simple: inside Canada, our national law is supreme. Other foreign investors doing business in Canada follow Canadian rules, and experience suggests that we would not face difficulties in compelling a foreign-owned firm to obey domestic law. Aspiring beyond legally-required conduct toward higher standards of good corporate citizenship is admirable; but since these standards are adopted voluntarily by Canadian firms, they can hardly be made legally obligatory ones for foreign investors to adopt.

By contrast, real grounds for rethinking current foreign investment rules arise in the special case of a foreign government's potential ownership or control of a Canadian firm. The first cause for concern is economic: while our free-market system sees competition and profit-maximizing behaviour as the best guarantors of economically efficient outcomes, a foreign government owning Canadian resources might choose to make an inefficient use of those resources for the sake of propping up government-controlled firms or sectors at home. This policy could undermine the efficient functioning of our economy, reducing Canada's economic health.

A further concern has to do with national interest and national security, given the possibility of a foreign government less than fully committed to free-market economics, law and liberalism. Such a company might attempt to tie politics and business, or might exert pressure to secure preferential treatment for a state-owned company operating in Canada.

In the face of these legitimate worries, the government might consider modifying the Investment Canada Act to require that foreign governments and firms controlled by foreign governments would be more carefully scrutinized if they invest in Canada. Alternatively, takeovers by foreign government-controlled firms could be restricted to a certain size or a certain percentage of a company's shares or be subject to a high level of required economic benefit. Yet if such amendments to the Act were made in order to address the concerns raised by the Minmetals case, they would have to avoid imposing any new and unnecessary restrictions on the vast majority of unproblematic foreign investments.

The Conference Board believes that future deals of the Minmetals-Noranda type pose a real dilemma for Canadian lawmakers. Our country needs foreign investment, but there are reasons to consider whether a state — as opposed to private foreign investors — should be allowed to buy a significant stake in the Canadian economy. The Investment Canada Act should be formally reviewed by Parliament, and amended if necessary, to address those concerns.

Source: Reproduced with permission from The Conference Board of Canada from http://www.conferenceboard.ca/press/2005/OpEds/041201_FDI_Op-ed.asp

QUESTIONS

1. How is the issue of globalization related to this article?

2. What is the author's point regarding foreign ownership in Canada?

3. What are the pros and cons of foreign ownership to Canada?

The Political Environment

Should the Canadian government take a more active role in the welfare of Canadian industry? The traditional relationship between government and business is clearly undergoing change. In this chapter, we will examine how government can intervene in business activity while fulfilling its role as both guardian of society and guardian of business. We will consider current and critically important trends regarding the shift toward reduced government involvement in the business sector. Specific attention will be paid to the issues of deregulation and privatization.

LEARNING OBJECTIVES

By the end of the chapter, you should be able to:

1. Describe the fundamental nature of the Canadian business enterprise system.
2. Discuss government's relationship with business with reference to government's guardianship of society.
3. Identify the purpose of Crown corporations.
4. Explain the notion of government as guardian of the private business sector.
5. Discuss government's role with regard to global business.
6. Describe the objectives and consequences of deregulation and privatization.

I am grateful to Professor Diane Jurkowski, who contributed Talking Businesses 8.1, 8.11 and Amy Bitton, who contributed Talking Business 8.3, to this chapter.

The Business World

Should Government Mind Its Own Business?

Canada is nothing. It's a zero, an empty shoebox, a vacuum of a country whose hopeless people, culture, economy and future would disintegrate into puffs of ozone were it not for government agencies and programs. Auto plants would cease to operate without subsidy, banks would disappear without ownership rules, airlines would not fly, cities would not exist and the mail would not get delivered. And of course, our cultural and telecom industries — films, television, cable, theatre — would vanish, leaving an impoverished nation of homeless primitives, wandering a wasteland, unable to look after themselves, and with nothing to do but watch American television on fading screens as the power went out.

Though few Canadians hold such ideas, they nonetheless periodically loom over the country, especially during election campaigns, and especially during election campaigns in which some of the champions of government aid and protection find their favourite recipients, usually themselves, at risk of losing support. Without the state, they — and presumably we — are nothing.

Celebrated Canadian fiction economist Margaret Atwood, writing in The Globe and Mail, contemplated the prospect of national nothingness this week as she envisioned a culture-less Canada ... Rattling off Statistics Canada numbers, Ms. Atwood reported that culture industries employ 740,000 people and account for $26-billion of GDP.

Without government aid and protection, what would there be? "Think of all arts events just disappearing from the face of the Canadian map. Poof. Gone. No more Stratford Festival, or Shaw Festival, or Annapolis Royal festival with its renowned costume ball, or Edmonton Symphony, or Royal Winnipeg Ballet, or Blue Metropolis, or poetry slams, or jazz singers, or Canadian literary publishing industry, or Alanis Morissette."

According to Ms. Atwood's economic model, none of this would exist without the "pump priming" of government programs. Any Conservative "nuking" of government aid would destroy Canadian culture. "You might as well mow it down," she said, adding that "if you're concerned, you should ask the Body Snatchers some direct questions about Culture, and those 740,000 jobs, and that $26-billion worth of GDP."

Only a strange character in an unlikely and unread novel about economics could carry on like this. It is so wildly at odds with the spirit of achievement behind any human activity, but perhaps especially culture. Do Canadians only act in plays, write books, produce films and invent video games because some politician or bureaucrat primes a money pump out of an office in downtown Ottawa?

Economies are the creations of individuals separately pursuing their own interests. Some are driven by greed, others by intellectual passion, most are out to make the very best of their lives. Some just want to have a good time. But it is individuals acting out their lives in freedom that produces the $26-billion in culture GDP. To propose that 740,000 people working in the industry would not be there without Ottawa is absurd and should be insulting to anyone in the industry.

Producers of culture like to think their work is a cut above the effort of the average person. Maybe it is, in some sense. But being an actor or a pop singer or a novelist does not in itself warrant subsidy. Government aid will certainly benefit the actual recipients. The cost, though, is borne by someone else. Also bearing the cost are the culture industries and individuals that do not receive aid. Money spent on one sector of the entertainment business creates artificial supply that attracts people who might otherwise have personally chosen some other form of entertainment.

With the artistic side of the industry comes the corporate side, a collection of protection-seeking operators who also claim that without government protection Canadians would be adrift in a sea of nothingness. The Conservative idea that the role of the Canadian Radio-television and Telecommunications Commission might be dramatically reduced, ending rules that protect their business interests, is portrayed as a national calamity.

If Canadian content and other broadcast rules were changed, including those governing satellite television, Canadian broadcasters would face the spectre of annihilation. It would be "an assault on the system," said the film association. "The entire edifice the industry is built on would probably come crashing down," an analyst said.

None of this is true, of course. Some parts of some industries might have to change the way they do business in a more deregulated market. Others would sell to the highest bidders, foreign or domestic. Most of the changes will happen anyway as broadband technology overtakes the business models of all Canadian companies. Changing technology, economic forces and the decisions of each individual Canadian about what to watch and when are already transforming the culture economy. With or without the CRTC and government programs, Canada's culture is in the good hands of individual Canadians. Canada is not a nothing; it is 30 million individuals who do what they do, mostly despite the government pump.

Source: Material reproduced from Terence Corcoran, "Canadian culture safe with Canadians," *National Post* (June 12, 2004) <http://www.friends.ca/News/ Friends_News/archives/articles06120404.asp> with permission of National Post Company, a CanWest Partnership.

THE CANADIAN BUSINESS ENTERPRISE SYSTEM: FUNDAMENTAL FEATURES

"The Business World" example highlights the importance of understanding the boundaries of what constitutes a legitimate relationship between business and government. What role should government play in business? Recent abuses of this relationship also underscore the powerful connection between government and business). As Diane Jurkowski, a professor at York University, Ontario, observes (see Talking Business 8.1), the recent "sponsorship scandal" offers an important cautionary note regarding the public sector–private sector interface.

TALKING BUSINESS 8.1   GOVERNMENT AND BUSINESS TOO CLOSE: THE SPONSORSHIP SCANDAL

For only the second time in Canada's history, has a sitting Canadian Prime Minister given testimony before a public inquiry — the Gomery Inquiry into the "Sponsorship Scandal."

The Gomery Inquiry was established to investigate and report on questions raised by the November 2003 Auditor General Report on the federal government sponsorship program and related advertising activities, including the management of the sponsorship program, how advertising agencies were selected, who received funds and how they were used. The Gomery Inquiry's mandate was to generate recommendations in order to prevent mismanagement of similar programs in the future.

In 2002, the federal Auditor General, Sheila Fraser, recommended that the Royal Canadian Mounted Police investigate how $1.6 million in federal government advertising contracts were handed out to a Montreal advertising agency. Furthermore, the Auditor General found that $100 million was paid to a variety of communications agencies in the form of fees and commissions. The program was basically designed to generate commissions for these companies rather than to produce benefits for Canadians. "Officials in Canada's Public Works Department 'broke just about every rule in the book' when it came to awarding contracts ..., Fraser said." (http://www.cbc.ca/news/background/groupaction/index.html) What emerged from the investigation, was a picture of the existence of a parallel system of underground and unreported fund-raising activities outside the party's control. (http://www.cbc.ca/news/background/groupaction/follow_the_money.html)

Essentially, the government advertising and sponsorship program that was set up to promote unity in the wake of the 1995 referendum in Quebec became, in fact, a vehicle to reward loyal Liberal party supporters. The fund was administered by the Public Works Department, headed by the then Prime Minister Jean Chretien's Quebec lieutenant, Alphonso Gagliano. Private sector advertising companies in Quebec were receiving not only federal government money, but also opportunity to gain access and influence of Cabinet by making donations to the Liberal Party.

continues

TALKING BUSINESS 8.1 (continued)

This case also highlights a much broader concern. For critics, this case reflects the potential power of business influence on government.

The issue is one of government accountability with regard to its relationship with business. Accountability emphasizes the structures of government. Accountability ensures political responsibility, whether in the formal structures of the constitution or the informal structures of constitutional conventions. It involves concern for the legal institutional and procedural devices by which Members of Parliament, Cabinet Ministers, including the Prime Minister and public administrators, are held accountable or answerable for their action.

Does society receive ample attention from the government in terms of preserving individual rights or does business wield more important power in terms of government decision making? Clearly this case was about patronizing business stakeholders who were in positions of offering ample support to the government. Is the government more interested in serving business stakeholders or societal stakeholders? These are important issues that are imbedded in the business-government relationship.

Source: Arnold Heidenheimer, *Political Corruption Readings in Comparative Analysis* (Rinehart and Winston, Inc., 1970); Donald J. Savoie, *The Politics of Public Spending in Canada* (University of Toronto Press, 1990); http://www.cbc.ca/news/background/groupaction/index.html; http://www.gomery.ca/en/termsofreference/

Historically, the government has played a critical role in the Canadian economy. From our very beginning as a nation, the government has taken responsibility for the success of business. It is useful to briefly consider the nature of our economic or business enterprise system, within which all business operates. The Canadian economic system has been described as a mixed system. This refers to the notion that while we possess a capitalist economy, government nonetheless plays an important role.

All developed countries have some sort of economic or **business enterprise system** that essentially determines the following:

1. what goods and services are produced and distributed to society.
2. how the goods and services are produced and distributed to society.

What kind of business enterprise system we have determines how or by whom these decisions are made. For example, the two decisions above might be made purely by business, or they might be determined by government, or perhaps by a combination of the two. To understand the basis of our Canadian business enterprise system, it is necessary to understand the nature of capitalist economic systems. So let's briefly explain what capitalism is.

Capitalism is a type of economic system that is based on a number of fundamental principles, including the following:

1. **Rights of the individual.** The notion of capitalism is based on the view that it is the individual who takes precedence in society, as opposed to institutions or the overall society. This implies that individuals have every right to pursue their own self-interest, which includes seeking to make profits from business enterprises. The notion of the individual as the most important element of society is not entirely representative of the ideology present in Canadian society. There are limits placed on individuals' right to pursue their self-interest. Government regulations enforce rules that affect how business owners conduct their affairs. For example, government guidelines regarding job candidate selection criteria may affect who is hired for a job, and may place emphasis on certain groups in society over others.

2. **Rights of private property.** As opposed to state ownership, capitalism asserts that individuals have the right to own land, labour and capital. In Canada, certainly, individuals are permitted to own their means of production, whether it is land, labour or capital. However, because there has been an uneven distribution of wealth in society, the government has intervened in a number of ways. For example, taxation is one approach that can be partly aimed at redistributing wealth among members of society. Much of the natural resources in Canada have still been retained by federal or provincial governments. The government may also decide that where a product or service is of a national interest, this product or service should be nationalized — e.g., government control of health care.

3. **Competition.** Capitalism advocates competition. The belief is that sufficient competition among business enterprises will ensure that business provides the goods and services required by society at a fair cost. Competition is the "invisible hand" (in the words of economist Adam Smith) that ensures the market works in this manner. In Canada, the notion of "perfect competition" does not exist in practice — there is no guarantee that an adequate supply of competitors exists across all industries.

4. **The role of government.** The view of government is reflected in the French term *laissez faire*, which means "let people do as they choose." This suggests minimal government interference in the business enterprise system. This notion of capitalism has also been referred to as the "free enterprise system," reflecting the notion of the right to private ownership of property, competition, and restricted government involvement.

Of course, the polar extreme of capitalism is another economic system referred to as communism. Whereas the capitalist system allows individuals or businesses the responsibility for the allocation of resources, the communist system places the responsibility for the allocation of society's resources into the hands of the government. There really are no societies today that are either purely capitalist or communist. In Canada, government does intervene in the affairs of business. Business is not left entirely to conduct its own affairs. When Canada first came into existence as a country, the federal government was granted the power to "regulate trade and commerce." And the fact is, throughout our history, the government has played a major role in fostering industrial development and continues to provide significant support to the business sector.

GOVERNMENT AS GUARDIAN OF SOCIETY ———

Exhibit 8.1 illustrates the variety of ways government can influence business activity, issues that we explore in the following sections.

The Tax Collector Role

Government plays many roles in relation to business. The most obvious role, and perhaps the least popular one, is that of government as tax collector, whether it is at the federal, provincial or local level. There are two broad forms of taxes: revenue taxes and regulatory or restrictive taxes. The intent of revenue taxes is to collect money in order to help fund government services and programs. *Revenue taxes* include individual taxes as well as corporate income tax, along with property tax and sales tax. *Individual income taxes* have provided the largest source of revenue for the federal and provincial governments. Individual income tax is levied on the income of individuals or on the net profits of proprietorships and partnerships. *Corporate income tax* has provided the second largest source of revenue for the federal government. Corporations are taxed on their net profit at a combined federal and provincial rate that can vary among provinces, and are subject to change based on government policy. Government policy may include an agenda of manipulating taxation to stimulate government investment or to raise more revenues.

Sales taxes are an important source of revenue for most provinces, as well as for the federal government. This tax is paid through retail stores, which act as collection agents when they sell their goods to consumers. The Goods and Services Tax (GST) that came into effect in 1991 provides substantial funds to the federal government. It is a value-added tax — a tax that is paid at each step of the manufacturing process. Consider, for example: a producer buys raw materials from a supplier, and the GST is charged by the supplier. The producer may then work on the raw materials and produce a part for sale to a manufacturer, who is then charged GST on that purchase. Everyone involved in

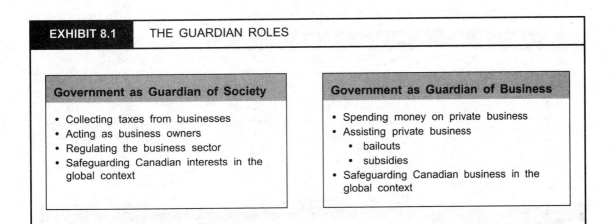

EXHIBIT 8.1	THE GUARDIAN ROLES

Government as Guardian of Society	Government as Guardian of Business

• Collecting taxes from businesses
• Acting as business owners
• Regulating the business sector
• Safeguarding Canadian interests in the global context
	• Spending money on private business
	• Assisting private business
	  • bailouts
	  • subsidies
	• Safeguarding Canadian business in the global context

the goods or services production pays GST, but only the final consumer, obviously, cannot pass the tax on to another party.

Finally, another well-known form of taxation is *property taxes*, which have been the largest revenue source for municipal governments. The revenue gained from this form of tax is typically used to fund the operating costs of the municipal government and the services that it generates.

As mentioned earlier, the second broad form of taxation is referred to as **restrictive or regulatory taxes**. There are two main types of regulatory taxes, referred to as excise taxes and customs duties or tariffs. Restrictive taxes are primarily aimed at controlling or curbing the use of specific products or services. *Excise taxes* typically are applied to goods or services that the government desires to restrict, such as products deemed to be potentially harmful (including tobacco and alcohol products). Excise taxes have been used as a deterrent to potential excesses — in fact, back in 1976, the federal government actually levied an additional tax on gasoline to discourage overuse in order to help conserve what was then a product in very short supply. Whatever the source, excise taxes are, essentially, selective sales taxes. **Tariffs** are also a form of restrictive tax, the purpose of which is detailed elsewhere in this book.

The Business Owner Role: Crown Corporations

What is a Crown corporation? A **Crown corporation** or public enterprise is an organization accountable, through a minister, to parliament for its operations. Crown corporations may be federal (e.g., Canada Post, the Canadian Broadcasting Corporation [CBC], the Canadian Wheat Board) or provincial (e.g., the Liquor Control Board of Ontario [LCBO]). (See Exhibit 8.2.)

Whether federal or provincial, why are Crown corporations established? Governments establish Crown corporations for a number of possible reasons:

- **To implement public policy that includes protecting or safeguarding national interests.** For example, federal Crown corporations, such as Air Canada and Petro-Canada, helped facilitate government policy in the area of cross-Canada transportation and Canadian ownership in the domestic oil industry.

- **To protect industries deemed to be vital to the economy.** The Canadian Radio Broadcasting Commission was established by the Canadian government in 1932 to administer a national broadcasting service in order to prevent Canadian broadcasting becoming inundated with material originating in the United States. Similarly, this was a reason for taking control of the Canadian National Railways. The CNR originated in 1919 in order to "safeguard the government's large investment in the railways" and "to protect Canada's image in foreign capital markets."[1] While few municipal governments have traditionally held significant corporate holdings, they have been owners of public transit systems, recreational centres and other facilities that are intended to enhance the quality of life in society.

- **To provide special services that could not otherwise be made available by private business.** For example, Trans Canada Airlines (Air Canada) was established in the

EXHIBIT 8.2	TOP CROWN CORPORATIONS

Rank	Company (Year End)	Group	Revenue		Profit	Employees
			$000	% Change	$	
Federal						
1	Canada Post	serv	6,365,000	3	253,000	66,500
2	Canada Mortgage and Housing	fin	4,430,000	7	667,000	1,799
3	Canadian Broadcasting Corp.	media	1,551,817	3	20,099	7,422
4	Export Development Canada	fin	1,524,000	−11	158,000	1,003
5	Canadian Commercial	serv	1,260,145	3	107	92
6	Atomic Energy of Canada	indust	576,952	15	−25,716	3,334
7	Farm Credit Canada	trans	572,116	2	96,833	900
8	Business Development Bank Can.	trans	565,960	1	31,880	1,250
9	Via Rail Canada	trans	470,046	1	15,503	3,054
10	Vancouver Port Authority	trans	103,860	8	24,544	150
Provincial						
1	Hydro-Quebec	util	11,454,000	−12	1,931,000	21,410
2	Caisse de dépot et placement du Québec	fin	7,559,000	1,343	11,524,000	712
3	Ontario Power Generation	util	5,386,000	−7	−491,000	11,000
4	B.C. Hydro & Power	util	4,493,000	−30	418,000	6,013
5	Hydro One	serv	4,065,000	1	396,000	3,970
6	Insurance Corp. of B.C.	p&c	3,230,121	9	224,807	4,750
7	Manitoba Hydro-Electric Board	util	1,980,000	0	71,000	5,800
8	Saskatchewan Power Corp.	util	1,370,000	20	187,000	2,350
9	Société de l'assur. automobile	p&c	1,012,812	−31	−160,485	3,000
10	SGF du Québec	mgt	992,740	−13	−510,728	211

Source: "Top 1000" Globe & Mail.com (http://www.globeinvestor.com/series/top1000/tables/crown/2004/). Footnotes omitted. Reproduced with permission from *The Globe and Mail*.

1930s, after observing that no private business was willing or able to provide domestic air services. Consider also the Bank of Canada. The Bank of Canada, created in 1935, was established to first serve as a control agent for the chartered banks: for example, requiring the banks to report regularly on their operations and to hold deposit reserves with the Bank of Canada. Second, the Bank of Canada is responsible for developing monetary policy and regulating monetary operations in Canada.

- **To nationalize industries that were considered to be "natural monopolies," including the generation and distribution of electricity.** It is not hard to imagine that in the early days of Canadian society the private sector was too small to undertake the creation of a national electricity supply grid. On the other hand, government was capable of raising the necessary capital, and, consequently, it took on the establishment of public utilities, including things like water supply, sewage treatment plants and electricity-generating plants, in addition to road construction and the like. In some cases, there were companies capable of building their own private utilities, which then became subject to government regulation, as we will discuss further.

Each Crown corporation is a legally distinct entity wholly owned by the Crown, and each is managed by a board of directors. The recent range of Crown corporations has been relatively diverse, with corporations operating in a variety of areas of the economy. Naturally, the corporations differ with regard to their public policy purpose, as well as in their size and in their relative need for government financial support.

Many observers suggested that, traditionally, there has been a great reliance on Crown corporations in the Canadian context. For example, by the late 1980s there were 53 parent Crown corporations (at the federal level) and 114 wholly owned subsidiaries, employing about 180,000 people, and maintaining assets worth approximately $60 billion. (For employment data, see Exhibit 8.3.)

The Liquor Control Board of Ontario (LCBO) is a provincial Crown corporation in the sense that it is owned by the province of Ontario. Technically, it is also an agency of the Ministry of Consumer and Commercial Relations. It receives its purchasing directives from the Cabinet's Management Board Secretariat, and it abides by the same regulations,

EXHIBIT 8.3	EMPLOYMENT IN CANADA — BY AGE, SEX, TYPE OF WORK, CLASS OF WORKER AND PROVINCES (MONTHLY)				
	April 2004	March 2005	April 2005	March–April 2005	April 2004– April 2005
		seasonally adjusted			
		employment in thousands		% change	
Canada — All ages	15,903.5	16,088.4	16,117.7	0.2	1.3
15 to 24 years	2,450.2	2,453.8	2,455.2	0.1	0.2
25 years and over	13,453.3	13,634.5	13,662.6	0.2	1.6
Men	8,454.2	8,553.8	8,549.9	0.0	1.1
Women	7,449.4	7,534.6	7,567.8	0.4	1.6
Full-time	12,970.1	13,088.3	13,137.9	0.4	1.3
Part-time	2,933.5	3,000.0	2,979.9	−0.7	1.6
Employees	13,456.9	13,579.3	13,616.1	0.3	1.2
Public sector[1]	3,030.2	3,106.3	3,144.1	1.2	3.8
Private sector[2]	10,426.7	10,473.0	10,472.1	0.0	0.4
Self-employed	2,446.6	2,509.0	2,501.6	−0.3	2.2

1. Those who work for a local, provincial or federal government, for a government service or agency, a Crown corporation, or a government-funded establishment, such as a school (including universities) or hospital.
2. Those who work as employees of a private firm or business.

Source: Statistics Canada, tables 282-0087 and 282-0089, <http://www40.statcan.ca/l01/cst01/labr66a.htm (Last modified: 2005-05-05).

laws and trade agreements that govern purchasing for all provincial government departments. For many years, the LCBO has been the largest single retailer (and the largest buyer) of alcoholic beverages in the world. By 2000 it had established five regional warehouses and was supplying 602 stores across Ontario with over 7,000 products.

The state-owned liquor outlet of the Société des Alcohols du Québec receives the same type of praise and criticism as the LCBO. It has been viewed as a well-managed business with excellent customer service. (See Talking Business 8.2.) On the other hand, critics also argue that private food retailers would like to be allowed to enter the alcohol sales industry more fully, given that the potential for profits is very lucrative. This sentiment also argues for privatization — the expansion of private industry into what has traditionally been the domain of the public sector.

TALKING BUSINESS 8.2   **TOASTING THE LCBO?**

Keep the LCBO As a Crown Corporation!

Ontario liquor boards employee union, http://www.olbeu.com/News%20Events/message_in_bottle.htm:

> The LCBO protects Ontario's grape and wine industry. "There are dozens of reasons not to privatize the LCBO, and the future of our grape and wine industry, in which the government of Ontario in the 1980s invested tens of millions of dollars, is one of the most important." — Jim Bradley, Legislative Assembly, April 28, 1997
>
> The LCBO protects the public. "[W]e fear that the privatization of that organization (the LCBO) will lead to increases in crime, drunk driving, alcohol abuse...." — Rick Bartolucci, Legislative Assembly, February 12, 1997
>
> The LCBO protects our children. "[T]he LCBO provides the best method of restricting the sale of liquor to minors in Ontario ..." — John Gerretsen Legislative Assembly, February 13, 1997
>
> Selling the LCBO makes no financial sense. "Why would [the Ontario] government ever consider letting go a safe, secure, successful operation and turning it over to the risky operation of those who, understandably so, only wish to make a profit from the sale of liquor in this province?" — Jim Bradley, December 4, 1996

National union of public and general employees, http://www.nupge.ca/news_2004/n25ja04b.htm:

> How much money does the Liquor Control Board of Ontario generate for the people of Ontario?
> The Ontario Liquor Board Employees Union (OLBEU/NUPGE) says the total is over $2.9 billion annually — including $2 billion in taxes and another $900 million in profits each year.

continues

And the total grows with every passing year. Without doubt, the LCBO is one of the most successful liquor retailers in the world.

Privatize the LCBO!!!

... criticism of the LCBO tends not to focus on its business acumen but rather focuses on the philosophical debate over whether state-owned enterprises should be operating in the domain of the private sector. In blunt terms, critics view the LCBO as another case of an unnecessary government-run monopoly. In fact, critics have asserted that improvements in their operations and continued expansion are aimed at preserving their monopoly power and avoiding privatization, rather than being aimed at helping the consumer. These sceptical views of the LCBO were summarized in an article by Terence Corcoran:

> With a few exceptions, nobody in Ontario can buy beer or liquor at any other retail outlet, not at corner stores nor in supermarkets. All alcoholic sales, therefore, must pass through an expensive system that keeps prices high and wages high and deprives entrepreneurs of the right to enter the business unless they join the large black market. The number of jobs that could be created by opening the market to competition is substantial. When Alberta privatized liquor retailing, employment in the industry tripled.... The monopolies also impose significant hidden costs on consumers.
>
> Even with the recent increase in the number of retail locations, buyers must make special trips, often involving many miles of travel and wasteful expenditures of time — costs that are not measured in the already high markups.... ("Ontario: Monopoly's Friend" *The Globe and Mail* [November 18, 1997]).

Source: Excerpts from Gilles Bisson, "'Message In a Bottle' Campaign Will Stop LCBO Fire Sale" (March 2004) from Ontario Liquor Boards Employee Union Web site <http://www.olbeu.com/News%20Events/message_in_bottle.htm>.

There are other examples, globally, of state-owned corporations that are struggling to avoid privatization as well as to compete with private businesses. For example, according to recent reports,[2] European post offices are making great efforts to upgrade themselves because their two basic businesses — delivering letters and delivering parcels — are both threatened by e-mail and competition from U.S. market leaders Federal Express Corp. and United Parcel Service Inc. At stake is the state post office's concern for control of Europe's $27-billion fast-growing parcel service. Observers note that Europe's big postal bureaucracies have continued to lose ground, and are also losing their domestic letter monopolies in 2003 because of European Union deregulation. Nex, we will discuss in more detail the issue of privatization and deregulation.

The Regulator Role

Government economic regulation has been defined as "the imposition of constraints, backed by the authority of a government, that are intended to modify economic behaviour in the private sector significantly."[3] As Exhibit 8.4 indicates, there has been a relatively wide scope for government regulation in business activity: for example, regulation focused on consumer protection, regulation aimed at environmental protection and regulation regarding the nature of competition. One obvious set of regulations exists fundamentally to protect the consumer, and the Canadian government has initiated a number of programs designed for consumer protection, many of which are administered by the Department of Consumer and Corporate Affairs — a body that plays a major role in regulating business in Canada. Among the numerous regulations, there is, for example, the Food and Drug Act, which was designed to protect the public from potential risks to health as well as from fraud or deception as it relates to food, drugs, cosmetics and the like. Similarly, the Hazardous Products Act serves to protect public safety by either banning products because they are deemed dangerous or requiring warning labels on products that might be considered hazardous. Ecological regulations are designed to protect the environment, and include things like the Environmental Contaminants Act, which creates regulations to limit any dangerous by-products of industrial production that could be harmful to individuals' health.

Why does the government need to intervene in the functioning of the business enterprise system? Consider the notions of competition and the public interest, discussed next. (See Talking Business 8.3, about critics of government regulation.)

Imperfect Competition

One fundamental shortcoming in the market system — the presence of imperfect, as opposed to perfect, competition — suggests the need for government involvement. If you recall our earlier discussion of the nature of the business enterprise system, we identified it as a system that essentially determines what goods and services are produced and distributed to society, and how they are produced and distributed. Ideally, such a system produces all the goods and services a society wants at a fair price. In very basic terms, on the demand side, decisions are made by individuals regarding their tastes or preferences for certain goods or services. On the supply side, businesses aim to meet the demands they face. The "invisible hand" of competition transforms these decisions of demand and supply into a system that uses scarce resources in the most efficient manner. In other words, business supply will be responsive to consumer demand: those products and services that are needed most will demand increased production, while those no longer in demand can only be sold with a drop in price; or, ultimately, businesses that do not serve any demand would go bankrupt. If a resource becomes scarce, its price will increase, and this may lead consumers to shift their preferences to a less costly alternative. In this sense, by allowing individuals and businesses to follow self-interest, the market system is responsive to consumer needs and to the capability of the environment. However, the system does not work flawlessly and, in fact, there are challenges to the effective functioning of this system. One such challenge is the notion of **imperfect competition**.

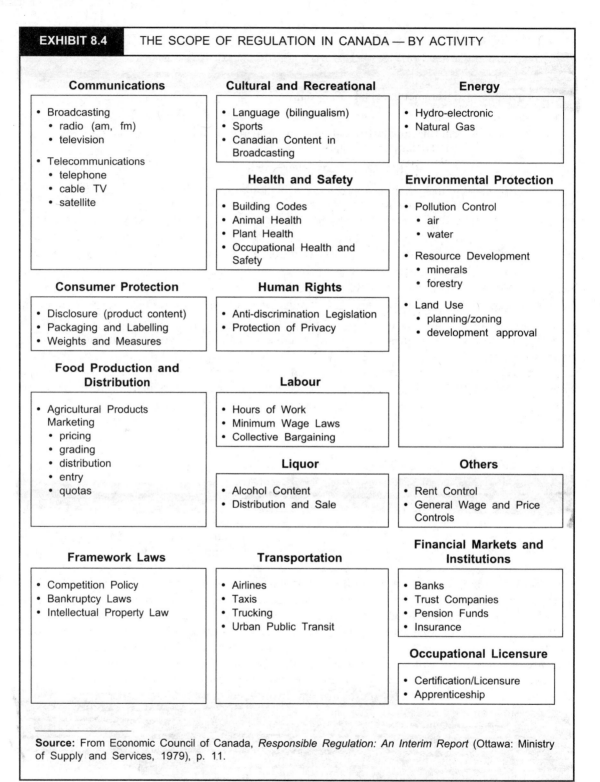

EXHIBIT 8.4   THE SCOPE OF REGULATION IN CANADA — BY ACTIVITY

Communications

- Broadcasting
  - radio (am, fm)
  - television
- Telecommunications
  - telephone
  - cable TV
  - satellite

Cultural and Recreational

- Language (bilingualism)
- Sports
- Canadian Content in Broadcasting

Energy

- Hydro-electronic
- Natural Gas

Health and Safety

- Building Codes
- Animal Health
- Plant Health
- Occupational Health and Safety

Environmental Protection

- Pollution Control
  - air
  - water
- Resource Development
  - minerals
  - forestry
- Land Use
  - planning/zoning
  - development approval

Consumer Protection

- Disclosure (product content)
- Packaging and Labelling
- Weights and Measures

Human Rights

- Anti-discrimination Legislation
- Protection of Privacy

Food Production and Distribution

- Agricultural Products Marketing
  - pricing
  - grading
  - distribution
  - entry
  - quotas

Labour

- Hours of Work
- Minimum Wage Laws
- Collective Bargaining

Liquor

- Alcohol Content
- Distribution and Sale

Others

- Rent Control
- General Wage and Price Controls

Framework Laws

- Competition Policy
- Bankruptcy Laws
- Intellectual Property Law

Transportation

- Airlines
- Taxis
- Trucking
- Urban Public Transit

Financial Markets and Institutions

- Banks
- Trust Companies
- Pension Funds
- Insurance

Occupational Licensure

- Certification/Licensure
- Apprenticeship

Source: From Economic Council of Canada, *Responsible Regulation: An Interim Report* (Ottawa: Ministry of Supply and Services, 1979), p. 11.

TALKING BUSINESS 8.3   CRITICS OF GOVERNMENT REGULATION

Opponents of government regulation have argued that Canada is guilty of overregulating its economy:

Case-in-point 1: Regulatory quotas placed on foreign automotive companies. The Canadian companies are perhaps being sheltered temporarily from the more powerful foreign corporations yet the majority, the consumers, will suffer the excessive costs. If Canadian auto industries receive such protection, there is a risk that the lack of pressure to improve and compete will eventually cause the Canadian automotive industry to stagnate.

Case-in-point 2: The story of a small business entrepreneur, Jazz Siekham, who attempted to establish a mini-bus company that accommodates 7 passengers at any one time and charges a flat rate of $3.50 for a ride anywhere within the city of Vancouver. In light of consumers' best interests, this more affordable, taxi alternative shuttle bus that offers the same door-to-door service should have been approved. This is especially true since there are similar shuttle companies in Miami and Seattle that are very successful in their operations. However, Canadian government regulation prevented this business from operating. Essentially, transportation regulations precluded more competition from entering the industry and protected the existing taxi drivers from facing cost-efficient competition in that region. This is an example of overregulation resulting in opportunities lost.

Overregulation can unfairly restrict competition and consequently many valuable innovations are never approved, and preventing them from ever coming to fruition.

Source: Based on "Do You Think Overregulation Is Strangling Canada's Economy?" *Reader's Digest Canada* (June 9, 2005) <http://www.readersdigest.ca/debate.html?a=v&di=79>

Generally, businesses aim to reduce competition as a means of succeeding and prospering. The fewer the competitors, the more secure a business becomes. Of course, on the consumer's side, the ideal scenario is perfect competition: where, essentially, there is an optimal number of competitors in any given industry to ensure fair pricing and distribution of the goods or services at the highest possible level of quality. In such a situation, those businesses unable to compete will be replaced by more efficient competitors. Imperfect competition occurs when fewer than the optimal number of competitors exist to ensure this type of situation. Where there are an insufficient number of competitors, there is less pressure on businesses to offer the best possible good or service at the lowest possible price. Businesses that are not worried about competition are also not worried about innovating, managing their operations at peak efficiency, improving product/service quality or offering their product/service at competitive prices. Consequently, inefficient businesses will remain, and consumers will be forced to accept those types of products or services, at prices dictated by those businesses. Overall, then, society is offered fewer of the goods and services citizens really want, as opposed to a situation where competition was stronger. This also leads to a less efficient use of society's resources, particularly compared to perfect competition, where resources are divided among various activities in a manner that generates the optimal combination of goods and services desired by consumers. For example, industries that lack sufficient competition may choose to restrict their output as a means to maintain higher prices, as opposed to the case of perfect competition, where businesses must accept prices determined by the market.

It is relatively easy to see, with an understanding of the notion of imperfect competition, that the market system itself will not necessarily guarantee the best and most efficient use of resources to generate the optimal mix of products and services for consumers at fair prices. Consequently, this is one fundamental rationale for government intervention in business.

The Public Interest

One of the central objectives of government regulation is to protect the public interest. Instead of having to establish its own public enterprise, government can control the operations of a private enterprise through regulations. Consequently, what we see in some areas of business is government regulation of businesses through commissions, tribunals, agencies and boards. National regulators include the Canadian Transport Commission, which judges route and rate applications for commercial air and railway companies. In terms of provincial regulatory bodies, like the provincial liquor boards, for example, provincial boards or commissions will assess and judge proposals from private business. Liquor boards, for example, are responsible for approving any price changes proposed by breweries within their province. The Canadian Radio-television and Telecommunications Commission (CRTC), under the auspices of the Department of Communications, regulates the telecommunications industry and its carriers, such as Bell Canada, and its traditional responsibilities have included accepting or refusing requests for rate increases among these carriers.

The government has also established a competition policy to control the nature of competition in the business sector. Earlier, we identified the importance of competition in our economy, given its ability to encourage the production and distribution of goods and services at the lowest possible cost. Consequently, the competition policy, set out in the Competition Act, is intended to stimulate open competition and eliminate any restrictive business practices with the aim of encouraging maximum production, distribution and employment opportunities. The role of the Competition Bureau is discussed in Talking Business 8.4.

We have, for example, government regulation in the area of public utilities, such as an electric power company or a telephone company. The government has regulated this industry because there has traditionally been an absence of competition there. Consequently, the public utilities boards or commission that regulates the industry will monitor the company's performance, as well as assess requests for rate increases and changes in the types of services provided. Consider, for example, the CRTC, which, among other things, regulates the Canadian broadcasting system. The CRTC is responsible for issuing broadcasting licences, and can require companies seeking such a licence to conform with standards regarding the type or content of programming they will provide. The

TALKING BUSINESS 8.4   THE ROLE OF THE COMPETITION BUREAU

What Is the Competition Bureau?

The Competition Bureau is an independent law enforcement agency responsible for the administration and enforcement of the *Competition Act*, the *Consumer Packaging and Labelling Act*, the *Textile Labelling Act* and the *Precious Metals Marking Act*. Its role is to promote and maintain fair competition so that all Canadians can benefit from competitive prices, product choice and quality services. Headed by the Commissioner of Competition, the organization investigates anti-competitive practices and promotes compliance with the laws under its jurisdiction.

The basic operating assumption of the Competition Bureau is that competition is good for both business and consumers.

Fair competition

- makes the economy work more efficiently;
- strengthens businesses' ability to adapt and compete in global markets;
- gives small and medium businesses an equitable chance to compete and participate in the economy;
- provides consumers with competitive prices, product choices and the information they need to make informed purchasing decisions; and
- balances the interests of consumers and producers, wholesalers and retailers, dominant players and minor players, the public interest and the private interest.

The types of anti-competitive activities investigated by the Bureau include:

Price fixing: When competitors agree on the prices that they will charge their customers.

Bid-rigging: When, in response to a call or request for bids or tenders, one or more bidders agree not to submit a bid, or two or more bidders agree to submit bids that have been prearranged among themselves.

False or misleading representations: When materially false or misleading representations are made knowingly or recklessly to the public.

Deceptive notice of winning a prize: When a notice, sent by any means, gives a recipient the impression of winning a prize and requires the recipient to incur a cost to obtain the prize.

Abuse of dominant position: When a dominant firm engages in anti-competitive practices that substantially lessen competition in a market, or are likely to do so.

Exclusive Dealing, Tied Selling and Market Restrictions: When a supplier requires or induces a customer to deal only, or mostly, in certain products; requires or induces a customer to buy a second product as a condition of supplying a particular product; requires a customer to sell specified products in a defined market.

Refusal to deal: When someone is substantially affected in his or her business, or is unable to carry on business, because of the inability to obtain adequate supplies of a product on usual trade terms.

continues

TALKING BUSINESS 8.4 (continued)

Mergers: When all or part of one business is acquired by another. The Bureau has the authority to review any merger, regardless of its size. However, the Bureau must be notified in advance of proposed transactions when the value of the assets or the target firm exceeds $50 million or the value of the amalgamated company exceeds $70 million, and when the combined dollar value of the parties and their respective affiliates exceeds $400 million.

Multi-level Marketing Plans and Schemes of Pyramid Selling: Multi-level marketing, when it operates within the limits set by the *Competition Act*, is a legal business activity, while a scheme of pyramid selling is illegal as defined by the law.

Deceptive Telemarketing: When a product's representation is false or misleading while promoting the supply of a product or a business interest during person-to-person telephone calls.

Deceptive marketing practices: When a product is advertised at a bargain price and is not supplied in reasonable quantities; when a product is supplied at a price above the advertised price; when retailers make "regular price" claims without selling a substantial volume of the product, or offering the product, at that price or a higher price in good faith for a substantial period of time; or when a contest, lottery, or game of chance or skill is conducted without making adequate and fair disclosure of facts that affect the chances of winning.

Source: Reproduced with permission from Competition Bureau Canada, 2005 <http://www.competition bureau.gc.ca/internet/index.cfm?itemID=18&lg=e>. The reproduction is not represented as an official version of the materials reproduced.

CRTC's responsibilities extend far beyond broadcasting, however, and also govern the nature of competition in the telecommunications and media industries. For example, in the telecommunications industry, there are regulations regarding the permissible amount of foreign ownership.

GOVERNMENT AS GUARDIAN OF THE PRIVATE BUSINESS SECTOR

Government Assistance to Private Business

In Canada, we have a long history of government involvement in business in the sense of promoting and protecting our industries. For example, tariff and non-tariff barriers on imported goods were designed to protect our domestic business by making foreign goods more expensive relative to Canadian goods. In fact, we could argue that a large portion of Canada's industrial development is due to protectionism through tariffs first imposed in 1879 by Sir John A. Macdonald's National Policy. Eventually, the government also offered direct incentives for industrial and resource development. Incentive programs were established to encourage managers to conduct business in a manner desired by the government. For example, it may be desirable for managers to invest in a new product development, or engage in greater export activities, or locate in an underdeveloped region. Consequently, incentives will be offered to engage in such activities. Receiving government financial support or reward for such activities would influence decisions to engage in these activities.

For example, provincial and municipal governments can encourage new employment opportunities by offering incentives to industry for locating in their areas. The municipal government might offer property tax incentives to attract industry to its jurisdiction, and the provincial government might even offer an outright grant to attract large-scale industry. Governments at all levels have provided both direct and indirect assistance for businesses, in the form of grants, loans, information, consulting advice, etc. Among the better-known and largest forms of government assistance to a business occurred in the 1980s, when both the Canadian and U.S. governments provided a loan guarantee to banks of over $1 billion in an effort to prevent the Chrysler Corporation from bankruptcy. Why the high level of assistance? If Chrysler had collapsed, hundreds of thousands of jobs would have been lost in both Canada and the United States.

The government also has tried to offer assistance to those industries deemed to be of particular importance. Industries with leading-edge technology, or those providing highly skilled jobs, or oriented toward exports, might be among the more likely recipients of government aid. The federal and provincial governments have also provided financial incentives in an effort to dissuade companies from moving their operations outside of Canada. For example, Pratt & Whitney Canada Corp. was given an $11.7-million interest-free loan from the Quebec and federal governments to encourage the company to retain the development of a new aircraft component within Canada. (See Talking Business 8.5 for another example of government assistance.)

Bailouts

Bailouts may involve a one-time financial assistance to combat significant financial troubles that a business may be experiencing. This financial assistance could also take the form of a loan or loan guarantee, for example. Bailouts were relatively common in the 1980s, involving such companies as Dome Petroleum, Chrysler Canada and Massey Ferguson. By the 1990s, while complete bailouts became rare, the government nevertheless did not refuse to offer some assistance in a bailout arrangement, as evidenced in the 1992 bailout of Algoma Steel, which involved government loan guarantees.

Subsidies

Government assistance to business in the form of subsidies has significant implications in the global business context. Subsidies have been identified as either cash payments, low-interest loans or potentially reduced taxes. Specifically, subsidies in the global context are

TALKING BUSINESS 8.5   WORKFARE BEATS TAX HANDOUTS

Earlier this month General Motors announced a $2.5 billion investment in several Canadian facilities, code-named the "Beacon Project." This investment is an incredibly important step forward for Canada's auto industry, both qualitatively and quantitatively.

By modernizing key production facilities in Canada, the Beacon Project solidifies GM's presence here, even as the company and the industry face coming challenges. But the benefits of this investment extend well beyond the plant gates at GM's Canadian manufacturing operations.

Indeed, through this project GM will add valuable Canadian content throughout the automotive value-chain — from designers imagining new models, right down to the smallest tool shop. GM already buys a stunning $17 billion worth of parts and services from Canadian suppliers every year (as much as all other automakers in Canada combined). Under Beacon it will increase those purchases further, including significant new buying in Quebec.

GM will also expand its engineering and development activity in Canada. For example, it was GM's Canadian engineers who dreamed up the hot-selling Equinox (the first Canadian-designed car since the Bricklin). Beacon will feature cutting-edge Canadian initiatives to improve the environmental performance of both manufacturing plants and finished vehicles. And the company will sponsor a long-overdue innovation in Canadian post-secondary education: Canada's first university degree program in automotive engineering.

So millions of Canadians will benefit one way or another from the Beacon Project, not just those directly associated with GM. Every job at an automaker like GM supports 7.5 jobs in total in the national economy: including upstream spin-offs through supply industries, and downstream spin-offs through consumer industries. Our economy badly needs the auto industry's exports and productivity — all the more so, given Canada's emerging specialization as a hewer of wood and pumper of oil for the world economy, rather than a producer of value-added products and services. Finally, governments need auto for the billions in tax revenues they collect each year from autoworkers, suppliers and their workers, the automakers themselves, and auto consumers.

It was in this context that the federal and Ontario governments decided to put up about one-sixth of the total cost of the Beacon Project. Does this constitute "corporate welfare," as some conservative critics call it? Not at all. I call it "corporate workfare."

In order to qualify for a single loonie under the new federal and Ontario auto programs, GM had to make firm commitments to Canadian investments and product programs. In other words: no work, no money. And government leveraged its influence to help "round out" the overall Beacon package, to encompass its cutting-edge educational, technological, and environmental features. Given the current reality of the global economy, there is zero chance that Canada could have won this investment without public participation.

Governments thus spent just over $20,000 each to help solidify the 20,000 jobs associated with GM's manufacturing operations in Canada (not to mention the several hundred new positions created through this project). Each of those jobs returns that much annually to provincial and federal coffers in direct income tax revenues alone — let alone the tax revenues generated by spin-off economic activity. Clearly, the public participation

continues

TALKING BUSINESS   8.5 (continued)

in the Beacon project represents a fiscal investment for government, not a handout — and a lucrative one, too.

Contrast this with the dubious corporate tax cuts handed down by federal and provincial governments in recent years — energetically supported by the same right-wing policy wonks who denounce the auto investments. The basic federal corporate tax rate has been cut seven points since 2001, with two more points of future relief announced in Finance Minister Goodale's February budget. Those tax cuts are worth $5 billion per year, and growing — but with no strings attached, in terms of what the private sector must do in return.

Have these blanket tax cuts stimulated the new investment we need in Canada? Hardly. In fact, measured as a share of GDP, new business investment spending (excluding the booming energy sector) has been weaker since 2001 than during the last recession. And measured as a share of after-tax corporate cash flow, it's the weakest in our history. Now that's what I call corporate welfare: tax handouts that demand nothing from the companies receiving them, and hence generate no visible improvement whatsoever in their economic behaviour. Yet those tax cuts cost Ottawa 25 times as much every year, as the federal government's one-time stake in the Beacon Project.

It's absolutely clear that Canada's high-value industries will fade away without focused, powerful policies to stimulate domestic investment and innovation. We'll be relegated to a supplier of resources for more successful countries — even including China — which recognize the value of stimulating domestic value-added. If it takes programs like the Beacon Project to help get Canada's corporations back to the work of developing our economy, then this is a form of workfare that I energetically support.

Source: Reproduced from "Buzz Hargrove Counterpoint — Workfare beats tax handouts" *National Post* (March 14, 2005) with permission of CAW/TCA — Canada. Available from CAW/TCA Canada Web site: <http://www.caw.ca/news/natpostbuzz/buzznat_031405.asp>.

---

intended to assist domestic industry to compete against foreign businesses, whether in the home country or through exports. One central argument against subsidies, whether in the domestic or global context, is that businesses should be required to manage their costs without external help, or "handouts," from the government. This is part of the requirement of fair competition, according to the critics. In addition, it is argued that consumers essentially pay for these subsidies. The government collects revenues through income and sales taxes, and it is these funds, collected from the general public, that are used to help some businesses. The question then is, Are subsidies to business an unfair drain on public funds? There is no clear resolution to this ongoing debate.

From the global perspective, there is a second central criticism aimed at companies that receive subsidies from their local government. The criticism asserts that subsidies are not merely harmless forms of assistance to businesses; rather, they constitute a form of trade barrier, just like tariffs, and they create unfair competition. (See Talking Business 8.6.) Why are subsidies viewed as non-tariff trade barriers, and how do they amount to

311

TALKING BUSINESS 8.6   THE SOFTWOOD-LUMBER DISPUTE:
                          A CASE OF GOVERNMENT SUBSIDIES?

One of the highest profile trade disputes between Canada and the United States has been the softwood lumber dispute. The origins of the dispute can be traced back to 2001 when Canada exported softwood lumber products to the United States (worth about C$10 billion). The U.S. lumber industry complained to the U.S. government that Canadian lumber producers were competing in an unfair manner since they received a hidden subsidy from their government. In retaliation for this "unfair trade," the United States imposed countervailing duties averaging 27% on Canadian lumber imports. This had a devastating effect on the Canadian lumber industry, particularly in British Columbia, which accounts for about half of the exports. Among the consequences were the closing of Canadian lumber mills, the laying off of thousands of workers and the crashing of profits.

Why was the Canadian lumber industry accused of receiving government subsidies? This claim and indeed the basis of this dispute arose due to the different traditions followed by the two countries. Most U.S. forests are privately owned, and consequently timber prices are set by private contracts or auctions. However, almost all Canadian forests belong to provincial governments. The Canadian government grants companies long-term cutting-rights simply in return for promises about employment numbers and sustainable forestry, while setting the cutting fees according to market conditions. The U.S. lumber industry feels that the Canadian government has given the Canadian lumber industry an unfair advantage and has aided in the competition against U.S. lumber producers. As of 2006, the dispute appeared to be nearing a resolution.

Source: Based on "A simple lesson in economics" *The Economist* (January 30, 2003).

---

unfair competition? Recently, the WTO has dealt with numerous international cases of allegedly unfair subsidies. The question is: Why should government subsidies to private industry be considered unfair? If the government deems it necessary, why shouldn't a domestic business receive some financial assistance? The answers to these questions have been subject to much debate. In the next section, we consider the issue of subsidies in the global context.

GOVERNMENT AS GUARDIAN OF BUSINESS IN THE GLOBAL CONTEXT

The pervasiveness of globalization has demanded that governments reconsider the extent to which they feel obligated to maintain a relationship with the private business sector. Thomas Friedman, in his book, *The Lexus and the Olive Tree*, asserts that globalization is, in fact, increasing the importance of government while changing the roles that it plays:

> The ability of an economy to withstand the inevitable ups and downs of the herd depends in large part on the quality of its legal system, financial system and economic management — all matters still under the control of governments and bureaucrats. Chile, Taiwan, Hong Kong and Singapore all survived the economic crises of the 1990s so much better than their neighbours because they had better-quality states running better-quality software and operating systems.[4]

Consequently, while governments may find their role increasingly challenged, and in some ways compromised, by the onslaught of multinationals and globalization, the need for government involvement in certain ways may be increased in this new, global context. The following section, illustrated in Exhibit 8.5, offers reasons for government support for Canadian business. Talking Business 8.7 offers arguments against such support.

Why Should Government Play the Role of Guardian of Business in the Global Context?

1.   Nurturing Young Industries

The notion that government must play a role in nurturing domestic industry was raised earlier in this chapter. The infant-industry argument asserts that the government should help a young industry to grow and develop by ensuring that the industry maintains a dominant share of the domestic market until it is mature enough to compete against foreign competition. Consequently, this philosophy is still applied, particularly among developing countries. The rationale is that the infant industry may be less competitive, particularly because of initially high output costs; however, with maturity, the production will become more efficient, and protection will no longer be necessary.

At least two risks have been associated with this form of government influence:

- Such protection can discourage domestic industry from increasing competitiveness and engaging in innovation. This is an argument that has been levelled at Canadian business.

- There is a question as to whether consumers are better or worse off from such practices. Not all Canadian parties want the Canadian steel industry to receive this type of protection from foreign rivals (see below). In fact, Canadian purchasers of any good or service arguably would want the lowest-cost supplier to be accessible and, consequently, may not appreciate the protection of infant industry if it comes at the expense of blocking access to cheaper foreign goods or services.

2.   Encouraging Direct Foreign Investment

The action of reducing foreign imports may result in the foreign business directly investing in the target country instead. That is, a foreign company can decide to set up business in the target country if it wishes to gain access to that country's consumer market and it is unable to achieve that with imports. Of course, from the domestic country's viewpoint, this

313

| EXHIBIT 8.5 | GOVERNMENT AS GUARDIAN OF BUSINESS IN THE GLOBAL CONTEXT |

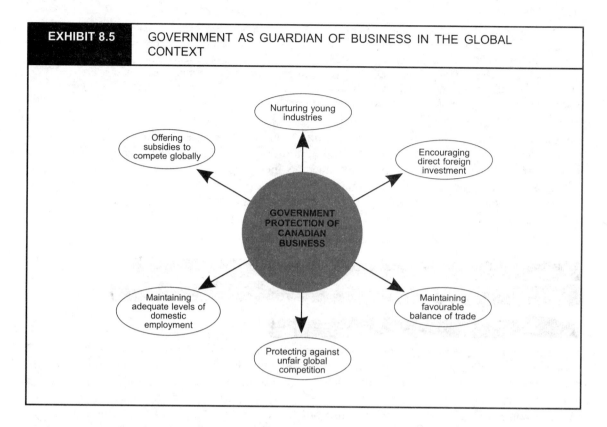

TALKING BUSINESS 8.7   WHY SHOULD GOVERNMENT NOT PLAY THE ROLE OF GUARDIAN OF BUSINESS?

Bombardier and its subsidiaries have received $772-million in federal government hand-outs since 1982, making the company the largest beneficiary of Ottawa's corporate welfare program. This week, the aerospace manufacturer is expected to confirm whether or not it will build a new regional jet.

The project will cost more than $2.5-billion and the company wants governments to pony up a third of the cost. Because Ottawa remains committed to providing business subsidies, Canadian taxpayers should brace themselves for another fleecing as Bombardier returns to the public trough.

Federal ministers will likely describe this giveaway as necessary, important, and a winner for Canada. They might even tell taxpayers the contributions will be repaid one day. But a quick review of Ottawa's collection record will put the lie to such propaganda — since 1996 less than 5 per cent of the tax money "invested" in business projects has been recouped. So in advance of the Bombardier subsidy announcement it is worth re-stating the case against corporate welfare:*

continues

TALKING BUSINESS 8.7 (continued)

i) Market decisions should be made by investors, not by politicians and bureaucrats. The proper function of the private capital market is to direct investment to projects, industries or firms that offer investors the best and/or most secure rate of return. The difference between a sound and poor investment for an individual can have profound implications yet there is no similar discipline for government officials when using other people's money.

ii) Corporate welfare is not driven by market imperatives. Investment decisions should be based on financial reward versus risk. Government investment decisions are driven by political imperatives. The top concern when offering subsidies is a preoccupation with the number of jobs created with little concern for profitability or sustainability.

iii) Picking market winners and losers is not a job suited for government officials. Corporate welfare decisions are most often made by individuals with little experience in private investing; moreover, decisions are often made in a politically charged environment. As a result, ensuring that taxpayer-financed projects meet geographical, industrial equity, and politically saleable criteria often become an end in itself. Governments have an abysmal record of picking winners, whereas corporate losers — like Bombardier — have a stellar record of finding government handout programs.

iv) Corporate welfare is unfair. Business subsidies create an uneven playing field as money is diverted away from successful companies to less successful, but politically connected ones. Worse still is those firms and their workers which do not receive government grants end up subsidizing their government-supported competitors through their taxes.

v) Corporate welfare undermines public confidence in our decision-makers. Despite assurances from politicians that subsidies serve an overall industrial policy, there is a growing sense among Canadians that government aid to business is about divvying up pork to favoured and politically connected constituencies.

vi) Corporate welfare runs contrary to free and open markets. Business owners lose sight of their competencies, namely to provide customers with a good or service and earn a profit. They become better lobbyists than businesspeople and morph from entrepreneurs into grantrepreneurs.

vii) Corporate welfare creates a culture of dependency. Business owners become so reliant on government assistance they build expectations of handouts into financial plans. This has the perverse effect of directing resources to less productive investment projects, which slows economic growth rather than enhancing it.

viii) Corporate welfare is not a public good. Tax money ought to be spent on projects that provide the largest societal benefits or on social programs that are a priority to citizens. For example, infrastructure such as roads and water treatment; services such as national defence, policing, border control and immigration; and social services like health care, assistance for the disabled and pensions. Business subsidies

continues

do not fit these criteria and most taxpayers realize subsidies routinely fail to achieve their public policy objectives.

ix) Corporate welfare leads to higher taxes. All taxpayers end up footing the bill for Canada's $4-billion business subsidy programs.

Taxpayers deserve better than to subsidize well-connected corporations and their shareholders. Ottawa should end corporate [subsidies] and create a business climate that rewards success, not sycophants.

* The nine points were adapted from the CTF report A Taxpayers Audit of Technology Partnerships Canada (Feb. 2002).

Source: Reproduced from John Williamson, The Canadian Taxpayers Association (March 14, 2005) <http://www.taxpayer.com/main/news.php? news_id=1954> with permission of the Canadian Taxpayer Federation.

foreign investment may be desirable if it increases job opportunities, contributes to the growth of industry and adds to the amount of capital.

3. Maintaining Favourable Balance of Trade

Government may seek to influence the relative status of exports and imports to avoid running a trade deficit. (Chapter 7 on globalization expands the discussion with regard to the importance of trade and the issue of trade surpluses and deficits.) **Trade surpluses** come about when a country's exports exceed its imports and, consequently, more money is entering the country (from foreign consumers buying these exports) than is leaving the country (from domestic consumers buying foreign imports). A **trade deficit** is the reverse — when a country imports more than it exports. Traditionally, governments intervened to ensure a trade surplus by imposing tariffs or quotas or by banning outright some foreign-imported commodities. Typically, the governments would also subsidize domestic industries in order to encourage growth in their exports.

4. Protecting Domestic Business from Unfair Competition

There is a concern among some businesses that foreign competitors will offer their products at extremely low prices as a means of monopolizing their share of the target country's market. The ultimate consequence would be that domestic producers could potentially be driven out of business and be replaced by the foreign imports. A foreign competitor who manages to export the products at such low prices may be accused of **dumping** — which is pricing the product below cost or below the cost of the target country's product. In other words, a foreign supplier who sells the product at a loss or for less than the price of the seller's domestic market would be considered guilty of dumping.

Traditionally, steel companies have been among the most avid users of anti-dumping legislation in Canada and the United States. Hamilton-based Dofasco Inc. lodged a dumping complaint against steel mills in Asia and South America. The aim was to seek government assistance, which in this case resulted in a decision by the Canadian federal government to place anti-dumping tariffs on low-cost imported steel from these foreign suppliers. In total, these anti-dumping tariffs were aimed at blocking the dumping of steel shipments from nine countries. This echoes similar action taken in the United States. Steel producers in both the United States and Canada have blamed the increasing foreign imports of steel for reducing demand for their product domestically and, consequently, reducing product prices and revenue. It is interesting to note that while Canadian steel producers welcome such government intervention, other domestic players are not happy with the implementation of anti-dumping tariffs, which effectively raise the price of these cheaper goods. Specifically, western Canadian manufacturers have claimed that the protectionist measures will reduce their ability to compete with Ontario steel manufacturers. Many western steel businesses argued that they will lose access to these cheaper foreign sources and now be forced to rely on costlier steel sources in Ontario. These businesses argue that they should have access to the lowest-cost sources of steel, whether these sources are from Canada or from foreign producers. In this regard, they are opposed to the government's protectionist policy of imposing anti-dumping tariffs.

5. Maintaining Adequate Levels of Domestic Employment

A government knows that society holds it responsible for ensuring the unemployment rates are not high. Imports that come to dominate an industry bring the threat of causing domestic industries to go bankrupt. Consequently, where businesses claim they are under threat of bankruptcy due to foreign competition, the government is forced to consider what action it can take to combat this threat. In the past, the government protected Canadian business and employment from the risk of foreign competition via the implementation of tariffs, as discussed in the previous chapter. Clearly, such an option is complicated by the fact that reducing imports is not necessarily feasible, for reasons also described earlier. Protectionist policies are not compatible with the sentiments of free trade, and thus governments are sometimes placed in the unenviable position of balancing the needs of the domestic economy with the need to honour the rules governing global business. A case in point is the issue of government subsidies.

6. Offering Subsidies to Compete Globally

Whether it is for the purpose of maintaining employment levels or of assisting businesses in the global marketplace, the issue of government subsidies to business has become much more controversial in the context of globalization. Whether it is cash payments, low-interest loans or tax breaks, such financial assistance is referred to as a subsidy. And in the case of the global context, such subsidies are intended to help domestic industry deal with global competition. In recent years, the WTO has been involved in many international disputes regarding whether a local government has given its domestic industry an unfair advantage through some form of subsidy. The risks of such subsidies, in addition to the potential conflicts they create with regard to facilitating free trade, include the notion that competitive industries should be able to absorb such costs themselves rather than relying on the government for these handouts. The lumber dispute highlighted in Talking Business 8.6 earlier in this chapter is an example of the difficulty in establishing the degree to which government should aid business in the global context. Other examples abound with regard to government aid to business in the global context.

SHOULD GOVERNMENT "MIND ITS OWN BUSINESS"?

Government intervention in the economy has traditionally been greater in Canada than in the United States. For example, government expenditures as a percentage of GDP are typically higher in Canada than in the United States, and public sector employment in Canada has been as much as 30% greater than in the United States. However, Canada has been following the trend of reducing government's involvement in the business sector. Why are we witnessing this reduction in government involvement, and what are the implications of this trend? These questions are addressed in the following sections. (See Exhibit 8.6.)

Deregulation

Earlier, we discussed the issue of government regulation. And, as we mentioned, government regulates the operation of businesses through commissions, tribunals, agencies and boards. Whatever the form, government directly regulates about one-third of the economy through more than 600 organizations. However, what we have witnessed since the 1980s is a trend toward **deregulation**. Deregulation, as the name suggests, involves a reduction in the number of laws or regulations affecting business activity. It also suggests a reduction of the powers of government enforcement agencies and other forms of government control or influence.

In recent years, the process of deregulation in the Canadian economy seems to have accelerated, particularly in industry sectors, such as transportation, telecommunications, financial services and energy services. While the telecommunications sector maintains varying degrees of regulations in different areas, it has created an increased level of competition through deregulation in areas such as overseas calling, domestic long distance, local, wireless and other services. In the Canadian electricity sector, deregulation has recently been applied, particularly in Alberta and Ontario.

EXHIBIT 8.6	QUESTIONS TO BE ADDRESSED REGARDING GOVERNMENT INTEREVENTION

Why has the government deregulated certain industries?

Why has the government engaged in privatization?

What areas of business has the government chosen to deregulate or privatize?

What are the benefits of deregulation?

What are the benefits of privatization?

What are the risks of deregulation?

What are the risks of privatization?

In fact, in a number of countries, we have witnessed economic deregulation among many industries, including airlines, trucking, railroads, financial markets, energy and telecommunications. At the same time, there has been an increase in regulations that are intended to govern such areas as health and safety and the environment. In order to understand the implications of economic deregulation, it is useful to briefly reconsider why, in fact, there is a need to regulate any industry at all.

As explained earlier in this chapter, regulation is aimed at correcting market failures and inequities that may arise for a variety of reasons, including insufficient competition. However, just as the market can fail, so, too, the government policy of deregulation may not always achieve the goals for which it was intended. While it may be an oversimplification, the significant consequences of deregulation fall into two categories: potential benefit and potential risk.

What's the potential benefit?

• The benefit to consumers of increased competition arising from the reduction of regulations that have formerly restricted the entry of new competitors.

What's the potential risk?

• The risk to consumers of exploitation — e.g., reduction in quality of product or service, increases in consumer fees or price increases as a result of the reduction in laws governing their operation.

The question is, Will deregulation accomplish the central objective of sufficiently loosening constraints in order to encourage the entry of more competitors? Or, will deregulation fail to encourage adequate competition, and will this loosening of constraints instead permit current competitors to abuse the system and exploit consumers in some way? (See Talking Business 8.8.)

Research evidence from U.S.-based studies has offered strong support for the benefits of deregulation among a variety of sectors, including railway, trucking, airline, telecommu-

---

***TALKING BUSINESS* 8.8   DEREGULATION OF UTILITIES**

Deregulating the Electrical Energy Industry

In order to understand deregulation, it is necessary to briefly explore the history of owner-ship and regulation of the electric industry in Canada and the United States:

Originally, groups of private investors controlled the ownership and production of electrical energy in both the United States and Canada.

- Over time, electrical energy came to be considered as a natural monopoly, where economies of scale and the importance of electrical energy led to public ownership of most generation facilities.
- In most cases public ownership was at the state or provincial level. In Canada, with the sole exception of Alberta, this was accomplished through the formation of Crown corporations, such as BC Hydro.
- The end result was vertical integration, where one utility generated, transmitted, and distributed electricity within a certain area.
- The utility had a monopoly over electrical production and distribution in a given area. Customers were unable to choose between different energy providers.
- The vertically integrated companies operated primarily under state or provincial regula-tions.

. . . .

Why Deregulate?

In general, proponents of electrical deregulation hope to gain some or all of the following benefits:

- Cheaper electricity rates for customers through competition, particularly industry and larger businesses who purchase wholesale electricity
- Improved service for some customers through competition
- Greater freedom for customers choosing between different types of energy, including environmentally friendly technologies such as solar energy and wind turbines
- Prevention of companies that gain market power by lowering the price of generation and making up for it by raising the cost of transmission and distribution, which can happen when the three systems are bundled together

---

Source: Excerpts from Mapleleafweb.com, Department of Political Science, University of Lethbridge, http://www.mapleleafweb.com/features/economy/deregulation/energy/industry.html

---

nications and financial industries. Comparisons have been made of the U.S. and Canadian railway industries between 1956 and 1974, when the U.S. railway industry was more heavily regulated than the Canadian. While both industries had access to the same tech-nology, productivity growth was much greater in the Canadian (3.3%) than in the U.S. railroads (0.5%). Studies have indicated that unit costs in the U.S. trucking industry decreased significantly in the period following deregulation in 1983. Similarly, the airline industry managed to reduce costs by 25% in the period following deregulation.

The U.S. telecommunications industry has also benefited from deregulation, according to recent studies. For example, by 1996 long-distance telephone rates in the United States had dropped by over 70%. A number of studies have also suggested that deregulation encouraged much more innovation, as reflected in the emergence of such profitable services as cellular telephony and voice messaging. It is interesting to note that the concept of cellular phones was discussed as early as the 1950s, and the technology had become available by the early 1970s, yet the Federal Communications Commission did not issue licences until 1983 — an illustration of the inhibiting effect of regulations on innovation.

Deregulation in the financial industries, including securities, investment and banking sectors, has also yielded some positive support from U.S.-based studies with regard to its consequences. For example, it has been estimated that partial deregulation of the banking and savings and loan industry contributed to a 300% increase in productivity, while deregulated brokerage fees resulted in a 25% decrease in rates.

Comparative studies have supported the benefits of deregulation. For example, by 1999, in industries such as the airline industry, the United States was clearly maintaining a significantly higher level of deregulation than many European countries. Advocates of deregulation have asserted that the benefits of deregulation were reflected in the fact that European airline fares were about twice as costly as U.S. airfares, while European companies were neither as efficient nor as profitable as the U.S. carriers. Consequently, supporters of deregulation claim that eliminating price and entry restrictions would increase competition and, ultimately, benefit consumers through lower airfares and better service. Comparisons of the relative differences in levels of regulation between Europe and the United States by the late 1990s drew similar conclusions. It was estimated that many European companies were paying about 50% more for their electricity than their U.S. counterparts. For example, the high level of regulation in Germany's electricity market, including the requirement to purchase electricity from regional producers rather than less expensive alternative sources, was viewed as inhibiting efficiency and productivity. In contrast, the U.K. greatly benefited from energy deregulation with regard to productivity gains, estimated at 70% subsequent to deregulation.

While the findings above certainly point to the potential benefits of deregulation, there is no doubt that support for deregulation is far from universal. While advocates claim that the beneficial impact on consumers and businesses outweighs any costs, opponents suggest the reverse — that the risks of deregulation are too high to enter into this venture. There is likely no area more mixed with regard to the reaction to deregulation than in its impact on developing countries. Nonetheless, there is, again, evidence that is very supportive of the policy of deregulation. For example, deregulation in the telecommunications industry among some Latin American countries has greatly encouraged private sector involvement and led to increased efficiency in services. By the late 1990s, telephone user rates were reduced by about 50% following the deregulation of entry requirements in the long-distance telephone market in Chile. At the same time, studies have pointed out the negative consequences of maintaining regulation in various sectors within developing countries. For example, in the late 1990s Brazil and Argentina's transportation regulations forced businesses to ship largely by road, even though the costs were significantly higher than rail charges.[5]

Example #1:
Deregulation in the Transportation Industry

As mentioned, the main objective of government regulation is to protect the public interest. The railroad industry was among the very first to have regulations applied, with the deal made in 1895 between Prime Minister Wilfrid Laurier and the CPR. Essentially, the government promised the CPR the financing it needed to complete a transcontinental line if the CPR would carry wheat produced by western farmers for shipping on a regular basis at a negotiated rate. Many years later, the National Transportation Act created the Canadian Transport Commission (in 1970), whose job it was to regulate and control the various means of transportation in Canada, including motor, air, water transport and railways, among other things. However, on January 1, 1988, the new National Transportation Act came into effect, and brought with it a new era of deregulation. What did this new legislation contain, and how did it bring about deregulation in the transportation industry? Well, just consider its impact on the trucking industry.

This act brought with it the passage of the new Motor Vehicle Transport Act. Prior to that time, anyone wanting to enter the trucking business was required to appear before the provincial licensing board and prove there was a public need for their service in order to get a licence to operate a truck. However, under the new act the prospective trucker must simply present proof that they are insurable and can pass some minimal safety criteria. So what is the result of all this? One of the major benefits of the reduction in requirements for new entrants was increased competition: more truckers entered the industry. Shippers gained from a wider choice of trucking services and more competitive rates. Following the passage of this Act, shippers could negotiate the level of service and price of any domestic movement with any carrier. Consequently, consumers benefited in terms of reduced costs arising from increased competition in highway carriers. In fact, a central aim of this deregulation was to encourage greater efficiency in Canada's over $2 billion transportation market. In a more recent report of the trucking industry in Canada, the following observation was made:

> What has emerged is a new breed of Canadian trucker — one that is more efficient, value-priced, eager to customize to shippers' needs and adept at filling specialized niches in a North American market dominated by huge and efficient American carriers.[6]

In the related railway shipping industry, recent reports have indicated that shipper rates dropped by 35% since deregulation, and were considered the lowest in the world — 60% below the international average.[7] However, there has been a downside for some. With increased competition, some trucking companies have been unable to compete effectively and have gone bankrupt, resulting in the loss of hundreds of jobs. In fact, in 1990 about 130 trucking companies declared bankruptcy — over twice as many as those in the previous year. A major threat has come from U.S. trucking companies, which have lower labour, equipment and tax costs and, consequently, lower operating costs. So there are winners and losers in the trend toward deregulation, and the issue of competition lies at the heart of this. Reducing regulations welcomes more entrants and creates more pressure on existing Canadian companies. During the years following deregulation, the Canadian carriers admitted that they were slow to adapt to new technologies such as electronic data interchange, bar coding and satellite tracking of trailers. For example, by 1997 almost all U.S. truckload tractors were equipped for satellite tracking, while only 50% of Canadian tractors were equipped.[8] More recently, and following the September 11, 2001, terrorist attacks, truckers have complained of increased regulation, which is hurting the trucking industry (see Talking Business 8.9).

TALKING BUSINESS 8.9   TRUCKERS, OTHERS FEAR TRADE BEING
                          OVERREGULATED

Following the terror attacks of Sept. 11, 2001, the federal government has sought to shore up border security, transportation security and the security of the nation's infrastructure.

Yet the problem that now confronts truckers and everyone else involved in trade of some kind, is to what degree catching terrorists is balanced with the free flow of trade and privacy rights, truckers and others said recently.

Randal Mullett, vice president of government relations for CNF Inc., said CNF vehicles cross borders "hundreds of times a day and [we] believe a threat to business [is] more from over-zealous government regulations than from a terrorist."

The rules and regulations have become a "security maze," said Carol West, president of the Canadian Society of Customs Brokers.

There are too many individual government departments and agencies acting independently, West added. She made the comments at a cargo security and trade conference sponsored by the Border Trade Alliance (BTA) Feb. 14–15 in Washington.

BTA heard from a host of government officials, company representatives and others on how to balance trade with security concerns.

When it comes to government regulations, many agreed that less is more. "Businesses can't absorb the cost of meeting [government] regulations in every country in which they do business," said West.

John Tomoney, director of corporate security for the Warnaco Group, which deals with products with names like Calvin Klein Jeans and Speedo, said the federal government is pushing technology when what they need is "due diligence" and communication with partners in the supply chain. Tomoney was speaking on behalf of the National Cargo Security Council.

"Technology is not the savior of the world ... people still flip the switch," agreed Mullett. "Homeland security is still a people problem."

Many speakers agreed that truckers and others are being confronted with too many rules and credentials, and that there should be one standard identification credential used throughout, be it hazardous materials, agricultural products, immigration or whatever.

Mullett urged trade associations like BTA and private companies to present a more united front to address their needs and concerns.

Source: Reproduced from Dorothy Cox, "Border Trade Alliance," *BTA in the News*, National Edition (March 1, 2005) <http://www.thebta.org/news/articles/03012005.cfm> with permission of The Trucker Newspaper.

Example #2:
Deregulation in the Insurance and Banking Industry

In the financial services industry, deregulation permitted banks to enter the brokerage business and allowed them to sell insurance. This has not yet received widespread approval. A case has been made for deregulating the insurance industry to allow banks to enter.[9] The banks have long served as an example of an industry with inadequate competition and that, consequently, requires rigorous government regulation. In fact, the recent pressure exerted on the government by banks to allow them to merge was faced with a public fear of the creation of a greater monopoly situation and the negative consequences of such a situation. Interestingly, on the other hand, there has been an opposite sentiment with regard to allowing banks to expand their services into the insurance industry through their branch networks.

Critics assert that the insurance industry and, specifically, the current insurance distribution system fail to meet the requirements of the Canadian consumer. Relatively lower sales and a distinct lack of insurance availability suggest the need for more competition within the insurance industry. The argument is that allowing banks to enter the insurance industry would be a great service, particularly to lower-income Canadians, who currently cannot afford proper insurance coverage. With present government regulation, banks are not permitted to enter the insurance field. However, as with the general notion of deregulation, permitting banks to enter the insurance industry would, allegedly, result in less costly, more comprehensive insurance service for Canadians, and create a more competitive, stronger, financial services industry.

In addition, advocates of deregulation in this industry offer examples of similar practices in other countries. For example, allowing integration of insurance services has occurred in France, where banks are allowed to sell insurance policies in their branches. The average expense ratio for bank insurance policies was under 5%, compared with almost 14% for other companies selling insurance. The lower cost structure contributes to lower policy costs for consumers of insurance obtained through the banks. Combining banking and insurance services for French consumers allowed those banks to offer to low-income persons small, standardized policies that, under normal circumstances, would not generate sufficient commissions for a typical insurance agent. The advantages of permitting banks to enter the insurance industry are also evident in New Zealand, where there is evidence that competition from the insurance subsidiaries of banks led to falling prices for term life insurance. Consumers also valued the convenience of one-stop shopping. Benefits in the Canadian context are noted in Talking Business 8.10.

Example #3:
Deregulation in the Airline Industry

Deregulation in the airline industry actually started around 1984. The passage of the new National Transportation Act in 1988 eliminated many restrictions in the airline industry, including restrictions related to routes, frequency of flights and type of aircraft. Among the loosening of restraints, airlines could offer any combination of scheduled and chartered services on their current routes, and were no longer restricted in offering discounts. Once again, the effects of deregulation made it easier for new players to enter the industry, as

---

***TALKING BUSINESS* 8.10   DEREGULATING INSURANCE**

A Canadian example of the benefits of allowing banks to sell insurance is provided by the Caisses Desjardins of Quebec, which is a not a chartered bank but, rather, is governed by provincial regulation and, consequently, is not restricted by insurance regulations.

Allowing Caisses Desjardins to sell in-branch insurance policies in Quebec has made the purchase of such policies much more accessible. In Quebec, 60% of insurance policies are purchased by people with annual incomes of less than $30,000, compared to 44% in the rest of Canada. In fact, critics note that Canadians overall are underinsured. Recent reports indicate that approximately 17% of all Canadians have no life insurance, and 25% feel they require more life insurance than they can afford.

The assertion is that by permitting banks to enter the insurance industry, they would significantly increase access through their network of more than 8,000 branches and 12,000 automated banking machines. In sum, advocates of deregulation believe that the insurance industry will improve its treatment of consumers if it is faced with competition from the banks. It would also improve the quality of service and, arguably, result in reduced costs.

---

well as allowing existing airlines greater ease in expanding routes and increasing or reducing fares. In 1990, measures were taken to remove Canada–U.S. government-imposed restrictions. The "open-skies" agreement completed in 1995 permitted Canadian and U.S. airlines to fly across the border on any routes they think will be profitable and, essentially, create one North American market for air travel.

Why did all this deregulation occur in the airline industry? For essentially the same reason that it may occur elsewhere — to encourage increased competition. The Canadian government initiated deregulation because it felt that Canadian companies needed to learn how to compete internationally. The government had been observing large numbers of Canadians taking advantage of lower airfares in the United States. It has been argued that deregulation was, in a sense, a push to force Canadian carriers to be much more competitive. Of course, as was the case with the trucking industry, consumers of the service also are winners: they now have more choice of carriers and more competitive prices. However, deregulation also means much more difficult times for carriers, which must now contend with more competition. Deregulation, like the reduction of trade barriers, has forced many companies to become more competitive in order to survive in a more crowded marketplace. Of course, the hope is that the Canadian airline industry will increase its competitiveness, and benefit the consumer with lower prices and better products and services.

To date, the positive results of deregulation do not appear to have materialized in the Canadian airline industry. The deregulation process initiated by the National Transportation Act encouraged fierce competition between Air Canada and Canadian Airlines, with each offering identical fares, seat sales, etc. However, by the latter part of the 1990s, still only the two airlines remained as dominant competitors in the industry, accounting for

325

about 80% of industry operating revenues. By 1999, only Air Canada dominated the industry, after acquiring Canadian Airlines. Consequently, in February of 2000, Canada's Ministry of Transport announced some degree of re-regulation of the airline industry. The proposed legislation was intended to increase the power of the Competition Bureau and Transport Canada to control fares, among other issues.

The Canadian press has carried many stories reporting the criticisms of Air Canada, an airline that is about 13 times larger than its closest competitor. Relatively smaller competitors have been viewed as not big enough to mount any real threat to Air Canada's monopoly power in Canadian skies.[10] Does it really matter that there is only one big player in the Canadian airline industry? Critics suggest that, as with any monopoly, consumers ultimately suffer from a lack of real competition. Consequently, critics also relate overbooked flights, air rage and high air fares as the consequences of the Air Canada monopoly.

Air Canada was once a Crown corporation, but was privatized in the late 1980s. Critics encouraged such privatization in order to improve efficiency by taking this airline out of the hands of "inefficient bureaucrats." Ironically, many critics suggest that those same inefficiencies are back because of the power of private ownership in a monopoly situation. So, what, if anything, should the government do to combat what critics view as unwieldy monopoly power? The government could regulate the behaviour of Air Canada. It could force Air Canada to agree not to overcrowd routes and to fly certain routes at certain times. And in fact, the government has re-imposed some regulations on Air Canada. However, in a climate of deregulation, this is not a popular choice. Consequently, in line with the philosophy of deregulation, the transport minister also recently warned, in a 2000 speech, that if domestic competition does not increase in the short term, U.S. airlines would be permitted to serve domestic routes in Canada, even though foreign airlines traditionally have been barred from owning more than 25% of a Canadian airline.

Example #4:
Deregulation in the Electricity Industry

The past 10 years or so have seen a great interest in deregulation in the energy sector: specifically energy supply, with Britain and Scandinavia largely initiating this practice in the early 1990s. Traditionally, electricity costs have been higher in Europe than in North America. After a number of European governments privatized their public utilities, the cost of electricity dropped in those regions. Deregulation also welcomed much more competition, which forced the power companies to become more efficient and improve customer service.

The Canadian government, seemingly drawing on the European experience, decided to initiate privatization and deregulation in the energy sector in Canada, beginning with Alberta in 1995. Unfortunately, the reaction to this transition has been mixed, with some observers criticizing the 1995 deregulation process in Alberta's electricity industry, and others adding that the purchase of electricity has become more complicated with the advent of deregulation.

Ontario has followed Alberta's lead in electricity deregulation, although it has proceeded somewhat more slowly, and, according to some, more cautiously. While advocates of deregulation feel that, ultimately, the benefits of increased competition will prevail, those opposed to deregulation believe that public ownership should continue to exist for essential services in order to ensure that all members of society will be guaranteed access to the same service at a reasonable price:

> Deregulation was fingered by presenters as the culprit during hearings by the U.S.-Canadian Power System Outage Task Force on the August 14, 2003 electricity blackout. They pointed out that the electricity system is run down because ... [t]here wasn't enough concern about controlling all these new deregulated companies. ... Prior to restructuring and deregulation, the goal of utilities was reliable service at minimum long-term cost. In contrast, the goal of newly restructured organizations in a deregulated environment is short-term profit with little concern for the overall system.[11]

Privatization

What does *privatization* mean? In broad terms, **privatization** refers to the divesting of government involvement in the operation, management and ownership of activities. Typically, privatization involves the transfer of activities or functions from the government to the private sector. Privatization might involve selling off a Crown corporation to the private sector. For example, Air Canada, formerly a Crown corporation, was sold to the private sector in 1988–1989. Also in 1988, the government sold Teleglobe Canada Inc., a handler of overseas satellite calls for the telephone and telecommunications companies, to private business.

Privatization might also involve contracting government jobs to private companies. For example, in some provinces private businesses contract to manage hospitals and other health care institutions previously managed by government employees. Other services that can be contracted out are things like garbage collection and road construction. In addition, public institutions have also contracted out services such as data processing and food and janitorial services to private sector corporations. The closing of some postal stations and the franchising of postal services in retail businesses is yet another example.

In recent years there has been a significant transformation of the organizational landscape across the world, as numerous state-owned monopolies, agencies and other public organizations have privatized. Government ownership in areas from airlines to electricity has been sold to either domestic or foreign investors. In fact, over 15,000 enterprises were privatized during the period from 1980 to 1992. By 1997, worldwide privatization proceeds reached $153 billion.[12]

Privatization has been implemented not only in advanced countries, such as the United States, Canada, the U.K., Australia, France, Germany and Japan, but also in transitional countries such as Poland, Chile, Brazil, Mexico and Argentina. In addition, developing countries have been implementing privatization — including Nigeria, Tunisia and Zimbabwe. It is also expected that privatization will continue to progress around the world and in most economic sectors over the coming decade.

Global privatization accelerated in the 1990s, particularly in Western Europe, with developing countries accounting for about one-third of the annual funds raised by privatization. In the economies of Eastern Europe, the transition to private ownership has reflected a particularly significant political transition, as recently observed:

The development of a large-scale privatization program is also a highly political act. Almost by definition, privatization represents an ideological and symbolic break with a history of state control over a country's productive assets. Nowhere is this symbolism more apparent than in the economies of Eastern Europe and the former Soviet Union, where privatization of state-owned enterprises has come to signal a nation's transition from communism to democratic capitalism. In Russia, the privatization of enormous petroleum (Lukoil), natural gas (Gazprom) and telecommunications (Syazinevest) companies represented a fundamental break from socialist state ownership.[13]

Why Do Governments Privatize?

Why have we observed the increased divestiture of government in business activities, including the sale of Crown corporations? What are the reasons for reducing the level of government ownership in business enterprises? Let's consider some of the popular arguments for privatization.

Reasons for Privatization

Belief in the power of competition as a control mechanism. Privatization is considered to be an expected outgrowth of the free enterprise system. That is, private enterprise should be allowed to expand into areas that were once monopolized by the government. Moreover, privatization programs are typically guided by the view that the force of market competition is best suited to fostering efficiency and innovation in an industry. Specifically, the view is that privatization of a state-owned monopoly will open an industry to competition and, consequently, encourage innovation, growth and efficiency. Moreover, where privatization opens an industry to foreign competition, this permits consumers to have access to goods or services developed in other parts of the world, and will stimulate innovation among domestic firms operating in the industry. In addition, opening an industry to foreign investors may also provide access to needed financial and technological resources, and create growth in the industry.

Belief that private business can operate more efficiently. A second, common view, is that transferring the management of organizations to the private sector will result in increased productivity. Studies conducted in a variety of countries have found evidence that the private production of goods and services is typically more efficient than public production. Why should this be considered to be true? Well, think back to our discussion of why Crown corporations were established: not for profit, but for a social policy consideration — i.e., serving public interests. Consequently, many observers feel that it is difficult for government-owned enterprises to reconcile the social goals of the enterprise with the economic-efficiency goals that must be of concern to any business. Moreover, efficient operation may be difficult given that there are political interests to be considered. Removing the political element of an enterprise allows it to focus on efficiency and avoid potential conflicts of interest. The Ontario government announced that its main goal for privatization was to improve economic efficiency of the underlying organization, as reflected in reduced prices and improved customer service. (See Exhibit 8.11.) As Professor Diane Jurkowski comments:

TALKING BUSINESS 8.11   THE PRIVATIZATION OF HIGHWAY 407

Upon coming to power in 1995, Premier Mike Harris proclaimed the end of subsidies. Handouts to "special interest groups" were at an end. The other buzzword was "partnerships" between government and private enterprise. A strange model of public–private partnerships can be found on the northern edge of Toronto, where the 407 Electronic Toll Road Highway cuts across the region.

The expensive project was inherited from the previous New Democratic Party government of Bob Rae. Before the highway was opened, millions in extra costs were incurred due to safety improvements deemed necessary by the Ontario Provincial Police, but when it opened for business in October 1997, the 407 became a revenue-generating machine operated in a partnership between the province, now run by the government, and Canadian Highways International Corp. (CHIC) of Mississauga.

Toll roads were introduced to Upper Canada from England in the early 1800s. The theory was simple: Charge those who use or benefit from the location of a road and use the revenue collected for maintenance and payment of construction loans. At one time, Dundas Street, Yonge Street, Kingston Road and Vaughan Road were all toll roads. Some economists and public policy experts have argued that transportation is too important to be left to government bureaucrats. "By allowing innovation and start-of-the-art technology to flourish free of government interference, the private sector can vastly improve transportation and thereby advance our standard of living. Others suggest that there is simply not enough public funding available, so the private sector might as well be allowed to operate roads and other transportation services." (http://www.lib.uwo.ca/business/toll.html)

The Ontario government, the municipal governments of Toronto and the surrounding Greater Toronto Area faced the problem of enormous growth of population and residential, commercial and industrial development. The population was growing at a rate of approximately 90,000 people a year. In twenty years, the number of licensed drivers had doubled and the number of licensed vehicles had more than doubled. Highway 401, the major existing east–west route was saturated, carrying approximately 350,000 vehicles daily. Government decision makers recognized the necessity to create another east–west corridor across Greater Toronto Area.

In February 1993, the New Democratic Party provincial government decided to accelerate the development of Highway 407 by using toll financing and involving the private sector. Three commercial groups presented proposals. Kiewit's proposal suggested a tolling core section of Toronto's heavily congested Highway 401 as a means of leveraging capital for Highway 407. The government decided that only new highways would be tolled; so, the Kiewit submission failed. There were two remaining consortia: the Canadian Highways International Corporation (CHIC) and the Ontario Road Development Corporation. Each was given $1.5 million from the province's job creation fund to develop engineering improvements on Ontario Ministry of Transportation concepts and designs for Highway 407. Of the two hundred changes and innovations proposed, the Ministry of Transportation of Ontario accepted 60 major ones, resulting in a $200 million reduction from the project's costs.

To facilitate the development and construction of Highway 407, the Ontario government established a Crown corporation, the Ontario Transportation Capital Corporation as a means of exploiting new financing given that there was a growth of private sector participation. The Ontario Transportation Capital Corporation invited private sector proposals

TALKING BUSINESS 8.11 (continued)

to develop, design, build, operate and maintain Highway 407. There were three consortia that responded. While initially revealed that taxpayer funding was not required, it was learned that the Ontario government decided to retain the financing risk for the highway and awarded the development, design and construction for Highway 407, worth $930 million to Canadian Highway International Corporation. The tolling system contract, worth $72 million was given to Hughes Aircraft of Canada Ltd., Bell Canada, Bell Syma and Mark IV. It appeared that a business/government partnership was created. However, the provincial Auditor General's Annual Report in 1996 stated that significant financial ownership and operation risks associated with Highway 407 remained with the province and a government–business partnership had not been established.

The 69-kilometre 407 describes itself as "the world's first all-electronic open toll highway." Its automated equipment, which tracks regular users electronically through transponders and picks up one-time users with cameras that capture license plates, tracks an average of 243,000 trips per weekday.

With the completion of construction in 1998, Highway 407 received safety inspection by the Professional Engineers Ontario. On April 13, 1999, the Cabinet Minister responsible for privatization announced the sale of the highway to a consortium led by Cintra Concesiones de Infraestructuras de Transporte (a Spanish company) and SNC-Lavalin of Montreal. The consortium purchased the right to own and operate the 407 and build east and west extensions. The selling price was $3.1 billion — the largest selling price for a public asset in Canadian history. According to the minister, the people of Ontario had doubled their investment.

Crown corporations are encouraged to be more revenue producing. For example, the Liquor Control Board of Ontario annually generates revenues in excess of a billion dollars and this assists the province of Ontario in delivering infrastructure and social services to its citizens. Hospitals and universities have contracted out linen and catering services to private sector companies. Many municipalities have contracted to private sector companies to provide legal services and management of solid waste. By establishing these private–public sector partnerships, the belief is that the private sector companies will be more efficient in their business practices to respond to their clientele base.[14]

No longer need public involvement in some sectors. Air Canada was established as a Crown corporation at a time when no private company had the resources to develop a transnational airline. In more recent times, there are both domestic and international airlines more than capable of conducting such business and, consequently, there is little need for government ownership in such sectors. Where the enterprise is no longer required by the government to achieve its initial public policy goals, then ownership can be handed over to the private sector. If private industry is willing to offer the same product or service in a reliable and cost-effective manner, why not allow it to do so? As we discussed, in Canada's earlier days, the creation of Crown corporations was deemed necessary, in part, by the "natural monopoly argument" in industries such as public utilities or communications, given that low unit costs of production could be attained only if output were sufficiently high. Consequently, a large government monopoly or a regulated, privately owned monopoly was acceptable and, perhaps, necessary. This argument has weakened in more recent times, when globalization has introduced large, worldwide competitors who may be bigger and more efficient than federal or provincial Crown corporations.

Financial benefits from selling government-owned assets. Another reason for selling off government-owned enterprises is that the money can be used on other, more needed, areas. Certainly money received from sales of Crown corporations or partial disposition of Crown-owned assets has been applied to government deficit reductions. In addition, opening an industry to private investors may attract, for example, an influx of foreign capital. Maintaining a Crown corporation can be an increasingly costly venture, particularly when high subsidies are made to inefficient state-owned enterprises. Privatization can remove this unnecessary financial burden from government and taxpayers. For example, in the U.K. over US$16.8 billion was raised between 1990 and 1995 through the privatization of two power generating companies, the 12 regional electricity companies and the National Grid. Similarly, Argentina raised over US$4 billion through the partial disposition of government-owned electricity assets and cut its level of debt. Here in Canada, the financial incentive for privatizing Ontario Hydro was based on estimates of a corresponding provincial debt reduction of at least Cdn$8 billion. As well, the initial public offering of shares in CNR in 1995 was Canada's largest stock market flotation at that time. However, during the 1980s and 1990s, privatizations in Canada were most likely to have been conducted through sales to private businesses rather than public share offerings. Revenues from sales of Canada's 10 largest federal corporations amounted to $7.2 billion in the period between 1986 and 1996. Proceeds to the federal government were over $3.8 billion from the sale of shares in CN and Petro-Canada alone.

Challenges to "Going Private"

Stakeholders and objectives. Governments in Canada began to privatize their corporate holdings in the mid-1980s for many of the reasons already cited, including efficiency objectives, financial concerns and the capability of the private sector to fulfill public policy objectives.

It is useful to point out that while these may be objectives of privatization, they are not held equally by all parties affected by a privatization. The objectives of various stakeholders in the privatization of a Crown corporation may be different and potentially conflicting. Consider, for example, the stakeholders affected by the privatization of public utilities, which may include, among others, government owners, other government parties (i.e., other levels of government), creditors, future shareholders of the organization, the unionized and non-unionized employees of the corporation, the regulators, the taxpayers, the consumers and other existing or potential competitors in the industry.

Employees' objectives. In effect, the objectives of privatization could all be considered as objectives of the government owners, but some may conflict with elements of the enterprise itself. For example, after initiation of the privatization plan for Ontario Hydro,

331

Hydro's senior management was also agreeable to the province's plan for privatization. In fact, their view was that rapid privatization was necessary in order to face the increasing competition from the United States and from other provincial utilities in the Ontario electricity market, since deregulation began to open up the market for competition. However, within Hydro there has been much disagreement — culminating in a number of strikes by employees opposed to the government's plans.

A possible cost of privatization is massive layoffs of public employees, particularly in developing and transition countries. For example, the privatization of Argentina's national rail company in 1991 involved laying off almost 80% of the company's total workforce as part of the restructuring. However, numerous studies suggest that aggregate employment remains largely unchanged subsequent to privatization efforts.

The public's objectives. Another possible conflict is between the objectives cited and the public's concern for their "protection." For example, in the case of Ontario Hydro, some citizens are concerned that private competitors may be less likely to serve the public's interests than a government-owned enterprise. Consequently, some fear that privatization will bring higher rates and safety concerns. Other issues may relate to foreign ownership. For example, there were no foreign ownership restrictions placed on the privatization of Canadian National Railways (which involved a public offering of a majority of shares), and, consequently, 40% of the $2.3 billion share issue was sold outside Canada, largely to U.S. organizations. For some critics, this sale left too much power out of Canadian hands, and there was some question whether the newly controlled enterprise would keep Canadian interests high on their agenda. On the other hand, the government did not restrict foreign ownership, given the view that the Canadian market was not large enough to allow for complete privatization in one attempt. There were, however, other restrictions: no investor could own more than 15% of the shares, and CN must remain headquartered in Montreal.

While privatization has been viewed as a means to generate higher levels of entrepreneurship and efficiency in an industry, simply transferring ownership to the private sector does not guarantee efficiency gains. At least one important qualification is the level of competition that exists subsequent to the privatization. For example, critics suggest that although Air Canada was privatized in the late 1980s, clear efficiency gains and benefits to the user did not readily materialize, because Air Canada continued to operate in an environment that lacked sufficient competition and, consequently, the airline maintained its monopoly status.

Ironically, the technical responsibilities of the government may increase after privatization, because governments are shifting from owning and managing individual companies to potentially regulating an entire sector or industry. Critics have asserted that if the government fails to implement effective regulation over the new private sector owners, then many of the benefits associated with privatization will not materialize. (See Talking Business 8.12.) This risk may be most apparent in the case of government transfer of ownership of natural monopolies, such as electricity or gas utilities, to a single private owner who takes over the monopoly. This was a criticism levelled at the British government when a number of utilities were privatized, yet monopolistic industries were not consistently restructured to facilitate competition. Consequently, some privatized utility companies continued to operate under monopolistic conditions.

TALKING BUSINESS 8.12   **PRIVATIZATION AND REGULATION**

The government is facilitating the transition from private or public monopolies in certain industries to ones that will ideally foster competition through deregulation. This has naturally changed the mandate of the Competition Bureau from being solely a watchdog of business. The following basic roles for the Competition Bureau and industry regulators have been emphasized as the atmosphere of deregulation and privatization spreads:

1.   Ensure Regulators Promote Competition

The Competition Bureau encourages specific regulators to play a clear role in promoting competition. The benefit of providing regulators with a role to promote competition is illustrated in the telecommunications industry. The Telecommunications Act is ultimately aimed at nurturing increased reliance on market forces. Consequently, the Act encourages the industry regulator, the CRTC, to open new areas of the telecommunications industry to competition, such as local telephone service and pay phones in recent years.

2.   Implement Regulatory Control over Excessive Pricing from Monopolies

Even in deregulated markets the Bureau recognizes the need for regulators to monitor industries in transition and, potentially, regulate excessive pricing due to the market power held by a competitor. For example, during the initial stage of deregulation in the telecommunications industry, the CRTC continued to regulate long distance rates of telephone companies until the establishment of sufficient competition in the market. Similarly, the Bureau has continued to support regulatory control over Ontario Hydro Generation Company's electricity prices until such time as the Ontario generation market becomes sufficiently competitive.

3.   Support Regulatory Control Concerning Essential Facilities

The Bureau advocates regulatory control over essential facilities in an industry — that is, any facilities that businesses require in order to compete in a market, and for which there is no effective competition. Examples of such essential facilities include: transmission and distribution systems in electricity and natural gas, and interconnection to the public switched telephone network by competitive long distance and local exchange carriers. An industry regulator is present in such cases in order to prohibit excessive pricing of essential facilities due to any monopoly power.

4.   Establish a Framework for Deregulation

It is recognized that where regulation is not productive for the industry, the aim becomes one that is geared toward creating mechanisms to remove that regulation. Such would be the case where an industry is clearly approaching the perfect competition ideal; that is, when the level of competition is sufficient to prevent any market participant from establishing or sustaining a significant and permanent price increase. On the other hand, even where a lower level of competition exists, deregulation may also be a goal if the costs of maintaining regulation outweigh the benefits.

Source: Based on A. Lafond, Deputy Commissioner of Competition, Civil Matters Branch, Competition Bureau, "The roles and responsibilities of the industry regulator versus the Competition Bureau as regulated industries become competitive," Address to the Conference Board Regulatory Reform Program Meeting, February 19, 1999.

▮ CHAPTER SUMMARY

We have noted the shift toward reduced government involvement in the business sector, reflected in the trends toward deregulation and privatization. Observers suggest that what we are witnessing is a marked decrease in government involvement as public preferences shift toward a more purely private market system. It seems that many observers view the decrease in the level of government influence in business as a positive change. However, some believe that there is good reason for advocating a continued and, perhaps, increased role for government in business. What kind of role should government play in the business sector?

The question of government involvement in business has been debated for years. Certainly, the trend toward reduced government in terms of deregulation, privatization and elimination of tariff barriers seems to reflect the ideology that "less government is better." However, scholars such as Michael Porter suggest that the government still has a critical role to play in the health and well-being of business. For some, the answer lies in the government's ability to work with industry in order to develop a long-term industrial strategy to lead the country out of its current problems and ensure a more secure future for working Canadians. Consequently, rather than simply taking a "hands-off" approach, it may be argued that what is required is a clear rethinking of the different types of roles that government can play, or how it may play its current roles in a different manner.

Helping the Canadian Auto Industry

The Ontario government is introducing a $500-million assistance program for Ontario automakers that is designed to attract leading-edge assembly plants and to compete with huge U.S. subsidies given to U.S. automakers in Alabama and Mississippi. The money, which will be available over five years, is a key part of Ontario's automotive policy.

It comes after years of pleading by Canada's auto-parts makers to help them compete against southern U.S. states that have won billions in new auto-assembly plants and gained thousands of jobs in recent years. Five new plants are operating or under construction in Alabama, Mississippi and Texas.

Automakers building new assembly plants in Ontario can apply for the money, but it is also designed to protect the 50,000 jobs at existing assembly plants by providing financing for further developing those sites. The program appears aimed initially at Ford Motor Co., which is proposing a $1-billion additional development of its assembly operations in Oakville, Ont., to improve it operations, by building a "flexible manufacturing" operation.

Flexible manufacturing is emerging as a key trend in the competitive North American auto industry because it allows companies to build multiple car models in a single plant and react more quickly to changes in consumer tastes. It is a departure from the traditional structure of an auto plant that has become focused on a slow, bureaucratic process of producing a narrow line of vehicles. This new approach is a re-thinking of the process of producing a variety of car models. It demands changes to the whole organizational structure and approach of auto manufacturing.

Ford is considering, for example, using a plant in Oakville to assemble minivans and at least two models of sport utility vehicles off the same platform, or basic auto underbody. Ford wants $200-million in financial help from Ottawa and Ontario. The Ontario move, which also comes after U.S. automaker DaimlerChrysler refused proposals to build plants in Ontario, puts the pressure on the federal government to participate in the incentive battle as well.

Automakers want Canadian governments to compete with southern states that have been offering hundreds of millions of dollars in subsidies in recent years to attract assembly plants to their regions. Automakers think Canada needs to participate in the "incentive game."

Ontario Economic Development Minister Joe Cordiano said the government would unveil "a new approach" to the Canadian auto industry that emphasizes investments to help the Canadian auto industry become more competitive. He suggested that this would centre on funding more training for auto workers and financial assistance with building a public infrastructure to support this industry (such as road systems, community colleges and other support for the construction of auto plants in new, underdeveloped regions of Ontario).

"Those things are going to be investments for the long term in Ontario, not short-term handouts," Mr. Cordiano told reporters. "It's about ensuring those companies are innovative and can compete with the rest of the world."

Source: Reproduced with permission from Murray Campbell, Greg Keenan and Simon Tuck, entitled, "Ontario to lure leading-edge auto plants," *The Globe and Mail* (April 14, 2004) [Edited].

QUESTIONS

1. Discuss the nature of the relationship that the Canadian government has with business in this situation. Discuss the role of "government as guardian of business in the global context" and how those issues might be reflected in this case. Your discussion should also make reference to the implication of this role for *all affected parties* (i.e., the Canadian auto industry, the U.S. auto industry, Canadian and U.S. employment, Canadian car consumers).

2. It "wrong" for the government to give the auto industry these huge "handouts" (financial subsidies and incentives) while other industries get no financial support from the government. Support this statement. Refute this statement.

3. Describe one course illustration that shows the benefits of government involvement in business. Describe one course illustration that shows the negative consequences of government involvement in business. What "lessons" do these illustrations offer for the auto industry (i.e., The pros or cons of government involvement in the auto industry)?

The Reel World

Government film tax credits are a waste of precious resources that could be better used elsewhere.

Walking down Richmond Street in downtown Toronto this summer, I felt I had entered a time warp. There before me was a large sign indicating I was in front of early-20th century Madison Square Garden in New York. No, it was not a trick of the mind — it was another U.S. film production using one side of the historic Bay department store as a stand-in.

For some reason, totally inexplicable to me, such blatant Americanization of Canadian cities does not seem to attract hordes of nationalists demonstrating against further encroachment on our culture. Even the beleaguered CRTC does not seem to have any rules prohibiting the Americanization of Canadian scenery. Perhaps most Canadians do not care that many film productions here are simply U.S. films produced with Canadian landscapes and buildings. After all, this is just good business and we get film production jobs to boot, right?

Not really. The dirty little secret is that our federal and most provincial governments are throwing millions of dollars in overly generous tax assistance to Canadian and foreign film and video producers. For example, the federal government provides a film and video production tax credit of 16%, and the Ontario government absorbs a further 11% of eligible labour costs. And who benefits? Actors, filmmakers and Hollywood producers who aren't exactly representative of the poorest members of society.

Defenders of these film tax credits will argue that Canada gains not just foreign movies but also Canadian production spinoffs that create jobs. And without the tax credits, most of the foreign production would go to lower-cost locations. They have a point: although a low Canadian dollar did a lot to bring production here, we would have had a smaller film industry if we did not provide Hollywood producers with tax support to set up their vans, shades and cameras in Canada.

But we should not only be concerned with jobs in the film industry. The federal cost of tax credits for all film production in 2003 was $261 million; provincial credits added many millions more to the kitty. With these sums we could cut corporate capital taxes substantially or fund more roads and bridges at the border. Yes, maybe we would have a smaller film industry, but we would have more thriving business elsewhere.

Which raises a major question — how best can Canadian governments grow the economy? One approach is to provide the right incentives for work, investment and risk-taking with lower taxes, letting businesses figure out who can best succeed through competition. The other approach is for governments to micro-manage the economy: pick "winning" businesses that supposedly create well-paying jobs.

Noted U.S. economist Arnold Harberger showed why well-intentioned governments are so bad at picking winners. Every decade has had a "star" industry — such as transportation in the 1950s, high tech in the 1990s and the latest craze, biotech. Within each industry, business performance varied widely. Many businesses were "dogs," only a few were "stars" — even in the very best-performing industries. In other words, it is very difficult (if not impossible) for government bureaucrats to really know which businesses are most able to succeed. Governments would be better off cutting tax rates and keeping tax bases broad without special exemptions. If they should fund anything, it should be infrastructure or research from which many businesses can benefit.

The film industry is profitable, so it begs the question why we need to throw money at it. The next time you go see a Hollywood movie, make sure you read the credits — you can take dubious pride in the fact that Canadian governments have overindulged an industry with unneeded tax support when the money could have been better spent elsewhere.

Source: By Jack Mintz from *Canadian Business* 77(18): 23. Reproduced with permission of Jack Mintz, President and Chief Executive Officer of CD Howe Institute.

QUESTIONS

1. Is the author of this article arguing for or against government involvement in the film industry? Discuss.

2. Should government offer aid to this industry? Why, or why not?

3. What role should government play in businesses? How do we decide which businesses are worthy of support?

PART 4

The Challenges of Change

Managing in a Changing Environment

9

To succeed in today's business environment requires the ability to quickly adapt to changing market conditions. Consequently, it is fitting that we devote specific attention to a discussion of the nature of change. What does change entail? What are the forces for change? We will examine the methods adopted to facilitate change. Within this discussion, the concept of the "learning organization" will be explored. In addition, we will consider how organizations may facilitate or impede change. The chapter ends with a discussion of the issue of change in the context of organizational mergers.

LEARNING OBJECTIVES

By the end of the chapter, you should be able to:

1. Consider the forces encouraging change in organizations.
2. Understand the value of Theory E and Theory change.
3. Examine the process of transformational change.
4. Explain the relationship of learning with organizational change.
5. Identify the role of "the tipping point" and its impact on change.
6. Explore change issues in the context of corporate mergers.

I am grateful to Karen Rabideau, Gillian Gurney, Chris Kirkpatrick for their contributions "IBM's Change Challenge," "Implementing Change through Tipping Point Leadership," and "The Case of Merger," respectively.

The Business World

Struggling for Change at Nortel

About three weeks ago, the new president and chief operating officer (COO) of Nortel Networks Corp., Gary Daichendt, dropped a bombshell on the board. He proposed an accelerated plan to overhaul Nortel's product strategy — and he would be in charge of driving that change.

It was seen as a direct challenge to the vision of CEO Bill Owens, the retired U.S. admiral who had taken command in early 2004, when Nortel was reeling from the ouster of its previous chief executive. But on June 10, Mr. Daichendt was gone after just three months at Nortel, having played his hand and lost ...

In a struggle between two Americans over a new vision for the troubled Canadian telecom icon, the Nortel board backed Mr. Owens, 65, who is also its vice-chairman. That left Mr. Daichendt, a 53-year-old former Cisco Systems Inc. executive, with no option but to leave. Having come to Nortel with expectations to be CEO, he learned that wasn't in the cards right away, and he didn't want to wait. This chronology has been pieced together from interviews with analysts and observers, and with a number of people with ties to Nortel.

Mr. Daichendt, who has a real estate business in Huntingdon Beach, Calif., did not respond to requests for an interview. The departure of Mr. Daichendt, along with his former Cisco colleague, chief technology officer Gary Kunis, has dealt a new blow to Nortel's recovery from a barrage of accounting, governance and financial blows, including a constant turnover in the ranks of top executives.

It also raises questions about how Mr. Owens sees his future. Outside observers say he is a transitional CEO, who moved from a director's role to the top executive job at the darkest hour — when former CEO Frank Dunn left amid allegations of accounting malfeasance at the company. But Mr. Owens has been vague about the length of his tenure. His ability to fight off Mr. Daichendt's challenge suggests he retains considerable authority on the board, which feels indebted to him for coming to Nortel's aid. Mr. Daichendt's exit also raises the expectation that when Mr. Owens does leave, his replacement will be Peter Currie, who returned to Nortel as chief financial officer just before Mr. Daichendt was hired. Mr. Currie is entering his third go-round with the telecommunications company, having left most recently in 1997 to serve as Royal Bank of Canada CFO. His return is seen as a psychological boost, assuring employees, suppliers and customers that Nortel has a future. He was appointed executive vice-president at the same time Mr. Daichendt joined the company.

Mr. Daichendt's résumé seemed equally suited for a future CEO of Nortel, a company that had fallen on hard times after riding the telecom bubble of the late nineties.

Brought to Nortel's attention by a headhunter, he's an industry veteran who in the 1990s became a top executive for San Jose, Calif.-based Cisco, whose aggressive sales approach contrasts sharply with the Canadian company's more relaxed culture.

But in fact, Mr. Daichendt had been out of the industry for five years when he joined Nortel. ...

Mr. Daichendt ... presented his change agenda, recommending increased emphasis on certain product areas. It was not radically different from Mr. Owens' strategic plan of last August when he took aim at the large-company and government markets. But under Mr. Daichendt, changes would have come more quickly.

In Nortel, there is a concern that customers, already buffeted by the company's recent history, needed a period of stability in relationships with their supplier.

In the end, the board rejected the accelerated strategy, and decided Mr. Daichendt would not get the CEO's job right away.

The view inside Nortel is that while the Daichendt-Kunis departure seems serious from the outside, it is not a crippling blow. It is far better that Mr. Daichendt's agenda surfaced in the early stages of his Nortel tenure, rather than in another six or nine months.

Even so, turnaround experts wonder about a recruiting process that would allow such a gap between the company's plans and the new recruit's expectations. "There clearly was a disconnect here," said corporate turnaround specialist William Aziz, who is now the chief restructuring officer at SR Telecom Inc. of Montreal....

Source: Reproduced with permission from Gordon Pitts, "The Story Behind the Nortel Divorce," *The Globe and Mail* (June 19, 2005), B1.

CHANGE AND THE ENVIRONMENT OF BUSINESS

"The Business World" article underscores the significant challenges organizations like Nortel face in their attempts to implement change. What are the sources of change directed at organizations? How do these changes affect the nature of organizations and work? In every chapter in this book, from management thought to business ethics, we have, often, recognized that just about every important area of business is undergoing some kind of change. How is the organizational environment changing? Consider a number of issues addressed in this book, including issues like globalization, free trade, deregulation, privatization, the changing emphasis on corporate social responsibility. Much of what we have addressed involves issues that are undergoing dramatic change.

In terms of planned change, organizations can attempt to focus on any of the internal forces as a target for change. That is, fundamentally, the change occurring may involve strategy, structure and/or people. For example, with regard to strategy (discussed elsewhere in this text), we can see that organizations must often change their strategic directions in order to compete effectively. With regard to structure, from re-engineering to downsizing to becoming virtual, we have witnessed a shift away from the traditional bureaucratic structure. Technological improvements can bring about more efficient work arrangements. With regard to people, change may involve getting employees to adopt different work approaches than in the past. A major challenge is to ensure that employees accept and adapt to the change. Regardless of the target for the change, it is critical to understand what factors in the organization's environment dictate the need for change.

Forces for Change

As discussed in Chapter 1, organizations are open systems that are in continual interaction with their external environment. Success and survival require organizations to continually develop a "fit" with their dynamic and evolving environment. Consequently, the ability to change, is central to the success of any organization. On the other hand, there is a paradox at play — while change is ultimately required in order to adapt to a changing environment, the success of any organization depends on the capability to maintain stable and reproducible organizational processes and outcomes. See Exhibit 9.1 for an illustration of the forces for change, which we discuss next.

1.   Economic Changes

Is the economy healthy or weak? Clearly, organizations must adapt to changing economic conditions. Downsizings are more likely to occur in lean times than in rich. Organizational expansion cannot occur in an economic vacuum, as the following indicates:

> We have watched what the new workplace rules mean in periods of economic expansion. The decade long boom of the 1990s occurred just as downsizing became de rigueur at American companies. The greater efficiency with which companies allocated their human resources spurred enormous gains in economic growth and pro-

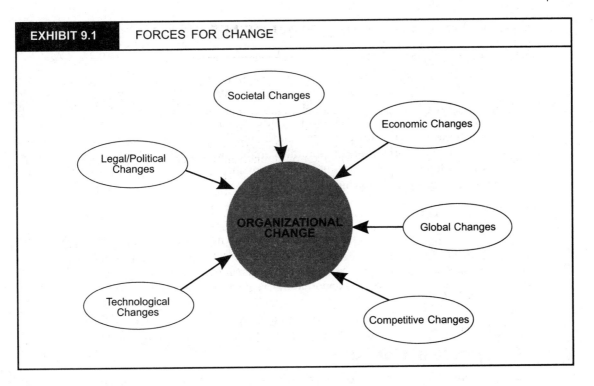

EXHIBIT 9.1 FORCES FOR CHANGE

ductivity. Companies hired contract consultants who could deliver specific expertise on a project, and they hired temporaries to handle the surge periods of the business day.[1]

This quote alludes to a few of the changes that resulted from changing economic circumstances. Certainly, such changes have also facilitated changes to the nature of the employer–employee relationship. Lifetime employment appears to be a thing of the past. Consider the 1950s or the 1970s: these were actually times where employment meant security. The dominant model was long-term employment — stability. However, a change to this implicit employment contract occurred sometime in the 1980s. And, as we identified in an earlier chapter, the age of downsizing began — with large, secure organizations beginning to lay off employees. Part-time and temporary work arrangements have become much more common than in the past:

> Organizations are typically responding to this challenging new organization world by becoming preoccupied with improving performance and bottom line results while losing sight of the importance of a people/performance balance in achieving lasting success. In these organizations, slashing costs, continuous restructuring, downsizing, trying endless quick fix programs and solutions, announcing new visions, values, and goals that everyone is expected to embrace, and lots of well intended talk about the importance of people and values is becoming common place. It is a push, cut, slash, slice, talk, quick fix management mentality and strategy that places a high emphasis on perfor-

345

mance and a low emphasis on people and often creates an illusion of doing well while the organization is regressing and in some cases unraveling! It appears to employees to be a "built to sell or built to fail" strategy that assumes that you can manage or shrink your way to success.[2]

We have also witnessed a change with regard to the pattern of career movement within an organization. Traditionally, employees attempted to move up the corporate hierarchy throughout their career. However, the flattening of many organizational hierarchies has tended to substitute horizontal or lateral career movement for the former vertical movement, so that you might move around an organization into different areas rather than directly up the hierarchy. The following quote reflects the new era of the "free agent":

> Employees and workers must view their careers in terms of what skills they can offer. As individual identity has become uncoupled from a particular company, people have focused on functional career areas, such as law, human resources, financial, sales and marketing, and manufacturing. In the 1990s, professional associations and functional groupings have seen explosive membership gains. More and more people have sought community and networking opportunities in the company of like-minded career professionals.[3]

2.   Competitive Changes

Chapter 6 underscored the importance of identifying how industries change or evolve over time. Competitive processes do evolve, and understanding what to expect and what drives evolution along the lifecycle of an industry is critical for surviving turbulent times. As we identified in Chapter 6, there are major phases and milestones that mark an industry's evolutionary path from emergence and shakeout to maturity and decline. At each stage of the industry lifecycle, the organizational skills and capabilities needed to survive and grow change in significant ways.

Organizations must adapt to change as competition evolves in markets from fragmented and fast-growing to concentrated and declining. In addition, competition, both domestic and foreign, certainly has demanded an acceleration in innovation among firms in many industries. Organizations, to compete effectively, must continually create new and better methods of serving customers. For example, while globalization has opened up larger markets for businesses, it has also facilitated much higher levels of competition. Globalization, as discussed elsewhere in this book, opened the floodgates for competitors. Clearly, the number of competitors and the nature of competition will dictate changes in organizational design and strategy.

3.   Technological Changes

Technology, as we will discuss, is both a continuously changing variable and one that permits and demands organizational change. One scholar observed the following:

> In recent years, there has been considerable discussion of whether the development and application of information and communications technology have changed the ... economy in a fundamental way, promising a golden future of rapid growth, low unem-

ployment and inflation, perpetual economic expansion, and a booming stock market. The change is sometimes called the "Information Revolution"; more commonly, it is called the "New Economy." ... As the economy absorbs any new technology, what typically happens first is that existing economic activities are performed at lower cost. E-commerce is no exception...Only a few firms have gone through the deep organizational changes needed to become web-based organizations, but those that have done so have achieved remarkable results, like cutting administrative costs by 75 percent.[4]

Technology has been a double-edged sword for members of the workforce — bringing both benefits and threats. Benefits from technology have included the ability to gain more flexibility in work arrangements such as the practice of telework:

> The idea of telecommuting isn't new, but companies still have a long way to go to fully exploit the benefits of a networked economy. Indianapolis pharmaceutical company Eli Lilly and Co. lets all its knowledge workers work from home occasionally, and a formal telework program lets a smaller number of employees keep their primary offices at home. Such telecommuting generally had been considered a concession to work-life balance, but these days, the company is also thinking about it as a means to drive productivity, says Candi Lange, director of workforce partnering. "We bring in such smart people who are responsible for so much important work in the company," she says. "Why not let them control their own schedules as well?"[5]

Part-time work has increased dramatically in recent years, and we also continue to see the increasing use of compressed workweeks and flex-time — all in all, this means that the nine-to-five job is certainly no longer a fixed rule.

4. *Legal/Political Changes*

Deregulation and privatization, discussed in an earlier chapter, are clear examples of the importance of considering governmental changes on business strategy. Are legal regulations facilitating, or restricting, certain strategies? The legal environment of business can dictate changes in how business competes, as well as what services it offers and how they can be offered.

> The deregulation of protected industries in the 1980s and 1990s created competition for companies where none had previously existed. The telecom, banking, energy, and aerospace industries were ruled by the change. As the dominant companies in these sectors were forced to compete in an open market, they started letting sizable numbers of people go. The breakup of the Bell System into AT&T, Lucent, and the seven Baby Bells unleashed a surge of technology inventiveness. It was not surprising that telecom, financial services, and aerospace dominated the list of industries experiencing the heaviest downsizing in the early to mid-1990s.[6]

In the workplace, we have witnessed an increasing emphasis on organizational justice — i.e., how employees are treated. This has translated into more laws governing fairness in the workplace. One such area that has been dramatically affected is compensation. Pay equity has been among numerous issues involved in redressing inconsistencies in pay treatment among men and women, for example. We have also witnessed an increasing emphasis on merit-based pay, and pay-for-performance, which all attempt to more closely link actual effort to performance (versus seniority-based pay, which bases pay on the number of years you have been with the organization).

5.   Societal Changes

Business must respond to society: consumer tastes change, for example, and business must adapt to such changes. Similarly, the types of organizations that service societal demands can change. The aging population suggests greater emphasis needs to be placed on such industries as the health care sector:

> The growing number of people with advanced educational degrees is another force hurtling knowledge forward at a higher rate. As more people become educated, knowledge expansion increases geometrically simply because there are more people to move the cutting edge of knowledge ahead. Geniuses emerge who could not have appeared in past eras because they did not have access to the then-current state of knowledge necessary to push the thought boundaries. Unprecedented numbers of people today are working at the cutting edge of research in a variety of fields. And the glass ceiling is breaking apart because young women are achieving the advanced degrees necessary for economic and social advancement.[7]

The increasing education level of the workforce has also generated changes to the nature of work. As we discussed in an earlier chapter, there has been, for some time, a movement away from high job specialization, where jobs are broken down into simple, distinct packages. The trend has been to generate jobs that demand employees be multi-skilled in order to handle more challenging and enriched work. Consequently, employees are also tending to work more in teams, and are responsible for a larger piece of the work, so to speak. Knowledge work (as we will discuss later in this chapter) demands a more highly educated workforce.

6.   Global Changes

As we observed in Chapter 7, globalization has been among the most pervasive forces affecting not only business in Canada but in almost every corner of the world. We also noted the tremendous growth of "borderless" corporations. The increasing ability of multi-national corporations to move freely across borders and set up business just about anywhere reflects the title "borderless corporation." The term *multinational* is a bit inaccurate, however, given that many of these companies do not claim any specific nationality but, in fact, gear their planning and decision making to global markets. For example, goods could be designed in one country, raw material obtained from a second country, manufactured in a third country and shipped to consumers in another country.

In a broader sense, globalization has also influenced profound changes in the relationship of business to its external stakeholders, reflected in the following comments:

> Employees and communities were once critical factors in companies' long-term strategic decisions. Moving factories and jobs to another area of the country was unthinkable because of the damage it would do to the local community. In recent years,

thousands of companies — including UPS, J.C. Penney, and Boeing — have moved their headquarters or operations from cities where they had deep roots. The old business structure — with a dominant CEO, a largely ceremonial board of directors, and employees willing to put the goals of the company first — is nearly extinct.... Several primary forces created systemic change in the American economy in the 1980s and 1990s, leaving the former system in shambles. One such factor was globalization, which forced the United States out of its isolation. Companies began to look for new markets overseas. Coca-Cola and McDonald's spread throughout the world. NAFTA, GATT, and free trade brought down barriers that had prevented the flow of goods and services and human resources around the world. The law of unintended consequences worked its way into the American economy. Protected industries such as auto manufacturing faced serious competition from overseas for the first time, with devastating consequences. Chrysler almost ceased operations, and General Motors cut 74,000 jobs in December 1991, one of the largest downsizings ever.[8]

WHY DO ORGANIZATIONS RESIST CHANGE?

Given that any or all of the six external forces are very likely undergoing some kind of change, it would seem critical that organizations be capable of continually adapting to a changing environment. How do organization fare with regard to adapting to the change forces of the environment? Do organizations embrace change? The simple answer is — no. Most organizations have a very difficult time adapting the change, and many organization eventually "die out" because of a failure to successfully promote organizational change.

Why are so many organizations incapable of effectively promoting and implementing change? The answer lies in understanding the inherent nature of organizations. Organizations are designed to produce goods or services in the most effective and efficient manner, so that this efficiency and effectiveness can be reproduced on a daily basis. That is — we learn how to do a job best and then we put mechanisms into place that ensure we can reliably reproduce this performance. This involves ensuring organizational stability in its operations and functions.

Given that any organization requires stability, changes to "core" structural features (e.g., mission, market strategy, core technology, etc.) disrupt the organization's routines and therefore can compromise its reliability and accountability. Substantive change is thus very disruptive, costly and rarely successful. Moreover, organizations are more amenable to stability than to change and many organizations exhibit a resistance to change. Why?

Henry Mintzberg raises a number of interesting issues regarding the ability, or rather inability, of organizations to change. Certainly, Mintzberg underscores the desperate need for organizations to change their ways, so to speak. So, what, exactly, does Mintzberg say about organizational change?

Mintzberg reminds us that we are a society of organizations. That is, think about any aspect of our society — from our schools to our hospitals to our government — and you are really thinking about organizations. So, how organizations are designed says a lot about how our society is designed. Consequently, how adaptive organizations are to change says a lot about how readily adaptive our society is to change. And Mintzberg argues

349

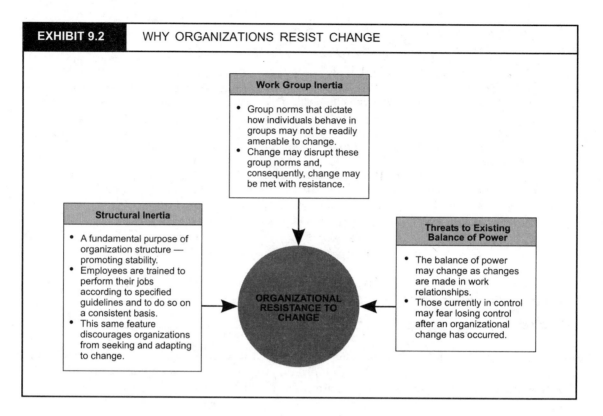

EXHIBIT 9.2   WHY ORGANIZATIONS RESIST CHANGE

Work Group Inertia

- Group norms that dictate how individuals behave in groups may not be readily amenable to change.
- Change may disrupt these group norms and, consequently, change may be met with resistance.

Structural Inertia

- A fundamental purpose of organization structure — promoting stability.
- Employees are trained to perform their jobs according to specified guidelines and to do so on a consistent basis.
- This same feature discourages organizations from seeking and adapting to change.

ORGANIZATIONAL RESISTANCE TO CHANGE

Threats to Existing Balance of Power

- The balance of power may change as changes are made in work relationships.
- Those currently in control may fear losing control after an organizational change has occurred.

that how our organizations are designed is still being led by one dominant and traditional view — that is, when it comes to organizations, we still think in terms of **machine bureaucracy**.

Recall the nature of the machine bureaucracy and when it is most suitable. For tasks that can be made simple and repetitive, as in mass production processes, the machine bureaucracy is very suitable: through its formalization of rules, its standardization of tasks, its emphases on efficiency. However, given this, why are so many organizations whose work is not based on simple, repetitive tasks still structured like a machine bureaucracy? Moreover, given the changes occurring in our environment, why would organizations wish to maintain these rigid bureaucracies? Mintzberg suggests that the dominance of the machine bureaucratic mentality really stems from an irrational need for control. In Mintzberg's words, organizations are "irrationally" rational — there is a focus on maximizing efficiency through rules and regulations without a real critical evaluation of the process of managing.

Finally, Mintzberg suggests rather ominously that organizations "sow the seeds of their destruction." In other words, Mintzberg believes that any preoccupation with control to the degree that it emphasizes the machine bureaucracy over other forms tends to eventually become too rigid to adapt to change. In addition to Mintzberg's comments, management scholars have identified a number of central sources of resistance to change at the organizational level. (See Exhibit 9.2.)

Change is not easily achieved in any organization even though it may be critical for survival. In order to successfully overcome resistance to change, managers must first understand the types of change that can occur and the nature of change as it impacts organizations. Next, we will explore these issues and consider the manner in which organizations go about trying to achieve change.

TYPES OF CHANGE

According to Dean Anderson and Linda Ackerman Anderson, organizations may confront three fundamentally different types of change: developmental, transitional and transformational.[9] Any organization must comprehend the nature of the change that it is attempting to undergo — this is a precursor to successfully managing any type of change.

1. **Developmental change.** This type of change attempts to improve upon what the business is currently doing, rather than creating something completely new. This may include the improvement of existing skills, processes, methods, performance standards or conditions. For example, increasing sales or quality of goods, interpersonal communication training, simple work process improvements, team development and problem-solving efforts may all be considered forms of developmental change.

2. **Transitional change.** This type of change actually replaces what already exists with something completely new and requires the organization to depart from old methods of operating while the new state is being established. Examples of transitional change include reorganizations, simple mergers or acquisitions, creation of new products or services that replace old ones, and information technology implementations that do not require a significant shift in culture or behaviour.

   There are two factors that largely distinguish transitional from transformational change:

   - It is possible to determine the final destination or state in detail before the transitional change is implemented. This permits the change to be managed.
   - Transitional change largely impacts employees only at the levels of skills and actions, but not at the more personal levels of mindset, behaviour and culture.

3. **Transformational change.** This type of change is far more challenging to manage compared to the other types of change for at least two reasons. First, the future state or destination caused by the change is unknown when the transformation begins. Rather, the final state is determined through trial and error as new information is gathered. Consequently, transformational change cannot be managed with predetermined, time-bound or "linear" plans. While an overarching change strategy can be created, the actual change process only really emerges, somewhat unpredictably, as the change is implemented. This means that managers and employees must operate in the "unknown" — where future outcomes are quite uncertain. Second, the future state is so dramatically different from the current operating state that employees and their culture must change in order to successfully implement this type of change. New mindsets and behaviours are required to adapt to this transformed state.

Methods of Change:
Theory E and Theory O Change

Whether it is the presence of new competitors, new technologies or changes to any of the other forces facing business, organizations often respond to the challenges of change with a variety of programs that might include the following:

- Structural change: e.g., mergers, acquisitions, etc.
- Cost cutting: e.g., eliminating nonessential activities
- Process change: e.g., re-engineering
- Cultural change: e.g., change approach to doing business or change the relationship between management and employees.

In broader terms, Beer and Nohria discuss two fundamentally different approaches to change. Each of these methods of change are based on different assumptions regarding what successful change tools must be employed in order to achieve a desirable final outcome for the organizations. These two different approaches are referred to as Theory E change and Theory O change:

> Two dramatically different approaches to organizational change are being employed in the world today, according to our observations, research, and experience. We call these Theory E and Theory O of change. Like all managerial action, these approaches are guided by very different assumptions by corporate leaders about the purpose of and means for change. In effect these two approaches to organizational change represent theories in use by senior executives and the consultants and academics who advise them. By "theory in use" we mean an implicit theory that one can deduce from examining the strategies for change employed.[10]

"Theory E has as its purpose the creation of economic value, often expressed as shareholder value. Its focus is on formal structure and systems."[11] The central goal of this approach to change is based on the notion of maximizing shareholder value. The methods used to achieve this goal are changes to organizational structure and systems. The planning for this type of change tends to emanate from the highest levels of the organization, making it a "top-driven," programmatic approach to change. Among the specific mechanisms employed to achieve such change are performance bonuses, personnel reduction, asset sales, strategic restructuring of business units.

An example of Theory E change can be seen in the changes implemented by Scott Paper, operating largely in the consumer package paper business. About a decade ago, Al Dunlap, CEO of Scott Paper, embarked on a series of changes. His main objective was to increase shareholder value by 200%. Among the changes were the following:

- 11,000 terminations were conducted throughout Scott Paper.
- Certain business units within Scott Paper were sold off.
- The location of the head office was moved.
- Financial incentives were given to executives that met new performance criteria.

The changes at Scott Paper were consistent with the spirit of Theory E change. While the short-term goal was achieved, the company did not achieve long-term viability and eventually was sold to Kimberly-Clark. There had been no lasting change achieved within the organization or its workforce.

"Theory O has as its purpose the development of the organization's human capability to implement strategy and to learn from actions taken about the effectiveness of changes made."[12] The central goal of Theory O change is to develop organizational capabilities. The focus is on developing an organizational culture that supports learning and a high-performance employee population. The planning for this type of change is essentially emergent and participative rather than programmatic and top-driven. The mechanisms employed to facilitate such change include the following: flatter structure (to increase involvement of employees); increased bonds between organization and employee; employee commitment to the change.

An example of Theory O change involves the case of Champion International, operating in the same industry as Scott Paper. In response to poor performance, CEO Andrew Sigler of Champion International initiated an organizational change effort aimed at altering the culture and behaviour of management, unions and workers. Sigler developed a vision of the new Champion, called the Champion Way, which reflected such values as involvement of all employees in improving the company, fair treatment of workers, support for the community around its plants and openness in the company. In the years that followed, Champion's management implemented one of the most effective organization development efforts witnessed in several decades. Champion used a high-involvement method called sociotechnical redesign to change its approach to organizing and managing people in all of its plants.

To support these changes, Champion improved its relations with its unions, and compensation systems were aligned with culture change objectives. A skill-based pay system was installed to encourage employees to learn multiple skills. A corporation-wide gains-sharing plan was introduced to help unify union workers and management with a common goal. Throughout this change effort, occurring over a decade, there were no layoffs. Ironically, this Theory O change did not actually result in any improvement in shareholder value.

The advice from the experts is clear — Theory E and Theory O must be combined in order to achieve successful, long-term change. As Beer and Nohria assert:

> Where the objective is to enable an institution to adapt, survive, and prosper in the long run, Theory E change must be combined with Theory O. In effect we are arguing for the and/also, for the management of a paradox. It is the way to get rapid improvements in economic value while also building sustainable advantage inherent in building organizational capability.[13]

THE PROCESS OF TRANSFORMATIONL CHALLENGE: AN ILLUSTRATION

The story of transformational change at IBM is clearly told in the book, *"Who Says Elephants Can't Dance?"* Specifically, it documents IBM's transformation from the period 1993 to 2002 under the leadership of Louis V. Gerstner, Jr. (also the author of the book). In the book's foreword, Gerstner writes that his reason for writing *"Who Says Elephants Can't Dance?"* is to "tell [the] story of the revival of IBM" in order to answer the questions posed by those who wanted to know how IBM was saved. Gerstner modestly acknowledges that he did not transform IBM alone, and maintains that "without the heroes among [his] IBM colleagues" and the "thousand of IBMers who answered the call," IBM would not have been restored to its former glory.[14]

1.   Understanding the Forces for Change

At a time when the external marketplace was changing rapidly, IBM had not realized that its customers, technology and competitors had changed; nor had it adapted to meet those changes. Gerstner writes that "IBM's dominant position had created a self-contained, self-sustaining world for the company"; however, by the early 1990s, it woke up to find itself perilously close to bankruptcy.

Gerstner accepted the job at IBM after being told that the company needed and wanted a "broad-based leader and change agent" who was "skilled at generating and managing change." IBM's management team, led by Gerstner, had to quickly assess and react to the rapidly changing external environment.

As part of Gerstner's orientation into the company, he went out into the field to learn about IBM, the IT industry and the external business environment. He quickly learned that IBM had lost touch with the outside world and the external forces that were changing as IBM stood still, lost in time. One distinct advantage Gerstner held over IBM's previous leaders was that he was from the outside and had been one of IBM's former customers; therefore, he had first-hand knowledge of IBM's lack of customer focus.

According to Beatty and Ulrich, mature organizations "establish a relatively fixed mindset."[15] This creates a huge resistance to change. Gerstner, essentially, had to attempt to implement *transformational change* within IBM. Among the fundamental changes that Gerstner initiated are the elements highlighted below.

2.   The Change Vision and Implementation

Gerstner had to develop and implement a program that would be accepted and adopted by the stakeholders (employees, customers and shareholders). Gerstner writes that restructuring the organization, implementing a new compensation program and consolidating its marketing plans was relatively easy compared to having to change the corporate culture and establishing strategies for the new business environment. Gerstner writes, "Fixing IBM was all about execution."

While management scholar, Todd Jick, warns that "change lists" and guidelines don't guarantee success, he nonetheless offers ten "rules" that can be used as a tool to assist in the implementation process.[16] It appears that Gerstner did in fact follow most of these rules in one sense or another:

- Analyze the organization and its need for change — Gerstner, as well as the business community knew that IBM needed to change just to survive.

- Create a shared vision and common direction — a common corporate focus was created — customer focus — which instilled a common direction.
- Separate from the past — At his first meeting, Gerstner told IBM executives that "there was no time to focus on who created [IBM's] problems."
- Create a sense of urgency — IBM's precarious cash flow problems made urgency a high priority.
- Support a strong leader role — Based on his previous leadership record, Gerstner was selected by IBM's search committee as the one who could lead the organization.
- Line up political sponsorship — Gerstner involved IBM senior management team from the beginning, even including them in Operation Bear Hug.
- Craft an implementation plan — "Win, Execute, and Team" became what Gerstner felt was what "all IBMers needed to apply in their goals."
- Develop enabling structures — Gerstner restructured the organizations and reset the compensation system to create a sense of ownership.
- Communicate, involve people, and be honest — Just six days after his arrival, Gerstner wrote a note to his employees. From there he continued with a strong, open, honest employee communication strategy.
- Reinforce and institutionalize change — Gerstner writes that "execution is all about translating strategies into action programs and measuring their results" and that "proper execution involves building measurable targets and holding people accountable for them."

3. The Need for Cultural Change

"Big Blue," an "institution" in its own right, had culture, behaviour and beliefs uniquely its own. Traditions ran deep at IBM and Gerstner candidly admits, "the company has been known as much for its culture as for what it made and sold."

Historically, IBM had been a paternalistic, family-oriented company, providing its employees with generous compensation and benefits packages, lifelong employment and plenty of opportunities for advancement; as a matter of fact, IBM was not the standard — IBM set the standards. According to Denise Rousseau, there are two ways to change the *psychological contract* — that is, the set of implicit assumptions that underlie the expectations of employees with regard to their employment status:

- Accommodation, which means to modify or alter the terms "within the context of the existing contract so that people feel the old deal continues despite the changes" or
- Transformation, which means a radical change that replaces the old mindset with new ones.[17]

By all accounts, the psychological contract had been "transformed" by Gerstner's predecessor, who had made significant alterations to the company's commitment to lifelong employment by laying off tens of thousands of employees and capping future medical benefits. Gerstner further transformed the psychological contract by implementing a new compensation program, which was based on *pay for performance* rather than on corporate loyalty, long service or entitlement.

By implementing a pay-for-performance compensation program, Gerstner followed the opinion of Bob Knowling, who says that "changing a culture from one of entitlement into a culture of accountability"[18] is a starting point for making a successful change.

According to Rousseau, "a core issue in the management of contract change involves how change is framed"; this means that the "reasons for the change" must be validated and communicated.[19] Gerstner knew and understood that it was "essential to open up a clear and continuous line of communications with IBM employees" and that the end result of a "successful corporate transformation" was to publicly acknowledge the "existence of a crisis." He felt that if the IBM employees didn't believe that there was a real threat, they wouldn't make or accept the need for the urgently needed changes.

Just in the manner in which Gerstner acknowledges the hard work and determination of the "thousands of IBMers who answered the call, put their shoulder to the wheel, and performed magnificently" and how he dedicates this book to acknowledge their efforts, it's evident that the IBMers responded to his plea for change. No stranger to change, Gerstner knew that "management doesn't change culture. Management invites the workforce itself to change the culture."

4.   Leading Change Through Communication

Instrumental to the change was Gerstner's acceptance that he needed to assume the role of chief communicator, which he did willingly and in an outstanding fashion. Gerstner's outstanding communication and leaderships skills were the most influential contributing factors in IBM's transformation. By becoming the change agent and the communicator Gerstner was able to express his passion about leading the company into a new era, visibly demonstrate that he was committed to the change, and ready to face the challenges along with the rest of his leadership team. Rosabeth Moss Kanter writes in her article "The Enduring Skills of Change Leaders" that leaders should be "offering a dream, stretching their horizons, and encouraging people to do the same" rather than just "announce a plan, launch a task force, and then simply hope that people find the answers."[20]

Gerstner also championed many of the other skills recommended by Kanter, such as "transferring ownership to a working team." Gerstner's belief is that "Great institutions are not managed; they are led," meaning that managers should set goals and objectives, and allow their teams to determine the most appropriate manner in which to attain these goals and objectives. Kanter also recommends perseverance; Gerstner admits that it takes time to implement large changes and that it took him "more than five years of daily attention" to transform IBM.

According to Mary Young and James E. Post, the most effective organizations are those that communicate openly, honestly, consistently and continuously. They also developed a list of factors that determine the effectiveness of employee communications.[21] It is evident that IBM's successful transformation was facilitated through Gerstner's adherence to these principles:

- The chief executive as the communications champion — Gerstner appointed himself to the position of chief communicator, realizing that this task could not be delegated to anyone else and that he had to personally set the example for others to follow.

- Matching the words to the actions — Gerstner led IBM by demonstrating his passion, his anger, his directness, which in his own words was "very un-IBM. Very un-CEO-like." Gerstner even went so far as to tell his team that he was "looking for people who make things happen, not who watch and debate things happening." Commitment to two-way communications — Gerstner went out into the field to listen to and solicit input from the field employees; he held customer focus sessions, used the internal messaging system to "talk to employees" as well as listen to their concerns, comments and advice.

- Emphasis on face to face communications — Gerstner met regularly with executives and senior members of management; however, he omits to mention how often employees had opportunities to speak with him "live, face-to-face." Face-to-face communication is important; however, with 90,000 employees in 44 countries, *what* is communicated is certainly more important then the medium in which it is communicated.

- The bad/good news ratio — Gerstner felt it was imperative that employees knew and understood that IBM was in crisis, otherwise they would continue to operate in the same manner; while he felt it was important to communicate the "crisis, its magnitude, its severity, and its impact," he also felt it was necessary to communicate "the new strategy, the new company model, the new culture."

- The employee communication strategy — Young and Post stress that communication is a process, not a product; communication should include the whys and hows, not only the whats; it should be timely, continuous, help employees understand their roles and should allow employees to formulate their own feelings and opinions. Based on his actions, Gerstner followed this advice and developed an effective communication strategy that helped in IBM's transformation.

5. Reinforcing the Change

After assessing and reacting to the external environment, creating a new corporate strategy and vision, implementing the change program, convincing sceptical and resistant stakeholders of the need to change, Gerstner's last challenge was to instill a culture that may not necessarily embrace change, but at the very least would not shun and avoid change at any cost.

Gerstner believes that "great companies lay out strategies that are believable and executable" but also writes that "these plans are then reviewed regularly and become in a sense, the driving force behind everything the company does." He also points out that "execution is all about translating strategies into action programs and measuring their results" and "holding people accountable for them."

Peggy Holman explains that "Change is a process, not an event" and that while "events can be helpful in focusing people's attention, they are only part of the change equation" and explains that "organizations and communities also need to focus on actively supporting the plans and improvements achieved during the event" otherwise "without such ongoing support, conditions may return to what they were before the event occurred."[22]

357

Unfortunately, making people accountable and measuring results makes them feel as if they are being tested or evaluated; however, when it comes to objectively evaluating a change program there is no other objective manner in which to assess the program other than to use quantifiable measures. It is a vital part of the change process and can help determine what further changes are needed, because there is always room for continuous improvement.

CREATING THE LEARNING ORGANIZATION

A view among many management scholars is that organizations that effectively change or adapt to changes in their environment are ones that have first "learned" — they have learned how to recognize the need for change, and they have learned what actions are necessary to adapt. This notion of the central role of change is reflected in one of the many definitions of a learning organization: "an organization that facilitates the learning of all its members and consciously transforms itself and its context."[23] Learning, in this sense, involves three aspects of learning:

- adapting to their environment
- learning from their people
- contributing to the learning of the wider community or context of which they are a part

Organizations, like individuals, need to develop and grow — not necessarily in size, but in their capacity to function effectively. Clearly, this demands organizational change. Organizational development has been defined as the following:

> a process of planned system change that attempts to make organizations (viewed as social-technical systems) better able to attain their short- and long-term objectives. This is achieved by teaching the organization members to manage their organization processes, structures, and culture more effectively.[24]

Chris Argyris and Donald Schon made a tremendous contribution to the management literature and to the topic of organizational change through their examination of the issue of **organizational learning**.[25] How do organizations learn? Do organizations learn from their mistakes? This seems to be an abstract notion, and yet it is a very real topic. Argyris and Schon suggested that organizational learning represents the collective experience of individuals within the organization and comes about when organizational procedures change as a result of what has been learned. In this sense, organizational learning has been defined as the detection and correction of error.[26] Organizations can learn through individuals acting as agents in an effort to critically examine the methods and functioning of their organization. Argyris and Schon make a distinction between two types of learning: single-loop learning and double-loop learning. It is the latter that constitutes genuine organizational learning, and that leads to significant organizational change. (See Exhibit 9.3.)

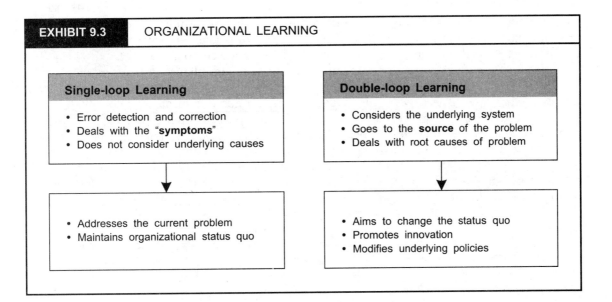

EXHIBIT 9.3   ORGANIZATIONAL LEARNING

Single-loop Learning

- Error detection and correction
- Deals with the "**symptoms**"
- Does not consider underlying causes

- Addresses the current problem
- Maintains organizational status quo

Double-loop Learning

- Considers the underlying system
- Goes to the **source** of the problem
- Deals with root causes of problem

- Aims to change the status quo
- Promotes innovation
- Modifies underlying policies

Single-loop learning involves the correction of errors that employees may find in organizational methods of performance in order to keep the system working. This approach assumes that the organization has the right systems established but simply needs to fine-tune the present system. For example, an organization may find that downsizing permits it to be more flexible with lower costs. However, does reducing the workforce achieve flexibility? Individuals engaging in single-loop learning or adaptive behaviour are essentially functioning within the boundaries or constraints of the presented problem. Single-loop behaviour typically results in making *incremental* improvements and improving efficiency. Such behaviour involves, at best, the modification of strategies or assumptions underlying the strategies in ways that maintain the existing organizational approaches to problems. That is, single-loop learning results in the organization continuing its present policies or achieving its current objectives.

Double-loop learning requires that individuals assess whether an error or problem exists in an organization because the systems themselves need to be changed. Changing organizational systems or assumptions requires a deeper level of examination, and typically is a precursor to significant organizational change. For example, if an organization wants to achieve "flexibility," is this achieved simply through a reduction in the workforce? Perhaps the objective itself of "flexibility" needs to be re-evaluated.

Double-loop learning leads to the organizations modifying its underlying policies or goals. The double-loop learning process requires innovation and involves challenging the status quo within an organization. Individuals engaged in double-loop learning are not bound by the constraints of the presented problem. Rather, double-loop learning involves an examination of the assumptions and values underlying an organization's functioning. This critical examination culminates in fundamental changes to the present system and in the recognition of new problems to be solved. These new problems and new solutions will ultimately transform current strategies and assumptions.

Single-loop learning results from addressing the *symptoms* of a problem, while double-loop learning results when individuals attempt to uncover the *root causes* of the problem — questioning why the problem arose in the first place.

What type of learning is dominant in most organizations? Many scholars have suggested that most organizations, at best, encourage single-loop, but not double-loop, learning. Moreover, it has been suggested that organizations typically create systems that, in fact, inhibit double-loop learning. For example, the bureaucratic nature of most organizations encourages employees to be methodical and disciplined and, consequently, less likely to question the basic assumptions of most organizational practices.

How do organizations change? According to Argyris and Schon, change is accomplished through double-loop learning. This demands that individuals increase their awareness of the nature of the status quo and of those elements that deserve and require change. What is the ultimate goal? As one scholar commented:

> [The] ultimate goal [is] to help individuals unfreeze and alter their theories of action so that they, acting as agents of the organization, will be able to unfreeze the organizational learning systems that also inhibit double-loop learning.[27]

Argyris and Schon assert that people tend to adopt a single-loop learning approach in organizations rather than developing double-loop learning skills.[28] Argyris stated that "We strive to organize our individual and organizational lives by decomposing them into single-loop problems because they are easier to solve and to monitor."[29]

Is the job of management one that demands learning? This is an interesting question. Some critics suggest that management, with its emphasis on concrete results (typically measured in profits, dollars, costs, etc.) has traditionally de-emphasized the importance of learning as a necessity of proper management. (See Talking Business 9.1.)

Double-Loop Learning and Shifting Paradigms

It would seem that radical organizational change can only come about when the members of an organization are encouraged to engage in double-loop learning — the concept we discussed above. It is akin to making a dramatic departure from the present way of doing things. This has also been referred to in the notion of *shifting paradigms*. Joel Barker, a management consultant and author, in his popular book *Paradigms* (1993), talks about the failure of many organizations to adapt to change. Consider the case of the Swiss watchmakers. Way back in 1968, who dominated the watch industry? Yes — the Swiss, with about 65% of the unit sales in the world. And in fact, back then, if anyone was asked to predict who would remain the leader even 20 or 30 years later, they would probably say the Swiss. However, by 1980, who came to dominate the world watch market? You may have correctly guessed Seiko of Japan. By that year, the Swiss share had fallen to 10% of the market, while Japan (who had held about 1% of the market in 1968) was the dominant force, with Seiko owning about 33% of the world market. From 1979 to 1981 about 50,000 of the 62,000 Swiss watchmakers lost their jobs — a huge disaster for Switzerland. What happened? Well, Japan had focused on electronic technology — the electronic quartz

---

TALKING BUSINESS 9.1   **THE LEARNING MANAGER**

Management scholar Steven Henderson noted the following:

> Why is it that managerial work is not generally as scientific, or learning-oriented, as it could be? In many ways, the process of scientific thinking would appear to be significantly different to that of management thinking, since managers rarely set knowledge as the prime target of their activity. Indeed, the so-called learning curve or learning effect is seen as a consequence of carrying out managerial activity (typically production) rather than prerequisite. Organizations structured along the lines of a "learning laboratory" remain isolated exceptions.

Source: Steven Henderson, "Black swans don't fly double loops: the limits of the learning organization?" *The Learning Organization* (1997) 4(3): 99. (Note omitted.)

---

was a natural outcome. Where did this technology come from that allowed Japan to demolish the Swiss's domination of the watch market? The technology came from the Swiss themselves — a research institute in Switzerland.

This story has a particularly ironic twist, because it suggests that the Swiss could have easily maintained their market leadership. However, when the Swiss researchers presented their new idea to Swiss manufacturers back in 1967, the manufacturers rejected it! They considered it inferior — who would want to buy a watch that didn't have a mainspring, didn't need bearings, nor, almost, any gears, and was electronic with battery power? So the manufacturers rejected it, but let their researchers display what they thought was useless technology at the world Watch Congress that year. Seiko, upon observing this invention, had a completely different view — and the result was a dramatic turnaround for Japan and a dramatic failure for the Swiss. What happened here, according to Joel Barker, was a failure to make a **paradigm** shift.

In Barker's view, change is all about adopting new paradigms. What is this strange concept called a paradigm, and how did it cause the downfall of the Swiss watch industry at that time?

The term *paradigm* can be considered as referring to our set of beliefs or mental framework for understanding how the world operates. We see the world through our paradigms. You might also think of a paradigm as our theories, our assumptions, our beliefs or customs. As Joel Barker writes: "A paradigm in a sense tells you that there is a game, what the game is and how to play the game according to the rules." Barker argues that overcoming resistance to change is all about being able to do two things:

1. Recognize the current paradigms that govern our behaviour.
2. Shift to a new paradigm.

So, how does this apply to our example of the Swiss watch industry?

You might consider the Swiss manufacturers as being prisoners of their old paradigm — they could not conceive of the watch industry as ever changing, so it was the old, traditional Swiss watches that would always dominate the market. However, the industry did, in fact, experience a paradigm shift, brought about by Seiko, which did adapt its thinking to recognize new consumer tastes: the paradigm governing the rules of the watch industry game changed, but the Swiss still thought they could play the game by the old rules, based on the old paradigm. Consequently, they were victims of failing to adapt to changing conditions, failing to shift away from their old paradigm. The ability to critically examine our paradigms, how we see the world, is very much a part of our ability to accept change, both at the individual and at the organizational level.

Why don't organizations encourage double-loop learning and, consequently, innovation? Clearly, innovation is a desirable objective, yet organizations tend to manifest rules and regulations that facilitate consistency and stability — qualities needed to function effectively on a day-to-day basis. Ironically, it is innovation and the ability to change that are the skills necessary for long-term survival. Unfortunately, organizations do not tend to encourage double-loop learning. If organizations are guilty of inhibiting genuine learning (double-loop learning) and, consequently, failing to generate real change, what are the sources of this dysfunction? We will consider those sources next.

Do Organizations Encourage or Discourage Learning and Change?

Peter Senge, in many ways, popularized the concept of the learning organization as one that encourages all employees to engage in the learning process through dialogue, experimentation and learning from each other.[30] It has been acknowledged that "learning organizations" cannot exist without "learning employees."[31] That is, organizational learning and development are facilitated through individual learning and development. The ability of organizations to adapt to, and change with, a changing environment is dependent on the ability of their members to change and adapt.

Individual change is really about learning — learning new skills, learning or developing new perspectives and new ways of dealing with everyday challenges. Do organizations facilitate individual learning and development? Can organizations provide a learning environment for their employees whereby employees can grow and develop throughout their careers? Given that the traditional bureaucratic organizational structures are rapidly being replaced with more organic structures, it would seem critical to similarly shift greater attention to a more adaptive, innovative type of employee, better suited to the changing needs of the new organization, and capable of changing and developing along with the organization.

Can Employees Learn?

Workplace experiences comprise a significant portion of people's lives and, consequently, it is understandable that the manner in which individuals experience their workplaces will have a considerable impact on their growth and development.[32] Adults continue to learn throughout their lifetimes, and their past experience can help or hinder this learning.[33] A number of developmental theorists have emphasized the presence of challenge and stimulation in the environment as a means to encourage learning and development. Environments or experiences that challenge individuals will help bring about development.[34] The workplace is an important element in adult development, with the power to foster or impede development of its members. For example, organizations that encourage self-exploration, and information-seeking, will facilitate individual growth and development.[35] The workplace's influence on individual development results from its ability to promote individual challenge and critical reflection through the introduction of new tasks and responsibilities.[36]

What is adult learning development? There is not one all-encompassing definition of adult learning or development. Among the streams of thought in adult learning and development theory is the notion that development grows out of the interaction of both internal/psychological events and external/social events.[37] Adult development is based on change rather than stability, and this change or growth occurs at a predictable rate and sequence.[38] Individuals can learn from their experience if they can effectively see what changes are involved and how they can be accomplished.[39]

Based on the views cited above, learning from experience essentially involves changing both what one does and how one see things. As we identified earlier, according to Argyris and Schon, learning in organizations involves the process of detecting and correcting "error."[40] When individuals begin to question or confront the underlying organizational norms and goals that relate to this process of error detection and correction, this constitutes double-loop learning. The questions of interest in this regard are, Do organizations contain elements that encourage or impede challenge, confrontation and enquiry as a means to facilitate double-loop learning or paradigm shifting in organizations among individuals? A consideration of the "institutional" nature of organizations offers some insights in this regard.

Bureaucracies and Roles

To understand the ability of organizations to influence individuals in the manner described above, it is useful to consider a theory of organizational behaviour that considers the institutional nature of organizations: **institutionalization theory**.[41] In order to determine what institutionalization theory has to offer in terms of understanding the influence of organizations on adult learning and development, it is necessary to understand what this theory says about the nature of organizations and their influence on individual behaviour.

Institutionalization involves the processes by which shared beliefs take on a rule-like status. *Institutionalization* has been defined as a social process through which individuals create a shared definition of what is appropriate or meaningful behaviour.[42] Meyer and Rowan suggested that organizations that incorporate societally legitimated elements in their formal structures maximize their legitimacy and increase their resources and survival capabilities.[43] Essentially, this perspective acknowledges that organizations often generate "accepted practices" that tend to govern how things are done. These practices may continue even when they are no longer functional, simply because they have become an "ingrained" part of the organization.

Single-loop learning would seem to be a natural consequence of adherence to institutionalized structures. Single-loop learning is emphasized in organizations governed by institutionalized structures — following organizational policy without critically examining behaviour or the policy that dictates behaviour. This is reflected in the image of the "mindless bureaucrat" who follows rules and regulations without considering the necessity of such rules. On the other hand, when individuals are not forced to conform with myriad rules and regulations, they are more likely to engage in thoughtful consideration of the utility of workplace policy in order to determine whether such policies are effective or ineffective. Consequently, organizations where institutionalized structures are deeply entrenched are less likely to provide an environment conducive to adult learning and development.

Cognitive Scripts

Organizational policy can discourage employees from thinking "outside the box," so to speak. This is also reflected in the notion of **cognitive scripts**. What are cognitive scripts? They are scripts we all carry with us in the performance of our jobs. Though they are not concrete or tangible, they are very real. That is, any organization possesses shared meanings regarding how its members should conduct themselves in the performance of their duties.[44] Cognitive scripts or schema have been described as mental pictures (most often unconscious) that serve to organize knowledge in some systematic fashion. Essentially, organizational members can function efficiently in organizations through the use of scripts or schema, to reduce the mass of information to be processed as a means to guide their performance. That is, cognitive scripts may guide thought and behaviour and are based on beliefs about people, situations, or behaviours. A script is a type of schema that serves to help understand and enact dynamic patterns of behaviour. A script provides knowledge about expected sequences of events, and guides behaviour for a given situation.

What are the implications of organizational scripts for learning and development in the workplace? Cognitive learning is one learning domain that assumes that people have characteristic ways of making sense of the world by organizing that world into abstract categories.[45] These categories change with age and, ideally, should be in the direction of growth. How do organizations impact cognitive learning? Individuals, within social settings, form and use categories in such processes as perception, decision making and conceptualization. As explained earlier, this categorization is intended to reduce the cognitive complexity of the environment. In other words, individuals within organizations often rely on pre-programmed methods of conduct (scripts) and cognitive pictures of their environment. In effect, scripts internalize a routinized approach to performance on the job. Similarly, the use of scripts to guide behaviour in the workplace can potentially discourage individuals from critically examining events and situations each time performance is required.

The reliance on cognitive scripts and schema in the workplace reduces the need to continually question and confront environmental cues. Rather, a pre-programmed approach to dealing with others in the workplace seems to be developed. To the extent that reliance is placed on these scripts and schemas, confrontation and change will be discouraged, and, consequently, learning and development will be impeded.

Employees can differ in the degree to which they rely on scripts or pre-programmed performance guidelines to govern their work conduct. Work behaviour that is largely scripted discourages employees from engaging in critical evaluation of how their work is conducted. Through their need to maintain reliability and consistency in employee performance, cognitive scripts that we use to function in our jobs can actually generate obstacles to individual-level change and learning. Organizations that encourage a critical evaluation of these scripts are more likely to motivate learning and development among members than are organizations that discourage the critique of established methods of work.

IMPLEMENTING CHANGE THROUGH TIPPING POINT LEADERSHIP

> What must underlie successful epidemics, in the end, is a bedrock belief that change is possible, that people can radically transform their behaviour or beliefs in the face of the right kind of impetus.[46]

What Is the Tipping Point?

Malcolm Gladwell's 2002 book, *The Tipping Point*, offers a unique and thought-provoking framework for understanding change and serves to explain some of the reasons for change when it happens in rather unexplained ways. Through the use of terminology borrowed from epidemiology, Gladwell describes change as seeing a virus when it reaches critical mass, or, as he references, "the boiling point." He develops this term to lend itself to an examination of what he refers to as "social epidemics." While the book speaks to many social phenomena dating back to the American Revolution, it also has great relevance to organizational change.

One of the ideas that he discusses is the phenomena of *word of mouth* and its ability to bring about change. As well, the book addresses the notion of change occurring as an epidemic within an organization, beginning at the periphery and moving to the core. Finally, contrary to the idea of slow and steady change, the premise of Gladwell's book is to understand change that happens quickly and successfully.

Three Rules of the Tipping Point

Gladwell has developed three rules of epidemics: (i) The Law of the Few — that is, there are exceptional people who possess social connections, personality, energy and enthusiasm to be able to spread "the word" (i.e., idea or product) in epidemic proportions; (ii) The Stickiness Factor — that is, there are specific ways to make a message memorable in terms of presenting and structuring information to influence the impact it will make; (iii) The

Power of Context — discussed in two parts, essentially that "...human beings are a lot more sensitive to their environment than they may think."[47]

The Law of the Few

The Law of the Few divides these "exceptional" people who essentially control the power of word-of-mouth epidemics into three categories. They are, as Gladwell has named them, Connectors, Mavens and Salesmen. **Connectors**, most simply put, know a lot of people. They are critical to the instigation of a word-of-mouth epidemic. Gladwell repeatedly uses the example of Paul Revere, who sparked the American Revolution by riding miles during the night to warn of Britain's impending attack. Gladwell contrasts the success of this word-of-mouth campaign with William Dawes, who, in collaboration with Revere, embarked on the same ride but with a lower success rate: fewer people were called into action by Dawes than by Revere. This, Gladwell explains, attests to the fact that Revere was a Connector, someone who had a great social network. Connectors, Gladwell describes, are so well connected because "...they manage to occupy many different worlds and subcultures and niches."[48] Hence, the ability to be able to diffuse an idea is greatly increased. Finally, he states, "...that the closer an idea or product comes to a Connector, the more power and opportunity it has."[49] Therefore, based on this explanation, had Dawes been a Connector his success rate would have been greater.

The second category of people in the Law of the Few are **Mavens**, from the Yiddish, meaning "...one who accumulates knowledge."[50] This term, also employed as a marketing concept, is important to economists analyzing Mavens's effect on the marketplace. Mavens are people who have information "on a lot of different products or prices or places."[51] Gladwell introduces a Maven by the name of Mark Alpert, whom he describes as pathologically helpful, even so far as writing to *Consumer Reports* to offer corrections. Mavens, he describes, are important in starting word-of-mouth epidemics because "...they know things the rest of us don't."[52] Mavens have the ability to start word-of-mouth epidemics not only because of their knowledge and social skills, but also because their motivation is pure, based on a desire to "help out" and therefore appeared to be unbiased, people accept their message or information more willingly.

The final category, **Salesmen**, have the skills to persuade those who are not convinced by the data provided by the Mavens or the message spread by the Connectors. Salesmen possess natural exuberance and are finely tuned (albeit often subconsciously) to non-verbal communication. Moreover, it is the subtle, hidden and unspoken communication that often hinges the Salesmen's success. While Salesmen are known for their persuasiveness, it is not through overt tactics that they are able to persuade. It is a genuine interest that makes them mesmerizing and, in turn, persuasive.

The Stickiness Factor

The second rule of epidemics is called the *Stickiness Factor* — that is, the quality of a message to ensure that it "sticks"; it is the method of presenting information in a memorable way. The tangible descriptor Gladwell uses is the television program *Sesame Street* and how it was created to cause an epidemic of literacy in children. The creators of the television program endeavored to create a program that would increase literacy in children through a medium that was not known to elicit such a reward. Gladwell describes a process of testing and reworking the program to arrive at a "sticky" version that accomplished its intended goal. The importance of "Stickiness" is that the idea needs to resonate with people so that it becomes memorable. Gladwell poses a question as he considers the notion of Stickiness in comparison to the importance of the messenger: "Is it so memorable, in fact, that it can create change, that it can spur someone to action?"[53] Although the Law of the Few states that it is the exceptional people who start the epidemics and all that is required is you find them, Stickiness has the same applicability — there is a simple way to present information to make it irresistible, and the only requirement is you find the right way. To sum: while the messenger is critical to spreading the message, the content of the message is equally important.

The Power of Context

The third rule of epidemics is called the *Power of Context*, which is described in two parts. The first part pertains to the environment: "epidemics are sensitive to the conditions and circumstances of the times and place in which they occur."[54] Gladwell illustrates this using the "Broken Windows" theory, borrowed from criminologists James Q. Wilson and George Kelling. The theory states that if a window is broken and left unrepaired, people will draw the conclusion that there is no place for authority and order, and in turn more windows will be broken, inviting a graduation in the severity of crimes committed.[55] He posits that the Broken Window theory and Power of Context are one and the same in that the smallest changes in the environment can lead to an epidemic that can be tipped or reversed. He states that behaviour is a "...function of social context" and that in this situation "...what really matters is little things."[56]

The second part of the Power of Context is the critical role that groups play in social epidemics. Gladwell introduces the notion of groups and their importance in initiating and sustaining change by creating a community to practice and support the change. Borrowing from cognitive psychology and research by anthropologist Robin Dunbar, Gladwell describes the Rule of 150, which asserts that human beings are most capable of having genuine social interaction with a maximum of one hundred and fifty individuals.[57] He describes an organization that uses this model and has had tremendous success. The strength behind this notion is that "...in order to create one contagious movement, you often have to create many small movements first."[58]

Applying the Tipping Point to Organizational Change

As mentioned previously, human interaction is of great importance in how we receive information, specifically information pertaining to change. Therefore, the concept of the Law of the Few has strong relevance to the organizational context.

"Word-of-mouth" change may seem like an unorganized and unconventional approach to implementing change within an organization. For an organization to draw upon hidden resources such as the Connectors, Mavens and Salesmen already within the ranks, there exists the potential to bring about a change epidemic.

Wanda Orlikowski and J. Debra Hofman discuss the need for change to be flexible and not based on a fixed beginning, middle and end point. To accomplish this they suggest being more open to the opportunities that arise during change.[59] A word-of-mouth change "epidemic" in an organization requires at least some prior commitment by the "few" key organizational members.

A second approach to change based on Gladwell's framework is implementing change from the periphery (i.e., small groups) in an organization and then moving to the corporate core, as is suggested by Beer, Eisenstat and Spector.[60] What the authors suggest is change that is mandated from the most senior levels within the organization and delivered in a "top-driven" fashion will not lead to success, as opposed to change that begins far from corporate headquarters and initiated by line managers and employees. The underlying rationale is that at the "grassroots" level there is a greater understanding of the individual roles and responsibilities and the changes that are required to bring about change. Instead, senior management should create a culture for change and support initiatives at the grassroots level, or the periphery, and allow it to move to the corporate core, as opposed to mandating change in the opposite direction.

Again, if we look at the Law of the Few and assume that an organization has a culture that encourages change, then it is possible that change can be initiated or "tipped" by either a Connector, Maven or Salesmen. This outside/in-driven philosophy could remedy the failures that organizations encounter when attempting top-driven change. Of course, this philosophy does require participation and awareness from the senior levels, primarily in understanding and seeking out, perhaps from the human resources function, these Connectors, Mavens and Salesmen and engaging them in an idea, or further allowing them to engage the organization with their ideas.

The concept of identifying and allowing the role of a change agent to move from a senior leadership function to a employee line-driven process for a change initiative to take hold and "tip" within an organization is a powerful notion. As suggested by Beer et al., the potential for change could be significantly increased if initiated by employees and if the processes of engagement is also employee driven. If employees see the value in the change and it is initiated by a respected peer (i.e., a Salesman or Connector), employee support for the change would increase significantly as opposed to a mandated or programmatic change that does not have employee "buy-in" or support.

The *Power of Context* also has relevance here as Gladwell states that groups also play a critical role in initiating and sustaining change. Further, as stated earlier, in order to have one contagious movement you often have to have many small movements first. Again, speaking to the power of change occurring at the *periphery* and moving inward, if there are many small movements started locally the power of these movements to grow into one large movement and eventually "tip" into large-scale change is a strong possibility and presents a compelling and lasting model for change.

If organizations are willing to accept some risk, to take some of the control away from senior management and place it in the hands of the Connectors, Mavens and Salesmen and place more emphasis on the impact that employees can have on one another, the potential for any change to "tip" (i.e., spread) within an organization is great. We must embrace the idea that change is possible, that people can change behaviour and that it can happen quickly. All we need to do is consider the right "triggers" to make it all happen.

MANAGING MERGER CHANGE

There are few organizational-related change events that have a more profound impact on the organization than mergers. Many scholars have observed that mergers of two organizations not only hasten growth, but provide opportunities for the establishment of corporate diversity[61] and consequently can be a powerful building block in organizational success. Several key successes can be realized as a result of merger activities and can include increased market power, increased sales, increased shareholder wealth and increased profitability.[62]

While there are many benefits to be gained, ironically much of the existing research shows that half or 50% of all attempted mergers fail to realize the efficiencies or synergies originally expected.[63] Why does this type of change so often fail? It has been estimated that as much as one-third to one-half of all failed mergers can be linked to employee issues[64] — the human side of mergers. Given the prevalence of mergers in today's global economy and the resulting people struggles that ensue, it's critical that we investigate this phenomenon further to establish a greater understanding and a model from which the people side of mergers and acquisitions can be understood and applied.

Imagine for a moment that you are an employee with 15 years service within an organization, representing significant tenure. Like any other organization, your organization has undergone change, but your employer always maintained its autonomy, its vision and core goals to become the number-one service provider in its industry. Then, without warning, based on your lack of knowledge or inclusion in the merger process, your organization announces a decision to merge with one of your competitors with whom you have spent the past 15 years competing.

This brief example helps to shape the reality that many employees must endure when their employer makes the decision to merge with another organization. This decision can cause employees to feel a sense of betrayal and anxiety due to the uncertainty associated with their unclear future. Carrying forward from the above example, one can understand the degree of uncertainty that such a predicament forces on an employee who has a great deal of familiarity and currency with the current employer with whom they "identify" given their 15-year history. Clearly the challenge here is of acceptance of a new organizational reality. How should this type of change be managed?

The model presented in Exhibit 9.4 and explained next highlights the fundamental change issues that must be addressed in order to successfully facilitate a merger and underscores the high level of human factors that must be managed in undergoing such a change.

Managing Identity Change

Employees naturally attach meaning to their employers, which helps them to establish an "identity."[65] "'Identity' is 'who we are.'"[66] Within the organizational context, identity is in part defined or shaped by one's membership within that organization — "I am an IBMer," "I am a member of the Molson family," etc. In the context of a merger, if the identification of employees with their organization is very strong, resistance to the change event will likely occur given that merger and acquisition (M&A) is perceived as a threat to their old identity, which is founded in their original employer.[67]

EXHIBIT 9.4   MANAGING MERGER CHANGE

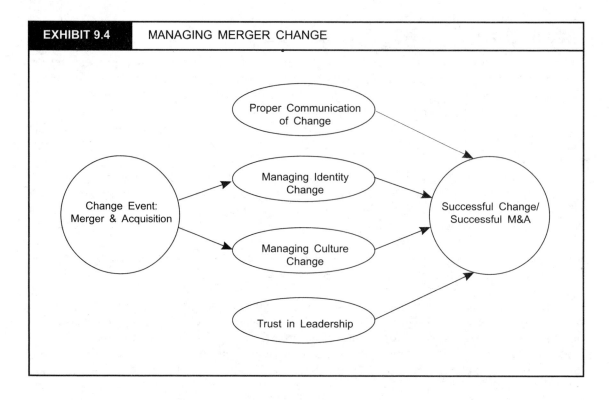

Individuals naturally categorize themselves into different social groups, which may include religion, nationality and, specific to this topic, organizational membership. This is a form of self-categorization within the context of Social Identity Theory.[68] Most of the existing research on identity defines this construct as "the perception of oneness with, or belongingness to the organization.[69] Moreover, it has been argued that identity within an organizational context can be reduced to "the degree to which a member defines him or herself by the same attributes that he or she believes define the organization."[70] Put simply, individuals may find meaning or belongingness within their organizations, and that, in part, helps to define their sense of self.

What are the implications of organizational identity in the context of M&A? A merger can have a very real and profound effect on one's sense of self or identity simply by confusing the lines of membership within a group. Members of merging organizations can experience a loss of purpose, self-worth and even pride. Within a merger situation, employees perceive their futures to be uncertain and their cognitive attachment with their original employer, strained. Employees' sense of individual and organizational identification is in part constructed by their ability to assign such things as esteem, efficacy and distinctiveness through their membership with their employer. However, during a merger, employees find it increasingly difficult to accomplish this given the inherent uncertainty. As a result of this conflict, they resort to activities of habit and familiarity, fostering an "us vs. them" attitude. This is counterproductive to generating a healthy transition into one common identity, as is the aim of any merger.

The reality is that a merger as a change event is an extremely tenuous situation fraught with a great deal of emotion. For example, many mergers sight "existing compatibilities" or "merger of equals" as the anchors on which the alliance is built.[71] However, it is crucial to understand that no two organizations are the same or so similar that alliance efforts will be immune to a "we vs. they" attitude. Moreover, it is certainly impossible for there ever to be a true "merger of equals."[72] This is specifically true in the perceptions of the members of each organization who will undoubtedly experience, at one point or another, feelings of unfairness and uncertainty as one group's initiatives are adopted over another's.[73] It follows that during times where perceived threats to identity are prevalent, members will again retreat to routines and customs that help to define their original membership within their employer of origin and reject all other initiatives in favour of their own.

The very nature of a merger calls for a reconstruction of identity given that there are two entities aligning, each with already well-established histories and customs. Social Identity theory teaches us that it is in these circumstances that members of the affected organizations will try to promote their own identity as the superior choice within the newly established organization by highlighting the differences between both groups.[74] Marks and Mirvis go on to point out that those attempts will generate high conflict within the organization as it will result in the creation of both "in-groups" and "out-groups" — the "us versus them" mentality.[75] Certainly this is not conducive to achieving a successful M&A transition.

One of the primary concepts that the research concerning identity reveals is the concept of *continuity*.[76] Continuity or the continuance of particular aspects of employees' previous connections to their employers help to ease the transition into the new alliance.[77] If employees are provided with the opportunity to retain some of their emotional or cognitive connections, this offers some security amid the chaos they may experience during the M&A.[78] In fact, the concept of *continuity* neither suggests a full departure from old identity constructs nor the need to craft a completely new identity, but rather an effort to create an identity based on the retention of fundamental components of old identities while attempting to embrace some components of new identities.[79] The process that employees go through when they cognitively separate either in part or wholly from their original employer's identity is referred to in the research as *de-identification*.[80]

Managing Culture Change

While *identity* reflects who we are, *culture* in turn reflects "how we do things."[81] However, culture is a great deal more in that it has been described as a "set of common understandings for organizing action and language and other symbolic vehicles for expressing these common understandings. It represents the collective, shared meaning of existence in the organization and how life in this setting is to proceed."[82] Other key components that are included in the establishment of culture are values, norms, symbols, rituals and activities.[83] Put simply, culture can be described as the nature in which an organization approaches its work, its direction and its sense of priority. Culture plays a significant role in any change event and most certainly within the context of a merger.

Often the challenge within M&A change is to somehow "merge" different cultures. *Acculturation* is referred to as "the changes in both groups that occur as a result of contact between cultural groups."[84] This is simply the process in which members of each organization begin to recognize the differences in each culture and ideally begin to embrace particular components within each. This can help form the basis for a new, commonly accepted culture or "way of doing things" for the newly merged organization. Specifically, these differences can include customs, rituals, routines, process methodologies and corporate ethics. Both entities may be required to recognize and adopt specific practices from each other's cultures in order to form one common culture. This is a very difficult and tenuous process, given all of the feelings, emotions and attitudes that members from both merging organizations experience.

Merging organizations typically experience conflict in the acculturation process. While organizations may recognize the need to merge in order to generate combined strength or "synergy," the need for cultural integration often creates much disagreement regarding the method or way in which this process is carried out.[85] In fact, this can often present the greater barrier to a successful transition.[86] This conflict can escalate when one or both of the merging organizations wishes to retain their unique culture even though one common culture is what the newly merged organization will require.[87] This conflict is commonly referred to as "culture clash."[88]

If the new organization falls short of addressing the "culture clash" issues, the consequences can include low morale, increased absenteeism, turnover and ultimately a decrease in productivity.[89] Some observers have used the analogy of marriage to illustrate the unique dynamics that often confront a new alliance or merger.[90] Within this context, one partner may feel as though her needs are considered secondary to the needs of her partner. Similarly, a merger, in the professional sense, may include one side of the merging alliance feeling "short-changed." This causes conflict and often motivates members within these circumstances to retreat to their established norms and activities that in part define their culture, as something they struggle to retain.[91]

Cross-cultural or global mergers accentuate the challenges of this type of change. For example, according to some observers, Canadian organizations tend to be more collaborative than those based in the U.S. Imagine the anxiety of employees of a Canadian-operated corporation merging with an American organization. They may assume that as a result of the merger, they are going to lose their autonomy and the culture within which they operate. In fact, this can sometimes be referred to as *cultural competitors*.[92] There may be specific services or amenities that an organization provides for its members (i.e., daycare, internal financial institutions, etc.) that help to define everyday culture within an organization and that are threatened by the merger.[93] The policies and practices that shape organizational culture, if eliminated, shake the reality that members have traditionally worked within. This causes a great deal of mistrust and anxiety among members and forces them to re-evaluate their place within the new organization and culture.

There are many initiatives that newly merged organizations can undertake to try and lessen the impact of a change transition. Some of the initiatives that address conflicts that arise as a result of culture clash include creating an atmosphere that promotes and advocates multiculturalism.[94] This can in part be established by crafting cross-cultural presentations that could serve to educate members of each merging partner about each other's cultures. This can serve to lessen the "degree of the unknown" and in turn decrease anxiety levels often associated with mergers.[95] These types of workshops are often evident within the diversity arena but also serve a worthwhile purpose within the context of a merger. These workgroups must represent members from both organizations in order to share cultural differences and provide a foundation on which to establish a new culture that has some degree of input from both merging entities.[96]

The Impact of Trust and Communication on Merger Change

Trust is a critical element in any change effort. A high level of trust among employees and their employer is a necessary condition if a change event such as a merger is going to succeed. *Trust* has been defined as "the willingness of a party to be vulnerable to the actions of another party based on the expectation that the other party will perform a particular action important to the trustor."[97] Put simply, it is the belief that one party can expect that the other party will and has the ability to fulfill an obligation.[98]

Trust has been considered as one of the primary components in ensuring organizational success when a change effort is initiated.[99] During times of uncertainty, employees engage in an exercise to re-evaluate their level of trust in management and in turn establish their corresponding level of commitment to the change effort. Therefore, it is within the context of a merger as a change event that trust can be either obliterated or re-affirmed.[100]

The decision to merge with another organization is obviously not entered into lightly by any organization. It demands a great deal of time, effort, analysis and forethought. However, often the announcement of such a decision is perceived by the recipients (employees) as poorly planned. In short, if the goal of the organization is to elicit feelings of commitment on the part of its employees, the organization must demonstrate that the decision to merge with another organization is a "quality" decision accompanied by a clear direction so that employees can internalize their role within the change effort.[101] To help achieve this requires both trust and communication.

Organizations must plan and execute a communication strategy that addresses two primary goals:

1. The organization must be perceived by those affected to be capable of the execution of the change effort.
2. The change must be seen as a reasonable and/or required need in order to solicit commitment.[102]

In fact, some observers go so far as to claim that if leaders are successful in conveying the need for change among their employees and if there is an existing degree of trust already present, employees can react by embracing decisions that may not seem advantageous.[103] This underscores an important element — employees are "hungry" for information in situations of significant change such as M&A's. Given the level of uncertainly among employees, they require clarification and knowledge or they will in turn, naturally "create" their own. This can be damaging in that the "reality" constructed in the absence of communicated facts can distort the actual reality of the change occurring. Employees may "frame" the change in very negative ways, and these perceptions may be difficult for an organization to reverse. Moreover, these perceptions can, in turn, create a "disconnection" between the employee and the change effort. This is why the concept of communication becomes so relevant during times of change.

Leaders who demonstrate a free exchange of information or go so far as to demonstrate the need for change during merger situations generally elicit a greater degree of trust among their employees.[104] Communication within the context of generating trust must be participative and/or collaborative.[105] It has been demonstrated that employees that have a greater degree of involvement within each phase of a change effort perceive their leaders to trust them as employees, and, in turn, they reciprocate that same level of trust toward their leaders.[106] Stemming from this concept is the notion that trust is something that is only given when received. Therefore, leaders who foster an open, sharing environment in which they project trust to their employees will in turn find their employees exhibit greater trust toward them in times of the M&A change — when trust is critical.

One of the key concepts in the existing research that speaks to the generation of trust is the notion of "procedural justice."[107] Simply put, this refers to an organization's ability to constantly and consistently apply its procedures fairly and free of any bias. Specifically, if employees perceive the organization to have consistently applied its procedures and decision-making processes to the change event of the merger, they will more likely trust in the wisdom of the merger and help facilitate successful change.[108]

Organizations must ensure that their communication campaigns and information sharing initiatives during the change event are constant and continuous.[109] The ongoing commitment to ensure information flow helps to minimize rumours while providing updates on any significant issues that often arise during a merger.[110] Consistent communication efforts should serve to constantly remind each member of the merging organizations that the prospect of the new union is far more appealing than that of each of their pre-merger organizations.[111]

This communication keeps leaders "connected" with their employees during turbulent change. Managers and leaders of change need to demonstrate a connection with their employees by being involved with them. In fact, it has been argued that "leaders promote change more effectively if they not only act as leaders of the group, but if they act as members of the group and speak as such to the followers."[112] Put simply, they need to convey the human element by establishing that they, too, as leaders, are entering into a new partnership and alliance with feelings of anxiety and cautiousness, while exhibiting a certain confidence as to the success that the merger will provide.

CHAPTER SUMMARY

Every organization must contend with a changing environment. These changes may stem from economic, competitive, legal/political, technological or societal sources. This chapter emphasized the importance of understanding how organizations facilitate or resist change. We considered the notion of double-loop and single-loop learning, and how organizations might effect these types of learning among their employees. We discussed the tipping point for change as a theory of how to spread change in an organization. Sources of resistance to change were specifically identified, as well as organizational responses to resistance. Finally, we considered the challenge of change in the context of mergers.

IBM Preparing Its Workers for an "On Demand" World

Changes At IBM

Chris Behonick had been in the same job at IBM for more than seven years. As a member of the services support center, he came in every day and supplied price quotes to various clients of IBM's Global Services business. He worked with the same clients on the same types of transactions. Understandably, he was ready for a new challenge.

Behonick occasionally looked for another job, but not aggressively. That's why he was so surprised when his manager approached him late last year about an opening in a different IBM business unit as a relationship manager for IBM's telecommunications clients. He would be able to work with different types of suppliers and clients.

Within a week, Behonick had started at the new job, but was still available to train his replacement. After three months, he says there is still a lot to learn, but he is grateful for the opportunity. "You can't grow if you stand still," he says.

Behonick's move, and the reasons behind it, are an example of how IBM is instituting its well-advertised "on demand" business strategy within its own ranks. The plan also illustrates a crossroads that many businesses face: Will they respond to a changing business environment by fundamentally transforming themselves, or will they just do what they've always done but at a faster clip? IBM chief executive Sam Palmisano is opting for transformation.

He first used "on demand" to describe the company's future at a 2002 meeting of IBM clients. Palmisano talked about how the company had to become a business that could immediately respond to its customers' needs and help them do the same for their clients.

During his speech, which was webcast nationwide to IBM employees, Palmisano pointed to the banking industry as an area in need of this kind of transformation. Banks, he said, have a huge array of information about their customers, but it is all separated into silos.

If they could integrate their business process and technology so that a mortgage processor could view the customer's entire financial picture, loan applications could be processed online within minutes and costs could be halved by reducing the use of paper.

While it all sounded nice in theory, Ted Hoff, IBM's vice president of learning, remembers wondering at the time whether this was "a warmed-up version of e-business." Over the next few months, Palmisano held a series of internal meetings to explain his idea, and it became clear that what Palmisano had in mind was not 1990s e-hype.

And to convince customers that IBM could transform their businesses, the company would have to transform itself, says Donna Biley, vice president of talent.

Changing Times

For a company as big as IBM, becoming more flexible is no small task. But in an environment where clients want services immediately, companies must adapt, says Susan Wehrley, president of Susan K. Wehrley & Associates, a consultancy in Brookfield, Wisconsin, that specializes in workforce planning.

Many firms are responding to this need for faster services by adopting new technology. Instead, says Frank Gillett, principal analyst at Forrester Research, companies first should identify how their industry is changing, then figure out how their workforce has to transform to accommodate the change.

In 2002, the stakes were high for IBM. Not only would it have to act as a role model for the "on demand" concept, it would have to convince potential clients that its technologies would actually make their businesses more successful.

"In 2002, we were deep in a recession in the IT business, and customers just weren't going to buy technology for technology's sake," says Pierre Fricke, vice president of applications and integration infrastructure at Ideas International, a Port Chester, New York-based research firm. To be a technology leader, IBM had to give its clients a reason to care about technology again.

The company has allotted a $700 million annual budget to revamp its workforce capabilities. Of that, it allocated $40 million to training its 10,000 executives and managers on the new business model and how to implement it. The rest of the budget was dedicated to training the lower-tier managers and rank-and-file employees.

To be more flexible and responsive to clients' demands, IBM had to create a system to quickly identify needed skills, spot areas in which those skills were in short supply, and put the right people into place to fill them. This would involve teaching workers new skill sets and getting them to work with other divisions. If there are always employees willing to take vacant positions within the company, the delays associated with being short-staffed become a nonissue.

The new structure also would reduce layoffs, which are a waste of resources, Riley says.

"It is the smart business thing to do to let employees grow rather than having to pay to replace them," she says.

IBM's performance last year may be a sign that its work has started to pay off. The company reported that net earnings for 2004 increased 11 percent to $8.4 billion. During that year, 56 percent of employees whose jobs were in danger of being eliminated were retrained and given new positions, according to Hoff.

The company says it has reduced layoffs by half from 2003, though it would not disclose actual numbers. Riley estimates that has saved IBM "tens of millions of dollars" in the past two years.

Source: Reproduced with permission from Jessica Marquez, "IBM Cuts Costs and Reduces Layoffs as It Prepares Workers for an 'On Demand' World," *Workforce Management* 84, 5 (May 10, 2005): 84–85.

QUESTIONS

1. What are the central forces for change acting on IBM? Explain.

2. Describe the nature of the changes occurring at IBM and suggest whether they are incremental or radical changes.

3. In what way do you think IBM is trying to be a learning organization? How does it encourage double-loop learning?

Change and Survival in Canadian Manufacturing

Canadian manufacturers say they are facing the most dire prospects in a decade, blaming rising energy costs and a strong dollar. The companies also pointed to other costs, such as shipping and insurance, as well as a shortage of skilled workers and high taxes, according to a survey of 1,000 companies across Canada.

"Canadian manufacturers and exporters have become more cautious about business prospects," says the management issues survey by the Canadian Manufacturers & Exporters (CME). "Forecasts for sales, production and profit performance, employment and investment are not as strong for 2005 and 2006 as expectations were last year."

While manufacturing costs are rising, the producers are not able to pass along the higher costs to their customers, and are having to absorb the higher costs themselves, the survey showed. Only 32 per cent of companies in the annual survey said they expected business conditions to improve in 2005, and 30 per cent foresaw improvements next year.

The number of companies expecting a deterioration of the business climate is on the rise, with 20 per cent forecasting a decline this year and 25 per cent in 2006. "This is the lowest level of confidence we've seen" since the survey was started 10 years ago, said Jayson Myers, chief economist for the CME. He presented the survey results yesterday at his association's annual meeting in Toronto. The survey found a big jump in the number of companies reporting weaker profits. As a result, about three-quarters of companies in the survey either expected a decline or the status quo in employment and investment.

"With your focus on cost, and all of these profit pressures eroding your cash flow, and eroding investment, how do you position yourself for growing competition?" Mr. Myers asked rhetorically. The companies said governments could help them by boosting political stability and adopting a more competitive tax system with better incentives for training and skills development. In that respect, Finance Minister Ralph Goodale gave them some hope yesterday. He firmed up his promise yesterday to introduce new tax cuts to be implemented over the next five years, and said he wants to see the overall tax burden for companies come down significantly in that time.

"Our intention is to proceed with a common-sense tax reduction plan to be implemented in a timely manner over the coming five years," Mr. Goodale told the Toronto business audience. "We will also maintain, for Canadian businesses, our strategic tax rate advantage over the United States," the Finance Minister said. But Mr. Goodale said he hopes to do more than lower corporate tax rates. He also wants to make sure the total tax bill faced by individuals and businesses is also competitive with the United States. "It's not just a matter of rates. It's also the marginal effective tax. And my objective, quite frankly, is by the end of that five-year period, to make sure that we have the advantage there," Mr. Goodale said in response to a question from the audience.

While some economists have forecast the demise of the Canadian manufacturing sector because of high energy costs, the high dollar and intensifying competition from Asia, a leading analyst said yesterday that there's no reason why Canadian manufacturers, with a little ingenuity, should not be able to compete.

Canadian companies need to turn their attention away from their traditional markets in industrialized countries, where growth is stagnating, and focus on the high-growth areas of Asia, said Ken Courtis, vice-president of Goldman Sachs Asia. Companies that develop the agility to deal with rapidly changing demand and complex supply chains will have an edge, Mr. Courtis said. Manufacturers would be wise to link their products with long-term service contracts, and put effort into design of customized products, he said. "There is no reason why things can't be great for us."

Source: Reproduced with permission from Heather Scoffield, "Factories see their bleakest prospects in 10 years: High costs, dollar cast gloomy pall," *The Globe and Mail* (November 2, 2005), B1.

QUESTIONS

1. What are the forces of change acting on this industry?

2. Why is it so difficult for organizations to adapt to change in this case?

3. Discuss the notion of a paradigm and how it influences actions in this case. What new paradigm must the Canadian manufacturers adopt?

Appendices

Appendices

Notes

Chapter 1

1. The Conference Board of Canada, "Executive Summary," *Canadian Outlook Long-Term Economic Forecast: 2005* (January 2005) at http://www.conferenceboard.ca/documents.asp?rnext=1153.
2. Mel Hurtig, "Canadian Democratic Movement, Foreign Investment? No. Foreign Ownership and Control? Yes!" (October 19, 2005) from Canadian Democratic Movement Web site: http://www.canadiandemocratic movement.ca/index.php?name=News&file=article& sid=757.

Chapter 2

1. D. Jones, 1997. "Doing the wrong thing: 48% of workers admit to unethical or illegal acts" *U.S.A. Today* (Apr. 4–6, 1997).
2. M. Mahar, "Unwelcome legacy: There's still a big unpaid tab for the S and L bailout" *Barron's* 72(48): 16.
3. L. Karakowsky, A. Carroll and A. Buchholtz, *Business and Society* (Toronto: Nelson Thomson, 2005), p. 66.
4. Ibid.
5. David Wheeler and Maria Sillanpää, *The Stakeholder Corporation: A Blueprint for Maximizing Stakeholder Value* (London: Pitman Publishing, 1997).
6. M. Friedman, *Capitalism and Freedom* (Chicago: University of Chicago Press, 1962); M. Friedman, "The social responsibility of business is to increase its profits" *New York Times Magazine* (September 13, 1970).
7. John Kenneth Galbraith, *The Affluent Society* (Boston: Houghton Mifflin Company, 1958).
8. K.E. Goodpaster, and J.B. Matthews, Jr., "Can a corporation have a conscience?" in T.L. Beauchamp and N.E. Bowie (eds.), *Ethical Theory and Business* (Englewood Cliffs, NJ: Prentice Hall, 1983).
9. L. Karakowsky, A. Carroll and A. Buchholtz, *Business and Society* (Toronto: Nelson Thomson, 2005).
10. Ibid.
11. Natasha Tarpley, "Levi's Mends the Social Fabric" *Fortune* (July 10, 2000). © 2001 Time Inc. All rights reserved.
12. A.Z. Carr, "Is business bluffing ethical?" *Harvard Business Review* 46: 127–34.
13. Ibid.
14. *The Economist* (November 17, 2001), p. 70.
15. A.B. Carroll, "Linking business ethics to behaviour in organizations" *SAM Advanced Management Journal* 43: 4–11.
16. A.Z. Carr, "Is business bluffing ethical?" *Harvard Business Review* 46: 127–34.
17. CBC Web site, "Car Owner Sues Shell for Bad Gas" (July 8, 2002): http://www.cbc.ca.
18. Simon Tuck, "Tribunal Hears First Allegations of 'Deceptive Marketing' by Sears," *The Globe and Mail* (October 28, 2003).
19. Megan Barnett, Margaret Mannix, and Tim Smart, "The New Regime; Corporate Reform Measures Are Forcing Boards of Directors to Clean Up Their Act," *U.S. News & World Report* (Vol. 136, No. 6, February 16, 2004), E.2.
20. D.D. Runes, *Dictionary of Philosophy* (Littlefields: Adams and Co., 1964).
21. T.L. Beauchamp and N.E. Bowie, *Ethical Theory and Business* (Englewood Cliffs, NJ: Prentice Hall, 1983).
22. Richard T. De George, *Business Ethics*, 5th Ed. (Upper Saddle River, NJ: Prentice Hall, 1999).
23. P.V. Lewis, "'Defining business ethics': Like nailing Jello to a wall" *Journal of Business Ethics* 4(5): 377–83.
24. J.R. Rest, *Moral Development: Advances in Research and Theory* (New York: Praeger, 1986).
25. T.M. Jones, "Ethical decision making by individuals in organizations: An issue-contingent model" *Academy of Management Review* 16(2): 367.
26. Richard T. De George, *Business Ethics*, 5th Ed. (Upper Saddle River, NJ: Prentice Hall, 1999).
27. Mark Pastin, *The Hard Problems of Management: Gaining the Ethics Edge* (San Francisco: Jossey-Bass, 1986).
28. Ibid.

29. Susan Pulliam, "Over the Line: A Staffer Ordered to Commit Fraud Balked, Then Caved — Pushed by WorldCom Bosses, Accountant Betty Vinson Helped Cook the Books — A Confession at the Marriott," *Wall Street Journal* (June 23, 2003) A1.

30. Gretchen Morgenson, "Wall Street Firms Endorse Ethics Standards for Analysts," *The New York Times* (June 13, 2001).

31. Mark Pastin, *The Hard Problems of Management: Gaining the Ethics Edge* (San Francisco: Jossey-Bass, 1986).

32. Richard T. De George, *Business Ethics*, 5th Ed. (Upper Saddle River, NJ: Prentice Hall, 1999).

33. L.D. Molm, "Affect and social exchange: Satisfaction in power-dependence relations" *American Sociological Review* 56(4): 475–93.

34. M.R. Buckley, D.S. Wiese and M.G. Harvey, "An investigation into the dimensions of unethical behaviour" *Journal of Education for Business* 73(5): 284–90.

35. Richard T. De George, *Business Ethics*, 5th Ed. (Upper Saddle River, NJ: Prentice Hall, 1999).

36. T.M. Jones, "Ethical decision making by individuals in organizations: An issue-contingent model" *Academy of Management Review* 16(2): 367.

37. B. Holstrom, "Moral hazard and observability" *Bell Journal of Economics* 10: 74–91.

38. G. Becker, *The Economic Approach to Human Behaviour* (Chicago: University of Chicago Press, 1976).

39. L.K. Trevino, "Ethical decision making in organizations: A person-situation interactionist model" *Academy of Management Review* 11(3): 601–17.

40. S.L. Grover, "Why professionals lie: The impact of professional role conflict on reporting accuracy" *Organizational Behaviour and Human Decision Processing* 55: 251–72.

41. W.H. Hegarty and H.P. Sims, "Some determinants of unethical decision behaviour: An experiment" *Journal of Applied Psychology* 63(4): 451–57.

42. M.L. Pava, "Religious business ethics and political liberalism: An integrative approach" *Journal of Business Ethics* 17(15): 1633–52.

43. J. Rawls, *Political Liberalism* (New York: Columbia University Press, 1993), p. 51.

44. L.K. Trevino and S.A. Youngblood, "Bad apples in bad barrels: A causal analysis of ethical decision making behaviour" *Journal of Applied Psychology* 75(4): 378–85.

45. S.L. Payne and R.A. Giacalone, "Social psychological approaches to the perception of ethical dilemmas" *Human Relations* 43: 649–65; L.K. Trevino, "Ethical decision making in organizations: A person-situation interactionist model" *Academy of Management Review* 11(3): 601–17.

46. A.M. Pettigrew, "On studying organizational cultures" *Administrative Science Quarterly* 24: 570–81.

47. Ibid.

48. J. Meyer and B. Rowan, "Institutional organizations: Formal structure as myth and ceremony" *American Journal of Sociology* 83: 440–63.

49. S.B. Knouse and R.A. Giacalone, "Ethical decision-making in business: Behavioral issues and concerns" *Journal of Business Ethics* 11: 369–77.

50. C.D. Stone, "The culture of the corporation" in W.M. Hoffman and J.M. Moore (eds.), *Business Ethics*, 2d Ed. (New York: McGraw-Hill, 1975).

51. G.B. Northcraft and M.A. Neale, *Organizational Behaviour* (Chicago: Dryden Press, 1994).

52. R.D. Gatewood and A.B. Carroll, "Assessment of the ethical performance of organizational members: A conceptual framework" *Academy of Management Review* 16: 667–90.

53. R.R. Sims, "The institutionalization of organizational ethics" *Journal of Business Ethics* 10: 493–511; L.J. Brooks, "Corporate codes of ethics" *Journal of Business Ethics* 8: 117–29.

54. K.E. Kram, P.C. Yeager and G.E. Reed, "Decisions and dilemmas: The ethical dimension in the corporate context" in J.E. Post (ed.), *Research in Corporate Social Performance and Policy*, Vol. 1 (Greenwich, CT: JAI Press, 1989), pp. 21–54.

55. J. Weber, "Manager's moral reasoning: Assessing their responses to the three moral dilemmas" *Human Relations* 43: 687–702.

56. L.J. Brooks, "Corporate codes of ethics" *Journal of Business Ethics* 8: 117–29.

57. R.S.J. Baumhart, "How ethical are businessmen?" *Harvard Business Review* 39: 6–31.

58. A. Higgins, C. Power and L. Kohlberg, "The relationship of moral atmosphere to judgments of responsibility" in W.M. Kurtines and J.L. Gewirtz (eds.), *Morality, Moral Behaviour and Moral Development* (New York: Wiley, 1984), pp. 74–106.

59. W.H. Hegarty and H.P. Sims, "Organizational philosophy, policies, and objectives related to unethical decision behaviour: A laboratory experiment" *Journal of Applied Psychology* 64(3): 331–38.

60. J. Weber, "Manager's moral reasoning: Assessing their responses to the three moral dilemmas" *Human Relations* 43: 687–702.

61. L. Kohlberg, "Stage and sequence: The cognitive developmental approach to socialization" in D.A. Goslin (ed.), *Handbook of Socialization Theory and Research* (Chicago: Rand McNally, 1969), pp. 347–480; B. Knouse and R.A. Giacalone, "Ethical decision-making in business: Behavioral issues and concerns" *Journal of Business Ethics* 11: 369–77; L.K. Trevino, "Ethical decision making in organizations: A person-situation interactionist model" *Academy of Management Review* 11(3): 601–17.

62. L.G. Zucker, "Institutionalization as a mechanism of cultural persistence" *American Sociological Review* 42(2): 726–42; Meyer and B. Rowan, "Institutional organizations: Formal structure as myth and ceremony" *American Journal of Sociology* 83: 440–63.

63. J. Meyer and B. Rowan, "Institutional organizations: Formal structure as myth and ceremony" *American Journal of Sociology* 83: 440–63.

64. J.G. March, and H.A. Simon, *Organizations* (New York: Wiley, 1958).

65. C.J.G. Gersick and J.R. Hackman, "Habitual routines in task-performing groups" *Organizational Behaviour and Human Decision Processes* 47: 65–97.

66. Ibid.

67. R. Jackall, *Moral Mazes: The World of Corporate Managers* (New York: Oxford University Press, 1988).

68. Ibid.

69. H. Tajfel, *Human Groups and Social Categories: Studies in Social Psychology* (Cambridge, England: Cambridge University Press, 1981); H. Tajfel and J.C. Turner, "The social identity theory of intergroup behaviour" in S. Worchel and W.G. Austin (eds.), *Psychology of Intergroup Relations*, 2nd Ed. (Chicago: Nelson Hall, 1985), pp. 7–24.

70. B.E. Ashforth and F. Mael, "Social identity theory and the organization" *Academy of Management Review* 14(1): 20–39.

71. J. Turner, "Towards a cognitive redefinition of the social group" in H. Tajfel (ed.), *Social Identity and Intergroup Relations* (Cambridge, England: Cambridge University Press, 1982), pp. 15–40.

72. H. Tajfel and J.C. Turner, "The social identity theory of intergroup behaviour" in S. Worchel and W.G. Austin (eds.), *Psychology of Intergroup Relations*, 2d Ed. (Chicago: Nelson Hall, 1985), pp. 7–24.

73. B.E. Ashforth and F. Mael, "Social identity theory and the organization" *Academy of Management Review* 14(1): 20–39.

74. R. Ricklee, "Ethics in America" *The Wall Street Journal* (October 31/November 3, 1985): 3; S. Milgram, *Obedience to Authority* (New York: Harper & Row, 1974).

75. E. Sutherland and D.R. Cressey, *Principles of Criminology* (Chicago: J.B. Lippincott, 1970).

76. Kahn et al., *Organizational Stress: Studies in Role Conflict and Ambiguity* (New York: John Wiley, 1964).

77. Merton, R.K. *Social Theory and Social Structure*, 2d Ed. (New York: Free Press, 1957).

78. R. Kahn et al., *Organizational Stress: Studies in Role Conflict and Ambiguity* (New York: John Wiley, 1964).

79. B.E. Ashforth and F. Mael, "Social identity theory and the organization" *Academy of Management Review* 14(1): 20–39.

80. John Locke, *Second Treatise on Civil Government* (Cambridge: Cambridge University Press, 1690).

81. Immanuel Kant, *Grounding for the Metaphysics of Morals*. [First published in 1785.] Trans. James W. Ellington. (Indianapolis, IN: Hackett, 1993).

82. Betsy Morris, "White-Collar Blues," *Fortune* (July 23, 2001).

Chapter 3

1. Rebecca Zicarelli, "The Military Advantage," *Across the Board* (2005) 42(1) <http://www.conference-board.org/articles/atb_article.cfm?id=296> [Date accessed: 2006-10-31].

2. W.F. Ulmer, Jr., "In focus/leadership styles: Comparing military and business leaders," *Leadership in Action*, 25(1): 18.

3. J.D. Eggensperger, "How far is too far? Lessons for business from ultra-high-performing military teams," *Team Performance Management*, 10(3/4): 53.

4. National Defence Web site, "The Profession of Arms": www.forces.gc.ca.

5. Ibid.

6. Ibid.

7. Ibid.

8. National Defence Web site, "Arm Forces Leadership Doctrine": www.cda.forces.gc.ca).

9. National Defence Web site, "Military HR Strategy 2020": www.cda.forces.gc.ca.

10. H.C. Sashittal, J. Berman, and S. Ilter, "Impact of trust on performance evaluations," *The Mid-Atlantic Journal of Business*, 34(2): 163.

11. S.S. Tzafrir, G.H. Harel (deceased), B. Baruch, and S.L. Dolan, "The consequences of emerging HRM practices for employees' trust in their managers," *Personnel Review*, 33(5/6): 628; N. Ferres, J. Connell, and

A. Travaglione, "Co-worker trust as a social catalyst for constructive employee attitudes" *Journal of Managerial Psychology*, 19(6): 608.

12. R. Lines, M. Selart, B. Espedal, and S.T. Johansen, "The Production of Trust During Organizational Change," *Journal of Change Management*, 5(2): 221.

13. As cited in F. Erdem, J. Ozen, and N. Atsan, "The relationship between trust and team performance," *Work Study*, 52(6/7): 337.

14. K. Hultman, "Let's Wipe Out Systemic Mistrust," *Organization Development Journal*, 22(1): 102.

15. J.A. Mello, "Profiles in leadership: Enhancing learning through model and theory building," *Journal of Management Education*, 27(3): 344.

16. Paul Hersey and Kenneth H. Blanchard. "Great Ideas Revisited: Revising the Life-Cycle Theory of Leadership," *Training and Development* (Jan. 1996), pp. 42–47.

17. J.C. Chen, and S. Silverthorne, "Leadership effectiveness, leadership style and employee readiness," *Leadership & Organization Development Journal*, 26(3/4): 280.

18. National Defence Web site, "Arm Forces Leadership Doctrine": www.cda.forces.gc.ca.

19. Ibid.

20. Ibid.

21. Ibid.

22. National Defence Web site: www.cda.forces.gc.ca

23. National Defence Web site: http://armyapp.forces.gc.ca/allc/aar/

24. National Defence Web site: http://armyapp.forces.gc.ca/allc/main.asp

25. P. Castka, C.J. Bamber, J.M. Sharp, and P. Belohoubek, "Factors affecting successful implementation of high performance teams," *Team Performance Management*, 7(7/8): 123.

26. P. Castka, C.J. Bamber, J.M. Sharp, and P. Belohoubek, "Factors affecting successful implementation of high performance teams," *Team Performance Management*, 7(7/8): 123.

27. J.T. Scarnati, "On becoming a team player," *Team Performance Management*, 7(1/2): 5.

28. Statistics Canada Web site: http://www40.statcan.ca/l01/cst01/demo34a.htm.

29. Human Resources and Social Development Canada Web site, "Manual — 2001 Employment Equity Data Report": http://www.hrsdc.gc.ca/en/lp/lo/lswe/we/ee_tools/data/eedr/annual/2001/toc.shtml.

30. Statistics Canada 2001 Census of Canada Web site: http://www12.statcan.ca/english/census01/Products/Analytic/companion/paid/canada.cfm

31. Statistics Canada Web site: http://www40.statcan.ca/l01/cst01/labor10a.htm

32. A. Tomlinson, "Wall Street Rougher than Bay Street," *Canadian HR Reporter* (March 11, 2002) 15(5): 1, 14.

33. Women's Executive Network, WXN Research on Workplace Issues, *Moving Forward — The Experiences and Attitudes of Executive Women in Canada* (July 2002) <http://www.wxnetwork.com/images/externalrpt_2002.pdf>; Asha Tomlinson, "Is There a War of the Sexes? It Depends on Who You Ask," *Canadian HR Reporter* (October 21, 2002) 15(18): 2–3.

34. Stelios Loizides, "Aboriginal Baby Boom a Challenge for Employment Prospects," *Canadian HR Reporter* (December 15, 2003) 16(22): 10.

35. Canadian Health Network Web site: <http://www.canadian-health-network.ca/servlet/ContentServer?cid=1045848 110489&pagename=CHN-RCS%2FPage%2FGTPageTemplate&c=Page&lang=En>.

36. Ibid.

37. Statistics Canada, *2001 Census — Analysis Series*, "The changing profile of Canada's labour force: Canada": http://www12.statcan.ca/english/census01/Products/Analytic/companion/paid/canada.cfm

38. Jean Lock Kunz, Anne Milan, and Sylvain Schetagne, *Unequal Access: A Canadian Profile of Racial Differences in Education, Employment and Income*. A report prepared for Canadian Race Relations Foundation by the Canadian Council on Social Development (Toronto: The Foundation, 2000).

39. Department of Justice, http://canada.justice.gc.ca/en/dept/pub/guide/appendix_C.htm.

40. Human Resources and Social Development Canada, *What is Employment Equity?* <http://www.hrsdc.gc.ca/en/lp/lo/lswe/we/information/what.shtml> [Date accessed: 2006-11-01].

41. Government of Canada Web site, "Minister Blackburn releases 2005 Annual Employment Equity Report" (Press release June 15, 2006) <http://news.gc.ca/cfmx/view/en/index.jsp?articleid=220479>.

42. *Employment Equity Act*, 1995, c. 44, s. 2. [Justice Canada Web site: http://laws.justice.gc.ca/en/E-5.401/238505.html

43. Human Resources and Social Development Canada, *History of Employment Equity* <http://www.sdc.gc.ca/asp/gateway.asp?hr=/en/lp/lo/lswe/we/information/history.shtml&hs=wzp> [Date accessed: 2006-11-01].

44. Stelios Loizides, "Aboriginal Baby Boom a Challenge for Employment Prospects," *Canadian HR Reporter* 16, 22 (December 15, 2003): 10.

Chapter 4

1. Gareth Morgan, *Images of Organization* (Sage: Newbury Park, 1986).
2. J. Pfeffer and G.R. Salancik, *The External Control of Organizations* (New York: Harper & Row, 1978).
3. K. Weick, "Educational organizations as loosely coupled systems" *Administrative Science Quarterly* 21: 1–19.
4. E. Goffman, *Interaction Ritual* (Garden City, NY: Doubleday, 1967).
5. L. Pondy et al. (Eds.), *Organizational Symbolism* (Greenwich, CT: JAI Press, 1983).
6. J.D. Thompson, *Organizations in Action* (New York: McGraw-Hill, 1967); D. Katz and R.L. Kahn, *The Social Psychology of Organization*, 2d Ed. (New York: Wiley, 1978).
7. A.D. Hall and R.E. Fagen, "Definition of system" *General Systems: The Yearbook of the Society for the Advancement of General Systems Theory* 1: 18–28.
8. Michael Hammer and James Champy, *Reengineering the Corporation* (New York, NY: HarperBusiness, 1993).
9. Varun Grover, William J Kettinger and James T.C. Teng, "Business process change in the 21st century" *Business and Economic Review* (Jan.–Mar. 2000) 46(2): 14–18. Reproduced with permission of the authors.
10. Ibid.
11. David Brown, "CIBC HR department halved as non-strategic roles outsourced" *Canadian HR Reporter* (June 4, 2001) 14(11): 1.
12. Kim Cameron, "Strategies for successful organizational downsizing" *Human Resource Management* 33 (Summer): 189–211 at 192.
13. Ibid., 189–211.
14. Dan Worrell, Wallace Davidson and Varinder Sharma, "Layoff announcements and shareholder wealth" *Academy of Management Journal* 34 (September): 662–78.
15. Peggy Lee, "A comparative analysis of layoff announcements and stock price reactions in the United States and Japan" *Strategic Management Journal* 18 (December): 879–94.
16. Wayne Cascio, "Downsizing? What do we know? What have we learned?" *Academy of Management Executive* 7 (February): 95–100.
17. Terry H. Wagar, "Exploring the consequences of workforce reduction" *Canadian Journal of Administrative Sciences* (December 1998) 15(4): 300–309.
18. Mark Mone, "Relationships between self-concepts, aspirations, emotional responses, and intent to leave a downsizing organization" *Human Resource Management* 33 (Summer): 281–98; Lisa Ryan and Keith Macky, "Downsizing organizations: Uses, outcomes and strategies" *Asia Pacific Journal of Human Resources* 36 (Winter): 29–45.
19. Jeffery A. Tomasko, *Downsizing: Reshaping the Corporation of the Future* (New York: AMACON, 1990); Wayne Cascio, "Downsizing? What do we know? What have we learned?" *Academy of Management Executive* 7 (February): 100; J. Brockner, "The effects of work layoff on survivors: Research, theory, and practice" *Research in Organizational Behaviour* 10(1): 213–56; Brockner et al., "Interactive effects of procedural justice and outcome negativity on victims and survivors of job loss" *Academy of Management Journal* 37 (June): 397–409; Sutton & D'Aunno, 1989; and K. McLellan and B. Marcolin, "Information technology outsourcing" *Business Quarterly* 59 (Autumn): 95–104.
20. Wayne Cascio, "Downsizing? What do we know? What have we learned?" *Academy of Management Executive* 7 (February): 100; Kim Cameron, "Strategies for successful organizational downsizing" *Human Resource Management* 33 (Summer): 189–211.
21. Connie Wanberg, Larry Bunce and Mark Gavin, "Perceived fairness of layoffs among individuals who have been laid off: A longitudinal study" *Personnel Psychology* 52 (Spring): 59–84.
22. Marjorie Armstrong-Stassen, "Downsizing the federal government: A longitudinal study of managers' Reactions" *Canadian Journal of Administrative Sciences* 15 (December): 310–21.
23. Stephen Havlovic, France Bouthillette and Rena van der Wal. "Coping with downsizing and job loss: Lessons from the Shaughnessy Hospital closure" *Canadian Journal of Administrative Sciences* 15 (December): 322–32.
24. Wayne E. Baker, "Bloodletting and Downsizing Executive Excellence" *Provo* (May 1996) 13(5): 20.
25. P. DiMaggio and W. Powell, "The iron cage revisited: Institutional isomorphism and collective rationality in organizational fields" *American Sociological Review* 48(1): 147–60; J. Meyer and B. Rowan, "Institutional organizations: Formal structure as myth and ceremony" *American Journal of Sociology* 83: 440–63.
26. P. DiMaggio and W. Powell, ibid.
27. John W. Meyer and B. Rowan, "Institutional organizations: Formal structure as myth and ceremony" *American Journal of Sociology* 83: 440–63.
28. P. DiMaggio and W. Powell, "The iron cage revisited: Institutional isomorphism and collective rationality in organizational fields" *American Sociological Review* 48(1): 147–60; W. McKinley, C. Sanchez and A. Schick, "Organizational downsizing: Constraining, cloning, learning" *Academy of Management Executive* 9(3): 32–41.

29. W. McKinley, C. Sanchez and A. Schick, "Organizational downsizing: Constraining, cloning, learning" *Academy of Management Executive* 9(3): 32–41.

30. Martin G. Evans, Hugh P. Gunz and R. Michael Jalland, "Implications of organizational downsizing for managerial careers" *Canadian Journal of Administrative Sciences* 14: 359–71.

31. W. McKinley, C. Sanchez and A. Schick, "Organizational downsizing: Constraining, cloning, learning" *Academy of Management Executive* 9(3): 32–41.

Chapter 5

1. Richard Blackwell, Media Reporter, "Movie Marriage Promises Blockbuster Savings," *The Globe and Mail* (June 22, 2005), B3. Reproduced with permission from *The Globe and Mail*.

2. S. Leung, "McDonald's Flips to Profit as Sales Provide the Sizzle," *Wall Street Journal (Eastern edition)* (January 27, 2004), A6.

3. E. Schlosser. *Fast Food Nation*. New York: Houghton Mifflin, 2001.

4. S. Leung, "McDonald's Flips to Profit as Sales Provide the Sizzle," *Wall Street Journal (Eastern edition)* (January 27, 2004), A6.

5. P. Gogoi and M. Arndt, "Hamburger Hell: McDonald's Aims to Save Itself by Going Back to Basics. But the Company Needs More Than a Tastier Burger to Solve Its Problems," *Business Week* (March 3, 2003) 3822: 104–106.

6. A. Zuber, "McD McShakeup? Mgmt., menu eyed," *Nation's Restaurant News* (March 3, 2003) 37(9): 1–3.

7. Anonymous, "Has McDonald's Lost the Plot?" *Strategic Direction* (April 2003) 19(4): 14–17.

8. P. Gogoi and M. Arndt, "Hamburger Hell: McDonald's Aims to Save Itself by Going Back to Basics. But the Company Needs More Than a Tastier Burger to Solve Its Problems," *Business Week* (March 3, 2003) 3822: 104–106.

9. S. Leung, "McDonald's Flips to Profit as Sales Provide the Sizzle," *Wall Street Journal (Eastern edition)* (January 27, 2004), A6.

10. N. Pachetti, "Back in the kitchen," *Money* (July 2003) 32(7): 44–45.

11. Anonymous, "Has McDonald's Lost the Plot?" *Strategic Direction* (April 2003) 19(4): 14–17.

12. N. Pachetti, "Back in the kitchen," *Money* (July 2003) 32(7): 44–45.

13. Anonymous, "Has McDonald's Lost the Plot?" *Strategic Direction* (April 2003) 19(4): 14–17.

14. S. Leung, "McDonald's Makeover; CEO Cantalupo's Focus on Improving Food and Service Sparks Turnaround; Catering to the Low-carb Crowd," *Wall Street Journal (Eastern edition)* (January 28, 2004), B1.

15. A. Garber, "Salad Days? McD Says Turnaround on Menu," *Nation's Restaurant News* (June 2, 2003) 37(22): 4–5.

16. Anonymous, "McD's Plots Supersized Ops, Menu Makeovers," *Restaurant Business* (May 1, 2003) 102(8): 12–14.

17. P. Gogoi and M. Arndt, "Hamburger Hell: McDonald's Aims to Save Itself by Going Back to Basics. But the Company Needs More Than a Tastier Burger to Solve Its Problems," *Business Week* (March 3, 2003) 3822: 104–106.

18. Anonymous, "McD's Plots Supersized Ops, Menu Makeovers," *Restaurant Business* (May 1, 2003) 102(8): 12–14.

19. S. Leung, "McDonald's Makeover; CEO Cantalupo's Focus on Improving Food and Service Sparks Turnaround; Catering to the Low-carb Crowd," *Wall Street Journal (Eastern edition)* (January 28, 2004), B1.

20. N. Pachetti, "Back in the kitchen," *Money* (July 2003) 32(7): 44–45.

21. P. Gogoi and M. Arndt, "Hamburger Hell: McDonald's Aims to Save Itself by Going Back to Basics. But the Company Needs More Than a Tastier Burger to Solve Its Problems," *Business Week* (March 3, 2003) 3822: 104–106.

22. N. Pachetti, "Back in the kitchen," *Money* (July 2003) 32(7): 44–45.

23. P. Gogoi and M. Arndt, "Hamburger Hell: McDonald's Aims to Save Itself by Going Back to Basics. But the Company Needs More Than a Tastier Burger to Solve Its Problems," *Business Week* (March 3, 2003) 3822: 104–106.

24. D. Stires, "McDonald's keeps right on cookin'," *Fortune* (May 17, 2004) 149(10), 174.

25. A. Garber, "Burger Giants Weigh in with More Healthful Menu Ideas," *Nation's Restaurant News* (May 26, 2003) 37(21): 1–2.

26. P. Gogoi and M. Arndt, "Hamburger Hell: McDonald's Aims to Save Itself by Going Back to Basics. But the Company Needs More Than a Tastier Burger to Solve Its Problems," *Business Week* (March 3, 2003) 3822: 104–106.

27. S. Leung, "McDonald's Makeover; CEO Cantalupo's Focus on Improving Food and Service Sparks Turn-around; Catering to the Low-carb Crowd," *Wall Street Journal (Eastern edition)* (January 28, 2004), B1.

28. S. Brooks, "Seeing the Lite," *Restaurant Business* (September 15, 2003) 102(15): 18–24.

29. C. Murphy, "Health Crackdown Hits Food," *Marketing* (February 20, 2003), 24–26.

30. Ibid.

31. "Client file: Salad days," *The Lawyer* (July 5, 2004), p. 11.

32. M.M. Mello, E.B. Rimm, and D.M. Studdert, "The McLawsuit: The Fast-food Industry and Legal Accountability for Obesity," *Health Affairs* (November/December 2003) 22(6): 207–16.

33. J.K. Nestruck, "Super Size Me: Would You Like Fries with Your Film?" *CanWest News* (May 5, 2004), p. 1.

34. S. Brooks, "Seeing the Lite," *Restaurant Business* (September 15, 2003) 102(15): 18–24.

35. Ibid.

36. R. Gibson, "Food: McDonald's to Drop 'Super Sizes' from Its Menu," *Wall Street Journal (Eastern edition)*, (March 3, 2004), D3.

37. S. Brooks, "Seeing the Lite," *Restaurant Business* (September 15, 2003) 102(15): 18–24.

38. A. Park, "Would You Like to Un-super Size That?" *Time* (Canadian edition) (March 15, 2004) 163(11): 65.

39. S. Gray, "McDonald's Feels the Heat and Offers Some Healthier Fare; Would You Like Some Apples with Your Happy Meal? Here's Your 'stepometer'," *Wall Street Journal (Eastern edition)* (April 16, 2004), A11.

40. The Corporation, "Fixing the Fat," *Business Week* (September 16, 2002) 3799: 67.

41. R. Gibson, "Food: McDonald's to Drop 'Super Sizes' from Its Menu," *Wall Street Journal (Eastern edition)*, (March 3, 2004), D3.

42. S. Gray, "McDonald's Feels the Heat and Offers Some Healthier Fare; Would You Like Some Apples with Your Happy Meal? Here's Your 'stepometer'," *Wall Street Journal (Eastern edition)* (April 16, 2004), A11.

43. S. Brooks, "Seeing the Lite," *Restaurant Business* (September 15, 2003) 102(15): 18–24.

44. C. Murphy, "Health Crackdown Hits Food," *Marketing* (February 20, 2003), 24–26.

45. S. Leung, "McDonald's Flips to Profit as Sales Provide the Sizzle," *Wall Street Journal (Eastern edition)* (January 27, 2004), A6.

46. S. Leung, "McDonald's Flips to Profit as Sales Provide the Sizzle," *Wall Street Journal (Eastern edition)* (January 27, 2004), A6.

47. M. Arndt, "McDonald's: Fries with that salad?" *Business Week* (July 4, 2004) 3890: 82–84.

48. S. Brooks, "Seeing the Lite," *Restaurant Business* (September 15, 2003) 102(15): 18–24.

49. Ibid.

50. M. Arndt, "McDonald's: Fries with that salad?" *Business Week* (July 4, 2004) 3890: 82–84.

51. N. Pachetti, "Back in the kitchen," *Money* (July 2003) 32(7): 44–45.

52. M. Arndt, "McDonald's: Fries with that salad?" *Business Week* (July 4, 2004) 3890: 82–84.

53. Ibid.

54. McDonald's Corporation, *2003 Financial Report* <http://www.rmhc.com/corp/invest/pub/annual_rpt_archives/2003Archive.RowPar.0004.ContentPar.0001.ColumnPar.0001.File.tmp/2003%20Financial%20Report.pdf [Date accessed: 2006-11-02].

Chapter 6

1. Marc C. Suchman, "Managing Legitimacy: Strategic and Institutional Approaches," *Academy of Management Review*, 20(3) (1995): 571–610 at 574.

2. Howard Aldrich, *Organizations Evolving* (California: Sage Publications, 1999); Michael T. Hannan and R. Carroll Glenn, *Dynamics of Organizational Populations: Density, legitimation and competition* (New York: Oxford University Press, 1992).

3. Phillip A. Anderson and Michael Tushman, "Technological discontinuities and dominant designs: A cyclical model of technological change," *Administrative Science Quarterly* 35 (1990): 604–33.

4. William J. Abernathy and James M. Utterback, "Patterns of Industrial Innovation," *Technology Review* 80(7) (1978): 40–47.; James M. Utterback, *Mastering the Dynamics of Innovation* (Boston: Harvard Business School Press, 1994).

5. Phillip A. Anderson and Michael Tushman, "Technological discontinuities and dominant designs: A cyclical model of technological change," *Administrative Science Quarterly* 35 (1990): 604–33.

6. R. Foster, "The S-curve: A New Forecasting Tool," *Innovation, The Attacker's Advantage* (New York, N.Y.: Summit Books, Simon and Schuster, 1986), pp. 88–111.

Chapter 7

1. Foreign Affairs and International Trade Canada, "Canada's International Policy Statement: A Role of Pride and Influence in the World" <http://itcan-cican.gc.ca/IPS/IPS-commerce01-en.asp>.
2. Department of Foreign Affairs and International Trade, "A Message from The Honourable Pierre S. Pettigrew, Minister for International Trade" <http://www.dfait-maeci.gc.ca/eet/research/nafta/nafta-en.asp>.
3. Philip Preville, "Exclusive Report: How to fix Canada — On the brink," *Macleans Magazine*, (November 27, 2006) <http://www.macleans.ca/topstories/business/article.jsp?content=20061127_137129_137129#>.
4. Offshore Outsourcing World Staff, "Spotlight India: Globalization," *Offshore Outsourcing World* (February 26, 2004 at 5:08 am) <http://www.enterblog.com/200402260508.php>
5. David Ticoll, "'Offshoring' will soon be making waves" *The Globe and Mail* (February 19, 2004). Reproduced with permission.
6. *Entrepreneur Magazine*, "Entrepreneur's top global franchises for 2004" <http://www.microsoft.com/smallbusiness/resources/startups/franchise/top_global_franchises.mspx>
7. Foreign Affairs and International Trade Canada, "Canada's International Policy Statement: A Role of Pride and Influence in the World" <http://itcan-cican.gc.ca/IPS/IPS-commerce01-en.asp>.
8. Michael Marth, Balance of Payments Division, Statistics Canada, "Cross-border acquisitions: A Canadian perspective" <http://www.statcan.ca/english/research/11-621-MIE/11-621-MIE2004013.htm>.
9. Anthony Spaeth, "Get Rich Quick,," *Time Magazine* (April 13, 1998) <http://www.time.com/time/magazine/article/0,9171,988175,00.html>
10. Harry Sterling, "Is free trade a realistic option for East Asia?" *National Post* (March 13, 2001).
11. David Crane, "Canada in a shifting world," *Foreign affairs Canada*, 2005 <http://www.dfait-maeci.gc.ca/canada-magazine/01-title-en.asp>
12. Government of Canada <http://www.dfait-maeci.gc.ca/can-am/menu-en.asp?act=v&did=2890&mid=46&cat=2132&typ=1>
13. Bruce Campbell, "NAFTA's Broken Promises," The CCPA Moniter (July 1, 2006) <http://www.policyalternatives.ca/MonitorIssues/2006/07/MonitorIssue1415/index.cfm?pa=DDC3F905>.
14. Ibid.
15. Philip Preville, "Exclusive Report: How to fix Canada — On the brink," *Macleans Magazine*, (November 27, 2006) <http://www.macleans.ca/topstories/business/article.jsp?content=20061127_137129_137129#>.
16. Ibid.
17. Bruce Campbell, "NAFTA's Broken Promises," The CCPA Moniter (July 1, 2006) <http://www.policyalternatives.ca/MonitorIssues/2006/07/MonitorIssue1415/index.cfm?pa=DDC3F905>.
18. Ibid.
19. Jeff Faux, "NAFTA at 10," *The Nation* (February 10, 2004) <http://www.thenation.com/doc/20040202/faux>

Chapter 8

1. Legislative Assembly of New Brunswick, Legislative Committees, "Looking Back:": http://www.gnb.ca/legis/business/committees/previous/reports-e/electricityfuture/look-e.asp
2. William Echikson with Jack Ewing, "Who'll get stomped in Europe's postal wars?" *BusinessWeek* (May 31, 1999).
3. Economic Council of Canada, *Responsible Regulation: An Interim Report* (Ottawa: Ministry of Supply and Services, 1979).
4. Thomas L. Friedman, *The Lexus and the Olive Tree* (New York, NY: Farrar Strauss Giroux, 1999).
5. J. Luis Gausch and Robert W. Hahn, "The cost and benefits of regulation: implications for developing countries" *The World Bank Research Observer* 14(1): 137–58.
6. Garrett Wasney, "A new road for Canadian truckers" *World Trade* 10(2): 50.
7. Anonymous, "Deregulations' real winner: The consumer" *Railway Age* 202(1): 20.
8. Garrett Wasney, "A new road for Canadian truckers" *World Trade* 10(2): 50.
9. Jordy Barnes, "Let banks fill low low-income insurance gap. Branch networks would make policies accessible, affordable" *National Post* (June 28, 2001).
10. Air Canada articles, *The Globe and Mail* (May 9, 2001).
11. Tom Campbell, Jack Casazza, Marjorie Griffin-Cohen, John Wilson and Carl Wood, "Another Blackout Looming: Gov't inaction could leave millions in the dark again soon" (March 1, 2005). Retrieved September 2, 2006 from BC Citizens for Public Power Web site <http://www.citizensforpublicpower.ca/articles/mt/archives/2005/03/another_blackou.html>.
12. Shaker A. Zahra and Carol Dianne Hansen, "Privatization, entrepreneurship, and global competitiveness in the 21st Century" *Competition Review* 10(1): 83–103.

13. William Megginson, "Privatization" *Foreign Policy* (Spring, 2000): 14.
14. Personal communication.

Chapter 9

1. John A Challenger, "The transformed workplace: How can you survive." Originally published in Nov./Dec. 2001 Issue of *The Futurist*. Used with permission from the World Future Society, 7910 Woodmont Avenue, Suite 450, Bethesda, Maryland 20814. Telephone: 301/656-8274; Fax: 301/951-0394; <http://www.wfs.org>.
2. D.D. Warrick, "The illusion of doing well while the organization in regressing," *Organization Development Journal* 20(1): 56–61.
3. John A Challenger, "The transformed workplace: How can you survive." Originally published in Nov./Dec. 2001 Issue of *The Futurist*. Used with permission from the World Future Society, 7910 Woodmont Avenue, Suite 450, Bethesda, Maryland 20814. Telephone: 301/656-8274; Fax: 301/951-0394; <http://www.wfs.org>.
4. Timothy Taylor, "Thinking about a 'new economy'," *Public Interest* 143: 3–19.
5. Diane Rezendes Khirallah, "The tug of more Informationweek," *Manhasset* 883: 32–40.
6. John A Challenger, "The transformed workplace: How can you survive." Originally published in Nov./Dec. 2001 Issue of *The Futurist*. Used with permission from the World Future Society, 7910 Woodmont Avenue, Suite 450, Bethesda, Maryland 20814. Telephone: 301/656-8274; Fax: 301/951-0394; <http://www.wfs.org>.
7. Ibid.
8. Ibid.
9. Dean Anderson and Linda Ackerman Anderson, "What Is Transformation? Why Is It So Hard to Manage?" *Workforce Performance Solutions* (April 2005) <http://www.wpsmag.com/content/templates/wps_section.asp?articleid=124&zoneid=29>.
10. Harvard Business School, Working Knowledge Web site: http://hbswk.hbs.edu/item/2166.html (Access 2006-11-21).
11. Ibid.
12. Ibid.
13. Ibid.
14. L.V. Gerstner, Jr., *Who Says Elephants Can't Dance* (New York, NY: HaperCollins Publishers Inc., 2002).
15. R.W. Beatty and D.O. Ulrich, "Re-energizing the Mature Organization" Organizational Dynamics 20(1): 16–30.
16. T.D. Jick, "Implementing Change" in T.D. Jick and M.A. Peiperl, *Managing Change: Cases and Concepts*, Second Edition (New York, NY: McGraw-Hill/Irwin, 2003), pp. 174–83.
17. D.M. Rousseau, "Changing the Deal While Keeping the People," *Academy of Management Executive* 10 (1996): 50–59.
18. N. Tichy, "Bob Knowling's Change Manual," *FastCompany Magazine* (April 1997): 76–99 <http://www.fastcompany.com/magazine/08/change2.html>.
19. D.M. Rousseau, "Changing the Deal While Keeping the People," *Academy of Management Executive* 10 (1996): 50–59.
20. R.M. Kanter, "The Enduring Skills of Change Leaders," *Leader to Leader*, 13 (Summer 1999). 15–22. Available on-line: <http://leadertoleader.org/leaderbooks/l2l/summer99/kanter.html>.
21. M. Young and J.E. Post, "Managing to Communicate, Communicating to Manage," *Organizational Dynamics*, 22(1) (Summer 1993): 31–43.
22. Peggy Holman, Draft of "Unlocking the Mystery of Effective Large-Scale Change," *At Work*, 8(3): 7–11. Available on-line: "A Change Agent's Quest," <http://www.opencirclecompany.com/thequest.htm>.
23. J. Pedler, R. Burgoyne, and A. Boydell, *The Learning Company* (Maidenhead, Surrey: McGraw-Hill, 1997), p. 3.
24. W.L. French, C.H. Bell, Jr., and R.A. Zawacki (eds.), *Organization Development and Transformation: Managing Effective Change*, 4th ed. (Burr Ridge, IL: Irwin, 1994), p. 7.
25. C. Argyris and D.A. Schon, *Organizational Learning: A Theory of Action Perspective* (Reading, MA: Addison-Wesley Publishing Company, 1978).
26. Ibid.
27. Ibid., p. 4.
28. Ibid.
29. C. Argyris, *Reasoning, learning, and action* (San Francisco: Jossey-Bass, 1982), p. xii.
30. P. Senge, *The Fifth Discipline: The Art and Practice of the Learning Organization* (New York: Doubleday, 1990).
31. M. Dogson, "Organizational learning: A review of some literatures" *Organization Studies* 14: 375–94.

32. J.S. Glaser, "Connecting the workplace and adult development theory: Self directed work teams as a petri dish for adult development." Paper presented at the 7th Annual Meeting of the Society for Research in Adult Development, Toronto, Canada, June 1992.

33. D.H. Brundage and D. Mackeracher, *Adult Learning Principles and Their Application to Program Planning* (Toronto: Ministry of Education, 1980).

34. J. Mezirow, "Perspective transformation" *Adult Education* 28(2): 100–10.

35. R. Kegan, *The Evolving Self: Problem and Process in Human Development* (Cambridge: Harvard University Press, 1982).

36. M. Basseches, *Dialectical Thinking and Adult Development* (Norwood, NJ: Ablex, 1984).

37. E. Erikson, "Identity and the life cycle" *Psychological Issues Monograph* 1(1) (New York: International Universities Press, 1968).

38. Ibid.

39. E. Cell, *Learning to Learn from Experience* (Albany: State University of New York Press, 1945).

40. C. Argyris and D.A. Schon, *Organizational Learning: A Theory of Action Perspective* (Reading, MA: Addison-Wesley Publishing Company, 1978).

41. J. Meyer and B. Rowan, "Institutional organizations: Formal structure as myth and ceremony" *American Journal of Sociology* 83: 440–63; L.G. Zucker, "Institutionalization as a mechanism of cultural persistence" *American Sociological Review* 42(2): 726–42

42. L.G. Zucker, "Institutionalization as a mechanism of cultural persistence" *American Sociological Review* 42(2): 726–42; Meyer and B. Rowan, "Institutional organizations: Formal structure as myth and ceremony" *American Journal of Sociology* 83: 440–63.

43. J. Meyer and B. Rowan, "Institutional organizations: Formal structure as myth and ceremony" *American Journal of Sociology* 83: 440–63

44. J.P. Sims, Jr., D.A. Gioia, and Associates, *The Thinking Organization* (San Francisco: Jossey-Bass, 1986).

45. J. Piaget, *The Construction of Reality in the Child* (New York: Basic Books, 1954); L. Kohlberg, "Stage and sequence: The cognitive developmental approach to socialization" in D.A. Goslin (ed.), *Handbook of Socialization Theory and Research* (Chicago: Rand McNally, 1969), pp. 347–480.

46. M. Gladwell, *The Tipping Point: How Little Things Can Make a Big Difference* (New York: Little, Brown and Company, 2002), p. 258.

47. Ibid., p. 29.

48. Ibid., p. 48.

49. Ibid., p. 55.

50. Ibid., p. 60.

51. Ibid., p. 62.

52. Ibid., p. 67.

53. Ibid., p. 92.

54. Ibid., p. 139.

55. Ibid., p. 141.

56. Ibid., p. 150.

57. Ibid., p. 179.

58. Ibid., p. 192.

59. W.J. Orlikowski and J.D. Hofman, "An Improvisational Model for Change Management," *Sloan Management Review* (Winter 1997): 11–21. Available on-line: <http://ccs.mit.edu/papers/CCSWP191/ccswp191.html>. [The article is directed at technological change; however, I am applying the model more broadly to beyond that type of change to change initiatives as I think it has great relevance.]

60. M. Beer, R.A. Eisenstat and B. Spector, "Why Change Programs Don't Produce Change" in T.D. Jick and M.A. Peiperl, *Managing Change, Cases and Concepts* (pp. 229–41) (New York: Mc Graw Hill/Irwin, 1990).

61. Afsanch Nahavandi and R. Ali Malekzadeth, "Acculturation in Mergers and Acquisitions," *Academy of Management Review*, 13(1): 79–90.

62. K.D. Brouthers, P.V. Hastenburg and J. Ven. "If Most Mergers Fail, Why Are They So Popular?" *Long Range Planning*, 31(3): 347–53.

63. S. Cartwright and S.L. Hudson, "Coping with merger and acquisitions," in R.J. Burke & C.L. Cooper (Eds), *The Organization In Crisis. Downsizing, Restructuring and Privatization* (Oxford: Blackwell, 2000), pp. 269–83.

64. J.A. Davy, A. Kinicke, J. Kilroy and C. Scheck, "After the merger: Dealing with people's uncertainty," *Training and Development Journal* (November 1988): pp. 57–61.

65. I. Dackert, P.R. Jackson, S. Brenner and C.R. Johansson, "Eliciting and analyzing employees' expectations of a merger," *Human Relations*, 56(6): 705–25.

66. S. Zaheer, M. Schomaker and M. Genc, "Identity Versus Culture in Mergers of Equals," *European Management Journal*, 21(2): 185–91.

67. C.M. Fiol, "Revisiting an identity-based view of sustainable competitive advantage," *Journal of Management*, 27: 691–99.

68. H. Tajfel and J.C. Turner, "The social identity theory of intergroup behaviour," in S. Worchel and W.G. Austin, (Eds), *Social Psychology of Intergroup Relations*, 2nd ed. (Chicago, IL: Nelson-Hall, 1985), pp. 7–24

69. B.E. Ashforth and F. Mael, "Social identity theory and the organization," *Academy of Management of Review*, 14: 20–39.

70. J.E. Dutton, J.M. Dukerich and C. Harquail, "Organizational Images and member identification," *Administrative Science Quarterly*, 30: 239–63.

71. S. Zaheer, M. Schomaker and M. Genc, "Identity Versus Culture in Mergers of Equals," *European Management Journal*, 21(2): 185–91.

72. Ibid.

73. Ibid.

74. P. Haunschild, R. Moreland and A. Murrell, "Sources of resistance to mergers between groups," *Journal of Applied Social Psychology*, 24:. 1150–78.

75. M. Marks and P.H. Mirvis, "Making mergers and acquisitions work: Strategic and psychological preparation," *Academy of Management Executive*, 15: 80–94.

76. L. Millward and O. Kyriakidou, "Linking pre and post merger identities through the concept of career," *Career Development International*, 9(1): 12.

77. Ibid.

78. Ibid.

79. J.M. Bartunek, "The multiple cognitions and conflicts associated with second order organizational change," in J.K. Murninghamm (Ed,), *Social Psychology in Organizations: Advances in Theory and Research* (Englewood Cliffs, NJ: Prentice-Hall, 1993), pp. 322–49.

80. J.M. Dukuerich, R. Kramer and J.M. Parks, "The dark side of organizational identification," in D.A. Whetten and P.C. Godfrey (Eds.), *Identity in organizations: Building theory through conversations* (Thousand Oaks, CA: Sage, 1998), pp. 245–56.

81. S. Zaheer, M. Schomaker and M. Genc, "Identity Versus Culture in Mergers of Equals," *European Management Journal*, 21(2): 185–91.

82. N. Nelson, and H. Liao, "On Acculturation of Business Acquisition: The Case of two Machine Tool Manufacturers in Taiwan," *Journal of American Academy of Business*, 4(1): 233.

83. C. Enz, "The Role of Value Congruity in Intra-organizational Power," *Administrative Science Quarterly*, 33: 284–304.

84. J.W. Berry, "Social and Cultural Change," in H.C. Triandis and R.W. Brislin (Eds.), *Handbook of Cross-Cultural Psychology*, Vol. 5 (Boston: Allyn & Bacon, 1980), pp. 211–79.

85. Afsanch Nahavandi and R. Ali Malekzadeth, "Acculturation in Mergers and Acquisitions," *Academy of Management Review*, 13(1): 79–90.

86. Ibid.

87. P. Elsass and J. Veiga, "Acculturation in acquired organizations: A force-field perspective," *Human Relations*, 47: 431–53.

88. S. Cartwright and C.L. Cooper, "The role of culture compatibility in successful organizational marriage," *Academy of Management Executive*, 7: 57–70.

89. S. Cartwright and C.L. Cooper, "The psychological impact of merger and acquisition on the individual: A study if building society managers," *Human Relations*, 46: 327–47.

90. S. Cartwright and C.L. Cooper, *Managing Mergers, Acquisitions and Strategic Alliances: Integrating People and Cultures* (Oxford: Butterworth-Heinemann, 1996).

91. Ibid.

92. E. Vaara, J. Tienari and R. Santti, "The international match: Metaphors as vehicles of social identity-building in cross-border mergers," *Human Relations*, 56(4): 419.

93. J. Ulrich, J. Wieseke and R. Van Dick, "Continuity and Change in Mergers and Acquisitions: A Social Identity Case Stude of a German Industrial Merger," *Journal of Management Studies*, 42(8): 1549–69.

94. P. Elsass and J. Veiga, "Acculturation in acquired organizations: A force-field perspective," *Human Relations*, 47: 431–53 (Note 27).

95. A.F. Buono and J.L. Bowditch, *The Human Side of Mergers and Acquisitions* (San Francisco: Jossey-Bass, 1989).

96. R. Larsson and M. Lubatkin, "Achieving acculturation in mergers and acquisitions: An international case survey," *Human Relations*, 54: 1573–607.

97. R.C. Mayer, J.H. Davis and F.D. Schoorman, "An integrative model of organizational trust," *Academy of Management Review*, 20: 709–34.

98. H.J. Lee, "The role of competence-based trust and organizational identification in continuous improvement," *Journal of Managerial Psychology*, 19(6): 623.

99. S.L. Robinson, "Trust and breach of the psychological contract," *Administrative Science Quarterly*, 41: 574–99.

100. R. Lines, M. Selart, B. Espedal and S.T. Johansen, "The production of trust during organizational change," *Journal of Change Management*, 5(2): 221.

101. Ibid.

102. A.A. Armenakis, S.G. Harris and K. Mossholder, "Creating organizational readiness for change," *Human Relations*, 46: 681–703.

103. J. Brockner and B.M. Wiesenfeld, "Living on the edge (of social and organizational psychology): The effects of layoffs on those who remain," in J.K. Murnighan (Ed.), *Social Psychology in Organizations: Advances in Theory and Research* (Englewood Cliffs, N.J.: Prentice-Hall, 1993), pp. 119–40.

104. H.J. Sapienza and M.A. Korsgaard, "Managing investor relations: the impact of procedural justice in establishing and sustaining investor support," *Academy of Management Journal*, 39: 544–74.

105. A.W. Gouldner, "The norm of reciprocity: a preliminary statement," American Sociological Review, 25: 161–78.

106. Ibid.

107. G.S. Leventhal, "Fairness in social relationships," in J.W. Thibaut, J.T. Spence and R.C. Carson (Eds.), *Contemporary Topics in Social Psychology* (Morristown, NJ: General Learning Press, 1976). pp. 211–39; G.S. Leventhal, "What should be done with Equity Theory," in K.J. Gergen, M.S. Greenberg and R.H. Willis (Eds.), *Social Exchanges: Advances in Theory and Research* (New York, NY: Plenum, 1980), pp. 27–55.

108. N. Bews and T. Uys, "The impact or organizational restructuring on perceptions of trustworthiness," *South African Journal of Industrial Psychology*, 28: 19–26.

109. M.N.K. Saunders and A. Thornhill, "Organizational justice, trust and the management of change: An exploration," *Personnel Review*, 32(3): 360.

110. Ibid.

111. O. Kyriakidou, and L.J. Millward, "A network model of change interpretation." Paper presented at the European Conference on Work and Organizational Psychology, Lisbon, May 2003.

112. J. Ulrich, J. Wieseke and R. Van Dick, "Continuity and Change in Mergers and Acquisitions: A Social Identity Case Stude of a German Industrial Merger," *Journal of Management Studies*, 42(8): 1549–69.

Glossary

administrative management Henry Fayol's philosophy of management, one of the three major classical approaches (the others being the scientific and the bureaucratic), and focusing on the principles of division of work, unity of command, subordination of employees' individual interests to the common good, and *esprit de corps*. *See* bureaucratic management and scientific management.

agency theory An ethical behaviour theory which argues that when agents (employees) possess more information than principals (employers), and their goals conflict, agents may behave in accordance with their self-interest and, thereby, such individuals may deceive the principal.

bailouts A type of government support of business, often in the form of a loan or loan guarantee. Common in the 1980s, but by the 1990s complete bailouts had become rare.

behavioural approaches to management Managerial perspectives that consider the social or human side of organizations and address the challenges of managing people. Assume that achieving maximum productivity requires understanding the human factor of organizations and creation of an environment that permits employees to fulfil social, not only economic, needs.

borderless corporations A new term for multinational corporations that is not linked with one specific home country. Such an enterprise thus has no clear nationality.

branch plants Subsidiaries (in one country, of companies in another country) that do not perform the complete range of functions necessary to offer a product in the marketplace. Typically, subsidiaries defer responsibility of higher-level strategic functions to the parent company.

bureaucratic management A classical approach to management (others including the scientific and the administrative) that focuses more broadly on the organization as a whole, and incorporates the ideas of rules and procedures, hierarchy of authority, division of labour, impersonality and selection and promotion. Associated with Max Weber. *See* scientific management and administrative management.

business enterprise system The system all developed countries possess that determines what goods and services are distributed to society, and how they are so produced and distributed. The decisions may be made by government or by business or by both.

business ethics Ethics is the study of morality or moral judgments, standards and rules of conduct. The notion of business ethics has been considered as comprising the rules, standards, principles, or codes giving guidelines for morally right behaviour in certain contexts.

capitalism An economic system based on the rights of the individual, on the rights of private property, on competition and on minimal government interference.

Categorical Imperative The assertion by the philosopher Immanuel Kant that moral actions are by definition actions that respect others.

centralization The degree to which decision-making authority in an organization is concentrated at the top level.

classical approaches of management The oldest of the formalized perspectives of management, which arose in the late 19th and early 20th centuries during a period of rapid industrialization of the U.S.

and European business sector. Includes scientific, administrative and bureaucratic management. *See* scientific, administrative and bureaucratic management.

cloning forces Pressure on organizations to imitate the behaviour of industry leaders. "Jumping on the bandwagon," "keeping up with the corporate Joneses."

cognitive heuristics An aspect of non-rationality in decision making, where simple rules or guidelines are generated and employed in making decisions. They are "cognitive shortcuts" to reduce the amount of information that must be collected or processed.

cognitive legitimacy The level of public knowledge of a new industry and its conformity to established norms and methods reflected in the extent to which it is taken for granted as a desirable and appropriate activity.

cognitive scripts Mental pictures, usually unconscious, that serve to organize knowledge in some systematic fashion. Scripts or schema used by organizational members to help them function efficiently by reducing the amount of information they need to process as a means to guide their performance. Can generate obstacles to learning and change.

collaboration In behavioural approaches to management (particularly as formulated by Mary Parker Follett), the consequence of the discovery of the importance of managers and workers viewing themselves as collaborators or partners. Also emphasized by Chester Barnard, who felt that authority of managers over subordinates had to be earned.

commoditization The process by which a good becomes saleable in the market. By making the good available to a broader audience, the process also lowers the class of "goods" on the other.

common market Economic integration that goes beyond free trade areas and customs unions, and includes, for example, freer flow of labour and capital across members' borders and a common trade policy regarding non-members. *See* free trade area, customs union and economic union.

compartmentalizing In scientific management, the result of Frederick Taylor's pursuit of the one best method of performing a job, also called specializing, and involving breaking the job down into its most fundamental steps or components.

connectors Individuals who know a lot of people and well connected socially and, therefore, are critical to the instigation of a word-of-mouth epidemic.

constraining forces Practices that come to define what are perceived as legitimate management structures and activities and that, consequently, place pressure on organizations to conform to these institutional roles.

contingency approach The acknowledgement that there is no one best way to manage, and that different conditions and situations require the application of different approaches or techniques. Includes consideration of organization size, environmental uncertainty, etc.

corporate codes of conduct Codes that are necessary because external laws cannot cover all possible situations. They may be irrelevant if ethical behaviour is not rewarded and unethical behaviour tacitly encouraged.

corporate language The potential use of language to de-couple behaviour from its evaluation. To maintain external legitimacy organizations may adopt commonly accepted language for appearance but not relate them to how activities are really conducted.

corporate memory Individuals who are a central part of an organization's knowledge base. They can be eliminated by downsizing, but at significant cost, especially to the organization's ability to innovate.

corporate social responsibility (CSR) Obligations or responsibilities of an organization to go beyond the production of goods or services at a profit, and beyond the requirements of competition, legal regulation or custom, thus acting in a way desirable in terms of the values and objectives of society.

creative destruction A term that explains how innovations swept away old technologies, skills, products, ideas and industries and replaced them with new ones.

Crown corporation Also called a public enterprise. An organization, federal or provincial, accountable, through a minister, to parliament for its operations. For example, Canada Post and the Liquor Control Board of Ontario.

customs union Economic integration with removal of trade barriers in international trade in goods and services among the member countries. A greater degree of integration than free trade areas, but with less member autonomy in how non-member countries are dealt with. *See* free trade area, common market and economic union.

decisional roles One of Mintzberg's three broad categories of roles that managers play, where information is processed and decisions made. Includes entrepreneur, disturbance handler, resource allocator and negotiator. *See* informational roles, interpersonal roles, entrepreneur, resource allocator and negotiator.

de facto standard A standard that arises by virtue of common usage and is not officially sanctioned by any authority. It is a standard "in fact" or "in practice," rather than in law.

de jure standard A standard that is legally mandated and enforced by a government or standards organization.

de-layering Flattening organizational hierarchies so that they have a wider span of control. *See* span of control. The elimination of hierarchical layers, often involving downsizing.

demographics Population trends, which have a significant effect on business planning and activities. Includes such phenomena as the baby boomers and the aging population.

deregulation Reduction in the number of laws or regulations affecting business activity. The potential benefit to consumers is increased competition, and the potential risk is exploitation in the form of reduction in quality of the product or service, or price increases.

discontinuance When an entrepreneur or owner ceases operation. Not the same as failure. *See* small business failures. There are two paths to discontinuance: the business can be sold, or it can be folded. The probability of folding rather than selling increases as profitability declines.

disseminator One of the three informational roles that managers play (the others being monitor and spokesperson), where the information obtained through monitoring is shared and distributed. *See* monitor and spokesperson.

disturbance handler One of the four decisional roles that managers play (the others being entrepreneur, resource allocator and negotiator), where the manager deals with and attempts to resolve conflicts, such as with a difficult or unco-operative supplier. *See* informational and interpersonal roles, entrepreneur, resource allocator and negotiator.

double-loop learning The assessment by individuals of whether an error or problem exists in an organization because the systems themselves need to be changed. Requires a deeper level of examination (than single-loop learning) and, typically, precedes significant organizational change. Uncovers root causes. *See* organizational learning and single-loop learning.

downsizing The planned reduction in breadth of an organization's operations, typically involving terminating relatively large numbers of employees and/or decreasing the number of products or services the organization provides.

dumping An accusation against an exporting country of pricing its product below cost or below the cost of the target country's product.

dynamic environment One of the two (the other being "static") broad classifications of environments of organizations, containing relatively more uncertainty and change. *See* static environment.

economic union A higher level of economic integration than a common market, with harmonization of fiscal, monetary and tax policies and, often, a common currency. There is comparably very little member autonomy. *See* free trade area, customs union and common market.

economies of scope The situation where the total costs for serving two markets or producing the products for two markets are less than the costs for serving them or producing them alone.

effectiveness The pursuit and achievement of goals that are appropriate for an organization. Part of the manager's process of administering and coordinating resources in an effort to achieve the organization's goals and, as such, sometimes confused with efficiency. *See* efficiency.

efficiency Using the fewest inputs to produce a given level of output. Part of the manager's process of administering and coordinating resources in an effort to achieve the organization's goals, and as such, sometimes confused with effectiveness. *See* effectiveness.

employment equity The treatment of employees in a fair and non-biased manner; a term that was develped by Judge Rosalie Silberman Abella, Commissioner of the Royal Commission on Equality in Employment (1984) to reflect a distinct Canadian process for achieving equality in all areas of employment.

end-point ethics *See* utilitarian ethics.

entrepreneur (1) One of the four decisional roles that managers play (the others being disturbance handler, resource allocator and negotiator), where the manager, for example, develops and initiates new projects. *See* informational and interpersonal roles, disturbance handler, resource allocator and negotiator. (2) Usually applied to the founder of a new business but, alternatively, may also be seen as encompassing anyone who buys an existing business or manages the growth or turnaround of an existing business. Originally from a French word meaning "to undertake."

entrepreneurial skills Skills required to start or expand a business, including creativity, innovativeness, risk-taking and independence.

entrepreneurship No agreed-upon definition, but the features most often cited are opportunity recognition, organizational creation and risk-taking.

environmental uncertainty The rate at which market conditions and production technologies change, producing dynamic or static environments. *See* dynamic environment and static environment.

esprit de corps In administrative management, generating organizational cohesiveness and unity by encouraging team spirit and harmony among workers.

expansion The second stage in the small business life cycle, consisting of exponential growth and then slower growth. The other two stages are formation and stability. *See* formation and stability, small business life cycle, formation and stability.

five-forces model A prescriptive model developed by Michael Porter (1980) that allow systematically assessment of the industry environment. The five forces include the threat of entrants, the bargaining power of suppliers, the bargaining power of the buyers, the threats of substitutes, and rivalry among existing firms.

figurehead One of the interpersonal roles that managers play (the others being leader and liaison). Typically ceremonial or symbolic, such as handing out "employee of the month" awards.

finance-related problems One of the three kinds of problems encountered by small businesses, the others being marketing-related and management-related. Usually, undercapitalization and locating financial resources. *See* management-related and marketing-related problems.

first mover advantage The benefits of being among the first to establish strong positions in important world markets.

fluid organizations Organizations that tend to be organic rather than bureaucratic and by avoiding rigid adherence to rules realize the flexibility needed to be able to adapt quickly to changing environments. May use just-in-time inventory principles, for example.

foreign direct investment The purchase of physical assets or an amount of ownership in a company from another country in order to gain a measure of management control.

formalization Rules, regulations, procedures and so on governing how work is performed; the standardization of jobs in the organization. The greater the degree of formalization, the lower the reliance on individual discretion, and the greater the assurance of consistent and reliable performance.

formation The first stage in the small business life cycle, initiated with the idea for a new business and culminating when products or services based on that idea are sold to customers in the marketplace. The other stages are expansion and stability. *See* small business life cycle, expansion and stability.

franchising A method of distribution or marketing where a parent company (the franchisor) grants to another individual or company (the franchisee) the legal right to sell its products or services, with exclusive rights to a particular area or location.

free trade area The lowest degree of regional economic integration, where tariffs and non-tariff trade barriers on international trade in goods and services among the member countries are removed. *See* customs union, common market and economic union.

functional specialization With social specialization, one of the two divisions of job specialization. The dividing-up of jobs into their smallest components, so that workers perform simple, specific and repetitive tasks. Job enrichment, on the other hand, requires a low degree of functional specialization. *See* horizontal differentiation and social specialization.

general environment The environment shared by all organizations in a society, such as the economic and political environments, and technological, societal and global forces. *See* specific environment, technological forces, societal forces and global forces.

global forces Forces that could be embedded in general economic, political, technological or societal forces, but are international in nature, such as international trade agreements. *See* technological forces and societal forces.

globalization No universally agreed-upon definition, but may be considered as a process involving the integration of national economies and the worldwide convergence of consumer preferences. The process of generating a single world economic system.

government economic regulation The imposition of constraints, backed by the authority of the government, to significantly modify economic behaviour in the private sector. The motive may include protection of the consumer or of the environment, or protection of fair competition among businesses.

gross domestic product (GDP) The total value of a country's output of goods and services in a given year.

habitual routines Commonly accepted methods for performing a task, with, potentially, both functional and dysfunctional consequences. For example, once a routine has been established in a group, the behaviour involved will submit to normative control, without regard to actual effects. Unethical behaviour could be a consequence.

Hawthorne Effect The discovery that human nature is such that productivity can be enhanced by motivating employees by giving them special attention rather than by simply improving their physical working conditions. This is a key component of the human relations school of behavioural management, marking the transition to it from scientific management.

horizontal differentiation The degree of differentiation between horizontal units of the organization, based on, for example, the orientation of the members, the nature of their jobs and their education or training. Includes job specialization, which is divided into functional and social specialization. *See* vertical differentiation, functional specialization and social specialization.

human relations movement One of the schools of behavioural management, developed by Elton Mayo, who emphasized that social factors had a greater impact on productivity than actual working conditions. Focuses on organizations as social systems. *See* Hawthorne Effect.

imperfect competition A fundamental shortcoming in the market system, necessitating government involvement. When fewer than the optimal number of competitors exist that are needed to ensure fair pricing and distribution of goods and services at the highest possible level of quality.

import quota Limitation on the amount of a product that can be imported to ensure that domestic producers retain an adequate share of consumer demand for their product.

industry lifecycle model An inverted U-shaped growth pattern that exhibits in almost all industries, given a long enough period of observation, with the number of organizations rising initially up to a peak, and then declining as the industry ages.

informational roles One of Mintzberg's three broad categories of roles that managers play, where managers are communication sources for the organization, whether between parties in the organization or to parties outside it. Include monitor, disseminator and spokesperson roles. *See* decisional roles, interpersonal roles, monitor, disseminator and spokesperson.

institutionalization The processes by which shared beliefs take on a rule-like status. A social process through which individuals create a shared definition of what is appropriate or meaningful behaviour. May generate "accepted practices" that continue even when they are no longer functional.

institutional theory The theory that organizations are driven to incorporate practices and procedures defined by current concepts of work and those accepted or institutionalized by society. Taken-for-granted means of "getting things done" and, as such, not necessarily rational.

integrated organizations Organizations that focus on teams of workers rather than on individuals, unity of command or clear lines of authority; also, organizations with closer connections to their external environment, such as suppliers or other companies, to the extent of interdependence or alliance.

interpersonal roles One of Mintzberg's three broad categories of roles that managers play. Those tasks that arise from the manager's formal authority base and involve relationships with either other organizational members or external parties. Include figurehead, leader and liaison roles. *See* decisional roles, informational roles, figurehead, leader and liaison.

joint venture An arrangement between two or more companies from different countries to produce a product or service together, or to collaborate in the research, development or marketing of that product or service. Also known as a strategic network or strategic alliance. *See* strategic alliance.

keiretsu The Japanese term for networking of major enterprises. Loosely affiliated collections of companies, common in Japanese industry and banking.

knowledge workers People employed in knowledge intensive industries such as the high-tech industries, where specialized and frequently changing knowledge is required. Knowledge work is thus harder to routinize than, for instance, service work.

398

laissez faire A term which meant that business or manufacturers should be free to make and sell what they please and, consequently, reflected the notion that government should not interfere with the economic affairs of business.

leader One of the three interpersonal roles that managers play (the others being figurehead and liaison), wherein the manager may serve as a motivator, communicator and coordinator of subordinates' activities, such as by conducting performance appraisals. *See* informational roles, interpersonal roles, figurehead and liaison.

learning forces Lessons that result from institutionalized management practices and that are taught to future managers and business leaders in the course of their formal education.

liaison One of the three interpersonal roles that managers play (the others being figurehead and leader), including developing relationships with members of the organization outside the manager's area of authority, such as with other departments. *See* interpersonal roles, figurehead and leader.

machine bureaucracy One of Mintzberg's five fundamental organizational configurations, the others being simple or entrepreneurial structure, the professional bureaucracy, diversified/divisional, and the adhocracy or innovative organization. An organization with the technostructure dominant. Its strength is its efficiency.

managerial skills Skills appropriate for maintaining the smooth running of an existing business, including skills in strategic and general management and in each of the functional areas, such as finance, marketing and human resource management.

Mavens Individuals who are knowledgeable and pathologically helpful and therefore many rely on them to make informed decisions.

mercantilism The trade theory that dominated economic thinking for the 15th, 16th and 17th centuries, where a country's wealth was believed to be a matter of its holdings of treasure, especially gold. The economic policy of accumulating this wealth through trade surpluses. *See* trade surpluses. In the modern era Japan has often been called a mercantilist country because of its high trade surpluses.

military ethos The foundation that encapsulates how the military operates on a daily basis; it comprises values, beliefs and expectations that reflect core Canadian values, the imperatives of military professionalism and the requirements of operations

modern behavioural science The discoveries of researchers with backgrounds in sociology, psychology and anthropology who studied the human element of organizations with particular attention to motivation, on the premise that motivating workers is preferable to controlling them. It has produced an enormous number of theories, including need-based and cognitive-based theories of motivation.

monitor One of the three informational roles that managers play (the others being disseminator and spokesperson), where the internal and external environments of the organization are constantly monitored for information useful in decision making. *See* disseminator, spokesperson, internal environment and external environment.

monopolistic competition When a large number of small firms have a product or service each of which is perceived as slightly different from the others, so that each firm has some influence on the price. Some retail operations are an example.

multinational corporations Business enterprises that control assets, factories, etc., operated either as branch offices or affiliates in two or more foreign countries. It generates products or services through its affiliates in several countries, and maintains control over their operation, managing from a global perspective.

negotiator One of the four decisional roles that managers play (the others being entrepreneur, disturbance handler and resource allocator), involving negotiation in all its forms, whether with customers, employees or other departments. *See* informational and interpersonal roles, entrepreneur, disturbance handler and resource allocator.

networking Organizations engaging in co-operative relations with suppliers, distributors or competitors, with the aim of improving efficiency and flexibility in meeting consumer needs. Japanese version called keiretsu. *See* keiretsu.

official goals The expression of the general aims of the organization, showing the organization's purpose. *See* operative goals.

oligopoly When a small number of producers have significant control over prices, and yet competition does play a role in the prices set. Car makers are an example.

open systems Organizations viewed as entities that are embedded in, and dependent on exchanges with, the environment within which they operate. The interdependence of elements means that the entity (the organization) is more than the sum of its parts; it interacts with its environment.

operative goals More specific and measurable than the official goals, and pertaining to the primary tasks of an organization. *See* official goals.

organic and mechanistic Opposite extremes in organizational design, as exemplified by, respectively, the adhocracy (or innovative organization), and the machine bureaucracy. *See* adhocracy or innovative organization and machine bureaucracy.

organizational learning The detection and correction of error (Argyris and Schon). The collective experience of individuals within the organization, resulting in changes in organizational procedure. Consists of single-loop learning and double-loop learning. *See* single-loop learning and double-loop learning.

organizational role theory The theory that organizational roles have a psychological reality to individuals occupying them, whereby they fulfil role requirements based on internalized expectations concerning responsibilities of the role. Incompatible expectations produce role conflict, where the individual occupies more than one role.

outsourcing Hiring external organizations to conduct work in certain functions of the company, such as accounting. May be employed by corporations engaged in downsizing. *See* downsizing.

paradigms Our mental framework for understanding how the world operates. Our theories, our assumptions, our sets of beliefs, our customs. Overcoming resistance to change means recognizing the current paradigms that govern our behaviour, and shifting to a new paradigm.

perfect competition A market situation where many firms all produce an indistinguishable product or service so that no single producer has the power to affect the price of that product or service.

piece-rate system In scientific management, motivating workers by tying compensation to performance, so that a standard level of performance produces a standard level of pay, and above-average performance produces above-average pay.

prioritizing role demands A means of rationalizing behaviour when there is a role conflict. A potential method of ignoring ethical conflicts. Also called compartmentalizing, although not in the sense in which the term is used in scientific management.

privatization Divesting of government involvement in the operation, management or ownership of business activities, involving transfer of activities or functions from the government to the private sector. May involve selling a Crown corporation.

pull factors Reasons a business would gain from entering the international context. Include the potential for sales growth and the opportunity of obtaining needed resources. *See* push factors.

punctuated equilibrium A study that holds, over long periods, technological discontinuities tend to appear at rare and irregular intervals in industries.

push factors Forces that act on all businesses to create an environment where competing successfully means competing globally. Include the force of competition, the shift toward democracy, reduction in trade business, and improvements in technology. *See* pull factors.

re-engineering The fundamental rethinking and radical redesign of business processes to achieve dramatic improvements in measures of performance. It often advocates the collection of individual tasks into a greater number of whole jobs.

resource allocator One of the four decisional roles that managers play (the others being entrepreneur, disturbance handler and negotiator), where it is decided how resources, such as money, equipment, personnel and time, will be allocated. *See* informational and interpersonal roles, entrepreneur, disturbance handler and negotiator.

restrictive or regulatory taxes One of two broad forms of taxes, the other being revenue taxes. Consist of two types, excise taxes and customs duties or tariffs. Excise taxes are applied to goods and services the purchase of which the government wants to restrict. *See* revenue taxes and tariffs.

revenue taxes One of two broad forms of taxes, the other being regulatory or restrictive taxes. Money collected to help fund government services and programs, including individual taxes, corporate income tax, property tax and sales tax. *See* restrictive or regulatory taxes.

rule ethics Judging actions to be right or wrong according to absolute rules regardless of the consequences. Such rules may be based on religious beliefs, family values, education, experience, etc. *See* utilitarian or end-point ethics.

Salesmen Individuals who are unusually charismatic and have the skills to persuade even those who are unconvinced by Connectors or Mavens.

scientific management Frederick Taylor's philosophy that the fundamental objective of management is "securing the maximum prosperity for the employer coupled with the maximum prosperity for each employee," by standardizing and compartmentalizing work practices. One of the three central classical approaches to management, the others being the administrative and the bureaucratic. *See* administrative and bureaucratic management.

self-management In behavioural approaches to management, the emphasis by Mary Parker Follett on the fact that the person doing a job is often the best one to decide how best to do it, rather than managers who are not familiar with it. One of three factors she highlights, the others being coordination and collaboration.

shakeout A large number of exits from the market at the same time as the aggregate output of the industry increases; a natural and healthy, though painful, process for an industry to purges and weed out the weaker competitors.

single-loop learning Simply, the correction of errors that employees find in organizational methods of performance in order to keep the system working. Assumes that the organization has the right systems established but simply needs to fine-tune them. Results in incremental improvements and improved efficiency. Addresses symptoms rather than root causes. *See* organizational learning and double-loop learning.

social context Acknowledgement of the fact that actions affect others and demand to be considered thus.

social contract ethics This model of ethics posits that the rules by which people live are those that they would agree to live if given the opportunity to make a choice based on reason or knowledge.

The idea of the social contract provided a basis for a new model of organizations that views them as networks of contracts.

social identity theory The theory that individuals classify themselves and others into social categories defined by typical characteristics of the members. Organizational identification is one form of social identification, with implications for ethical behaviour.

social specialization With functional specialization, one of the two divisions of job specialization. Specialization of individuals rather than specialization of jobs, accomplished through employment of professionals whose skills cannot be easily routinized. *See* functional specialization.

societal forces A wide range of influences, including, for example, changes in public opinion on ethical issues such as organizational justice (how employees are treated), that affect all organizations and to which business must respond.

sociopolitical legitimacy The endorsement of an industry, activity or organizational form by key stakeholders and institutions such as the state and government officials, opinion leaders or the general public.

span of control The number of employees reporting to a supervisor. It determines vertical differentiation. *See* horizontal and vertical differentiation.

specific or task environment The environment within which a particular organization operates, ultimately shaped by the general environment, and including stakeholders, customers, competitors, suppliers, etc. *See* general environment and stakeholders.

spokesperson One of the three informational roles that managers play (the others being monitor and disseminator), where information is transmitted to individuals outside the manager's area of authority. *See* decisional and interpersonal roles, monitor and disseminator.

stability The third and last stage in the small business life cycle, where daily operating practices become routine and institutionalized. Preceded by the stages of formation and expansion. *See* small business life cycle, formation and expansion.

stakeholders Individuals or groups who bear some kind of risk, whether financial, physical or other, as a result of a corporation's actions. Include such parties as suppliers, the government, and society in general. There are ethical as well as practical reasons to attend to all of their interests, even when they conflict. *See* general environment.

standardization In scientific management, the establishment of clear rules regarding how to perform the job, leaving little or no room for individual discretion, thus assuring consistent performance.

static environment One of the two (the other being dynamic) broad classifications of environments of organizations, exhibiting little, if any, change. *See* dynamic environment.

strategic alliance An alignment of different businesses meant to extend or enhance the core competencies of the businesses involved, obtain access to the expertise of another organization, and create new market opportunities for all parties involved. *See* joint venture.

strategic management An ongoing process that requires managers of a firm constantly analyze their external and internal environments, make decisions about what kinds of strategies they should pursue, implement the strategies and evaluate the outcomes of the implementations to make any change if necessary in order to create and sustain its competitive advantages.

strategic planning The process by which an organization creates its own future. A function of the board, but not limited to board members and not necessarily including all of them. Often involves a SWOT analysis. (See SWOT analysis.)

SWOT analysis Analysis of strengths and weakness of the organization and of external opportunities and threats. In its light the strategic planning team needs to re-examine the mission statement.

tariff A tax on imported goods traditionally employed with the intent to ensure that they are not less expensive than domestically produced goods. *See* restrictive or regulatory taxes.

technological forces The technological environment that exerts influence across industries, playing a central role in how an organization functions, obtains resources, and competes, and changes in which permit and demand organizational change. *See* general environment.

time and motion studies In scientific management, the scientific analysis of work, often using a film taping and a stopwatch to closely scrutinize the elements of performing a task. *See* scientific management.

trade protectionism Protecting a country's domestic economy and businesses by restricting imports to prevent domestic producers from losing business to producers of low-priced foreign goods, and to prevent a trade deficit, where more money leaves the country than enters it because imports exceed exports.

trade deficit When a country imports more than it exports to the degree that the value of its imports exceeds the value of its exports.

trade surpluses When a country's exports exceed its imports, so that more money enters than leaves.

transactional leader A type of leadership role in a basically stable and knowable framework, with the aim of organizational maintenance. *See* transformational leader.

transformational leader A type of leadership role, particularly important in times of organizational change, that communicates a vision and inspires employees. *See* transactional leader.

unity of command In administrative management, avoiding confusion and conflicting instructions by having each employee report to only one boss, preferably at the upper levels of the organization. *See* administrative management.

utilitarian or end-point ethics Assessing the rightness or wrongness of an action by its outcomes. Its modern counterparts are cost-benefit and risk-benefit analysis. Can lead to taking the view that good ends justify bad means. *See* rule ethics.

vertical differentiation The number of managers and levels in the organizational hierarchy. *See* horizontal differentiation.

work specialization One of the six defining elements of organizational structure, the others being chain of command, centralization, span of control, formalization and departmentation. Work is divided into horizontal differentiation, functional specialization and social specialization in order to achieve organizational goals. *See* horizontal differentiation, functional specialization, social specialization, chain of command, centralization, span of control, formalization and departmentation.

zero-sum gain The assumption of mercantilism that the world's wealth is a fixed amount, so that a nation can only increase its share by forcing other nations to reduce theirs. *See* mercantilism.

Bibliography

Abernathy, William J., and James M. Utterback. 1978. "Patterns of Industrial Innovation," *Technology Review* 80(7): 40–47.

Adams, J.S. 1965. "Inequity in social exchanges" in L. Berkowitz (ed.), *Advances in Experimental Social Psychology*, pp. 267–300. New York: Academic Press.

Aldrich, H. 1979. *Organizations and Environments*. Englewood Cliffs, NJ: Prentice Hall.

Aldrich, Howard. 1999. *Organizations Evolving*. California: Sage Publications.

Alpert, M., and H. Raiffa. 1982. "A progress report on the training of probability assessors" in D. Kahneman, P. Slovic, and A. Tversky (eds.), *Judgment under Uncertainty: Heuristics and Biases*, pp. 294–305. New York: Cambridge University Press.

Anderson, Phillip A., and Michael Tushman. 1990. "Technological discontinuities and dominant designs: A cyclical model of technological change," *Administrative Science Quarterly*, 35: 604–33.

Andreasen, A.R. 1996. "Find a corporate partner." *Harvard Business Review* 74: 47–56.

Anonymous. 1999. "The privatization of public services." *The Worklife Report* 11(4): 13–14.

Argyris, C. 1982. *Reasoning, learning, and action*. San Francisco: Jossey-Bass.

Argyris, C., and D.A. Schon. 1989. *Theory in Practice: Increasing Professional Effectiveness*. San Francisco: Jossey-Bass.

Argyris, C., and D.A. Schon. 1978. *Organizational Learning: A Theory of Action Perspective*. Reading, MA: Addison-Wesley Publishing Company.

Armstrong-Stassen, Marjorie. 1998. "Downsizing the federal government: A longitudinal study of managers' Reactions." *Canadian Journal of Administrative Sciences* 15 (December): 310–21.

Ashforth, B.E., and F. Mael. 1989. "Social identity theory and the organization." *Academy of Management Review* 14(1): 20–39.

Bandura, A. 1977. "Self-Efficacy: Toward a unifying theory of behavioral change." *Psychological Review* (May): 191–215.

Barker, J. 1993. *Paradigms: The Business of Discovering the Future*. New York: Harper Business.

Barlett, C. A., and S. Ghoshal. 2002. "Building competitive advantage through people," *MIT Sloan Management Review*, 43: 34–41

Barny, J. B. 1991. "Firm resources and sustained competitive advantage," *Journal of Management*, 17: 99-120.

Beer, Michael, and Nitin Nohria. 2001. *Breaking the Code of Change*. Boston, MA: HBS Press.

Barnard, C. 1938. *The Functions of the Executive*. Cambridge, MA: Harvard University Press.

Barnard, C.I. 1976. "Foreword" in H.A. Simon, *Administrative Behaviour*, 3d Ed. New York: Free Press. (Original work published 1945.)

Basseches, M. 1986. "Cognitive-structural development on the conditions of employment." *Human Development* 29: 101–223.

Basseches, M. 1984. *Dialectical Thinking and Adult Development*. Norwood, NJ: Ablex.

Bateson, G. 1972. *Steps to an Ecology of Mind*. New York: Ballantine Books.

Baumhart, R.S.J. 1961. "How ethical are businessmen?" *Harvard Business Review* 39: 6–31.

Bazerman, M.H. 1998. *Judgment in Managerial Decision Making*, 4th Ed. New York: John Wiley.

Bazerman, M.H. 1990. *Judgment in Managerial Decision Making*, 2d Ed. New York: John Wiley.

Bazerman, M.H., J.R. Curhan, D.A. Moore, and K.L. Valley. 2000. "Negotiation." *Annual Reviews Psychology* 51: 279–314.

Beauchamp, T.L., and N.E. Bowie. 1983. *Ethical Theory and Business*. Englewood Cliffs, NJ: Prentice Hall.

Becker, G. 1976. *The Economic Approach to Human Behaviour*. Chicago: University of Chicago Press.

Becker, N. 1992. *Shifting Gears: Thriving in the New Economy*. Toronto: HarperCollins.

Berger, I.E., and M.E. Drumwright. 2000. "The role of marketing in the development and distribution of social capital." Special Topic Session proposed for Marketing and Public Policy Conference 2001, Washington, DC.

Bird, B.J. 1989. *Entrepreneurial Behaviour*. Glenview, IL: Scott, Foresman.

Blau, P.M. 1970. "A formal theory of differentiation in organizations." *American Sociological Review* 35: 201–18.

Brockner, J. 1992. "The escalation of commitment to a failing course of action: Toward theoretical progress." *Academy of Management Review* 17(1): 39–61.

Brockner, J. 1988. "The effects of work layoff on survivors: Research, theory, and practice." *Research in Organizational Behaviour* 10(1): 213–56.

Brockner, J., M. Konovsky, R. Schneider, R. Folger, M. Christopher, and R. Bies. 1994. "Interactive effects of procedural justice and outcome negativity on victims and survivors of job loss." *Academy of Management Journal* 37 (June): 397–409.

Brooks, L.J. 1989. "Corporate codes of ethics." *Journal of Business Ethics* 8: 117–29.

Brown, T.J., and P.A. Dacin. 1997. "The company and the product: Corporate association and consumer product responses." *Journal of Marketing* 61: 68–84.

Brundage, D.M. 1986. *The Maturation Process and Learning*. Proceedings of the Annual Conference of The Canadian Association for Studies on Adult Education, Winnipeg.

Brundage, D.H., and D. Mackeracher. 1980. *Adult Learning Principles and Their Application to Program Planning*. Toronto: Ministry of Education.

Buckley, M.R., D.S. Wiese, and M.G. Harvey. 1998. "An investigation into the dimensions of unethical behaviour." *Journal of Education for Business* 73(5): 284–90.

Bunner, P. 1999. "The next wave of privatization." *Report/Newsmagazine* (Alberta Edition) (December 6) 26(43): 10.

Burak, R. 1997. *Building the Ontario Public Service for the Future: A Framework for Action*. Toronto: O.P.S. Restructuring Secretariat, Government of Ontario.

Burgelman, R.A. 1983. "Corporate entrepreneurship and strategic management: Insights from a process study." *Management Science* 29(12): 1349–64.

Burgelman, R.A. 1985. "Managing the new venture division: Research findings and implications for strategic management." *Strategic Management Journal* 6(1): 39–54.

Burns, T., and G.M. Stalker. 1961. *The Management of Innovation*. London: Tavistock.

BusinessWeek. 1990. "The stateless corporation." (May 14), pp. 98–104.

Busenitz, L.W. 1999. "Entrepreneurial risk and strategic decision making: It's a matter of perspective." *Journal of Applied Behavioral Science* 35(3): 325–40.

Busenitz, L.W., and G.B. Murphy. 1996. "New evidence in the pursuit of locating new businesses." *Journal of Business Venturing* 2: 221–31.

Cameron, K. 1994. "Strategies for successful organizational downsizing." *Human Resource Management* 33 (Summer): 189–211.

Cameron, K., S. Freeman, and A. Mishra. 1991. "Best practices in white-collar downsizing: Managing contradictions." *The Academy of Management Executive* 5(3): 58.

Canada and the World Backgrounder. 2001. "Small is beautiful: Going further than deregulation, a major trend in government has been to sell off publicly owned assets in the hope of raising cash to help offset deficits." *Canada and the World Backgrounder* (March) 66(5): 12–15.

Carr, A.Z. 1968. "Is business bluffing ethical?" *Harvard Business Review* 46: 127–34.

Carroll, A.B. 1978. "Linking business to behaviour in organizations." *SAM Advanced Management Journal* 43: 4–11.

Carter, N. 1975. *Trends in Voluntary Support for Non-Governmental Social Service Agencies*. Ottawa: Canadian Council on Social Development.

Carter, N., W.B. Gartner, and P.D. Reynolds. 1996. "Exploring start-up events sequences." *Journal of Business Venturing* 2: 151–66.

Cascio, W. 1993. "Downsizing? What do we know? What have we learned?" *Academy of Management Executive* 7 (February): 95–104.

Cell, E. 1945. *Learning to Learn from Experience*. Albany: State University of New York Press.

Chandler, A.D. Jr. 1962. *Strategy and Structure: Chapters in the History of the Industrial Enterprise*. Cambridge, MA: M.I.T. Press.

Clark, C. 1996. "Privatization and industrial policy as U.S. competitiveness strategies: Lessons from East Asia." *ACR* 4(1): 101–28.

Clark, P.B., and J.Q. Wilson. 1961. "Incentive systems: A theory of organizations." *Administrative Sciences Quarterly* 6: 129–66.

Clegg, S. 1990. *Modern Organizations*. Newbury Park, CA: Sage.

Cooper, A.C., W.C. Dunkelberg, and C.Y. Woo. 1988. "Entrepreneurs' perceived chances for success." *Journal of Business Venturing* 3: 97–108.

Craig, S.C., and J.M. McCann. 1979. "Assessing communications effects on energy conservation." *Journal of Consumer Research* 5: 82–88.

CUPE Report. 1999. "The privatization of public services." *Worklife* 11(4): 13–14.

Cyert, R.M., and J.G. March. 1963. *A Behavioral Theory of the Firm*. Englewood Cliffs, NJ: Prentice Hall.

Daft, R.L. 2001. *Organizational Theory and Design*, 7th Ed. Cincinnati, OH: South-Western College Publishing.

Daniels, J.D.J., and L.H. Radebaugh. 1998. *International Business: Environments and Operations*. Reading, MA: Addison-Wesley.

Deal, T., and A. Kennedy. 1982. *Corporate Cultures: The Rites and Rituals of Corporate Life*. Reading, MA: Addison-Wesley.

De Castro, J.O., and K. Uhlenbruck. 1997. "Characteristics of privatization: Evidence from developed, less developed, and former communist countries." *Journal of International Business Studies* 28(1): 123–43.

Deci, E.L. 1975. *Intrinsic Motivation*. New York: Plenum.

De George, R.T. 1999. *Business Ethics*, 5th Ed. Upper Saddle River, NJ: Prentice Hall.

DiMaggio, P., and W. Powell. 1983. "The iron cage revisited: Institutional isomorphism and collective rationality in organizational fields." *American Sociological Review* 48(1): 147–60.

Dogson, M. 1993. "Organizational learning: A review of some literatures." *Organization Studies* 14: 375–94.

Doherty, N., and J. Horsted. 1995. "Helping survivors to stay on board." *People Management* 1 (January): 26–31.

Dollar, D. 1993. "What do we know about the long-term sources of comparative advantage?" *AEA Papers and Proceedings* (May): 431–35.

Drucker, P.F. 1973. *Management: Tasks, Responsibilities and Practices* (Chapter 7). New York: Harper & Row.

Drucker, P.F. 1967. *The Effective Executive*. New York: Harper & Row.

Drucker, P.F. 1954. *The Practice of Management*. New York: Harper & Row.

Duchesne, D. 1989. *Giving Freely: Volunteers in Canada*. Statistics Canada, Labour Analytic Report, Cat: 71-535 No. 4. Ottawa: Minister of Supply and Services, Canada.

The Economist. 1994. "The global economy" (October 1): 3–46.

Ellen, P., L. Mohr, and D. Web. 1997. "Can retailers benefit from cause marketing?" Working Paper, Georgia State University.

Erikson, E. 1968. "Identity and the life cycle." *Psychological Issues Monograph* 1(1). New York: International Universities Press.

Erikson, E.H. (ed.). 1976. *Adulthood*. New York: W.W. Norton.

Evans, B., and J. Shields. 1998. *Reinventing the State: Public Administration 'Reform' in Canada*. Halifax: Fernwood Publishing.

Evans, M.G., H.P. Gunz, and R.M. Jalland. 1997. "Implications of organizational downsizing for managerial careers." *Canadian Journal of Administrative Sciences* 14: 359–71.

Fayol, H. 1930. *Industrial and General Administration*. New York: Sir Isaac Pitman and Sons.

Ferrell, O.C., and L.G. Gresham. 1985. "A contingency framework for understanding ethical decision making in marketing." *Journal of Marketing* 49: 87–96.

Fiol, C., and M. Lyles. 1985. "Organizational learning." *Academy of Management Review* 10: 803–13.

Fischhoff, B., P. Slovic, and S. Lichtenstein. 1977. "Knowing with certainty: The appropriateness of extreme confidence." *Journal of Experimental Psychology: Human Perception and Performance* 3: 552–64.

Flynn, J.P., and G.E. Web. 1975. "Women's incentives for community participation in policy issues." *Journal of Voluntary Action Research* 4: 137–45.

Follett, M.P. 1942. "Dynamic administration" in H. Metcalf and L.F. Urwick (eds.), *Dynamic Administration: The Collected Papers of Mary Parker Follett*. New York: Harper & Row.

Follett, M.P. 1934. *Creative Experience*. London: Longmans, Green.

Foster, M.K., and A.G. Meinhard. 1996. "Toward transforming social service organizations In Ontario." Presented at Babson Conference on Entrepreneurship, Seattle, WA.

Foster, R. 1986. "The S-curve: A New Forecasting Tool," *Innovation, The Attacker's Advantage*, pp. 88–111. New York, N.Y.: Summit Books, Simon and Schuster.

Fredrickson, J.W., and A.L. Iaquinto. 1989. "Inertia and creeping rationality in strategic decision processes." *Academy of Management Journal* 32(3): 516–42.

French, W.L., C.H. Bell, Jr., and R.A. Zawacki. (eds.). 1994. *Organization development and transformation: Managing effective change*, 4th Ed. Burr Ridge, IL: Irwin.

Friedman, M. 1962. *Capitalism and Freedom*. Chicago: University of Chicago Press.

Friedman, T.L. 1999. *The Lexus and the Olive Tree*. New York, NY: Farrar Strauss Giroux.

Fulford, D. 2000. Personal communication, Director of Business Planning, Management Board Secretariat, Queen's Park, Toronto.

Gagnon, L. 1997. "In praise of state-owned liquor outlets." *The Globe and Mail* (December 27).

Galbraith, J.K. 1958. *The Affluent Society*. Boston: Houghton Mifflin Company.

Galbraith, J.R. 1977. *Organization Design*. Reading, MA: Addison-Wesley.

Galbraith, J.R. 1973. *Designing Complex Organizations*. Reading, MA: Addison-Wesley.

Garten, J.E. 1998. "Cultural imperialism is no joke." *BusinessWeek* (November 30).

Gatewood, E., K. Shaver, and W. Gartner. 1995. "A longitudinal study of cognitive factors influencing start-up behaviors and success at venture creation." *Journal of Business Venturing* 10: 371–91.

Gatewood, R.D., and A.B. Carroll. 1991. "Assessment of the ethical performance of organizational members: A conceptual framework." *Academy of Management Review* 16: 667–90.

Gausch, J.L., and R.W. Hahn. 1999. "The cost and benefits of regulation: implications for developing countries." *The World Bank Research Observer* 14(1): 137–58.

Gersick, C.J.G., and J.R. Hackman. 1990. "Habitual routines in task-performing groups." *Organizational Behaviour and Human Decision Processes* 47: 65–97.

Gidron, B., R.M. Kramer, and L.M. Salamon. 1992. *Government and the Third Sector: Emerging Relationships in Welfare States*. San Francisco: Jossey-Bass.

Gilbreth, F.B. 1911. *Principles of Scientific Management*. New York: Van Nostrand.

Gilmore, T.N., and R.K. Kazanjian. 1989. "Clarifying decision making in high-growth ventures: The use of responsibility charting." *Journal of Business Venturing* 4: 69–83.

Gioia, D.A. 1986. "Symbols, scripts, and sensemaking: Creating meaning in the organizational experience" in H.P. Sims, Jr., D.A. Gioia, and Associates, *The Thinking Organization: Dynamics of Organizational Social Cognition*, pp. 49–74. San Francisco: Jossey-Bass.

Gladwell, M. 2002. *The Tipping Point: How Little Things Can Make a Big Difference*. New York: Little, Brown and Company.

Glaser, J.S. 1992. "Connecting the workplace and adult development theory: Self directed work teams as a petri dish for adult development." Paper presented at the 7th Annual Meeting of the Society for Research in Adult Development, Toronto, Canada (June).

Gluck, R. 1975. "An exchange theory of incentive of urban political party organization." *Journal of Voluntary Action Research* 4: 104–15.

The Globe and Mail. 2001. "Who's minding the Crown corporations?" (March 5).

Goffman, E. 1967. *Interaction Ritual*. Garden City, NY: Doubleday.

Goodpaster, K.E., and J.B. Matthews, Jr. 1983. "Can a corporation have a conscience?" in T.L. Beauchamp and N.E. Bowie (eds.), *Ethical Theory and Business*. Englewood Cliffs, NJ: Prentice Hall.

Goold, M. and K. Luches. 1993. "Why diversify? Four decaded of management thinking," *Academy of Management Executive*, 7: 7–25.

Greider, W. 1997. *One World, Ready or Not: The Manic Logic of Global Capitalism*. New York: Simon & Schuster.

Griffin, R.W., and M.W. Pustay. 1998. *International Business: A Management Perspective*, 2d Ed. Reading, MA: Addison-Wesley.

Grover, S.L. 1993. "Why professionals lie: The impact of professional role conflict on reporting accuracy." *Organizational Behaviour and Human Decision Processing* 55: 251–72.

Hall, A.D., and R.E. Fagen. 1956. "Definition of system." *General Systems: The Yearbook of the Society for the Advancement of General Systems Theory* 1: 18–28.

Hall, R.H. 2002. *Organizations: Structures, Processes, and Outcomes*. Upper Saddle River, NJ: Prentice-Hall.

Hambrick, D.C., and L. Crozier. 1985. "Stumblers and stars in the management of rapid growth." *Journal of Business Venturing* 1(1): 31–45.

Hambrick, D.C., and S. M. Schecter. 1983. "Turnaround strategies for mature industrial product business units," *Academy of Management Journal*, 26: 231–48.

Hammer, M., and J. Champy. 1993. *Reengineering the Corporation*. New York, NY: HarperBusiness.

Hannan, Michael T., and R. Carroll Glenn. 1992. *Dynamics of Organizational Populations: Density, legitimation and competition*. New York: Oxford University Press.

Havlovic, S., F. Bouthillette, and R. van der Wal. 1998. "Coping with downsizing and job loss: Lessons from the Shaughnessy Hospital closure." *Canadian Journal of Administrative Sciences* 15 (December): 322–32.

Heath, C., and A. Tversky. 1991. "Preferences and beliefs: Ambiguity and competence in choice under uncertainty." *Journal of Risk and Uncertainty* 4: 5–28.

Hegarty, W.H., and H.P. Sims. 1979. "Organizational philosophy, policies, and objectives related to unethical decision behaviour: A laboratory experiment." *Journal of Applied Psychology* 64(3): 331–38.

Hegarty, W.H., and H.P. Sims. 1978. "Some determinants of unethical decision behaviour: An experiment." *Journal of Applied Psychology* 63(4): 451–57.

Heracleous, L. 1999. "Privatisation: Global trends and implications of the Singapore experience." *The International Journal of Public Sector Management* 12(5): 432–44.

Hertzberg, F., B. Mausner, and B. Snyderman. 1959. *The Motivation to Work*. New York: John Wiley.

Higgins, A., C. Power, and L. Kohlberg. 1984. "The relationship of moral atmosphere to judgments of responsibility" in W.M. Kurtines and J.L. Gewirtz (eds.), *Morality, Moral Behaviour and Moral Development*, pp. 74–106. New York: Wiley.

Hirschhorn, L., and T. Gilmore. 1992. "The new boundaries of the 'boundaryless' company." *Harvard Business Review* (May/June): 104–15.

Hogarth, R.M. 1987. *Judgement and Choice: The Psychology of Decisions*. New York: John Wiley.

Holstrom, B. 1979. "Moral hazard and observability." *Bell Journal of Economics* 10: 74–91.

Huber, V.L., and M.A. Neale. 1987. "Effects of self and competitor's goals on performance in an interdependent bargaining task." *Journal of Applied Psychology* 72: 197–203.

Hunt, S.D., and S. Vitell. 1986. "A general theory of marketing ethics." *Journal of Macromarketing* 6(1): 5–16.

Industry Canada and Statistics Canada. 1998. *Small Business Quarterly Report* (Summer).

Industry Canada. 1991. *Small Business in Canada*.

Jackall, R. 1988. *Moral Mazes: The World of Corporate Managers*. New York: Oxford University Press.

Janger, A.R. 1979. *Matrix Organizations of Complex Businesses*. New York: The Conference Board.

Janis, I.L., and L. Mann. 1977. *Decision Making: A Psychological Analysis of Conflict, Choice, and Commitment*. New York: Free Press.

Jick, T.D. and M.A. Peiperl. 2003. *Managing Change, Cases and Concepts*. New York: McGraw Hill/Irwin.

Jones, T.M. 1991. "Ethical decision making by individuals in organizations: An issue-contingent model." *Academy of Management Review* 16(2): 366–95.

Kahn, R., D. Wolfe, R. Quinn, J. Snoek, and R. Rosenthal. 1964. *Organizational Stress: Studies in Role Conflict and Ambiguity*. New York: John Wiley.

Kahn, W.A. 1992. "To be fully there: Psychological presence." *Human Relations* 45(4).

Kahn, W.A. 1990a. "Toward an agenda for business ethics research." *Academy of Management Review* 15(2): 311–28.

Kahn, W.A. 1990b. "Psychological conditions of personal engagement and disengagement at work." *Academy Management Journal* 33(4): 692–724.

Kahneman, D. 1992. "Reference points, anchors, norms, and mixed feelings." *Organizational Behaviour Human Decision Process* 51: 269–312.

Kahneman, D., and D. Lovallo. 1993. "Timid choices and bold forecasts: A cognitive perspective on risk taking." *Management Science* 39(1): 17–31.

Kahneman, D., P. Slovic, and A. Tversky. (eds.) 1982. *Judgment under Uncertainty: Heuristics and Biases*. New York: Cambridge University Press.

Kahneman, D., and A. Tversky. 1979. "Prospect theory: An analysis of decision under risk." *Econometrica* 47: 263–91.

Kant, I. 1785. *Grounding for the Metaphysics of Morals*. Trans. James W. Ellington [1993]. Indianapolis, IN: Hackett.

Karakowsky, L. 1994. "The Influence of Organizational Context on Ethical Behaviour in the Workplace: Linking Institutionalization Theory to Individual-Level Behaviour." *Proceedings of the Administrative Sciences Association of Canada* 15(12): 21–30.

Karakowsky, L., and A.R. Elangovan. 2001. "Risky decision making in mixed-gender terms: Whose risk tolerance matters?" *Small Group Research* 32(1): 94–111.

Karakowsky, L., A. Carroll, and A. Buchholtz. 2005. *Business and Society*. Toronto: Nelson Thomson.

Katz, J.A. 1992. "A psychosocial cognitive model of employment status choice." *Entrepreneurship Theory and Practice* 17(1): 29–37.

Katz, D., and R.L. Kahn. 1978. *The Social Psychology of Organization*, 2d Ed. New York: Wiley.

Kegan, R. 1982. *The Evolving Self: Problem and Process in Human Development*. Cambridge: Harvard University Press.

Kegan, R. 1979. "The evolving self: A process conception for ego psychology." *The Counselling Psychologist* 8: 5–34.

Kikeri, S., J. Nellis, and M. Shirley. 1994. "Privatization: Lessons from market economies." *World Bank Research Observer*, 241–72.

Kohlberg, L. 1969. "Stage and sequence: The cognitive developmental approach to socialization" in D.A. Goslin (ed.), *Handbook of Socialization Theory and Research*, pp. 347–480. Chicago: Rand McNally.

Kolb, D.A. 1984. *Experiential Learning: Experience as the Source of Learning and Development*. Englewood Cliffs, NJ: Prentice Hall.

Kotler, P., and R.E. Turner. 1995. *Marketing Management*, Canadian 8th Ed. Toronto: Prentice Hall.

Knouse, S.B., and R.A. Giacalone. 1991. "Ethical decision-making in business: Behavioral issues and concerns." *Journal of Business Ethics* 11: 369–77.

Knox, A.B. 1977. *Adult Development and Learning*. San Francisco: Jossey-Bass.

Kohlberg, L. 1969. "Stage and sequence: The cognitive developmental approach to socialization" in D.A. Goslin (ed.), *Handbook of Socialization Theory and Research*, pp. 347–480. Chicago: Rand McNally.

Kram, K. 1985. *Mentoring at Work*. Glenview, IL: Scott Forseman.

Kram, K.E., P.C. Yeager, and G.E. Reed. 1989. "Decisions and dilemmas: The ethical dimension in the corporate context" in J.E. Post (ed.), *Research in Corporate Social Performance and Policy*, Vol. 1, pp. 21–54. Greenwich, CT: JAI Press.

Krueger, N., and P. Dickson. 1994. "How believing in ourselves increases risk taking: Perceived self-efficacy and opportunity recognition." *Decision Sciences* 25: 385–400.

Krugman, P.R., and M. Obstfeld. 1997. *International Economics: Theory and Policy*. Reading, MA: Addison-Wesley.

Kuhnle, S., and P. Selle. 1992. *Government and Voluntary Organizations: A Relational Perspective*. Aldershot: Avebury.

Latham, G.P., and G.A. Yukl. 1975. "A review of research on the application of goal setting in organizations." *Academy of Management Journal* (December): 824–45.

Lawrence, P., and J. Lorsch. 1969. *Developing Organizations: Diagnosis and Action*. Reading, MA: Addison-Wesley.

Lawrence, P.R., and J.W. Lorsch. 1967a. *Organization and Environment*. Boston: Graduate School of Business Administration, Harvard University.

Lawrence, P.R., and J.W. Lorsch. 1967b. "Differentiation and integration in complex organizations." *Administrative Science Quarterly* (June): 1–47.

Lee, P. 1997. "A comparative analysis of layoff announcements and stock price reactions in the United States and Japan." *Strategic Management Journal* 18 (December): 879–94.

Leontief, W. 1954. "Domestic production and foreign trade; The American capital position re-examined." *Economia Internationale* (February): 3–32.

Levac, M., and P. Wooldridge. Financial Markets Department. 1997. "The fiscal impact of privatization in Canada." *Bank of Canada Review* (Summer): 25–40.

Levering, R., M. Moscowitz, and M. Katz. 1985. *The 100 Best Companies to Work for in America*. Scarborough, New York: New American Library.

Levinson, D.J., C.N. Darrow, E.B. Klein, M.H. Levinson, and B. McKee. 1978. *The Seasons of a Man's Life*. New York: Ballatine Books.

Lewin, K. 1951. *Field Theory in Social Science*. New York: Harper & Row.

Lewis, P.V. 1985. "'Defining business ethics': Like nailing jell-o to a wall." *Journal of Business Ethics* 4(5): 377–83.

Lichtenstein, S., B. Fischhoff, and L. Phillips. 1982. "Calibration of probabilities: The state of the art to 1980" in D. Kahneman, P. Slovic, and A. Tversky (eds.), *Judgment under Uncertainty: Heuristics and Biases*, pp. 306–34. New York: Cambridge University Press.

Lipman, J. 1990. "When its commercial time, TV viewers prefer cartoons to celebrities any day." *The Wall Street Journal* (Feb. 16): B1, B4.

Locke, E.A. 1968. "Toward a theory of task motivation and incentives." *Organizational Behaviour and Human Performance* (May): 157–89.

Locke, E.A., L.M. Saari, and G.P. Latham. 1981. "Goal setting and task performance." *Psychological Bulletin* (January): 125–52.

Locke, John. 1690. *Second Treatise on Civil Government*. Cambridge: Cambridge University Press.

Low, M.B., and I.C. MacMillan. 1988. "Entrepreneurship: Past research and future challenges." *Journal of Management* 14(2): 139–61.

Luthans, F. 1973. "The contingency theory of management: A path out of the jungle." *Business Horizons* 16 (June): 62–72.

March, J.G., and H.A. Simon. 1958. *Organizations*. New York: Wiley.

Masi, D.A. 1981. *Organizing for Women: Issues, Strategies, and Services*. Lexington, MA: Lexington Books.

Maslow, A. 1954. *Motivation and Personality*. New York: Harper & Row.

McGregor, D. 1960. *The Human Side of Enterprise*, pp. 33–58. New York: McGraw-Hill.

McKinley, W., C. Sanchez, and A. Schick. 1995. "Organizational downsizing: Constraining, cloning, learning." *Academy of Management Executive* 9(3): 32–41.

McLellan, K., and B. Marcolin. 1994. "Information technology outsourcing." *Business Quarterly* 59 (Autumn): 95–104.

McMillan, C.J., and E.M.V. Jasson. 2001. "Technology and the new economy: A Canadian strategy" in T. Wesson (ed.), *Canada and the New World Economic Order*, 2d Ed. Toronto: Captus Press.

McMurdy, Deirdre. 1995. "Rummage sales." *Maclean's* (July 24) 108(30): 32.

Mertens, B. 1998. "The push for privatization." *Asian Business* 34(6): 42–45.

Merton, R.K. 1957. *Social Theory and Social Structure*, 2d Ed. New York: Free Press.

Meyer, J., and B. Rowan. 1977. "Institutional organizations: Formal structure as myth and ceremony." *American Journal of Sociology* 83: 440–63.

Mezirow, J. 1978. "Perspective transformation." *Adult Education* 28(2): 100–10.

Miles, R.E., and C.C. Snow. 1978. *Organizations: Strategy, Structure and Process*. New York: McGraw-Hill.

Milgram, S. 1974. *Obedience to Authority*. New York: Harper & Row.

Mill, J.S. 1861. *Utilitarianism*. Edited by Oskar Piest. [1948] New York: Liberal Arts Press.

Mill, J.S. 1859. *On Liberty*. Edited by Oskar Piest. [1975] New York: Norton.

Miller, D., and P.H. Friesen. 1984. *Organizations: A Quantum View*. Englewood Cliffs, NJ: Prentice Hall.

Mintzberg, H. 1979. *The Structuring of Organizational Structures*. Englewood Cliffs, NJ: Prentice Hall.

Mintzberg, H. 1974. "The manager's job: Folklore and fact." *Harvard Business Review* (July/August): 49–61.

Mintzberg, H. 1973. *The Nature of Managerial Work*. Englewood Cliffs, NJ: Prentice Hall.

Mitroff, I.I. 1983. *Stakeholders of the Organizational Mind: Toward a New View of Organizational Policy Making*. San Francisco: Jossey-Bass.

Molm, L.D. 1991. "Affect and social exchange: Satisfaction in power-dependence relations." *American Sociological Review* 56(4): 475–93.

Mone, M. 1994. "Relationships between self-concepts, aspirations, emotional responses, and intent to leave a downsizing organization." *Human Resource Management* 33 (Summer): 281–98.

Morgan, G. 1986. *Images of Organization*. Sage: Newbury Park.

Morrison, C. 2000. "Beyond booze." *Summit* 3(4): 21–22.

Murray, V. 1995, "Improving board performance." *The Philanthropist* 13(4).

Neale, M.A., and M.H. Bazerman. 1991. *Cognition and Rationality in Negotiation*. New York: Free Press.

Newell, A., and H. Simon. 1981. "Computer science as empirical inquiry: Symbols and search" in J. Haugeland (ed.), *Mind Design*. Cambridge, MA: MIT Press.

Nicolini, D., and M. Mezner. 1995. "The social construction of organizational learning: Conceptual and practical issues in the field." *Human Relations* 48(7): 727–47.

Northcraft, G., and M. Neale. 1994. *Organization Behaviour: A Management Challenge*. Chicago: Dryden Press.

Northcraft, G., and M. Neale. 1987. "Experts, amateurs, and real estate: An anchoring perspective on property pricing decisions." *Organizational Behaviour and Human Decision Processes* 39(1): 84–87.

Novelli, W.D. 1981. "Social Issues and direct marketing: What's the connection?" Paper presented at the Annual Conference of the Direct Mail/Marketing Association, Los Angeles, California, March 12.

Ogilvy, D., and J. Raphaelson. 1982. "Research on advertising techniques that work and don't work." *Harvard Business Review* 60 (July–August): 14–18.

Ohlin, B. 1933. *Interregional and International Trade*. Cambridge, MA: Harvard University Press.

Olson, M. 1965. *The Logic of Collective Action; Public Goods and the Theory of Groups*. Cambridge: Harvard University Press.

Osborne, D., and T. Gaebler. 1993. *Reinventing Government: How the Entrepreneurial Spirit Is Transforming the Public Sector*. New York: Plume.

Ottesen, O. 1977. "The response function" in M. Berg (ed.), *Current Theories in Scandinavian Mass Communications Research*. Grena, Denmark: GMT.

Pal, L.A. 1997. "Civic re-alignment: NGOs and the contemporary welfare state" in Raymond B. Blake, Penny E. Bryden and J. Frank Strain (eds.), *The Welfare State in Canada: Past, Present and Future*. Concord, Ontario: Irwin Publishing.

Parson, H.M. 1974. "What happened at Hawthorne?" *Science* 183: 922–32.

Pastin, M. 1986. *The Hard Problems of Management: Gaining the Ethics Edge*. San Francisco: Jossey-Bass.

Pava, M.L. 1998. "Religious business ethics and political liberalism: An integrative approach." *Journal of Business Ethics* 17(15): 1633–52.

Payne, S.L., and R.A. Giacalone. 1990. "Social psychological approaches to the perception of ethical dilemmas." *Human Relations* 43: 649–65.

Pedler, J., R. Burgoyne, and A. Boydell. 1997. *The Learning Company*. Maidenhead, Surrey: McGraw-Hill.

Perrow, C. 1979. *Complex Organizations*, 2d Ed. Glenview, IL: Scott, Foresman.

Perry, W.G., Jr. 1970. *Forms of Intellectual and Ethical Development in the College Years*. New York: Holt, Rinehart, and Winston.

Peters, T.J., and R.H. Waterman. 1982. *In Search of Excellence*. New York: Harper & Row.

Pettigrew, A.M. 1979. "On studying organizational cultures." *Administrative Science Quarterly* 24: 570–81.

Pfeffer, J. 1982. *Organizations and Organizational Theory*. Boston: Pitman.

Pfeffer, J., and G.R. Salancik. 1978. *The External Control of Organizations*. New York: Harper & Row.

Piaget, J. 1954. *The Construction of Reality in the Child*. New York: Basic Books.

Pondy, L.R., P. Frost, G. Morgan, and T. Dandridge. (eds.) 1983. *Organizational Symbolism*. Greenwich, CT: JAI Press.

Porter, M.E. 1998. "Clusters and the new economics of competition." *Harvard Business Review* (November/December): 77–90.

Porter, M.E. 1990. *The Competitive Advantage of Nations*. New York: Free Press.

Porter, M.E. 1980. *Competitive Strategy: Techniques for Analyzing Industries and Competitors*. New York: Free Press.

Porter, M.E., and Monitor Company. 1991. A study prepared for the Business Council on National Issues and the government of Canada, October.

Pritchard, R.D., K.M. Campbell, and D.J. Campbell. 1977. "Effects of extrinsic financial rewards on intrinsic motivation." *Journal of Applied Psychology* (February): 9–15.

Rawls, J. 1993. *Political Liberalism*. New York: Columbia University Press.

Rawls, J. 1971. *A Theory of Justice*. Cambridge, MA: Harvard University Press.

Rumelt, R. 1974. *Strategy, Structure, and Economic Performance*. Cambridge, MA: Harvard University Press.

Ray, D.M. 1994. "The role of risk-taking in Singapore." *Journal of Business Venturing* 9(2): 157–77.

Rein, I., P. Kotler, and M. Stoller. 1987. *High Visibility: How Executives, Politicians, Entertainers, Athletes and Other Professionals Create, Market and Achieve Successful Images*. New York: Dodd, Mead.

Rest, J.R. 1986. *Moral Development: Advances in Research and Theory*. New York: Praeger.

Reynolds, P., and B. Miller. 1992. "New firm gestation: Conception, birth, and implications for research." *Journal of Business Venturing* 7: 405–17.

Ricardo, D. 1996. *The Principles of Political Economy and Taxation*. [Originally published London, New York: J.M. Dent & Sons, 1911.] Amherst, NY: Prometheus Books.

Rogers, C.R. 1961. *On Becoming a Person*. Boston: Houghton Mifflin.

Runes, D.D. 1964. *Dictionary of Philosophy*. Littlefields: Adams and Co.

Ryan, L., and K. Macky. 1998. "Downsizing organizations: Uses, outcomes and strategies." *Asia Pacific Journal of Human Resources* 36 (Winter): 29–45.

Salamon, L.M. 1987. "Partners in public service" in W.W. Powell (ed.), *The Nonprofit Sector: A Research Handbook*, pp. 107–17. New Haven: Yale University Press.

Salamon, L., R. List, W. Sokolowski, S. Toepler, and H. Anheier. 1999. *Global Civil Society: Dimensions of the Nonprofit Sector*. Baltimore: John Hopkins University, Centre for Civil Society Studies.

Schein, E.M. 1985. *Organizational Culture and Leadership*. San Francisco: Jossey-Bass.

Schumpeter, J. 1936. *The Theory of Economic Development*. Cambridge: Harvard University Press.

Schwenk, C.R. 1988. "The cognitive perspective on strategic decision making." *Journal of Management Studies* 25(1): 41–55.

Scott, W.R. 1981. *Organizations: Rational, Natural, and Open Systems*. Englewood Cliffs, NJ: Prentice Hall.

Seidle, F.L. 1995. *Rethinking the Delivery of Public Services to Citizens*. Montreal: Institute for Research on Public Policy.

Selznick, P. 1943. "An approach to a theory of bureaucracy." *American Sociological Review* 8: 47–54.

Senge, P. 1990. *The Fifth Discipline: The Art and Practice of the Learning Organization*. New York: Doubleday.

Sethi, S.P. 1982. *Against the Corporate Wall*. Englewood Cliffs, NJ: Prentice Hall.

Shapira, Z. 1995. *Risk Taking: A Managerial Perspective*. New. York: Russell Sage Foundation.

Simon, H. 1957. *Models of Man*. New York, NY: Wiley.

Simon, H.A. 1945. *Administrative Behaviour*. New York: Free Press.

Sims, J.P. Jr., D.A. Gioia, and Associates. 1986. *The Thinking Organization*. San Francisco: Jossey-Bass.

Sims, R.R. 1991. "The institutionalization of organizational ethics." *Journal of Business Ethics* 10: 493–511.

Smalhout, James. 1999. "Keep the state out of business." *Euromoney* (March) 359: 36–41.

Smith, A. 1937. *The Wealth of Nations*. Edited by E. Cannan. [First Modern library edition 1937.] New York: Modern Library.

Smith, D.H. 1982. "Altruism, volunteers, and voluntarism" in J. Harmon (ed.), *Volunteerism in the Eighties: Fundamental Issues in Voluntary Action*. Washington DC: University Press of America.

Sonnenfeld, J.A. 1985. "Shedding light on the Hawthorne studies." *Journal of Occupational Behaviour* 6: 111–30.

Spence, A. M. 1981. "The learning curve and competition," *The Bell Journal of Economics*, 12: 49–70

Starbuck, W.H. 1976. "Organizations and their environments" in M.D. Dunnette (ed.), *Handbook of Industrial Psychology*, pp. 1069–123. Chicago: Rand McNally.

Staw, B.M. 1981. "The escalation of commitment to a course of action." *Academy of Management Review* 6: 577–87.

Staw, B.M., and J. Ross. 1987. "Behaviour in escalation situations: Antecedents, prototypes and solutions" in L.L. Cummings and B.M. Staw (eds.), *Research in Organization Behaviour* 9: 39–78. London: JAI Press.

Steers, R.M., and L.W. Porter. 1979. *Motivation and Work Behaviour*, 2d Ed. New York: McGraw-Hill.

Stene, E.O. 1940. "An approach to a science of administration." *American Political Science Review* 34: 1129ff.

Sternthal, B., R.R. Dholakia, and C. Levitt. 1978. "The persuasive effect of source credibility: Test of cognitive response." *Journal of Consumer Research* 4: 242–50.

Stewart, W. 1996. *The Charity Game: Waste and Fraud in Canada's $86-Billion-a-Year Compassion Industry*. Toronto: Douglas & McIntyre.

Stone, C.D. 1975. "The culture of the corporation" in W.M. Hoffman and J.M. Moore (eds.), *Business Ethics*, 2d Ed. New York: McGraw-Hill.

Stryker, S., and R.T. Serpe. 1982. "Commitment, identity salience, and role behaviour: Theory research example" in W. Ickes and E.S. Knowles (ed.), *Personality, Roles and Social Behaviour*, pp. 199–218. New York: Springer-Verlag.

Suchman, Marc C. 1995. "Managing Legitimacy: Strategic and Institutional Approaches," *Academy of Management Review*, 20(3): 571–610.

Sutherland, E., and D.R. Cressey. 1970. *Principles of Criminology*. Chicago: J.B. Lippincott.

Sutton, R., and T. D'Aunno. 1989. "Decreasing organizational size: Untangling the effects of money and people." *Academy of Management Review* 14(2): 194–212.

Tajfel, H. 1981. *Human Groups and Social Categories: Studies in Social Psychology*. Cambridge, England: Cambridge University Press.

Tajfel, H., and J.C. Turner. 1985. "The social identity theory of intergroup behaviour" in S. Worchel and W.G. Austin (eds.), *Psychology of Intergroup Relations*, 2d Ed., pp. 7–24. Chicago: Nelson Hall.

Taylor, D.W., and A.A. Warrack. 1998. "Privatization of state enterprise: Policy drivers and lessons learned." *International Journal of Public Sector Management* 11(7): 524–35.

Taylor, D.W., A.A. Warrack, and M.C. Baetz. 1999. *Business and Government in Canada: Partners for the Future*. Scarborough, Toronto: Prentice Hall Canada, Inc.

Taylor, F. 1991. *Principles of Scientific Management*. New York: Harper & Row.

Taylor, F.W. 1947. *Scientific Management*. New York: Harper & Row.

Taylor, F.W. 1913. *Principles of Scientific Management*. New York: Harper & Brothers.

Taylor, M., J. Langan, and P. Hogget. 1995. *Encouraging Diversity: Voluntary and Private Organisations In Community Care*. Hampshire, England: Arena.

Teece, D., G. Pisano, and A. Shuen. 1997. "Dynamic Capabilities and Strategic Management," *Strategic Management Journal*, 18(7): 509–33.

Theil, Rita. 1996. "Learning to apply the lessons of privatization." *International Financial Law Review* (April) 15(4): 51ff.

Thoits, P.A. 1983. "Multiple identities and psychological well-being: A reformulation and test of the social isolation hypothesis." *American Sociological Review* 48: 174–87.

Thompson, J.D. 1967. *Organizations in Action*. New York: McGraw-Hill.

Tolbert, P., and L.G. Zucker. 1983. "Institutional sources of change in the formal structure of organizations: The diffusion of civil service reform, 1880–1935." *Administrative Science Quarterly* 28(1): 22–39.

Tomasko, R. 1990. *Downsizing: Reshaping the Corporation of the Future*. New York: AMACON.

Trevino, L.K. 1986. "Ethical decision making in organizations: A person-situation interactionist model." *Academy of Management Review* 11(3): 601–17.

Trevino, L.K., and S.A. Youngblood. 1990. "Bad apples in bad barrels: A causal analysis of ethical decision making behaviour." *Journal of Applied Psychology* 75(4): 378–85.

Tsalikis, J., and D.J. Fritsche. 1989. "Business ethics: A literature review with a focus on marketing ethics." *Journal of Business Ethics* 8: 695–743.

Turner, J. 1982. "Towards a cognitive redefinition of the social group" in H. Tajfel (ed.), *Social Identity and Intergroup Relations*, pp. 15–40. Cambridge, England: Cambridge University Press.

Tversky, A., and D. Kahneman. 1974. "Judgment under uncertainty: Heuristics and biases." *Science* 185: 1124–31.

Tversky, A., and D. Kahneman. 1973. "Availability: A heuristic for judging frequency and probability." *Cognitive Psychology* 5: 207–32.

Tversky, A., and D. Kahneman. 1972. "Subjective probability: A judgment of representativeness." *Cognitive Psychology* 3(3): 430–54.

Tversky, A., and D. Kahneman. 1971. "The belief in the 'law of small numbers'." *Psychological Bulletin* 76: 105–10.

Useem, M. 1987. "Corporate philanthropy" in W.W. Powell (ed.), *The Nonprofit Sector: A Research Handbook*. New Haven: Yale University Press.

Utterback, James M. 1994. *Mastering the Dynamics of Innovation*. Boston: Harvard Business School Press.

Van Til, J. 1988. *Mapping the Third Sector: Voluntarism in a Changing Social Economy*. New York: Foundation Center.

von Finckenstein, K. 1999. Q.C. Commissioner of Competition Bureau, Statement to the "Meet the Competition Bureau," Forum Insight Conference, Toronto, May 3.

Vroom, V.H. 1964. *Work and Motivation*. New York: John Wiley.

Wahba, M.A., and L.G. Bridwell. 1976. "Maslow reconsidered: A review of research on the need hierarchy theory." *Organizational Behaviour and Human Performance* (April): 212–40.

Wanberg, C., L. Bunce, and M. Gavin. 1999. "Perceived fairness of layoffs among individuals who have been laid off: A longitudinal study." *Personnel Psychology* 52 (Spring): 59–84.

Wasney, G. 1997. "A new road for Canadian truckers." *World Trade* 10(2): 48–50.

Weber, J. 1990. "Manager's moral reasoning: Assessing their responses to the three moral dilemmas." *Human Relations* 43: 687–702.

Weber, Joseph. 1998. "Does Canadian culture need this much protection?" *BusinessWeek* (June 18). Online: <http://www.bwarchive.businessweek.com>.

Weber, M. 1979. *Economy and Society*, eds. G. Roth and C. Wittich. Berkeley: University of California Press.

Weber, M. 1947. *The Theory of Social and Economic Organizations*. Edited and Translated by A.M. Henderson and T. Parsons. New York: Free Press.

Weber, M. 1946. *From Max Weber: Essays in Sociology*, eds. H.H. Gerth and C.W. Mills. New York: Oxford University Press.

Weber, M. 1927. *General Economic History*. Transl. F.H. Knight. London: Allen & Unwin.

Weick, K. 1979. *The Social Psychology of Organizing*. Reading, MA: Addison-Wesley.

Weick, K. 1976. "Educational organizations as loosely coupled systems." *Administrative Science Quarterly* 21: 1–19.

White, J.P., and R. Janzen. 2000. "The industrial relations implications of privatization: The case of Canada Post." *Industrial Relations* (Winter) 55(1): 36–55.

Whyte, G. 1993. "Escalating commitment in individual and group decision making: A prospect theory approach." *Organizational Behaviour and Human Decision Process* 54(3): 430–55.

Wild, J.J., K.L. Wild, and J.C.Y. Han. 2000. *International Business: An Integrated Approach*. Upper Saddle River, NJ: Prentice Hall.

Williamson, O.E. 1975. *Markets and Hierarchies: Analysis and Antitrust Implications*. New York: Free Press.

Winston, C. 1993. "Economic deregulation: Days of reckoning for economists." *Journal of Economic Literature* 31: 1263–89.

Woodward, J. 1965. *Industrial Organization: Theory and Practice*. London, NY: Oxford University Press.

World Bank. 1997. "Privatization revenue statistics by regions." Online: <http://worldbank.org/ecsp/finl/html/priv-regions.htm>.

Worrell, D., W. Davidson, and V. Sharma. 1991. "Layoff announcements and shareholder wealth." *Academy of Management Journal* 34 (September): 662–78.

Wren, D. 1979. *Evolution of Management Thought*, 2d Ed. New York: Wiley.

Zahra, S.A., and C.D. Hansen. 2000. "Privatization, entrepreneurship, and global competitiveness in the 21st Century." *Competition Review* 10(1): 83–103.

Zajac, E.J., and M.H. Bazerman. 1991. "Blind spots in industry and competitor analysis: Implications of interfirm (mis)perceptions for strategic decisions." *Academy of Management Review* 16(1): 37–56.

Zucker, L.G. 1977. "Institutionalization as a mechanism of cultural persistence." *American Sociological Review* 42(2): 726–42.

Index